MODERN
ENGLISH

MODERN ENGLISH

A Glossary of
Literature
and
Language

ARNOLD LAZARUS, ANDREW MACLEISH, AND H. WENDELL SMITH

GROSSET & DUNLAP, INC.
A NATIONAL GENERAL COMPANY

Publishers • New York

The authors wish to thank the following for their courtesy in granting permission to reprint from copyrighted material:

Brandt and Brandt: From "John Brown's Body," in *The Selected Works of Stephen Vincent Benét.* Published by Holt, Rinehart and Winston, Inc. Copyright 1927, 1928, by Stephen Vincent Benét. Copyright renewed 1955, by Rosemary Carr Benét. Reprinted by permission of Brandt and Brandt.

Jonathan Cape: From *The Bestiary,* by T. H. White.

J. M. Dent and Sons, Ltd.: "Song of the Open Road." From *Family Reunion,* by Ogden Nash.

Faber and Faber, Ltd.: From *Murder in the Cathedral,* by T. S. Eliot. Reprinted by permission of Faber and Faber Ltd.

————: "Paysage Moralise," by W. H. Auden. Reprinted by permission of Faber and Faber Ltd. from *Collected Poems 1927–1957.*

————: "Langue d'Oc," by Ezra Pound. Reprinted by permission of Faber and Faber Ltd. from *Personae.*

Since this page cannot accommodate all the copyright notices, the following page constitutes an extension of the copyright page.

Preface

ANYBODY WHO USES ENGLISH will find in this book an index to, and a summary of, concepts that writers, critics, and scholars have used to describe and discuss the language and its literature. We offer this glossary not as a last-word textbook, but as a tool which we believe students, writers, teachers, critics, and the general public will find useful and up to date.

We also believe that this is the first glossary to include the terminology of the three major branches of English studies — literature, rhetoric, and linguistics. Each of these fields of study during the past few years has developed scores of new concepts — and has brought new significance to many old ones. We have included as many terms as our own scholarship embraces — and to the depth permitted by a glossary that does not try to be encyclopedic.

Both students and general users of this glossary will find that its articles are adjuncts to, not substitutes for, deeper study of the concepts here defined and illustrated. To help with such deeper and broader studies, we have concluded most of the major articles with selected bibliographies, citing not only classic and celebrated works but also books and articles of comparatively recent vintage.

In line with "what's happening" in modern language and literature studies this book adopts a "now" approach to English. And wherever contemporary practice conflicts with the traditional, we have moved intrepidly toward the contemporary. Yet we all know that *now* has grown out of *then,* so that the scholarship of the 1970s must blend the traditional with the "mod," the normative with the permissive, the analytical with the intuitive — emphasizing each as may be appropriate. In short, we have tried to put the language and its literature in contemporary perspective without forsaking those traditions that remain valid — and we have tried to do so without making our book a hodgepodge of all things to all men.

Properly this glossary belongs not on the reference shelf but at the elbow, ready for instant use. Its aim is to aid in what is essentially a private enterprise — the sharpening of both zest and competence in the social enterprises of reading, writing, talking, listening, and reasoning.

A. L.
A. MacL.
H. W. S.

Acknowledgments

We wish to thank our many friends and colleagues who have given us their advice during the preparation of this book, especially those in the English Departments at Purdue University, the University of Minnesota, and Santa Monica College. We are also gratefully indebted to Professors John Block Friedman of Sir George Williams University, Montreal; J. N. Hook of the University of Illinois; Robert Hapgood of the University of New Hampshire; and James Runnels, of Carthage College, Wisconsin. Librarians who have helped us include Mary Anne Black, Mary Gibbs, Margo Hayes, Amy Johnson, Barbara Pfrogner, Elaine Puckett, Helen Schroyer, Pat Vann, and Reta Weintraub.

CONTENTS

A
GLOSSARY
OF
LITERATURE
AND
COMPOSITION

A

abbreviation   Brevity and conciseness are a virtue in composition, but the needless abbreviation of words is a form of discourtesy to the reader and should be avoided. In a reference book, where the intention is to convey the most information in the least space, abbreviation is freely used; in the Armed Forces and in businesses a stringent abbreviation, almost to the point of shorthand, is also used; and in the sciences and in technical writing the conciseness of abbreviation and the precision of symbols speed communication. But in standard prose abbreviation should be used only when it is customary or conventional. Deciding what is customary or conventional is the crux of the writer's problem. The answer almost always depends on context, but a general solution is never to abbreviate if the reader will be puzzled or stymied in discovering the intended meaning.

Since abbreviation is an aspect of spelling, deciding the literal appearance of an abbreviation is easily done: a good dictionary usually provides lists of abbreviations. But decisions about the *form* of an abbreviation pose greater difficulties: (1) Should the initial letter, or all the letters, be capitalized? (2) Should the abbreviation be italicized? (3) Should the abbreviation be written with or without period or periods? General answers, which are helpful but not invariable, are (1) Capitalize an abbreviation that would be capitalized when spelled out. Thus *Mr., Dr., St.,* when used as titles preceding names; *U.S.A., AFL-CIO,* and similar all-initial abbreviations. (2) Italicize an abbreviation if the spelled-out word or words would be italicized. (3*a*) Punctuate any abbreviation that is pronounced in full, as if the complete spelling were present, with the appropriate number of periods: *Mr.* (read *mister*); *n.d.* (read *no date*); *e.g.* (read *for example*). (3*b*) An all-initial abbreviation *should* be punctuated if the letters are pronounced individually — *U.S.A., C.O.D., A.D., B.C.* — but to this there are many exceptions. (3*c*) Any abbreviation that is read as a complete word (thus, an ACRONYM) should not be punctuated; *NATO, UNESCO, CORE, SNCC. Note:* Words like *don't* and *we'll* are contractions, not abbreviations; they never take periods.

Standard American English does use the following abbreviations:

1. For titles before names: *Mr., Mrs., Dr., St.* (and sometimes the more formal *M., Messrs., Mlle., Mlles., Mme., Mmes.,* and *Monsig.*).

2. For certain designations after names: *Jr., Sr., M.P.* (Member of Parliament), *B.A.* (Bachelor of Arts), *M.A.* (Master of Arts), *Ph.D.* (Doctor of Philosophy), *M.D.* (Doctor of Medicine), *D.D.S.* (Doctor

of Dental Surgery), *LL.D.* (Doctor of Laws), and for all other academic degrees.

3. For initialized terms more widely used in speech than their full forms: A.D. and B.C. (with dates), *C.O.D.* (the periods usually retained), *D.C.* (for District of Columbia), *f.o.b.*, *P.S.*, *R.S.V.P.* (the periods usually retained). *SOS, FCC, NAM, AMA, UN, UNESCO, CIO, YMCA, FBI, UCLA, NBC, TVA, TV, FM, AP.*

4. For names of radio and television stations: *WGN, KCBS, KTLA.*

5. For certain terms used in DOCUMENTATION or in parenthetical reference to such documentation: *p.* (*page*), *pp.* (*pages*), *ch.* (*chapter*), *col.* (*column*), *No.* (*number*), *Nos.* (*numbers*), *sec.* (*section*), *supp.* (*supplement*), *et al.* (*et alii* — "and others"), *etc.* (*et cetera*), *ca.* (*circa* — "about"), *cf.* (*confer* — "compare"), *f.* ("and the following page"), *loc. cit.* (*loco citato* — "in the place cited"), *MS* (*manuscript*), *n.d.* ("no date"), *op. cit.* (*opere citato* — "in the work cited"), *passim* ("throughout"), *q.v.* (*quod vide* — "which see"), *viz.* (*videlicet* — "namely").

Currently the trend in scholarly work is toward less Latin, more English — and thus fewer abbreviations even in footnotes and scholarly asides. Such terms as *op. cit.* and *loc. cit.* are being dropped altogether in contemporary scholarship; *q.v.* and *viz.* are appearing as "see. . ." and "namely."

6. For certain address designations *after* names of streets, avenues, boulevards, drives: *St., Ave., Blvd., Dr.* (But these are giving way to spelled-out forms — even in business offices and newspapers.)

7. For certain commercial terms after names of companies and corporations: *Co., Corp., Inc., Ltd.* (These, too, are giving way to spelled-out forms, and should be written only when a firm itself uses the abbreviation on its letterhead.)

8. For initials in names: *T. S. Eliot, H. G. Wells, Winston S. Churchill.* (Names should be written as their owners prefer — always *W. Somerset Maugham,* never *William S. Maugham;* always *George Bernard Shaw* or *G.B.S.,* never *George B. Shaw.*) When an initial is strictly a letter and stands for no name in particular, it usually is written without a period: *Harry S Truman.* No periods are used after nicknames or foreshortened names like *Jim, Sam, Fred,* or *Al,* for those are not abbreviations.

In standard American usage the names of days, months, states, cities, and countries (except *U.S.A., USSR, UK* and certain other special designations) are spelled out rather than abbreviated.

abstract   See PRECIS.

abstraction   The process of separating attributes from their physical structures or "referents." As a device of semantics, abstractions name classes of things rather than individual things. The semanticist imagines an "abstraction ladder" upon which the successively higher rungs are the more and more general terms. An abstraction is a word whose referents are many (the more referents, the more abstract the word). An example is *animal,* which has such referents as cats, dogs, impalas, monkeys, and so on. (See SEMANTICS.)

abstraction ladder   See SEMANTICS 3.

accentual verse   Verse measured by a set number of accents (heavily stressed syllables) in each line, rather than, as in other poetry, a regular alternation of accented and unaccented syllables. The unstressed syllables vary in number and placement from one line to the next. Anglo-Saxon poetry (for example, *Beowulf* or "The Seafarer") was not only accentual, but also ALLITERATIVE, and provided the model for subsequent poetry which followed the same rhythmical pattern. Thus poetry of the Middle English alliterative revival was at the same time accentual; for example, the anonymous *Gawain and the Green Knight,* William Langland's *Piers Plowman,* and *Morte d'Arthur.* Frequently the alliterative consonants fall on the stressed syllables, as in a typical line from *Piers Plowman* (slightly modernized): "Wíves and wídows wóol and flax spínneth." By and large, accentual verse was unrhymed, but some Middle English examples—notably *Gawain* and the York CRAFT CYCLE PLAYS—employ rhyme in addition to alliteration, showing the influence of French literature. Among the modern poets who have written accentual verse, Gerard Manley Hopkins is perhaps the best known (see SPRUNG RHYTHM).
REFERENCE: J. C. Pope, *The Rhythm of Beowulf.*

acronym   A word in which each letter stands for another word. In the acronym "laser," the *l* stands for *light,* the *a* for *amplification,* the *s* for *stimulated,* the *e* for *emission,* and the *r* for *radiation.* In acronyms articles, conjunctions, and prepositions are usually not assigned letters. Thus a fuller "translation" of "laser" would read: "light amplification *by* stimulated emission *of* radiation." (Compare PORTMANTEAU WORDS.)

act   1. In a play, a major division in action or story-line, in a theater usually marked by the drawing of a curtain, but in printed copy simply by the words "Act One," "Act Two," and so on. (The smaller divisions within an act are called SCENES.) Sixteenth-, seventeenth-, and eighteenth-century plays usually had five acts. According to Renaissance commentators on Aristotle's *Poetics,* the five acts were supposed to correspond to five divisions of the action—*introduction, rising action, climax, falling action,* and *catastrophe* (see DRAMATIC STRUCTURE).

Except for Ben Jonson, the Elizabethans did not pay much attention to acts in that sense. Shakespeare's plays, for example, were originally produced in scenes and were posthumously divided into five acts in a thorough way by the editor Nicholas Rowe (1674 – 1718). Rowe was a product of the age of NEO-CLASSICISM, in which dramatists were very much concerned with the problems of the classical UNITIES. Nineteenth-century plays (especially those of Barrie, Ibsen, and Shaw) consist usually of four acts. Contemporary plays tend to consist of two or three acts. The one-act play, which developed with the Abbey Players of Dublin, Ireland, and with the Provincetown (Massachusetts) Players (and also with the early twentieth-century little theater movement), is a genre of its own, corresponding to the SHORT STORY in unity of impression and brevity of time-span. 2. One of the key terms in Burke's pentad (see DRAMATISM).

REFERENCES: Richard Corbin and Miriam Balf, "How to Read a Play," *Twelve American Plays 1920-1960;* Eric Bentley, *In Search of Theater;* Gustav Freytag's "Graph" in Jackson Barry, *Dramatic Structure.*

adage   An old and supposedly wise saying, like the proverb and APHORISM. Adages are brief and memorable ("A stitch in time saves nine") and have thus become a part of folklore, transmitted orally and in writing. The adages or "morals" at the ends of Aesop's *Fables* (sixth century B.C.) are generally believed to have had oral currency in one form or another before he used them. About A.D. 1500 there appeared a collection of adages and proverbs, *Adagia,* by the Dutch humanist Erasmus. There is little definable difference between an adage and a proverb, though the latter label has a more reputable connotation. If pointlessly used too often, either may become little more than an old *saw.* A MAXIM is usually literary in origin and somewhat restricted in meaning.

REFERENCES: Desiderius Erasmus, *Adagia;* Funk & Wagnalls *Standard Dictionary of Folklore, Mythology, and Legend.* For distinctions between *adage, proverb, aphorism,* etc., see *Webster's Dictionary of Synonyms.*

ad captandum or **ad captandum vulgus**   The deliberate use of unsound reasoning in an attempt to deceive the crowd. Using this device, an advertiser says, "More people buy Poofy – so Poofy is the best buy." The lack of connection between the two statements will probably not be noticed by more than a few. (Compare BANDWAGON.)

ad hominem   In ARGUMENTATION, any appeal to the personal feelings and prejudices of the reader or audience (the Latin phrase means "to the man"). The device may also be used to refute an opponent's argument by reasoning through propositions that he already accepts. This sort of argument was the technique of Clarence Darrow in the Scopes trial of 1925, when he called his opponent, William Jennings Bryan, to the stand. Starting with Bryan's belief in the Bible as absolute truth, Darrow led Bryan to untenable positions; that is, he used Bryan's own beliefs to humiliate him.

Argument *ad hominem* is not the same thing as ARGUMENT AGAINST THE MAN, which attempts to discredit a proposition on the grounds that it is asserted by a discredited person. (Compare NAME-CALLING.)

ad ignorantiam   In ARGUMENTATION, the contention that a proposition is true because an opponent (or the audience) can offer no evidence to the contrary. The device takes advantage of the ignorance of the audience. The arguer may, for example, assert that there is no such thing as infinity, and offer as "proof" that his opponent cannot prove otherwise.

ad misericordiam   An appeal to the sense of pity or to the sympathy of an audience. An example is the use of photos of a crippled child to inspire gifts to research funds; another, the "send an underprivileged boy to camp" appeal to sell newspaper subscriptions. These appeals may often be justified, of course.

ad populum   In ARGUMENTATION, an appeal to the emotions of the masses. The device is exemplified by the rabble-rouser who avoids presenting rational evidence against a proposition and shouts instead, "Are we going to let them do that to us?"

ad verecundiam   Snob appeal or an appeal to one's sense of prestige. Advertisers use this device when they suggest that their product is the one to "step up" to "when you can afford the best." In ARGUMENTATION the appeal is to pride, rank, sense of status.

aesthetic distance   The theory that once an author has created a piece, it goes forth on its own and is to be understood on its own terms. In its extreme form, the theory holds that any reference to the author's intentions or to cultural and historical backgrounds is irrelevant, misleading, or premature.

REFERENCES: W. K. Wimsatt, "The Intentional Fallacy," *The Verbal Icon;* Meyer Abrams, *The Mirror and the Lamp*; René Wellek, "The Mode of Existence of a Literary Work of Art," *The Southern Review* (Spring, 1942); Bernard Berenson, *Aesthetics and History*.

affirming an alternative   See FALSE DILEMMA and SYLLOGISM 3.

affirming the consequent   See SYLLOGISM 2.

African literature   See BLACK LITERATURE.

agent   1. In Burke's rhetoric, the third term of DRAMATISM. 2. In conventional rhetoric, the performer of an action. This performer may be subject of a predication ("That *newspaper* misled us") or object in a prepositional phrase ("We were misled by that *newspaper*"). Notice that both examples identify the agent, so that the distinction between "active" and "passive" is not here in question, although the first example emphasizes "newspaper" while the second emphasizes "we." When a reader or listener must ask, "Who is doing what?" the writer had better recast. A vague utterance, like "There will be a visitation tonight," for example, prompts the reader to ask, "Who is going to do the visiting?" An agent-verb statement, like "The inspector will be visiting," is clearer and more direct, unless the writer deliberately intends for "visitation" to connote "plague." Finally, agent-verb constructions clarify and refine ambiguous strings of -ations and -icities, strings known as "NOUNIFICATIONS." For example, an ambiguous phrase like "the correction of the administration" leaves the reader asking, "Who corrected whom?" An agent-verb-object pattern can rescue the meaning here: "The administrators corrected the voters" or "The voters corrected the administrators." (Compare REIFICATION.)

Alexandrine   In English poetry, an iambic hexameter line, usually in a stanza of iambic pentameter lines; for example, the last line of the SPENSERIAN STANZA. The term derives from the *Roman d'Alexandre,* a twelfth-century French romance that used the twelve-syllable line. Since its use by the poet Ronsard (sixteenth century) and by the playwrights Corneille and Racine (seventeenth century) the Alexandrine has been as standard in French poetry as the dactyllic hexameter in Latin and the iambic pentameter in English. But whereas the French Alexandrine, especially that of the nineteenth-century poet Verlaine, can be measured in syllables, the English Alexandrine is more accurately measured in metrical feet. A classic example of the English six-foot line is Alexander Pope's "That like / a wound / ed snake / drags its / slow length / a long," which pokes fun at the form. (Pope regarded as freakish any line longer than five feet.) But the Alexandrine need not drag: it may be an artistic triumph, as it is in certain lines of W. H. Auden's poem "In Memory of W. B. Yeats"—notably the line "Now Ireland has her madness and her weather still." In oral interpretation the Alexandrine, like other six-beat lines, tends to break into three-beat lines, as John Hollander observes in "Metrics," in Edward Gordon (ed.), *Writing and Literature.*

alienation   1. A condition in which a person is rejected or feels cut off from friends, community, or society. 2. An archetypal theme in literature (see ARCHETYPE), especially in such works as Dostoevsky's *Notes from Underground,* Kafka's *Metamorphosis,* Joyce's *Portrait of the Artist as a Young Man,* Baldwin's *Another Country,* and most of Brecht's plays.

REFERENCES: Hannah Arendt, *The Human Condition;* Timothy O'Keefe (ed.), *Alienation;* Gerald Sykes (ed.), *Alienation: The Cultural Climate of Our Times.*

allegory   A kind of extended metaphor in which characters or PERSONI-FICATIONS represent something other than themselves—virtues, vices, causes, issues. There are two main kinds of allegory: those that use personifications, as in Bunyan's *Pilgrim's Progress;* and those that use a special kind of symbolism, as in Dante's *Divine Comedy.* In *The Pilgrim's Progress* the main character, Christian, who "trudged through the Slough of Despond," represents the Christian soul on its pilgrim-age through the world. Christian is not a real person, of course, nor is the Slough of Despond a real place; they are rather concretizations of abstract ideas made real and vital to the reader by their dramatic presentation. In *The Divine Comedy* a real man, Dante, meets the ghost of a real person, the Roman poet Vergil, who serves him as a guide through Hell. Aside from their literal roles as pilgrim and guide, Dante and Vergil represent mankind led by human reason to an under-standing of the nature of evil and the spiritual consequences of sin. Such a representation is *symbolic allegory.*

Allegorical writing was quite common in early didactic literature (see DIDACTICISM), as reflected in numerous FABLES and PARABLES. Some major works that are allegorical in one respect or another are *Everyman* (a morality play), *Piers Plowman, The Parliament of Fowls* (Chaucer), *The Faerie Queene* (Spenser), and *A Tale of a Tub* (Swift). In modern literature, allegorical LEVELS OF MEANING tend to be more veiled and thus less susceptible to explicit interpretation, as in *Moby-Dick* (Melville), *Animal Farm* (George Orwell), and *Tiny Alice* (Ed-ward Albee). There is, in fact, some controversy over whether such works should be called allegorical at all.

REFERENCES: C. S. Lewis, *The Allegory of Love;* R. W. Frank, Jr., "The Art of Reading Medieval Personification Allegory," *E*[nglish] *L*[iterary] *H*[is-tory] (December, 1953) 237–250; Edwin Honig, *Dark Conceit: The Making of Allegory;* Arnold Williams, *Medieval Allegory.*

alliteration (Also called **head rhyme**)   The close-order repetition of initial consonants in a series of words, as in Poe's "ghastly, gaunt, ungainly bird," Alliteration deftly used may contribute to EUPHONY; but excessive use of alliteration can degenerate into EUPHUISM. Al-literation also serves as a MNEMONIC device; advertising copywriters often use it to catch attention and impress the memory. Our heritage abounds in alliterative utterances: "Fifty-four forty or fight," 'Tippe-canoe and Tyler too," "right as rain," "kith and kin," "time and tide," "might and main." (Compare CONSONANCE and ASSONANCE.)

alliterative verse The accentual, unrhymed verse of Old English poetry, especially of *Beowulf:*

> There was laughter of heroes, the heroes high,
> Words were winsome. Waltheow went forth,
> Hrothgar's queen, in courtly costume. . .
> Then there came forth from the moors under the mists,
> Grendel creeping; he bore God's anger;
> The dreadful serpent drew near the sires. . . .

Old English poetry relied on ALLITERATION and on a certain number of accented syllables to each line. The line was broken into two HEMIS-TICHS with a CAESURA in between.

An alliterative revival took place in the fourteenth century, as evidenced in *Sir Gawain and the Green Knight* and *Piers Plowman.* Certain of the York CRAFT CYCLE PLAYS (ca. 1340) are also written in alliterative verse, for example, the first one, on the creation and fall of Lucifer. But these plays also use rhyme, perhaps reflecting a French influence.

REFERENCES: Margaret Williams (ed.), *Word Hoard: A Treasury of Old English Literature;* Neil Isaacs, *Structural Principles in Old English Poetry.*

allusion Loosely, any reference — direct or indirect; strictly, an allusion is an *indirect* reference to anything the writer feels should be well known in literature, history, and the arts. By tapping the reader's memory, the writer or speaker brings the import of an experience — with all its associations — to bear upon a present meaning. He thus says much in few words, allusion being a striking device for economy, as Reuben Brower observes in *Alexander Pope: The Poetry of Allusion.*

Allusions may range from the universal to the obscure and momentary. What is necessary is that they be recognized by the audience. How much does the reader or listener know of the culture around him — of history, of art, of science, of yesterday's headlines, of philosophy, of great men and women, of great books and poems and plays? The more he knows of all these, the more he will derive from his current reading and listening, as Ronald Christ suggests in *The Narrow Act: Borges' Art of Allusion.*

If a speaker or writer mentions "a visit to England in the cruellest month," the line would mean much to those of his audience familiar with the opening line of T. S. Eliot's *The Waste Land:* "April is the cruellest month, . . ." Those familiar with the Eliot poem know that he, in turn, alludes "to England in April" — and they also understand that the whole background of Eliot's poem bears upon the present "visit to England." For some the reference will take on still further implications because they recall another line of poetry—Browning's "Oh, to be in England / Now that April's there!" And the contrast of attitudes between the pleasurable April and the cruel April will further condition the understanding of "a visit to England in the cruellest month."

What happens in the mind of the reader or listener who does not "pick up" those allusions? He misses the full sense of the line as well as the delight of "getting it" for himself.

Depending as they do on shared knowledge, allusions are truly successful only when the audience does share the knowledge. The wider the audience, the more universally known must be the thing alluded to. Literature (as well as daily speech) abounds with allusions to the Bible and to Shakespeare, perhaps the two most widely shared literary experiences of English-speaking people. If the audience is small and local, however, an allusion may call up specific knowledge of something very immediate—something, let us say, that would be unknown to those who had not attended a certain baseball game or read a certain news story yesterday. Local or ephemeral allusions obviously do not make good material for the writer who hopes to appeal to the wider, general audience.

REFERENCES: Most dictionaries, collegiate or larger, identify proper name (i.e., direct) references. For identifying a quotation or an allusion to one, even when only a few key words are given, the following dictionaries can be useful: (1) *Bartlett's Familiar Quotations*, (2) *The Oxford Dictionary of Quotations*, and (3) Bergen Evans's *Dictionary of Quotations*. A celebrated work that actually identifies allusions as well as more direct references is S. A. Allibone, *Critical Dictionary of English Literature and British and American Authors* (1899), which, of course, is obviously limited to the classics and to literature published before the turn of the century. In the end, nothing will help the reader so much as his own wide reading.

alter ego   Literally, "other I." **1.** Another person, a close friend, who is very much like oneself; e.g., Damon's Pythias; Achilles' Patroclus; Gertrude Stein's Alice B. Toklas. **2.** Another side of oneself, as in a "split personality" or "schizophrenia"; e.g., Dr. Jekyll may be thought of as Mr. Hyde's alter ego. **3.** A character who shares another character's manifest or suppressed traits; e.g., in Conrad's *Secret Sharer* the narrator-Captain and Leggatt; and in Hesse's *Demian* Demian and Emil. In that context the alter ego is close to the German *Doppelgänger* (literally, "doublegoer") since one of the two characters seems to be a ghostly manifestation or re-incarnation of the other. (Strictly the German term refers to a pair of persons of whom one is flesh, the other spirit.)

REFERENCE: William Gillis, "Doppelgänger," CEA *Critic* (February, 1969).

ambiguity   Multiple meaning. Whatever has more than one possible meaning is ambiguous. When ambiguity is not intended, it is usually considered a flaw. But intentional ambiguity may enhance.

To consider these two aspects separately:

1. In unintended ambiguity the uncertainty may be caused by careless syntax, spelling, punctuation, or word choice. Here are ambiguous statements: "We all know that woman is fickle." (Are *all* women fickle, or just *that* woman? Is *that* a connective or a demonstrative? In speech the proper stress would no doubt clarify the meaning.) "We boarded the *Elizabeth II* for our ocean voyage in New York." (The misplaced modifying phrase does the damage.) "The little valley made a perfect site." (Spelling trouble: was *sight* intended?) "We saw her play last night." (Did she play tennis? Did she act in a play? Did she write the play we saw?) "He's an old coin collector." (A hyphen might clarify things: though young, he's an old-coin collector.) Context often clarifies such ambiguities as those above, but careful speakers and writers know that the way into the minds of their audience is difficult at best, and that unintended ambiguity makes contact still more difficult. Among unintentional yet meaningful ambiguities is the FREUDIAN SLIP: "I was sure I heard a burglar downstairs, and I lay there wild awake."

2*a*. Occasionally, ambiguity is deliberate. EQUIVOCATION, giving "equal voice" to two meanings, is an intention to mislead or deceive. It may appear when the speaker wants to avoid taking either of two stands. Politician, diplomat, barrister, parent—almost anyone—may equivocate to avoid commitment; the student may equivocate in his essay examination, hoping to appear in agreement with whatever the teacher believes. Equivocation is considered at best unethical.

2*b*. Desirable ambiguity occurs when a context yields two or more meanings to enrich, rather than obscure. Most writers of poetry and other imaginative literature use such ambiguity. Cleanth Brooks says, "The tendency of science is necessarily to stabilize terms, to freeze them into strict denotations; the poet's tendency is by contrast disruptive." The poet consciously "disrupts" the normal uses of words, both to pack much meaning into a few words and to startle the reader into a sharper attention to a turn of thought. Shakespeare often boldly directs our attention to the double-flip that words may take. Says Othello as he enters Desdemona's bedchamber with intent to kill her: "Put out the light, and then put out the light." He extinguishes the lamplight—and then Desdemona's life. PUNS and other sorts of DOUBLE-ENTENDRE are common in everyday speech but are especially useful to the poet, as is virtually "any verbal nuance, however slight, which gives room for alternative reactions to the same piece of language," as William Empson puts it in *Seven Types of Ambiguity*. Laurence Perrine has said of desirable ambiguity: "The poet needs a multi-dimensional language, and creates it partly by using a multi-dimensional vocabulary. . . . The poet, we may say, plays on a many-stringed instrument. And he sounds more than one note at a time." Those who play the violin know that Perrine has in mind, here, something like the "double stop." (See Ruth Krauss, *There's a Little Ambiguity Over There Among the Blue Bells*.)

ambivalence 1. In Freudian psychology, simultaneous love and hate. 2. In literature, especially fiction and drama, a pair of contrasting (often contradictory) characteristics within a single character. The classic example is Stevenson's Dr. Jekyll, who is also Mr. Hyde; the first good, the second evil. Freudian ambivalence is manifest in such characters as Melville's John Claggart (*Billy Budd*), Dostoevsky's Raskolnikov (*Crime and Punishment*), Conrad's Mr. Kurtz (*Heart of Darkness*), and Henry James's John Marcher (*The Beast in the Jungle*).

REFERENCE: W. Eugene Davis, "Tess . . . Some Ambiguities," *Nineteenth Century Fiction* (March, 1968).

amphibole An utterance that can be taken in opposite senses. For example, "Feed a cold and starve a fever" can mean (*a*) "If you have a cold, eat; if you have a fever, fast" and (*b*) "If you eat when you have a cold, you will get a fever." In ancient Greek literature such ambiguous predictions were attributed to the Pythian priestesses and oracles at Delphi.

amphibrach See METER.

anachronism The use of any character, incident, artifact, or language at a time or place inconsistent with historical fact. The striking of a clock in Shakespeare's *Julius Caesar* is a case in point, since the Roman setting of the play antedates the invention of this kind of clock by hundreds of years. Such archaic language as "thee," "thou," "thy," and similar words in would-be contemporary poetry is quite anachronistic. Most anachronisms are unintentional. Occasionally, anachronisms may be deliberate, as they are in *A Connecticut Yankee in King Arthur's Court*. Here the comic IRONY emerges to a large degree from Twain's deliberate joining of modern with medieval language, customs, and technologies. Similarly, George Bernard Shaw has his Joan of Arc, his Cleopatra, and his Androcles speak in a modern idiom, the better to show the human characteristics they share with contemporary people.

A person is anachronistic if he seems to be living in the wrong age, one in which his is an alien personality. A famous example is Cervantes' Don Quixote, who attempts to live according to an outdated code of chivalry.

anacoluthon   Failure to follow through a syntactical structure once begun. Some examples: "To tell the truth, I found the book rather dull and ends with an anticlimax"; "He couldn't find a parking place, had to run late to his exam, and which undoubtedly spoiled his performance"; "This is what I hope to do myself, so far as it is proper and the people who will meet within a few short weeks to take over the direction of the campaigns, I am ready to do my part." Anacoluthon is the term Fowler uses to castigate such befuddlements as FRAGMENTS, DANGLERS, and MISPLACED MODIFIERS. Anacoluthon is also a kind of slipping on such banana peels as FAULTY PARALLELISM and WHICH-MIRES. (See SYLLEPSIS and ZEUGMA.)

REFERENCE: George Starbuck, "Anacoluthon All Over Again," *Papers of the Midwest MLA* (1969).

anacrusis   Literally, "up-beat." A kind of grace note or extra unaccented syllable (or syllables) at the beginning of a line of poetry. Longfellow's "Psalm of Life," for example, whose lines begin mostly with heavy-stressed (trochaic) syllables ("Learn to labor and to wait"), starts *one* of its lines with the anacrusis, "There is a Reaper." *Note*: The context does not call for a heavy fingerpointing stress on *there*.

anadiplosis   The ending of an utterance deliberately repeated at the beginning of the next. The repetition emphasizes: "And now for *the dessert — the dessert* so lovingly prepared by my wife." "Spare me your *words; words* are not what I need." "Wanly he *sings, / Sings* of the day now lost."

analogy   A comparison of two things that are essentially unlike but which can be shown to have some similar properties. When construed loosely, analogy may cover all sorts of figurative comparisons — METAPHOR, SIMILE, ANTONOMASIA. But in its more restricted sense, analogy is a more fully developed comparison than any of the other sorts of similitude. Its use is among the most effective ways to explain, describe, or convince.

When used to describe or explain, an analogy clarifies some new concept by comparing it to a better-known one. Hobbes's *Leviathan*, for example, compares political governments to a great whale, showing that both have structure, organization, power. The comparison goes beyond metaphor and simile, for it points up a larger number of similarities between the two unlikes. The more points of similarity, the stronger the analogy. These points of similarity are made explicit, not left to the reader's imagination.

Alexander Pope used analogy to explain something about the variety of human opinion: " 'Tis with our judgments as with our watches; none go just alike, yet each believes his own." The figure is analogy rather than simile because Pope points explicitly to the ways in which the two things, judgments and watches, are alike. Without his clause of explanation, the clause of assertion would only puzzle us. A simile, on the other hand, would be clear enough without explanation.

In ARGUMENTATION analogy is both useful and dangerous. It is useful as a shortcut, for it draws upon accepted knowledge to establish new, and as yet unaccepted, theory. But reasoning by analogy is dangerous because it may claim or suggest fundamental similarity between two things whose similarities are only superficial. To say that peaches are lemons, for example, because both have roundness, skins, and seeds is, of course, a FALSE ANALOGY — one that ignores differences in favor of superficial likenesses. (See INDUCTIVE REASONING 4.)

REFERENCE: Randall Decker, "Analogy as an Expository Device," *Patterns of Exposition;* Monroe Beardsley, "Analogies," *Practical Logic.*

anapest   In poetry, a unit of rhythm consisting of two lightly stressed syllables followed by one heavily stressed syllable. Here is an example from Alfred Noyes's "The Highwayman": "And he taps with his whip on the shutters, but all is locked and barred." Notice that the last three feet of this line are iambic and not anapestic. Verse that is purely anapestic tends to become monotonous. It is a mark of the skillful poet that he uses occasional substitutes interestingly and appropriately. Algernon Swinburne is known for his heavy reliance on anapests.

anaphora   Repetition of a word or group of words in successive clauses, sentences, or lines of poetry. "War is cruel. War is evil. War is stupid." (Compare the similar devices of REPETITION and ANADIPLOSIS).

anecdote   Literally, "not for publication." 1. A confidential tale or bit of gossip. 2. An episode or event worked in as a kind of parenthesis to the main story-line in a work of fiction (as in Sterne's *Tristram Shandy* and Dickens's *Pickwick Papers*) or in a long narrative poem (as in *The Iliad* and *The Aeneid*). The didactic anecdotes in Chaucer's "Nun's Priest's Tale" are a delightful parody of anecdotal digressions.

REFERENCE: Edmund Fuller (ed.), *Thesaurus of Anecdotes.*

animism   1. Ancestor worship, in several Oriental cultures, whose assumption is that the spirits of ancestors live on in the universe. 2. The investing of animals and inanimate objects in nature with human characteristics, as do children, classical poets, and primitive cultures. Thus, in several mythologies, trees and bodies of water, for example, have human personalities and even divine doubles (dryads, nymphs).

REFERENCES: James Frazer, *The Golden Bough;* Bronislaw Malinowski, *Magic, Science, and Religion;* Robert Redfield, *The Primitive World;* William G. Sumner, *Folkways;* William Butler Yeats, *The Celtic Twilight.*

annotated bibliography   See DOCUMENTATION.

antagonist   The villain or chief negative character in a plot; it is he who opposes the protagonist. In Shakespeare's *Othello,* for example, Othello's chief antagonist is Iago. But Othello himself is also his own enemy. Thus, Othello's own "green-eyed jealousy"—his TRAGIC FLAW —may also be considered an antagonistic force. (See DRAMATIC STRUC-TURE.)

anthology   A collection (literally, a "bouquet") of selected pieces; —e.g., Palgrave's *Golden Treasury.* The chief purpose of most anthologies is to delight or entertain. A secondary purpose, especially in school anthologies (e.g., *Adventures in Modern Literature*), is to whet the appetites of readers so that they will read more of a given author's works or more works of a certain literary type. In this sense an anthology is also called a *sampler* or a *reader. Note:* Just as appetizers are not intended as substitutes for complete meals, anthologies are not intended as substitutes for authors' whole books.

antibacchius   See METER.

anticlimax   1. Any event or scene (usually at the end of a play) that is less crucial than what precedes it; in classical drama and early fiction, the spelling out of minor details and the tying up of loose ends. (See DÉNOUEMENT.) The climax, or high point of a play or story, is at the end, so that the anticlimax, if any, which can come only after the climax, is very close indeed to the end. Anticlimax may be a blemish only when it is structurally irrelevant. Early popular fiction was usually marred by it, for writers tried to satisfy sentimental readers by explaining every last detail of the characters' "fates." 2. Anticlimax is also a stylistic device that may occur within as small a unit as the sentence: something trivial following something of importance: "As a serious young man, I loved Beethoven, Keats, and hot dogs." Intentional anticlimax can be first-rate humor. Advertising writers sometimes fall into anticlimax unintentionally by placing too much value on a product: "Look gay and beautiful! Let romance enter your life! Spray your hair with Sheen!" Intentional anticlimax is a favorite device of the satirist. It can be seen in Pope's title "The Rape of the Lock," for example, and in these two lines from Canto V: " 'Now meet thy fate,' incensed Belinda cried, / And drew a deadly bodkin from her side. . . ."

antimasque   See MASQUE.

antinovel   A kind of fiction which de-emphasizes (if not disregards) plot, and instead emphasizes psychological introspection into human motivations and feelings—into all the thousands of little things that fill time. (Compare STREAM OF CONSCIOUSNESS.) In this respect such works as James Joyce's *Finnegans Wake,* Virginia Woolf's *Orlando,* Marcel Proust's *Remembrance of Things Past,* and William H. Gass's

Omensetter's Luck may be called antinovels. The term first gained prominence when it was used by Jean-Paul Sartre in his review of *Portrait of a Man Unknown* by Nathalie Sarraute, the Russian-born French novelist. Such writers as Robert Walser, Jorge Luis Borges, and Donald Barthelme have published distinguished fiction that is plotless. The revolt of certain contemporary novelists against traditional forms and conventions is comparable to the revolt of contemporary playwrights in the THEATER OF THE ABSURD and in the IMMEDIATE THEATER.

REFERENCES: Jean-Paul Sartre, *Literary Essays;* Ruth Temple, *Natalie Sarraute;* Alain Robbe-Grillet, *For a New Novel;* Raney Stanford, ". . . When a Not-a-Hero Is a Hero," *Journal of Popular Culture* (Winter, 1967).

antiphrasis   Any use of a word in a sense contrary to its meaning; for example, "Let's slap a *mandate* on him" for "Let's slap an *injunction* on him." (Compare MALAPROP and IRONY.)

antistrophe   See ODE.

antithesis   1. An idea opposed to another idea or THESIS. 2. The balancing of one thing against another opposing or contrasting thing. What is contrasted may be words, phrases, clauses, sentences—even paragraphs or whole sections of a literary work; but antithesis most often consists in the contrast between two parts of a sentence: "Art is long; life is short." The second clause of an antithesis may omit the verb if that verb can be assumed the same as the first: "The early writers are in possession of nature, and their followers of art."—Samuel Johnson. Antithesis, as one form of rhetorical balance, was used to extreme in the oratory of the Sophists of ancient Greece. In English it became almost an obsession of John Lyly, whose markedly artificial style became known as EUPHUISM. Antithesis also lent itself especially well to expression in the HEROIC COUPLET of the age of Dryden and Pope. Antithesis turns easily to the EPIGRAM. As a device of contrast, antithesis is related to IRONY, OXYMORON, PARADOX, AMBIVALENCE, FOILS, ANTAGONIST. (See also DIALECTIC 3.)

antonomasia   The substitution of the name of an individual for that of a class. Call a person an Izaak Walton and you have indirectly called him an expert fisherman. This device is a sort of METONYMY, or cross-naming: a lover becomes a *Romeo,* an orator a *Cicero,* a poet a *Milton.* Another kind of antonomasia is the substitution of an EPITHET for a person's name: "Your Honor" for Judge Jones; "Officer" for "Patrolman McDougal."

aphorism   Any terse statement of doctrine or of acknowledged principle. Examples include such pithy assertions as "Education is learning to take pleasure in the right things" (Aristotle), "Whatever is, is right" (Alexander Pope), and even the remark of a character in a modern cartoon, "Happiness is a warm puppy" ("Peanuts"). Like these examples, the brief attempt at defining the indefinable often becomes an aphorism. If it happens also to be startling or paradoxical, it may be called an *apothegm:* "History is bunk" (Henry Ford).

When such a brief assertion is widely known and the author forgotten, it is called a PROVERB: "There's no fool like an old fool." If generally accepted as a truth, it becomes an ADAGE: "Handsome is as handsome does."

If an aphorism turns to advice on how to live, it becomes a MAXIM: "Give every man thy ear, but few thy voice" (the advice of Polonius to Laertes in *Hamlet*). A maxim of ethical content or purpose is a *precept,* a term that may also apply to any instructional *adage:* "Don't change horses in mid-stream." Aphorisms, proverbs, and maxims in verse are known as GNOMIC POETRY. (Compare EPIGRAM.)

REFERENCES: W. H. Auden and Louis Untermeyer (eds.), *The Viking Book of Aphorisms;* "Prose Forms: Apothegms," in Arthur Eastman *et al.* (eds.), *The Norton Reader.*

apocalypse   From the Greek word meaning "that which is uncovered or revealed." 1. A synonym for the Book of Revelation, the last book of the New Testament. In this work are found the Four Horsemen of the Apocalypse—Conquest, Slaughter, Famine, and Death. They ride white, red, black, and pale horses respectively. It is to Death that Katherine Anne Porter alludes in *Pale Horse, Pale Rider. The Four Horsemen of the Apocalypse,* a novel by the Spaniard Vicente Blasco-Ibáñez, was based on the horrors of World War I. 2. Sometimes the word is used for any literary work or vision of experience which, like the classic Judaeo-Christian apocalypses, is cast in the form of a dream or several dreams in which a superior authority reveals the imminent end of the world. The apocalypse usually constitutes a warning to, and criticism of, contemporary society and hints that a chosen people (the Israelites, the Christians, and so on) will triumph over an oppressor. The imagery of the apocalypse is often rife with fires, floods, storms, mysterious signs, and symbolic portents. 3. Viewed in a much more special "comic vision," the "apocalyptic world of the Bible" consists, according to Northrop Frye, of these equivalents:

Divine world   = society of gods = One God
Human world   = society of men = One Man
Animal world   = sheepfold   = One Lamb
Vegetable world = garden or park = One Tree of Life
Mineral world   = the city   = One Building or Temple

REFERENCES: Northrop Frye, "Archetypal Criticism," *Anatomy of Criticism;* Norman Cohn, *The Pursuit of the Millenium.*

apocope   See CLIPPED FORM.

apocrypha   A group of books traditionally associated with the Old Testament but not accepted as part of the CANON by Jews and Protestants because they were not written in Hebrew. The apocryphal books were not included by the translators of the Authorized (King James) Version of the Protestant Bible, but were made a part of the Catholic Bible at the time of Saint Jerome's Latin translation (see VULGATE). In spite of their disputed authenticity, the Apocrypha have had a great influence on art and literature. The best-known of the apocryphal books are Esdras, Tobit, Judith, part of Esther, the Wisdom of Solomon, Ecclesiasticus, Baruch, parts of Daniel, and Maccabees.

REFERENCES: Harold Watts, *The Modern Reader's Guide to the Bible; The Apocrypha* (Oxford World Classics); Charles C. Torrey, *Apocryphal Literature;* Millar Burrows, *The Dead Sea Scrolls;* Hugh Schonfield, *Readers' A to Z Bible Companion;* James Hastings, *Dictionary of the Bible.*

apophasis   In rhetoric, the making of an assertion while pretending to deny it. A classic example is Antony's address in *Julius Caesar:* ". . . If I were dispos'd to stir / Your hearts and minds to mutiny and rage, / I should do Brutus wrong, and Cassius wrong, / Who, you all know, are honorable men."

However annoying it may be to hear a tedious introduction to a speaker "who needs no introduction," the device of saying something by denying that you will say it has long been a staple of RHETORIC. Apophasis usually begins with such phrasing as "needless to say," "not to mention . . . ," "I need not point out . . . ," "Surely this audience need not be reminded . . . ," or the timeworn "It goes without saying . . . ." Apophasis is often a means of informing an unknowing audience while at the same time complimenting that audience by courteously asserting that it already knows. It is essentially a device of IRONY, not to mention its kinship to the COUNTER WORD.

aposiopesis   From a Greek root meaning "to be silent." A sudden interruption of thought in mid-sentence, conveying emotion or suggesting irony. In writing, the sudden silence is usually marked by a dash: "My last visit to that campus left me—well, I shall not go again."

a posteriori reasoning   Reasoning from effect to cause. (See INDUCTIVE REASONING 3; compare A PRIORI REASONING.)

apostrophe   1. In rhetoric, a brief turning aside to address a person who is not present or to address a personified object or abstraction: "Milton! thou shouldst be living at this hour." "Oh, Eden!" Ben Jonson apostrophizes his late contemporary:

> Yet must I not give nature all; thy art,
> My gentle Shakespeare, must enjoy a part.

George Peele, also a contemporary of Shakespeare, apostrophizes (in a PERSONIFICATION) his shadow:

Shadow, my sweet nurse, keep me from burning.

Today's poets are less likely to address someone (or something) not present. Apostrophe as rhetoric is now considered old-fashioned.

2. In punctuation, the apostrophe (') was originally — and in some uses still is — a mark of elision: It takes the place of something that has been omitted. Its use to form the possessive of nouns, for example, perhaps developed through elision of a syllable, so that Chaucer's line "Our hoste seyde, and swoor by goddes bones" is now written, "Our host said, and swore by *God's* bones. . . ." The Elizabethan habit of writing "his" for the possessive ("William Shakespeare his Tragedie of Macbeth") became, at least according to some historians of language, simply " 's" ("William Shakespeare*'s* Tragedy of Macbeth"). But these historical matters are of small concern to anyone bent on learning how today's English uses the apostrophe. The system is almost entirely arbitrary, and therefore can be more readily learned if the learner accepts the arbitrary without too much chafing under illogic.

The apostrophe suffers widespread abuse by those who have neglected to learn the system, and the abuses tend somewhat to affect the system, though it is not likely that competent printers and editors will adopt such errors as "Book's for sale" or "Henrys Hamburger Haven." Recent practice has, however, tended to drop the possessive inflection from many words (*baby carriage* and *executive car*); if the trend continues (from *goat milk* to *boy shoes* and *driver license*), the apostrophe may become obsolete. So far, however, the trend seems to apply mostly to possessives in which there is no clear possession: The carriage does not really belong to the baby; the goat does not now own the milk. Apostrophes have already been declared officially obsolete in many institutional names: The Veterans Administration, the Lions Club, State Teachers College, Citizens National Bank. It is also disappearing from signs: Esquire Mens Wear, Ladies Shoes, and — Henrys Hamburger Haven. And the names of post offices, by administrative fiat, are uniformly spelled without the apostrophe: Snedens Landing, Harpers Ferry, Prides Crossing.

To form the possessive of nouns, observe the following rules:
FOR THE PLURAL
(1) If the noun does not end in *s*, add *'s*.
    men : men's   children : children's
(2) If the noun ends in *s*, add ' only.
    Joneses : *Joneses'   girls : girls'   citizens : citizens'*

FOR THE SINGULAR

(3) If the noun does not end in an *s* or *z* sound, add *'s*.

  cat : *cat's*   *child* : *child's*

(4) If the noun ends in an *s* or *z* sound,

  (*a*) and it has only one syllable, add *'s*.

  James : *James's*   *boss* : *boss's*

  (*b*) has two or more syllables, and the accent is on the last syllable, add *'s*.

  Hortense : *Hortense's*

  (*c*) has two or more syllables, and the last syllable is preceded by an *s* or *z* sound, add *'* only.

  Moses : *Moses'*   *Jesus* : *Jesus'*

  (*d*) has two or more syllables, and the last syllable is *not* preceded by an *s* or *z* sound, add *'s*.

  Thomas : *Thomas's*   *Dickens* : *Dickens's*

(5) If the noun ends in an *ez* sound, and the accent is on the penultimate syllable, add *'* only.

  Achilles : *Achilles'*   *Archimedes* : *Archimedes'*

The apostrophe is also used to indicate the omission of letters, numbers, or sounds:

  we'll *can't* *o'clock* *g'bye* *'most* (for almost) *KO'd* *'39* (for 1939)

The apostrophe is also used to form plurals of figures, abbreviations, and words used as words (although some writers prefer to omit the apostrophes in such cases):

  6's *YMCA's* *if's, and's, and but's* *ABC's* *p's and q's*

If this style is followed, and two apostrophes are called for, because of a contraction and a plural, then omit the second apostrophe:

  Roaring '20s   *too many don'ts*

Note: No apostrophe is used in forming the possessive of personal pronouns: yours, its, ours, theirs, whose. The possessive of indefinite pronouns is regularly formed with the apostrophe: everybody's, someone's.

apothegm   See APHORISM.

appropriateness of illustration   An inexperienced preacher, intent on illustrating the idea that we often hurt ourselves when we cast aspersions on our enemies, told this ANECDOTE: "A soldier walked into a room of an abandoned house, where he thought he saw an enemy soldier. He fired, but *only* shattered a mirror." What the preacher had intended to imply was that the killer is his own worst enemy, as reflected in the mirror. But the soldier's success in eliminating "only" the mirror all too readily suggests that he might have been more successful had he eliminated another soldier. Confronted with this ambiguity, the horrified preacher conceded that the illustration was not appropriate.

a priori reasoning   Reasoning from cause to effect; also, reasoning from "fixed causes" or premises. (See DEDUCTIVE REASONING; compare A POSTERIORI and INDUCTIVE REASONING 3.)

archaism   1. An ancient expression, one older than just obsolete; for example, "Methinks" for "it seems to me." In *The Faerie Queene* Spenser used archaisms deliberately. 2. Conscious or unconscious imitation of the archaic or obsolete: "It behooves us to pay heed, as it were, to his every word."
REFERENCE: *The Shorter Oxford English Dictionary on Historical Principles.*

archetype   1. In mythology, the Bible, and imaginative literature, a character with whom readers readily identify because he seems to re-enact familiar experiences, especially ordeals. Thus Sisyphus, the mythological character condemned in Hades to roll uphill a boulder that always rolls down again, is an archetype. So is the biblical Job. When we read about such characters, we experience a kinship with their human condition, and we hear in their utterances echoes of our own. Among other archetypes are the stranger or outsider (Ruth), the hero who risks his life to bring progress to mankind (Prometheus), the initiate (young David), the scapegoat (Isaac), the sorceress (Circe). Some of the reader's identification may be unconscious — the collective racial unconscious described by Carl Jung. 2. According to Northrop Frye, an archetype may be not only a character but also a MODE. In the "archetype of romance," for example, there are such myths and "myth-phases" as *dawn, spring,* and *birth; birth of the hero; revival and resurrection; defeat of the powers of darkness; winter and death.*
REFERENCES: Northrop Frye, "The Archetypes of Literature, "*Fables of Identity;* Carl Jung, *Archetypes and the Collective Unconscious;* Maud Bodkin, *Archetypal Patterns in Poetry;* Joseph Campbell, *The Hero with a Thousand Faces;* J. B. Friedman, *Orpheus in the Middle Ages.*

architectonics   Structural design in works of art and literature. (See DRAMATIC STRUCTURE.)

argument   1. In logic, an ordered series of statements including the premises (or "reasons") and a conclusion drawn from those premises. (See LOGIC.) 2. In expository writing, a major reason in support of a THESIS. 3. In literature, especially that before 1800, a SYNOPSIS prefixed to a canto or a section of a long poem (such as Milton's *Paradise Lost)* and intended to give the reader an overview of what is in the piece itself.

argument against the man   Argument in which it is asserted that a proposition is false because a certain person says it is true. The validity of the assertion depends upon the man's being a "reliable anti-authority"; that is, one who is almost always wrong in his statements on the topic at hand. (See EMOTIONAL APPEALS and PROPAGANDA DEVICES.)

argument from authority   A form of ARGUMENTATION in which it is asserted that A is true because a certain person says it is. Chaucer's Chauntecleer and Pertelote, in the *Nun's Priest's Tale,* parody this form of argument, each citing a long list of authorities to support them in their views that one should (or should not) put much stock in dreams.

argumentation   Presentation and support of a thesis or proposition; one of the traditional four forms of discourse. It may employ any or all of the other forms (EXPOSITION, DESCRIPTION, and NARRATION), but it subordinates them to its own purpose, to convince.

Since argumentation must support a proposition, its method is chiefly logical. Yet because its audience is the human mind and not a computer, argumentation often benefits from emotional warmth, as long as it does not fall into fallacy or unjustified appeals to emotion. (See EMOTIONAL APPEALS.)

Good argumentation has these virtues—and avoids the opposing dangers:

Economy: The writer uses no unnecessary words.

Clarity and order: Good argumentation makes its premises clear and its conclusion unmistakable. It avoids EQUIVOCATION and AMBIGUITY. An argument that confuses an issue with the unclear or irrelevant is a failure.

Validity and thoroughness: The writer of sound argumentation carefully observes the rules of reasoning (see LOGIC) and checks his premises for accuracy of fact. He deals justly with opposing arguments, being careful not to overlook points that might invalidate his own. An argument that draws an unjustified conclusion or ignores alternatives cannot stand against challenge.

Balance: Good argumentation does not overstate its case. It neither overcomplicates an issue nor oversimplifies it. Its tone is temperate, not invidious—and though argumentation is usually based upon opinion, it is not merely opinionated.

REFERENCES: "Argument and Persuasion," in Francis Connolly and Gerald Levin (eds.), *The Art of Rhetoric;* Lee A. Jacobus (ed.), *Issues and Response.*

Arthurian romance   Any of the numerous legends, chiefly in verse, about King Arthur and the Knights of the Round Table. Among the most celebrated versions: Malory's *Morte d'Arthur* (prose version, 1471), Spenser's *Faerie Queene* (1589–96), and Tennyson's *Idylls of*

the King (1859 ff.). Chief characters in these legends are the brave King Arthur (with his magic sword Excalibur and his wizard, Merlin); his beautiful but unfaithful wife, Queen Guinevere; the knight Sir Lancelot and his FOIL, Sir Galahad; and the lovers Tristan and Isolde.
REFERENCES: E. K. Chambers, *Arthur of Britain;* Roger S. Loomis, *The Development of Arthurian Romance* and *Arthurian Literature in the Middle Ages;* J. D. Bruce, *Evolution of the Arthurian Romance;* Madeline Cosman, *The Education of the Hero in Arthurian Romance;* A. B. Ferguson, *The Indian Summer of English Chivalry;* William Matthews, *The Ill-Framed Knight;* Charles Moorman, *A Knyght There Was.*

article   A short prose piece that informs or persuades. (See ESSAY.)

aside   **1.**   A digression or a parenthetical remark sometimes figuratively called "a footnote." **2.** In drama, part of a character's dialogue intended for the audience only, and not for the play's other characters. Examples abound in William Wycherly's *Country Wife* (1675). At the beginning of the play, when Sir Jaspar Fidget asks Horner to "salute" (kiss) Lady Fidget, and the professed woman-hater Horner declines ("I have taken eternal leave, Sir, of the Sex"), Sir Jaspar in an aside to the audience says, "So the report is true . . . his coldness or aversion to the Sex; but I'll play the wag with him."

Most modern playwrights have abandoned the aside, although in Eugene O'Neill's *Strange Interlude* (1928) one or another of the characters reveals his thoughts to the audience only (usually in ironic contrast with his spoken lines) by means of prerecorded lines electronically reproduced on a public address system concealed in the trappings over the stage. Such "interior monologue" is a combination of the aside and of the STREAM-OF-CONSCIOUSNESS technique used by certain novelists. (Compare SOLILOQUY.)

assertion   An affirmation or declaration; a positing (hence a positive statement). In LOGIC either a PREMISE or a CONCLUSION may be an assertion, though in ordinary usage an assertion is presented without supporting evidence. Mere assertion is not evidence.

assonance   The repetition of internal vowel sounds usually for aesthetic effect—"*a* r*ai*n-t*i*r*a*ded cl*ay*"—or for humorous effect—"H*ow* n*ow*, br*ow*n c*ow!*" and "the r*ai*n in Sp*ai*n st*ay*s m*ai*nly in the pl*ai*n."

In poetry such sound effects as assonance, ALLITERATION, CONSONANCE, and ONOMATOPOEIA are associated with the works of Algernon Swinburne, Gerard Manley Hopkins, and Edith Sitwell in England; and with the works of Edgar Allen Poe, Sidney Lanier, and Vachel Lindsay in the United States. But poems that rely solely or mainly on these sound effects seem now to be going out of fashion, especially in poems that rhyme, in favor of the quieter and subtler effects of METAPHOR and PARADOX, as Henry Rago has observed.

assumptions   Ideas taken for granted. Practically every assertion a speaker or writer makes is based on one or another of his assumptions. Such assumptions may be explicit or implicit, conscious or unconscious; they may be susceptible to logical and factual analysis or they may be explicable only in the context of a milieu or philosophical system or point of view. Assumptions about the purpose of man, the human condition, man's place in the universe, are least often clearly stated in a work, and a deep reading may be necessary to reveal them. Assumptions in this sense may be considered the equivalent of anschauung or VIEWPOINT.

Assumptions in the sense discussed here are usually amenable to logical and factual analysis. When a speaker says, "The study of grammar does not transfer to competence in writing," he *implies* "Throw grammar out," but he *assumes* that the study of grammar should contribute to competence in writing, an assumption not accepted by most linguists.

The thoughtful listener or reader tries to identify assumptions and to ask whether they are valid. Assumptions, when stated, are often qualified by words like *all* and *some*. "Most men are rational" does not mean "All men are rational." Furthermore, the *some*ness of a statement may lie hidden or obscured. To say, "Citizens are *often* voters" is practically the same as saying "*some* citizens are voters." Something tantamount to a *some*-statement is also made when, in place of *some*, there appears a verb modifier like *sometimes, usually, often,* or *seldom*.

Conversational English freely uses the pattern "All. . .is not. . ." even though precision would call for the pattern "Not all. . .is. . ." Consider, for example, the statement "All men are not voters." It is reasonably safe to assume that the speaker meant, "Some men do not vote," rather than "All men do not vote." (See EVERY-ALL FALLACY.) *Note*: It is a good plan for the writer of an article or essay to level with his readers immediately (first paragraph, if possible) by stating one or two of his chief assumptions relating to the subject of the article. (Compare *illicit presumption* under BEGGING THE QUESTION 1.)

asterisk   A mark shaped like a little star (*), used most often to draw attention to a footnote. In some printed works, especially in earlier centuries, the asterisk was used in series to indicate an ELLIPSIS or an omission from a text; today it is seldom used for that purpose, except in poetry when a complete line or more is omitted. Its use as a censoring ellipsis was satirized by Laurence Sterne in *Tristram Shandy* (1761): "and all the world as usual, gave credit to her evidence — 'That the nursery window had not only * * * * * * ; but that * * * * * * * * * *- * * 's also.' "

asyndeton   The omission of conjunctions (chiefly *and*) between parts of a compound; literally, "lack of *and*'s." This form of ELLIPSIS, because it departs from the expected, often lends a sense of rapid movement. *Time* magazine, for example, adopted asyndeton as one of the marks of its famous Time style: "As a boy, he recalls, he tried to break up a fight, got a drubbing for his pains" (*Time,* March 20, 1964). The example omits *and* between the verbs of a compound predicate; but asyndeton can also result from omission of the conjunction between independent clauses ("I came, I saw, I conquered"). Where formal punctuation demands a semicolon, informal usage (especially that of journalists) prefers the comma. Thus asyndeton may sometimes produce what may look at first like a COMMA FAULT. Effective asyndeton is a mark of sophistication; overused, it may seem an annoying mannerism. (See POLYSYNDETON.)

Attelan comedy   See COMMEDIA DELL'ARTE.

attitude   1. The author's way of looking at his subject (material, content, topic, and so on); usually implicit in the mode — satire, comedy, tragedy, romance — and an essential clue to meaning. 2. The imagined speaker's or narrator's attitude toward unfolding experiences may be different from the author's attitude. (See PERSONA.)

REFERENCE: Walker Gibson, "Writing for Attitude," *Persona.*

aubade (also called **alba**)   Literally, "dawn song." A lyric poem dealing with the parting of lovers after a night spent together. The famous aubades of the Provençal TROUBADOURS contain these traditional elements: the watchman's song waking the lovers and telling of first light; the need for secrecy for fear of discovery by the lady's husband; chastisement of the sun for returning too soon; complaint at the need to part; the lovers' pledge of mutual fidelity. Here is Ezra Pound's "Alba" from *Langue D'oc:*

> When the nightingale to his mate
> Sings day-long and night late
> My love and I keep state
> In bower,
> in flower
> 'till the watchman on the tower
> Cries:
>> 'Up! Thou rascal, Rise,
>> I see the white
>>> Light
>>> And the night
>>> Flies.'

Other examples are Donne's "The Sunne Rising"; the "Hark, the lark, the herald of the dawn" speech in Shakespeare's *Romeo and Juliet;* and William Empson's "Aubade" with the refrain, "The heart of standing is you cannot fly."

audience   1. In communications theory, the intended receivers of the message and one of the three major polarities, the others being the "sender" and the message, or "signal." These three poles represent only the skeleton of the model, however, since rather complex processes of "encoding" take place on the sender's end and similarly complex processes of "decoding" take place on the receiver's end. There has been a ferment, in recent years, in attitudes about the importance of the audience as compared with the importance of the message — or, rather, of the medium for transmitting the message. To hear Marshall McLuhan, strongly influenced as he has been by the NEW CRITICS' tenet that in any literary work the manner is more significant than the matter, the "medium *is* the message." Critics of contemporary mass media have accused producers and publishers of irresponsible use of the media and of callous disregard of audiences. Nevertheless, publishers and disseminators of cinema and television productions do consider the preferences of the audiences, as reflected in sampling polls and in film ratings. In the end, the controversy comes down to the philosophical question of whether the audience should receive "what it wants" or whether its tastes should be constantly "elevated."

     2. In SEMANTICS, a more or less mythical entity, on the general principle that most audiences are likely to share very few referents with the speaker. The implication is that the careful speaker or writer, to avoid talking to himself, will use concrete examples that are not only pertinent to his communication but also as close as possible to the experience of his audience. There is, of course, a limit to the practicability of that procedure; its efficacy diminishes quickly: consider the classical writers' enthusiasm for EPIC SIMILE and, in "The Nun's Priest's Tale," Chaucer's satire of the exasperating narrator who proliferates his examples when he should be making a point or getting on with the story.

     3. In literary criticism certain contemporaries who are also teachers (among them Louise Rosenblatt) contend that the audience plays, or should play, an active role in "completing" any literary work; that just as a drama remains a mere "script" until experienced by a theater audience, so a poem or a narrative remains a mere script until experienced by readers in a kind of author-reader "transaction."

     4. In rhetoric the audience has long played an important role. One of the traditional guidelines of speakers and writers has been "Respect your audience." The writer who postures — "I write to please myself, and let the audience be damned" — is in the misguided minority. The novelist William Styron has said, "Look, there's only one person a writer should listen to, pay any attention to . . . the reader. The writer must criticize his own work as a reader. Every day I pick up the story . . . and read it through. If I enjoy it as a reader, I know I'm getting

along all right." Admirable as this practice may be as a beginning, the final proving ground requires the receiver and the sender to be different persons.

In recent studies of rhetoric and linguistics, especially those of Martin Joos and Walker Gibson, audience *size* has been identified as a controlling consideration in the speaker's or writer's choice, not only of vocabulary, but also of usage and PERSONA—with larger audiences eliciting more formal, smaller audiences eliciting more informal, choices.

5. In school and college composition classes an instructor may specify the audience (e.g., "myself," "your classmates," "the senior citizens of this community," "the men of this community," "the women of this community," and so on). It is obviously important to decide early upon the audience one intends to address. The writer may well ask himself, "Who will my audience be? How large will it be? What are my audience's ages, sexes, professions? What is its mood? What are its cultural biases?" The writer or speaker who asks himself these questions before he begins to write will find several related problems comparatively easier to solve—for example, decisions about vocabulary, usage, ATTITUDE, and TONE. (See PERSONA and SLANTING.)

REFERENCES: Bernard Berelson and Morris Janovitz (eds.), *A Reader in Public Opinion and Communication;* Marshall McLuhan, *Understanding Media;* S. I. Hayakawa, *Language in Thought and Action;* Louise Rosenblatt, *Literature as Exploration,* Second Edition; William Styron, [Interview in] *Writers at Work: Paris Review Interviews, 1958;* Walker Gibson, *Tough, Sweet, and Stuffy;* Martin Joos, *The Five Clocks;* William Riley Parker, "The Question of Audience," *MLA Style Sheet;* Robert Graves and Alan Hodge, *The Reader over Your Shoulder;* T. E. Pearsall, *Audience Analysis for Technical Writing;* Robert Hapgood, "Shakespeare and the Included Spectator," *Reinterpretations of Elizabethan Drama.*

audience analysis   See AUDIENCE and SLANTING.

Augustan age   See CLASSICISM and NEO-CLASSICISM.

autobiography   The story of the writer's life. The *Autobiography* of Benjamin Franklin and the *Autobiography of Lincoln Steffens* are two well-known examples. Notable experiments with this form are *The Education of Henry Adams,* in which the writer speaks of himself as "he" instead of "I"; James Joyce's *Portrait of the Artist as a Young Man,* in which the autobiographer uses PSYCHOLOGICAL INTROSPECTION and occasionally some POLYPHONIC PROSE; and Gertrude Stein's *Autobiography of Alice B. Toklas,* in which the narrator, Miss Stein's companion for twenty-five years, reveals as much about Miss Stein as about Miss Toklas. (See BIOGRAPHY.)

REFERENCE: Roy Pascal, *Design and Truth in Autobiography.*

B

babbittry   Used to describe the non-intellectual attitude exemplified by the leading character in Sinclair Lewis' novel *Babbitt*; materialistic "go-getting"; lack of sensitivity toward cultural values and things aesthetic. (Compare PHILISTINISM.)

bacchius   See METER.

balance   A symmetrical arrangement of ideas in which word matches word, phrase matches phrase, or clause matches clause. By its repetition of rhythms, as well as by its usual repetition of words and word-patterns, balance achieves a marked emphasis, and places two or more ideas in similar syntactical form. Balance occurs when the speaker or writer says *this is that, this and that, this or that,* or *this but not that;* in other words, balance may display two or more ideas as *parallels,* as *alternatives,* or as *contrasts.* To illustrate each: (1) balance of parallels: "As *ye sow,* so shall *ye reap";* "*To be great* is *to be misunderstood";* (2) balance of alternatives: "*Give me liberty,* or *give me death!*" "We must indeed all *hang together,* or, most assuredly, we shall all *hang separately";* (3) balance of contrasts: "This nation cannot exist *half slave, half free";* "Say *what you have to say,* not *what you ought.*" (For more on balance of contrasts, see ANTITHESIS.) Though balance appears most often as symmetry of clauses in a sentence, it may apply to larger elements: the parts of a paragraph or the sections of a whole work may balance one another. Like any artifice of discourse, balance may be overdone, as it was by the Greek Sophist orators and by certain Elizabethans. (See EUPHUISM.)

ballad   1. An anonymous narrative song transmitted orally; often called a *folk ballad.* The stories told by ballads are sometimes authentic historical events important to a clan or nation, sometimes adventures dealing with romantic love. A few are humorous, and many are concerned with the supernatural—seduction by supernatural figures, visitations by ghosts, detentions by evil persons or spirits, and the eruption of irrational evil into the world, as in the "demon lover" ballads where a young man takes his love for a walk and kills her for no evident reason. Whatever the subject, folk ballads are narrated with little comment or intrusion by the teller. The action and dialogue are presented for their own sake, the stress being on the situation rather than on the motivation behind it, character or development, or questions of morality. Indeed, a moral tag at the end of a folk ballad suggests a later reworking of the text.

The ballad stanza usually rhymes *abcb* and alternates a four-stress line (lines *a* and *c*) with a three-stress line (lines *bb*). Here is an example from "Little Musgrave and Lady Barnard":

> She cast an eye on Little Musgrave,
>> As bright as the summer sun;
> And then bethought this Little Musgrave,
>> This lady's heart I have won.

Two frequently mentioned stylistic features of folk ballads are their "incremental repetition" and "leaping and lingering." The first takes place when a formula introduced in one stanza, perhaps in the form of a question, is repeated in the next, but with something added or changed. In "Little Musgrave," for example, Lord Barnard asks his foot-page:

> "What news, what news, my little foot-page,
>> What news do you bring to me?
> Oh are my castle walls torn down
>> Or are my towers three?

And the foot-page replies, repeating the formula:

> "Your castle walls are not torn down,
>> Nor are your towers three,
> But Little Musgrave is in your house,
>> In bed with your gay lady."

"Leaping and lingering" refers to the tendency of the ballad to omit details we might expect—for example, a description of an ocean voyage between two points where the action takes place—and to linger over seemingly unimportant matters, such as details of a dress or the food served at a banquet.

The best-known English folk ballads include "Lord Randal," "Lord Lovel," "Sir Patrick Spens," "Barbara Allen," "King Orfeo," "Robin Hood and Maid Marian," "The Braes of Yarrow," and "Get Up and Bar the Door." The best-known American folk ballads include "Frankie and Johnny," "John Henry," "Jesse James," and "Shenandoah."

2. A literary poem written in the style of the folk ballad or in an adaptation. One of the best-known literary ballads is Coleridge's "Rime of the Ancient Mariner." Here is one of Coleridge's several different stanza forms:

> The western wave was all aflame.
> The day was well-nigh done!
> Almost upon the western wave
> Rested the broad bright Sun;
> When that strange shape drove suddenly
> Betwixt us and the Sun.

REFERENCES: G. H. Gerould, *The Ballad of Tradition;* Albert B. Friedman,

The Ballad Revival; Matthew Hodgart, *The Ballad;* Francis J. Child, *English and Scottish Popular Ballads;* Bertrand H. Bronson, *The Traditional Tunes of the Child Ballads, with Their Texts according to the Extant Records of Great Britain and America* (as the subtitle implies, this work contains careful comparisons and discussions of variant texts, including recent American variants); Bartlett J. Whiting (ed.), *Traditional British Ballads;* Arthur Quiller-Couch (ed.), *Oxford Book of Ballads;* John and Alan Lomax (eds.), *Folk Song U.S.A.: The 110 Best American Ballads* and *American Ballads and Folk Songs;* David Fowler, *Literary History of the Popular Ballad;* Bertrand Bronson, *The Ballad as Song; Harvard Catalogue of English and American Ballads.*

ballade   A French verse form consisting typically of three eight-line stanzas and a four-line *envoy*. Each of the first three stanzas rhymes *ababbcbc;* the envoy, *bcbc*. The envoy repeats the REFRAIN, which is introduced in the last line of the first stanza and repeated with or without variation in the last line or two of each of the other stanzas. As a general rule only three or four rhymes are used in the whole poem, with no rhyming-word repeated except in the refrain lines. A representative example is W. E. Henley's "Ballade of Dead Actors":

> Where are the passions they essayed,
> And where are the tears they made to flow?
> Where the wild humors they portrayed
> For laughing worlds to see and know?
> Othello's wrath and Juliet's woe?
> Sir Peter's whims and Timon's gall?
> And Millamant and Romeo?
> Into the night go one and all.
>
> Where are the braveries fresh or frayed?
> The plumes, the armors—friend and foe?
> The cloth of gold, the rare brocade,
> The mantles glittering to and fro?
> The pomp, the pride, the royal show?
> The cries of war and festival?
> The youth, the grace, the charm, the glow?
> Into the night go one and all.
>
> The curtain falls, the play is played:
> The Beggar packs beside the Beau;
> The Monarch troops, and troops the Maid;
> The Thunder huddles with the snow.
> Where are the revelers high and low?
> The clashing swords? The lover's call?
> The dancers gleaming row on row?
> Into the night go one and all.
>
> *Envoy*
> Prince, in one common overthrow
> The hero tumbles with the Thrall;

As dust that drives, as straws that blow,
Into the night go one and all.

REFERENCE: Nigel Wilkins (ed.), *One Hundred Ballades, Rondeaux, and Virelais from the Late Middle Ages.*

bandwagon   An appeal to the human readiness to "jump on the bandwagon"; that is, to approve what those around us seem to approve. This "Everybody's doing it" appeal is especially effective in PROPAGANDA. Advertisers use this device when they claim that their products are "the nation's best selling," "the most popular in the West," "the one all the kids are going for." Candidates use it when they hire opinion pollsters to establish that a majority of voters favors so-and-so. The purpose of the appeal, of course, is to attract customers or voters to do or think as "most" are said to do or think.

barbarism   1. A particular kind of SOLECISM reflecting an uncivilized or illiterate background — "the sort of thing one might expect from a foreigner," says Henry Fowler, somewhat snobbishly, in *Modern English Usage* (Second Edition). The ancient Greek noun for foreigner was indeed *barbaros,* and according to one theory of its origin (the onomatopoetic theory) the noun was applied to outsiders (that is, to non-Athenians) who, to the Athenian ear, could only babble "bar, bar, bar." From this early meaning — one who doesn't know the language — *barbarism* came to mean the misuse or mistaken combination of roots and affixes from different languages (originally, Greek and Latin languages) in the creation of new English words. Classical scholars, like Fowler, who have abhorred such hybrid creations as *electrocute, bureaucracy,* and *finalize,* have ceased to resist such coinages, regarding the process as beyond their control. Many so-called barbarisms are well established in modern English. 2. By extension, barbarism has come to mean any expression that indicates the user does not know how to use the language, or how to use it gracefully; the use of grammatical structures not found in standard speech; the use of words or phrases inappropriate to the tone, purpose, or audience. (See CATACHRESIS and SOLECISM.)

REFERENCE: J. R. Masterson and W. B. Phillips, *Federal Prose: How to Write in and/or for Washington.*

bard   1. A poet, especially one of the early itinerant Celtic poets. 2. "The Bard" — William Shakespeare.

REFERENCES: Marchette Chute, *Shakespeare of London;* Oscar James Campbell (ed.), *The Reader's Encyclopedia of Shakespeare.*

baroque   An ornate or grotesque style. Deriving from the name of a rough or irregularly shaped pearl, the term has been used to describe certain kinds of architecture, painting, music, and literature produced mainly in Europe during the seventeenth and early eighteenth centuries. Things baroque are characterized by redundance, floridness, and sometimes distortion. In architecture a baroque ceiling, for example, may be ornamented with small sculptured cherubs, personified winds and seasons, figures from classical mythology, and the like. In baroque (also Mannerist) painting, the artist strove to say something in an abnormal manner, preferring the artificial and the affected to the plain and natural. An example of the baroque in music is Bach's Toccata and Fugue in D Minor, in which the opening phrases suggest to some listeners the bloodcurdling shriek of a Hunchback of Notre Dame about to jump from the cathedral. A less prejudicial description would say that the toccata opens with a startling treble, repeats it twice, then shifts down to the organ's lowest notes, from whence it makes a return climb punctuated by heavy and grandiose chords. Of baroque style Jorge Luis Borges has said, "It exhausts its possibilities and borders on its own caricature."

In the 1960s baroque artifacts, clothing, and decor constituted one aspect of the revolt against classical (i.e., Establishment) restraints. In contemporary criticism the epithet "baroque" remains derogatory. For baroque literature is characterized by startling or farfetched imagery, excessive ALLUSION, and contorted syntax. Such characteristics were often employed self-consciously in the GOTHIC NOVEL of the middle eighteenth and early nineteenth centuries. But it was perhaps in the prose and verse of the seventeenth century that baroque was most conspicuous. The prose of Milton and Sir Thomas Browne has often been called baroque, as have the sermons of John Donne and the verse of certain METAPHYSICAL POETS, especially Richard Crashaw. Here is the first stanza of Crashaw's "The Weeper," a poem in praise of Mary Magdalene:

> Hail, sister springs,
> > Parents of silver-footed rills,
> Ever bubbling things,
> Thawing crystal, snowy hills!
> > Still spending, never spent; I mean
> > Thy fair eyes, sweet Magdalene.

REFERENCES: Wylie Sypher, *Rococo to Cubism in Art and Literature;* Rosemond Tuve, *Elizabethan and Metaphysical Imagery;* Gilbert Highet, "A Note on Baroque," "Baroque Prose," and "Baroque Tragedy," *The Classical Tradition;* Morris W. Crooll, "The Baroque Style in Prose," *Studies in Honor of Frederick Klaeber;* René Wellek, "The Concept of Baroque in Literary Scholarship," *Journal of Aesthetics and Art Criticism,* V (1946).

bathos Literally, "depth." Unconscious humor; intended loftiness; PATHOS that has failed. A classic example is the couplet in which the speaker says, "Advance the fringed curtains of thy eyes / And tell who comes yonder." See Alexander Pope, "Peri Bathous."

Beat poets   Such poets as Allen Ginsberg (author of *Howl*), Lawrence Ferlinghetti (author of *A Coney Island of the Mind*), Gregory Corso, Gary Snyder, Paul Blackburn, Kenneth Rexroth, Brother Antoninus, and Jack Kerouac (who was better known as a novelist). Ginsberg is sometimes described as "neo-Whitmanesque"; Ferlinghetti, as "neo-surrealist"; and Corso, as "neo-romanticist." The ideological forbears of the Hippies, the Beat poets, with individual differences, subscribe to antimaterialism, radical Christianity ("Make love, not war"), and certain adaptations of ZEN Buddhism. They stress oral presentation of their poems, often to the accompaninent of jazz and Oriental percussion instruments. Beat poetry usually avoids rhyme and meter and relies heavily on confession, catalog, and radical graphics, including unusual punctuation or no punctuation at all.

"Beat," a shortened version of "beatific" or "beaten down," served to describe the state of mind which the social-economic-political Establishment had allegedly induced in the generation that came of age in the late 1940s and early 1950s. At least a part of this generation —the part Jack Kerouac depicted in *On the Road* and *The Dharma Bums*—chose to disengage itself from the Cold War, from the "Establishment's spiritual bankruptcy," and from conventional society in general and to adopt its own conventions of dress, religion, sex, and drugs.

REFERENCES: Lawrence Lipton, *The Holy Barbarians;* Elias Wilentz (ed.), *The Beat Scene;* W. B. Fleischman, "Those 'Beat' Writers," *America* (September 26, 1959); Seymour Krim (ed.), *The Beats, Evergreen Review* (No. 2, 1957); Donald M. Allen (ed.), *The New American Poetry (1945–1960)*; Stephen Berg and Robert Mezey (eds.), *Naked Poetry* (this anthology contains poems by almost all of the Beat poets); "Bang, Bong, Bing," *Time* (September 7, 1959); Gene Feldman and Max Gartenberg (eds.), *The Beat Generation and the Angry Young Men.*

begging the question   An unsupported assumption of something that has yet to be proved (also called *petitio principii*). It is also known as "arguing in a circle," since it asserts (even if only by indirection) a premise and then returns to the same premise as a conclusion. Such fruitless argument takes several forms.

1. *Illicit presumption:* In arguing on one side of a question, the arguer improperly uses words prejudicial to the other side; that is, he smuggles into his premises an assumption of his conclusion. For example: "The ridiculous belief that Jones is qualified for office should be questioned seriously." (The arguer has asked us to question something—but he has already labeled that something "ridiculous" and so has prejudiced our questioning.)

2. *Circular reasoning* (or vicious circle): In attempting to establish conclusion A, the arguer supports it with premise B; but the evidence

for B lies in, or depends upon our acceptance of, conclusion A. For example: "My check is perfectly good; you may ask my friend Jack to vouch for it – and I assure you that Jack can be trusted."

3. *Tautological argument:* In the belief that he is establishing proof of something, an arguer may actually only be restating that "proof" in different words. For example: "This is the finest symphony Haydn ever wrote, because none of his others approaches it in quality." (The arguer has not offered evidence to support his statement that "none of his others approaches it in quality" – which is really the same thing as saying that the symphony in question is "the finest.")

In an interpretive essay on *Macbeth* a student was developing the thesis, "Lady Macbeth functions less as a believable woman than as Macbeth's own evil self." To this thesis he had put the question "How do we know this?" and he answered, "Because she seems more an evil spirit than a flesh-and-blood woman." But that was not an answer to the thesis question, for it repeated the thesis, as in a tautology.

belles lettres   1. Imaginative literature. In the United States, usually, poetry, drama, and fiction. 2. In England it includes items in (1) but extends to literary criticism and to "familiar essays" – e.g., Lamb's *Essays of Elia* and DeQuincey's *Confessions of an English Opium Eater*. In American usage the latter are called simply "essays" or "nonfiction prose."

bestiary   A medieval work about animals, which mingles natural history with fables and Christian ALLEGORY. Bestiaries contained chapters of varying lengths, often illustrated, treating birds, animals, fish, and sometimes a few stones and plants. Among the animals described were many fabulous ones like the manticore, chimera, phoenix, yale, and unicorn. Here is an account of the unicorn from T. H. White's *Book of Beasts; Being a Translation from a Latin Bestiary of the Twelfth Century:*

He is a very small animal like a kid, excessively swift, with one horn in the middle of his forehead, and no hunter can catch him. But he can be trapped by the following strategem. A virgin girl is led to where he lurks, and there she is sent off by herself into the wood. He soon leaps into her lap when he sees her, and embraces her, and hence he gets caught.

Our Lord Jesus Christ is also a Unicorn spiritually, about whom it is said: "And he was beloved like the Son of the Unicorns." . . . The fact that it has one horn on its head means what he himself said: "I and the Father are One." Also, according to the Apostle: "The head of Christ is the Lord." It says that he is very swift because neither Principalities, nor Powers, nor Thrones, nor Dominations could keep up with him, nor could Hell contain him, nor could the most subtle Devil prevail to catch or comprehend him; but, by the sole will of the Father, he came down into the virgin womb for our salvation. . . .

The Unicorn often fights with elephants, and conquers them by wounding them in the belly.

REFERENCES: E. and J. Lehner, *A Fantastic Bestiary;* Peter Lum, *Fabulous Beasts;* Thomas Browne, *Pseudodoxia Epidemica;* Norman Douglas, *Birds and Beasts of the Greek Anthology.*

bibliography   See DOCUMENTATION.

Bildungsroman   A novel depicting the spiritual growth or education of the hero—usually a young man—as he faces various moral and intellectual crises and meets characters representing different attitudes toward life. Some examples of the Bildungsroman are *Wilhelm Meister's Apprenticeship* (Goethe), *Joseph Andrews* (Henry Fielding), *Huckleberry Finn* (Mark Twain), *Look Homeward, Angel* (Thomas Wolfe), *Catcher in the Rye* (J. D. Salinger), and *A Separate Peace* (John Knowles). A synonymous term is *Entwickelungsgeschichte.* Another synonym is *Kunstlerroman,* the development of the artist, as, for example, *A Portrait of the Artist as a Young Man* (James Joyce) and *Tropic of Capricorn* (Henry Miller). (Compare DIDACTIC NOVEL.)

biographical fallacy   The interpretation of a literary work all too naively in the light of the author's life. While any author is in certain ways influenced by his own environment (MILIEU) and experiences, the literary piece he creates has a life and logic of its own. (Compare AESTHETIC DISTANCE.) The NEW CRITICS and other contemporary critics tend to discredit literary interpretations and explications that rely too heavily on biography. (See LEVELS OF MEANING.)

REFERENCE: W. K. Wimsatt, "Genesis: A Fallacy Revisited," in Peter Demetz (ed.), *The Disciplines of Criticism.*

biography   An exposition of a person's life. Though primarily informational, certain biographies tend to support theories or teach moral lessons. Among the latter, "DIDACTIC," biographies are the Biblical portraits of Ruth, David, and Joseph; the lives of the saints (*Acta Sanctorum,* written by the Bollandists); and the well-known Plutarch's *Lives* (of Eminent Greeks and Romans). Plutarch's biographies were also called *The Parallel Lives;* for in attempting to prove his various ethical and political theories, he often compared pairs of prominent Greeks and Romans of the same calling (e.g., Demosthenes and Cicero, orators). Plutarch's biographies in Lord North's translations provided the bases for Shakespeare's *Julius Caesar, Antony and Cleopatra, Coriolanus,* and *Timon of Athens.* What makes Plutarch readable, if not always factually reliable, is his human touch and his use of ANECDOTE. He remains not only one of the most charming of biographers but also the pioneer of collective biography.

His example was followed in such collections as Suetonius' *Lives of the Caesars*, Giorgio Vasari's *Lives of the* [Renaissance] *Artists*, Thomas Fuller's *Lives of the Worthies of England*, Izaak Walton's *Lives*, Samuel Johnson's *Lives of the Poets*, Walter Scott's *Lives of the Novelists*, William Thackeray's *Four Georges*, Lytton Strachey's *Eminent Victorians*, Hendrik Van Loon's *Lives*, Paul de Kruif's *Microbe Hunters*, Louise Tharp's *Peabody Sisters*, Jacques Barzun's *Darwin, Marx, and Wagner*, and John F. Kennedy's *Profiles in Courage*.

Another kind of biography, one's life story written by oneself, is known variously as AUTOBIOGRAPHY, DIARY, JOURNAL, memoir, and the like. One of the earliest and best known, St. Augustine's *Confessions*, illustrates by content as well as by title one of the therapeutic purposes of this genre. But most autobiographers have admitted that they could not or would not confess everything. Among the most celebrated autobiographies have been those of Benvenuto Cellini, Samuel Pepys (*Diary*), Jean-Jacques Rousseau (*Confessions*), John Stuart Mill, John Woolman (*Journal*), J. W. von Goethe, Benjamin Franklin, John Henry Cardinal Newman, Mark Twain, Maxim Gorky, Booker T. Washington, T. E. Lawrence (of Arabia), Henry Adams (*The Education of Henry Adams*), William Butler Yeats, Anne Frank (*The Diary of Anne Frank*), Simone de Beauvoir (*Memoirs of a Dutiful Daughter, The Force of Age, The Force of Circumstances*); Jean-Paul Sartre (*The Words*); and André Malraux (*Anti-Memoirs*).

Biography has perhaps yet to win recognition as an art form in its own right. It is still classified for the most part as reportage or EXPOSITION rather than as BELLES LETTRES or imaginative literature. Yet if there is a single biography that comes close to the art of re-creating a subject in as well-rounded a portrait as possible, it is James Boswell's *Life of Samuel Johnson* (1791). Even though Boswell was not a close associate, and not always a friend, he nevertheless was able to capture at first hand an in-the-flesh portrait and to quote almost verbatim Johnson's most sententious and characteristic pronouncements. These the biographer took down either immediately (to Johnson's *professed* annoyance) or soon after their utterance. Boswell also introduced in his biography certain insights that, in a later age, were hailed as "psychological introspection."

Psychological introspection, which is after all more art than science, characterized nineteenth- and twentieth-century biographies, as reflected in such well-known works as those of Lytton Strachey (mentioned above), Ernest Renan's *Life of Jesus*, Gamaliel Bradford's *Lee the American* (and many another of Bradford's "psychographs"),

Sigmund Freud's *Leonardo da Vinci*, Emil Ludwig's *Napoleon*, André Maurois' *Disraeli*, Amy Lowell's *John Keats*, Marchette Chute's *Ben Jonson of Westminster*, and A. L. Rowse's *William Shakespeare*.

Two modern biographies that combine readability with thorough scholarship are Carl Sandburg's *Abraham Lincoln* and Catherine Drinker Bowen's *Yankee from Olympus* [Justice Oliver Wendell Holmes].

Biographical dictionaries, which make no claims to art but which are useful to students, are the multivolume (British) *Dictionary of National Biography* (the *DNB*), *The Dictionary of American Biography* (the *DAB*), and *Current Biography*, the latter being chronicles of prominent people who make the news. One-volume biographical reference works are *The Concise Dictionary of American Biography*, *Who's Who* (British), *Who's Who in America*, *Directory of American Scholars*, Webster's *Biographical Dictionary*, and *American Authors*.

The use of biography and autobiography as keys to interpreting literary works has been for the most part disparaged by the NEW CRITICS. (See BIOGRAPHICAL FALLACY.) Viewed strictly as fact, biography and history may provide meaningful background, as reflected in Louis Bredvold's *Intellectual Milieu of John Dryden* and Leon Edel's life of Thoreau, which exposes *Walden*.

REFERENCES: Catherine Drinker Bowen, *Biography: The Craft and the Calling;* John A. Garraty, *The Nature of Biography;* Louis Kaplan *et al., A Bibliography of American Autobiographies;* James Clifford, *Biography as an Art;* Philip Daghlian (ed.), *Essays in Eighteenth-Century Biography;* R. H. Costa, "The Rashest Art: A Forum on Literary Biography," *Quartet* (Fall, 1969).

black humor   1. Works that are superficially humorous but at bottom gruesome and terrifying. An example is Frederic Dürrenmatt's *Physicists*. 2. A comic treatment of events that might seem pathetic or painful to other writers. The hero of a novel using black humor is usually an ingenue figure, hopeless and helpless in the grip of events but still portrayed with much satire, as is the world that crushes him. Black humor can be found in Kafka's novels and stories, Nathaniel West's *Cool Million*, Evelyn Waugh's *Decline and Fall* and *The Loved One*, and in Terry Southern's *Candy*, to name only a few. Recent novels employing black humor are much dependent upon the topical and impermanent world of popular culture. Their authors strive to give scene, dialogue, and narrative structure a light, transitory, "throw-away" quality.

REFERENCE: B. J. Friedman (ed.), *Black Humor*.

black literature   A term pertaining to literary works written by or about black people in the United States. It is generally conceded to refer to American as opposed to African works. (Thus Alan Paton's *Cry, the Beloved Country*, Leonard Boob's collection of poetry, and such fiction as that of Achebe, Senghor, and Tutuola would not be included.) Several writers of different skin colors (among them poet Robert Hayden and novelist Mark Harris) question the logic and appropriateness, in America, of classifying literature along racial separatist lines. They argue that American literature consists, rather, of GENRES. It consists, they maintain, of fiction whether written by William Faulkner or Ralph Ellison; of poetry whether written by Robert Lowell or Langston Hughes; of essays whether written by Henry Thoreau or James Baldwin; of plays whether written by Arthur Miller or LeRoi Jones. This argument aside, it is a fact that, until the 1960s, the literature of black American authors was little known, and the Negro in literature was primarily the creation of white authors. Perhaps the best-known portrayals are in *Uncle Tom's Cabin* (Harriet Beecher Stowe), *Uncle Remus* (Joel Chandler Harris), *The Adventures of Huckleberry Finn* (Mark Twain), *Strange Fruit* (Lillian Ross), *Intruder in the Dust* (William Faulkner), and, more recently, *To Kill a Mockingbird* (Harper Lee), *Black Like Me* (John Howard Griffin), and *The Confessions of Nat Turner* (William Styron).

With the emergence of increased racial consciousness and of pride in the black cultural heritage, the situation has changed. Heretofore the black writer was heard mainly through small literary magazines. Now contemporary writers are finding a broader and better informed audience, as well as a more open market for their works, and earlier black authors are being rescued from oblivion. Many of these earlier works, in particular, are being reassessed and reissued, although it would seem that most will remain of interest primarily to scholars and historians. Among the most celebrated works by black authors are *Up from Slavery* (Booker T. Washington), *The Life and Times of Frederick Douglass, The Souls of Black Folk* (W. E. B. DuBois), *Autobiography of an Ex-Colored Man* (James Weldon Johnson), *Native Son* (Richard Wright), *Invisible Man* (Ralph Ellison), *The Fire Next Time* (James Baldwin), *A Raisin in the Sun* (Lorraine Hansberry), *The Autobiography of Malcolm X, Soul on Ice* (Eldridge Cleaver), and the poetry of Paul Lawrence Dunbar, James Weldon Johnson, Countee Cullen, Langston Hughes, Gwendolyn Brooks, and LeRoi Jones.

REFERENCES: Arna Bontemps, *Golden Slippers: An Anthology of Negro Poetry;* John Henrik Clarke (ed.), *American Negro Short Stories;* James Emmanuel and Theodore Gross (eds.), *Dark Symphony;* Milton Meltzer (ed.), *In Their Own Words;* William L. Katz (ed.), *Eye Witness;* Sterling Brown, "A Century of Negro Portraiture in American Literature," *Massachusetts Review* (Winter, 1966); Dorothy Sterling, "The Soul of Learning," *English Journal* (February, 1968); Charlemae Rollins, *We Build Together;* Abraham Chapman, *The Negro in American Literature;* Addison Gayle (ed.), *Black Expression;* Robert Hayden (ed.), *Kaleidoscope;* John Henrik Clarke (ed.), *Ten Black*

Writers Reply to Styron's "Nat Turner"; Alan Lomax and Raoul Abdul (eds.), *3000 Years of Black Poetry* [includes Africans].

blank verse   Unrhymed iambic pentameter. This verse form, used by Shakespeare in his plays (although the first English play to use it was Norton and Sackville's *Gorboduc,* 1561), was the most widely used verse form in the history of English poetry and drama up to the twentieth century. In 1557 Henry Howard, Earl of Surrey, published a blank verse translation of Vergil's *Aeneid* (the original Latin having used dactyllic hexameters), and in the same year Surrey and his contemporary Sir Thomas Wyatt (who had imported the sonnet form — at least, the Petrarchan form — into England from Italy) published blank verse in *Tottel's Miscellany.* Wyatt and Surrey thus established the trend that modern English verse was to follow for more than four centuries. Here is an excerpt from Surrey's translation of Vergil:

> The Greeks' chieftains, all irkëd with the war
> Wherein they wasted had so many years,
> And oft repulsed by fatal destiny,
> A huge horse made, high raisëd like a hill, . . .

In reading this blank verse, one tends to drop one's voice at the end of each line, a phenomenon that suggested the label "end-stopped" and George Saintsbury's "single moulded line," as distinguished from ENJAMBEMENT, the effect produced by the kind of line whose sense flows into the next line without a logical or phonological break. Such run-on lines in blank verse were to be developed first by Christopher Marlowe. Although a study of Marlowe's blank verse reveals that only about a fourth generates enjambement, most of his lines do demonstrate an ingenious variety of stresses within the line. Here, for example, is Marlowe's Mephistopheles in *The Tragical History of Doctor Faustus:*

> Hell has no limits, nor is circumscribed
> In one self place; for where we are is hell,
> And where hell is there must we ever be.

It was Shakespeare, however, who demonstrated a remarkable virtuosity with blank verse. A comparative study of his earlier plays, for example, *Two Gentlemen of Verona* and *Love's Labour's Lost,* with such later plays as *Macbeth* and *The Tempest* reveals an increased number of run-on lines, along with a host of other developments beyond the scope of this article. Compare these lines from *Two Gentlemen*

> Here can I sit alone, unseen of any,
> And to the nightingale's complaining notes
> Tune my distresses and record my woes.

with these lines from *The Tempest*

> Where should this music be? i' th'air or th'earth?
> It sounds no more! And sure it waits upon
> Some god o' th'island. . . .

Notice, incidentally, the conventions and cliché statements in the *Verona* lines as contrasted with the disarming questions and the invention in the lines from *The Tempest*. Shakespeare has yet to be surpassed in blank verse.

The tradition of enjambement in blank verse was carried forward by John Milton in *Paradise Lost* (1667). Milton also demonstrated talent in varying the stresses within lines. In defending his use of blank verse, he called it

English Heroic Verse without Rime . . . Rime being no necessary Adjunct or true Ornament of Poem or good Verse, in longer Works especially, but the Invention of a barbarous Age, to set off wretched matter and lame Meeter [sic]

but he also resorted to an artificially poetic line (see POETICISM), distorting modern English syntax and sound patterns while echoing Vergil:

> Of man's First Disobedience, and the Fruit
> Of that Forbidden Tree, whose mortal tast[e]
> Brought Death into the World, and all our woe,
> With loss of Eden, till one greater Man
> Restore us, and regain the blissful Seat,
> Sing Heavnly Muse. . . .

Milton's laureate successor, John Dryden, deprecated blank verse (*Essay of Dramatic Poesy,* 1668), although he used it himself in the play *All for Love* (1671). Dryden and Pope preferred to cultivate rhymed iambic pentameters, especially the HEROIC COUPLET, and their brilliance seems to have outshone even posthumously the blank verse of poets like James Thomson ("The Seasons," 1726), Edward Young ("Night Thoughts," 1742), and William Cowper ("The Task," 1785).

But with the publication of William Wordsworth's *Prelude* (1850) blank verse was once again vindicated, and all its most admirable possibilities revived. Aside from natural syntax and sound patterns Wordsworth accommodated it to an appropriate lexicon—"a selection of language really used by men," as he observed in the Preface to the second edition of *Lyrical Ballads* (1800). (Although *The Prelude* was not published until 1850, he had been working on it since the turn of the century and had practically completed it by 1805.) Here is a representative passage from *School-Time,* Book Two:

> We ran a boisterous course; the year span round
> With giddy motion. But the time approached

That brought with it a regular desire
For calmer pleasures, when the winning forms
Of Nature were collaterally attached
To every scheme of holiday delight
And every boyish sport. . . .

Almost every major poet of the nineteenth century—among them Keats, Tennyson, and Browning—used blank verse, especially in such longer poems as *Hyperion* (1820), *Idylls of the King* (1859), and *The Ring and the Book* (1868). In the twentieth century blank verse was used by T. S. Eliot (notably in *The Waste Land,* 1922), by Robert Frost, and by W. H. Auden. But even these poets used less blank verse than FREE VERSE and rhymed forms. After 1950 blank verse suffered a decline, and it now seems to be giving way to free verse and to more experimental forms.

REFERENCES: Alex Preminger, *Encyclopedia of Poetry and Poetics;* George Saintsbury, *A History of English Prosody;* John Thompson, *The Founding of English Metre;* Roy Harvey Pearce, *The Continuity of American Poetry.*

bluestocking   An eighteenth-century term for an intellectual woman; for example, Fanny Burney, author of *Evelina,* and Lady Mary Wortley Montagu, traveler, writer, and introducer of smallpox inoculation into England.

bombast   Pompous language or stuffy style or both. Bombast is noise overstuffed with words, words overstuffed with pretentiousness. It is "rhetorical" in the worst sense (see RHETORIC); the overuse of devices of speech when the occasion demands a light and sparing use. Its chief marks are long words (when short ones would do); circumlocution (see DEADWOOD), EUPHEMISM, and stock EPITHETS. When learned men use bombast, it is pedantic; when unlearned men use it, it tends to be full of MALAPROPISM and MIXED METAPHOR. (See GOBBLEDYGOOK.)

bon mot   A witty remark.

book review   A brief invitation to read a book that the reviewer has enjoyed. By "brief" is meant anywhere from a hundred to five hundred words, depending on space limitations of the newspaper or magazine that has agreed to look at, and perhaps publish, what has been written. One reviewer's enjoyment of the book is indispensable, for more often than not the newspaper or magazine that will print a review prefers (*a*) to educate, if possible elevate, its reader's tastes; and (*b*) to avoid, if possible, attacking a shoddy book, to say nothing of even reviewing it. An adequate review gives only such factual elements as will suffice to identify the book—not such factual elements as may tend to substitute for a reading of the book itself (not, that is, the whole plot of a novel). The reviewer should settle on one interesting aspect that may whet the reader's curiosity or appetite. One of the best ways to do this — assuming a first-rate book — is to quote a key short passage, then suggest how this quoted piece reflects a major theme, characterization, issue, or even the writer's style. One caution: a reviewer must check with the publisher on how many words may be quoted (the limit for a review is liberal, but there is a limit).

REFERENCES: "Book Reviews," in John Crowe Ransom (ed.), *The Kenyon Critics;* Anne Davis, "The ABC's of Book Reviewing," in A. S. Burack (ed.), *The Writer's Handbook; The Book Review Digest; Publishers' Weekly; The New York Review of Books; The Saturday Review.*

bowdlerized   Expurgated or "cleaned up"; after Thomas Bowdler (1754–1825), editor of *The Family Shakespeare* (1818), from which he deleted certain words that he felt were appropriate for adults only.

REFERENCES: Noel Perrin, *Dr. Bowdler's Legacy: A History of Expurgated Books in England and America;* Bertrand Russell, "Mr. Bowdler's Nightmare," *Nightmares of Eminent Persons;* Marvin Rosenberg, Appendix: "A Kind Word for Bowdler," *The Masks of Othello.*

brackets   The pairs of square-cornered marks, [   ], that are so easily confused with PARENTHESES. Their uses are almost entirely scholarly:

1. To enclose editorial addition or comment within matter being quoted: "You may observe [said Sir Arthur Wardour, speaking of Jonathan Oldbuck] that he never has any advantage of me in dispute. . . ." — Sir Walter Scott. "To err is humane [*sic*]; to forgive, divine."

2. To enclose the correction of an error in matter being quoted: "The Roosevelt inauguration on January 20 [March 4], 1933, launched a whirlwind program."

3. To enclose information supplied by the editor: "He was a lifelong admirer of [Teddy] Roosevelt's."

4. To enclose parenthetical matter within parentheses: "An age of scientific discovery gave rise to defenders of literature (including John Stuart Mill [see p. 90] and Matthew Arnold)."

5. To enclose symbols in phonetic transcription: "By assimilation, [ŋ] has become [n] in *congress* [kɑngrəs]."

brief   An abridged statement, summary, or abstract of the content of a written work. (See PRÉCIS.) In law, a brief is either a short statement of a legal argument or a formal, documented outline of the argument.

broad reference   See FAULTY REFERENCE.

broadside ballads   The most popular of all ballads and songs during the Tudor and Stuart reigns. These ballads were usually of anonymous authorship, especially when politically risky. They were printed on one side of a printer's unfolded sheet and introduced with a large title and sometimes an attractive woodcut. Purchasers used them not only for entertainment, very much as purchasers used sheet music during the early 1900s, but also for decoration of walls, much as people today decorate walls with posters. One of the most popular in its day, and well known even today, was the broadside ballad "Greensleeves" (1580), whose chief repeated stanza went (in a slightly modernized spelling):

> Greensleeves was all my joy,
> Greensleeves was my delight;
> Greensleeves was my heart of gold,
> And who but my Lady Greensleeves?

The royal court intrigue reflected here, if any, is now for the most part lost to us. But consider the possibilities of veiled meanings in this broadside ballad that was hawked in the streets, possibly in alleys, of London during the reign of Henry VIII (occasionally married, occasionally divorced, occasionally a widower):

> The hunt is up, the hunt is up,
> And it is well-nigh day;
> And Harry our king is gone hunting
> To bring his deer to bay!

Among the subjects of ballads—besides politics, court intrigue, and gossip—were current events, personal feuds, and the last words of criminals before execution.

REFERENCES: Charles H. Firth, "Ballads and Broadsides," *Shakespeare's England;* "Broadside Ballads," in J. William Hebel and Hoyt H. Hudson (eds.), *Poetry of the English Renaissance (1509–1660).*

bromide   A dull, stereotyped remark offered as if it were an original thought. "It isn't *what* you know—it's *whom* you know," says the spouter of bromides. The bromide may be obviously true (see TRUISM) or open to question; in either case it lacks originality. (See CLICHÉ, PLATITUDE, STEREOTYPE, and TRITENESS.)

Brook Farm   A nineteenth-century New England intellectuals' club and experiment in practicing the kind of life advocated by TRANSCENDENTALISTS, Unitarians, and other liberal Christians. As members or guests, at one time or another, there worked at Brook Farm, in West Roxbury, Massachusetts, such celebrities as Ralph Waldo Emerson, Nathaniel Hawthorne, Horace Mann, William Channing, Charles Dana, Bronson Alcott, Washington Allston, Margaret Fuller, and Elizabeth Peabody.

REFERENCES: Van Wyck Brooks, *The Flowering of New England,* Chapter XII; Henry Sams (ed.), *Autobiography of Brook Farm.* For a fictional portrait: Nathaniel Hawthorne, *The Blithedale Romance.*

burlesque   1. A form of "strip-tease vaudeville" or "follies" popular in

English and American music halls before the era of television. **2.** In literature, an extended farce or take-off, usually an extravaganza, in which the characters are caricatures (persons with exaggerated features) of fictional or real-life counterparts. By its use of exaggeration, burlesque resembles PARODY; but the two forms differ, since burlesque has to do with subject or character and parody with form or manner of expression. In a burlesque, hilarity usually exceeds bitterness, if any. The operettas of Gilbert and Sullivan, for example, are burlesques of several nineteenth-century empire-builders. Among the most celebrated burlesques is John Gay's *Beggar's Opera* (1728), in which the vices of certain public officials under England's King George I (d. 1727) are ridiculed, as are the follies of a society that idolized highwaymen and other criminals even when it punished them with hanging.

buskin   In ancient Greece, the bootlike footwear of actors in a tragedy. (Compare SOCK.)

C

cacophony   The result of a disagreeable combination of sounds, although its use is not always a flaw. Unintended cacophony, however, when not suited to the sense of its context, mars expression; but skilled writers often employ cacophony deliberately to emphasize a discordant idea or unpleasant image.

Whatever is difficult to pronounce is likely to be cacophonous—jawbreaking juxtaposition of sound. Jingles that use excessive ALLITERATION, hissing sibilants, unintended rhymes, or needless repetitions of a word may produce cacophony. Though no sounds in English are themselves essentially unpleasant, an insistence upon any one sound may tax the ear—especially a close piling-on of explosive *stops* (*p, t, k, b, d, g*) or of the harsher *fricatives* (*ch, j*). Cacophony consists in what Sir Walter Raleigh called the "unfit or untuneful phrase." (Contrast EUPHONY.)

cadence   The rise and fall of a person's voice as he reads a passage aloud. Though most poets, in "counting syllables," assign either a heavy or a light stress to each syllable, they do not intend that the reader echo this counting; neither do they intend that the reader drop his voice automatically at the end of every line. Rather, the intention is that the oral reading be as natural and contextual as possible. In "Stopping by Woods on a Snowy Evening," for example, Frost may have counted out "He will not see me stopping here," but many a reader says, "HE will not see me STOPping here." Similarly, the sensitive reader does not drop his voice at the end of the line "The only other sound's the sweep," but, rather, reads, "the sweep / of easy wind and downy flake."

As early as 1894, in a letter to editor Susan Hayes Ward, Robert Frost observed, "I have not succeeded in revising my poem ['My Butterfly'] . . . the line, 'These were the unlearned things,' is wretched . . . the would-be cadence may be incorrect also . . . when once I doubt an idiom, my ear hesitates to vouch for it thereafter."

caesura   A pause taken by an oral interpreter in reading literature, especially poetry. Thus, in the line "This is the forest primaeval, the murmuring pines and the hemlocks," the comma marks the caesura. There is also a caesura, although a weaker one, after "pines." Caesura is essentially what linguists mean by "pause" or "juncture."

Calvinism   1. The system of theological thought expounded by the Frenchman John Calvin (born Jean Chauvin) in *The Institutes of the Christian Religion* (1536) and adopted by his Protestant followers. His doctrinal descendants in England, Scotland, Holland, and America were known variously as Puritans, Presbyterians, Separatists, and Congregationalists. Departing from Luther, who had believed in the subordination of church to state, Calvin argued for a theocratic state, the kind of society that came in fact to dominate Geneva (Switzerland), parts of Holland, and Puritan New England in the sixteenth and seventeenth centuries. The five chief tenets of Calvinism, along with their corollaries, were (*a*) total depravity of mankind ever since Adam's fall ("In Adam's fall / we sinned all," said the hornbook studied by seventeenth-century children in New England): even infants were subject to eternal damnation; (*b*) limited atonement: man's hereditary corruption only partially atoned for by Christ; no automatic redemption; salvation only for those infused with the Holy Spirit; (*c*) irresistible grace: grace available only to the elect of God; (*d*) predestination: absolute power of the will of God, man's inability to exercise free will, and the superiority of faith over good deeds; (*e*) perseverance of saints by predestination, election, and conversion: even a saint might not recognize his good fortune (his election) until he experienced a regeneration, an "inner light."

Unlike the damned, who, unaided by God, were incapable of suppressing their evil natures, the elect by nature lived a righteous life. Nevertheless, to determine God's will on specific matters of daily existence, they had to consult God's revealed word, the Bible. And the correct interpretation of the Scriptures required a literate and educated mind. Thus the fostering of education, particularly among New England Calvinists, became a religious duty. Moreover, a deep concern for moral conduct and an earnestness about this life, the prelude for the next, encouraged a sense of thrift and hard work. The so-called Protestant ethic of perseverance and industry owes much to Calvinism. On the other hand, Calvinism could also give rise to a strait-laced, sanctimonious way of life and impelled some leaders to attempt what now would be considered an unwarranted control of the personal lives of others and a rigid suppression of various entertainments and fashions no longer considered evil. Although the Five Points comprised the main doctrine of Protestant reformed churches originally, their intractable austerity gradually gave way to some of the rationalism of the eighteenth and nineteenth centuries.

2. In English and American literature Calvinism and anti-Calvinism have had a profound influence. Calvinistic puritanism outlawed the comic muse from the English stage and sent it underground from 1649 to 1660. In America Calvinism undergirded such theological and historical works as Michael Wigglesworth's *Day of Doom* (1662), Cotton Mather's *Magnalia Christi Americana* (1702), and Jonathan Edwards's

Sinners in the Hands of an Angry God (1741). These works were faithful to the letter and spirit of the Five Points. Other works hazarded revisionist interpretations of one or another of the original tenets, or were inspired by the liberalization. Regeneration or conversion is a well-known example. Conversion—experiencing an inner light—could turn out in practice to be possible for ordinary parishioners, not just ministers and saints. Annie Bradstreet secular, for example, could become Mistress Anne Bradstreet the divine after she looked into her heart and versified her discoveries about "Flesh and the Spirit." Her collected poems, *The Tenth Muse Lately Sprung Up in America* (1650), echoed the sacred/profane conflicts and ambivalences in John Donne's poems, especially "The Extasie" and "Of the Progress of the Soul," but hardly competed with his metaphysical wit and invention.

Meanwhile, back in the Mother Country, where the Colonists' archetypal poet was John Milton, the Fall of Man was being celebrated in *Paradise Lost,* the epic poem Milton published in 1667. But in justifying God's ways to Man, Milton argued that free will, not absolute predestination, has a good chance of prevailing. (Milton—like Locke, Newton, and Franklin—was quite unorthodox in this respect.) Later, in *Samson Agonistes* (1671), Milton tried to reconcile in an almost autobiographical context (he had his own Delilah and his blindness) reformed Protestantism with certain antithetical orthodoxies, among them conflicting doctrines of backsliding, atonement, and redemption.

Man's precarious mission in this life—to shun evil, pray for grace, seek salvation—was graphically outlined in *The Pilgrim's Progress* (1678), perhaps the most popular allegory of all time. It was written by the Puritan preacher John Bunyan while he was imprisoned by the Stuart regime.

All Five Points, especially the practical consequences of their elaborations, their "laces and bows," were irreverently lampooned by Jonathan Swift in *A Tale of a Tub* (1704). Swift's *Tub* elicited a spate of essays pro and con, among them Anthony Ashley Cooper, Third Earl of Shaftesbury's *Characteristics of Men, Manners, Opinions, and Times* (1711, 1713). The 1713 edition contained the essay "An Enquiry Concerning Virtue," which in turn elicited from Bernard Mandeville *An Enquiry into the Origins of Moral Virtue, the Fable of the Bees, or Private Vices, Public Benefits* (1714). In the *Fable of the Bees,* Mandeville downgraded do-goodism and "good works," as had Calvin, but went on to discourage all virtue and religious restraints as delusions. In fact, he satanically championed selfishness as responsible for all human progress and nationalistic empire building.

If England was to lose its American colonies in one sense, however, nobody could ever take away the contributions made by the English

Dissenters to colonial and early national culture—especially the impact made by such families as the Cottons, the Mathers, the Edwardses, and their descendants. For example, Timothy Dwight (1752–1817), the grandson of Jonathan Edwards, was one of the most prominent Calvinists in America during the beginning decades of the United States. Aside from serving as pastor of the Congregational Church at Greenfield Hill, Connecticut, he collaborated with John Trumbull and other "Connecticut Wits" in introducing contemporary English literature into the Latinate curriculum of Yale College, of which he eventually became president. One of his famous sermons, later published as the pamphlet *Folly, Guilt, and Mischief of Duelling* (1805), was inspired by the duel between his cousin Aaron Burr and Alexander Hamilton. But Dwight is remembered most for his Calvinist convictions on theocracy and federalism, as expounded in *The True Means of Establishing Public Happiness* (1798).

Public vs. private happiness was a major issue and theme in the prose and poetry of the late 1700s and early 1800s, especially of three such romanticists as Percy Bysshe Shelley (1792–1822), author of *Prometheus Unbound* (1820); his father-in-law William Godwin, a Calvinist minister who later defected and who, in *An Inquiry Concerning Political Justice and Its Influence on General Virtue and Happiness,* denied the whole notion of innate depravity; and the Godwins' and Shelleys' friend and relative (through marital ties without benefit of clergy) George Gordon, Lord Byron (1788–1824). Byron is not generally associated with Calvinism, although often with Satan and Satanic themes. *Don Juan,* an uncompleted satirical poem which he began in 1818, is full of guilt-ridden intrigues that the hero undertakes after his mother banishes him from Seville because of liberties he has taken with Donna Julia. (The legendary libertine Don Juan, incidentally, appears in a dream of Tanner's in George Bernard Shaw's play *Man and Superman* and insists, with typical Calvinist misogyny, that far from pursuing women, *he* is the pursued. Such a posture comes close to representing the real-life Byron.) Again, in Byron's *Manfred* (1817) the protagonist, a haunted recluse, dies in his attempt to resist evil and fails to atone for some unspeakable and unrevealed sin. Byron, whose mother was a strict Calvinist, never outgrew the Calvinistic influences of his childhood. As Bertrand Russell has put it, "Calvinism, which he never shook off . . . made him feel that his manner of life was wicked." Of course, Byron did lead an unconventional life, judged by any standards, but "wickedness, he told himself, was a hereditary curse in his blood, an evil fate to which he was predestined by the Almighty."

But perhaps the most unmistakable Calvinist influences in the nineteenth century are reflected in the stories and novels of Nathaniel Hawthorne and Herman Melville. Hawthorne's stories "The Minister's Black Veil" (1836) and "Young Goodman Brown" (1856) and his novels *The Scarlet Letter* (1850) and *The House of the Seven Gables* (1851) are exhibits in point. The brooding dark guilt feelings of Hawthorne's Reverend Mr. Hooper, Goodman Brown, and the Reverend Mr. Dimmesdale are matched only by the depraved obsessions of Melville's Captain Ahab in *Moby Dick* (1851) and Petty Officer Claggart in *Billy Budd* (written in the late 1800s; published 1924). Of Hawthorne, Melville wrote: "This great power of blackness in him derives its force from its appeals to that Calvinistic sense of Innate Depravity and Original Sin." But perhaps Hawthorne was less critical of Puritanism than of the Puritans who failed to practice what they preached. Of Melville, F. O. Matthiessen wrote: "Though deeply impressed by the . . . Puritans' conception of evil, his mind moved away from a fixed system of theology." (As for Hawthorne's and Melville's contemporary Edgar Allan Poe, his macabre tales about murderers, ghouls, and graves are not rooted in Calvinism but rather in the kind of ROMANTICISM that undergirds the GOTHIC NOVEL.)

A nineteenth-century American dropout from Calvinism was Harriet Beecher Stowe (1811–96), daughter of the celebrated Calvinist minister Lyman Beecher. She gained fame for her novel *Uncle Tom's Cabin* (1852), which aroused millions of readers against slavery and unwittingly contributed an ironic epithet to the lexicon of the 1960s, although paradoxically enough she herself was not an Abolitionist. But in a less well-known novel, *The Minister's Wooing* (1859), she attacked the injustices of Calvinism and thus obliquely explained her eventual apostasy.

As for Total Depravity—that motif has been subject and object of hundreds of novels, plays, poems, and essays. The depravity of the human heart and that "moral sense" which somehow accommodates tortures, hypocrisies, inequalities, and other inhumanities, are depicted not only in the works of Hawthorne and Melville but also in such well-known works as Mark Twain's *Adventures of Huckleberry Finn* (1884) and "The Mysterious Stranger" (1916); Henry James's "Beast in the Jungle" (1903); Joseph Conrad's "Heart of Darkness" (1905); Ford Maddox Ford's *Good Soldier* (1915); W. Somerset Maugham's "Miss Thompson" (1921); Theodore Dreiser's *American Tragedy* (1925); Sinclair Lewis's *Elmer Gantry* (1927); and George Santayana's *Last Puritan* (1928).

But to this power of blackness certain American and Scottish–American Calvinists in the late 1800s (among them, Andrew Carnegie and Anthony Comstock) opposed the powerful light of industry and perseverance, reviving the ethos that had enabled Puritan and Pilgrim to endure and prevail. Carnegie, for example, wrote *The Gospel of Wealth* (1889) and founded the Carnegie public libraries. Comstock, a self-appointed censor, as reflected in *Traps for the Young* (1883), policed what went into those libraries, organized YMCA cultural improvement groups and the New York Society for the Suppression of Vice. This Protestant Ethic became the staple of many dime novels, especially those of Horatio Alger, Jr. (1834–99), which by the early 1900s had sold over twenty million copies. On a higher plane of literary excellence a champion practitioner of this ethos was the hero of Mark Twain's fantasy *A Connecticut Yankee in King Arthur's Court* (1889).

Over the years "perseverance of saints" has been dramatized in novels and plays (to say nothing of melodramas), notably in versions of the sainthood of the Maid of Orleans. Mark Twain's fictionalized Joan of Arc (1896), in which the heroine is a kind of impeccable maiden schoolteacher, is much less credible than George Bernard Shaw's *Saint Joan* (1923). Shaw's Joan is a real saint complete with Irresistible Grace. Although the historical Joan was born a Catholic a century before Calvin, she was in many respects "one of the first Protestant martyrs and one of the first apostles of nationalism," as Shaw observed in the Preface to this play. Nor was Shaw as ironic about Joan's Irresistible Voices as he was about her enemies, the corrupt cartel of Feudal Lords and Organization Bishops. Both Shaw and Clemens thus personified in Joan some of the nobler aspects of Calvinistic Protestantism, notably the rights and responsibilities of the individual.

But the Perseverance of Saints was not minted without an obverse side—the reality of Satan. Just as saints were the elect of God, so witches and heretics were the chosen representatives of Satan. As such, they were not to be spared for Hell-fire if they could be burned at the stake in the upper world. (Calvin himself had set the example by putting the torch to the heretical Dr. Michael Servetus in 1553.) It is a witches' sabbath, a veritable WALPURGISNACHT, that lures Hawthorne's Goodman Brown away from home; and in *The House of the Seven Gables* the atmosphere is permeated with the curse pronounced on the narrator's family, the Pyncheons, when his great grandfather was a judge in the Salem witchcraft trials. Witch-hunting, by no means the exclusive preserve of the Salem orgies and Calvinist New England, has been the subject of many literary works, one of the more recent being Arthur Miller's play *The Crucible* (1953).

Among other modern plays that have grappled with Calvinist, anti-Calvinist, and existentialist issues are Samuel Beckett's *Waiting for Godot* (1954) and Archibald MacLeish's *J.B.* (1958).

REFERENCES: J. T. McNeill, *The History and Character of Calvinism;* James Holly Hanford and James W. Taaffe, *A Milton Handbook,* Fifth Edition;

F. M. Krouse, *Milton's Samson and the Christian Tradition;* F. R. Leavis, "John Bunyan," *The Common Pursuit;* George Lyman Kittredge, *Witchcraft in Old and New England;* Vernon L. Parrington, *The Colonial Mind;* John Berryman, *Homage to Mistress Bradstreet;* Ralph Barton Perry, *Puritanism and Democracy;* Howard Mumford Jones, *O Strange New World;* A. T. Davies, *John Calvin and the Influences of Protestantism on National Life and Character;* Leslie Stephen, "Godwin and Shelley," *Hours in a Library;* Bertrand Russell, "Byron," *History of Western Philosophy;* Herman Melville, "Hawthorne and His Mosses," in Jay Leyda (ed.), *The Viking Portable Melville;* T. Walter Herbert, "Calvinism and Cosmic Evil in Moby Dick," *PMLA* (October, 1969); F. T. Matthiessen, "The Vision of Evil," *American Renaissance,* or in Walter Sutton and Richard Foster (eds.), *Modern Criticism;* Harry Levin, *The Power of Blackness;* Van Wyck Brooks, "New England at Large," *The Flowering of New England;* C. H. Foster, *Rungless Ladder: Harriet Beecher Stowe and New England Puritanism;* James M. Cox, "The Muse of Samuel Clemens," in Justin Kaplan (ed.), *Mark Twain, a Profile;* Lionel Trilling, "Huckleberry Finn," *The Liberal Imagination;* Mark Twain, "Andrew Carnegie," in Bernard De Voto (ed.), *Mark Twain in Eruption;* Burton Hendrick, *The Life of Andrew Carnegie;* Richard Henry Tawney, *Religion and the Rise of Capitalism;* Heywood Broun and Margaret Leech, *Anthony Comstock, Roundsman of the Lord;* Herbert Mayes, *Alger, a Biography Without a Hero;* Norman O. Brown, "The Protestant Era," *Life Against Death;* W. K. Wimsatt, "Poetry and Morals," in Eliseo Vivas and Murray Krieger (eds.), *The Problems of Aesthetics.*

camp   A cult name for a style characterized by elegant artifice, extravagance, theatricality, outlandishness, dandyism, hedonism, and innocent revolt against stereotyped sex patterns, high seriousness, and boredom. In the 1960s such a style was observable in certain clothing, furniture, movies, plays, novels, and rock 'n' roll music. In this sense the term first appeared in Christopher Isherwood's novel *The World in the Evening* (1954) and gained popularity after its discussion by Susan Sontag in a *Partisan Review* article in 1964. Miss Sontag listed, among other examples of Camp, Tiffany lamps, lighting fixtures shaped like flowering plants, Scopitone films, Gaudi's architecture, Aubrey Beardsley's drawings, Oscar Wilde himself, Greta Garbo and Mae West, *King Kong, Vanessa, Zuleika Dobson,* Jean Cocteau's plays, beaded dresses, long hair on men, and trousers on women. (Compare BAROQUE.)

REFERENCE: Susan Sontag, "Notes on Camp," *Against Interpretation.*

canon   1. A critical standard. 2. The authorized books of the Bible. 3. A catalogue or official list of an author's works. The Shakespeare canon, for example, consists of (*a*) works verified to be Shakespeare's, (*b*) works verified to be those on which he collaborated, and (*c*) works ascribed to him but not verified as his. (Compare APROCRYPHA.)

REFERENCES: David V. Erdman (ed.), *Evidence for Authorship: Essays on Problems of Attribution, with an Annotated Bibliography of Selected Readings;* Richard Altick, *The Art of Literary Research.*

cant   **1.** The special vocabulary used by a group to conceal meaning from outsiders; e.g., thieves' cant. **2.** The use of stock words or phrases that produce an affectedly pious, insincere tone; the hypocritical use of religious or moralistic JARGON.

canto   From *cantus,* "song." A book or a section of a book written in verse; a major division of a long poem, as in Dante's *Divine Comedy* and in Scott's *Lady of the Lake.*

capa y espada   See CLOAK AND SWORD.

capitalizing   Capital letters developed from two aims: to beautify and to emphasize. The first capitals, or head letters, were the ornamental initials of hand-lettered books. All letters other than the first of a page or chapter were of the same size and were unadorned; indeed, in such manuscripts almost no punctuation was used, and spacing between words was rare. Reading became easier when punctuation was added to mark stops—and easier again when capital letters came to be used to begin each new sentence.

Desire for emphasis led to the use of capitals to begin proper names, in some places the device being extended to all nouns. Common nouns have seldom been capitalized in English, however, except during the eighteenth and nineteenth centuries—and then not by all writers. The heavy capitalizing by Samuel Johnson and Thomas Carlyle was never consistent.

Generally, lower-case letters are easier to read than capitals, except such a short and thin letter as *i.* The use of capital *I* for the first-person pronoun in English developed because of the tendency of the single *i* to get lost on the printed page.

Currently, the trend, particularly in newspapers, is toward a "down-style," the use of fewer capitals. Some newspaper stylebooks call for lower-case letters even in such things as Main *street,* Presbyterian *church,* and U.S. *army.* Standard usage, however, still dominates the printing industry as well as the schools, and the most-used forms are Main *Street,* Presbyterian *Church,* and U.S. *Army.*

The use of capitals for special emphasis is now quite unpopular and is confined almost entirely to PERSONIFICATION, as in, "We quail when Politics speaks, for its voice is the voice of Taxation."

In Standard American usage capitals are used:

1. To begin utterances:
    a) full sentences: Men say that a stitch in time saves nine.
    b) minor sentences: Why not? In a minute.
    c) full sentences after a colon: We have one complaint: The air in here is stifling.

d) full sentences used as complements of verbs: The difficulty is, How does one find the time for writing?

e) full sentences following item-markers: By definition: (1) Method is the order to be observed in any series of operation. (2) Demonstration is the deducing of a new truth from two known truths.

f) full or minor quoted sentences: He asked, "Where is my book?"

2. To begin each line of formal poetry, although some poets use lower-case letters to produce a special effect.

3. To begin a formal resolution or question: *Resolved,* That this organization acknowledge. . . .

4. To begin proper names:

a) persons: Abraham Lincoln, Ernest Hemingway

b) places and special geographical features: Europe, Brazil, the South, New York, Fifth Avenue, Rocky Mountains, Grand Canyon, Pacific Ocean, Missouri River, Yosemite National Park, the Orient

c) organizations and institutions: University of Chicago, American Legion, Lutheran Church, General Motors

d) buildings, ships, aircraft, trains, and brand names: Chrysler Building, Eiffel Tower, Ile de France, Starjet, Super Chief, Pennzoil

e) special time designations: Monday, Tuesday, May, September, Memorial Day, Hallowe'en, Stone Age, Renaissance, Christian Era

f) special events, historical or other: Reign of Terror, Reconstruction, Battle of the Bulge, Olympic Games, World Series

g) special documents and treaties: Magna Carta, Declaration of Independence, Alliance for Progress

h) languages: German, Latin, Russian, Sanskrit

5. To begin adjectives derived from proper names: American, Chinese, Legionnaire, Shakespearea 1, Californian, Democratic. Certain other adjectives are not capitalized: oriental, southern, italic, platonic. Names that have become common nouns by METONYMY are *not* capitalized: quisling, java, martini, gerrymander, boycott

6. To begin nouns or abbreviations that are followed by numerals: Room 24, Chapter 10, Psalm 23, Article V, No. 6. Minor literary subdivisions are not capitalized: p. 123, ll. 12–14, verse 12.

7. To begin titles before proper names: Mr. Danley, Dr. Carruthers, Senator Towne, Professor James, Captain Ellis. Such titles are not capitalized when used appositively after names, except in reference to the President of the United States: Jacob Javits, senator from New York; Richard M. Nixon, President of the United States

8. To begin first and last and all principal words in titles except short conjunctions, short prepositions, and *a, an,* and *the: How Thinking Is Written, The Way of All Flesh, War and Peace, Il Trovatore,*

"Stopping by Woods on a Snowy Evening," *Los Angeles Times, The New York Review of Books*

9. To name language courses and numbered or lettered courses, and courses with special titles: Greek, French, History 7A, Philosophy 21, The Age of Pope and Dryden, Contemporary Economics. Names of studies are not otherwise capitalized: "She's taking history, philosophy, biology, and literature."

10. For the pronoun *I* and the interjection *O:* O when will I listen to experience!

11. To begin the name of the Deity and all nouns and pronouns referring to Him: God, the Father, the Source of all creation; and the names of sacred books: Bible, Koran, Talmud; of religions: Judaism, Buddhism, Christianity; of persons belonging to religions or denominations: Jews, Buddhists, Christians, Mohammedans, Unitarians; and of all deities other than the pagan: Jehovah, the Prophet

12. To begin words of family relationship when they do not follow a possessive: "What did Mother say?" "This is Father." *But* "This is my father."

13. To begin abbreviations of titles, academic degrees, eras, and proper nouns: Mrs., Dr., Ph.D., B.C., A.D., Wash., Calif.; and for all-initial abbreviations: TVA, UCLA, UN, JFK

14. To begin nouns used as personifications: How firmly Virtue replies to the error of Vice; how Faith overcomes Despair!

15. To begin epithets that substitute for or are attached to proper names: Catherine the Great, the Scripture, Holy Writ, Honest Abe

16. To name specific academic classes when they refer to an entire class in a specific school: the Freshman class at Yale, the UCLA Senior class; but not when freshman, sophomore, junior, and senior are general designations or when they refer to an individual: a freshman, the sophomore year, senior studies; Knowles, the junior

17. For the foreign particles *le, la, de, du, di* when they do not follow a name or title: D'Artagnan, De Gaulle, La Rochefoucauld, "L'Allegro," Du Bartas. Do not capitalize these particles when they follow a first name or title: Charles de Gaulle, the Duc de la Rochefoucauld, Gabriele d'Annunzio. Foreign names fully naturalized in English are exceptions, although some families prefer to follow foreign usage: Thomas De Quincey, but Alfred I. du Pont.

18. To begin scientific names of phyla, classes, orders, families, and genera: Chordata, Mammalia, Carnivora, Castoridae, Panthera. Not capitalized are the names of species or English derivatives from scientific names: leo, sapiens; chordate, mammal, carnivorous

19. To begin the salutation and the complimentary close of a letter: Dear Mr. Brown, Very truly yours. Do not capitalize adjectives in

salutations or any word but the first in the close: My dear Sir, Yours sincerely

20. To distinguish letters used to indicate form or shape: T bar, I beam, U turn; or to differentiate phenomena: X ray, Vitamin B

card-stacking   Biased argument in which pertinent evidence for one's own view is emphasized and pertinent evidence against it is suppressed. The device also includes any biased interpretation of evidence, biased statistics, and biased choice of words. Card-stacking is also a fallacy in statistical induction. (See INDUCTIVE REASONING 2.)

caricature   An exaggerated representation of a person or action. (Compare BAROQUE and THEOPHRASTAN CHARACTERS.)

carmen figuratem   A poem printed in a pattern that signals part of the poem's meaning. "The long tail of the Mouse" in *Alice in Wonderland* (Chapter III) is a well-known example. (See CONCRETE POETRY 2.)

carol   1. A dance; also spelled *carole*. 2. A song sung at such a dance; e.g., the folk carol, "Here We Go Round the Mulberry Bush." 3. A literary song; e.g., Charles Wesley's Christmas carol, "Hark, the Herald Angels Sing."
REFERENCES: Percy Dearmer *et al.* (eds.), *The Oxford Book of Carols;* Roger L. Green (ed.), *The Early English Carols;* E. K. Chambers and F. Sidgwick (eds.), *Early English Lyrics;* David Cecil (ed.), *The Oxford Book of Christian Verse;* Carleton Brown, *Religious Lyrics of the Fifteenth Century.*

carpe diem   Literally, "Seize the day"; or "Make hay while the sun shines" or "Make the most of your opportunities." In literature, especially poetry, a prevalent theme; e.g., Herrick's "Gather ye rosebuds while ye may" and Marvell's "But at my back I always hear / Time's winged chariot hurrying near," in which the poets urge the ladies addressed to become more active lovers before it is too late.

casuistry   1. In modern RHETORIC, a kind of right-and-wrong ambiguity arising out of issues of conscience, although more often than not the term has a derogatory connotation. 2. In medieval literature, a lovers' code of conduct also known as "love casuistry." (See COURTLY LOVE.) 3. In seventeenth-century literature, a devout Christian's code of conduct also known as "case casuistry" and "case divinity." This code embraced rules of behavior to be adopted by a person in dealing with himself, with other persons, and with God. The classic piece spelling out how to behave in church and out is George Herbert's poem "The Church Porch," widely reprinted in anthologies of seventeenth-century verse.
REFERENCES: H. J. C. Grierson, *Metaphysical Poetry of the Seventeenth Century;* Louis Martz, *The Meditative Poem;* Joan Bennett, *Five Metaphysical Poets;* Hugh Kenner, *Seventeenth Century Poetry;* Alexander Witherspoon and Frank Warnke (eds.), *Seventeenth Century Prose and Poetry.*

catachresis The misuse of words, by carelessness rather than by design. It may include almost any verbal mistake, or SOLECISM, such as the use of *infer* for *imply,* "nucular" for *nuclear,* or *except* for *accept.* Catachresis may also include MALAPROPISM and MIXED METAPHOR, as in Sheridan's *Rivals* and Smollett's *Humphrey Clinker.* Since popular misuse of a word tends to "catch on," catachresis often contributes to language change and development.

catastrophe Literally, "downfall." In tragic drama, the final scene, in which most of the characters die or are dying. (While dying, incidentally, they give long speeches: *Hamlet:* "O good Horatio . . . / Absent thee from felicity awhile, / And in this harsh world draw thy breath in pain, / To tell my story" — this some dozen lines *after* he has said, for the second time, "Horatio, I am dead.") The term catastrophe is appropriate not only because it describes a theater stage strewn with the mighty fallen but also because it describes the culmination of the plot action, which has been "falling" since the CLIMAX. (See DRAMATIC STRUCTURE.)

categorical syllogism See SYLLOGISM I.

catharsis The "purging" or cleansing of a spectator's or reader's emotions by means of emotional agitations. The term, used by Aristotle in *The Poetics* in the description of TRAGEDY, has been much debated and analyzed. It is generally taken to mean that the play-goer who hangs on every word and action of a drama and who is stirred to pity and terror may say to himself, "I'd never want to get into *that* kind of mess!" Such a spectator has experienced *catharsis;* he leaves the theater a better person (at least for a few hours) than he was when he entered. Catharsis, while usually a phenomenon experienced by the spectator, may also be experienced by one of the few characters who do not die in a tragic drama. Thus, Horatio in *Hamlet* will undoubtedly "absent" himself "from felicity [death] awhile."

REFERENCES: Aristotle, *The Poetics;* Lily Bess Campbell, *Shakespeare's Tragic Heroes;* "The Power of the Word," in Margot Astrov (ed.), *American Indian Prose and Poetry;* D. M. Hill, "Catharsis," *Essays in Criticism.*

causal induction See INDUCTIVE REASONING.

causal reasoning Reasoning about causes and effects. *This need not be fallacious,* though it often is. The general fallacy in causal reasoning is that a supposed result ("effect") is mistakenly ascribed to one or another innocent "cause." This fallacy, in which the effect turns out on close examination not really to have followed from the alleged cause, is called a NON SEQUITUR. ("The fault [cause], dear Brutus, is not in our stars / But in ourselves.") More often, non sequiturs do not need elaborate examination — they are perfectly obvious: "Something the Lastradonians ate caused them to make war." Among several kinds of non sequiturs there is a special kind involving an immediate time factor, the fallacy known as POST HOC.

cavalier From the Latin, "horseman." Having the characteristics of libertinism, elegance, wit, and high spirits. Specifically, one of the followers of the Cavalier party of Charles I. (See CAVALIER POETS.)

Cavalier poets. A group of witty and clever young poets—chiefly Thomas Carew, Sir John Suckling, and Richard Lovelace—who served as courtier-soldiers at the court of Charles I (1625–49) and so were identified with the King's Cavalier (Royalist) party. Their lyrical verse, written for the entertainment of the court and marked by grace, elegance, high spirits, and wit, often sounded the note of CARPE DIEM. Their themes turned generally on love and chivalry. Though not courtiers, such other seventeenth-century poets as Robert Herrick and Edmund Waller are usually classed with the Cavalier poets because their verse is characterized by the same lyrical sensuousness. The oft-recited Cavalier lines "Gather ye rosebuds while ye may" are from Herrick's "To the Virgins to Make Much of Time." And perhaps the most famous Cavalier poem of all is the same poet's "On Julia's Clothes":

> Whenas in silks my Julia goes,
> Then, then, methinks, how sweetly flows
> That liquefaction of her clothes.
> Next, when I cast mine eyes and see
> That brave vibration each way free,
> Oh, how that glittering taketh me!

REFERENCES: J. William Hebel and Hoyt H. Hudson (eds.), *Poetry of the English Renaissance* (1509–1660); John F. Danby, *Poets on Fortune's Hill.*

censorship See OBSCENITY.

central intelligence See FOCUS OF NARRATION.

chapbook A small penny book or pamphlet sold by "chapmen" or peddlers, mostly in Elizabethan England. Even more so than BROADSIDE BALLADS, chapbooks were anonymous or pseudonymous, especially those that contained political attacks on people in high places. A celebrated exception, a *signed* chapbook, was Robert Greene's *Groatsworth of Wit Bought with a Million of Repentance* (1592), containing an envious slur on Shakespeare as "that Shakescene." REFERENCE: *Harvard Catalogue of English and American Chapbooks.*

characters See THEOPHRASTAN CHARACTERS, DRAMATIC STRUCTURE, SPEAKING VOICE.

chiaroscuro "Light and shade." In painting, and by extension architecture, sculpture, music, poetry, and so on, representation by means of contrasts—light and dark, loud and quiet (*fortissimo* and *pianissimo*), fast and slow, and so on. Yeats said that in poetry he preferred "silences" between substantive words (including contrast words) in order that the latter might count for more.

REFERENCES: William Butler Yeats, "The Cutting of an Agate," *Essays and Introductions;* Paul Valéry, "On Literary Technique," *The Art of Poetry;* Eugene Delacroix, *The Journal;* Henry Adams, *Mont St. Michel and Chartres.*

chiasmus   A rhetorical device in which the two end-words and the two inner-words share respectively common parts of speech; for example, "handsome lads and maidens fair" (adjective noun and noun adjective). Chiasmus also produces a contrast of ideas by a sort of reverse parallelism. In "She would be *always true, false never,*" the contrasted elements appear in reverse order. Phrases or clauses may be reversed to produce chiasmus: "Vigor is the way of youth; the way of age is wisdom"; "We succeed if we persevere; if we falter, we fail." (See also ANTITHESIS, BALANCE, and PARALLELISM.)

chivalric romance   A metrical or a prose narrative with a backgound of court, kings, knights, ladies, love, adventure, intrigue, and religious fervor. The term is a synonym for medieval romance. From the eleventh to the fifteenth century many French romances were translated into English. Two of the most celebrated were *Guy of Warwick* (ca. 1300) and Malory's *Morte d'Arthur* (fifteenth century). The exaggerated prowess attributed to the hero of romances in the 1300s was parodied in the portrait of Sir Thopas, in *The Canterbury Tales* (1387). (See also COURTLY LOVE and METRICAL ROMANCE.)

choriamb   See METER.

chorus   1. In Greek drama, the group of actors who, while participating in the action to some extent, serve mainly as observers of the other characters. The Greek chorus spoke in unison, as one character, and usually moved in unison as well, in the slow stylized motions by which the tragedies were "danced." In Sophocles' *Oedipus Rex,* the Theban Elders, a collective body, participate by advising the king of the citizens' point of view, greeting newly entered characters, questioning the messenger, and so on. Their more important function, however, is to witness and comment upon Oedipus's curse on the unknown polluter of Thebes and his gradual discovery that the accursed person is himself. Traditionally, the chorus represents the Greek middle way— "nothing overmuch"—and mistrusts extremes of feeling or action on the part of the protagonist. In its role of witness it is able both to intensify the audience's reactions by giving them audible expression and to raise questions which the playwright wishes his audience to think about—for example, the forces behind Oedipus's downfall, the possible absence of a consistent and ordered rule of divine beings. With ancient Greek formalities, but with Christian ideology, T. S. Eliot used the chorus in his play *Murder in the Cathedral* (1935).

2. In modern popular songs, the repeated verse or refrain between the "story" verses; usually it is the chorus that is the memorable part of the song.

3. In the modern theater, especially in musical comedy, the girls who sing and dance and punctuate the story-line with thematic, often feisty, comment. Such interruptions by the chorus (or chorus line) in modern musical comedy are designed more to entertain than to enlighten the audience. In the fiction of F. Scott Fitzgerald, Ring Lardner, and Sinclair Lewis, the chorus girl is stereotyped as (*a*) coming from the lowest socio-economic stations, (*b*) rising fast in the glamorous worlds of theater, fashion, and finance, (*c*) stealing the affections of other women's fiancés and husbands, whose intentions are originally dishonorable, and (*d*) failing to win social acceptance even after marrying into the upper classes.

REFERENCES: H. D. F. Kitto, *Greek Tragedy;* Friedrich Nietzsche, *The Birth of Tragedy.*

circular reasoning   See BEGGING THE QUESTION 2.

circumlocution   Roundabout statement (See DEADWOOD 3.)

classic   1. A work of art so universal in appeal that it has transcended the boundaries of time and place; it has survived the "tests of time." 2. One of the GREAT BOOKS. *Note.* A *classic* should not be confused with a *classical work,* which is a work written in Greek or Latin before the fall of the Roman Empire, or with *classic* (standard) examples.

classical   Pertaining (1) to things Greek and Latin or (2) to classicism.

classicism   The spirit of art characterized by traditional form, with greater emphasis on reason than on emotion. A good deal of balance, of bilateral symmetry, characterizes classical furniture, music, and rhetoric. Such taste especially characterized eighteenth-century France and England (the age of Voltaire, Pope, and Johnson.) Eighteenth-century England was called the "Augustan" age because many statesmen and writers of the time imagined England to be a kind of recreation of the age of the Roman emperor Augustus and the Roman poets Vergil and Horace. In literature and art, classicism reflects the standards and models of Greek and Roman antiquity and thus inclines toward order, repose, symmetry, and an intellectual, objective view of life. Classicism is often contrasted with ROMANTICISM, the two supposedly corresponding to contrary impulses in man's nature. On the one hand, man desires solid traditional values and perhaps needs to have his emotions controlled and his thoughts positive and clear. On the other hand, he loves individual expression, intoxication, and passion, and he yearns for the faraway and the unobtainable. From age to age, the pendulum of fashion has swung between classicism and romanticism — most notably, toward classicism in the seventeenth and eighteenth centuries and toward romanticism in the nineteenth. But it is a misconception that any writer can be classed exclusively as a classicist or as a romanticist. Even the most "classical" of classical writers sometimes express profound emotion. Perhaps it can only be said that they tend to purify their emotions by subjecting them to the simplicity of universal designs.

The major principles of classicism may be summarized as follows:

1. *Imitation of the ideal.* Because he sets high value on order and stability, the classical artist seeks to portray what he considers to be lasting and universal in life, to represent what is typical and essential in man or nature rather than what is individual, transitory, or accidental. He strives, in short, to present life in its essential purity or idealized form. The classic Greek hero, for example, whether in drama or in marble art, is simple in form and appears almost godlike, lifted above the level of everyday life to superhuman stateliness.

2. *Practical-mindedness.* Even in idealizing, however, the classical artist's chief concern is with life present and observable, with things essentially as they are. Because his outlook is highly objective, it does not proceed far beyond the horizon to things exotic, faraway, ethereal, or mysterious. Even so great a flight of the imagination as Jonathan Swift's *Gulliver's Travels* has a rational, sobering air of truth in its acid criticism of contemporary human society.

3. *A taste for civilization.* The classicist tends to favor the town over the countryside, civilized society over primitive life — even in pastorals his shepherds and shepherdesses are likely to have an urbane air. And his novels of country life usually focus on the cultivated gentry, with scant attention paid to the raw farmhand (except, perhaps, when he is ridiculed). The refined products of society are more interesting to him than are the effusions of wild nature — he prefers formal parks and forums to the irregularities of jagged mountains and untamed fields and forests. Madame de Staël's château on Lake Geneva, for example, faced landward onto formal, harmoniously proportioned gardens, as the antiromantic T. E. Hulme observes.

4. *Moderation.* Self-control, restraint, the "golden mean," "nothing to excess" all describe the classicist's handling of his art. His products of high seriousness are marked by repose, graceful symmetry, and harmony of parts. He avoids emotionalism, discordance, romantic embellishment, and individualism. In satire and comedy — modes in

which he is usually more successful than the romanticist—his critical targets are extremism, pretension, pettiness, bigotry, pedantry, and the other forms of excess that he finds intolerable.

5. *Adherence to traditional form.* A deep respect for tradition and a desire to communicate clearly within a framework familiar to everyone incline the classical artist toward the use of traditional literary and artistic forms. He rejects innovations and complexities of design, for these might puzzle his audience. Thus, the eighteenth-century English poets wrote chiefly in HEROIC COUPLETS, a traditional English verse form that is sonorous, clear, and neatly rounded. (Greek and Roman EPIC POETS had used the DACTYLIC HEXAMETER; the French, the ALEXANDRINE.) In drama the classicist adheres to the traditional UNITIES. (Compare ROMANTICISM.)

REFERENCES: Gilbert Highet, *The Classical Tradition;* Walter Jackson Bate, *From Classic to Romantic.*

cliché   When a bit of FIGURATIVE LANGUAGE becomes widely repeated, it is on its way to becoming a cliché—an expression too worn to bear fresh meaning. Because it comes to mind too easily, the cliché ordinarily falls short of exactness; it lures the user into the rut when his topic demands that he explore the higher ridges. Thus, because he never pushes his thought to its possibilities, the user of clichés produces only triteness and platitude; he neglects his responsibilities and leaves the reader's mind as numb as his own.

Repeated use alone does not make a cliché, for many phrases occur repeatedly in speech and writing and do not offend: *the only way, the same thing, if you please, more often than not* have not become clichés; they say what they mean. But *the shadow of a doubt* and *a bee in your bonnet* are used when there is no thought of shadows or of apiary headgear. Clichés are usually figurative in basis, and under analysis prove impertinent to the context. It is inexactness of expression, not repetition, that makes the cliché.

For a discussion of some nonfigurative language that offends by overuse and inexactness, see also BROMIDE, PLATITUDE, STEREOTYPE, TRUISM.

REFERENCES: Eric Partridge, *A Dictionary of Clichés;* William Sparke and Clark McKowen, *Montage;* Barnet Kottler and Martin Light, *The World of Words;* Herbert Reed, *English Prose Style.*

climax   The highest point; the culmination of a rising suspensive action within a scene or within the over-all plot of a story, novel, or play. (See DRAMATIC STRUCTURE.)

clipped form   A word made by clipping off one of its parts; e.g., *intro* for introduction. The clipping of an initial sound is *apheresis;* the clipping of a final sound is *apocope;* the clipping of a middle sound is *syncope.* Examples of apheresis, syncope, and apocope: *specially,* for especially; *gen'ral* for general; *supposin'* for supposing.

cloak and dagger   A label for the fiction and drama of espionage and intrigue. British examples include John Buchan's *Thirty-Nine Steps* (1915); Graham Greene's *Stamboul Train* (1932) and *Our Man in Havana* (1958); Ian Fleming's "James Bond" series; and the spy stories of Len Deighton. (Compare CLOAK AND SWORD.)

cloak and sword   A label for the fiction and drama of swashbuckling romance and adventure, whether historical or pseudo-historical, usually revolving around aristocracy, athletic heroes, perspicacious ladies, and a chivalric code that leads to sword or pistol duels or both. The expression is a translation of the Spanish [*comedia*] *capa y espada,* the cloak and sword having been part of the attire of the nobility and upper middle class in the sixteenth and seventeenth centuries. The master playwrights of cloak-and-sword comedy in Spain were Lope de Vega (1562–1630) and Pedro Calderón (1600–81). In modern times some cloak-and-sword romances have been *The Three Musketeers* (1844) and *The Count of Monte Cristo* (1845) by the French novelist Alexandre Dumas; and *Cyrano de Bergerac* (1897) by the French playwright Edmond Rostand. British examples include Anthony Hope's *Prisoner of Zenda* (1894) and Daphne Du Maurier's *Jamaica Inn* (1936). American examples include Charles Major's *When Knighthood Was in Flower* (1898) and George Barr McCutcheon's "Prince of Graustark" series (1901–1914). (Compare CLOAK AND DAGGER.)

close reading   See DEPTH READING.

closed   1. "Complete in itself," as in reference to a line, a COUPLET, a verse, a QUATRAIN, or any other STANZA. (Contrast ENJAMBEMENT.) 2. Of a literary work, one that seems to have only one level of meaning. (Contrast OPEN BOOK.)

coherence   The quality of effective relation among the elements of a discourse—the "sticking together" of those elements. Clear connection among the parts of an utterance (from the phrase up to the long literary work) depends upon the care given to (1) sequence of ideas—a proper arrangement in time, space, or logic; (2) consistency of subject—a constant focus upon the central element as the grammatical subject of most sentences; (3) repetition of key words; (4) clear reference of pronouns to key nouns; (5) parallelism—the use of similar structures for ideas of similar function; (6) careful transition—words and phrases that lead clearly from one idea to the next.

colon   A mark of punctuation (:) used chiefly as an introducer, an indication that an example, explanation, or division of what went before is about to follow. The colon is used:

1. To announce an example or list of examples:

What danced through her mind were pictures: last year's Christmas tree, the mud on Jamie's shoes, the grocer's frown as he weighed the turkey.

2. To announce a restatement in apposition to what has gone before:

Art is long: it comes only to him who persists.

3. To announce an explanation of what has gone before:

She could hardly invite him to dinner: there was nothing but ice in the refrigerator.

4. To announce the body of a statement after a conventional salutation or introduction:

Dear Sir: We hereby resolve:

5. To announce a list of parts or members of what has been generally named:

The whole family went: mother, father, son, daughter, and pet turtle.

In addition, the colon is used conventionally for miscellaneous technical problems.

6. To separate hours from minutes in writing the time of day, to separate chapter from verse in Biblical references, to separate volume number from page numbers in bibliographical references:

6:24 P.M.   Matthew 5:20   *Atlantic* 209:73–77

7. To separate place of publication from name of publisher in a formal bibliographical entry:

Chicago: Follett Publishing Company, 1965

8. To separate a cue line from the speech in a dramatic script:

ALGERNON: Oh! it is absurd to have a hard-and-fast rule about what one should read and what one shouldn't. More than half of modern culture depends on what one shouldn't read.

9. To separate the terms in a mathematical ratio:

$$5 : 19 = 32 : x$$

Should a capital letter follow a colon? Yes, if what follows the colon would ordinarily be capitalized or if what follows the colon is capitalized in an original that is being quoted. (See CAPITALIZING.)

When a colon is used with quotation marks, the colon always goes outside:

Two things can be said about "style": It is indefinable, and it is unmistakable.

Any colon that appears at the end of quoted matter is dropped, so the colon never appears just before a quotation mark.

comedy   1. One of the major MODES. 2. A play, not necessarily humorous, designed primarily to amuse, as distinguished from TRAGEDY, which is designed to evoke such emotions as pity and terror. The protagonist of a comedy almost always solves his major problem (instead of being overcome by it, as is the protagonist in tragedy). But such a solution may not necessarily be happy as far as society is concerned. (Compare, for example, some of the comedies of George Bernard Shaw.) Nevertheless, most comedies do engage both protagonist and audience in more laughter than tears, more satire than reportage, more thought than emotion.

The earliest Greek comedy consisted of loose episodes, choruses, and ritual dialogues in honor of Dionysus, the god of fertility. (*Comedy* is the Greek term for Dionysian revel.) It was not until the advent of Aristophanes (died ca. 388 B.C.) that Greek Old Comedy developed plot structure along with brilliant wit, repartee, and SATIRE. Celebrated plays by Aristophanes are *The Clouds* (a satire on sophists), *The Knights* (a satire on politicians), and *Lysistrata* (a comedy in which the Athenian women boycott their husbands to end a war). The Greek New Comedy, chiefly the plays of Menander (died ca. 291 B.C.), was characterized by much less wit and satire and by more clichés of plot and characterization, especially the character of humours. There now appeared such stereotypes as the braggart soldier, the libertine master, and the insolent slave. This kind of play, along with the stereotyped comedy-of-errors plot, was soon imitated by the Roman playwrights Plautus and Terence, who flourished in the second century B.C.

During the early Christian era, classical comedy practically disappeared, no doubt because the early Church fathers regarded the theater as frivolous and irreverent. Nevertheless, comedy managed to survive in certain folk plays and festivals, especially in the FARCES and MORALITY PLAYS of the Middle Ages. Nor was this comedy always as crude as is usually supposed, even if crudity and slapstick did characterize a few of the best-known CRAFT CYCLE PLAYS (the Wakefield *Noah* and the Chester *Deluge*) and later, in the sixteenth century, the Italian COMMEDIA DELL'ARTE.

During the English renaissance, comedy revived, and was developed in several forms. John Heywood wrote some of the best-known INTERLUDES, especially *The Playe of the Four P's* (ca. 1521). Nicholas Udall and John Lyly revived the classical New Comedy, as did Shakespeare in *The Comedy of Errors*. Ben Jonson developed the comedy of humours — creating characters, later to be stereotyped, like the parasite (in *Volpone*) and the woman-hater (in *Every Man in His Humour*). Shakespeare also created such humour-characters as the glutton-souse Falstaff and the egregious fool Malvolio. But both Jonson and Shakespeare raised their characters above classical stereotypes by adding a good many individualistic traits and bringing in much local London color. Shakespeare's genius prompted him to range even further, in a repertoire that included, as well, tragicomedy and such romantic comedies as *The Tempest, Twelfth Night,* and *As You Like It.* The last play represents typical Shakespearian virtuosity in realizing the double vision of romance and anti-romance, or comic realism.

The closing of the London theaters by the Puritans in 1642 produced an eighteen-year hiatus in comedy, but it resumed with éclat at the restoration. Such comedies as George Etherege's *Man of Mode* (1674), William Wycherly's *Country Wife* (1675), and William Congreve's *Way of the World* (1700) were marked by wit, brilliant repartee, and much sexual innuendo. Because restoration comedies satirized contemporary manners, mores, sports, and pastimes, they came to be called "comedies of manners." Because of their urbane wit, they also became known as "high comedy," to distinguish them from the "low comedy" and buffoonery of the interlude. The comedy of manners retained its popularity through most of the eighteenth century, especially with the often-produced plays mentioned above and with Oliver Goldsmith's *She Stoops to Conquer* (1773) and Richard Brinsley Sheridan's *School for Scandal* (1777).

Comedy suffered an eclipse at the beginning of the nineteenth century, especially during the early years of Queen Victoria's reign. But after the middle of the century it returned, at first somewhat cautiously, and then hilariously, in the operettas of W. S. Gilbert and A. S. Sullivan (*H. M. S. Pinafore,* 1878, and *The Pirates of Penzance,* 1880) and in the sophisticated plays of Oscar Wilde (*The Importance of Being Earnest,* 1895) and George Bernard Shaw (*Candida,* 1898, *Man and Superman,* 1905, and *Pygmalion,* 1913). At the same time there appeared the sentimental comedies of James M. Barrie (*Peter Pan* and *What Every Woman Knows*) and the Irish comedies of J. M. Synge (*The Playboy of the Western World*) and of Sean O'Casey (*Juno and the Paycock* and *The Plough and the Stars,* the latter surcharged with tragic irony).

Celebrated comedies, including musical comedies, of the first half of the twentieth century include *The College Widow* (1904) by George Ade; *Abie's Irish Rose* (1922) by Anne Nichols; *Showboat* (1927) by

Edna Ferber, Jerome Kern, and Oscar Hammerstein; *See Naples and Die* (1929) by Elmer Rice; *Bittersweet* (1929) by Noel Coward; *The Green Pastures* (1930) by Marc Connelly; *Of Thee I Sing* (1932) by George Kaufman and George Gershwin; *The Time of Your Life* (1940) by William Saroyan; *South Pacific* (1948) by Richard Rodgers and Oscar Hammerstein II; *The Matchmaker* (1954) by Thornton Wilder, a revision of an earlier play and the basis of the musical *Hello, Dolly!* (1963).

Recent experimental comedy includes the BLACK HUMOR of playwrights like Samuel Beckett (*Waiting for Godot*) and Eugene Ionesco (*Rhinoceros*). Nevertheless, most plays and cinemas continue to be comedies; tragedy, with some few exceptions, seems to have been left to another time, another place. (See DRAMATIC STRUCTURE.)

REFERENCES: F. M. Cornford, *Origins of Attic Comedy;* Hazelton Spencer (ed.), *Elizabethan Plays;* Dougald MacMillan and Howard Mumford Jones (eds.), *Plays of the Restoration and Eighteenth Century;* Charles M. Gayley (ed.), *Representative English Comedies;* M. C. Bradbrook, *Growth and Structure of English Comedy;* Joseph Wood Krutch, *Comedy and Conscience after the Restoration;* George Meredith, *The Idea of Comedy and the Uses of the Comic Spirit;* Northrop Frye, "Comic Fictional Modes," *The Anatomy of Criticism;* John J. Enck *et al.* (eds.), *The Comic in Theory and Practice;* Henri Bergson, "Laughter," in Wylie Sypher (ed.), *Comedy;* R. W. Corrigan (ed.), *Comedy: Meaning and Forms;* Paul Lauter (ed.), *Theories of Comedy;* C. L. Barber, *Shakespeare's Festive Comedy;* W. K. Wimsatt (ed.), *The Idea of Comedy;* Louis Kronenberger, *The Thread of Laughter;* James Feibleman, *In Praise of Comedy.*

comedy of humours   See HUMOURS.

comic relief   In drama and fiction, the humorous scenes or episodes presented between tragic or serious scenes in order to relieve the audience's tensions. A classic example is the scene in *Macbeth* in which the wry porter chatters his earthy speculations about the people knocking at the gate as he goes to answer them. His soliloquy delays the opening and aggravates the knocking, but the low comedy serves as a relief after the more intense episodes of murder.

REFERENCE: Thomas De Quincey, "On the Knocking at the Gate in Macbeth," in Philip Stern (ed.), *Selected Writings of Thomas De Quincey.*

comma   A mark of punctuation (,) that aids understanding by separating elements in a written utterance. Rife as it is with ambiguity, the English language has great need of the comma to do in writing what intonation often does in speech: sort and separate, group and array the elements of thought. If the writer's ear is bad, his commas (or lack of them) will reflect his failure to "hear" the sense-bearing intonations of his own speech, and his writing will continually send the reader off on false leads. Today's written English tends toward fewer commas than were used a century ago. But to suppose that the trend proves commas are not needed, or to suppose that the trend is in every instance right, is wrong. The teacher who tells his students of the comma, "When in doubt, leave it out," is after all offering only a rule of thumb on the stipulation that they have first of all seen no reason for putting the comma in. The rule for sense supersedes all other rules. Thus one cannot learn the effective use of the comma without also learning something of ideas and how they fit together. Fundamentally, the comma (*a*) separates elements that have equal form or status in an utterance, (*b*) sets off elements that are subordinate to the main idea, (*c*) sets off elements that, although worthy in themselves, could be removed without damage to the main idea, and (*d*) separates elements that, if not separated, might be misread. The comma is also used conventionally for certain technical matters, such as grouping figures (1,000, etc.). In accordance with the four functions mentioned, use the comma:

1. To separate independent clauses that are linked by *and, or, nor, but, so, for,* or *yet.*

Sister Mary rapped quietly on the desk, and her pupils aligned themselves like filings near a magnet.
Swans glided toward our crumbs, but the quicker ducks got most of the food.

The comma is sometimes omitted when the clauses are very short.

We rang twice and the door swung open.

2. To separate words, phrases, or clauses in a series.

Words, phrases, or *clauses* may form a series.
He has distinguished himself *in poetry, in drama,* and *in criticism.*
Theirs is the toil, theirs is the blood, and *theirs is the victory.*

Some writers, particularly journalists, omit the comma between the last two items in a series. To omit the comma, however, often leads to distortion of meaning: "In his oddly manful squeak, T. R. advised all boykind: 'Don't flinch, don't foul and hit the line hard!' " (*Time,* February 7, 1964, p. 49). Did T. R. mean "don't . . . hit the line"? The comma before *and* in a series should be omitted only when the last two items are to be understood to form a unit: "Give me *eggs, toast, coffee and cream.*"

3. To separate consecutive modifiers that apply to a single element.

His *broad, heavy* hand pushed against the wall.
Our little Swedish visitor has such a *shy, appealing* smile.

(Since no one would say, "Our little *and* Swedish visitor . . . ," there is no comma between *little* and *Swedish.*)

4. To set off an introductory adverb clause.

While you're up, get me another toothpick.
If trouble develops in the lab, the alarm will sound automatically.

Although the sky is dark, no rain is expected.
Once we gain the summit, the view will prove worth the climb.

5. To set off an introductory verbal modifier.

Smashing a fist into the bag, Kayo gave the workout all the energy he had.
Taken at its best, the work of the young artist shows remarkable promise.
To protect his lead, Marsh took every turn at full throttle.

Introductory verbal phrases are not set off when they are not used as modifiers.

To protect his lead was Marsh's only thought.

6. To set off an appositive (renaming element) that is not needed to *identify* what it renames.

Karl Pippin, *the boy who won the contest,* said he would enter again next year.
His father, *Major Pippin,* just laughed.
It was an astounding performance, *a masterpiece.*

7. To set off an adjective clause that could, without damage to the main, be omitted.

Karl, *who plays as well as most professionals,* has never had a lesson.
His games, *which always thrill the spectators,* are classics of form.
In Minneapolis, *where he was born,* they are already calling him "The Champ."

Adjective clauses *that could not be omitted without damage to the sense* are not enclosed or set off by commas (the italics here marking an example).

8. To set off an adverb clause that could, without damage to the meaning of the sentence, be omitted.

Wertz was ineligible, *since he had gained too much weight.*
Joe may be interested, *although golf is not his game.*
The third question, *while it lasted,* held the audience in suspense.

Adverb clauses that are essential to the import of the sentence are not enclosed or set off by commas: "The game will be canceled *if the rain persists*" (in which omission of the *if* clause would leave the statement not necessarily true); "Harry didn't lose his job *because he was inefficient*" (in which we are led to infer that he lost his job for some *other* reason).

9. To set off absolutes that substitute for adverb clauses.

The hour being later than midnight, she skipped.
The slipper falling from her foot, she limped toward the pumpkin coach.
The prince caught by her beauty, romance was inevitable.

10. To set off such transitions as *however, therefore, on the other hand, of course.*

We cannot, *of course,* ignore the possibility of engine failure. *On the other hand,* we should not exaggerate its likelihood. Let us, *therefore,* be calm.

11. To set off interjections and such absolutes as *yes* and *no.*

"*Oh,* you saw him yesterday?"
"*Yes,* I did. *Gosh,* did he look good!"
"*Well,* then he is fully recovered?"

12. To set off nouns of direct address.

"*Mother,* where are you?"
"Come out, *Jim,* and quit that idiotic hiding."
"Your friend Oliver is here to see you, *Son.*"

13. To set off such elements in written dialogue as *he said, she replied,* and *Johnny shouted.*

"Please come out," *his mother pleaded.*
"I don't want to see Oliver," *snarled Jim* from under the bed.
"Listen," *said Oliver,* "I brought you a new frog."

14. To take the place of an omitted verb in certain elliptical structures.

In the ballad the first and third lines have four feet; the second and fourth lines, three feet.

15. To avoid awkward run-on reading of words when misunderstanding might result.

Whatever *is, is* right.
In the *morning, glory* seems most glorious.
All over the *ground, squirrels* had disturbed the leaves.

16. To set off the salutation and complimentary close in a friendly, informal letter, and the complimentary close even in a business letter.

Examples: Dear Harry,   Sincerely,

17. To separate the two clauses of an "echo" question.

"Frank didn't have a chance, did he?"
"Drop in to see Aunt Ellen, will you?"

18. To set off an introductory prepositional phrase that is very long or that deserves special emphasis.

On the morning after his first visit to the downtown section of the biggest city in Brazil, Parker sat down to write.
In view of the time, it will be wise to adjourn.

19. To separate the elements in dates, titles, and geographical names.

Thursday, November 24, 1966.
Francis T. Harriman, director, personnel division.
Omaha, Nebraska.

20. To separate groups of figures.

Congress appropriated $14,657,330 for a new water project.

When commas are used with quotation marks, the comma always goes inside the end quotation mark:

"Just now," he said, "I had a twinge."
He had read "Il Penseroso," but not "L'Allegro."

Faulty use of the comma grows from negligence in observing the practice of effective writers and editors. For discussion of ways in which the comma is frequently misused, see COMMA FAULT and COMMA SPLICE.

comma fault   The use of a comma in a misleading way. Because he is uncertain of the sense-making sound, or INTONATION, of what he writes, the salt-and-pepper punctuator is as likely to use a comma in the wrong place as he is to omit one from the proper place. He commits a *comma fault* when he puts a comma where a clear reading of the sentence demands none.

Perhaps the most notorious of comma faults is the COMMA SPLICE — the use of only a comma between independent clauses, where a semicolon or period would give the reader an easier clue to sense.

Other comma faults are:

1. A single comma between subject and verb in a clause or sentence: "Several heavy *trunks, sat* on the dock." "The *man* in the gray flannel suit, suddenly *raised* his hand." (But a *pair* of commas may enclose parenthetical matter between subject and verb: "Several heavy trunks, *each with a brass lock,* sat on the dock.")

2. A single comma between a verb and its object or other complement: "Jim dragged from under the bed, *a green frog.*" "What I want to know *is, the answer* to that first question." (Again, a *pair* of commas may enclose parenthetical matter; but the single comma is misleading.)

3. A single comma between *two* words or phrases that are joined by *and, or,* or *nor:* "We enjoy *Beethoven, and Brahms.* We first heard their music when we were *young, and impressionable.* That's when you either *like it, or leave it.*" (But if *three or more* such items are used in a series, commas would be proper: "We enjoy *Beethoven, Brahms, and the Beatles.*")

4. A comma that sets off a modifying clause or phrase that is es-

sential to the full sense of its sentence: "There goes the policeman, *who stopped us last week.*" (The comma implies that the modifying clause is not needed, as if "There goes the policeman" would be clear enough by itself; but the statement would leave the reader asking, "What policeman?") Other examples of this comma fault: "I didn't eat, *because I was hungry.* I ate, *because everyone else did.*" "The little fellow, *in the red jacket,* has a cold." (In each example the comma misleads the reader.)

5. A comma that sets off a short introductory prepositional phrase: "*In the morning,* we awoke early." "Between meals, he eats like a horse." (The comma tends to overemphasize the prepositional phrase; it may be proper when such emphasis is wanted, or when the phrase is long and could become unwieldy.)

6. A comma that sets off an introductory verbal noun: "*Staying on the horse,* is the idea of the event." (This comma fault is the same as (1), but the careless writer may commit it because he believes that a comma is required after an introductory verbal phrase.)

comma splice   The result of the omission of a conjunction from a compound sentence so that the clauses have only a comma to separate them: "The day was stifling, we suffered for want of the old swimming hole." Considered an illiteracy by most teachers of formal writing, the comma splice can be corrected either by supplying the conjunction (in this case *and*) or by using a semicolon rather than the comma. An apparent comma splice, however, may actually be a deliberate omission of *and*—a practice now in some vogue among even skilled writers (see ASYNDETON). The omitted *and* produces, for these writers, an emphasis upon the close connection—whether of sequence or of BAL-ANCE—between the ideas in the two clauses. Some examples: "There is no such thing as general education, there are only specific individual educations" (Howard Mumford Jones); "You circle in what seems an endless regular dance, you provide for us not only a place to live but also a magnificent spectacle for our enjoyment" (Joseph Wood Krutch); "They know it's a movie, they know it must be fake, still, they are weeping" (William Saroyan).

commedia dell'arte   Literally, "comedy of the profession." A kind of theatrical entertainment performed by troupes of professional actors. It was popular in Italy from the sixteenth through the eighteenth centuries and was characterized by pantomime, stock situations, and such stock characters as Harlequin, Columbine, and Pantaloon. Some of the conventions of this art form originated in ATTELAN COMEDY (as reflected in the *Fabulae Attelanae* of early Rome)—such conventions, for example, as the stock plots, the *concetti* (stock responses for certain emotions), and the *lazzi* (stock stage business). The character Harlequin (compare English "harlequinade") usually wore a black mask and a costume spangled with diamond-shaped patches of red, blue, and green; he also carried a wooden sword, forerunner of the SLAPSTICK. His sweetheart was the servant Columbine. None of the female characters wore a mask, nor did those males assigned to more speaking than pantomiming. The character Perolino, forerunner of the clown Pagliaccio and of the French Pierrot, acted the part of a dreamer with a sad, whitened face. The character Pulcinella, a villainous girl-chaser, was the forerunner of Punch in the English Punch-and-Judy shows. Aside from the influence that the *commedia dell'arte* had on later mimes, it proved to be the source of many character types subsequently appearing in the comedy of HUMOURS. The commedia with certain adaptations, including improvisation, is still kept alive today in several cities of Europe, notably in Copenhagen's outdoor theater at the Tivoli Gardens.

REFERENCES: K. M. Lea, *The Italian Popular Comedy;* Pierre L. Ducharte, *The Italian Comedy;* Allardyce Nicoll, *Masks, Mimes, and Miracles;* Giacomo Oreglia, *Commedia dell' Arte.*

complication   In any RISING ACTION the tension in a scene arises from the conflict or prospective conflict between a character and his obstacles. Often, in a given scene or episode this conflict is only partially resolved. In *Macbeth,* for example, there is a partial resolution when Macbeth overcomes the first obstacle, Duncan, by murdering him. But this solution is temporary and incomplete, since Duncan's two sons, Malcolm and Donalbain, who are sure to seek revenge, escape. This development is called a complication. A similar complication arises when Macbeth kills Banquo, only to learn that Banquo's son and avenger, Fleance, has fled. Each complication thus tends to be more suspensive than its predecessor since it contributes to a cumulative force (in *Macbeth,* the Battle of Birnam Wood).

Another kind of complication in the plot, or STORY-LINE, of fiction and drama is a suspensive incident or development that confronts characters with crucial decisions; for example, the unexpected return of the husband, Ford, in *The Merry Wives of Windsor;* in Henry James's *Ambassadors,* Strether's realization that he prefers to stay in Paris rather than return to America with young Chad, although Strether had originally undertaken the mission in order to win the hand of Chad's widowed mother, Mrs. Newsome.

REFERENCE: Carolyn Gordon, *How to Read a Novel.*

comstockery   Moralistic censorship. After Anthony Comstock (1844–1915). (Compare BOWDLERIZED; see OBSCENITY.)

conceit **1.** In general contemporary usage, egotism or exaggerated self-importance. **2.** In sixteenth- and seventeenth-century poetry (especially that of Shakespeare, Donne, and the METAPHYSICAL POETS) a fanciful notion; something *conceived,* or created, or "dreamed up" out of the imagination (for example, Donne's imagination of his own autopsy, in which the face of his lady would be discovered in his heart). **3.** Strained or farfetched imagery, for example, in *Romeo and Juliet* I, 4, where Mercutio says to Romeo, "O, then I see Queen Mab hath been with you. / She is the fairies' midwife, and she comes / In shape no bigger than an agate stone / On the forefinger of an alderman / Drawn with a team of little atomies / Over men's noses as they lie asleep." (See METAPHYSICAL POETS.)
REFERENCE: K. K. Ruthven, *The Conceit.*

conclusion **1.** In a SYLLOGISM, the third and last statement. **2.** In a composition, a formal close, now outmoded and to be distinguished from *conclusions,* which constitute the formal close of a scientific paper, study, or experiment. **3.** The third section of an oversimplified outline (Introduction, Body, Conclusion). **4.** In an informal essay—to say nothing of poetry, drama, and fiction—no formal conclusion is nowadays expected, as it often was in the past, when classicists demanded "a beginning, a middle, and an end." The modern essayist more often than not allows the reader to draw his own conclusions.

concrete poetry **1.** Loosely, any poetry emphasizing imagery as opposed to philosophic (i.e., abstract) statement. **2.** More specifically, poems whose arrangement on the page re-creates such concrete graphics as a Christmas tree, a cornucopia, a comma, a question mark, a lightning bolt, a wine goblet, a crucifix, or any other concrete configuration. In 1968 concrete poetry occupied an entire issue of the *Beloit Poetry Journal.* (See CARMEN FIGURATEM.)
REFERENCES: M. E. Scott (ed.), *Concrete Poetry;* Eugene Wildman (ed.), *Anthology of Concretism.*

concrete universal A synonym for ARCHETYPE.

conditional syllogism See SYLLOGISM 2.

confessional verse Verse in which the poet painfully publicizes private aspects and episodes of his experience, the self-expression serving as a kind of confession, therapy, or exorcism. Anglo-Saxon (*The Wanderer*) and medieval poets (Chaucer and Jean de Muin) used the confession as a device to reveal the feelings and beliefs of a character; confession made directly to the audience, without the use of a PERSONA, is observable mainly in such poets as Sylvia Plath, Anne Sexton, W. D. Snodgrass, and Robert Lowell (especially in the latter's "At the Altar"). (Compare EXPRESSION and PROJECTIVE VERSE.)

conflict   In drama and fiction the impact of the PROTAGONIST, or hero, on his antagonist, or obstacles. (See DRAMATIC STRUCTURE.)

connotation   Whatever is *suggested* beyond what is actually said. "A violet by a mossy stone" *denotes* a certain kind of flower next to a stone and the colors violet and moss green. But the same phrase in the context of Wordsworth's poem "She Dwelt Among the Untrodden Ways" *suggests* such images and ideas as death, a shy and unaffected girl, and so on. Even out of context "slithers" connotes more than does "goes": "slithers" suggests a snake or a snakelike movement. Connotations arise from experience, both individual and general (or widely shared) acquaintance with things and words. Every person, because of unique experience, has private associations with words—his feelings about what they name—and these become part of the meaning of the words for him. And every person shares with his society some associations with words—some connotations beyond the literal meanings. Semanticist S. I. Hayakawa (in *Language in Thought and Action*) has distinguished two sorts of connotation—*informative* and *affective*. Informative connotations include socially agreed upon definitions and denotations; affective connotations are the partly private, partly shared suggestions of words. It is affective connotation that makes *politician* quite different from *statesman*, or *slender* more complimentary than *thin*. Speakers and writers must attend to the connotations of their words if they are to communicate effectively, for affective connotations often speak louder than dictionary meanings do. (Contrast DENOTATION; see also DICTION and TONE.)
REFERENCES: Richard Altick, *Preface to Critical Reading;* Judson Jerome, *Poetry: Premeditated Art;* X. J. Kennedy, "Connotation and Allusion," *An Introduction to Poetry.*

consonance   1. A sound effect arising from repetition or close occurrence of consonants within words; for example, "an e*dg*er for fu*dge*"; "li*k*e the sound of the ony*ch*a / When the pho*c*a has the pi*c*a" (Edith Sitwell). 2. The occurrence of identical consonant sounds in stressed syllables whose vowel sounds differ; for example, "a *frail* a*ll*iance of *laugh*ing *l*ilies," in which the *f* and *l* sounds in words are repeated in an irregular pattern of initial, internal, and final position. It is the irregularity of position that distinguishes consonance from ALLITERATION, which is usually of initial sounds and need not be in stressed syllables. Some poets use consonance as a subtle variation from RHYME, as air / fire or rule / sail. (Contrast ASSONANCE.)

context   An oral or written continuum that is more meaningful as a whole than is any single fragment thereof. Thus "apple" has different meanings in the context of "apple of the King's eye" and in the context of "Adam and Eve ate the apple of knowledge," and still different meanings when by itself. Quoting out of context must be guarded against by both the transmitter and the receiver of a communication.

REFERENCES: Richard Altick, *Preface to Critical Reading;* Mortimer Adler, *How to Read a Book;* I. A. Richards, *How to Read a Page;* Donald Sears, *The Sentence in Context.*

contraposition   See SYLLOGISM 2.

contrast   Comparison of opposites often helps dramatically to clarify the attributes of a thing or one's attitudes toward a thing. Thus, *contrast* is among the major methods of EXPOSITION. Contrasts may be presented in brief or at length: in the two-word phrase (see OXYMORON) or in the full essay of extended contrast. Rhetorical forms employing contrast include (in addition to OXYMORON) PARADOX, ANTITHESIS, and CHIASMUS. In school and college examinations the word *contrast* (used as a verb) means to compare the differences between two or more things.

controlling question   See THESIS QUESTION.

controlling statement   See THESIS STATEMENT.

convention   1. In literature, any accepted practice, style, or structure; for example, invoking the blessings of a deity or muse, as did the writers of EPICS; using ALLITERATION rather than RHYME for poetry, as did the Anglo-Saxons; or furnishing COMEDY with a pair of minor as well as major lovers, as do most playwrights. 2. More broadly, a climate of taste, manners, and morals. Thus, as reflected in medieval romances, knights and ladies practiced a set of conventions known as COURTLY LOVE. 3. STYLE, as, for example, the BAROQUE styles and influences characterizing the arts, including literature, during most of the seventeenth to nineteenth centuries. Eras of CLASSICISM have prevailed between eras of ROMANTICISM. 4. During the 1960s the prevailing method of teaching literature in prestigious colleges and preparatory schools, as reflected in the examinations of the College Entrance Examination Board, was to follow such leading conventions of the NEW CRITICS as close reading of the text, resistance to biography and history as relevant to the interpretation of a text, and the assumptions underlying the theory of AESTHETIC DISTANCE.

REFERENCES: John Livingston Lowes, *Convention and Revolt in Poetry;* F. R. Leavis, *The Great Tradition;* Frederick A. Pottle, *The Idiom of Poetry;* Robert Hapgood, "Dramatic Conventions in *All's Well,*" *PMLA* (March, 1964).

coordination   The proper tying together of language elements that have equal rank. The underlying principle is that two or more things that are equal in relation to other elements must have equal form of grammar and syntax. Within a sentence the coordination of these equal-rank elements usually calls for such conjunctions as *and, or, nor, but;* or such conjunctive adverbs as *however, therefore, nevertheless.* Careful writers give equal form to coordinated elements even to the extent of not mixing active and passive voices, abstract and concrete ideas, or ideas from different spheres of thought. Faulty coordination occurs in these sentences: (1) "Oscar is *a European,* but Larry is *a college graduate*"; (2) "The moon *rose,* and the stars *were seen*"; (3) "He acquired *a bride* and *much happiness.*" (See also BALANCE, ANTITHESIS, PARALLELISM, and SYLLEPSIS.)

copyright   The exclusive right of the creator or author of an original literary or artistic work to benefit from his own creation, either by publishing the work himself or by licensing publication. Two kinds of copyright are recognized—common-law copyright, which resides in the author before publication, and statutory copyright, which *may* reside in the author after publication if specific actions are taken in accordance with law. The term of statutory copyright in the United States is twenty-eight years, with a renewal for another twenty-eight years if the author applies for it. At publication—the offering of the work for sale to the public—the work *must* bear a notice of copyright, as and where demanded by law. (This notice and its placement vary from category to category—maps, sheet music, etc.). For most literary works, the copyright notice must appear on the verso of the title page; and it is usually worded (for the broadest possible protection): "Copyright" c in circle, year date of publication, and the name of the copyright holder, followed by the words "All rights reserved." Immediately after publication, two copies of the work "shall promptly be deposited" with the Register of Copyrights in the Library of Congress, accompanied by a completed application for registration and the required registration fee. After copyright expires, or is voided (for certain actions or oversights will void a copyright), the work passes into the "public domain"; that is, anyone may publish the work.

In the United States the copyright laws are quite complex, and legislation to revise the statutes has been pending in Congress for several years. Under the proposed law the period of copyright would be, as it now is in Great Britain, the life of the author plus fifty years.

These points should be noted by the aspiring writer: (1) In the quotation of passages from copyrighted works, the use of more than five hundred words (and sometimes less) from a single source requires the consent, or permission, of the publisher or author and, often, the payment of a fee determined by the extent of the quotation. (In the case of poetry, permission should be asked if more than two lines are used.) (2) The mechanical reproduction of a copyrighted work in any way without permission of the copyright holder is an infringement of copyright. (3) Certain works cannot be copyrighted, including, specifically, the official publications or documents or papers of the United States government and its officers. (4) An author who circulates his manuscripts among friends or who mechanically reproduces them for submission to publishers retains his common-law copyright in them—so long as he does not offer the copies for sale to the public. Such manuscripts need not bear the usual copyright notice, but should perhaps carry a legend like this: "For confidential use only—not for circulation, distribution, or publication. All rights in this work are the property of. . . ."

REFERENCES: Margaret Nicholson, *Manual of Copyright Practice for Writers, Publishers, and Agents,* Second Edition; Richard C. DeWolf, "Note on American Copyright Law," in Sir Paul Harvey (ed.), *The Oxford Companion to English Literature;* Barbara A. Ringer and Paul Gitlin, *Copyrights.*

Corpus Christi Day   See HOLIDAYS.

counter words   Vague and general words used when the speaker or writer is too lazy to search out the more precise words. In current English every level of usage has its counter words, ranging from the handy but unimaginative terms of approval or disapproval in conversation (*fine, awful, fabulous*) to the catchall usage of the young (*like, far out*) and the empty echoes of the intellectuals (*adjusted, area, aspect, factor,* and anything ending with *-wise*). Counter words, akin to jargon and slang, lack the precision of the most useful jargon and the color of the best slang. When vagueness does no harm, counter words are appropriate enough; they are best avoided in serious writing.

couplet   1. Two rhyming lines of verse. 2. HEROIC COUPLETS are in iambic pentameter: "Know then thyself; presume not God to scan; / The proper study of mankind is Man" (Alexander Pope). (See METER.)

courtesy books   Renaissance etiquette books like the ones imported from Italy—e.g., Castiglione's *The Courtier* (1528). Courtesy books suggest what the gentleman should wear and how he should behave around ladies, horses, and fencing companions. After Sir Thomas Hoby's translation of Castiglione in 1561, Italian fashions, manners, and pastimes were reflected not only in the "Italianate gentleman," but also in plays which at first aped and later lampooned these conventions.

courtly love   A set of conventions in manners, morals, and pastimes of knights and ladies in medieval England and on the Continent, especially in Provence. These sports and pastimes are described and reflected in the works of Chrétien de Troyes (twelfth century), in the thirteenth-century love allegory *Roman de la Rose,* and in CHIVALRIC

ROMANCE such as Chaucer's *Troilus and Criseyde* (1385), Malory's *Morte d'Arthur* (1471), Spenser's *Faerie Queene* (1590), and Tennyson's *Idyls of the King* (1859). Among the doctrines of courtly love were humility, courtesy, adultery (for the lady was usually married), chivalry, and the religion of love. (See CHIVALRIC ROMANCE and METRICAL ROMANCE.)

REFERENCES: C. S. Lewis, *The Allegory of Love;* Sidney Painter, *French Chivalry;* Jean Froissart, *Chronicles;* W. C. Meller, *A Knight's Life in the Days of Chivalry;* Andreas Capellanus, *The Art of Courtly Love;* F. X. Newman, *The Meaning of Courtly Love;* Wallace Fowlie, *Love in Literature;* Denis de Rougemont, *Love in the Western World.*

craft cycle plays   A series of plays presenting the story, or cycle, of Christian history from the Creation to the Last Judgment; also known as mystery plays because they dramatized events of Christian history that could not be explained but had to be taken on faith. These plays were enacted on Corpus Christi day during the fourteenth, fifteenth, and sixteenth centuries by members of local craft guilds in various English towns. The most complete surviving cycle, a series of forty-eight plays, is from the town of York. The Wakefield cycle (also called the Towneley plays because the scripts were kept at Towneley Hall) consists of thirty-two plays, five of which are variations of York plays. Other plays exist from the towns of Coventry and Chester. Each play was performed on its own pageant, or wagon-stage — an ark on wheels for the play of Noah, a garden of gilded trees perhaps for Paradise, a gaping gargoyle mouth issuing smoke and flame for the entrance to Hell. The use of very literal props and settings provided opportunities for the guilds producing the plays to show off their particular crafts. Thus, the armourers traditionally produced the expulsion of Adam and Eve from Paradise, which called for a two-edged sword; the chandlers were charged with the Shepherd's play with its dazzling star of Bethlehem; the bakers prepared quite an edible Last Supper. The plays are simply constructed, each composed of two or three scenes, with extraneous details either reported or remembered. As the audience surely knew the outcome of these scenes, having heard the stories many times in church, their enjoyment consisted partly in the DRAMATIC IRONY of knowing what was going to happen.

The authors of the English cycle plays are unknown to us, but the evidence in the plays shows these authors to have been well-read, witty, sensitive to what would make "good theatre" and that at least one of them was a master of versification. There are twenty-two different stanzaic forms in the forty-eight plays comprising the York cycle, all employing the same northern dialect. Many of these stanza forms are French, handled with skill and sophistication. Some are in the English tradition of ACCENTUAL VERSE, and are heavily alliterative. Other plays are in metrical verse, but still somewhat alliterative. Here is an example of this sort of stanza from Play No. VII, on the sacrifice of Cain and Abel:

> *Angel* Thowe cursyd Cayme, where is Abell?
> Where hais thowe done thy broder dere?
> *Cayme* What askes thowe me that taill to tell?
> For yit his keper was I nere.
> *Angel* God hais sent thee his curse downe,
> Fro hevyn to hell, *maldictio dei.*
> *Cayme* (hitting the angel) Take that thyself, evyn on thy crowne,
> *Quia non sum custos fratris mei,* To tyne.
> *Angel* God hais sent thee his malyson,
> And inwardly I geve thee myne.

REFERENCES: (For more general references regarding medieval religious drama, see MIRACLE PLAYS.) H. F. Westlake, *The Parish Guilds of Medieval England;* Martial Rose (ed.), *The Wakefield Mystery Plays;* Lucy T. Smith (ed.), *York Mystery Plays;* E. K. Chambers, *The Medieval Stage.*

cretic   See METER.

crisis   In fiction and drama a crucial moment in a scene or in the entire work in which the PROTAGONIST faces a dilemma and must make a decision. In Ibsen's *A Doll's House* the crisis of one scene is Torvald's reading of the letter incriminating his wife, Nora; in the play the chief crisis (the CLIMAX) comes just at the moment before Nora decides to leave Torvald, to walk out of the doll's house forever.

critic   A writer who evaluates literature and other works of art. The German playwright Gotthold Lessing observed that "Critics create rules, and artists create literature." While it is true that artists create literature, most critics do not create rules, but rather try to discover in masterworks the rules by which artists have been consciously or unconsciously guided. Critics thus serve not only as evaluators, but also—and perhaps primarily—as interpreters. They also enrich our understanding of a difficult work, or jog us into re-examining our own notions about it. The fact that a critic spends time (sometimes his life) in studying, interpreting, and writing about certain works implies immediately that he has placed great value on them. (See NEW CRITICS.)

Among the world's great critics and their masterpieces of criticism have been Plato (*ca.* 427–347 B.C.), *The Republic;* Aristotle (384–322 B.C.), *The Poetics;* Horace (65–8 B.C.), *The Art of Poetry;* Longinus (*ca.* 213–273), *On the Sublime;* Dante (1265–1321), *The Banquet;* Sidney (1554–86), *An Apology for Poetry;* Corneille (1606–84), *On the Three Unities;* Dryden (1631–1700), *An Essay of Dramatic Poesy;* Pope (1688–1744), *An Essay on Criticism;* Johnson (1709–84), *Preface to Shakespeare;* Buffon (1707–88), *Discourse on Style;*

Lessing (1729–81), *Laocoön;* Goethe (1749–1832), *Conversations with Eckermann;* Coleridge (1772–1834), *Biographia Literaria;* Shelley (1792–1822), *A Defence of Poetry;* Sainte-Beuve (1804–69), *What Is a Classic?;* Poe (1809–49), *The Poetic Principle;* Flaubert (1821–80), *The Correspondence;* Arnold (1822–88), *The Function of Criticism;* Henry James (1843–1916), *The Art of Fiction;* Croce (1866–1952), *Aesthetics;* Eliot (1888–1964), *Essays;* and Edmund Wilson (1895–), *Axel's Castle.*

See also David Daiches, *Critical Approaches to Literature;* J. H. Smith and E. W. Parks, *The Great Critics;* René Wellek, *Concepts of Criticism;* Stanley Edgar Hyman, *The Armed Vision;* Lawrence S. Hall, *A Grammar of Literary Criticism.*

culture shock   The reaction of a reader (or listener) to a situation foreign to his own cultural patterns, even if the shock-producer is quite conventional within its own culture or ethos. For example, a Western reader may gasp when he learns that in certain Oriental countries both sexes share common bathing facilities simultaneously. Even within Western culture a reader may experience shock when first learning that within certain subcultural areas there are no indoor plumbing facilities.

REFERENCES: Lewis Mumford,*The Culture of Cities;* Ruth Benedict, *Patterns of Culture;* Margaret Mead, *Male and Female;* Conrad M. Arensberg and Solon T. Kimball, *Culture and Community;* Edward Hall, *The Silent Language;* Alvin Toffler, *The Future as a Way of Life.*

cycle plays   See CRAFT CYCLE PLAYS.

D

dactyl   In verse, a word or word-group consisting of one heavily stressed syllable followed by two lightly stressed syllables; e.g., *múr-muring*. (See METER.)

dangler   In a sentence, a modifier lacking its intended substantive. No fault of sentence structure is more notorious than the dangling participle — but an element does not have to be a participle to be a dangler. The chief types:

1. *Dangling participle: "Sitting up in the stands,* our team looked pretty flashy." (Was the team sitting in the stands?) *"Aroused* from my slumber, my day was ruined." (Was my day aroused from slumber?)

2. *Dangling gerund:* "After *taking* the exam, our grade average improved." (Did the grade average take the exam?)

3. *Dangling infinitive phrase: "To lose weight,* starches should be avoided." (Are the starches expected to lose weight?)

4. *Dangling prepositional phrase: "At the age of nine* my father took me on an African safari." (A nine-year-old father?)

5. *Dangling elliptical clause: "Although wealthy,* nobody would honor his check." (Who was wealthy? Nobody?) The construction is called an elliptical clause because subject and verb have been elided: "Although [he was] wealthy. . . ." (When the subject and verb are supplied, there is no dangler.) (See also ELISION.)

Repairing a dangler is not difficult. Usually the repair can be accomplished in either of two ways: (*a*) by making a full clause of the dangling phrase: *"From where we were sitting in the stands,* our team looked pretty flashy"; *"After we took the exam,* our grade average improved"; *"When I was nine years old,* my father took me on an African safari"; or (*b*) by supplying for the main clause a subject that is properly modified by the phrase in question: "To lose weight, *you* should avoid starches"; "Although wealthy, *he* could find no one to honor his check."

Dartmouth Conference   Also known as the Anglo-American Seminar, a meeting of English and American teachers and professors of English at Dartmouth College, New Hampshire, in 1966. The meeting was sponsored by the (British) National Association for the Teaching of English and by the (American) Modern Language Association, the Carnegie Foundation, and the National Council of Teachers of English. The purpose of the Conference was an international exchange of experience and opinion (CULTURE SHOCK) on the improvement of the language arts curriculum in the schools and colleges. Among the major issues (What is English? What is continuity? What are language standards and attitudes?) the greatest and most widespread impact in the United States since 1966 seems to have been made by the issue over appropriate and relevant kinds of writing that young people (mostly in the schools) should be involved in. Before the Dartmouth Conference, most composition teachers in the United States had subscribed to a writing curriculum that stressed the mundane kinds (i.e., investigative) as opposed to the more imaginative kinds (interpretive exposition and "creative writing,"), although they "allowed" creative writing if it was done with "discipline." Creative writing as an undisciplined flow of self-expression and "free association" had generally been discouraged except under the guidance of a professional writer-in-residence. The British members of the Dartmouth Conference, however, seem to have changed the minds and moods of the American members on this particular issue. The American members and their associates now seem inclined to acknowledge that writing as taught in our American schools has been too restrictive and unimaginative. Thus, thanks to the Dartmouth Conference the idea and practice of "creative writing" have become increasingly encouraged.

REFERENCES: Herbert Muller, *The Uses of English;* John Dixon, *Growth Through English;* Lois Josephs, "A Disciplined Approach to Creative Writing," *English Journal* (October, 1962); Geoffrey Summerfield (ed.), *Creativity in English;* Gary Tate and E. P. J. Corbett (eds.), *Teaching High School Composition;* J. N. Hook, *Writing Creatively;* Walker Gibson, *Persona.*

dash   Like other marks of punctuation, the dash (−) is not to be sprinkled upon the page — though many untutored writers use it slapdash, letting it fall wherever they are not quite sure what punctuation is needed. Properly used, the dash helps to organize thoughts and display them effectively; it separates, it emphasizes, it lends suspense or irony, it lends informality, it lends — dash.

Properly, the dash is used:

1. To set off an appositive when commas would not do enough and parentheses would do too much: "Brucie growled back at all the animals — lions, leopards, llamas, and linxes."

2. To mark a suspension of thought — whether the thought simply stops unfinished, takes off on a new tack, or continues with some repetition or twist:

"Ah, I see you've — ."

"Arrived early? Yes, I wanted to be sure — well, you know how it is."

"Of course, I've done it myself often — more often than you'd guess."

3. To enclose parenthetical matter when commas would lack the desired emphasis or would cause difficulty in reading: "Men — not children — are what this work requires." "Those piercing eyes — hard, sharp, unrelenting — were unforgettable."

4. To set off a summarizing clause that follows a listing of things in apposition: "Clarity, economy, variety—these are marks of style." "He had dawdled, he had delayed, he had put off, he had procrastinated —in short, he hadn't done the assignment."

5. To create a feeling of suspense before a sudden revelation or afterthought: "The choice at last was—Mozart!" "Drop that revolver—or else!"

6. After a quotation, to set off the title or the name of the author: "If music be the food of love, play on!"—*As You Like It*.

Dashes do not usually appear next to commas, semicolons, colons, or periods. When the dash is used, other marks—even those that might otherwise be expected—are ordinarily omitted. Sometimes even a terminal period is omitted when a dash shows a suspended thought: "Please, Uncle Sam, I'd rather—" (What follows then begins a new paragraph.)

dead metaphor   See FADED METAPHOR.

deadwood   Whatever can be removed from a statement without altering its meaning or reducing the effectiveness of style; it is sometimes called *redundancy*. Deadwood repeats ideas in different words (as in *pleonasm* and *tautology*), or it labors the obvious (as in the several forms of *verbosity: circumlocution, periphrasis, prolixity, verbiage*).

1. *Pleonasm* repeats what is implicit by adding a word or phrase that could be cut away:

as of yet	later *on*
both alike	*make a* study *of*
chairman *in charge*	*make a* survey *of*
continue *on*	near*by* the lake
defeated *by a score of 2–1*	*new* beginner
equally as	*old* adage
fall *down*	oldest *one of them all*
first *of all*	*only* just arrived
Ford *car*	*past* experience
have *got*	*past* history
his *or her*	plan *on*
inside *of*	raise *up*
invited guests	rarely *ever*
invited *to attend*	*take a* look at

2. *Tautology* repeats what is explicit, as if the writer were unaware of the import of his words:

adequate *enough*	*needed* prerequisites
and etc.	now *at this time*
bibliography *of books*	petite *little* girl
combines *together*	red *in color*
consecutive times *in a row*	*round* circle
consensus *of opinion*	short *in length*

different varieties	square *shape*
few *in number*	*still* persists
gathered *together*	vocabulary *words*
heavy *in weight*	*wild* savage
modern times of today	*youthful* teen-ager
necessary requirements	

3. *Circumlocution* is "talking around" a topic. Words dilute the thought by *overphrasing* (expanding a word into a phrase):

was	*becomes*	acted as
many		a number of
now		at the present time
when		at which time
named		by the name of
meet		come in contact with
because		due to the fact that
stated		made a statement
by		on the part of
visited		paid a visit to
appear		put in an appearance

or by *overpredication* (expanding words and phrases into clauses):

library books	books *that are* in the library
classes in session	classes *that are* in session
teacher in charge	teacher *who is* in charge
broken window	window *that is* broken

4. *Periphrasis* is a form of circumlocution, but more thoughtfully used and often allowable. It uses indirect forms of expression, often wordier than the direct. As a device of EUPHEMISM, periphrasis may be defended on grounds of courtesy ("Gentlemen of the Jury" instead of "Jurors") or on grounds of effectiveness of rhythm ("the house of Mr. Pennington" instead of "Mr. Pennington's house"—and other such PERIPHRASTIC GENITIVES). Unfortunately, periphrasis has recently become one mark of OFFICIALESE and GOBBLEDYGOOK.

5. *Prolixity* is the tedious proliferation of detail. Not content with getting to the point, the prolix writer or speaker must make the point abundantly clear—and often wanders into the irrelevant. The fellow who can't tell about his vacation without supplying the exact dates and times of arrival and the names of the bellboys is prolix.

6. *Verbiage* is words that say nothing—a sort of meaningless prattle.

Deadwood is not the same as REPETITION, though some forms of deadwood are indeed repetitive. While repetition often reinforces utterance, deadwood weakens. By violating the principle of ECONOMY, deadwood taxes a reader's patience—and often so dilutes a thought that it precludes communication. An occasional bit of deadwood will not offend; but a pervasive wordiness does. Speech will bear more deadwood than writing, since the ear is less attentive than the eye and less readily absorbs lean sentences.

decadence 1. In literary criticism, a relaxing of critical standards — especially the standards upheld by the critics in fashion. 2. The moral and economic deterioration of once socially prominent families, as depicted in the fiction of Faulkner and Steinbeck and in the plays of Tennessee Williams. 3. The literary movement of the DECADENTS.

Decadents, the A late nineteenth- and early twentieth-century group of French and English writers who revolted against majority CONVENTION, regarded art as its own reward, and developed a cult of necroaesthetics — of finding beauty in death, decay, and evil. (Baudelaire's *Flowers of Evil* is a representative work by one of its devotees.) In France the group included Verlaine, Rimbaud, and Baudelaire. In England four of the Decadents were Oscar Wilde, Ernest Dowson, Aubrey Beardsley, and Frank Harris.

REFERENCES: Frank Harris, *Oscar Wilde;* G. L. Roosbroeck, *Legend of the Decadents;* H. Jackson, *The 1890s;* Yvor Winters, *Primitivism and Decadence;* Oscar Cargill, "The Decadents," *Intellectual America;* Graham Hough, *The Last Romantics;* Enid Starkie, *Baudelaire.*

deductive reasoning Reasoning from the general to the specific; a form of logical argument beginning with a generalization and leading to an assertion of its application to special or particular cases. Deduction follows rigid forms and rules prescribed to ensure the validity of the conclusion. The formal deductive argument is the SYLLOGISM, which has four chief forms: the *categorical,* the *conditional,* the *alternative,* and the *disjunctive.* Each of these forms, in turn, has its own rules for validity. Each, when valid, produces a conclusion that is absolute and certain — not just a probability. (Contrast INDUCTIVE REASONING; see also SYLLOGISM.)

REFERENCES: Jeremy Pitt and Russell E. Leavenworth, *Logic for Argument;* John Sherwood, *Handbook of Logic and Semantics;* Randall Decker, *Patterns of Exposition.*

deep image Just as contemporary grammarians (especially transformationists) speak of "deep structure" beneath the surface features of an utterance, so certain contemporary poets and critics (among them May Swenson and Robert Bly) speak of images that come from the poet's subconscious and from SURREALISM. These images, even when translated into recognizable levels of meaning, retain a mysterious, universal, archetypal quality. Such images may be found in the surrealist poems of May Swenson, as, for example, in "Sightseeing in Provincetown": "If your elbow were an eagle's head / and your loins / the mouth of a cat / its tongue / many ripped tongues of flame. . . ." (See SURREALISM and PROJECTIVE VERSE.)

REFERENCES: Archibald MacLeish, *Poetry and Experience;* Robert Bly, *The Sixties;* X. J. Kennedy, "Imagery," *An Introduction to Poetry.*

defining   Explaining the meanings of words or the nature of concepts or processes. Defining is a refined logical process, at least on the formal level. The student who hopes to understand his dictionary or to make his own terms clear needs to be aware of several kinds of defining — and of some of the pitfalls. Definitions are essentially *ad hoc;* that is, they define for a given purpose or situation. Thus one cannot assume that a definition can apply always and everywhere. We define in several ways: (1) by *showing* or *pointing* (ostensive definition): *"This* is a horse"; (2) by citing *examples:* "The *moon* and *Sputnik* are satellites"; (3) by listing *properties:* "A paddle is a *small, rounded, flat* piece of wood *with a handle";* (4) by telling what something *does* (operational definition): "The heart *pumps* blood to the arteries"; (5) by citing *purpose:* "Compass: an instrument *for ascertaining direction";* (6) by citing *process from origin:* "Coffee is a beverage made from the roasted and ground seeds of beans found in the fruit of a tropical evergreen shrub. . . .";* (7) by citing *cause:* "Steam is the gas or vapor into which *water is changed by boiling."* And occasionally we define (8) by *stipulation,* usually only for the purposes of a given discourse: "By *recall* we shall mean *restoration."* In stipulative definition both writer and reader agree that the term defined probably means something else in another context. The following are major guidelines in defining:

A. A definition should be clearer than the term being defined: its terms must be better known than the term in question, and without obscurity or AMBIGUITY; a definition should thus avoid repeating the term being defined. "Truth is the quality of being true" is not a useful definition. (Compare BEGGING THE QUESTION 3.)

B. A definition should be positive, saying what a word *means* or a thing *is,* not what it does *not mean* or *is not,* although such a dimension may be a useful *additive.*

C. A definition should be properly limited: it should include all that lies within the limits of what is defined, but nothing outside those limits.

REFERENCES: Harold Martin and Richard Ohmann, *The Logic and Rhetoric of Exposition;* Robert McDonnell and William E. Morris (eds.), *Form and Focus, a Rhetorical Reader;* Alfred North Whitehead, "Contrast between Accurate Definition and Importance," *Symbolism;* Randall Decker, *Patterns of Exposition;* Walker Gibson, *The Limits of Language.*

denotation   The specific meaning of a word, or the object (the referent) that the word names, is the *denotation* of that word. The denotation of a word, of course, depends always upon context; in one context *dog* may refer to Fido; in another, *dog* may refer to a despicable person; but in neither case does the denotation have much to do with further associative meanings of the word, its CONNOTATIONS. Usually, only concrete nouns are thought of as having denotations. In this sense denotation is one kind of extensional meaning. (Compare CONNOTA-TION.)

REFERENCE: Richard Altick, *Preface to Critical Reading.*

dénouement   Literally, "unraveling" or resolution; the end of a comedy or story, in which every character, even the most minor, and every complication, even in a subplot, is accounted for. Thus, by the end of Act V in *The Tempest,* not only are the major conspirators against Prospero exposed, with their conflicts resolved, and the lovers Ferdinand and Miranda engaged, but also such comparatively minor characters as Stephano, Trinculo, Caliban, and Ariel are disposed of or set right.

dependence   See INFLUENCE

depth psychology   See PSYCHOANALYSIS.

depth reading   1. In expository prose, reading for meaning beyond what is said in so many words; "reading between the lines"; understanding most of the total context of a literary work as well as just parts or details; identifying the writer's assumptions and implications. (See Mortimer Adler, *How to Read a Book,* and I. A. Richards, *How to Read a Page.*) 2. In BELLES LETTRES, a kind of intellectual skindiving beneath the surface (the manifest STORY-LINE) for an examination of secondary, tertiary, and other currents of meaning, based strictly, however, on actual images and symbols floating in the diver's view; understanding the place that the work has in the artist's vision of life. In Emily Dickinson's poem "Bring Me the Sunset in a Cup," for example, the first-stanza line, "Tell me how far the morning leaps," can be read superficially to mean the speaker's request for a report from the reader. A depth reading reveals that "tell" is a challenge (almost impossible to fulfill) that has been used in the bank-teller sense of "counting"; that the speaker, the banker, may be God, or Zeus, or even the poet herself as a trustee on the board of the Nature Savings and Loan Association; that the person addressed may be Ganymede or a kind of sexton in the halls of heaven. In this context the imperatives ("Bring me . . ." "Tell me . . ." "Reckon . . .") turn out to be not only "dares" but also arguments that one cannot measure Nature's aesthetic riches.

REFERENCES: I. A. Richards, *Practical Criticism;* Ezra Pound, *ABC of Reading;* Stanley R. Hopper and David L. Miller (eds.), *Interpretation: The Poetry of Meaning;* Edgar Roberts, *Writing Themes about Language.*

description   One of the four forms of discourse, description sets out to make a reader or listener see, hear, feel, taste, and smell something — at least in his imagination. At its best it does not talk about, but rather re-creates, sensory experience. (Compare RENDERING.)

Seldom appearing as an end in itself, or in its pure form, description usually serves to orient a NARRATIVE or realize its characters, to lend detail to an EXPOSITION, to support some bit of ARGUMENTATION. In contemporary writing description is usually unobtrusive; it is not presented in long, concentrated passages, but unfolded bit by bit as a story, an explanation, or an argument moves on.

Good description is never random. It is always guided by a purpose, controlled by some clear order; it is never without specific sensory detail and freshness of diction. Lack of purpose, order, detail, and style will make a description both useless and dull—the "part most likely to be skipped." More than any of the other forms of discourse, description concerns itself with what exists physically, concretely— with people, places, objects.

Differing methods and purposes lead writers to take several approaches to description: scientific, literary, and journalistic.

Scientific description is objective, thorough, precise. It measures, analyzes, and classifies accurately, deliberately avoiding attitude or bias. It uses literal (and therefore often abstract) words, but never vague words. (Compare operational DEFINING.)

Literary description is guided by a special purpose: the mood, the theme, or the thesis of the work in which it appears. It is subjective, attempting to re-create not merely what is to be seen, but also the attitudes through which the writer wishes it seen. It seeks to emphasize an impression and leave the reader with that impression unmistakably. Thus, literary description is highly selective: the writer selects those details of his subject that will enhance that impression, and he omits or subordinates other details. Literary description is often as much figurative as literal in its choice of words: it draws upon SIMILE and METAPHOR, and deploys words for their connotative values.

Journalistic description combines some of the methods of both other kinds. Like scientific description, its purpose is to inform, to be accurate, to be unbiased. Yet, like literary description, it selects details that point toward a dominant impression, interprets through attitude (though a general and unbiased one), and employs much FIGURATIVE LANGUAGE to bring the subject into the reader's experience.

REFERENCES: Walker Gibson, *Seeing and Writing;* Hart Leavitt and David Sohn, *Stop, Look, and Write!;* John Nist, *Speaking into Writing.*

determinism   The philosophic and literary position that every event is the inevitable result of (unalterable) antecedents and that human choice is predetermined by heredity and environment; the opposite of "free will." (Compare FATALISM and CALVINISM.) Thomas Hardy's novels are said to be deterministic or fatalistic in this sense. (Compare NATURALISM.)

deus ex machina   Literally, "god out of a machine." In Greek drama, a device by which a mythological god descends to rescue the hero from himself, if necessary, as is the case in Euripides' *Orestes,* when "the god Apollo suddenly appears *ex machina* above the palace" and commands Orestes *to marry* Hermione instead of *killing* her. This is such an unconvincing solution that the device has since been avoided by most writers, except those of MELODRAMA. Critics use the term as a derogation of shoddy plot construction.

dialectic   1. Broadly, the art of argumentation or debate. 2. In classical literature, especially in Plato's *Dialogues,* the tradition of the perennial debate or "continuing conversation"; that is, of forever open, unsettled issues and polarities such as "good vs. evil," "the individual vs. society," and so on.

REFERENCES: Robert Hutchins, *The Great Conversation;* Mortimer Adler, *Great Ideas from the Great Books.*

3. In philosophy, especially Hegel's, a systematic analysis of an idea or problem in the order of (*a*) *thesis,* (*b*) *antithesis,* and (*c*) *synthesis,* on the assumption that life's contradictions can be resolved. Thus, for example, if slavery (as reflected in *Uncle Tom's Cabin*) were the *thesis* and Black Power (as reflected in *The Autobiography of Malcolm X*) the *antithesis,* the reconciliation urged by Martin Luther King, Jr.—if it came about—would be a *synthesis.*

REFERENCES: G. W. F. Hegel, *The Science of Logic;* Norman O. Brown, "Instinctual Dialectics," *Life Against Death;* William Bache, *Measure for Measure as Dialectical Art.*

4. In RHETORIC, an adaptation of (3) in which the writer starts with a thesis statement, then qualifies it with an opposing (if minor) objection or two, then arrives at a compromise, which is nevertheless close to his original thesis.

REFERENCES: Sheridan Baker, *The Practical Stylist;* Leslie Fiedler and Jacob Vinocur (eds.),*The Continuing Debate;* Robert Knoll (ed.), *Contrasts.*

dialogue   1. A synonym of DIALECTIC or discussion; some reconciliation between antagonistic views may or may not emerge. ("Progress in civilization sometimes emerges out of intelligent dialogue between opposing powers.") 2. In fiction and narrative verse, the speeches of the characters. 3. In drama, the same as in (2), but also the chief means by which the development of plot is communicated. (See MONOLOGUE, SOLILOQUY, and STICHOMYTHY.) Unlike real-life conversation, literary dialogue is organized toward a purpose and thus usually presents a controlled conflict of ideas in a directed sequence. Except by design (for example, in the plays of Pinter, who deliberately uses small-talk and simulated silences), dialogue is generally free of the deadwood of real-life conversation. 4. A specific genre, as in *The Dialogues of*

Plato and certain interviews called "Conversations," in which literary celebrities talk informally with editors and other literary persons. REFERENCES: *The Dialogues of Archibald MacLeish and Mark Van Doren; Writers at Work,* The Paris Review Series; Rozanne Knudson, "Conversation with May Swenson," *Quartet* (Winter, 1969).

diary   A JOURNAL or day-by-day record of the writer's experiences. Most diaries are kept for personal satisfaction, and are not intended to be published. Among the diaries that did get published whether or not in accordance with the authors' intentions, perhaps the most famous are those of Samuel Pepys (from 1659), William Byrd (from 1700), Sarah Knight (from 1704), Eugene Delacroix (from 1822), and Anne Frank (from 1942).

dicho   An expression that lends itself to its *vice versa* with little loss of general truth. For example, "Creativity is the enemy of old age." "Old age is the enemy of creativity." Ernest Hemingway is said to have been fond of inventing *dichos*. (Compare PALINDROME.)
REFERENCE: A. E. Hotchner, *Papa Hemingway.*

diction   Choice and arrangement of words. The diction of speech or writing contributes importantly to TONE and STYLE. The chief mark of "good diction" is appropriateness to the author's purpose. Good diction is also consistent, avoiding mixtures of JARGON with standard vocabulary or of informal with formal expressions, unless deliberately.
REFERENCES: Richard Altick, *Preface to Critical Reading;* Barnet Kottler and Martin Light, *The World of Words;* Hans Guth, *Words and Ideas.*

didactic novel   1. In general, any novel more intent on teaching a lesson than on telling a story, more devoted to character development in the moral sense than to characterization with psychological introspection; for example, Horatio Alger's *Struggling Upward.* 2. In particular, one or another of the eighteenth-century fictionalized works embodying an ideal education for the young gentleman. Influenced in some few instances by the Elizabethan COURTESY BOOKS, but in most instances by Rousseau's *Emile* (1762), a fictionalized plan to make young people morally and intellectually self-reliant, the didactic novel enjoyed immense popularity in England during the late 1700s. The most popular included Henry Brooke's *Fool of Quality* (1766–70), which emphasized the advantages of physical as well as moral training; Thomas Day's *Sandford and Merton* (1783–89), which urged young people not only to practice the cardinal virtues but also to study astronomy, botany, ethnography (especially the black man and the American Indian), geography, political economy, and zoology; Elizabeth Inchbold's *Simple Story* (1791), which advised against boarding schools; the first part of William Godwin's *Caleb Williams* (1794), which was on the whole more sentimental than didactic; Maria Edgeworth's *Parents'*

Assistant, which was issued in a series in the 1790s; and parts of Thomas Holcroft's *Hugh Trevor* (1794), although the latter was essentially a BILDUNGSROMAN. (In the latter kind of novel—loosely called "pedagogical"—didactic elements appear more or less incidentally.)

The didactic novel was the forerunner of the modern pedagogical novel, which, even when it propagandizes or argues a thematic issue—for example, the exploitation of children, as in Dickens's *Nicholas Nickleby* (1839) and John Hersey's *Child Buyer* (1960)—attends much more to characterization and narrative development than did the early prototypes. The best-known nineteenth-century pedagogical novel, after Dickens, was Edward Eggleston's *Hoosier Schoolmaster* (1871), which set the pattern for the frontier method of handling young bullies, a sterotype situation in scores of later novels, among them Faulkner's *Hamlet* (1940).

In the 1900s the best-known pedagogical novels have been: F. Scott Fitzgerald, *This Side of Paradise* (1920); Thomas Wolfe, *Look Homeward, Angel* (1929); James Farrell, *Young Lonigan* (1932); George Santayana, *The Last Puritan* (1936); John Marquand, *Wickford Point* (1939); William Maxwell, *The Folded Leaf* (1945); J. D. Salinger, *The Catcher in the Rye* (1945); Ivy Compton-Burnett, *Two Worlds and Their Ways* (1949); Mary McCarthy, *The Groves of Academe* (1952); Jessamyn West, *Cress Delahanty* (1953); C. P. Snow, *The Masters* (1953); Frances Patton, *Good Morning, Miss Dove* (1954); Evan Hunter, *The Blackboard Jungle* (1954); Kingsley Amis, *Lucky Jim* (1954); Herman Wouk, *Marjorie Morningstar* (1955); Howard Nemerov, *Homecoming Game* (1957); Vladimir Nabokov, *Pnin* (1957); John Knowles, *A Separate Peace* (1959); John Updike, *The Centaur* (1962); and Bel Kaufman, *Up the Down Staircase* (1964).

REFERENCES: Wilbur Cross, *Development of the English Novel;* Ian Watt, *Rise of the Novel;* Arnold Lazarus, "Educational Thought in Modern Fiction," in G. F. Kneller (ed.), *Foundations of Education.*

didacticism   From the Greek verb "to teach." The tendency to emphasize instruction or moralizing; in contemporary literary criticism a derogation, since the assumption is that literary works are essentially descriptive (Aristotelian) rather than prescriptive (Platonic). (The DIDACTIC NOVEL is treated in a separate article.) Examples of didactic poetry are Ella Wheeler Wilcox's "Laugh and the world laughs with you; / Weep and you weep alone"; Kipling's "If" and "Ballad of East and West"; and Longfellow's "Psalm of Life." (Ironically, lines from the last two poems are frequently quoted out of context so that the lesson intended in each poem as a whole is reversed.) Examples of didactic drama include MELODRAMA in general and, in particular, such eighteenth-century sentimental plays as Richard Steele's *Conscious Lovers* (1772); George Lillo's *London Merchant* (1731) and *The Christian Hero* (1735); and Hugh Kelley's *False Delicacy* (1768). All of these are clear-cut examples of didacticism, reflecting intentions that few critics today would disagree over. But the above-mentioned criteria that distinguish a didactic from a nondidactic work remain all too simplistic; the problem is actually more complex. When, for example, is the theme of a poem, novel or play a *descriptive* philosophic observation and when is it a *prescriptive* "moral"? Whether or not a theme is stated in the grammatical imperative (for example, "Don't go near the water") is after all a trivial distinction. Although such critics as Matthew Arnold and T. S. Eliot must have cringed at overt didacticism, they did insist respectively on moral "high seriousness" and on the social and moral function of literature. And to hear George Bernard Shaw, one would think that even intentional didacticism on the part of an author is no literary crime. In the Preface to *Pygmalion,* for example, he says

It [Pygmalion] is so intensely and deliberately didactic . . . that I delight in throwing it at the heads of the wiseacres who repeat the parrot cry that art should never be didactic. It goes to prove my contention that art should never be anything else. — *Complete Plays,* Vol. I, p. 194.

But Shaw was a notorious iconoclast, and *Pygmalion* remains less memorable for its didacticism than for its wit, its entertaining situations, and its charming characterizations. (See ALLEGORY, APHORISM, GNOMIC, MORAL, PHILOSOPHIC STATEMENT, and THEME 2.)

REFERENCES: Matthew Arnold, *Culture and Anarchy;* T. S. Eliot, *The Use of Poetry and the Use of Criticism;* George Bernard Shaw, Preface to *Pygmalion;* W. K. Wimsatt, "Poetry and Morals," in Eliseo Vivas and Murray Krieger (eds.), *The Problems of Aesthetics.*

dieresis   A mark (¨) placed over the second of two successive vowels to indicate that it is to be sounded separately. The mark has fallen from favor in American orthography, its function having been assumed by the hyphen or not at all. In such a word as *naïve,* it serves a valuable purpose, indicating two syllables are to be pronounced; but *coöperate* has given way to *co-operate* or *cooperate, preëmpt* to *pre-empt* or *preempt.* In poetry the dieresis is still sometimes used to mark a sounded syllable that in normal speech would not be sounded:

A huge horse made, high raisëd like a hill

dilemma   A form of DEDUCTIVE REASONING that presents a pair of alternatives, one of which must be faced and both of which are usually, though not necessarily, unpleasant. For example, "Here we are at a crucial fork in the road. One route leads through a treacherous swamp;

the other skirts dangerously close to a precipice. Which route shall we take? We must take one or the other, because everything behind us is burned out." Notice that dilemma poses a real and legitimate pair of alternatives ("horns") and is thus to be distinguished from FALSE DILEMMA or DISJUNCTIVE DILEMMA.

dimeter   In verse, a line with two major stresses; for example, *Laughing waters*. (See METER.)

dirge   In poetry, a lament, or wailing, or "keening" (Irish) for a dead person. Unlike an ELEGY, a dirge has no prescribed forms.

discovery   1. In literature, an unfolding in which a character proceeds from ignorance and innocence to knowledge and experience. Thus, in Sophocles' *Oedipus* the protagonist is initially ignorant of his real parentage and gradually becomes informed. Such "unfoldings" are also basic to the short stories called *epiphanies*. Many of the stories in James Joyce's *Dubliners* are superb examples. 2. When a protagonist discovers something that the reader or audience already knows — and especially when the audience knows what the protagonist has yet to discover — the situation is called DRAMATIC IRONY. 3. In logic, exposition, and learning, discovery is an inductive process in which the reader makes general inferences from given data. Such discovery is the opposite of *deductive instruction,* in which the general principle is given, and the reader or student then seeks specimen data to support the generalization.
REFERENCE: Caroline Gordon, *How to Read a Novel.*
   4. A writer often "discovers" what he wants to say when he allows himself to be disciplined by the *form,* the technique, the way he says it. (Compare INVENTIO.)
REFERENCE: Mark Schorer, "Technique as Discovery," in James Miller, Jr. (ed), *Myth and Method.*

disjunctive dilemma   A specious argument which asserts that two possible things cannot both pertain at the same time, as in "It can*not* be *both* raining *and* snowing." Such a statement is of course false — and if used in a disjunctive syllogism. (see SYLLOGISM 4) would constitute a false premise. (Compare FALSE DILEMMA.)

disjunctive syllogism   See SYLLOGISM 4.

dissertation   See THESIS I.

dissociation of sensibility   See SENSIBILITY 2.

dissonance   A clashing combination of sounds. The dissonance may be deliberate and purposeful, or it may be the result of the author's "tin ear." (Compare CACOPHONY.)

distich   Literally, "two-lined." A COUPLET; any two-lined stanza;

a pair of rhyming lines written in the same METER. For example, "Anthologies and lecture tours and grants / Create a solvency which disenchants" (Donald Hall).

distributed term   See SYLLOGISM I G.

dithyramb   1. Originally, in Greek verse, an extravagant paean to, or song in praise of, Dionysus, the god of creative intoxication. 2. Now a more general label, usually derogatory, for any extravagantly emotional passage of prose or verse. Thus, in Thomas Wolfe's novel *Look Homeward, Angel* the final paragraph of Chapter 30 may be called a dithyramb: "O lost and by the wind grieved, ghost come back again, as first I knew you in the timeless valley. . . ."
REFERENCE: Jane Harrison, *Themis*.

ditrochee   See METER.

ditto marks   The paired marks (″) used to indicate that material printed directly above is to be repeated. Ditto marks are used in classroom notes, but not in formal writing.

division of words   See SYLLABICATION.

documentation   In research work the set of conventions the writer follows when citing his authorities and acknowledging his indebtedness. Documentation is achieved through *bibliography* and *footnotes*.

Bibliography is a formally arranged list of books and articles pertinent to a given topic. A researcher's *working bibliography* is a compilation of cards, each citing a work *to be* consulted as the researcher seeks information; his *final bibliography* is a list of works that *have been* consulted. If the final bibliography lists all works consulted for the project, it is a *full* bibliography; if it lists only the works actually referred to in the text and cited in the footnotes, it is a *selected* bibliography.

1. *The working bibliography.* After the researcher has tentatively defined his topic, so that he knows what subjects (or topic headings) to consult in reference works, he is ready to begin compiling his bibliography. As he finds reference to a possible source of pertinent information, he notes that source (using a formal order) on a 3″ × 5″ card. Such cards facilitate later arrangement of the materials as his project requires them, and they provide for final arrangement into alphabetical order.

Using the most complete available reference library, the researcher first consults the standard reference works—dictionaries and encyclopedias—and pertinent specialized reference works, to prepare himself for his later intensive study. But these reference works are not usually considered useful sources for a term paper, for in a sense they *are* term papers (though on topics not sufficiently limited). The researcher's attempt is to bring together materials that have not already appeared in reference works.

He next attempts a systematic search for books and articles that may contain information on his topic. He begins with his library's card catalogue, searching through several subject headings that could lead him to useful books. As he finds a catalogue card citing an apparently useful book, he transcribes onto a 3″ × 5″ card the information he needs: author's name, title, city of publication, publisher's name, and date of publication. It is advisable at this step that the researcher use the precise form that must appear in his final bibliography, in order to avoid later waste of time and to diminish the chance of error.

Most widely used among scholarly forms for bibliography is the *MLA Style Sheet,* published by the Modern Language Association. Other style guides are available and are sometimes required by a school or teacher; but mastery of the MLA style will help establish habits of accuracy. The researcher-student can easily switch to some other style, if he is called upon to do so. Precision and, above all, consistency in the order of information and in punctuation are indispensable. Following the *MLA Style Sheet,* the researcher will use these forms for his bibliography:

(*a*) Book with one author

Flesch, Rudolf.
The Art of Plain Talk.
New York: Harper & Brothers, 1946.

(*b*) Book with two authors

Wellek, René, and Austin Warren.
Theory of Literature.
New York: Harcourt, Brace and Company, 1956.

(*c*) Book with three or more authors

Bloom, Edward A., and others.
The Order of Poetry: An Introduction.
New York: The Odyssey Press, Inc., 1961.

(*d*) Book (anthology) with editor

Burnshaw, Stanley, ed.
Varieties of Literary Experience.
New York: New York University Press, 1962.

(*e*) Book in several volumes

Marchand, Leslie A.
Byron: A Biography. 3 vols.
New York: Alfred A. Knopf, 1957.

(*f*) Book (edited)

Melville, Herman.
Pierre. Ed. by Henry A. Murray.
New York: Farrar, Straus, 1949.

or

Murray, Henry A., ed.
Pierre, by Herman Melville.
New York: Farrar, Straus, 1949.

When using the library's card catalogue, the researcher will be wise to note on each of his cards the *call number* of the book referred to. This will facilitate his finding the book on the shelves and checking it out for use, and will preclude a wasteful return trip to the catalogue.

Since much of the most recent as well as the most valuable material on many topics appears not in books but in periodicals, the researcher must next turn his attention to magazines and newspapers. There are several indexes, regularly published, that catalogue by topic (and often by author) many of the thousands of articles published in periodicals, both general and specialized. A good research library will have available at least some of these indexes:

Readers' Guide to Periodical Literature (indexes articles in a selected group of American magazines—from 1900 to the present)
Poole's Index to Periodical Literature (indexes general interest articles in magazines—from 1802 to 1906)
International Index to Periodicals (indexes American and some foreign articles, especially in scholarly journals—from 1907 to the present)

Specialized indexes:

Agricultural Index (from 1916 to present)
Art Index (from 1929 to present)
Dramatic Index (from 1909 to 1950)
Education Index (from 1929 to present)
Engineering Index (from 1892 to 1906) and *Engineering Index Annual* (from 1906 to present)
Index Medicus (from 1879 to present, indexing medical periodicals, books and pamphlets)
Index to Legal Periodicals (1908 to present)
Industrial Arts Index (from 1913 to present)
National Geographic Index (limited to articles in a single publication)
New York Times Index (from 1913 to date, indexing only articles that appeared in *The New York Times,* but often useful for locating national interest stories in other newspapers by date)
PMLA [Publications of the Modern Language Association] (an annual listing of books and articles dealing with the literature of all modern languages)
Public Affairs Information Service Bulletin (from 1915 to present, indexing periodicals, books, documents, and pamphlets in economics, political science, and sociology)

In most of these indexes the researcher will find entries in this form:

(*a*) Subject entry   Sabotage in Springfield: Webster's third edition.
                             W. Follett. Atlan 209:73–7 Ja '62

(*b*) Author entry   FOLLETT, Wilson
                             Sabotage in Springfield. Atlan 209:73–7 Ja '62

The form used in *Readers' Guide* (and most other periodical indexes) is much abbreviated, and the researcher must "translate" the information into the proper *MLA Style Sheet* (or other) form. Under the subject entry, where the researcher initially finds the information, the author is listed as "W. Follett"; but because the single initial is improper for bibliography, the researcher must look under "Follett," the author entry, to find the author's full name. The title of the magazine is abbreviated, and if the researcher does not recognize the title, he must turn to the list of "Abbreviations of Periodicals Indexed" (just inside the front cover of *Readers' Guide*). He must also understand that the numbers "209:73-7" mean Volume 209: Pages 73 through 77. "Ja" means January, and "'62" means 1962. Now he is ready to make out a bibliography card in proper *MLA Style Sheet* form:

Follett, Wilson.
"Sabotage in Springfield."
Atlantic, CCIX (January 1962), 73–77.

Some variant forms of periodical entries:

(*a*) Two authors   Durkin, Dolores, and W. D. Sheldon.
"Should the Very Young Be Taught To Read?"
NEA Journal, LII (November 1963), 22.

(*b*) Magazine without   Wheeler, J. H.
     volume number   "Banker With a Mission."
Business Week, May 16, 1964, p. 56.

(*c*) Newspaper article   Kamm, Henry.
     (with byline)   "Parisians Dance on Bastille Day."
New York Times, July 15, 1964, p. 13, col. 1.

(*d*) Newspaper article   "Paul Marks First Year as Pope."
     (unsigned)   *New York Times,* July 1, 1964, p. 14, col. 4.

If the researcher finds pamphlets among materials he will use, he will ordinarily show the sponsoring agency or corporation in author position, then, in order, the pamphlet's title (underlined), the name of the *author* (if known), the *series* and *number* of the pamphlet (if pertinent), the *edition* number, the *place* of publication, the *date,* the number of *pages* in the pamphlet. A sample:

American Association of School Administrators.
Year-Round School.
Washington, D.C., 1960. 26 pp.

After compiling the bibliography cards, the researcher is ready to consult the books and articles themselves, using his cards as a directory to locations in the library. His "notetaking" then begins. (See RESEARCH PAPER.)

2. *The final bibliography.* When he has finished writing his paper,

the researcher appends a list of works used in its preparation. He must decide whether to list *all* the works consulted (*full bibliography*) or only those actually referred to in his text and footnotes (a *selected bibliography*). He alphabetizes the pertinent bibliography cards and transcribes from them all their information, using a hanging indention format, i.e., authors' names flush to the left margin of the sheet. His final bibliography may look something like this:

BIBLIOGRAPHY

Bloom, Edward A., and others. *The Order of Poetry: An Introduction.* New York: The Odyssey Press, Inc., 1961.

Burnshaw, Stanley, ed. *Varieties of Literary Experience.* New York: New York University Press, 1962.

Durkin, Dolores, and W. D. Sheldon, "Should the Very Young Be Taught To Read?" *NEA Journal,* VII (November 1963), 22.

Flesch, Rudolf. *The Art of Plain Talk.* New York: Harper & Brothers, 1946.

Follett, Wilson, "Sabotage in Springfield." *Atlantic,* CCIX (January 1962), 73–77.

Kamm, Henry, "Parisians Dance on Bastille Day." *New York Times,* July 15, 1964, p. 13, col. 1.

Marchand, Leslie A. *Byron: A Biography.* 3 vols. New York: Alfred A. Knopf, 1957.

Melville, Herman *Pierre.* Ed. by Henry A. Murray. New York: Farrar, Straus, 1949.

"Paul Marks First Year as Pope." *New York Times,* July 1, 1964, p. 14, col. 4.

Wellek, René, and Austin Warren. *Theory of Literature.* New York: Harcourt, Brace and Company, 1956.

Wheeler, J. H. "Banker With a Mission." *Business Week,* May 16, 1964, p. 56.

Note that the final bibliography is a single alphabetical listing: books are *not* separated from articles. Every item is listed in its alphabetical place according to the first letter of the entry, whether that be an author's name or a title.

Footnotes are immediate citations of sources. Everything taken from a printed source must be credited to that source. The footnotes provide the necessary credit and the authentication.

The following should be footnoted: (1) all statements of opinion (it is usually assumed that the researcher does not report his own opinions, though he may draw *conclusions* from cited evidence); (2) all facts not well known to the intended readers of the paper; (3) all facts (even if well known) upon which any part of the paper's thesis may depend.

As the term implies, footnotes usually appear at the *foot* of the page on which the cited material appears. Some publishers and teachers ask that footnotes be compiled in a list at the end of the paper, but the foot-of-the-page method is still more widely used.

Footnotes in a research paper follow a single sequence, every footnote with its own number. A new numbering sequence is not begun on every page, but a new sequence is begun for each chapter in a thesis, dissertation, or book.

Footnote form differs from bibliography form in several ways: (1) footnotes are not alphabetized; therefore, the authors' names are not reversed; (2) footnotes are assumed to be abbreviated sentences; therefore, commas are used in some instances in which bibliography notes use periods — after authors' names and titles; (3) footnotes do not include names of publishers; (4) footnotes do include page numbers, since they refer to specific points within a book or article, rather than to the entire book or article.

Footnotes are not properly used for "asides" to the reader. They are, in most scholarly work, strictly citations of sources.

Repetitive sequences of footnotes may employ some abbreviations — for example, *ibid., op. cit., loc. cit..* Except *ibid.,* however, the use of these terms is discouraged by the *MLA Style Sheet,* since the author's name and page number will usually tell enough. But the student-researcher must learn how to use these Latin-term abbreviations so he can use them with precision when necessary — and the knowledge will help him to interpret other scholarly, documented works.

Here is a sample sequence of footnotes, with explanation of the devices properly used:

[1]René Wellek and Austin Warren, *Theory of Literature* (New York, 1956), p. 128.

[2]*Ibid.*

[3]Wilson Follett, "Sabotage in Springfield," *Atlantic,* CCIX (January 1962), 75.

[4]*Ibid.,* p. 76.

[5]"Paul Marks First Year as Pope," *New York Times,* July 1, 1964, p. 14, col. 4.

[6]Wellek, *loc. cit.*

[7]Follett, p. 76.

[8]"Paul Marks First Year," *loc. cit.*

[9]Wellek, *op. cit.,* p. 129.

Explanation of footnote sequence: (1) First reference to a book; (2) repeat of immediately preceding footnote; (3) first reference to a magazine article; (4) Repeat of immediately preceding footnote, with change of page number; (5) first reference to a newspaper article; (6) second (or later) reference to a book, same page as last time mentioned; (7) second reference to a magazine article, with change of page number; (8) second (or later) reference to a newspaper article; (9) second (or later) reference to a book, with change of page number (the *op. cit.*

could be omitted without ambiguity, as is recommended by the *MLA Style Sheet*).

Some students complain that, when typing the final draft, they cannot plan ahead for the space that footnotes will require. They will find this method helpful: In writing the first draft of a research paper, stop immediately when a footnote number has been written in the text; type the footnote at that point, rather than at the foot; after typing the footnote, go ahead with the text until another footnote number is reached, type it in; when typing the final draft, simply skip the footnotes, and when the last line of text has been typed, there will be just enough space left for the footnotes on that page.

REFERENCES: *MLA Style Sheet;* D. F. Bond, *A Reference Guide to English Studies;* James Thorpe, *Literary Scholarship;* Milton Byrd and Arnold Goldsmith, *Publication Guide for Literary and Linguistic Scholars;* Donald Sears, *Harbrace Guide to the Library and Research Paper.*

doggerel   1. Trivial, singsong verse; e.g., "Jack and Jill go down the hill to get their bread at Baker's Mill." 2. Doggerel is also a derogatory epithet applied to unintentionally bad verse. (See Wyndham Lewis and Charles Lee [eds.], *The Stuffed Owl: An Anthology of Bad Verse.*)

donnée   The "given" — such factual elements of a literary work as setting, manifest story-line (or plot), and at least the names and apparent attributes of the characters. The term, introduced by the novelist Henry James, is based on the analogy of a geometry problem, in which certain elements are "given"; the reader then takes it from there, trying to solve the puzzle, to get at meaning. The donnée may include THEME, if by that is meant something general like "alienation," "retribution," and so on. But such a factual element is to be distinguished from any PHILOSOPHIC STATEMENT implicit in the deeper structure of a literary work. (Compare VISION OF LIFE.) More often than not, the donnée consists mainly of the cast of characters (*dramatis personae*) with their most overt identifications (names, ages, sexes, outward appearances, and so on), the setting (time, place, socio-economic condition, and so on), and the manifest story-line. (See LEVELS OF MEANING.)

REFERENCE: Henry James, "The Art of Fiction," in James Miller, Jr. (ed.), *Myth and Method;* C. S. Brown, "Difficulty and Surface Value," in Peter Demetz (ed.), *The Disciplines of Criticism.*

Doppelgänger   See ALTER EGO.

double dactyls   Also known as **jiggery-pokery.** Light verse consisting of two four-line stanzas in which the last line of the first stanza rhymes with the last line of the second stanza and in which each line consists of two DACTYLS, for example, "Higgledy, piggledy." Although the METER is ancient, the verse form is a modern invention of the poets

Anthony Hecht and John Hollander, authors of the collection *Jiggery-Pokery*.

double entendre   An utterance with two intended meanings, the less obvious of which suggests something indelicate or risqué. When Hamlet tells Ophelia, "Get thee to a nunnery . . . Or if thou wilt needs marry, marry a fool; for wise men know well enough what monsters you make of them," his "monster" suggests not only a fierce creature but also the pitiable creature with horns, a cuckold. PUNS are double entendres, though not all double entendres are puns. An AMBIGUITY arising from a verbal — e.g., "She enjoys exciting dates" — is also often a double entendre. "Exciting," understood as a transitive gerund rather than as a participle or adjectival, suggests a rather aggressive subject-agent.

Careful speakers and writers do not confuse double entendre with double-entente, which idiomatically takes an adjectival position: "He's always making double-entente remarks."

double negative   The use of two negative words ("There wasn't nothing we could do") when only one negation is intended. The double negative is not used in standard English, but its absence is a matter of fashion rather than of logic, since two negatives in an utterance do not, after all, make an affirmative. Certainly, no one hearing a child say, "I've *never* had *no* black shoes," will honestly believe that the child *has* had black shoes. If two negatives really made an affirmative, would *three* negatives restore the appropriate logic? Probably not, for "I have*n't never* had *no* black shoes" remains negative and nonstandard.

A troublesome double negative often occurs in nonstandard usage with "scarcely" or "hardly": "I *can't hardly* do that." Standard usage calls for "I *can hardly* do that," meaning "I cannot easily do that" or "I cannot do that at all." When two negations are intended, then two or more negative words are used properly: "We could *not* understand why he did *not* speak up," or even "I was *not* sure that the letter had *not* been sent for *no* good purpose." But when multiple negations are used, the style becomes involved and the message unintelligible. Revision to the clearer affirmative may well be the wiser alternative.

drama   See DRAMATIC STRUCTURE.

dramatic irony   A situation, chiefly in drama, in which a character says or does something that has more meaning than he is aware of, a meaning known to another character or to the audience or both. In the last act of Shaw's *Caesar and Cleopatra,* Caesar, preoccupied with the logistics of moving on from Egypt with most of his army, forgets all about taking formal leave of Cleopatra. Hoping perhaps for an embrace, she asks, "Has Cleopatra no part in this leavetaking?" Caesar replies absentmindedly, "Ah, I *knew* there was something." But he then goes on to talk about her mourning clothes, so that the "something" Caesar had in mind was not exactly the "something" that Cleopatra and the audience were anticipating. (See IRONY 3.)

dramatic monologue   A poem in which one character, frequently revealing his own personality, speaks for all the other characters; that is, he speaks his own lines and reports what the other characters say and do. The result is a purposely limited FOCUS OF NARRATION. An example is Browning's "My Last Duchess," in which the Duke speaks for the entire cast of characters. This kind of speaker is manifestly a member of the cast, of the *"dramatis personae."* (Compare PERSONA.)

dramatic structure   A combination of the following: (1) rising suspensive action or conflict between the PROTAGONIST and his obstacle(s), the latter being another character or one of the protagonist's traits; (2) the protagonist's success or failure in overcoming these obstacles, each one larger and more complicated than its predecessor; (3) the protagonist's confronting the most crucial obstacle (in the CLIMAX) and either overcoming it (in COMEDY) or being overcome by it (in TRAGEDY). In *Macbeth,* the protagonist's goal is to gain clear, uncontested title to the Throne of Scotland. His first obstacle is King Duncan. By killing Duncan, Macbeth gets this obstacle out of the way, but creates a larger, three-headed obstacle in the persons of the suspicious General Banquo and Duncan's sons, Malcolm and Donalbain, who get away. Macbeth cannot do anything about Duncan's sons for the moment; but he has Banquo murdered. Overcoming this obstacle is not wholly successful either, since Banquo's son, Fleance, gets away. Meanwhile, Duncan's sons have been able to muster the help of Lord Macduff. Macbeth's brutal slaughter of Macduff's wife and children only motivates the climactic action: the victims' relatives and other enemies of Macbeth combine against him in the Birnam Wood battle, which he fails to overcome, and which in fact overcomes him. Thus in dramatic structure each obstacle (or scene built on an obstacle) is tied to its predecessor or successor in a cause-and-effect chain.

Contrasted with dramatic structure is *episodic structure,* in which one scene is tied to another only loosely, usually because what happens, happens to the main character (as in a PICARESQUE NOVEL like *Anthony Adverse*) or to the main personage (as in a BIOGRAPHY like *Always the Young Strangers*). Any suspense or excitement in episodic structure is limited to, and bounded by, a given episode or scene, with little or no reference to other episodes or scenes.

In dramatic structure, on the other hand, the suspense (rising suspensive action) grows cumulatively up to the most crucial scene or climax. If the protagonist overcomes the climactic obstacle, the play turns out to be a comedy, and the *falling action* (the action from the climax to the end) is called the DÉNOUEMENT. If the protagonist is overcome by the climactic obstacle, the play is a tragedy, and the falling action is, or culminates in, the CATASTROPHE.

Because of long speeches and even COMIC RELIEF, the falling action of tragedy tends to be longer than that of comedy. Most comedies are built around a very hectic climax, followed by a brief dénouement.

REFERENCES: Norman Friedman, "Forms of the Plot," *Journal of General Education* (July, 1955); Arnold Lazarus, "Plot Graph," *Adventures in Modern Literature,* Fifth Edition; Caroline Gordon and Allen Tate, "Notes on Fictional Techniques," *The House of Fiction;* Alan Downer, *The Art of the Play;* Georges Polti, *The Thirty-six Dramatic Situations;* Richard Corbin and Miriam Balf, "How to Read a Play," *Twelve American Plays, 1920–1960;* Robin Farquhar, "Dramatic Structure in the Novels of Ernest Hemingway," *Modern Fiction Studies* (Autumn, 1968); D. M. Church, "Structure and Dramatic Technique in Gide's *Saul*," *PMLA* (October, 1969); Frederic Litto, "Introduction," *Plays from Black Africa;* Jackson Barry, *Dramatic Structure;* John Taylor, *Rise and Fall of the Well-Made Play.*

dramatism   One of Kenneth Burke's systems for the analysis of literature and human motivation. It is based on the premise that literature, language, and thought are primarily modes of action. ("Somebody is always doing something to somebody else.") Burke's theoretic model is so close to the basic sentence patterns of Western languages, especially English, that he calls his two chief books dealing with dramatism, among other matters, "a grammar" and "a rhetoric." The notion that "someone is doing something" is the "S-V-O" (subject-verb-object) sentence pattern, while the observation that there may be a recipient of this action calls to mind the "S-V-iO-O" (subject-verb-indirect object-direct object) pattern.

Some such dramatistic model is also common to most plays, short stories, novels, epics, and narrative poems. Burke subsumes under his "S-V-O" model the notion that "something is this or that" — what some structural linguists call the "S-LV-C" (subject-linking verb-complement) pattern. Within this last frame one can order the main themes or thematic motifs or philosophic implications, not only of the literary genres just mentioned, but also of such genres as lyric poems, familiar essays, and essays in literary criticism.

The five key terms ("pentad") in Burke's dramatism are *act, scene, agent, agency,* and *purpose. Act* seeks to answer "What happened?" (in thought as well as in deed). Burke's inclusion here of *thought,* as well as of overt deed, makes his concept more complex than the roughly synonymous "plot" or "manifest story line." *Scene* answers "Where did it happen?" *Agent* seeks to answer "Who did it?" Answers to "Who did it?" may range from a solution in an ephemeral "Whodunit" to the most complex unmasking of a PERSONA. *Agency* answers "How was it done?" The answers would include not only the instruments used, but also the author's tone and attitude toward his material. *Purpose* seeks to answer "Why?" It is in answer(s) to this last question that Burke as virtuoso orchestrates the contributions of anthropology, sociology, linguistics, SEMANTICS, psychology, and PSYCHOANALYSIS.

REFERENCES: Kenneth Burke, *A Grammar of Motives* and *A Rhetoric of Motives;* Stanley Edgar Hyman (ed.), *Terms for Order;* David W. Thompson and Virginia Fredericks, *Oral Interpretation of Literature: A Dramatistic Approach;* James Mullican, *Kenneth Burke's Rhetorical Theory.*

dramatis personae   The cast; a list of characters. To be distinguished from PERSONA.

E

eclogue   Literally, "choice selection," "morsel," or "tidbit." Originally, a short poem or section of a poem dealing with pastoral themes. From earliest times the eclogue was associated with pastoral poetry; that is, with poetry of the countryside, of shepherds, flocks, peacefulness. Classic examples are the *Idylls* of the Greek Theocritus (third century B.C.) and the *Eclogues* of the Roman Vergil (first century B.C.). The most celebrated eclogues in English literature are Edmund Spenser's *Shepheardes Calendar* (1579), with one poem for each month. Eclogues are characterized by (*a*) singing contests, (*b*) playful dialogue, with boasting about one's flocks or sweethearts, (*c*) formal courtship, and (*d*) laments for the dead. According to Barriss Mills, in the introduction to his verse translation of *The Idylls of Theokritos,* eclogues "invite us to forget for a while man's destiny . . . and to indulge ourselves in a daydream of rustic simplicity and romantic love."

REFERENCES: Patrick Cullen, "Imitation and Metamorphosis: The Golden Age Eclogue in Spenser, Milton, and Marvell," *PMLA* (October, 1969); Walter W. Greg, *Pastoral Poetry and Drama.*

economy in writing   Brevity is courtesy—and self-defense. A writer cannot grasp a reader by the lapels to force an audience, and none will stay to be bored; so that he who has much to say must be brief. But economy in expression is an achievement, not a gift. It comes to him who studies the language, refines his thought, and respects the reader's quickness of mind. To gain economy the writer must sharpen and extend his own vocabulary, to know how much or how little a word will do, for the weak or watery vocabulary leads to wordiness; the writer who knows, for example, what the prefix *re-* imports will not burden "return" with a REDUNDANCY ("Return the book *back* to the library"). He must analyze his thought and trim from it all the fat, for only such tough RENDERING will rescue the work from flabbiness. He must trust the reader's quick intelligence while not overrating his information, for the reader may be confused by the omission of some key fact unknown to him. (For advice on avoiding faults that destroy economy, see DEAD-WOOD, GOBBLEDYGOOK, and PARSIMONY.)

eiron   See IRONY.

elegant variation   The use of pretentious synonyms in the mistaken belief that repetition must always be avoided. (See VARIETY.)

elegy   A poem in an elevated style, written in praise of, and mourning for, a specific dead person. An elegy sometimes contains general reflections on death, often with a rural or pastoral setting—in which case it is called a pastoral elegy. The elegy is to be distinguished from the general poem on death, which speaks primarily about the typicality of death. Among the most celebrated elegies are Chaucer's *Book of the Duchess,* Milton's *Lycidas,* Gray's "Elegy in a Country Churchyard," Shelley's *Adonais,* Tennyson's *In Memoriam,* Whitman's "When Lilacs Last in the Dooryard Bloomed," and Rilke's *Duino Elegies.* More restrained, less dithyrambic than a DIRGE, an elegy dispenses as quickly as possible with its lament and gets on with an idea, observation, or meditation. Three of the most moving modern elegies, which do just that, are Dylan Thomas's "A Refusal to Mourn the Death, by Fire, of a Child in London," John Crowe Ransom's "Bells for John Whiteside's Daughter," and W. H. Auden's "In Memory of W. B. Yeats."

REFERENCE: Thomas P. Harrison, *The Pastoral Elegy.*

elision   In poetry, the omission of an unstressed vowel or syllable from a word to preserve the meter; for example, "is't" for "is it"; "i'th'earth" for "in the earth"; "th'expense" for "the expense"; " 'twas" for "it was." In modern poetry, such elisions are shunned as "poeticisms." Other elisions, such as "t'other" for "the other," are peculiar to backwoods DIALECTS.

Elizabethan   Pertaining to the era and reign of Elizabeth I (1558–1603). The Elizabethan Age, noted for religious controversy, world exploration, expansion of trade and sea power, was accompanied by a flowering of literature—especially lyric poetry and drama. During this RENAISSANCE, which reached England much later than it reached the countries of the Continent, flourished such poets and playwrights as William Shakespeare, Sir Philip Sidney, Samuel Daniel, Thomas Campion, Ben Jonson, John Donne, Christopher Marlowe, John Lyly, Robert Greene, Thomas Kyd, George Chapman, John Marston, Thomas Heywood, and Thomas Dekker.

REFERENCES: John E. Neal, *Queen Elizabeth I;* Maxwell Anderson, *Elizabeth the Queen;* Hazelton Spenser (ed.), *Elizabethan Plays;* J. William Hebel and Hoyt H. Hudson (eds.), *Poetry of the English Renaissance (1509–1660);* A. L. Rowse, *The England of Elizabeth;* E. M. W. Tillyard, *The Elizabethan World Picture;* Paul J. Alpers (ed.), *Elizabethan Poetry: Modern Essays in Criticism;* Norman Kotker and L. B. Smith (eds.), *The Horizon Book of the Elizabethan World;* E. K. Chambers, *The Elizabethan Stage;* G. Gregory Smith (ed.), *Elizabethan Critical Essays;* David Bevington, *Tudor Drama and Politics.*

ellipsis   1. The omission of any element from a sentence so that the grammatical structure is incomplete although the sense is clear. Conversational English is especially elliptical: "Hi!" "Morning!" "Got troubles?" "Sure have." "Lost a friend?" "No, just tired." "Up late last night?" "Yeah. Big party." (The conversation communicates even though no full sentence appears.) Even formal English uses ellipsis and the MINOR SENTENCE, which, however, must be distinguished from the FRAGMENT, in which the sense is unclear and the unfinished structure awkward. Ellipsis is a characteristic of the LACONIC style; it appears often in EPIGRAM, APHORISM, proverb, and maxim. One special sort of ellipsis is the purposeful omission of *and* (see ASYNDETON). 2. The omission of elements from quoted material — usually in formal writing — may be indicated by the use of three "dots" (. . .); the mark is called an ellipsis. The use of ellipsis calls for a careful and honest study of the quoted material so that nothing essential to sense or intent is omitted. The ellipsis mark may also be used to indicate a suspension of a remark ("The fellow was . . . oh, I don't know what") or an implied continuation of a sequence ("So it went, day and night, day and night . . . "). (See APOSIOPESIS.)

emotional appeals   Most of these are treated in separate articles in this handbook under the following entries: AD CAPTANDUM (bandwagon); AD HOMINEM (appeal to personal prejudices); AD IGNORANTIAM (appeal to ignorance); AD MISERICORDIAM (appeal to pity); AD POPULUM (appeal to popular prejudices); AD VERECUNDIAM (snob appeal); FRIEND OF THE ENEMY (guilt by association); RED HERRING (smokescreen; smoked herring); TU QUOQUE ("You did it, too!"). (See also PROPAGANDA DEVICES and FALLACIES OF REASONING.)

empathy   A reader's or spectator's feeling of identification ("That could be me") with a character. Empathy is involuntary, and should be distinguished from *sympathy,* which is voluntary. Empathy is part of the "transaction" between actor and audience, between author and reader, which some critics insist is elicited by a masterwork.

REFERENCE: Northrop Frye, *The Educated Imagination.*

emphasis   A principle of organization by which the elements of an utterance or a composition are clearly placed as to their importance. Elements may be emphasized by (1) pointing at them with direct statement ("most important is . . . ," "Foremost . . ."); (2) placing them at beginning or end (in a sentence, a paragraph, or a full discourse); (3) giving them fullness of treatment (more space than is given to less important elements); (4) repeating them; (5) setting them apart (as in a very short paragraph that draws attention by contrast with longer ones); (6) couching them in terse independent clauses or sentences.

Proper emphasis cannot be achieved by such hackneyed devices as false exaggeration, underlining, italicizing, or exclamation-marking.

end-stopped   A synonym for "closed line." (Contrast ENJAMBEMENT.)

enjambement   In poetry, the continuation of a sentence from one line into the next, or of two lines or more into the next; respectable "run-on lines." In Edwin Arlington Robinson's "Richard Cory": "In fine, we thought that he was everything / To make us wish that we were in his place." In Stephen Vincent Benét's *John Brown's Body:* "And bleak New England farms, so winter-white / Even their roofs look lonely, and the deep / The middle grainland where the wind of night / Is like all blind earth sighing in her sleep."

enthymeme An elliptical argument in which one or more elements of a SYLLOGISM are implicit. For example, "Nice girls don't go there" implies (1) "there" is not respectable, (2) you are a nice girl, and (3) therefore you won't go there. In argumentation the enthymeme is often used to make the audience draw its own conclusions.

envoy (envoi) See BALLADE.

epanadiplosis The repetition of a word or phrase at the beginnings of successive lines, clauses, or sentences. Examples: *"My day* begins rapidly; *my day* moves toward its usual frenzy." *"Come now,* Molly! *Come now,* I say!" Poets have made much use of the emphasis supplied by epandiplosis. Thus, Emily Dickinson:

Our share of night to bear—
Our share of morning—
Our blank in bliss to fill
Our blank in scorning—

epic A long narrative poem unified by a hero who reflects the customs, mores, and aspirations of his nation or race as he makes his way through legendary and historic exploits, usually over a long period of time. The celebrated epics of world literature include the *Shah Namah* (Persia), *The Mahabharata* (India), *The Kalevala* (Finland), the *Niebelungenlied* (Germany), *The Cid* (Spain), and Camõens' *Lusiads* (Portugal). Perhaps the best-known epics in Western literature are Vergil's (Latin) *Aeneid* and his ancient Greek models, *The Iliad* and *The Odyssey*. The latter two are usually attributed to Homer, but they are also called folk epics because of possible group authorship and because of their oral transmission over many generations. *The Iliad, The Odyssey,* and *The Aeneid* were written in dactyllic hexameter.

The best-known epic poems in English are the Anglo-Saxon folk epic *Beowulf,* written in ALLITERATIVE VERSE, and Milton's *Paradise Lost,* written in BLANK VERSE. The American poet Longfellow attempted, in *Hiawatha,* an epic poem of the American Indian. And the modern American poet Stephen Vincent Benét attempted, in *John Brown's Body,* an epic poem of the War Between the States.

An epic poem will exhibit most of the following CONVENTIONS: the invocation of a MUSE appropriate to the theme; the appearance of supernatural forces; the use of the IN-MEDIAS-RES narrative technique; the cataloging of genealogies and battle equipment; the delivery of formal, often pretentious, speeches; and the elaboration of long, drawn-out similes. (See EPIC SIMILE.)

REFERENCES: E. M. W. Tillyard, *The English Epic and Its Background;* Jan Devries, *Heroic Song and Heroic Legend;* Charles M. Gayley and Benjamin P. Kurtz, *Lyric, Epic, and Allied Forms of Poetry;* Gilbert Highet, *The Classical Tradition;* Gilbert Murray, *The Rise of the Greek Epic;* W. P. Ker, *Epic and Romance;* James Justus, "Epic Design of *Absalom, Absalom,*" *Texas Studies in Literature and Language* (Summer, 1962).

epic simile   An extended and elaborate simile conventional in EPIC poetry. An example from John Milton's *Paradise Lost* (Book II, lines 284–290):

> He scarce had finished, when such murmurs filled
> Th'Assembly, as when hollow Rocks retain
> The sound of blustring winds, which all night long
> Had roused the Sea, now with hoarse cadence lull
> Sea-faring men orewatcht, whose Bark by chance
> Or Pinnace anchors in a craggy Bay
> After the Tempest. . . .

Long before the Bark has anchored in the Bay we smile (perhaps *with* Milton) at the "blustring winds," for it is to these sounds that he compares the applause of the fallen angels for their comrade Mammon. Epic simile is not always humorous, but it is almost always open to PARODY.

epicurean   1. The term originally pertained to the cult of the Greek philosopher Epicurus (342–270 B.C.), who taught that the goal of man is lasting rather than fleeting pleasure; that he can find this only in temperance and in cultivating the intellect, morality, and serenity. 2. More loosely, in conversation, pertaining to a cultivated taste for things exotic, especially luxurious food, beverages, and other indulgences of the senses.

epigram   A brief, witty saying, often in verse. In classical literature one of the most prolific writers of epigrams was the Roman Martial. One of Martial's celebrated epigrams in an eighteenth-century English translation goes like this: "I do not love you, Dr. Fell. / The reason why I cannot tell. / But this I know, and know full well: / I do not love you, Dr. Fell."

The epigram incarnates the soul of wit: brevity. Though to the Greeks the epigram was but an "inscription" or a short, solemn poem, the Romans took the solemnity out of it and added a barb, employing the epigram usually as LAMPOON or SATIRE. Today the epigram is more often prose than verse, and it may be either satire or philosophical observation, but it remains brief, clever, pointed. Its favorite device is ANTITHESIS. Some examples: "The trouble with living it up is that it's so hard to live down"; "You can take the boy out of the country, but you can't take the country out of the boy." A writer whose work is larded with epigrams may be said to have an *epigrammatic style.* Among such writers: Alexander Pope, Ralph Waldo Emerson, George Eliot, Mark Twain, Ambrose Bierce, H. L. Mencken, J. V. Cunningham, and many columnists and reviewers.

REFERENCE: Barriss Mills (trans.), *The Epigrams of Martial;* J. V. Cunningham, *The Exclusions of a Rhyme.*

epigraph   A brief quotation or motto prefixed to a written work and used to suggest its theme. For example, Ernest Hemingway uses as an epigraph to *For Whom the Bell Tolls* the passage from John Donne beginning "No man is an island," which contains the title of the novel. An epigraph that suggests particularly well the theme of Roger Shattuck's *Banquet Years* is from Plato's *Symposium,* in which Socrates suggests that "the genius of comedy is the same as that of tragedy" and that "the writer of tragedy ought to be a writer of comedy also."

epilogue   A short conclusion to a work; formerly, to a play. In the epilogue to *The Tempest* Prospero makes a poetic bid for applause: "Now my charms are all o'erthrown / . . . so release me from my bands [bonds] / With the help of your good hands!"

epiphany   See DISCOVERY.

epistolary novel   Prose fiction narrated through personal letters exchanged by the characters. This device allows the author to remain in the background while re-creating each character-narrator's thoughts and feelings with a sense of immediacy. (See FOCUS OF NARRATION.) The device also affords the author the opportunity for some keen play of IRONY and DRAMATIC IRONY, inasmuch as one character's letter can reflect a frame of reference utterly opposed to that of another character. Among the best-known examples are Aphra Behn's *Love Letters Between a Nobleman and His Sister* (1683), Samuel Richardson's *Pamela* (1740) and *Clarissa Harlowe* (1748), Tobias Smollett's *Humphrey Clinker* (1771), and Fanny Burney's *Evelina* (1778).

REFERENCES: Natascha Wurtzbach (ed.), *The Novel in Letters;* R. H. Costa, "The Epistolary Monitor in *Pamela," Modern Language Quarterly* (March, 1970).

epitaph   **1.** Any brief inscription in prose or verse on a tombstone. **2.** A short formal poem of commemoration, often a credo written by the person who wishes it to be placed on his own tombstone. Perhaps the most celebrated epitaph is Shakespeare's: "Good friend, for Jesu's sake forbear / To dig the dust enclosed here. / Blest be the man that spares these stones. / Cursed be he that moves my bones." Well known also is Robert Louis Stevenson's "Here he lies where he longed to be; / Home is the sailor, home from the sea / And the hunter home from the hill." (Compare ELEGY.) **3.** The epitaph as a conventional form is sometimes used for ironic and humorous verse, as it is, for example, by David McCord in "Epitaph on a Waiter": "By and by / God caught his eye."

epithalamion   A formal poem in honor of a marriage, one of the loftiest and best known being Spenser's *Epithalamion* (1595), commemorating his own marriage. Spenser succeeds in re-creating the tension between patience and impatience by means of such lofty Platonic lines as these:

> Behold whiles she before the altar stands
> Hearing the holy priest that to her speakes
> And blesses her with his two happy hands. . . .

and the impatient lines:

> Ah! when will this long weary day have end,
> And lende me leave to come unto my love?

epithet   1. An adjunctive or descriptive phrase attached to a person's name with either complimentary or disparaging effect: *Honest Abe, William the Conqueror, Alfred the Great, Philip the Bold, Stonewall Jackson, broad-shouldered Bunyan, rare Ben Jonson, Leo the Lip, the incomparable Max* [Beerbohm], *Scarface Al.* Compare *robin redbreast* and Milton's *resplendent Eve.*

2. *Homeric epithet* is used repeatedly in *The Iliad* and *The Odyssey: rosy-fingered dawn, cloud-gathering Zeus, Poseidon the Earth-shaker.* The Homeric epithet is akin to the Anglo-Saxon KENNING.

3. Epithets are sometimes also METONYMS, especially the formal circumlocutions for simple, less formal nouns: *finny tribe* for *fish,* and *briny deep* for *ocean.* Such phrases used repeatedly are called *stock epithets.* Sometimes the pompousness of these circumlocutions is somewhat softened by intended humor. Dr. Samuel Johnson probably kept tongue in cheek when he called chickens "gallinaceous fowl." At other times a stock epithet like *long, last sleep* for death is intended as a EUPHEMISM.

4. *Transferred epithet* is a poetic device in which an adjective is transferred from the noun it would ordinarily precede to another noun, thus giving a pleasant shock-effect. In "Fern Hill," for example, instead of a "lilting boy about the house," Dylan Thomas sings the praises of a boy about the "lilting house"; instead of "whinnying horses," "whinnying . . . stable." This transfer enables the poet to suggest that the building is practically shaking with sound.

5. *Ironic epithet* is (*a*) an obvious twisting of facts or meaning (compare OXYMORON) or (*b*) a satire on a common, well-known epithet. To

satirize "audio-visual aids," Patrick Hazard has used for the word *books* the ironic epithet "printed aids." Similarly, "to hurl epithets at [someone or something]"—"fellow traveler," "pinko," "fascist," "beatnik"—is the same as NAME-CALLING.

epitrite   See METER.

epode   See ODE.

equivocation   Hedging or misleading by giving "equal voice" to two meanings so that the utterance can be taken either of two ways. (Compare AMBIGUITY.) In logic, equivocation also arises when a term within an argument has more than one meaning and its established meaning changes in the course of the argument. For example:

> Someone loves me.
> Mary is someone.
> Therefore Mary loves me.

The conclusion is invalid, for the meaning of *someone* (a person) in the major premise has shifted to *Mary* (a specific person) in the minor premise.

essay   From the French *essai,* literally "attempt." Brief nonfiction reflections in prose; developed, though not originated, by Michel de Montaigne (1533–92) and Francis Bacon (1561–1626); popularized by Joseph Addison (1672–1719) and Richard Steele (1672–1729). In *The Spectator* and *The Tatler* Addison and Steele did not try to conceal their editorializing under the guise of reporting (or the other way around). They indulged a tongue-in-cheek humor and exploited the leisurely mood of their times—as did many of their successors, in this genre, during the eighteenth and nineteenth centuries: Samuel Johnson, Charles Lamb, William Hazlitt, Thomas De Quincey, Oliver Wendell Holmes, Ralph Waldo Emerson, Henry David Thoreau, Walter Pater, Matthew Arnold, Andrew Lang, Robert Louis Stevenson, G. K. Chesterton, and Max Beerbohm. Most essays written before the 1940s reflected the tranquillity of clouds on a summer's day or the fireside easy chair of a winter's evening. When essays were not poking fun at contemporary manners and mores (as in the humorous, sometimes satirical essays of Stephen Leacock, H. L. Mencken, Robert Benchley, James Thurber, E. B. White), they were extolling the pleasures and inspirations of Nature with a capital N (as in the essays of E. V. Lucas, Walter Pritchett, Christopher Morley, Donald Culross Peattie, Rachel Carson, Joseph Wood Krutch, Loren Eiseley).

As distinguished from the ARTICLE or *feature story,* both of which, however informal, are devoted mostly to informing, the essay (also known as *familiar essay* and *personal essay*) is devoted to entertaining, or reflecting, or inspiring. It tends to be relaxed and philosophic, or witty, or poetic, or all of these at once. And it is comparatively brief—approximately five hundred words but rarely longer than a thousand. It takes such a commonplace ("familiar") subject as "pigs," for example, and treats it in an original manner; for example, "Pigs as Pets." The style of an essay is both informal and urbane—the voice of a civilized speaker in conversation with a civilized audience, an audience well-read enough to recognize and appreciate ALLUSIONS.

In writing an essay, no matter how commonplace the topic, the writer strives for unusual treatment. He may start with an anecdote or a personal experience ("narrative hook") or with an appropriate quotation. As he expresses his feelings and opinions, he illuminates and supports them with appropriate examples. Above all, he leads his reader to discover the main drift, attitude, theme. To qualify as an essay, in fact, the piece of writing must make a point expressly or by implication.

REFERENCES: Robert Scholes and Carl Klaus, *Elements of the Essay;* William T. Moynihan (ed.), *Essays Today;* Alton C. Morris *et al.* (eds.), *The Modern Essay;* Alfred Kazin (ed.), *The Open Form;* Paul Jorgensen and Frederick Shroyer (eds.), *The Informal Essay;* David Daiches (ed.), *A Century of the Essay;* Houston Peterson (ed.), *Great Essays;* Mordecai Marcus and Henry F. Salerno (eds.), *Cross Section: Essays on Contemporary America;* W. O. S. Sutherland and Robert L. Montgomery (eds.), *The Reader: A Study of Form and Content;* Arthur Mullin (ed.), *The Questing Mind;* Leslie Fiedler (ed.), *The Art of the Essay;* Brock Brower, "The Article," in Paul Engle (ed.), *On Creative Writing.*

euphemism   The substitution of a mild or inoffensive expression for one that might shock or offend; e.g., "You almost passed" instead of "You failed the course." George Orwell, in "Politics and the English Language," deplores politicians' irresponsible use of such euphemisms as "clean bomb" and "relocation center" (for concentration camp).

In the climb up the socio-economic ladder many trades and professions have sought to promote themselves, often with unconsciously ridiculous euphemisms. Cases in point are *sanitary engineer* for *garbage collector, mortician* for *undertaker,* and *hospital* for *repair shop.*

Obviously useful in everyday conversation, where it helps us avoid giving offense, euphemism in its less commendable forms may disguise error or deception. Fowler calls euphemism "slurring over badness by giving it a good name." It is one of the prime characteristics of GOBBLE-DYGOOK, a style that generally obscures thought and hides purpose (as the charlatan may hide his purpose from the crowd). Especially useful in achieving euphemism are UNDERSTATEMENT and LITOTES, which tone down expression by choosing words with mild connotations. The "Newspeak" of Orwell's *1948* never used the word *bad,* but always *ungood.*

Some representative euphemisms: a *slender* girl (skinny), a *conservative* man (stingy), a *liberal* spender (wasteful), *man of leisure* (bum), an *untruth* (lie), *people's democracy* (communist dictatorship), *went to his reward* (died).

Euphemism became a mark of the verbal delicacy of the nineteenth century, when legs were *limbs*, undergarments were *unmentionables*, and even the breast of a chicken was *white meat*. Modern usage generally calls for a simple, natural, direct recognition of facts. But euphemism will probably never go out of popular style, nor will politicians fail to exploit its infinite possibilities.

REFERENCES: H. L. Mencken and Raven McDavid, *The American Language;* George Orwell, "Politics and the English Language," *A Collection of Essays.*

euphony   The pleasing combination of the sounds of language. Euphony is a quality that resists precise analysis, since it is essentially in the ear of the listener. Yet certain contributory principles may be identified.

Vowel sounds are generally considered to be more pleasing to the ear than consonants, and the "long" vowel sounds (and diphthongs) more so than the "short." Among consonants, the *resonants* (*m, n, ng, l, r, w, y*) are the most euphonious, as Poe observed. Runners-up, perhaps, are the *fricatives* (*f, v, th, s, sh, z*). Usually the least agreeable to the ear are the *stops* (*p, t, k, b, d, g*); but even the stops contribute generously to euphony when they are combined with resonant long vowels or diphthongs.

Repetition of sounds, as well as a harmonious variety of them, contributes to euphony. The echoing devices of ONOMATOPOEIA, ALLITERATION, ASSONANCE, and CONSONANCE are usually observable in euphonious prose, and RHYME often enhances the sound of verse; but these must be used with discretion lest they produce a sauce to drown in.

It is by no means certain that sound alone makes for euphony. Rhythm—or INTONATION (pitch, stress, and pause)—may also contribute; and of nearly equal importance is the choice of words with pleasing referents—since a harsh name for a revered object may seem more euphonious than a melodious name for something hated.

Since euphony, like all pleasure, is more felt than defined, most writers do not strive consciously to produce it. Rather, it is often achieved by negative means—the avoidance, or careful excision of, the harsh and clumsy. The careful writer avoids sound-effects that bend the sense to the sound. He heeds Alexander Pope's advice: "The sound should seem an echo to the sense." (Contrast CACOPHONY.)

euphuism   A kind of rhetoric characterized by excessive ANTITHESIS, ALLITERATION, ALLUSION, and DIDACTICISM. The label derives from the prose romance *Euphues* by John Lyly (1554–1606). An example: "Be merry but with modesty; be sober but not too sullen; be valiant but not too venturesome; let your attire be comely but not too costly." Although some of Lyly's contemporaries (among them, John Lodge and Robert Greene) admired and imitated this style, Shakespeare must have regarded it as egregious, as reflected in his putting euphuisms into the mouth of one of his most egregious characters, Polonius. Compare Polonius's exhortations to his son, Laertes: "Be thou familiar but by no means vulgar. . ."(*Hamlet,* I, iii). A more satirical slap at euphuism appears in Walter Scott's character Sir Piercie Shafton in *The Monastery* (1820).

evading the issue   See RED HERRING, AD HOMINEM, and ARGUMENT AGAINST THE MAN.

"every and all" fallacy   The mistaken assumption that "every" implies "all"; that is, the assumption that since every member of the family eats one slice of bread, the whole family eats one slice of bread. Ambiguity also mars a statement like "Our club collects ten dollars from all the members." How much does each member pay?

evidence   1. Facts and statistics interpreted as reasonably as possible; the testimony of unbiased, reputable experts (not just *any* "authority"). 2. In literary scholarship, primary texts and original documents. The careful citer does not offer mere assertion or ANALOGY as evidence. REFERENCE: W. W. Little et al., "Evaluation of Evidence," *Applied Logic.*

exclamation mark   An abrupt outcry is indicated in writing by an exclamation mark (!). Newspapermen call the mark the "screamer," a nickname that reveals why it should be used rarely and with discretion. Competent writers never use the mark when adequate force of utterance can be conveyed without it.

1. Use the exclamation mark after an emphatic exclamatory utterance or an emphatic command:

> Wow! Has Charlie got a sunburn! Charlie, you darned fool!
> Hit the dirt!
> Get 'em, Casey!
> Hurry!

2. An ironic or sarcastic statement may also be pointed up by an exclamation mark:

> A fine friend you are!
> And for this malarky he received one thousand dollars!

Rarely, and in parentheses, an exclamation mark may be used to make an ironic comment:

Phil got out of bed on time (!) and managed to drag himself to breakfast.

When it appears next to a closing quotation mark, the exclamation mark goes inside if what is quoted is an exclamation; otherwise it goes outside:

The sergeant yelled, "Get in line!" Then everybody "fell in"!

(See QUOTATION MARKS.)

existentialism   A comparatively modern philosophic movement (not a philosophic system) in revolt against traditional philosophies. Nor is this movement organized; in fact, there are several different kinds of revolt—some religious, some secular—and most writers either repudiate or resist the label "existentialist." Certainly Karl Jaspers (b. 1883), Martin Heidegger (b. 1889), and Jean-Paul Sartre (b. 1905), who appear on most lists of existentialists, are far apart on several of their convictions. Perhaps the one emphasis they share is a fierce individualism. In the view of an existentialist, Hamlet's dilemma—"To be or not to be?"—becomes "To overcome the forces of depersonalization or to be overcome?" This is, in fact, the central question of *Either/Or* by Søren Kierkegaard (d. 1855). Existentialist writers also stress the need for (*a*) the individual's self-actualization through self-expression, (*b*) coping rationally and realistically with human dilemmas, although Kierkegaard would add the need for passion as well as reason, (*c*) finding ways toward morality that have their foundation in the human condition rather than in theological dogma, and (*d*) becoming committed to, and involved in, whatever is good in society without doing violence to the individual's integrity. Kierkegaard, who was originally church-affiliated, developed in several books (especially in *Fear and Trembling*) his conviction that each individual needs to find Christ in himself rather than in organized religion and the forces of depersonalization. Other celebrated religious existentialists include Martin Buber (Jewish), Jacques Maritain (Catholic), and Paul Tillich (Protestant).

The leading secular existentialist (and one who does not deny the label) is Jean-Paul Sartre. His best-known work, *Being and Nothingness,* exposes the meaninglessness of one's existence unless one actively assumes moral responsibility. In fiction, drama, and essay—and in his autobiography, *The Words*—Sartre has developed the conviction that moral codes are man-made, not divine, and that man must be responsible to man. This tenet is shared by HUMANISM (among other philosophic movements); and several authors usually called existentialists have preferred to be called humanists, among them Sartre's companion Simone de Beauvoir and the Nobel Prize winner Albert Camus (d. 1960). (One of Sartre's essays is titled *Existentialism Is a Humanism.*) Existentialist approaches to the problems of good and

evil are reflected in the works of such writers as Nietzsche, Dostoevsky, Melville, Rilke, Kafka, Brecht, and Arthur Miller.

REFERENCES: Walter Kaufmann, *Existentialism from Dostoevsky to Sartre;*
Maurice Friedman, *The Worlds of Existentialism, a Critical Reader;* Frede-
rick J. Hoffman, *The Mortal No;* Erich Heller, *The Disinherited Mind;*
George F. Kneller, *Existentialism and Education;* George W. Morgan, *The
Human Predicament;* William Barrett, *What Is Existentialism?*

expatriates   Writers, artists, and patrons of the arts who leave home for
various reasons to live in other countries. Among the best-known
modern writers who became expatriates are Henry James, who left
New York for Paris and London; James Joyce, who left Dublin,
Ireland, for the Continent (chiefly Italy, Switzerland, and France);
T. S. Eliot, who was born in St. Louis but gave up American citizenship
and became a British subject; Ezra Pound, who left the United States
to live for several years in Rapallo, Italy, where he sympathized with
Fascism; Henry Miller, who lived in France and Greece before settling
in Big Sur, California; and Katherine Anne Porter, who lived in Mexico
for a number of years. But perhaps the most celebrated group of expatriates is "the lost generation," which included Ernest Hemingway,
F. Scott Fitzgerald, and Malcolm Cowley, who frequented the salon
of Gertrude Stein. Miss Stein, who was born in San Francisco, had
set up her salon on the Left Bank of the Seine in The City of Man.
Among more recent expatriates are James Jones and James Baldwin.

REFERENCES: Ernest Earnest, *Expatriates and Patriots: American Artists,
Scholars, and Writers in Europe;* Leon Edel, *Henry James;* James Joyce,
Exiles; Ezra Pound, *Patria Mia* and *Letters, 1907–1941;* Ford Madox Ford,
Memories and Impressions and *Thus to Revisit;* Richard Ellmann, *James
Joyce;* Gertrude Stein, *The Autobiography of Alice B. Toklas;* Ernest Heming-
way, *A Moveable Feast* and *The Sun Also Rises;* Harold Loeb, *The Way It
Was;* Malcolm Cowley, *Exile's Return;* Arthur Mizener, *The Far Side of
Paradise;* Henry Miller, *The Colossus of Maroussi;* James Baldwin, *Notes
of a Native Son.*

explication de texte   A systematic study of a literary work; a close
analysis of its words and images and its LEVELS OF MEANING and
AMBIGUITY. This kind of literary study was popularized in France at
the end of the 1800s and in the early 1900s, especially by the symbolists
and by the poet-critic Paul Valéry (1871–1945). It was carried forward
by Ezra Pound, T. S. Eliot, and the NEW CRITICS. The chief tenets of
this approach to literary study are that (1) the meaning or meanings of a
literary work reside mostly inside, not outside, the work, the primary
text; (2) each literary work has a logic or integrity of its own; its form
and content are right for each other, and each is inextricable from the
other; (3) as Dante pointed out, a masterwork has several levels of
meaning operating simultaneously. In this country the New Critics,

who adopted these tenets, adapted them to what they called close reading. Because they resisted direct evaluation of a work, the New Critics regarded themselves less as critics, more as explicators or interpreters. (See DEPTH READING, AMBIGUITY, AESTHETIC DISTANCE, BIOGRAPHICAL FALLACY, INTENTIONAL FALLACY, LEVELS OF MEANING.)

REFERENCES: Cleanth Brooks and Robert Penn Warren (eds.), *An Approach to Literature;* Ezra Pound, *ABC of Reading; The Explicator* Magazine; Monroe Beardsley, "The Logic of Explication," *Aesthetics;* I. A. Richards, *Practical Criticism;* Stanley R. Hopper and David L. Miller, *Interpretation; The Poetry of Meaning;* C. S. Singleton (ed.), *Interpretation: Theory and Practice.*

exposition   **1.** That form of discourse which presents and explains facts and ideas. *Investigative exposition* deals with facts and ideas in relatively straightforward prose, unadorned with FIGURATIVE LANGUAGE. It appeals more to the understanding than to the imagination. Such exposition (for example, an article on how something works) identifies, defines, classifies, illustrates, compares, and contrasts. Well-known examples are T. H. Huxley's "On a Piece of Chalk" and Rachel Carson's *The Sea Around Us.* **2.** *Interpretive exposition,* or EXPLICATION, is concerned with interpreting a difficult piece of literature. Examples are Allen Tate's essay on his own "Ode for the Confederate Dead"; Cleanth Brooks's "Case of Miss Arabella Fermor" explicating Pope's *Rape of the Lock;* Robert Heilman's explication of Henry James's "Turn of the Screw"; F. M. Boldereff's *Reading Finnegans Wake.* **3.** In fiction and drama *exposition* is that part of the story-line which introduces facts that the audience must know to appreciate what happens next. The conventional method of sharing this information with the audience is via a messenger, a talkative servant, or an old friend of the family. In plays of the early 1900s the chief instrument for communicating exposition was a telephone in the hands of a maid or a butler; contemporary playwrights convey exposition more subtly, without delaying the action of the play.

REFERENCES: Harold Martin and Richard Ohmann, *The Logic and Rhetoric of Exposition;* Susan Sontag, "Against Interpretation," *Partisan Review Reader;* Israel J. Kapstein, *Expository Prose;* William G. Leary *et al., Thought and Statement;* William F. Smith and Raymond D. Liedlich, *From Thought to Theme;* Gerald Levin, *Prose Models;* Jerome W. Archer, *Exposition;* Morris H. Needleman, *Handbook for Practical Compositions;* J. N. Hook, *Guide to Good Writing;* Richard Dodge and G. S. Wykoff, *The Harper Handbook.*

expression, self-expression   **1.** In general, the free, uninhibited flow of one's thoughts and feelings in prose or verse. **2.** In Aristotelian rhetoric, disciplined delivery. **3.** In contemporary RHETORIC, (*a*) a derogatory term contrasting with *communication* and connoting a lack of discipline ("Easy writing makes devilish hard reading"); (*b*) a therapy for writers of CONFESSIONAL VERSE; (c) as necessary as "breathing" for writers of PROJECTIVIST VERSE; (d) pedagogy endorsed by most of the leaders of the DARTMOUTH CONFERENCE.

expressionism   An artistic movement of the 1920s, in which painters, dramatists, novelists, and poets went a step further than did advocates of the IMPRESSIONISM of the previous decades in "expressing" their most subjective, often private, impressions of experience. Thus Kafka, in "The Metamorphosis," turns his protagonist into an actual cockroach rather than just suggesting, as an impressionist would have done, that the young man feels like a cockroach in his father's house. The expressionists also reflected Marxian revolt against the mechanization of labor and life, as in Elmer Rice's play *The Adding Machine,* in which the protagonist is Mr. Zero. Studies in Freudian and Jungian psychology also influenced the expressionists. Thus in Eugene O'Neill's play *The Emperor Jones,* the black protagonist relives—now consciously, now subconsciously—the history of his race. Most of the psychological, social, and cultural influences on the expressionists unite in James Joyce's novel *Finnegans Wake.*

REFERENCES: B. S. Myers, *Expressionism;* Max Brod, *Franz Kafka;* E. A. Engel, *The Haunted Heroes of Eugene O'Neill;* Eric Bentley, *The Playwright as Thinker;* Ronald Gray, *Bertolt Brecht;* Frances Boldereff, "The Poet Speaks," *Reading Finnegans Wake.*

eye dialect   A literary approximation of what the speech of a character sounds like. To quote Mr. Dooley (the creation of Finley Peter Dunne): "As th' pote says, Opporchunity knocks at ivry man's dure wanst." (Compare EYE RHYME.)

eye rhyme   A pair of words that rhyme in spelling but not in pronunciation: seat, great; [hot] wind, kind. Some rhymes that are eye-rhymes today (love, prove) were once actual rhymes; similarly, "historical rhymes" like Pope's "sign / join" reveal the way certain words were once pronounced. (Much evidence can be adduced that in Pope's day "join" was pronounced "jine.")

REFERENCE: H. C. Wyld, *Studies in English Rhymes from Surrey to Pope.*

F

fable   A brief narrative, more often in prose than in verse, usually about animals with human attributes and concluding with a memorable moral; e.g., "Nothing ventured, nothing gained." In world literature one of the earliest collections of fables, *The Panchatantra,* came from India. The best-known collection in Western literature, though no doubt with borrowings from the East, is that of the Greek slave Aesop (620–560 B.C.). Aesop's sources were largely FOLKLORE.

During the Middle Ages the wily fox became the subject of many fables and tales, including two "animal epics" of which he was the central character, the German *Reineke Fuchs* and the French *Roman de Reynard.* Fox stories appear in all the fable collections of that time, perhaps the best-known collections being those of Walter of England (based on the work of the Latin fabulist Romulus) and of Marie de France. The story of Chaunticleer, which Chaucer borrowed for *The Nun's Priest's Tale,* is a product of this tradition, as are later reworkings of Reynard material by Goethe and Lessing. Jean de la Fontaine (1621–95), a friend of Racine and Molière, collected and rewrote what remains the most celebrated collection of fables in verse, *The Fables of La Fontaine.* (An especially delightful translation is that of the American poet Marianne Moore.)

In the tradition of Aesop and La Fontaine, who enhanced their fables with wit and humor, the American writer Joel Chandler Harris (1848–1909) created his Uncle Remus fables, celebrating the exploits of "Br'er Rabbit." Two other American humorists, George Ade (1866–1944) and James Thurber (1894–1962), wrote, respectively, *Fables in Slang* and *Fables for Our Times.*

REFERENCES: Jean Shepherd (ed.), *The America of George Ade;* Philip Robinson, *The Poets' Birds;* Willy Ley, *The Lungfish, the Dodo, and the Unicorn;* Daniel Hoffman, *Form and Fable in American Fiction;* Donald Sands (ed.), *The History of Reynard the Fox.*

fabliaux   Short bawdy stories in octosyllabic couplets, popular in France during the late Middle Ages. Fabliaux usually concerned intrigue, adulterous husbands and wives caught out and punished, the trickster tricked, and so on. These verses also satirized clerics, doctors, and lawyers and seemed to appeal to the rising mercantile class of the day. They served Chaucer as a model for some of *The Canterbury Tales,* notably the tales of the Reeve and the Miller, sometimes called fabliaux. More strictly, there is only one fabliau in English—"Dame Sirith." Balzac used the fabliau frame of reference in *Droll Stories.*

REFERENCES: E. K. Chambers, *English Literature at the Close of the Middle*

Ages; Robert Hellman and Richard O'Gorman (trans.), *Fabliaux; Ribald Tales from the Old French;* J. A. Bennett and G. V. Smithers (eds.), *Early Middle English Verse and Prose.*

faded metaphor   A comparison, implied or express, the meaning of which is now taken for granted, its original novelty or freshness having faded; e.g., "running brook." Slang metaphor often fades in this way. "Square shooter," for example, has lost its association with actual "shooting irons," as have "table-leg" and "bottleneck" with the human body. Any word whose origin lies in metaphor but which has come to be used literally with no awareness of the metaphor, is a faded metaphor. The forgotten comparison that led to the word's first use is now known mainly to those interested in word origins. An example in everyday usage is the word *magazine,* used by most to mean a periodical publication. The word's original meaning (from Arabic), a *storehouse,* is seldom thought of; yet it is clear enough upon reflection, especially when another use of the word, *powder magazine,* is compared. Faded metaphors are also referred to as *dead* metaphors.

fallacies of reasoning   Most of the logical fallacies are treated in this handbook under the following entries: AD CAPTANDUM, AD HOMINEM, AD IGNORANTIAM, AD MISERICORDIAM, AD POPULUM, AD VERECUNDIAM, ARGUMENT AGAINST THE MAN, ARGUMENT FROM AUTHORITY, ASSERTION, ASSUMPTIONS (mistaken), BEGGING THE QUESTION, CARD STACKING, CAUSAL REASONING, DISJUNCTIVE DILEMMA, EQUIVOCATION, "EVERY" AND "ALL" FALLACY, FALLACY OF COMPOSITION, FALLACY OF DIVISION, FALSE ANALOGY, FALSE DILEMMA, FALSE PREMISE, FRIEND OF THE ENEMY, GENETIC FALLACY, GLITTERING GENERALITY, HALF-TRUTH, HASTY GENERALIZATION, INDUCTIVE REASONING, IPSE DIXIT, NON SEQUITUR, POST HOC, RED HERRING, SWEEPING GENERALIZATION, SYLLOGISM, TU QUOQUE, UNDISTRIBUTED MIDDLE. (See also EMOTIONAL APPEALS and PROPAGANDA DEVICES.)

fallacy of composition   In logic, the confusion of collective with distributive and individual characteristics. Given the premise that every member of a class has a certain characteristic, it does not necessarily follow that the class collectively has that characteristic. Consider:

> Every member of the church owns property.
> Therefore the church owns property.

The conclusion may not hold up. We have attributed to the *whole* a characteristic of *each* of its members. The fallacy of composition is also known as "garbled syllogism." (Contrast FALLACY OF DIVISION.)

fallacy of division   In logic, the confusion of distributive with collective characteristics. Given the premise that a class as a whole has a certain characteristic, it does not necessarily follow that every member of that class has that characteristic. Consider:

The school board is rich.
Johnson is a member of the school board.
Therefore Johnson is rich.

Obviously the conclusion may not hold up. We have confused a *collective* characteristic with a *distributive* characteristic. We have attributed to *each* the characteristics of *all*. (Contrast FALLACY OF COMPOSITION.)

falling action   See DRAMATIC STRUCTURE.

false analogy   In ARGUMENTATION a comparison of two things or situations that purports to establish a belief that because the two things are alike in some ways, they are also alike in other ways. The reasoning is fallacious because it ignores some very clear differences in favor of some superficial likenesses.

false dilemma   In ARGUMENTATION the "either/or" premise; the presentation of a choice between two alternatives while assuming (or hoping that the audience will assume) that these two alternatives are the only ones available, and neglecting to note that it might not be necessary to accept either. For example: "Are we going to teach our children spelling or are we going to teach them basket-weaving?"

false premise   In DEDUCTIVE REASONING a nonfactual or not necessarily acceptable statement from which a conclusion is drawn. If a premise in a SYLLOGISM is false, then the conclusion is necessarily false, even though the conclusion may nevertheless be valid in itself. For example, a conclusion like "Grissom was a brave astronaut," though quite valid in itself, is fallaciously drawn from a premise like "All brave astronauts die by incineration."

fancy   1. In Elizabethan literature, especially Shakespeare's plays, a synonym for FANTASY or ILLUSION, also for a spookish supernatural phantasm. Compare, for example, the Duke's speech at the opening of *Twelfth Night*, ". . . so full of shapes is fancy / That it alone is high fantastical" with the physician's speech in *Macbeth*, ". . . she [Lady Macbeth] is troubled with thick-coming fancies / That keep her from her rest." 2. In modern usage, a synonym for taste or judgment; for example, in the utterance "That kind of movie is not to my fancy" or "I don't fancy that." 3. In modern literature, an ingenious image, invention, or idea (compare CONCEIT) or quality of mind, often whimsical or extravagant or both. When Milton used the term in "L'Allegro" ("sweetest Shakespeare, Fancy's child"), he intended a compliment. From the 1900s on, however, the term became somewhat *déclassé*. (Compare IMAGINATION.)

fantasy   1. In psychology, the imagining of an object or event in concrete images whether or not the object or event is actually there. 2. In literature, a character's experience of an object or event, usually supernatural, which may or may not be there and which the author usually leaves more or less open as an AMBIGUITY. Less open, for example, are Hamlet's experience of the ghost in *Hamlet* and Scrooge's experience of the ghosts in Dickens's *Christmas Carol*. More open, perhaps, is the governess's experience of Mr. Quint and Miss Jessel, the "apparitions," in James's *Turn of the Screw*. 3. In Shakespeare's diction and that of his contemporaries "fantasy" is often a synonym for FANCY. 4. A kind of fiction in which the author creates his own wild, whimsical, and folkloristic world, as does J. R. R. Tolkien in *The Hobbit* and *The Lord of the Rings*.

REFERENCE: Mark Hillegas (ed.), *Shadows of Imagination*.

farce 1. Broad humor, often satirical. 2. A play, or elements in a play, using humor along with SLAPSTICK and STICHOMYTHIA. Examples range from Aristophanes' *The Frogs* to Kaufman and Hart's *Of Thee I Sing* (1931). In the latter, for example, the candidate for Vice-President of the United States is given the job of licking stamps, to exaggerate the trivial and ridiculous functions fulfilled by Vice-Presidents of that era.

REFERENCES: Eric Bentley, *The Life of Drama;* Leo Hughes, *A Century of English Farce*.

fatalism The pessimistic belief that man has no control over his destiny; that everything is predetermined or predestined. (Compare CALVINISM, DETERMINISM, EXISTENTIALISM, and NATURALISM.)

Fates, the In classical mythology, the three sister goddesses who determined human destiny: Clotho (spinner of the threads of life), Lachesis (caster of lots), and Atropos (cutter of life threads); also called the Weird Sisters. Compare THE GRACES.

REFERENCES AND READINGS, see under MYTH.

faulty reference The use of pronouns that, in context, do not clearly stand for nouns — that is, whose reference is uncertain. In current usage the personal pronouns (*he, she, it, they*), the relative pronouns (*which, that*), and the demonstratives (*this, that, these, those*) are the most carelessly used without clear reference. "I don't like music, which my friends cannot understand." (Does *which* stand for *music* — or for *I don't like music?*)

Ambiguous reference occurs when a context introduces two or more possible nouns for the pronoun to refer to: "His grandfather took him to Europe when *he* was on vacation." (Is *he* the grandfather or the grandson?) *Broad reference* occurs when a pronoun refers to an idea that is not actually expressed. For example, "She had little ambition; *this* made her seem lazy." *This* refers rather loosely to the whole idea, *she had little ambition*.

Faulty reference causes little difficulty in conversation, since the proper antecedent can usually be inferred from intonation or clarified by question and restatement. In writing, however, the fault is more troublesome, since the writer is not present to offer the clarification.

festschrift Literally, "festival writing." A term borrowed from the German to denote a collection of scholarly ariticles, critical essays, or biographical testimonials in honor of an esteemed scholar-teacher. The writers are usually the scholar's colleagues and former students, and the occasion is usually the retirement or death of the person honored. Some examples: Vittorio Gabrieli (ed.), *Friendship's Garland: Essays Presented to Mario Praz on His Seventieth Birthday;* Paul Sweezey *et al., F. O. Matthiessen;* Ray Browne and Donald Pizer (eds.), *Themes and Directions in American Literature: Essays in Honor of Leon Howard.*

ficelle In fiction, a minor character or a non-participating observer whose chief function is to help the reader understand what is going on. An example of this device, as Henry James admits in his *Notebooks,* is Maria Gostrey in *The Ambassadors.*
REFERENCE: Wayne Booth, *The Rhetoric of Fiction.*

fiction See NOVEL, NOVELLA, NOVELLETTE, SHORT STORY, SHORT-SHORT STORY.

fictive audience An audience (as distinguished from the reader) that a writer creates for a specific occasion or effect, much as he creates a PERSONA. In Emerson's "Concord Hymn," for example, the fictive audience addressed by the speaker is the "spirit that made those heroes [the embattled farmers] dare." (Compare APOSTROPHE.)

fictive character Legendary character; in legend and fiction, a character whose traits reflect somewhat romantically the real person he is supposed to represent or with whom he is usually associated. Natty Bumppo, for example, is a fictive character of the early American wilderness pioneer; similarly, Chingachgook represents certain of the noble traits of the American Indian. "George Catlin in paint and James Fenimore Cooper in the novel had fixed for the American imagination," writes Leslie Fiedler, "the *fictive* Indian and the legend of the ennobling wilderness . . . where the Noble Savage confronted Original Sin." (Emphasis added.) Whatever or whoever is represented in a fictive character, the faithfulness to history, biography, and reality is on a high, usually romanticized, level of abstraction. Though all fictive characters have fictional characteristics, not all fictional characters are fictive; many fictional characters are individualistic. (Compare STOCK CHARACTER and see BIOGRAPHICAL FALLACY.)
REFERENCES: Leslie Fiedler, "Montana: or The End of Jean-Jacques Rousseau," *An End to Innocence;* Lowry Nelson, "The Fictive Reader," in Peter Demetz *et al.* (ed.), *The Disciplines of Criticism.*

figurative language   Apt and imaginative language intended to mean something other than what it says (as opposed to LITERAL LANGUAGE). Figurative language arises when the mind associates one thing with another—another that is somehow (*a*) *related* in common experience, (*b*) *opposite* in one or more respects, or (*c*) *similar* in one or more respects. Figures of relationship include ALLUSION, EPITHET, PUN, METONYMY, and SYNECDOCHE. Figures of opposition include IRONY, PARADOX, OXYMORON, and (in the sense of expressing an extreme) HYPERBOLE, UNDERSTATEMENT, and LITOTES. Figures of similarity—the most widely prevalent figurative language—include SIMILE, METAPHOR, and PERSONIFICATION.

In all figurative language (as, indeed, in all language in general) appropriateness counts; inappropriate use of any of the mentioned figures of speech wearies the reader. An example illustrating inappropriate and unimaginative figures: "His television contract calls for more coin of the realm than any other artist has ever nailed down." The expression "coin of the realm" is a CLICHÉ; the expression "nailed down" is a FADED METAPHOR and in relation to "coin" and "artist" contributes to MIXED METAPHOR. Such artless language is almost always inappropriate. But appropriateness of figures also depends upon one's purpose, audience, and PERSONA or speaking voice. For example, such a comparison as "The road curves like an S" or "The road is S-shaped," however unimaginative, is perfectly appropriate (perfectly clear and useful) in exposition, in an engineer's instructions intended to inform, let us say, a demolition crew. For an imaginative piece like a poem, however, a more appropriate comparison might be something like Alfred Noyes's "The road was a ribbon of moonlight" or a figure in which the two things compared are as far as possible from being alike in actuality; for example, "The road was a ribbon-snake."

figure of speech   See FIGURATIVE LANGUAGE.

fin de siècle   Literally, "end of the century." The 1890s, characterized by the "new woman" seeking political and social emancipation, by the iconoclastic plays of George Bernard Shaw, and by such DECADENTS as Oscar Wilde and Frank Harris. (In France the artist Toulouse-Lautrec, who painted an unflattering portrait of Wilde, was also a prominent figure associated with "*fin de siècle*.")

REFERENCES: Mario Praz, *The Romantic Agony;* Thomas Beer, *The Mauve Decade.*

First Folio   The first authentic collection of Shakespeare's plays. It was published in 1623 by his friends Heming and Condell.

REFERENCES: Charlton Hinman, *The Printing and Proofreading of the First Folio;* Walter W. Greg, *A Bibliography of the English Printed Drama to the Restoration.*

flashback   A narrative technique in which the writer orders EXPOSITION and even dramatic scenes in a sequence other than strict chronology. Given a chronology of scenes 1, 2, 3, 4, 5, and 6, for example, the writer may start with scene 3, then flashback to scenes 1 and 2, then resume with scenes 4, 5, and 6. Or he may start with the final scene, or with a middle scene, then flashback to strategic portions of the preceding scenes, revealing only what is necessary for an unfolding of his story. Flashbacks are used by Dickens in *A Tale of Two Cities,* by Ford Madox Ford in *The Good Soldier,* and by Arthur Miller in *Death of A Salesman.* (Compare IN MEDIAS RES.)

REFERENCES: Caroline Gordon, *How To Read a Novel;* Jean B. Mosley, "Triple-Threat Flashback," in A. S. Burack (ed.), *The Writer's Handbook;* Hans Meyerhoff, *Time in Literature.*

flatting   UNDERSTATEMENT.

Fleshly School   A Victorian critic's (Robert Buchanan's) derogatory EPITHET for Swinburne, Rossetti, Morris, and other poets whose works, in revolt against restraints of the era, emphasize the beauties of the body. Swinburne lashed back in *Under the Microscope* (1872).

focus of narration   A synonym for "point of view" in the sense peculiar to fiction and other narrative forms. Regardless of who is telling the story (an all-knowing behind-the-scenes author or one of the major or minor characters), it is almost always told from the point of view of only one person or "central intelligence." This technique is among the chief ways in which a masterwork achieves its unity. In some few exceptions—e.g., Browning's *Ring and the Book* and Lawrence Durrell's *Alexandria Quartet*—a story is deliberately told from several different points of view. But most novels, stories, and plays use a single focus of narration, so that audience and readers soon know (in fact, often identify with) the chief character, through whose eyes, thoughts, and feelings, the action unfolds. This chief character is called the PROTAGONIST, or hero, though he may not always be heroic in the traditional sense.

In order to have the reader re-create experience through the eyes, thoughts, and feeling of one major character, the author may tell the story in the third person, focusing upon one character, one central intelligence, as the chief "he" or "she." This focus is said to be *omniscient* or, more strictly, *limited omniscient,* since very rarely does an author use "pure" or unlimited omniscience; to do so would be to focus on no one character in particular and thus eliminate a truly "chief" character. An alternative is to have one character, acting as "narrator," tell the story—a focus called the *participating point of view.* In participating focuses the narrator (the "I" speaking) may be either the chief character or an observer. As an observer the narrator may be a major or a minor character. He may be impartial ("objective") or emotionally involved ("subjective").

As Brooks and Warren have suggested (in *Understanding Fiction*), the traditional dichotomy between the "omniscient" and the "participating" narrator is oversimplified. Actually, the narrator may be located on a *participation continuum,* which, though anchored to the extremes of omniscient non-participation on one end, and autobiographical participation on the other, allows for degrees of participation (involvement) in between. Some examples should make these degrees of participation clear.

Defoe's *Robinson Crusoe* ("I was born in the year 1632 . . .") is obviously at the autobiographical extreme of the continuum. And aside from the autobiographical "first person grammar," the whole story is told from the point of view of the narrator and hero, Robinson Crusoe. Not at this extreme but close to it, Hemingway's *Farewell to Arms* is told from the point of view of the protagonist, Frederic Henry ("In the last summer of that year we lived in a house in the village that looked across the river . . ."); notice the narrator's "we."

At the other extreme of the continuum, or close to it, is Dickens's *Tale of Two Cities,* in which the narrator is the author himself. And though he is not purely objective and omniscient, he is sufficiently all-knowing to describe what is happening concurrently in London and in Paris. (This omniscience is sometimes called *panoramic.*) Except in quoted conversation, he uses "third person grammar" ("She looked so beautiful in the purity of her faith") and focuses mainly on Lucie Manette. Similarly, in Eliot's *Silas Marner* the author-narrator is omniscient, and though she obtrudes occasionally (as does Dickens) with some philosophic comment, the chief focus of narration—the chief point of view—is that of the protagonist, Silas. It is *his* story, just as *A Tale of Two Cities* is Lucie Manette Darnay's story.

Between these extremes or near-extremes on the continuum, and regardless of whether the story is told in the third person or the first, *the narrator may participate as a character in various degrees of involvement.* He may participate as an *objective observer* (as does Poe's Visitor in "The Fall of the House of Usher"). He may participate as a more *subjectively involved* but still minor character (as does Conrad's Marlowe in *Lord Jim*). He may participate as one of the *major characters, though still not the protagonist* (as does Ford Madox Ford's Dowell in *The Good Soldier.*)

REFERENCES: Carolyn Gordon and Allen Tate, "Notes on Fictional Technique," *The House of Fiction;* Cleanth Brooks and Robert Penn Warren, *Understanding Fiction;* Percy Lubbock, *The Craft of Fiction;* Henry James, "The Art of Fiction," *Critical Essays and Prefaces.*

foil   In drama and fiction, a character whose traits are contrasted with those of another character; e.g., Falstaff and young Hal (Shakespeare's *Henry IV,* Part I), Godfrey and Dunstan (Eliot's *Silas Marner*), Mr. Leggatt and the Captain (Conrad's "Secret Sharer"), Demian and Emil (Hesse's *Demian*), Gene and Phineas (Knowles's *Separate Peace*).

folklore   LEGEND, FABLE, PROVERB, riddle, joke, APHORISM, BALLAD, CAROL, MYTH, fairy tale, tall tale, charm, hex, and the like that have been orally transmitted for many generations before being recorded; hence of cumulative authorship and multiple versions. The term *folklore* was introduced in 1846 by William John Thoms in an issue of *The Atheneum* magazine. In the nineteenth century a revival of interest in collecting folklore occurred in England under the stimulus of (Thoms's) Camden Society and later the London Folklore Society. Folklore societies seek to collect, identify, and compare the survivals of ancient beliefs, customs, and tradition. (See also BESTIARY, FOLK SONG, FOLK TALE.)

REFERENCES: Funk and Wagnalls *Standard Dictionary of Folklore;* Stith Thompson (ed.), *Motif Index to Folk Literature;* B. A. Botkin (ed.), *A Treasury of American Folklore;* Richard Dorson (ed.), *American Folklore;* R. D. Abrahams, *Jump-Rope Rhymes: A Dictionary;* Iona and Peter Opie, *Children's Games.*

folk song   A poem of unknown original authorship, transmitted orally for many years in several different versions and ultimately recorded in one or more of its versions. Often the words or music or both migrate from one country to another; for example, "Foggy Foggy Dew" migrated to the United States from England via Australia and New Zealand. The folk song is characterized by brevity, simplicity, and the repetition of certain lines or phrases, especially the incremental repetition in such "rounds" as "Three Blind Mice" and "Row, Row, Row Your Boat." Unlike literary songs and poems, which are more or less "frozen," folk songs continually undergo changes, each generation adding its version, each interpreter varying the nuance, as reflected in the alternative versions in printed collections like Thomas Percy's *Reliques of Ancient English Poetry* (1765) and John and Alan Lomax's *Folk Song U.S.A.* (1948). This characteristic of *cumulative* authorship (as in "Green Grow the Rushes") is no doubt a more accurate description than the "communal authorship" often ascribed to folk songs and other folk genres. For "communal authorship" implies an original collaboration, which, though not impossible, is in most instances unlikely. It was no doubt the phenomenon of cumulative authorship that prompted the celebrated folklorist and philologist Jacob Grimm (1785–1863) to say that "a folk song composes itself."

The best-known English folk songs include "Scarborough Fair," "Greensleeves," "Pop Goes the Weasel," "London Bridge Is Broken [Falling] Down," "Once I Loved a Maiden Fair," "The British Grenadiers," "The Twelve Days of Christmas," "Good King Wenceslas," and even "God Save the King." Best-known Scottish folk songs include "Auld Lang Syne" [not originally composed by Robert Burns], "Blue Bells of Scotland," "Weel May the Keel Row," and "Leezie Lindsay." Best-known Irish folk songs include "Londonderry Air," "The Rose of Tralee," "Cockles and Mussles," and "Green Grow the Lilacs."

In the United States the best-known Negro folk songs (often called "spirituals") include "Swing Low, Sweet Chariot," "Nobody Knows De Trouble I've Seen," "Go Down, Moses," and "Joshua Fit De Battle of Jericho." The best-known songs of cowboys, sailors, railroad and steel workers include "The Old Chisholm Trail," "Home on the Range," "Git Along, Little Dogies," "Bury Me Not on the Lone Prairie," "The Erie Canal," "Yo, Heave Ho!" "John Henry" [aside from several ballad versions], "I Been Wukkin on de Railroad," "Casey Jones," and "Big Rock Candy Mountain." Other American folk songs include "Yankee Doodle," "Blue Tail Fly," "Turkey in the Straw," "Skip to My Lou," "Lil Liza Jane," "Old Smoky," "Clementine," "There Is a Tavern in the Town," "Down in the Valley," "Red River Valley," "Blow the Man Down," "She'll Be Comin' Round the Mountain," "John Brown's Body," and "The Man on the Flying Trapeze." (See BALLAD, CAROL, FOLKLORE.)

REFERENCES: Margaret Boni (ed.), *The Fireside Book of Folk Songs;* Leonard Deutsch (ed.), *Treasury of the World's Finest Folk Songs;* R. M. Lawless, *Folksingers and Folksongs in America;* Bruno Nettl, *An Introduction to Folk Music in the United States;* Carl Sandburg, *The American Songbag.*

folk tale   A narrative originally handed down by word of mouth with each narrator usually contributing some variation of his own; hence a story of cumulative authorship. Different versions of a basic story (for example, the abused orphan who ultimately marries a prince) migrate in different versions from country to country. From earliest times folk tales have survived first in the oral, then in the literary tradition of practically every nation and culture. Such ancient Greek epics as *The Iliad* and *The Odyssey* (ca. 800 B.C.), for example, include many a folk tale from an earlier Greece and Persia. And although the writing of these EPICS is attributed to one author, Homer, their authorship in pre-written (oral) stages of transmission must have been multiple and cumulative. Similarly, *The Thousand and One Nights, or Arabian Nights' Entertainments,* translated into English first by Edward Lane in 1839–41 and by Sir Richard Burton in 1855–88, derive from Persian and Egyptian prototypes of the fourteenth and sixteenth centuries. And the Arabian stories of "Sinbad the Sailor" and "Ali Baba and the Forty Thieves" have counterparts in the folk tales of ancient India, especially those collected in the *Panchatantra* (A.D. fifth century).

Except for some of Chaucer's retelling of talk tales and fables as incidental parts of his original works (for example, Chaunticleer the cock and Reynard [or "Russel"] the fox in "The Nun's Priest's Tale"), medieval English writers were given less to retelling secular folk tales, more to Biblical stories. Of course, the Judaeo-Christian Bible—like the sacred book of every other religion—is full of folk tales, as Sir James Frazer showed in *Totemism* (1887) and in his monumental twelve-volume study, *The Golden Bough* (1890–1915). One hastens to add that the folk origin of these tales need not make them unbelievable; even when they cannot be "scientifically true," they contain much truth on a higher level of abstraction. "Humble folk tale," observes Harold Watts, "is but myth that has lost its mooring in rite."

Perhaps the first influential collector of secular folk tales in modern times was the Frenchman Charles Perrault (1628–1703). In 1697 he surreptitiously published his *Contes de ma mere l'Oye,* addressed to children and containing such folk tales as "Cinderella," "Bluebeard," "Sleeping Beauty," and "Little Red Riding Hood." Whether it was Charles Perrault himself or his son Pierre who wrote (that is, retold) these traditional tales is a purely academic matter, since all of them have since been traced to ancient sources (for example, by Elizabeth Mure, as early as 1831, in an unpublished manuscript in the Toronto, Canada, Public Library).

During the late eighteenth and early nineteenth centuries, concomitant with the new interest in philology, there developed a revival of interest in collecting and recording folk tales. To collect their famous *Märchen* (1812) Jacob Grimm (1785–1863) and his brother William (1786–1859) interviewed peasants who had been retelling stories that had been told in their families for several generations.

The dividing line between genuine folk tales and literary tales based on a folk tradition is often tenuous. Little folklore is reflected in such essentially original tales as "The Emperor's New Clothes," "The Ugly Duckling," "The Red Shoes," and "The Little Mermaid" by Denmark's Hans Christian Andersen (1805–75). But because of his enchanting creations (reflected in much of the statuary in Copenhagen) and because of his visits to other Scandinavian countries and to England from 1840 to 1857, he inspired many folk collectors and collections—among them Anthony Montalba, *Fairy Tales of All Nations* (1849); Anne and Eliza Keary, *The [Norse] Heroes of Asgard* (1857); Mary Frere, *Old Deccan [Hindu] Days* (1868); and, above all, the celebrated *Blue Fairy Book* (1889) by Andrew Lang (1844–1912). Lang, a writer and scholar of amazing versatility, was one of the leading members of the London Folklore Society and in 1888 had translated and edited *Perrault's Popular Tales.* Two of Lang's best-known reconstructions were "Tom Thumb" and "Jack and the Giant Killer."

In the United States, meanwhile, aside from such highly original treatments of folk stories as Longfellow's *Hiawatha* and Washington Irving's "Legend of Sleepy Hollow" and "Rip Van Winkle," many Negro folk tales were retold by Joel Chandler Harris in *Tales of Uncle Remus* (1880). But perhaps the best-known American folk tales came from the frontier, the "tall" tales about Paul Bunyan, Tony Beaver, Johnny Appleseed, Mike Fink, John Henry, and Pecos Bill. These were first collected by Thomas Thorpe, in *The Mysteries of the Backwoods* (1846), and by W. B. Laughead, in *Paul Bunyan and His Big Blue Ox* (1914). (See also LEGENDS, MYTH, FOLKLORE, BALLAD, FOLK SONG.)

REFERENCES: Milton Rugoff (ed.), *A Harvest of World Folk Tales;* Stith Thompson (ed.), *Tales of the North American Indians* and *One Hundred Favorite Folk Tales;* Walter Blair, *Tall Tale America;* Richard Dorson (ed.), *American Folklore;* Martha Pappas (ed.), *Heroes of the American West;* Peter Poulatis (ed.), *American Folklore;* Mentor Williams (ed.), *Schoolcraft's Indian Legends;* Harold Watts, *The Modern Reader's Guide to Religions;* Donald M. Winkelman, "Three American Authors as Semi-Folk Artists," *Journal of American Folklore* (April-June, 1965).

footnotes   See DOCUMENTATION.

foreshadowing   In fiction and drama, a device to prepare the reader for the outcome of the action; "planting" to make the outcome convincing, though not to give it away. In *Macbeth,* for example, Shakespeare uses the various witch scenes in part to foreshadow Macbeth's doom: "Thou shalt get kings, though thou be none."

foreword   PREFACE; a statement by the author or another person preceding the text of a book. (Compare INTRODUCTION.)

REFERENCE: Jacques Barzun, *The Modern Researcher.*

four-term fallacy   See SYLLOGISM IH.

fragment   An utterance that lacks subject or verb or both; still generally considered unsatisfactory unless the missing element is clearly implied or is supplied by context. The unsatisfactory incomplete utterance is called a fragment, and it is among the most common weaknesses of inept writing.

When a fragment appears, the fault may usually be repaired by attaching the loose limb to the preceding full sentence, so that the offender no longer offends. Fragments usually occur in one or another of these patterns:

1. *Subordinate clause:* "Harvey was still at the table. *While all the other guests had retired to the drawing room.*" ("Harvey was still at the table, while. . . .")

2. *Prepositional phrase:* "She said she would meet him in the library. *After the exam.*" ("She said she would meet him in the library after the exam.")

3. *Verbal phrase:* "All the players jumped from the bench. *Shouting their disapproval.*" ("All the players jumped from the bench, shouting their disapproval.")

4. *Appositive:* "We had to memorize the Gettysburg Address. *One of the world's great speeches.*" (". . . the Gettysburg Address, one of the world's great speeches.")

5. *Absolute element:* "The little party decided to make camp. *It being nearly sundown.*" ("It being nearly sundown, the little party decided to make camp.")

Not every incomplete utterance is an offending fragment, however. Acceptable incomplete sentences abound in conversation (and dialogue), in highly informal writing, and in modern prose in which the attempt is to suggest the tentative workings of the mind (as in STREAM OF CONSCIOUSNESS). (For discussion of acceptable incomplete sentences, see MINOR SENTENCE and ELLIPSIS.)

REFERENCES: Alan Casty, *The Art of Writing and Reading;* Richard Dodge and George Wykoff, *Handbook of College Composition.*

frame story   A group of stories that would be unconnected if they were not tied to some central framework or situation, such as a pilgrimage (*The Canterbury Tales*), a plague (*The Decameron*), or the threat of execution (*The Arabian Nights*). In each of these the element in which the author establishes the setting and situation is called the frame. The stories within this frame are the frame stories. It is in this sense that a frame story is sometimes defined as "a story within a story."

free verse   Poetry in which regularity of line and rhyme are avoided; for example, Walt Whitman's *Leaves of Grass*. Robert Frost observed that the writing of free verse (as distinguished from the challenge of writing the more restrictive forms) is "like playing tennis with the net down." But this remains a minority view. An example of free verse is this stanza from Whitman's "Grass":

Tenderly will I use you, curling grass.
It may be you transpire from the breasts of young men,
It may be if I had known them I would have loved them,
It may be you are from old people; or offspring taken too soon
out of their mothers' laps.

It can be seen that despite the absence of meter and rhyme, here Whitman reiterates certain clauses ("it may be") in parallel structure (a rhetoric usually avoided by contemporary writers of free verse). Poets who have used free verse include Matthew Arnold, Stephen Crane, Edgar Lee Masters, Amy Lowell, Ezra Pound, T. S. Eliot, Archibald MacLeish, Conrad Aiken, William Carlos Williams, W. S. Merwin, John Logan, Allen Ginsberg, William Stafford.

REFERENCE: John Ciardi, "How Free Is Free Verse?" in A. S. Burack (ed.), *The Writer's Handbook*. For examples of an even more open form of verse—a form sometimes called "organic" in the sense that the nature of the poetic experience dictates an integration of form and content—see Stephen Berg and Robert Mezey (eds.), *Naked Poetry*.

Freudian slip   Any inadvertency of speech or writing, any "slip of the tongue," that can be taken as revealing a state of mind or "hidden motive." Sigmund Freud (1856–1939), the originator of psychoanalysis, held that every such "mistake" is caused, whether or not the speaker is aware of the cause. An example: "Would you care for an olive, branch—I mean Blanche!"

REFERENCE: Sigmund Freud, *Psychopathology of Everyday Life*.

friend of the enemy   In ARGUMENTATION, an emotional appeal in which the speaker, to avoid a rational analysis of the issue, says, in effect, "But the *bad guys* are in favor of this proposal!" thus implying "You are a friend of our enemies!" and, by extension, "You, too, are an enemy." This appeal is familiarly known as "guilt by association." In a different context a writer may strengthen his argument by quoting his opposition's friends: "Even my opponent's *friends* agree with me!"

REFERENCE: Harry H. Crosby and George Estey, *The Rhetorical Imperative*.

G

Gallicism   **1.** An IDIOM or expression peculiar to the French language but used in another language. Many French words and expressions have been transplanted into English and are thoroughly at home in it; others are resisted or rejected. The worst of Gallicisms is the use of French in English to affect superior knowledge. **2.** An English expression fractured to sound like French idiom; e.g., "It is to laugh, Baby!" (English is also sometimes fractured to sound like German: "We are already gepooped!") Compare the Anglicized treatment of borrowings from other languages; e.g., "Don Kwixit" for *Don Quixote*.

REFERENCE: H. L. Mencken and Raven McDavid, "Loan Words and Non-English Influences," *The American Language*.

genetic fallacy   The mistaken assumption that an idea is false or a discovery worthless because it was originated by someone we do not like. To avoid this fallacy, one must be certain that there is indeed a relevant connection between the idea or discovery and the disrepute of its originator. This same fallacy, of course, may occur in ARGUMENT FROM AUTHORITY. Normally the origin of an idea or discovery is irrelevant; its reliability or worth depends rather upon the weight of the evidence for or against it.

genre   **1.** A literary form, as, for example, NOVEL, SHORT STORY, PLAY, POEM, ESSAY, and the like. In each of these major genres there are subgenres; for example, there are such subgenres of the poem as the BALLAD, the SONNET, the MADRIGAL, these three being lyrical as distinguished from dramatic poems. **2.** Kenneth Burke regards genre somewhat more loosely as "any form which artistically arouses and satisfies appetites."

REFERENCES: Kenneth Burke, *The Philosophy of Literary Form* and *Terms for Order;* Northrop Frye, "Theory of Genres," *Anatomy of Criticism;* Mark Schorer (ed.), *Galaxy: Literary Modes and Genres;* Alton C. Morris *et al.* (eds.), *College English, The First Year;* W. O. S. Sutherland and Robert L. Montgomery (eds.), *The Reader: A Study of Form and Content.* (The last three are anthologies containing representative genres.)

gestes   From the Latin for "[heroic] deeds." A literary form, popular in the Middle Ages, in which heroic deeds or tales of these exploits are recounted. Three representative examples are the *Chanson de Roland* (eleventh century), *The Pilgrimage of Charlemagne* (twelfth century), and *The Gest Historie of the Destruction of Troy* (ca. 1350). These works were also known as *chansons de gestes* and are to be distinguished from *jestes,* the Elizabethan word for *jokes. Note:* Despite what the title suggests, the *Gesta Romanorum* (ca. 1300) is a collection of moralized tales used by medieval preachers.

REFERENCE: E. K. Chambers, *English Literature at the Close of the Middle Ages.*

glittering generality   When arguing in favor of a point, the arguer (or propagandist) may, whether consciously or not, attach complimentary terms, or EUPHEMISMS, to that point and thus make it seem attractive. He is avoiding the troublesome task of presenting supporting argument and is, in each such attachment of "good" words to his side of the matter, producing a *glittering generality*. The technique is the reverse of NAME-CALLING, which attaches unfavorable words to an opponent or his side of the matter. The complimentary terms are usually vague or otherwise too slippery to pin down; they seem to glitter but may not be gold, after all. "My plan for this city's *welfare* is *honest* and *scientifically trustworthy,* and would bring a *fair* and *democratic order* to a citizenry that deserves the *best.*" (See SWEEPING GENERALIZATION.)

gnomic   1. In early Greek literature (sixth century B.C.) the "Gnomic Poets" wrote a kind of verse full of APHORISMS or MAXIMS. Since then, the term "gnomic verse" (meaning moralistic or DIDACTIC) has become a derogation. 2. In FOLKLORE, pertaining to *gnomes,* a race of hunchbacked or otherwise misshapen dwarfs who were supposed to live deep in the earth, guarding its treasures. Their literary identification, along with their relationship to such similar spirits as sylphs, nymphs, and salamanders, is variously credited to the medieval Rosicrucians and to Dr. Theophrastus Paracelsus (1493–1541), a Faustlike person about whom Robert Browning wrote his narrative poem *Paracelsus* (1835). Gnomes and "little people" appear in various shapes under various names in the folklore and folkloristic literature of several nations. For example, compare the Norse trolls and troll-imps in Ibsen's *Peer Gynt;* the Irish leprechauns in *Finian's Rainbow.*

gobbledygook   Stuffy, pretentious, wordy, roundabout language. Senator Maury Maverick of Texas coined the word *gobbledygook* (also spelled *gobbledegook*) to name, and in a sense describe, the prose style so often found in government documents and in other official communications. Reflective of the twentieth-century rise of technology and breakdown of individualism, gobbledygook results from a paradoxical approach to subject matter and audience: the writer or speaker is at once timid (fearing to say anything too bold) and pompous (striving for a scientific-sounding tone of rightness). Characteristics of gobbledygook are (1) prolixity — much DEADWOOD, especially redundancy; (2) pedantry — obscure terms, jargon, and makeshift words like *actualize, regulationed, societality, personalwise;* (3) hedging — the protective covering of EQUIVOCATION, which provides an "out" for the writer should he be challenged ("Some experiments might seem to indicate. . . ," "One could possibly say . . . ," "It is not impossible to assume that. . . ."); (4) abstractness—big and obscure words where short and direct words would do; (5) EUPHEMISM—the glossing over of whatever may offend; the softer, roundabout expression in place of the harsh or straight-on; (6) fuzzy thought; (7) stale expression—many CLICHÉS and ready-cut phrases; (8) impersonality—the deliberate avoidance of reference to the first person (*I* or *we*) in favor of a neutralized and unemotional third person (usually *one,* or *a person,* or *an individual*) or in favor of an even more impersonal passive voice.

Gobbledygook may arise from several motives. The self-suspicious student, uncertain of his facts or ideas, may adopt gobbledygook to hide his weakness of thought and make his work "sound more important." The politician may adopt it, hiding unpopular ideas behind verbiage and doubletalk. The writer of office bulletins or official announcements may adopt it to make his work seem more dignified, impressive, or objective (and his prose is often called *officialese*).

REFERENCES: William Safire, *An Anecdotal Dictionary of Catchwords, Slogans, and Political Usage;* J. R. Masterson and W. B. Phillips, *Federal Prose: How to Write in and/or for Washington.*

Goliardic verse   Satirical Latin verse of a kind popularized by an irreverent "Bishop" Golias in the twelfth century. The chief theme was CARPE DIEM: Eat, drink and be merry today, for who knows what tomorrow will bring? During the Middle Ages university students and clerics (among them the popular Walter Map) wandered through Germany, France, and England composing and singing Goliardic verses very much in the manner of contemporary "protest" singers. The *Carmina Burana,* a collection of Goliardic poems, has become well known through the choral setting of the composer Carl Orff. (Compare TROUBADOUR.)

REFERENCES: Helen Waddell, *The Wandering Scholars;* George F. Whicher (trans.), *The Goliardic Poets.*

Gothic   1. The East Germanic language used by Bishop Ulfilas (fourth century) to translate the Bible. 2. The kind of medieval church architecture characterized by verticality; tall, pointed windows; steeply arched, vaulted roofs; flying buttresses; gargoyles side by side with saints; and so on. 3. In literature, the GOTHIC NOVEL or SOUTHERN GOTHIC.

gothic novel   A kind of mystery novel intended to shock or titillate and dependent for its psychological effects on Gothic architecture, bleak old castles with secret passageways, medieval armor, ghosts or rumors of ghosts, and decadent lone survivors of once proud families that are desperate for fresh young blood to stave off further decay. The writers of this genre assumed, perhaps justifiably, that their readers would accord it a willing suspension of disbelief. The gothic novel was developed in eighteenth-century England by Horace Walpole, with *The Castle of Otranto* (1764). Other popular "gothics" were *Vathek* (William Beckford, 1786), *The Monk* (M. G. Lewis, 1795), *Mysteries of Udolpho* (Ann Radcliffe, 1795), and *Frankenstein* (Mary Shelley, 1818). In America this genre had its representative in *Weiland* (Charles Brockden Brown, 1798). Aside from the impact that the gothic novel has made as an art form in its own right, it influenced the poetry of Keats (in "The Eve of St. Agnes"), Shelley (in *The Cenci*), and Byron (in *Manfred*); and the fiction of many a subsequent author. Gothic elements abound in the short stories of Poe (especially "The Fall of the House of Usher"), Hawthorne's *Marble Faun,* Charlotte Brontë's *Jane Eyre,* Emily Brontë's *Wuthering Heights,* and Henry James's *Turn of the Screw.* The gothic novel refurbished with subtler mysteries and revelations—the tunnels and cellars of the psyche—has been revived by the contemporary British writer Iris Murdoch. In *A Severed Head,* for example, the incestuous Honor Klein hovers like a black cloud over all the extramarital intrigues. Miss Murdoch's fiction is also a PARODY of the gothic novel. For aside from re-introducing standard gothic trappings, she re-examines some of them as hitherto repressed sexual symbols. She has her characters act out gothic sexual episodes, which in the eighteenth-century prototypes remained half-conscious stirrings or fantasies.

REFERENCES: Wilbur Cross, *Development of the English Novel;* Lowry Nelson, "Night Thoughts on the Gothic Novel," in Elearnor T. Lincoln (ed.), *Pastoral and Romance.*

Grace   See CALVINISM.

Graces, the   In classical mythology, the three sister goddesses who bestowed charm, beauty, and joy on nature and humanity: Thalia (abundance), Euphrosyne (mirth), and Aglaia (elevation). (Compare the FATES.)

graffiti   Literally, "inscriptions," especially those scratched into rocks and walls. For the most part graffiti are anonymous, satirical (often pornographic and scatological) comments in prose and verse scribbled on the walls of public and institutional rooms. The comments range from the childish to the bitter remarks of social protest.

REFERENCE: Albert Kalson, "The Theatre of Graffiti," *Journal of Popular Culture* (Summer, 1967).

grand tour   A tour through two or more countries of Europe ("the Continent") usually by walking or (in modern times) cycling for the purpose of "finishing" one's formal education. Since the Elizabethan era

Oxford and Cambridge graduates have traditionally taken such a tour, and in modern times American graduates and undergraduates have emulated this practice. In these tours, which usually take several weeks or longer (sometimes months), the traveler tests his knowledge of the "target" language(s); studies art, architecture, and historical monuments; and observes, at first hand, people, places, customs, mores, and pastimes. Such experiences John Stuart Mill categorizes as "The End of Education and the Beginning of Self-Education" in his celebrated *Autobiography*. The grand tour is more elaborately described in other biographies and is reflected in much modern fiction.

REFERENCES: John Addington Symonds, "Foreign Travel," *Sir Philip Sydney;* John Milton, "Italian Tour, 1638–1639," *Second Defence of the English People;* Laurence Sterne, *A Sentimental Journey through France and Italy;* Chauncey B. Tinker, *Young Boswell;* Frederick A. Pottle (ed.), *Boswell's Journals;* William Wordsworth, *Descriptive Sketches* [of a Walking Tour through France and Switzerland]; Jacques Barzun (ed.), "Traveler and Poet: Aetat. 21–26," *Selected Letters of Lord Byron;* André Maurois, "A Six Weeks' Tour," *Ariel: The Life of Shelley;* Aileen Ward, *John Keats: The Making of a Poet;* Henry Adams, *The Education of Henry Adams;* Lincoln Steffens, *Autobiography;* Harrison Smith (ed.), "Travel on Two Continents," *From Main Street to Stockholm;* Richard Haliburton, *The Royal Road to Romance;* Paul and Elizabeth Elek (eds.), *The Age of the Grand Tour;* Janet Mandelstam, "The Grinds on the Grand Tour," *Saturday Review* (February 21, 1970).

Graveyard school   A group of eighteenth-century poets—among them, Thomas Gray, Robert Blair, Thomas Parnell, and Edward Young—who wrote on funereal subjects.

Great Books, the   1. Certain classics of literature selected by such educators as Charles W. Eliot, for the "Harvard Classics" or "Five-Foot Shelf"; John Erskine, for the Columbia Great Books Course; Stringfellow Barr, for St. John's College, Maryland; and Robert Hutchins and Mortimer Adler, for the University of Chicago program in General Education. 2. An adult-education society organized by Hutchins and Adler in many communities across the country, with leaders who meet small groups every other week to discuss an assigned classic. For a list of these classics, see the Appendix to Adler's *How to Read a Book*. (See also Adler, *The Great Ideas* and *The Syntopicon,* an index to the ideas and issues in the Great Books.) 3. The chief instructional materials of an educational philosophy known as "perennialism," the major tenet of which is that education is essentially a continuing dialectic.

REFERENCES: Robert Hutchins, *The Great Conversation;* Mortimer Adler, *The Syntopicon;* Quentin Anderson and Joseph Mazzeo (eds.), *The Proper Study.*

great chain of being   The idea that all the components of the universe are arranged in a chain, or hierarchy, with each thing or creature occupying a God-given place. At the bottom of the chain is inanimate matter; farther up, things that grow but do not reason; then rational man, "a creature in a middle state," as Pope described him; above man, the angels; finally, at the top, God. The idea of the chain is said to have come from Milton — "hanging in a golden chain / This pendent world" — while the concept of orderly links derives from Plato's theories of the relations between mind and matter in the *Timaeus* and his "idea of the good" in *The Republic*. Plato's concepts were elaborated in the *Enneads* of Plotinus (A.D. 204–269), who more directly inspired the Neo-Platonists of both the Italian and the English RENAISSANCE. Most of these writers — among them Edmund Spenser, in his *Hymnes in Honour of Love and Beauty* (1596), and Henry More, in his *Platonical Song of the Soul* (1642) — emphasized the beauty of the universe and the aesthetic character of the relations between man and God. Such ideas were easily accommodated to the Judaeo-Christian belief in God's love for man as a binding-principle or covenant. To this principle in its Neo-Platonic version Shakespeare made frequent reference, especially in *Troilus and Cressida* (1609). Certain seventeenth-century poets who could find no unity in the physical world turned inward in an attempt to unify themselves, their own sensibilities. Given to fanciful CONCEITS and the invention of God-man links that seemed to the man of "New Science" to be too far removed from scientific reality, they were ridiculed as METAPHYSICAL (literally, "beyond nature") by John Dryden and by Samuel Johnson. But all seventeenth- and eighteenth-century writers were very much concerned with man's place in the world of nature. And next to the word *nature,* according to A. O. Lovejoy, the phrase "great chain of being" was the most sacred utterance of the eighteenth century. For as astronomers continued to discover a much more immense universe than had previously been realized, making Milton's "pendent world" look like a child's bauble, poets responded to the deeply felt human need of spiritualizing what might otherwise seem harshly impersonal and irrational. And poets like Pope and Thomson sought for rational rather than just aesthetic or mystical bonds between the earthly and the heavenly. In the long poem *Essay on Man* (1732–34) Pope reverently addressed himself to the "Vast chain of being":

> Vast chain of being! which from God began,
> Nature's ethereal, human, angel, man,
> Beast, bird, fish, insect, what no eye can see,
> No glass can reach; from Infinite to thee,
> From thee to nothing. — On superior pow'rs
> Were we to press, inferior might on ours;
> Or in full creation leave a void,
> Where, one step broken, the great scale's destroyed:

> From Nature's chain whatever link you strike,
> Tenth, or ten thousandth, breaks the chain alike.

Unlike the metaphysical poet George Herbert, who in his poem "The Pulley" (1633) had been concerned with a more personal and direct bond between himself and his God, the Neo-Platonist James Thomson in the long poem *The Seasons* (1726–1730) re-created—in stones, plants, beasts, men, and angels—a more rational chain to the All-Perfect. The great chain of being assumed, finally, the following three tenets: (*a*) plenitude, or infinite supply, (*b*) continuity and linked or shared attributes, and (*c*) hierarchy, or orderly arrangement of the links.

REFERENCES: A. O. Lovejoy, *The Great Chain of Being;* Frederick A. Pottle, "Dogma, Science, and Poetry," *The Idiom of Poetry;* Louis Martz, *The Poetry of Meditation;* E. M. W. Tillyard, *Elizabethan World Picture.*

H

hackneyed usage   See TRITENESS.

haiku (Hokku)   A classic Japanese verse form in three unrhymed lines of, respectively, five, seven, and five syllables. An example:

> In all the May rains
> there is one thing not hidden —
> Bridge at Zeta Bay.

Almost always a haiku establishes the season, usually in the first line. Like the TANKA, haiku are characterized by compression, restraint, and suggestion rather than explicit statement or description. The images are OBJECTIVE CORRELATIVES, which contribute to a tight unity of mood and tone. Occasionally, haiku are written in pairs or in related series (*"garlands"*). An example of a pair:

> *Decorations on a Japanese Fan**
>
> *Side 1*
>
> Wearing autumn reds
> and golds of maple driftings
> ladies live in leaves
>
> *Side 2*
>
> Limbs turn lovelier
> when leaves attach themselves to
> trees and dress the woods

REFERENCES: Harold Henderson (ed.), *Haiku: An Anthology from Bashō to Shiki;* Glenn Swetman, "The Haiku, the Sonnet, and the English Language," *Quartet* (Summer, 1964).

half-truth   A kind of misrepresentation which gives the audience the truth in part but not the whole truth, or which withholds saying anything about aspects that may be damaging to the persuader's case. (Compare CARDSTACKING.)

REFERENCES: Vance Packard, *The Hidden Persuaders;* John Kenneth Galbraith, *The Affluent Society;* C. Northcote Parkinson, *The Law and the Profits.*

hamartia   Tragic flaw. (See TRAGEDY.)

hanging indention   See BIBLIOGRAPHY.

hasty generalization   A fallacious conclusion resulting from a failure

*Reprinted from *College English* by permission.

to compile sufficient data (especially in statistical INDUCTIVE REASON-ING) or from a failure to examine the available data.

head rime   See ALLITERATION.

Hebraism and Hellenism   As codified by Matthew Arnold, the spirit of Hellenism is "life as it is"; of Hebraism, "life as it ought to be." Thus the Hebraic emphasis is essentially moral; the Hellenic, aesthetic. REFERENCES: Matthew Arnold, "Culture and Anarchy" in Lionel Trilling (ed.), *The Portable Matthew Arnold;* essays by Eliot, Trilling, Burke, Farrell *et al.* in Bernard Oldsey and Arthur Lewis, Jr. (eds.), *Visions and Revisions . . . ;* David DeLaura, *Hebrew and Hellene in Victorian England.*

hemistich   A half line of poetry, two of which make up a metrically complete line, as in Anglo-Saxon verse (see ALLITERATIVE VERSE). The modern poet W. H. Auden uses the hemistich in the poem "Always in Trouble."

hendiadys   An idea normally expressed in a phrase (*try to win, very ready, far away*) and presented instead with *and* (*try and win, good and ready, far and away*). This rhetorical device was much used in Greek and Latin poetry as a refinement.

heptameter   See METER.

heroic couplet   Also called **riding rhyme**. Rhymed pairs of iambic pentameter lines. Chaucer introduced this verse form into English, having developed it in 17,000 lines of *The Canterbury Tales* (ca. 1387). The heroic couplet, along with the Chaucerian style of dramatic narrative, was used by Spenser in the satirical "Mother Hubberd's Tale" (1590) and by Marlowe in the erotic poem "Hero and Leander" (1598). Marlowe preferred blank verse for his plays (as did Shakespeare and many other Elizabethan playwrights) and used heroic couplets in them only sporadically. The heroic couplet was developed to perfection, however, by Dryden and Pope. In Dryden's satirical *Absalom and Achitophel* (1682) the heroic couplets, while retaining Chaucer's narrative flow, also demonstrated the sophistication of EPIGRAM. Compare, for example, these couplets from Chaucer's "Wife of Bath's Prologue"

> I know that Abr'am was a holy man
> And Jacob too, as far as is my ken;
> And each of them had spouses more than two
> (As many another holy man did, too).
> When did you ever see in any age
> Our God on high forbidding marriage
> By express word? Please do enlighten me;
> Or where did he demand virginity?

with these couplets from *Absalom and Achitophel,* Part One

> In pious times, ere priestcraft did begin,
> Before polygamy was made a sin;
> When man on many multiplied his kind,
> Ere one to one was cursedly confined;
> When nature prompted, and no law denied
> Promiscuous use of concubine and bride. . . .

Chaucer's influence on Pope is reflected in the latter's "Paraphrases from Chaucer" (ca. 1709). But Pope's brilliance shines with its own light in such epigrammatic couplets as these from his *Essay on Criticism* (1701):

> True ease in writing comes from art, not chance,
> As those move easiest who have learned to dance.
>
> Men must be taught as if you taught them not,
> And things unknown proposed as things forgot.
>
> A little learning is a dangerous thing;
> Drink deep, or taste not the Pierian spring.

The above excerpts also illustrate Pope's art of the *closed* heroic couplet; that is, the couplet containing one complete sentence. But Pope was also a master of the *open* heroic couplet; that is, verse in which a sentence flows from one couplet into another, as, for example, these lines from his *Essay on Man* (1733–34):

> Let us, since life can little more supply
> Than just to look about us, and to die,
> Expatiate free o'er all this scene of man;

in which the main exhortation is "Let us . . . expatiate." Those same lines illustrate Pope's virtuosity with varying the CAESURA, a device that serves to prevent sing-song effects.

Another virtuoso of the varying caesura and the open couplet was Robert Browning, whose poem "My Last Duchess" (1842) begins,

> That's my last duchess painted on the wall,
> Looking as if she were alive. I call
> That piece a wonder, now; Fra Pandolfo's hands
> Worked busily a day, and there she stands.

Heroic couplets were used by such poets as Byron, Keats, Shelley, Swinburne, and William Morris, but gradually waned in fashion toward the end of the nineteenth century.

REFERENCES: John A. Jones, *Pope's Couplet Art;* W. B. Piper, *The Heroic Couplet;* W. K. Wimsatt, "On Relationship of Rhyme to Reason," *The Verbal Ikon.*

heterography   Spelling in which the same letter represents several sounds. Only a strictly phonetic alphabet could avoid it. In English, heterography plagues the schoolboy, who is both annoyed and amused that *c* should sound different in *call* and *cell,* that *g* should sound different in *gum* and *gem,* and that the combination *gh* should be so erratic in a *rough fight.* (See SPELLING.)

hexameter   See METER.

hiatus   In writing or speech, a break in continuity, such as a missing part of a manuscript or a brief vocal pause in midword, as between the successive vowels in *preempt.*

historical novel   A novel based on historical events and on one or more historical personages, but shaped otherwise by the novelist's imagination. Some of the most celebrated historical novels are *War and Peace* (Tolstoy), *Ivanhoe* (Scott), *Vanity Fair* (Thackeray), *A Tale of Two Cities* (Dickens), *The Last Days of Pompeii* (Bulwer-Lytton), *The Cloister and the Hearth* (Reade), *Northwest Passage* (Roberts), and *Gone with the Wind* (Mitchell).

Critics have argued about whether an historical novel is really fiction. Perhaps the tenet most widely accepted by authors and critics is that liberties may be taken with comparatively obscure or unverified historical events, but that violence must not be done to major historical events and personages; this tenet was developed by, among others, Lessing in his *Hamburgische Dramaturgie* (1767). Thus, whether a minor character like Dr. Manette (in *A Tale of Two Cities*) was imprisoned or actually existed is comparatively unimportant; it is perfectly plausible that a person like him could have been imprisoned. What Dickens could not have afforded to take liberties with, however, is the major circumstances of the French Revolution, the Reign of Terror, the tumbrils, and the guillotine. He might well have slipped into a tumbril a fictional character or two, but he could not very well have tampered with the recorded executions of well-known historical personages.

REFERENCES: For a bibliography of historical novels arranged according to events and periods (as well as by authors and titles), see Ernest Baker, *A Guide to Historical Fiction.* For another, select list of historical novels and short stories and for the view of historians on the value of such works, see Oscar Handlin *et al., Harvard Guide to American History.*

history as literature   In a broad sense, history may be taken to comprehend any record purporting to give facts about events and men's actions and to draw conclusions from those facts. Thus, articles, reports, memoranda, diaries, and the like may be construed as history;

but most often they are not literature, though they may be the materials of either history or literature. (In this sense, a scientist's report on an experiment may be taken as a micro-history of a micro-event.) In a narrower sense, history as literature comprehends those writings — annals, chronicles, memoirs, journals, diaries, narratives, and the like — that are presented with imaginative style. The writer of history, unlike the writer of an historical novel, may take few liberties with the facts; but he may combine all the skills of the novelist in the dramatic presentation of his materials. The writing of history as a discipline or profession is a development of comparatively recent times; but over the centuries many distinguished histories meriting attention by the student of literature have been written.

In classical antiquity the celebrated examples include the *History* [of Greece and Persia], by Herodotus, "the Father of History"; *The History of the Jews*, by Josephus; *The History of the Peloponnesian Wars*, by Thucydides; *The Anabasis*, by Xenophon; and the *Histories* and *Annals* [of Rome], by Tacitus.

In medieval times the most famous history was Jean Froissart's *Chronicles* [of France, Spain, Portugal, and England].

During the English Renaissance the two most famous histories were *The History of the World*, by Sir Walter Raleigh, and the *Chronicles* [of England, Scotland, and Ireland], by Raphael Holinshed, the latter being the source for several of Shakespeare's plays.

In modern times histories celebrated for their literary style include *The Decline and Fall of the Roman Empire* (Edward Gibbon), *The History of Charles XII* [of Sweden] (Voltaire), *The French Revolution* (Thomas Carlyle), *The Rise of the Dutch Republic* (J. L. Motley), *The History of England* (Thomas Macaulay), *The Civilization of the Renaissance in Italy* (Jacob Burckhardt), *The Renaissance* (John Addington Symonds), *The Conquest of Mexico* and *The Conquest of Peru* (both by William Prescott), *The Epic of America* (James Truslow Adams), *The Tragic Era* (Claude Bowers), *The Rise of American Civilization* (Charles and Mary Beard).

Recent notable histories include *The Story of Civilization* (Will and Ariel Durant), *The History of the English-Speaking Peoples* (Winston Churchill), *The Rise and Fall of the Third Reich* (William Shirer), *Red Star over China* (Edgar Snow), *History of the Russian Revolution* (Leon Trotsky), *Ten Days That Shook the World* (John Reed), *The Guns of August* (Barbara Tuchman), *Black Lamb and Grey Falcon* (Rebecca West), *Hiroshima* (John Hersey), and *The Armies of the Night* (Norman Mailer). (Compare HISTORICAL NOVEL and BIOGRAPHY.)

REFERENCES: Edmund Wilson, *To the Finland Station: A Study of the Writing and the Acting of History;* Arnold Toynbee, *A Study of History;* H. G. Wells,

An Outline of History; Oscar Handlin *et al., The Harvard Guide to American History;* Herbert Butterfield, *The Historical Novel.*

holidays mentioned in literature

Advent.   See *Christmas.*

All Hallows.   See *Hallowe'en.*

All Saints' Day, November 1, commemorates in particular Pope Boniface IV's converting the heathen in A.D. 834 and in general honors all Christian martyrs.

All Souls' Day, November 2, is a day of prayers and alms-giving to alleviate the suffering of souls in Purgatory.

Arbor Day, date varies, has been since 1872 a day devoted to the planting of trees, usually by schoolchildren.

Armistice Day, November 11, commemorates the day World War I ended officially (the eleventh hour of the eleventh day of the eleventh month). Now called *Veterans Day.*

Ascension Day, the fortieth day after Easter, commemorates Christ's ascension to Heaven on the fortieth day after His resurrection.

Ash Wednesday, the first Wednesday in Lent, signifies the beginning of Lent and Christian humility. The custom of sprinkling ashes on the forehead was popularized by Pope Gregory the Great, who had adapted it from an old Roman and Jewish custom.

Christmas, December 25, commemorates the birth of Christ. The French word for Christmas, *Noël,* and the Scandinavian *Jul* (Yule) are also used in English. The burning of the yule log, the decoration of the tree, the hanging of stockings, the placing of shoes and other receptacles for gifts — these customs had their origins in pre-Christian societies. The Angles of Britain, for example, celebrated December 25 as a combination New Year's Day and Mother's Day. As with many other holidays, several of the pre-Christian rites and customs of this day were merged with the Christian rites. In 1644 the English Puritans abolished most of the "pagan" aspects of Christmas, but these were restored by Charles II. The Christmas feast, celebrated sometimes on Christmas Day and sometimes on Christmas Eve, traditionally included a roast goose, as in Dickens's *Christmas Carol.* Groups of young people going from house to house to sing carols on Christmas Eve is also an adaptation of a pre-Christian custom.

Columbus Day, October 12, commemorates Columbus's discovery, in 1492, of what is now thought of as the Latin American West Indies.

Corpus Christi Day, the Thursday after Trinity Sunday, which is the Sunday after Pentecost, commemorates the Eucharist (the Lord's Supper of Holy Communion, which uses bread wafer and wine symbolically for the body and blood of Christ). It was on this day that the medieval English trade guilds of York, Coventry, and Chester produced their mystery and MIRACLE PLAYS.

Decoration Day, May 30, commemorates all American soldiers killed in all past wars; also called *Memorial Day.*

Easter, the first Sunday after the first full moon of the spring (March 21 or any of the twenty-eight days thereafter; hence not earlier than March 21 nor later than April 25), was originally a pagan Teutonic festival celebrating the spring equinox, in honor of the dawn goddess. (The Germanic *oestre* is a linguistic relative of several comparable words meaning *dawn.*) When the Church Fathers converted the Angles and Saxons, along with other Teutonic and Celtic peoples, they amalgamated into the Christian holiday many pre-Christian rites and customs.

Election Day, in the United States the first Tuesday after the first Monday in November of even-numbered years; also called *General Election Day.*

Empire Day, May 24, in the British Commonwealth honors Queen Victoria; also called *Victoria Day.*

Epiphany, January 6, commemorates the appearance (*epiphane* is Greek for *appearance*) of the Star of Bethlehem to the Three Wise Men.

Fathers' Day, the third Sunday in June. See also *Mothers' Day.*

Flag Day, June 14, commemorates the adoption in 1777 of the American flag; it is not a legal holiday.

Good Friday, the Friday preceding Easter Sunday, commemorates Jesus' crucifixion by the Romans. "Good" is a transliteration of the Anglo-Saxon word for "holy"; in folklore anyone born on Good Friday (or on Christmas) has the power to see spirits and to give them orders.

Hallowe'en, October 31, among the Old Celts was the last day of the year, when witches and warlocks were supposed to celebrate their rites; when the pagans were Christianized, this holiday was converted to the Eve of All Hallows' or All Saints'.

Hannukkah, the end of the third or the beginning of the fourth Jewish month, commemorates the victorious revolution, under the Maccabee patriots, against Antiochus IV of Syria, and the dedication of the Temple in Jerusalem in 165 B.C. It is also called the *Feast of Lights.* Hannukkah usually comes around Christmastime, and since it, too, is a time when gifts are exchanged, it is sometimes, all too loosely, called "the Jewish Christmas."

Holy Thursday.   The day before *Good Friday.*

Independence Day, July 4, commemorates the signing in 1776 of the Declaration of Independence.

Labor Day, the first Monday in September, commemorates, and gives a day of rest to, wage-earners.

Lent, the forty weekdays from Ash Wednesday to Easter, commemorates Jesus' fasting in the wilderness. Devout Christians, in self-abnegation, give up some personal indulgence, especially some food like meat, which they enjoy during the rest of the year. The night, or the few nights, before Lent is usually celebrated as a kind of "feast before the famine" with a Mardi Gras (as in New Orleans) or a Carnival (as in Europe). A *mardi gras* is, literally, "fat Tuesday"; *carnival* derives from *vale* and *carne* — "farewell to meat."

Mardi Gras.   See *Lent.*

May Day, May 1, is an ancient holiday rooted in spring fertility rites, especially in India and Egypt. In medieval England, and later in the United States, it was the custom on May Day to decorate a Maypole and then to dance around it (as, for example, in Hawthorne's "May-Pole of Merry Mount"). Freudian critics regard the Maypole as a phallic symbol. In the U.S.S.R., May Day is a legal holiday devoted to political speeches and to demonstrations of military might.

Memorial Day.   See *Decoration Day.*

Michaelmas, September 29, is the Festival of St. Michael, who fought dragons and now weighs the souls of the risen dead. In England the day is noted for (*a*) roast goose feasts, (*b*) election of magistrates, and (*c*) collection of rents. (Dickens refers to Michaelmas in the opening passage of *Bleak House.*)

Mothers' Day, the second Sunday in May, honors all mothers. The pre-Christian Angles and Saxons celebrated a mothers' day of sorts on December 25. The medieval Europeans, who thought of "mother" as the Virgin Mary, had numerous days in her honor — not only as an intercessor ("paraclete") on their behalf but also and more generally, according to Henry Adams (see "The Dynamo and the Virgin," in *The Education of Henry Adams*), as a deeply respected and loved exemplar of matronly fertility and strength.

New Year's Day, January 1 in Western cultures; various other dates in other cultures, such as the Jewish Rosh Hashana, the Chinese New Year's and so on. For fascinating information on various New Year celebrations, see James Frazer, *The Golden Bough.*

New Year's Eve, December 31.

Noel.   See *Christmas.*

Palm Sunday, the Sunday before Easter, commemorates Jesus' entry into Jerusalem, when palm branches were strewn in his path.

Paschal time, the Easter season. *Paschal* pertains to the lamb that was ritually killed and eaten at Passover; in Christian symbolism, the Paschal Lamb is Jesus (*Agnus Dei,* the Lamb of God).

Passover, beginning at sundown on the fourteenth of Nisan, the Jewish seventh month, is observed for eight days. It commemorates the Exodus from Egypt, the story of which is recounted at the Seder (Passover Supper) as it is read from the *Haggada.* Eating only unleavened bread (Matzoth) and refraining from any other leavened food products is a requirement for the observance of the holiday. It commemorates not only the Exodus but also the Angel of Death's "passing over" the Jewish homes the night before. Having marked their door posts with lamb's blood, the Jews were spared death by plague — the Tenth Plague — which killed the Egyptian first-born.

Pentecost, the sixth and seventh days of Sivan, the Jewish ninth month, is the Jewish Festival of Shavuoth, which commemorates Moses' receiving on Mount Sinai the tablets inscribed with the Ten Commandments. The Christian holiday, the seventh Sunday after Easter, commemorates the descent of the Holy Spirit over the Apostles; also called *Whitsunday.*

Purim, the fourteenth day of Adar, the Jewish sixth month, is the Jewish Feast of Lots, which commemorates the day on which the Jews of Persia were to be annihilated, the order to be determined by the drawing of lots. Queen Esther, the Jewish wife of King Ahasuerus, managed to save the Jews with the help of her uncle Mordecai. Haman, the mastermind of the anti-Jewish plot, was hanged. Celebration of the holiday involves hearing a reading of the "Megilla" (*Scroll of Esther,* recording the events of the holiday), the sending of gifts of food to friends and the poor, and merrymaking.

Rosh Hashana, the first of Tishri, is the Jewish New Year, which is reckoned from 3761 B.C., the traditional date of the Biblical Creation.

St. Agnes' Eve, January 20, is the holiday on which a girl, on performing certain rites, was supposed to have a vision of her future husband. See Keats's "Eve of St. Agnes."

St. Nicholas' Day. St. Nicholas is the patron saint of Russia, of scholars, of sailors, of pawnbrokers, and of little boys. He was the original Santa Claus. Many Eastern Orthodox people still celebrate St. Nicholas' Day; the Dutch people also celebrate this day, but they have tended to merge it with Christmas Eve.

St. Patrick's Day, March 17, commemorates the saint who, though not Irish himself, converted the pre-Christian Irish and rid Ireland of snakes and vermin. In explaining the Holy Trinity, St. Patrick used a shamrock.

St. Swithin's Day, July 15, celebrates the saint vaguely associated with rain: "If it rains on St. Swithin's Day, it will rain for forty days."

St. Valentine's Day, February 14, commemorates the Roman priest who gave aid and comfort to the persecuted Christians. This is

"lovers' day," when even the birds choose their mates for the year, as Chaucer observes in *The Parliament of Fowls*. In England on this day young people draw lots and exchange gifts, a modification and extension of an ancient pagan rite honoring Juno or Venus.
Shrovetide, the three days preceding Ash Wednesday.
Thanksgiving, the fourth Thursday in November in the United States, was originally any day of thanks-giving, but is now traced to the day of thanksgiving when the Pilgrims commemorated their survival during the first harsh winter in New England, thanks in part to gifts of food from the native Indians. The turkey feast is traditional, and the thanks offering has developed into a more general reverence for all blessings. Canadians celebrate a similar day of thanksgiving, the second Monday in October.
Trinity Sunday, the Sunday after Pentecost.
Veterans' Day.   See *Armistice Day.*
Whitsunday.   See *Pentecost.*
Yom Kippur, the tenth day of Tishri, the Jewish first month, is the Jewish Day of Atonement. Since the Jewish day is always reckoned from sundown to sundown, the holiday actually begins the evening before. Fasting and praying for forgiveness of sins mark the observance of this day.
Yuletide, Christmas.
REFERENCES: Mary Haseltine, *Anniversaries and Holidays;* George W. Douglas, *The American Book of Days;* Sir James Frazer, *The Golden Bough;* Robert Chambers, *The Book of Days;* E. O. James, *Seasonal Feasts and Festivals;* A. J. Nevins (ed.), *The Maryknoll Catholic Dictionary.*

homeric epithet   See EPITHET 2.

homily   1. Originally, a sermon or moral story, such as the Anglo-Saxon *Blickling Homilies*. 2. Generally, a derogatory term for a sermon or sermonlike lecture.

homographs   Words with the same spelling but different origins, meanings, and pronunciations: "He *wound* a bandage about the *wound*." Since pronunciation and meaning tend to change more rapidly than spelling, words that were once HOMONYMS may become only homographs (as did *wind,* which once rhymed with *behind* whether it meant "an air current" or "to coil.").

homonym   Two words spelled alike and pronounced alike which have far different meanings and derivations; each is the other's homonym. *Pitch* black and wild *pitch,* for example, have no connection in meaning, though they look and sound alike. The word *homonym* is often used loosely to mean the same thing as *homophone.* (Compare HOMOPHONE and HOMOGRAPH.)

homophone   Two words that sound alike but have different spellings, origins, and meanings. A *piece* of music and a lasting *peace* are examples. (See also HOMOGRAPH and HOMONYM.)

horn book   **1.** In seventeenth-century New England a child's primer consisting of a single sheet of paper protected by a transparent piece of horn and mounted on a small board. From horn "books" children learned the alphabet, numbers, the Lord's Prayer, and much of their earliest catechism ("In Adam's fall / We sinned all."). In England from the sixteenth to the eighteenth centuries the horn book was used for similar purposes. **2.** Thomas Dekker's *Gull's Horn Book* (1609) was a satirical primer for the young fop or Italianate gentleman, who was beginning to be smiled at in Elizabethan comedies and who was to be lampooned in RESTORATION comedies.

hubris   Excessive pride; one of the tragic flaws. (See TRAGEDY.)

Humanism   **1.** A generality often used too loosely, as Howard Mumford Jones has observed, for "humaneness" and for "the humanities"; that is, for studies in literature and the arts. **2.** A movement of enlightenment championed by Desiderius Erasmus (1466–1536) and others in reaction to medieval scholasticism. Although both the humanists and the scholastics were interested in Greek and Roman studies, the humanists emphasized matters of human, as distinguished from ecclesiastical, interest. (See RENAISSANCE 2.) **3.** A modern religious movement which, like Unitarianism, emphasizes rational, as opposed to mystical, beliefs. Its official publication is *The Humanist*. **4.** In contemporary literature and thought, a kind of secular existentialism. (See EXISTENTIALISM; compare NEW HUMANISM.)

REFERENCES: Howard Mumford Jones, *One Great Society;* Ernst Cassirer, *An Essay on Man;* Erwin Panofsky, *Meaning in the Visual Arts;* Georges Simenon, *The Novel of Man.*

humor   **1.** A "pleasant disappointment of expectation" – Max Eastman. **2.** Loosely, a synonym for pleasantry or WIT, though the latter is generally more conscious and sophisticated while humor is broader and unconsciously rooted in idiosyncrasy of personality. Thus the amusing behavior (speech as well as actions) of Bottom the Weaver, in Shakespeare's *Midsummer Night's Dream,* is generally regarded as humorous, whereas the amusing utterances of Professor Higgins, in Shaw's *Pygmalion,* are generally regarded as witty.

REFERENCES: Max Eastman, *The Sense of Humor* and *The Enjoyment of Laughter;* Walter Blair, *Native American Humor;* James Agee, "Comedy's Greatest Era," in Irving and Harriet Deer (eds.), *The Popular Arts.*

humours   **1.** The four body fluids assumed by most medieval and some RENAISSANCE writers to govern people's dispositions – (*a*) blood, (*b*) choler, (*c*) black bile, and (*d*) phlegm. In a healthy person the humours were thought to be in balance, with no one fluid predominating. If a person's metabolism went out of balance, it was thought that one of the humours was "stirring up an ascendancy." Thus a person suffering from an imbalance of one of the humours could be diagnosed as (*a*) sanguine or overly cheerful, (*b*) choleric or grumpy, (*c*) melancholy or lovesick, or (*d*) phlegmatic or stolid. 2. The humours were not only the four standard psychosomatic symptoms mentioned in (1) but also more individualistic psychological traits motivating certain characters in comedy, especially the comedy of humours. Thus, aside from the stock melancholy of a Jacques, in *As You Like It,* or the sanguine conceitedness of a Malvolio, in *Twelfth Night,* humours were also such individualistic human foibles as possessiveness, self-righteousness, affectation, misogyny, and the like. Some classic examples occur in Ben Jonson's play *Every Man in His Humour* (1598). In this comedy the choleric old merchant Kitely's individualistic humour is possessive jealousy of his pretty young wife, who he suspects is having an affair with the young Edward Knowell. Edward's father, phlegmatic and stolid, is obsessed with the individualistic humour of excessive concern for his son's morals. After a series of farcical intrigues involving such St. Paul's Church bench-warmers as the stock braggart Captain Bobadill and the young Knowell's cronies, the chief obsessed characters are somewhat disabused of their humours by the compassionate Justice Clement. *Every Man in His Humour* is celebrated not only because Shakespeare acted in it, but also because its Prologue ends with Jonson's theory of what good comedy should consist of:

. . . deeds and language such as men do use
And persons such as . . .
. . . would show an image of the times.
It should sport with follies, not with crimes;
Except we make 'em such, by loving still
Our popular errors, when we know they're ill.
I mean such errors as you'll all confess,
By laughing at them, they deserve no less;
Which when you heartily do, there's hope left, then,
You, that have so graced monsters
May like men.

Humours or human foibles, then, and the therapy of laughing at them are the obverse analogues of TRAGIC FAULTS and the therapy of CATHARSIS.

REFERENCES: C. H. Talbot, *Medicine in Medieval England;* J. B. Priestly, *The English Comic Characters;* John Palmer, *Comic Characters of Shakespeare;* James Parton, *Caricature and Other Comic Art;* William F. Fry, *Sweet Madness;* Francis Fergusson, *The Idea of a Theater.*

hymn   See LYRIC.

hyperbole (hy-per′-bo-le). Gross exaggeration for rhetorical effect — e.g., "I'm dead." We find it natural to say, "I've been waiting for *hours*" (though it has really been ten minutes), "His face fell *a mile*" (he showed mild disappointment), or "Your jokes really *kill* me" (they bring a smile), or "She was *hysterical* over that new dress!" (she said she liked it). American speech abounds in hyperbole, inherited perhaps from the early settlers, who found the mountains, rivers, and plains bigger than could be described in restrained words. Such national heroes as Davy Crockett, Daniel Webster, and the legendary Paul Bunyan were celebrated for their size, shrewdness, skills, and zest for life — they were big "as all outdoors." Exaggeration became a prime device of the frontiersman's language, perhaps because he needed to build himself up to the requirements of the vast frontier. His famed "tall tales" have become an American art form, still cherished. The national Liars' Club each year awards a prize for the most astounding "whopper." So common is hyperbole in American speech that even our least exciting ideas may be described as *great, stupendous, terrific.* Advertising, now a fixture that creates as well as expresses the American way of life, uses hyperbole as a standard means of luring attention. Every product is the *best* of its kind, of course, the biggest, the longest-lasting, the "most." But hyperbole has its dangers. Like the boy who cried "Wolf!" the constant user of hyperbole soon finds his remarks taken lightly, or nearly ignored. He may find need for a balance of hyperbole's opposites, UNDERSTATEMENT and LITOTES.

hyphen Though often thought of as a mark of punctuation, the hyphen serves chiefly as a device of spelling. It is a means of linking or of separating words or word parts to reduce the likelihood of misreading. The mark (-) is an appreciable help in adapting English speech to the printed page: it often does in writing what intonation does in speech. For example, *high-school grades* may mean something quite different from *high school-grades.* The difference is signaled in speech by intonation, in writing by the hyphen. The hyphen is generally used:

1. To link words that form a compound adjective:

red-hot stove	*fast-moving* train
blue-green water	*sit-down* strike
leveling-off period	*come-as-you-are* party
Watson-Prager Bill	*twenty-two*
three-eighths	

2. To indicate the breaking of a word from one line of print to the next. (See SYLLABICATION.)
3. To separate prefixes from roots whenever

a) a meaning other than the usual is intended:

> Please *re-form* the line.
> They *re-sent* the gift.

b) the root word begins with a capital letter:

> pro-British   non-Catholic   pre-Neanderthal   anti-Semitic

c) the prefix *semi-* is used with a word that begins with i:

> semi-independent   semi-infinite

d) the prefix is *ex-, cross-, half-, self-, vice-*:

> ex-sailor   cross-country   half-awake   self-confidence   vice-consul

4. To stand for the word "to" in certain phrases:

> the Chicago-Philadelphia jet   pp. 44–46

5. To indicate prefixes, infixes, suffixes, or syllables written alone:

> Of course, *un-* is not the same as *dis-,* so one cannot be dissatisfied if he is unsatisfied.

6. In typing, to indicate a dash (--); in this instance, two hyphens are necessary.

hysteron proteron   The rhetorical device (sometimes, the error) of putting the last thing first, as the effect before the cause, or the end of a story before the beginning. For example, "It was easy getting down after we got up." Now and then a striking freshness can be brought to a stale expression by reversing the order of its elements: "Man is forever chasing *tide and time*"; "Don't *chew* more than you can *bite off.*" In telling a story, the writer may start with the ending and then relate the events that led to it. In logic one may, in the *conditional* SYLLOGISM, commit the fallacy of hysteron proteron by asserting a consequent and then inferring an antecedent: "If the water is cold, Phil won't swim; Phil will swim—therefore the water isn't cold." (See *affirming the consequent* under SYLLOGISM 2.)

I

iamb   See METER.

idiom   1. An expression peculiar to a language; this expression may or may not make sense literally, but it is in common currency and quite respectable. An example: "What are you up to?" 2. In literature and the other arts, a style of expression peculiar to an artist: "In the *idiom* of Faulkner — mankind will survive, endure, prevail."

illusion of reality   That which *seems* real even though it may not be; the results of SELECTIVE REPRESENTATION as distinguished from random or candid representation; that is, a portrait as opposed to a photograph; one, but only one, of the aspects of Aristotle's MIMESIS or "imitation of life."

In the theater, for example, if the audience seems to be more aware of Hamlet than of the Richard Burton or John Gielgud performing the role, then the actor (as well as the playwright) can be said to have successfully created an illusion of reality.

Similarly, if the reader of *War and Peace* finds that in the Napoleonic sack of Moscow "he is there," then Tolstoy may be said to have successfully created an illusion of reality.

Illusion of reality is thus almost always "a transaction between author and audience" (as Louise Rosenblatt has put it). As such, it is a hypothesis subject to retesting in each new age or milieu. Hence, one of the tests of a classic is its ability to create an illusion of reality for its ever-new readers. (Compare SELECTIVE REPRESENTATION.)

REFERENCES: Eric Auerbach, *Mimesis;* Hazard Adams, "Imitation and Creation," *The Interests of Criticism;* Allen Tate, "Techniques of Fiction," in B. S. Oldsey and A. O. Lewis, Jr. (eds.), *Visions and Revisions;* Louise Rosenblatt, *Literature as Exploration.*

imagery   1. Traditionally, a verbal representation of objects appealing primarily to the sense of vision. 2. More broadly today, language that appeals to any or all of the senses. In Frost's poem "Out, Out . . . ," for example,

> The buzz saw *snarled and rattled* in the yard
> And made *dust* and dropped *stove-length sticks of wood,*
> *Sweet-scented stuff* when the *breeze* drew across it. [Emphasis added.]

Snarled and *rattled* are auditory images; *dust* is at once visual, tactile, and olfactory; *stove-length sticks of wood* appeal visually until Frost turns them to *sweet-scented stuff;* then *breeze* adds its tactile impression.

Thus, every concrete noun, along with many verbs, adjectives, or adverbs related to concrete nouns, is an image. When images and sensuous appeals are deliberately mixed, as in "a land, sour green," the resulting device is SYNESTHESIA.

In poetry, which usually contains more imagery than does prose, the image is a basic building block in a kind of image-metaphor-symbol complex. Thus, Frost's imagery "And miles to go before I sleep" is also a FADED METAPHOR for "much to accomplish," as is "before I sleep" for "before I lie down on the job"; and the whole context may be symbolic of the "journey toward death."

REFERENCES: "Image, Metaphor, Symbol, Myth," in René Wellek and Austin Warren, *Theory of Literature;* Philip Rahv, *Image and Idea;* Catherine Spurgeon, *Shakespeare's Imagery;* Rosemond Tuve, *Elizabethan and Metaphysical Imagery;* John Ciardi, "Single and Multiple Imagery," *How Does a Poem Mean?;* Martha Cox (ed.), *Image and Value;* Robert Gessner, *The Moving Image;* X. J. Kennedy, "Imagery," *An Introduction to Poetry.*

imagination   1. In general, the talent for making original interpretations of facts, original syntheses of raw data. By no means a talent exclusively displayed by writers, imagination is attributed to scientists as well, Helmholtz and Einstein, for example, having been praised for their "imaginative leaps." *Lack* of imagination in this sense, conversely, is what second-raters suffer from, according to *The Dialogues of Archibald MacLeish and Mark Van Doren* (pp. 116–18).

2. In literary criticism imagination can be a term of judgment, as in (1), but more often has another, special sense—"the ability to make an image in one's mind," according to the poet May Swenson. This is also the NEO-CLASSICAL sense expounded by Joseph Addison in "The Pleasures of the Imagination," a more acceptable notion today than that of the RENAISSANCE writers, who only distinguished imagination from reason. Francis Bacon, for example, observed that "imagination is to poetry what reason is to philosophy." A more discriminating distinction, which was to prove provocative for over a hundred years, was that of Samuel Taylor Coleridge (and of other ROMANTIC poets)— the distinction between imagination and fancy. While FANCY is merely an "associative power" or "mode of memory," imagination is a "shaping and modifying," a "re-creating power." The Victorian critic Sir Leslie Stephen, along with George Santayana, also assigns a higher niche in the poetic hierarchy to imagination than to fancy. Stephen, after slapping Coleridge's wrist for not living up to Victorian "morals," concedes to him the best touchstone for imagination in any literary work—"total dynamic effect [on the reader]." (This somewhat circular criterion foreshadows the "transaction" theory and the "experience of literature" approach now gaining attention.) Santayana's view is

that "imagination rediscovers deep ARCHETYPES and meanings beneath fanciful re-creations" as distinguished from fancy, which "only superficially reassembles images." An example of contemporary literature that comes very close to meeting all the above-mentioned criteria for imagination is J. R. R. Tolkien's *Lord of the Rings*.

3. Technically, "imaginative literature" is understood to consist of such genres as poetry, drama, and fiction, although this does not rule out the possibility that such expository genres as article, essay, and biography can be written with imagination.

REFERENCES: M. H. Abrams, "Coleridge's Mechanical Fancy and Organic Imagination," *The Mirror and the Lamp;* R. L. Brett, *Fancy and Imagination;* Rozanne Knudson, "Conversation with May Swenson," *Quartet* (Winter, 1969); Samuel Taylor Coleridge, "Imagination and Fancy," *Biographia Literaria;* Leslie Stephen, "Coleridge," *Hours in a Library;* George Santayana, "Imagination," in Arthur Eastman *et al.* (eds.), *The Norton Reader;* Alton C. Morris *et al.* (eds.), *Imaginative Literature;* James Heffernan, *Wordsworth's Theory of Poetry: The Transforming Imagination;* Benjamin DeMott, *Supergrow;* J. P. Houston, *The Daemonic Imagination.*

imagism   See IMAGISTS.

imagists, the   A group of poets, notably T. E. Hulme, HD (Hilda Doolittle), Richard Aldington, and Ezra Pound, who decided around 1912 to write a new kind of poetry, chiefly free verse characterized by concrete, jewel-like imagery, direct treatment of subject matter, little or no authorial comment on the thing being treated, and the use of no word that did not contribute to the effect or meaning of the poem. Many of these ideas were characteristic of Chinese and Japanese poetry, of the lyrics of the ancient Greek poet Sappho, and of the work of certain nineteenth-century French poets, particularly Gautier and Laforgue. The particular kind of poetry the imagists wrote was referred to as *imagism*. Here is a representative imagist poem by Ezra Pound, titled "In a Station of the Metro":

> The apparition of these faces in the crowd;
> Petals on a wet, black bough.

Among the best known of the poets whose work exhibits the characteristics of imagism are, besides Pound, T. S. Eliot and William Carlos Williams. The term was adopted by or applied to other poets as well, whose work was often far from the original conceptions of the movement. Among those poets the most notable is Amy Lowell, especially in her collection *A Dome of Many-Colored Glass*.

REFERENCE: Wallace Martin, "The Sources of the Imagist Aesthete," *PMLA* (March, 1970).

Immediate Theater   A mode of dramatic presentation featuring much improvisation and audience participation. Similar to the THEATER OF

THE ABSURD, with which it shares a dislike for plot, the Immediate Theater (also called Living Theater) has given a home to the most experimental kinds of plays, especially those with a minimum of "script." The improvisation is not restricted to minor stage business (as is allowed the insane inmates, for example, in Peter Weiss's *Marat/ Sade*) but extends (as in Jack Gelber's *Connection* and *The Apple*) to the audience. The rationale for audience participation is that play-acting is or properly should be role-playing; that the role of the audience has all too long remained passive, when it should have been active; that the roles of actors and spectators need to be switched as in psychodrama.

As early as 1958 directors Judith Malina and Julian Beck began to follow in their Living Theater the poet Antonin Artaud's advice to throw away the script. In the 1960s the Immediate Theater achieved serious development under the Polish playwright and director Jerzy Grotowski, the British director Joan Littlewood, and the American director Peter Brook. Off-Broadway productions included such plays as *Paradise Now; Dionysus in 69; Massachusetts Trust; Claudius; Philadelphia, Here I Come;* and Paul Foster's *Tom Paine*. According to the drama critic Walter Kerr, the Immediate Theater often alienates rather than integrates audience and actors. (Compare THEATER OF THE ABSURD.)

REFERENCES: Peter Brook, "The Immediate Theater," *Atlantic* (November, 1968); Walter Kerr, "The Theater of Say It! Show It! What Is It?" *New York Times Magazine* (September 1, 1968); Jan Kott, *Theatre Notebook: 1947–1967;* Robert Brustein, *The Third Theater;* Elenore Lester, "The Final Decline and Total Collapse of the American Avant-garde," *Esquire* (May, 1969); *The Drama Review.*

impressionism 1. An aesthetic movement which developed in France at the end of the 1800s and flourished in the early 1900s. The impressionists strove to paint, not objects, but light reflected from objects. This is why their paintings, however imprecise in outlines of things, are light and airy and full of ethereal colors. Since light is constantly changing, any object reflects different colors at different times. Thus Monet painted series of one object (a cathedral, a river bank, a haystack) at different times of the day, capturing changing qualities of light as these qualities appeared to him. In fact, such impressionists as Degas and Renoir strove to objectify their personal experiences of light and color. In his paintings of ballet dancers, for example, Degas avoided stock photographic details in favor of his impressions of certain effects the dancers made on him. Unlike the EXPRESSIONISTS of later decades, who carried impressionism deep into their private SYMBOLISM (sometimes into distortion), the impressionists demonstrated a respect for communication with spectators. 2. In literature, the rendering of details as they appear immediately to the senses. Imagination developed among the IMAGISTS and among such novelists as Virginia Woolf and John Dos Passos. In the trilogy *U.S.A.*, for example, Dos Passos used the impressionistic device of "the camera eye," which paradoxically enough was not photographic but rather a kind of quick brush stroke—the novelist's subjective impression of one element of experience, one point in space and time, followed by his impression of another point—very much as an impressionist painter offers dots and strokes to be blended by the eye of the beholder.

REFERENCES: John Rewald, *The History of Impressionism;* Bernard Berenson, "Introduction," *Aesthetics and History;* Monroe Beardsley, "The Object and Its Presentations," *Aesthetics.*

incunabula   Books printed before 1500 (in the "cradlehood" of printing). Classed as incunabula are the Gutenberg Bibles and about thirty thousand editions of books from the early presses of such other printers as William Caxton, Nicolas Jenson, and Aldus Manutius. Notable collections can be seen in the British Museum, The Hague, the Oxford (Bodleian) Library, the Library of Congress, and the Huntington Library (San Marino, California).

REFERENCE: Margaret B. Stillwell, *Incunabula and Americana 1400–1800.*

indefinite reference of pronoun   The careless use of a pronoun whose antecedent might be any of several nouns in a given context. (See FAULTY REFERENCE and AMBIGUITY.)

indention   The leaving of space between the margin and the first letter of a line of print or handwriting. Usually indented are (1) first lines of paragraphs (in typing, usually five spaces), (2) certain lines of poetry (ordinarily the rhyming lines being equally indented), (3) all lines of a blocked quotation inserted in a discourse, and (4) the subordinate items in an outline (the items of equal rank being equally indented).

index   An alphabetical list of the topics (whether discussed or merely mentioned) in a written work; each item is shown with a list of the pages on which the topic is referred to. A *bibliographical index* is a guide (arranged by topic and sometimes by author) to published works; for example, the *Readers' Guide to Periodical Literature* and the card catalog of any library. (See DOCUMENTATION.)

Index librorum prohibitorum   A list of books that a Roman Catholic Church committee of cardinals, the Congregation of the Index, has put off-limits to faithful Church members. A secondary list, *Index Expurgatorius,* allows certain titles if expurgated or BOWDLERIZED. Each of these lists is often referred to as "The Index." (See OBSCENITY.)

REFERENCES: Anne Haight, *Banned Books;* J. A. Farrer, *Books Condemned to Be Burned;* Noel Perrin, *Dr. Bowdler's Legacy.*

induction   1. Reasoning that draws inferences from given data or specimens. **2.** In literature, the characteristic method of most fiction, in which the specific incidents that unfold lead the reader to a (general) conclusion, PHILOSOPHIC STATEMENT, or THEME. **3.** A RENAISSANCE equivalent of the modern word *introduction,* as, for example, the Induction in Shakespeare's *Taming of the Shrew* and the philosophic Induction (Preface) to Sackville's *Mirror for Magistrates.* REFERENCE: Thelma Greenfield, *The Elizabethan Induction.*

inductive leap   In INDUCTIVE REASONING, the necessary act of arriving at a conclusion without having at hand all the pertinent facts or evidence.

inductive reasoning   Reasoning from the specific to the general; the examination of particular facts and the attempt to account for them in a generalization. If a veterinary doctor observes a white Persian cat and finds it is deaf, then observes another white Persian cat and finds it also deaf, then observes another white Persian cat, then another and another—he may infer that *all* white Persian cats are deaf. He has reasoned from a series of particular facts to a general INFERENCE, or conclusion. But his conclusion is not absolute truth; it is only *probable* —and more or less probable, depending upon how accurate his observations and how adequate their number.

1. *Perfect induction.* If we observe all possible cases, the conclusion is a perfect induction. This is possible only when the number of cases is limited and all have been observed. These are some examples of perfect induction:

All puppies in this litter have brown eyes.
All members of the math class are present today.
All of Mrs. Oliver's children are girls.
You have always been late to our appointments.

These perfect inductions are of limited usefulness. They do not go beyond the observed facts; thus, they are often tautological, seldom significant.

2. *Statistical induction.* The number of possible cases is often limited, but too large to make convenient an examination of every one. On the morning after a frost, we may discover that all the oranges on a certain tree have been frozen and spoiled. Because we know that the cause (the frost) obtained with all the other trees in the grove, we may justifiably conclude that *all* the oranges in the grove also suffered the effect—all have been frozen and spoiled. This extension of the perfect inductive method is reliable enough to justify our drawing the conclusion as if *all* cases had been observed.

Statistical induction in general produces valid inferences only if care is taken to ensure that the statistics are of sufficient number and are truly representative. The fallacies that often appear are those of (*a*) insufficient data or statistics (sometimes called HASTY GENERALIZATION) and (*b*) biased statistics (sometimes called CARD-STACKING). For example, we may see one elderly driver ignore a red light; we then conclude that all elderly drivers are careless breakers of traffic regulations (a *hasty generalization*); and at the same time we ignore the fact that we have seen dozens of elderly drivers properly obeying red lights (*card-stacking;* ignoring pertinent evidence).

The statistical syllogism arrives at a conclusion with a probability of less than 100 per cent. If investigation has shown us that 80 per cent of the voters in a certain town are Republicans, and we learn that Mr. G. is a voter in that town, we may conclude that Mr. G. is a Republican—and our conclusion has a *probability* of 80 per cent. This sort of statistical reasoning underlies much of what is today used as basis for life insurance rates, gamblers' odds, and opinion-poll predictions of election results.

A special form of the statistical syllogism is *argument from authority,* in which we assert that A is true because a certain person says A is true. Obviously, the reliability of such a conclusion depends upon to what degree that person is a reliable authority concerning A. If we know that most of his statements on that general topic are reliable, then we know that his statement about A is probably true. We reason thus:

Most of this man's statements are true.
"A is true" is one of this man's statements.
Therefore, A is true—probably.

The validity of the conclusion depends upon our avoiding certain fallacies: *Unreliable authority* (we must be certain that the man actually is an authority on the topic and that his statements in the past actually have been true)*; misquotation* (we must be sure that the man is accurately quoted and his remarks properly interpreted).

A reverse of the argument from authority is ARGUMENT AGAINST THE MAN, in which we assert that A is false because a certain person says A is true. This time the validity of our conclusion depends upon the man's being a "reliable *anti-authority"* —which is not the same thing as being an "unreliable authority." We must know that the man is almost always wrong in his statements on the general topic; if we know he is usually wrong, we may reason:

Most of this man's statements are false.
"A is true" is one of this man's statements.
Therefore, A is false—probably.

Again fallacies must be avoided: the man must actually be a habitual non-authority on the topic, and he must not have been misquoted or misinterpreted. Similarly to be avoided is the GENETIC FALLACY.

3. *Causal induction.* Much scientific and everyday knowledge is concerned with causes and their effects. We observe footprints on wet sand and infer that someone has recently walked there; that is, we observe the effect and infer the cause—*we reason from effect to cause.* We can do this validly, of course, only about things whose causes are generally known. When causes are not known, we must follow a careful procedure of observing effects, putting forth an assertion of possible cause (a *hypothesis*), then testing experimentally by producing that cause—carefully eliminating other possible causes—to see whether that cause does indeed produce those effects. Such inductive reasoning is a part of the "*scientific method.*"

In ARGUMENTATION a speaker or writer may use causal induction as the basis of his order of presentation. He may assert the existence of one thing (a cause) and then attempt to demonstrate that certain other things (effects) must follow. His method is called *a priori*—reasoning from cause to effect. On the other hand, he may assert the existence of certain things (effects) and then demonstrate that a certain other thing must be their cause. His method is then called *a posteriori*—reasoning from effect to cause.

Both kinds of argument are subject to difficulties. In reasoning *a priori*, we must be certain that the known cause is sufficient to produce the supposed effect and that nothing has intervened (or can intervene) to prevent its producing that effect. In reasoning *a posteriori*, we must be certain that the known effect is always the result of the supposed cause and that no other cause could produce that effect. These certainties are, of course, difficult to achieve.

One possible error in reasoning either *a priori* or *a posteriori* is that of assuming that because one thing seems always to occur before another, the first must be a cause of the second. This is the *post hoc* fallacy—more fully, *post hoc, ergo propter hoc,* or "after this, therefore because of this." The rooster always crows before the dawn, but it is certainly fallacious to assume that the rooster's crowing causes the sun to rise.

4. *Reasoning by analogy.* Much scientific induction as well as everyday argument proceeds by drawing comparisons between things of different types. That is, it asserts that two things are alike in certain ways and therefore are probably alike in certain other ways too. This *reasoning by analogy* follows this pattern:

Both A and B have the properties *p, q,* and *r.*

A has the property *s*.
Therefore, B also has the property *s* . . . probably.

It is this sort of reasoning that underlies the scientist's use of rats or other animals to test the effects of certain drugs. He reasons that rats are like men in certain significant ways; if the drug cures disease X in rats, it will *probably* also cure disease X in men.

Obviously, reasoning by analogy has its pitfalls. The reliability of an analogy depends heavily upon the relevancy of the ways in which the things compared are similar, and upon the number of similarities as compared to the number of dissimilarities. If the things compared in the analogy are more unlike than they are alike, or if they are alike in ways that have no bearing upon the matter at hand, the argument is weak because it relies on FALSE ANALOGY.

REFERENCES: Jeremy Pitt and Russell E. Leavenworth, *Logic for Argument;* John Sherwood, *Handbook of Logic and Semantics;* Randall Decker, *Patterns of Exposition.*

inference 1. Loosely, a synonym for "implication." 2. More strictly, what the reader (or listener) draws from a written or spoken communication where he reads (listens) beneath the lines, beneath what is said in so many words. Thus, in a statement like "Fifty thousand buyers can't be wrong," the speaker *implies* "You wouldn't be wrong to follow suit." And some such implication decoded by the reader (listener) is an inference. Notice the need not only for making inferences but also for examining their validity. 3. In logic, the drawing of conclusions from real or tentative evidence.

REFERENCES: Edgar Dale, *How to Read a Newspaper;* Mortimer Adler, *How to Read a Book.*

influence In literary history and criticism, the effect, real or apparent, of one writer on another, especially in the latter writer's youth; also, the effect of a school of writers on an individual writer. The influence of one writer or school on another, as Milton on Wordsworth or the Symbolists on T. S. Eliot, may be undeniable, but when many sources can be said to have influenced the creation of a new work, most of the borrowing is unconscious. The tracing of influence was a vogue in the early 1900s and resulted in some farfetched claims. But not all was nonsense. One of the most scholarly works was John Livingston Lowes's *Road to Xanadu* (1927), which traces almost all the literary influences on the poet Coleridge.

Another kind of influence, sometimes referred to as *dependence,* can be claimed when a particular literary work seems to have been influenced by a work written by another author, especially when parallel passages in the two works indicate a dependence of one writer on the other. But first it must be proved that one writer has read the other writer's work. Then a close similarity of thought or imagery must be demonstrated; then a clear structural similarity. (Compare PLAGIARISM.)

REFERENCES: Gilbert Highet, *The Classical Tradition* (page 202); "Epilogue," *The Concise Cambridge History of English Literature.*

in medias res Literally, "into the midst of things." A narrative technique, used in the Homeric epics and in Vergil's *Aeneid,* by which an author, bypassing a chronological beginning, introduces his readers to a sensational moment or scene. To catch the reader's attention, many a novelist uses this technique in the opening chapter, then reserves for the second chapter or for subsequent FLASHBACKS such narration and exposition as the reader needs for the complete picture. James Baldwin's *Another Country* is an example. Some writers (e.g., Joyce and D. H. Lawrence) prefer to have revelations unfold gradually and incrementally.

inns-of-court plays Plays produced (and sometimes written) by members of one or another of the four legal societies of London — Lincoln's Inn, Gray's Inn, the Middle Temple, and the Inner Temple — which could admit candidates to the practice of law ("the bar"). From the Middle Ages to the nineteenth century these inns of court served as universities or cultural centers. (Today they are mainly clubs.) In the sixteenth and seventeenth centuries, when they were quasi-universities, they fostered all sorts of literary and theatrical ("Thespian") interests. It was the "fellows" of the Inner Temple, for example, who produced *Gorboduc* (ca. 1561), the first English tragedy, before Queen Elizabeth at Whitehall. And in 1594 the fellows of Gray's Inn produced Shakespeare's *Comedy of Errors.* Inns-of-court productions are to be distinguished from productions in inn courtyards; the latter were performed by professional companies for the entertainment of travelers and other guests at the inn.

REFERENCES: E. K. Chambers, *The Elizabethan Theater;* Lily Bess Campbell, *Scenes and Machines on the English Stage.*

innuendo A subtle implication of something derogatory. An innuendo may arise from the tone of an utterance, though nothing derogatory appears in the literal meaning; or an innuendo may arise from a subtle IRONY, an utterance whose words can be taken to mean their opposite. Much ironic innuendo occurs in Jonathan Swift's *Modest Proposal* and in Mark Twain's *Mysterious Stranger.*

intention The general intentions or purposes of writers are (1) to inform or instruct, (2) to explain or interpret, (3) to convince, (4) to persuade or move to action, (5) to entertain or delight, (6) to inspire or elevate, (7) to express or relieve oneself.

Although communicating for the sake of communicating is a worthy human activity needing no apology, communicating in an expository paper (as in a formal speech) more often than not achieves success when the sender decides initially what his chief purpose is. Does he intend to inform, or delight, or . . . ? Of course, he may have more than one purpose. If so, he improves his chances of contact with his audience if he decides which purpose is primary, which secondary. (See AUDIENCE.)

Whereas articles, academic papers, and other forms of EXPOSITION characteristically state the specific intentions ("It is the intention of this paper to show that . . ."), a work of literature — POETRY, DRAMA, FICTION, imaginative PROSE — like any other work of art more often *implies* its intention. Occasionally an author, spurred by critics who he feels may have misconstrued his intentions, may state them in a formal reply. George Bernard Shaw did this in his defense of *Major Barbara,* where the *general* purposes are to entertain (shock, perhaps) and convince. But in the preface to a late edition Shaw says that his *specific* intention is to show through Undershaft, the play's hero, that one of the worst of crimes is poverty. (Compare Samuel Butler's *Erewhon.*)

A specific statement of intention may also be ironic. Consider Swift's *Modest Proposal:* "For preventing the Children of Poor People from being a Burden to their Parents and Country, and for making them beneficial to the Public." (In which one way to achieve this end is to butcher the children for food and hides.)

Just as any writer heightens the effectiveness of his work by deciding on how to limit his subject (what the emphasis shall be, who the audience is, what tone or attitude will be taken toward the material, and the like), so he may also heighten its effectiveness by writing down — if only for his own clarification — the specific purposes or intentions. Whatever the writer's intention, however, the acid test for successful communication is the actual *effect* of the written piece on the reader, as Morris Finder observes.

REFERENCES: Monroe Beardsley, "The Artist's Intention," *Aesthetics;* James McCrimmon, *Writing with a Purpose;* Thomas S. Kane and Leonard J. Peters, *Writing Prose: Techniques and Purposes;* William Riley Parker, "The Question of Audience," *MLA Style Sheet;* Morris Finder, "Comprehension: An Analysis of the Task," *Journal of Reading* (December, 1969).

intentional fallacy   In literary criticism, the theory that it is a mistake to assume that (*a*) the author has only one intention; (*b*) the author always creates what he intends to create or says what he intends; (*c*) a literary work succeeds or fails according to whether it fulfills or does not fulfill the author's intention; (*d*) the author of a work is the best authority on its meaning and value.

Thus readers are likely to be betrayed if they take at face value the intentions stated in the prefatory "Notice" to *The Adventures of Huckleberry Finn:* "Persons attempting to find a motive in this narrative will be prosecuted; persons attempting to find a moral in it will be banished; persons attempting to find a plot in it will be shot." That celebrated critics have disagreed over Twain's real intentions in this masterpiece is on record in such a contrariety of speculations as those by William Dean Howells (*My Mark Twain,* 1910); Bernard de Voto (*Mark Twain's America,* 1932); T. S. Eliot (Introduction to the Cresset edition of *Huckleberry Finn,* 1950); Van Wyck Brooks (*The Ordeal of Mark Twain,* 1920); Lionel Trilling (essay in *The Liberal Imagination,* 1950); and Leslie Fiedler (*Love and Death in the American Novel*).

An intention generally accepted in one era or place or milieu may be rejected in another. One of the best-known cases in point is John Milton's intention in *Paradise Lost.* Even though Milton was regarded as something of a heretic in his own milieu (as Cleanth Brooks has observed), it was generally understood by Puritan and non-Puritan alike in the seventeenth century and for two centuries thereafter that Milton's intention in *Paradise Lost* was "to justify the ways of God to man." Over the years the scholars and critics who re-examined this EPIC to see whether it really did, for them, reflect this intention delivered negative verdicts. Along with such critics the contemporary reader does not generally accept the notions that Adam and Eve's sexual knowledge is shameful, that children and hard work are a curse, or that a vindictive God deliberately creates floods, tornadoes, and earthquakes. Cleanth Brooks believes Milton intended rather to show that self-knowledge is part of man's destiny and his "predicament in which he experiences alienation and yet must strive for wholeness." Brooks adds that the modern reader may do better to think of Milton as a great poet, who, "whatever his beliefs as a man, is committed to a dramatic presentation of them . . . who does his reader the honor of letting him infer the meaning from the drama rather than preaching down to him" (from the Introduction to the Modern Library edition of Milton).

"A poet's primary concern," says Northrop Frye, "is to produce a work of art, and hence his intention can only be expressed by some kind of tautology" (*Anatomy of Criticism,* p. 86). See also "The Intentional Fallacy," in W. K. Wimsatt, *The Verbal Ikon.*

interior monologue   See STREAM OF CONSCIOUSNESS and ASIDE.

interlocking rhyme   A design in which an unrhymed line in one stanza signals the rhyme in the following stanza. (See TERZA RIMA.)

interlude   1. A comic skit, a form popular in late medieval and early Renaissance England. It was addressed, in simple plot and coarse language, to the uneducated. Representative is John Heywood's

Four P's (ca. 1520), in which a pedlar, a palmer, a pardoner, and a 'pothecary vie with one another in a contest of tasteless slander against women. **2.** The court interlude, designed for more genteel and sophisticated audiences, was a short comic play, topical, mundane, and aristocratic. It was usually presented at court, in schools, or at the homes of nobles between the banquet and the nightcap of spiced wine. The court interlude approached, at least in language and tone, the MASQUE. The earliest of these plays, first acted at Lambeth Palace in 1497, is *Fulgens and Lucrece,* by the Tudor dramatist Henry Medwall. The Tudor interludes characteristically embodied elements of ALLEGORY, SLAPSTICK humor and low comedy, songs, witty dialogue, and even debates. Two well-known and still stageable interludes are Nicholas Udall's *Ralph Roister Doister* (ca. 1553), written for students at Eton, and John Still's *Gammer Gurton's Needle* (ca. 1566), written for students at Christ's College, Cambridge.

REFERENCES: John Quincy Adams (ed.), *Chief Pre-Shakespearian Dramas;* Tucker Brooke, *The Tudor Drama;* Frederick S. Boas, *An Introduction to Tudor Drama;* A. W. Reed, *Early Tudor Drama;* Charles M. Gayley, "Historical View of the Beginnings of English Comedy," *Representative English Comedies.*

internal rhyme   See RHYME.

introducing quotations   See QUOTATIONS, INTRODUCING.

introduction   A statement, usually a chapter, that precedes and leads into a long written work. An introduction serves to provide the essentials of the subject under discussion and often delimits the scope of the work. Shorter works tend to dispense with formal introductions.

inventio   Literally, "invention" or "discovery." In classical rhetoric, one of the three major powers requisite to an accomplished speaker or writer (the other two being *dispositio,* or effective arrangement of one's material, and *elocutio,* or effective presentation). Today *inventio* is still invoked much as it was in ancient Greece — as the power of finding one's subject, of finding something to say that is worth saying because one knows it well as a part of one's own experience.

REFERENCES: Aristotle, *Rhetoric;* Plato, *Phaedrus;* Scott Elledge, "Inventio," The CEEB Commission on English: Film Series on Writing.

inversion   The transposing of a sentence part from its normal order, especially in verse, to achieve emphasis (and sometimes just to accommodate a rhyme). Thus, instead of saying, "The gunner went down," the song-writer said, "Down went the gunner!" And instead of "The wrinkled sea crawls beneath him," Tennyson wrote, in "The Eagle," "The wrinkled sea beneath him crawls." He inverted the natural word order, no doubt, to get a rhyming word for "walls" and "falls."

investigative paper   See RESEARCH PAPER.

invocation   In EPIC poetry, the convention of calling upon a muse for inspiration and guidance. In the *Aeneid,* Vergil, after announcing his theme — "Of arms and the man . . . I sing" — calls upon Calliope, the muse of epic poetry, to tell him "Why . . . did the Queen of Heaven urge on such a good man . . . to circle through all these afflictions?"

In *John Brown's Body* Stephen Vincent Benét begins, "American muse, whose strong and diverse heart / So many men have tried to understand / But only made it smaller with their art / . . . Where the great huntsmen failed, I set my sorry / And mortal snare for your immortal quarry."

Invocations, along with epics and long serious poems, seem to be out of harmony with the contemporary mood.

ionic   See METER.

ipse dixit   Literally, "He himself said [so]." An assertion made without any evidence — in fact, in lieu of evidence — of its truth or validity.

irony   1. *Verbal irony.* Saying the opposite of what is meant — e.g., "Tiny" as a nickname for a gigantic person; also Mark Antony's "And Brutus is an honorable man," when he meant the opposite. Irony as a manner of expression has not usually been admired. Since the early Greeks, the term has connoted slyness, foxlike cleverness, sometimes hypocrisy. In the comic theater of the Greeks the *eiron* was the quiet deadpan whose ironic remarks seemed to mean much more than they said — comments that tended to deflate the *alazon,* or braggart, and show him up as an impostor. This kind of irony is close to UNDERSTATE-MENT. Verbal irony lends itself to humor. Washington Irving describes the Old Dutch burgomaster Wouter Van Twiller as "a model of lordly grandeur" — and follows with a dimensional picture to prove it: "He was exactly five feet, six inches in height and exactly six feet, five in circumference." Verbal irony is often, but not always, tinged with SARCASM or a biting tone. But irony may also be so gentle as to be nearly overlooked.

2. *Socratic irony.* Socrates always understated his own knowledge and wisdom; indeed, he often pretended complete ignorance. He taught his young students, not by telling them *his* thoughts, but by asking and goading them for *theirs,* so that they seemed to be teaching themselves. Socrates was, in a sense, a real-life *eiron,* teaching by leading real-life *alazons* to reveal their own pretentiousness and thus to discover their own logic and illogic. Socratic irony thus received its name, with Aristotle defining it in a complimentary sense as Socrates' dialectic technique, from the pretending of ignorance while eliciting enlightenment from others.

3. *Dramatic irony.* A device by which the audience is made aware

of things that certain characters do not know. The characters' lines thus seem to mean far more to the audience than they do to those who speak them. When Oedipus vows revenge on the murderer of his father, the audience is horrified, because it knows, as Oedipus does not, that he himself is the murderer. Outside the theater, dramatic irony often occurs in everyday situations. We see dramatic irony in the words of friends whenever their remarks bear upon things about which we know facts, or secrets, that the friends do not know. Dramatic irony may be classified into three subcategories: *irony of speech* (words contrast with the facts); *irony of character* (outward appearance and behavior contrast with real nature); and *irony of events* (expectations contrast with fulfillment), which is but the stage version of real-life *irony of fate*.

4. *Irony of fate.* Close kin to dramatic irony, it is a matter of event rather than of language. Like all irony, it depends upon the unexpected, a twist of events that produces what is contrary to the foreseen, or shockingly opposed to beliefs or desires. The astronaut survives the hazards of space only to break an elbow when he slips in the bathtub at home. The young soldier survives many months of front-line battle without a scratch; on leave at home he is permanently disabled in an auto accident. The famed swimming champion drowns in his own backyard pool. Because they know the fascination of the unexpected, news reporters seek these ironies—and the newspapers almost daily record examples of the irony of fate.

5. Broadly, any ANTITHESIS, especially as depicted on the large canvases of such writers as Thomas Hardy, Henry James, and Katherine Anne Porter.

REFERENCES: Robert Penn Warren, "Katherine Anne Porter, Irony with a Center," *Kenyon Review* (Winter, 1942); Richard Poirier, *The Comic Sense of Henry James;* Anthony E. Dyson, *The Crazy Fabric: Essays in Irony;* D. C. Muecke, *The Compass of Irony;* R. B. Sharp, *Irony in the Drama;* Robert Scholes, "The Anti-Metaphorical Language of Irony," *Elements of Poetry.*

Italianate gentleman   See COURTESY BOOKS.

italics   Inspired by the cursive, slanted lettering of tenth-century Italian monks, Aldus Manutius (1450–1515), a Venetian scholar and printer, created the printing type now called italic. Today italics are used chiefly to mark some brief matter that deserves special distinction—certain titles; foreign phrases, words, or abbreviations; emphasized words or phrases; and words used as words. In the preparation of a manuscript for printing, the writer indicates italics by underlining, and the compositor sets the underlined matter in italics. (See UNDERLINING.)

J

Jacobean Pertaining to the era of "Jacobus" (the Latin name for James), in this instance James I of England (reigned 1603–25), who sponsored the first "authorized" English translation of the Bible; hence, King James Version. The Jacobean period marked the climax of the English RENAISSANCE, when there appeared the greatest plays of Shakespeare, Jonson, Chapman, Webster, Middleton, and Beaumont and Fletcher. It was during the Jacobean period that John Donne published much of his poetry, Francis Bacon his major works, and Robert Burton *The Anatomy of Melancholy*. METAPHYSICAL POETRY appeared at this time, and a kind of prose fiction in the character sketches by Joseph Hall and Sir Thomas Overbury.

REFERENCES: Basil Willey, *The Seventeenth Century Background;* Douglas Bush, *English Literature of the Early Seventeenth Century;* Marjorie Nicholson, *The Breaking of the Circle . . . Seventeenth Century Poetry;* John R. Brown and Bernard Harris (eds.), *Jacobean Theatre;* Joan Webber, *The Eloquent "I": Style and Self in Seventeenth Century Prose;* F. P. Wilson, *Elizabethan and Jacobean;* G. E. Bentley, *The Jacobean and Caroline Stage.*

jargon The specialized vocabulary or language of a restricted group, as of a trade, a profession, a sect, or a class. When used among members of the group, jargon is appropriate; but when used in general discourse, it defeats unity of tone and purpose of communication. Jargon is one characteristic of GOBBLEDYGOOK.

REFERENCES: Katherine Anne Porter, "Against Jargon," *Paris Review Interviews,* Second Series; Arthur Quiller-Couch, "Interlude: On Jargon," *The Art of Writing.*

jest books Late medieval and early Renaissance joke books containing ribald and often coarse slurs on women, friars, foreigners, doctors, students, courtiers, and tradesmen. The earliest of English jest books was *A Hundred Merry Tales* (1526). Certain jest books were devoted to shady stories about one person—John Skelton, for instance, or Ben Jonson.

jeu d'esprit Literally, "play of the spirit or wit." A witty remark, a quip, or a *bon mot.*

journal 1. A DIARY; a daily record of a writer's experiences, especially his reactions to them in impromptu prose and verse; his reactions to persons, places, events, books, and other works of art; and his designs-in-embryo of literary pieces for future development. Among the most celebrated journals are those of Da Vinci, Goethe, Samuel Pepys, James Boswell, Eugène Delacroix, John Woolman, Feodor Dostoevski, Henri Amiel, Herman Melville, Charles Darwin, Joseph

Conrad, Henry James, the Goncourts, André Gide, Arnold Bennett, Sherwood Anderson, Katherine Mansfield, Virginia Woolf, Juan Jiminez, F. Scott Fitzgerald, W. Somerset Maugham, and Anne Frank. **2.** A periodical publication. (See REVIEW.)

REFERENCES: Robert Freier *et al.,* "Writers' Notebooks," *Adventures in Modern Literature,* Fifth Edition; Arthur Eastman (ed.), "Journals," *The Norton Reader;* William Sparke and Clarke McKowen, *Montage.*

journey   **1.** A basic story-line for many works of mythology and folklore, as represented in the journeys of Jason, Hercules, Ulysses, and Aeneas. **2.** The basic structure (*framework*) for such masterpieces as *The Divine Comedy, The Canterbury Tales, The Pilgrim's Progress,* and *Gulliver's Travels.* **3.** An allegory of the human condition; that is, man's fate to journey through life, through "hell and high water," as dramatized by Ulysses, Aeneas, and Christian. Some critics interpret this journey symbolically in the context of Carl Jung's "racial unconscious," the theory that all of us vaguely remember our evolutionary journeys and those of the archetypal characters with whom we identify. (See ARCHETYPE and MYTHOPOETICS.)

REFERENCES: Northrop Frye, "The Archetypes of Literature," *Fables of Identity;* Carl Jung, *Archetypes of the Collective Unconscious;* Norman O. Brown, *Life Against Death.*

K

katharsis   See CATHARSIS.

kenning   An Anglo-Saxon metaphorical compound used instead of a single noun; e.g., "whale-road" instead of "ocean." (Compare EPITHET.)

REFERENCE: Margaret Williams (ed.), *Word-Hoard, a Treasury of Old English Literature;* Roger Fowler (ed.), *Old English Prose and Verse.*

kinetic imagery   Any image or images appealing to the sense of motion — riding, flying, climbing, falling, etc.

kitsch   1. Bric-a-brac, whether junk or junque. 2. Trivial would-be literature; in this sense, a term used by Gilbert Highet in *A Clerk of Oxenford.*

REFERENCES: "Kitsch," in Irving and Harriet Deer (eds.), *The Popular Arts;* Clement Greenberg, "Avant Garde and Kitsch," *Art and Culture.*

L

laconic style   Habitual brevity and terseness. Laconism was typical of the speech of ancient Laconia, whose capital was Sparta. It was the Spartans who, when warned that if their city were captured it would be burned to the ground, responded: "If." Laconism is typical of the EPIGRAM and the APHORISM.

lay (lai)   **1.** Short narrative verse made popular by Marie de France (twelfth century) and the Breton minstrels. The content was mostly Arthurian legend. **2.** More broadly, any short narrative song or BALLAD. See, for example, Macaulay's *Lays of Ancient Rome*.

REFERENCE: Mortimer Donovan, *The Breton Lay.*

lampoon   **1.** A satirical attack, in prose or in verse, against a person or system. (Contrast PARODY.) **2.** The title of a humor magazine published at Harvard College.

laureate   See POET LAUREATE.

leaders   A series of dots (periods) used in printing to lead the eye from one place to another. Leaders were once much used in tables, but the trend is to avoid using them except in dense, small-type statistical tabulations.

legend   **1.** Loosely, a caption or an explanatory comment under a map or picture. The legend, in this sense, was formerly distinguished from the caption, which appeared *above* the picture; now caption is used in both senses. In cartography, legend retains the original sense. **2.** A narrative transmitted orally and rooted more in the historical than in the supernatural, although it may be distorted history. Legends reflect a national spirit. Washington Irving's "Legend of Sleepy Hollow" reflects Dutch lore of the kind transplanted to the New Netherlands. (Compare MYTH and FOLKLORE.)

levels of meaning   As the Italian poet Dante, author of *The Divine Comedy,* pointed out in 1304 in *The Banquet* (I, 1), a masterwork of literature contains simultaneously four or more *levels of significance* (layers of meaning): (1) the literal, (2) the allegorical, (3) the moral, and (4) the anagogical. By *literal level* he meant, as is ordinarily meant today, the manifest story-line. By *allegorical level* he meant the one-for-one representations observable in medieval and early renaissance MORALITY PLAYS, in which such virtues and vices as Kindness and Greed are personified. By *moral level* he meant an author's vision of life or at least the moral values stated or implied in a given work. By *anagogical level* he meant the deepest, most "mystical" (Dante's term) possibilities of interpretation, especially those inherent in Christian symbols.

For centuries Dante's multiple-levels theory was subscribed to by major writers and critics as basic to intelligent reading. But most readers, then as now, read superficially; and even if they sometimes dug beneath to ALLEGORY and symbolic mystery, they erroneously assumed that a work could have only one interpretation. (See INTENTIONAL FALLACY.)

In modern times one of the first artists and critics to call attention to levels of meaning was the novelist Henry James. In *The Art of Fiction* he decries the notion that there can be only one "correct" interpretation and urges the reader not to stop after apprehending the mere DONNÉE or "given." As in any other problem, puzzle, or game, what is given—important as it is—is only a base. The fun begins where the donnée ends.

The NEW CRITICS, among them Allen Tate, posit three major levels of meaning: (1) the literal, (2) the allegorical, and (3) the symbolic. Along with most other contemporary readers, they concede that a writer leads us inductively to a main theme, which in turn reflects his vision of life in a particular work, but they categorize this contribution to CONTEXT as one of the writer's "thematic values," rather than as a "level" or "layer of meaning." The New Critics also assign a broader role to allegorical meaning. While they concede Dánte's definition of allegory to be the first and most easily recognizable kind of SYMBOLISM, they regard ALLEGORY as metaphor capable of extending beyond the STEREOTYPE of The Good Guy and The Bad Guy, as it extends, for example, in Archibald MacLeish's play *J.B.*

It is perhaps the symbolic levels that contemporary critics—thanks to such depth psychologies as those of Freud and Jung—have explored most. Thus any object or experience suggesting the sex drive is called a Freudian symbol. And any object, experience, or character echoing the history, MYTHOLOGY, or rituals of mankind is called a Jungian ARCHETYPE. The emphasis, incidentally, is on the *individual* in Freudian symbolism; on the group, race, or culture, in Jungian symbolism. (See Carl Jung, *Archetypes and the Collective Unconscious,* and Northrop Frye, *Fables of Identity.*)

How these three major levels of meaning (the literal, the allegorical, and the symbolic) interact in a given work can be illustrated by a brief analysis of Edward Albee's play *Who's Afraid of Virginia Woolf?* (1962). On the surface the two major characters, Martha and George, are on such destructive terms with each other and with themselves as to make Virginia Woolf's suicide look tame by comparison. In most of their talk during the three acts (respectively entitled "Fun and Games,"

"Walpurgisnacht," and "The Exorcism") these characters mercilessly flay each other and their vapid guests Honey and Nick, who serve as FOILS. On this literal level we thus see a murderous power-play between George and Martha.

Extended to the allegorical level, this feud also represents the vying for power by Man and Woman, although the man in this particular case is impotent. But the play contains more complex allegory and symbolism than this. As a son, George has killed his parents; later, as a parent, he has killed an imaginary son. This counterpoint, along with references to Jesus both at the beginning and at the end, gives meaning to the play as a Christian allegory, in which the Son represents the son killed during "The Exorcism."

When these clues go deeper than a one-to-one representation of the Son as the son (the allegorical formula), into the more mystical (if not mysterious) possibilities of meaning, the reader is confronted with complex symbolism. Aside from the Freudian symbolism in George's patricide and in the impotence of George and Honey, all the characters echo the torments of man burdened with guilt, seeking redemption (integrity) either in Christian terms, through the Son of God or, in terms of secular EXISTENTIALISM, through rejection of supernatural responsibility for man's behavior toward man.

Because symbolism is so complex a ramification of Freudian and Jungian possibilities of interpretation, most contemporary EXPLICATION is concerned almost entirely with this third level. Readers may thus assume that the first and second levels (the literal and the allegorical) are readily understood. This assumption seems to undergird hundreds of interpretive essays on such works as *Moby-Dick, The Catcher in the Rye,* and *Lord of the Flies.* Although several different interpretations may well be tenable, each within certain limits, a contrariety of critical approaches can be applied *ad absurdum* by the overzealous, as Frederick Crews demonstrates in *The Pooh Perplex.*

In addition to these three major levels of meaning, the last of which, the symbolic, subsumes multiple sublayers, other elements of a literary work control and contribute to its meaning: the structure of the GENRE itself, its MODE, TONE, and FOCUS OF NARRATION.

Most contemporary critics assume that the meaning of a literary work emanates from what is *in* that work much more than from what is outside the work. They therefore de-emphasize the author's biographical background as an element in the interpretation of a work's meaning. (See BIOGRAPHICAL FALLACY and AESTHETIC DISTANCE.)

One group of contemporary critics and teachers, among them Louise Rosenblatt, author of *Literature as Exploration,* maintains that a so-called literary work is only a "text," that it does not become "a poem" ("a play," "a novel") until it is "experienced by the reader." (See "The Poem as Event," *College English*, November, 1964). Most critics discourage such subjectivity. While allowing leeway for a contrariety of interpretations, most critics limit the validity ("viability") of any interpretation to a test against "what is there" in the work or text. Despite their diametric emphases, however, these critics cannot escape sharing a certain amount of both subjective and objective process in wresting meaning from literature.

REFERENCES: Northrop Frye, *The Anatomy of Criticism;* William Empson, *Seven Types of Ambiguity;* Stanley R. Hopper and David L. Miller (eds.), *Interpretation: The Poetry of Meaning;* Arnold Lazarus, "Playing the Piano with More than One Finger," *The CEA Critic* (February, 1965); Caroline Gordon, *How to Read a Novel;* Cleanth Brooks and Robert Penn Warren, *Understanding Fiction* and *Understanding Poetry.*

library classification systems   The numbers and letters on the spines of books (also the same notations on catalog cards that locate and identify books) according to the *Dewey Decimal System* or the *Library of Congress System,* or one of the more specialized systems mentioned below.

The Dewey Decimal System, used by most public libraries in this country and by many school and college libraries, was developed in 1876 by Melvil Dewey, a New York librarian and one of the founders of the modern public library movement in the United States. The system consists of ten major categories of books as follows:

000–099	General works (including bibliography and library science)
100–199	Philosophy
200–299	Religion
300–399	Social Sciences (including education)
400–499	Philology (including languages)
500–599	Pure Sciences
600–699	Useful Arts (including medicine and engineering)
700–799	Fine Arts
800–899	Literature (including poetry, drama, and literary criticism, but not fiction, which is catalogued and shelved according to authors' last names, without numbers)
900–999	Biography (though many libraries now use "B" instead of the "920s"), history, geography, travel.

Each of these ten major categories is broken down into subcategories — e.g., the 900s into the 910s (geography and travel), the 920s (biography), the 930s (ancient history), the 940s (Europe), the 950s (Asia), the 960s (Africa), the 970s (North America), the 980s (South America), the 990s (Pacific Ocean Islands). A third digit identifies a more specialized category. Thus, under the subcategory of the 370s (education) the 371s are assigned to the special category "teaching." The system is called "decimal" because — aside from its ten main categories — a decimal point and an expandable number of digits to the right of this point allow for identifying individual titles within categories. Thus an individual title, *The Advancement of Teaching,* has the Dewey Decimal identification of "371.3."

Library of Congress Classification. The Library of Congress (established in 1800 in Washington, D.C.) and many large university libraries catalogue and identify titles by a combination of letters and numbers according to the following system:

A   General Works
B   Philosophy and Religion
C   Auxiliary Sciences of History
D   Universal History and Topography
E, F American History
G   Geography and Anthropology
H   Social Sciences
J   Political Science
K   Law
L   Education
M   Music
N   Fine Arts
P   Language and Literature
Q   Science
R   Medicine
S   Agriculture
T   Technology
U   Military Science
V   Naval Science
Z   Library Science

Following each of these initial letters is a second letter that represents a subcategory. Under General Works (A) come encyclopedias (AE) and general reference works (AG). Under philosophy and Religion (B) come metaphysics (BD), esthetics (BH), ethics (BJ), etc. Under Language and Literature (P) come Classical (PA), Romance (PC), Germanic (PD), Slavic (PG), Oriental (PJ), English (PR), and American (PS) language and literature. Psychology, reflecting its ancient origin, remains a subcategory (BF) under Philosophy and Religion (B). Judaism (BM) is accorded a subheading parallel with that for Religions (BL). But Christianity shares, along with Mohammedanism [*sic*], Bahaism, and Theosophy, the one berth, BP. Biography appears as a subcategory (CT) under the Auxiliary Sciences of History (C), following such auxiliaries as Numismatics (CJ), Heraldry (CR), and Genealogy (CS).

After the second, subcategorical, letter there occur numbers for which the following, under Biography (CT), seem to be representative: 210–3150, National biographies; 3200–2830, Biographies of women;

and 9960–9998, Miscellaneous, including biographies of impostors and cripples. (See *Outline of the Library of Congress Classification,* Washington, D.C.: The Library of Congress, 1955.)

Special Systems. Important, if less common, classification systems for organizing library materials include the following: (1) *the Universal Decimal Classification,* (2) *the Bliss Classification,* (3) *the Colon Classification,* (4) *the Classification of the Harvard Graduate School of Business Administration,* (5) *the Lamont Library Classification of Harvard College,* (6) *the Union Theological Seminary Classification,* and (7) *the Glidden Classification.*

library paper   See RESEARCH PAPER.

light verse   Verse designed or intended to amuse or question rather than to transport; verse that appeals more to urbanity and the intellect than to one's sense of beauty. Whether witty enough to evoke laughter, ingenious enough to win a smile, or satirical enough to sting (though not to wound), light verse almost always succeeds through its social relevance. (Much light verse is in fact *vers de société.*) This social and contemporary quality, however, tends to make it more perishable than serious poetry. Indeed, for certain dictionaries of poetry, light verse seems beneath notice, even if poets like Horace, Chaucer, Shakespeare, Marvell, Herrick, Pope, Byron, Browning, Oliver Wendell Holmes, T. S. Eliot, e. e. cummings, and W. H. Auden have written light verse that has as yet not perished. Among their "entertainments" have been EPIGRAMS, SATIRES, PARODIES, PUNS, RIDDLES, LIMERICKS, and even ACROSTICS. Auden sees no really basic difference between serious poetry and the best light verse. Among the most widely published contemporary light versifiers are Ogden Nash, Richard Armour, and Phyllis McGinley.

REFERENCES: W. H. Auden (ed.), *The Oxford Book of Light Verse;* David McCord (ed.), *What Cheer;* Oscar Williams (ed.), *The Silver Treasury;* William Cole (ed.), *The Fireside Book of Humorous Poetry;* Louis Untermeyer, *Play in Poetry;* Richard Armour, *Writing Light Verse.*

limerick   A five-line nonsense verse in ANAPESTS rhyming *aabba;* with the first, second, and fifth lines having three stresses, the third and fourth lines two; and with an unexpected twist in the last line:

> There was an old man who said, "Hush!
> I perceive a young bird in the bush."
> When they joked, "Is it small?"
> He replied, "Not at all.
> It is five times as big as the bush!"

That limerick is one of hundreds attributed to Edward Lear (1812–88), the English bird watcher and painter. Other masters of this form are

Lewis Carroll, Robert Louis Stevenson, Gilbert and Sullivan, Oliver Wendell Holmes, Rudyard Kipling, Eugene Field, and Gelett Burgess. There is no evidence for the notion that limericks originated in County Limerick, Ireland, though Irish and English devotees have transmitted limericks orally along with other folk literature. The limerick is frequently devoted to humorous treatment of erotic subjects.

REFERENCES: Bennett Cerf (ed.), *Out on a Limerick;* Louis Untermeyer (ed.), *Lots of Limericks;* G. Legman (ed.), *The Limerick.*

lingua franca   **1.** A Frankish (Romance) language, with admixtures of Greek and Arabic, spoken chiefly in Mediterranean ports. **2.** Loosely, a hodgepodge or a hybrid language comparable to pidgin English. **3.** In criticism, the phrase is often used to describe certain current CONVENTIONS: " 'Boy-meets-girl' is the *lingua franca* of Hollywood." "Strategy-wise, the *lingua franca* of Madison Avenue is now the 'soft-sell.' "

literal language   Words used in their commonly accepted meanings, as *house* is used when it means "a dwelling place" or *knife* when it means "a tool for cutting." These same words are nonliteral, or FIGURATIVE, when used to mean something other than the most common denotation, as *house* is sometimes used to mean "the audience in a theater" or *knife* to mean "go through sharply" (e.g., "to *knife* through the Alabama line"). Words often originate figuratively, through imitation of natural sounds, comparison of the new to the old, or association of the unknown with the known; but they tend to become literal by long use: their picturesque qualities wear away until the figurative basis is forgotten. (See FADED METAPHOR.) For example, *comet* began as a Greek word meaning "long-haired," the name thus picturing the appearance of the astronomical body. But today *comet* is used in English with no thought of hair, and thus no figurative sense: the word has become literal. Heavily literal language tends toward ABSTRACTION, since the abstract word least arouses the imagination; it tends to narrow meaning to the DENOTATION rather than the CONNOTATIONS. (Contrast FIGURATIVE LANGUAGE and SYMBOLIC LANGUAGE.)

literary prizes and grants   Among the hundreds offered *annually* (unless otherwise stated) the following represent opportunities of interest, in most instances, to college students. Applications and particulars can be obtained from the address following each entry.

Atlantic Firsts ($750 and $250). For a first published story between 2,000 and 8,000 words. *Atlantic Monthly,* 8 Arlington St., Boston, Mass. 02116.

Balch Poetry Prizes ($500 and two of $250). *Virginia Quarterly Review.* 1 West Range, Charlottesville, Va. 22902.

Book-of-the-Month Club Writing Fellowships (fourteen at $3,000).

For talented or promising college seniors nominated by professors in their English departments. College English Association, 280 Park Avenue, New York, N.Y. 10017.

Brandeis Creative Arts Awards (eight at $1,000). For promise in literature, music, theater arts, fine arts. Brandeis University, Waltham, Mass. 02154.

Dutton Animal Book Awards ($10,000 and $5,000). For adult books and children's books about animals, fiction or nonfiction. E. P. Dutton & Co., 201 Park Ave., New York, N.Y. 10003.

Follett Award ($3,000). For fiction or nonfiction for young readers. Follett Publishing Co., 201 N. Wells St., Chicago, Ill. 60606.

Gauss Award ($1,000). For an outstanding book of literary scholarship or criticism. Phi Beta Kappa, 1811 Q St., N.W., Washington, D.C. 20009.

Grolier Award ($1,000). To a school or community librarian who has stimulated and guided reading by young people. Grolier, Inc., 575 Lexington Ave., New York, N.Y. 10022.

Guggenheim Fellowships (several in various amounts). For artists, writers, and scholars of high ability regardless of sex, race, color, creed, or marital status. Guggenheim Foundation, 90 Park Ave., New York, N.Y. 10016.

Hillman Award ($500). For fiction or nonfiction on race relations, civil liberties, and world understanding. Hillman Foundation, 15 Union Sq., New York, N.Y. 10003.

Houghton Mifflin Literary Fellowships ($5,000). For fiction or nonfiction by promising writers needing financial assistance to complete their works. Houghton Mifflin Co., 2 Park St., Boston, Mass. 02107.

Loveman Award ($1,000 and two at $200). To undergraduate students attending a U.S. college, who have won local contests for best student personal libraries. *Saturday Review,* c/o Miss Frieda Browne, 208 E. 28th St., New York, N.Y. 10016.

Mademoiselle Awards. For fiction ($500) and poetry ($100) by college students. Also Mademoiselle College Board Competitions (ten cash prizes along with salaried guest editorships) for college undergraduates in writing, arts, fashions, etc. *Mademoiselle* Magazine, 420 Lexington Ave., New York, N.Y. 10017.

National Book Awards ($1,000 each). For the year's most distinguished books of fiction, poetry, translation, history and biography, etc. National Book Committee, 1 Park Ave., New York, N.Y. 10016.

O. Henry Awards ($300, $200, $100). For best short stories published in American magazines. Doubleday & Co., 277 Park Ave., New York, N.Y. 10017.

P. E. N. Translation Prize ($1,000). For the best translation into English from any foreign language published in the U.S. P.E.N. American Center, 156 Fifth Ave., New York, N.Y. 10010.

Poetry Magazine Awards (several). *Poetry* Magazine, 1018 N. State St., Chicago, Ill. 60610.

Poetry Society of America Awards (several from $300 to $3,500). For various kinds of poems—single, groups, and book-length collections. Poetry Society of America, 15 Grammercy Park, New York, N.Y. 10003.

Pulitzer Prizes ($1,000 each). To American authors for a distinguished novel, play, biography, book of verse, etc. Trustees of Columbia University, Morningside Heights, New York, N.Y. 10027.

Seventeen Magazine Prizes (several from $25 to $500). For short stories by students under age twenty. *Seventeen* Magazine, 320 Park Ave., New York, N.Y. 10022.

Yale Series of Younger Poets (book publication with usual royalties). For a 46- to 64-page collection of poems previously unpublished as a collection. Open to writers under age forty. Yale University Press, 149 York St., New Haven, Conn., 06511. (See also NOBEL PRIZE.)

REFERENCES: "Literary Prizes and Awards," *Literary Market Place* (New York: R. R. Bowker Co., annually); "Fellowships and Grants," *Midwest MLA* (annually).

litotes   A kind of understatement, the method of which is to deny the opposite of what is intended. We use litotes (a three-syllable word: li'-to-tēs) when we say that the shrewd young man is *no fool* or when we describe Mount Everest as *not exactly a foothill.* If the speaker means that something is memorable, he may instead say that it is *unforgettable.* What is extremely urgent may become a matter *not unworthy of our attention.* Sir Winston Churchill, like many British speakers, made litotes a common mark of his speech. Addressing the Congress of the United States, he once referred to his own remarkable career as "My life, which has been long and *not entirely uneventful.*" Though litotes may produce an ironic tone, it is not to be confused with irony; for irony *states* the opposite of what is meant, while litotes *denies* the opposite of what is meant.

little magazines   When W. H. Auden in his poem "Under Which Lyre" speaks of "Our intellectual marines / Landing in the Little Magazines," he pays homage to one of the most vital movements in contemporary literature. Little magazines, even if individually short-lived or flickering, continue as a group to carry the torch for the new, the fresh, the experimental in poetry and fiction. In England, F. R. Leavis' *Scrutiny* (1932–1953), Wyndham Lewis's *Blast* (1914–1915), Ezra Pound and others' *The Egoist* (1914–1919), and Margaret Andersen's *Little Re-*

view (1914–1929) provided the pages in which many celebrities-to-be (among them, Joyce, Eliot, and Hemingway) were first published. In the United States the new voices found hearings in Harriet Munro's *Poetry, a Magazine of Verse,* and in the late 1920s in Marianne Moore's *Dial.* In fact, a poet like William Carlos Williams had to "prove himself" in the early *Kenyon* before being recognized and accepted by such Establishment magazines as *The Atlantic, Harper's, The New Yorker, The Saturday Review,* etc. Most "little mags," as they are called by the up-and-coming young writer, who relies on them for his first public hearing, are short-lived because (*a*) they are underfinanced by their patron-subscribers or by their sponsoring colleges and universities; and (*b*) the editors edit by avocation, most of them having other commitments. Nevertheless, most of these editors are dedicated men and women who encourage the experimental and sometimes share critical suggestions with young writers that show promise. At the time this handbook went to press, the following little magazines were being published and distributed to major American college and university libraries: *American Weave, Ante, Apple, Approach, Arion, Audit, Beloit Poetry Journal, Bitterroot, Bluestone, Boss, Burning Deck, Caravel, Centering, Chelsea, Choice, Cresset, Dalhousie Review, December, Descant, Discourse, Dust, Edge, Elizabeth, Epos, Essence, Fiddlehead, Gamut, Galley Sail, Generation, Genesis West, goodly co, The Goliards, Grist, Imago, Intermission, kayak, Kumquat, Literary Review, Lyric, Mad River, Maelstrom, Massachusetts Review, Michigan Quarterly, Midwest, Minnesota Review, Minority of One, Monocle, Mutiny, New, Nightshade, Nimrod, Northwest Review, nosegay in black, Opus, Orbit, Oyez, Perspective, Per Se, Plume & Sword, Poet and Critic, Poetry, Poetry Northwest, Potpourri, PS, Prairie Schooner, Quagga, Quarterly Review of Literature, Quartet, Radar, Satire NL, Shenandoah, The Sixties, The Smith, Smoky Hill Review, Snowy Egret, South & West, Southwest Review, Sparrow, Symptom, Synapse, Tamarack Review, things, Trace, Tri-Quarterly, Unicorn, University Review, Weed, Wormwood Review.*

REFERENCES: "Little Magazine," *Encyclopaedia Britannica;* Leonard Fulton (ed.), *Directory of Little Magazines;* Frederick J. Hoffman *et al., The Little Magazine, A History and a Bibliography;* Lionel Trilling, "The Future of the Little Magazine," *The Liberal Imagination;* Felix Stefanile, "The Imagination of the Amateur," *Trace* (May, 1966); Reed Whittemore (ed.), *The Little Magazine and Contemporary Literature.*

Living Theater   See IMMEDIATE THEATER.

local color   The characteristics, artifacts, clothing, dialects, manners, morals, and pastimes of a region or subculture. In Mark Twain's *Adventures of Huckleberry Finn,* for example, the local color depicted

along the Missouri shore of the Mississippi, especially in the environment of the Widow Douglas and Judge Thatcher, is distinctly different
from that of the feuding Grangerfords and Shepherdsons farther south.
REFERENCE: Harry Warfel and G. Harrison Orians (eds.), Introduction, *American Local Color Stories.*

locating information   In any library the four basic and first places to
look for information are (1) encyclopedias; (2) the card catalog under
the subject if you do not know authors or titles; (3) *The Readers'
Guide to Periodical Literature* (for magazine articles), again under
subject if you do not know authors or titles; and (4) the metal ("ver-
tical") file cabinets that contain pamphlets, leaflets, and similar unbound materials usually kept up to date. (See RESEARCH PAPER.)
REFERENCES: Donald F. Bond, *A Reference Guide to English Studies;* Ronald
B. McKerrow, *An Introduction to Bibliography for Literary Students;* Charles
Alexander and A. J. Burke, *How to Locate Educational Information; Information, Please, Almanac;* Encyclopedia Americana; Encyclopeadia Britannica;
Richard D. Altick, *The Scholar Adventurers.*

logic   A system of reasoning with *validity,* not necessarily with abstract *truth.* INFERENCE, the drawing of conclusions from real or supposed evidence, plays a large role in human discourse; thus logic, with
its formulation of principles of valid inference, has certain connections
with language and is indispensable to most GENRES of speaking and
writing. Reference to the principles of logical inference gives writer
and speaker, reader and listener, a check upon the validity of what is
said – at least when what is said depends upon reason.

Methods of reasoning. Ordered reasoning (that is, logic) follows one
of two methods, depending upon the nature of the material or the concepts to be reasoned about and upon the nature of the inferences to be
drawn. These methods are (1) induction and (2) deduction.

1. INDUCTIVE REASONING begins with the observation of particular
facts, then works toward assertion of a general inference that accounts
for, or at least *probably* accounts for, those facts.

2. DEDUCTIVE REASONING begins with the assertion of a general law,
or acceptable "truth," and works toward the explicit assertion of a
particular fact that is implicit in that generalization.

These methods of reasoning are complementary, not antithetical.
The chief distinction between induction and deduction lies in this: the
conclusion reached by induction is limited by *probability,* but the conclusion reached by deduction is *absolute.* It is by inductive reasoning
that much of experimental science proceeds. By observing past and
present phenomena, the scientist is able to draw inferences to predict
future phenomena with high probability; his conclusion adds to human
knowledge. On the other hand, deductive reasoning does not add to

knowledge; rather, its usefulness lies in allowing us to make proper applications of knowledge already possessed but never before applied to a specific instance.

For the speaker or writer and his audience no thorough grounding in SCIENTIFIC METHOD may be necessary. But valid ARGUMENTATION, like valid science, depends in large measure upon the care and honesty with which facts are observed, the adequacy of those facts as grounds for inference, and the avoidance of FALLACIES—errors in reasoning. (See INDUCTIVE REASONING, DEDUCTIVE REASONING, SYLLOGISMS, and FALLACIES OF REASONING.)

REFERENCES: John Sherwood, *Discourse of Reason: Brief Handbook of Logic and Semantics;* Monroe Beardsley, *Thinking Straight;* Irving M. Copi, *Introduction to Logic;* Jeremy Pitt and Russell E. Leavenworth, *Logic for Argument;* Morris R. Cohen and Ernest Nagel, *An Introduction to Logic.*

Lollards   The intellectual ancestors of the Puritans; followers of John Wycliffe (1320–84); members of a popular religious movement in England during the late fourteenth century. The Lollards, most of whom were low in the socio-economic and ecclesiastical scale, opposed the materialism of the Church rulers. The Lollards contributed portions of the Wycliffe Bible and, in 1395 presented to Parliament an unsuccessful petition for Church reform. This petition anticipated many of the tenets of the sixteenth-century Protestant Reformation. One of the tenets, no doubt the one for which many a Lollard was burned at the stake, was that war should be declared unchristian. Lollardism is mentioned or reflected in medieval literature, notably in Chaucer's *Canterbury Tales* (in the "Prologue" the host accuses the Country Parson of being a "Loller") and in Piers Plowman's *Creed.*

REFERENCE: James Gairdner and William Hunt, *Lollardy and the Reformation in England.*

loose sentence   A sentence in which the main idea comes early, the subordinate ideas or modifiers following usually in a string, as ducklings tag after their mother. The loose sentence may, in the hands of a careless writer, lack discipline; for it keeps a loose leash upon ideas. But to suppose that there is no control at all is a great mistake. The loose sentence, after all, is the normal English sentence. It has the flow of conversation, a quieter subtlety than has its rhetorical opposite, the PERIODIC SENTENCE. When carefully made, the loose sentence ranges but does not wander; the ducklings do not get lost, and no ugly one appears.

The loose sentence was first cultivated as the basis of a literary style during the seventeenth century, when Ciceronian and anti-Ciceronian writers vied to create a memorable prose by following classical models. The Ciceronians, whose model was the ornate and formal style of the

Roman orator Cicero, tried to construct their sentences so that the main idea always came near the end. (See PERIODIC SENTENCE.) The anti-Ciceronians, who felt that a prose style should at least appear natural, even if carefully constructed, modeled their work on Seneca's moral essays and Tacitus's histories, some preferring a curt manner with brief sentences and no connections, others building long leisurely sentences and paragraphs out of short clauses, informally connected, and with little symmetry. The English masters of this loose style were Sir Thomas Browne and Robert Burton. They employed both compound and complex sentences, often using prepositions and conjunctions without strict attention to their formal properties, or separating by a mere comma what we would probably set off by a semicolon, if not a period. (See COMMA SPLICE.) The effect of such a style upon the reader is one of intimacy, of being present in the writer's mind as he considers an idea and its associations for the first time. Here, for example, is Sir Thomas Browne:

Light that makes things seen makes some things invisible; were it not for darkness and the shadow of the earth, the noblest part of the creation had remained unseen and the stars in heaven as invisible as on the fourth day when they were created above the horizon with the sun, or there was not an eye to behold them. —*The Garden of Cyrus,* Chapter IV.

Compound sentences are usually classed as loose, since one independent clause might have ended the sentence, yet another has been attached. Simple sentences may also be loose, having modifying phrases added after the essential subject and verb, and possible object or other complement (this sentence itself being an example). Complex sentences may be loose if their subordinate (and nonrestrictive) clauses follow the main clause. The loose sentence consisting of a main generalization (e.g., *Odysseus crossed the seas*) followed by one or more amplifying and RENDERING phrases (e.g., *his men working the oars, the water dripping from the wood*) is called a cumulative sentence, and it enriches the TEXTURE of an utterance.

The loose sentence reflects a mind *at* work; the periodic sentence, a mind that *has* worked. But despite its being abusively named, the loose sentence can reflect a civilized informality. The following is an example by the Victorian writer Walter Pater:

One of the most beautiful passages of Rousseau is that in the sixth book of the *Confessions,* where he describes the awakening in him of the literary sense. An undefinable taint of death had clung always about him, and now in early manhood he believed himself smitten by mortal disease. He asked himself how he might make as much as possible of the interval that remained; and he was not biased by anything in his previous life when he decided that it must be by intellectual excitement, which he found just then in the clear fresh writings of Voltaire: "Well! we are all *condamnés* as Victor Hugo says: we are all under sentence of death but with a sort of indefinite reprieve."—*Studies in the History of the Renaissance.*

love casuistry   See COURTLY LOVE.

lower case   Small letters as opposed to capitals. (See CAPITALIZING.)

lyric   1. According to Elder Olson, a poem in which "a single perception or feeling is overtly expressed." More broadly, any song or short subjective poem with songlike qualities; hence, such forms as the AUBADE, BALLAD, BALLADE, hymn, MADRIGAL, ODE, RONDEL, serenade, SONNET, and VILANELLE. 2. In contemporary popular songs, the words as distinguished from the music. 3. In contemporary musical comedy, the songs as distinguished from the book, or story.

REFERENCES: Elder Olson, "The Lyric," *Papers of the Midwest Modern Language Association* (No. 1, 1969); C. Day Lewis, *The Lyric Impulse;* G. L. Brook (ed.), *The Harley Lyrics;* Katherine Ing, *Elizabethan Lyrics;* Herbert Grierson (ed.), *Metaphysical Lyrics and Poems;* F. T. Palgrave (ed.), *The Golden Treasury of the Best Songs and Lyrical Poems.*

M

macaronic   Pertaining to a kind of light verse, often DOGGEREL, that mixes languages (for example, Latin and English). A classic example, attributed to William Drummond of Hawthornden (1585-1649), begins "Cane carmen Sixpence, pera plena rye," obviously a mixed Latin and English version of the Mother Goose rhyme "Sing a song of sixpence, a pocket full of rye."

madrigal   A short LYRIC intended to be sung by several voices, usually four. Early Italian experiments with the form ("motets") appeared in Petrarch's *Rime* (ca. 1350). The more consistently developed forms that appeared in Pietro Bembo's *Rime* (1530) consisted of six to thirteen lines with no more than three rhymes, although he himself practiced and expressly invited variation. Luca Marenzio (1553-99) wrote twenty-three books of madrigals, which circulated all over Europe, several in English translation. The native English adaptations varied widely but had in common, as did their Italian models, planned repetition of words and phrases, affording singers the chance for echolike sound effects. A classic example is Shakespeare's "Crabbed Age and Youth," which appears in *Measure for Measure:*

> Take, O take those lips away
>   That so sweetly were forsworn,
> And those eyes, the break of day,
>   Lights that do mislead the morn!
> But my kisses bring again,
>   Bring again—
> Seals of love, but sealed in vain
>   Sealed in vain!

The madrigal was characterized not only by the CONVENTIONS noted above but also by CONCEITS and erotic or PASTORAL content. It was usually sung to the accompaniment of a lute, a pear-shaped stringed instrument. (Compare the twentieth-century revival of madrigal singing to the accompaniment of the guitar.) The madrigal enjoyed tremendous popularity in ELIZABETHAN England not only among poets but also among singers, amateur and professional, and composers—especially such court favorites as Edward Fairfax and Thomas Morley. The popularity of the madrigal is reflected in its frequent appearance in poetry anthologies—for example, in *The Bower of Delights* (1591), *The Phoenix Nest* (1593), and in the many editions of Richard Tottel's miscellany *Songs and Sonnets* from 1557 to 1587. The madrigals in Tottel's collection were often unsigned or anonymous, but according to

Hebel and Hudson many of them were almost certainly the work of such poets as Edmund Spenser, Philip Sidney, Thomas Lodge, and Thomas Campion.

Madrigals and mock madrigals occur in the operettas of Gilbert and Sullivan. *The Mikado* (1885), for example, contains the mock madrigal beginning "Brightly dawns our wedding day," for four tearful voices.

REFERENCES: E. H. Fellows (ed.), *English Madrigal Verse 1588–1632;* H. W. Janson and Joseph Kerman, "The Madrigal," *A History of Art and Music;* J. William Hebel and Hoyt H. Hudson (eds.), *Poetry of the English Renaissance (1509–1660)*; B. Pattison, *Music and Poetry in the English Renaissance.*

major premise   See SYLLOGISM (opening illustration).

major term   See SYLLOGISM IA.

malapropism   From *mal à propos,* "inappropriate." An inappropriate word or expression that only sounds something like the one intended. Some representative malapropisms: "We stuff your pay envelopes with *incendiaries*" (for *incentives*); "I like the man, but I am *contemptible* of his ideas" (for *contemptuous*); "It's simply *incredulous*" (for *incredible*); "Never had I suffered such *humility!*" (for *humiliation*). Richard Brinsley Sheridan's famed Mrs. Malaprop in *The Rivals* is the classic user of such near-miss words, and Fowler calls her "the matron saint of all those who go wordfowling with a blunderbuss." Except when used deliberately for humor, malapropism results from a careless acquaintance with words and a confusion about their meanings.

manifest story-line   See DRAMATIC STRUCTURE.

masque   A semidramatic aristocratic entertainment, allegorical in structure, accompanied by music, dancing, elaborate symbolic costume, and stage props. Early masques were usually pantomimes; and even if speaking-lines were added they were subordinated to the spectacle itself. The first court masque, Samuel Daniel's *Vision of the Twelve Goddesses* (1604), was an allegorical celebration of the blessings bestowed on England by the new monarch, James I. The masque was a very perishable art-form, lasting from 1604 only until the closing of the theatres in 1642. For the Jacobean masques Inigo Jones (1573–1652), the artist and architect, designed elaborate costumes and intricate stage sets, some of them with working fountains. Such stage props were often found ready-made, however, when masques were performed on the estates of the wealthy.

Among the conventions of the masque, especially when it was given as part of a garden party, was audience participation, the actors dancing with the guests. (Compare this convention with its counterpart in the IMMEDIATE THEATER.) Another convention was to fill the intermission with an optional extra known as an *antimasque,* a playful PARODY of the main plot.

The masque had its origins in agricultural ritual and popular dramatic entertainments like the St. George sword dances and plays, which involved costumed and masked persons, music, sudden appearances of the dancers, and the like. These sword dances were much more PASTORAL than militaristic — in most respects unlike the (Japanese) Samurai sword plays and dances.

For many years the best masque in English literature was considered to be John Milton's *Comus* (produced in 1634, published in 1637). (The Greek word *komos* means dance, incidentally, and is also the root from which the word *comedy* derives.) Though originally titled "A Masque," Milton's *Comus* is often regarded as a PASTORAL entertainment. Ben Jonson is perhaps the best-known writer of masques. Among his best are *Hymenai* (1606), *The Masque of Beauty* (1608), *The Hue and Cry after Cupid* (1608), *The Masque of Queens* (1609), and *Oberon* (1611).

REFERENCES: Enid Welsford, *The Court Masque;* Allardyce Nicoll, *Stuart Masques and the Renaissance Stage;* J. C. Meagher, *Method and Meaning in Jonson's Masques;* J. S. Diekhoff (ed.), *A Maske at Ludlow.*

mass literature   Popular ("pop") and low-brow literature; such popular pieces as comic books, newspaper comic strips, newspapers themselves (with some few exceptions like the New York *Times,* the Manchester *Guardian,* and the *Christian Science Monitor*), magazines like *Look* and *Reader's Digest,* and the most superficial paperbacks. (Compare KITSCH; contrast TOUGH LITERATURE.)

REFERENCES: Bernard Rosenberg and David M. White (eds.), *Mass Culture;* Irving and Harriet Deer (eds.), *The Popular Arts;* Reuel Denny, *The Astonished Muse;* Milton Klonsky, "Along the Midway of Mass Culture," *Partisan Review* (April, 1949); Kingsley Amis, *New Maps of Hell;* Jules Feiffer, *The Great Comic Book Heroes;* Eugene McNamara (ed.), *The Interior Landscape;* Walker Ong, *The Barbarian Within.*

mass media   Television, radio, cinema, and the popular press that publishes MASS LITERATURE.

REFERENCES: Marshall McLuhan, *Understanding Media* and *The Medium Is the Massage;* James Agee, *Agee on Film; Media and Methods* magazine.

maxim   A general truth, usually a rule of conduct, expressed concisely; for example, "Care for the pennies, and the dollars will care for themselves." (See APHORISM.)

medieval romance   See CHIVALRIC ROMANCE.

melodrama   Literally, a "play with music." A crude play, often self-satirizing, that invites the audience to hiss at the villain. The villain usually represents greed, while the heroine represents chastity. Among the other stereotypes of the melodrama are the drunken father, the beautiful daughter, the lecherous mortgage holder, and the heroine's handsome, honest, but penniless fiancé. Virtue ultimately triumphs over Vice. Played in "opera houses" to the accompaniment of a tinny piano in the pit, the melodrama has entertained music-hall London as well as the American frontier since the early 1800s. *East Lynne, The Drunkard,* and *M'Liss* have been among the most popular.

REFERENCE: Frank Rahill, *The World of Melodrama;* Eric Bentley, *The Life of Drama.*

metaphor　1. An utterance treating one thing as if it were something quite different, so that a resemblance not normally assumed is pointed up; a poetic comparison of two apparently unlike things; for example, "A rapier of light pinned him to the wall." Such a comparison draws attention to the similarity between a searchlight *beam* and a *rapier,* so that the reader gets an immediate image of straightness, thinness, length, and sharpness, and an impression of the beam's function in relation to the victim. Some other examples: "The wind is a whetted knife"; "The wind cuts"; "The man barks"; "The conversation ping-pongs"; "The road was a ribbon of moonlight." Through metaphor man discovers much of his world. Certainly the use of metaphor as discovery is of great importance to children, whose quick and natural making of metaphors often astounds their elders. (See Richard Lewis [ed.], *Miracles, Poems by Children of the English-Speaking World.*) Children come to understand new things, however inaccurately, by comparing the new to something already known.

But metaphor is not just *any* comparison. To say that a cannon is a giant pistol is hardly metaphor; the two things are too much alike (in structure and function) to begin with. Metaphor occurs when a surprisingly imaginative connection is made between two images that are in actuality dissimilar. The comparison of objects not actually unlike (for example, "The road was S-shaped") is prosaic, not metaphoric. Even "wind" and "knife" in our example have lost much of their original poetic edge and may be considered FADED METAPHOR. Traditionally, metaphor has been distinguished from *simile,* the latter being a comparison using "like" or "as": "The wind cut *like* a knife."

2. Broadly, metaphor is any fresh, imaginative comparison, whether expressed or implied; it is basic to the concrete universal, the essence of poetry. Aristotle was sure that metaphor is something a poet is born with.

3. In expository prose, a method of defining or explaining; e.g., "A deponent verb is an active wolf in passive sheep's clothing." Unconscious humor results when the writer mixes metaphors (or CLICHÉS);

e.g., "Swimming against the tide may pave the road to success."

REFERENCES: Christine Brooke-Rose, *A Grammar of Metaphor;* Archibald MacLeish, "Metaphor," *Poetry and Experience;* Herbert Read, "Metaphor," *English Prose Style;* Owen Thomas, *Metaphor and Related Subjects;* R. W. Winterowd, "Metaphor and Symbol," *Rhetoric: A Synthesis.*

metaphysical poets   A school of seventeenth-century poets, among them Crashaw, Donne, Herbert, and Vaughan, who were inspired by religious as well as secular experiences and who expressed them in intellectual, imaginative, often extended, METAPHORS and PARADOXES. Herbert's "The Pulley" (with God and man at opposite ends) and Donne's compass, in "A Valediction Forbidding Mourning," are examples of the extended intellectual metaphors at the heart of the metaphysical CONCEIT and WIT. The metaphysical poets had a considerable influence on twentieth-century poets, especially T. S. Eliot. The epithet *metaphysical* (literally, "beyond nature") was originally a derogation applied by Samuel Johnson to poets he regarded as too far removed from rational assumptions about Nature and the GREAT CHAIN OF BEING. But the metaphysical poets, intellectual though they were, having failed to find very much rationality in the universe, looked inward and tried to unify themselves, their own sensibilities; or, looking outward, sought more direct, personal, perhaps mystical bonds with the Creator.

REFERENCES: Edwin Honig (ed.), *The Major Metaphysical Poets of the Seventeenth Century: An Anthology;* T. S. Eliot, "The Metaphysical Poets," *Selected Essays;* Herbert Grierson (ed.), *Metaphysical Lyrics and Poems;* Douglas Bush, *English Literature in the Earlier Seventeenth Century;* Alfred Alvarez, *The School of Donne;* Rosamund Tuve, *Elizabethan and Metaphysical Imagery;* George Williamson, *The Donne Tradition;* J. B. Leishman, *The Monarch of Wit;* Alexander Witherspoon and Frank Warnke (eds.), *Seventeenth Century Prose and Poetry.*

meter   The measurement of poetry; the rhythmic patterns resulting from combinations of heavy and light stresses on words and syllables. The simplest basic stress pattern, corresponding in music to a "measure" or "bar," is called a *foot*. The following kinds of feet, especially the ones printed in italics, are generally encountered in English and American poetry:

Name of Foot (Adjectival form in parentheses)	Stresses [⌣ = light stress; ⁄ = heavy	Examples
Two-syllable feet		
iamb (iambic)		a·gain
trochee (trochaic)		never

spondee (spondaic)   péll-méll

pyrrhic (pyrrhic)   in a

Three-syllable feet

anapest (anapestic)   in the dárk

dactyl (dactylic)   yés·ter·dăy

amphibrach (amphibrachic)   to·mór·row

cretic (cretic,
    also called amphimacer)   síl·ver-tóngues

bacchius (bacchiac)   a déath·blów

antibacchius (antibacchiac)   críme-fíght·er

molossus (molossic)   gréat whíte chíef

tribrach (tribrachic)   and in the

Four-syllable feet

ditrochee (ditrochaic)   fór·túne-téll·er

choriamb (choriambic)   súg·ar and spíce

paeon, 1st class (paeonic)   wóm·an·li·ness

paeon, 2nd class   com·pár·i·son

paeon, 3rd class   an in·vá·sion

paeon, 4th class   in·to the bréach

Ionic major (ionic)   hárd-héad·ed·ness

Ionic minor   at a snáil's páce

Epitrite, 1st class   the cóld, cóld gróund

Epitrite, 2nd class   é·víl-éyed wítch

Epitrite, 3rd class   thréad·báre and tórn

Epitrite, 4th class   fúll-léngth nóv·el

Each *line* of a poem contains a certain number of the above *feet*. A poetic (or "metrical") line can thus be measured or "scanned" for its *number and kind of feet*. The following are representative samplings of metrical lines:

Metrical lines

monometer (one foot)
    Mȳ Bén! (iambic)
    chíldrĕn (trochaic)

dimeter (two feet)
    Tŏ·mór-/ rŏw díes (iambic)
    Máry / Máry / (trochaic)

trimeter (three feet)
No̮ tăw- / dry̆ rule / o̮f kings (iambic)
Caught in the / spell of the /mel·o·dy (dactylic)

tetrameter (four feet)
Come live / with me / and be / my love (iambic)
Then the/ lit·t·tle/ Hi·a /wa·tha (trochaic)
Like the leaves / of the for- / est when sum-/ mer is green (anapestic)

pentameter (five feet)
The cur- / few tolls / the knell / of part-/ ing day

hexameter (six feet)
She knelt, / So pure / a thing, / so free/ from mor- / tal taint

heptameter (seven feet)
All fun- / ny fel- / lows, com- / ic men, / and clowns / of pri- /vate life

octameter (eight feet)
Let it / fall on / Locks·ley / Hall, with / rain or / hail, or / fire
or / snow

Usual combinations of foot-lines:

Kinds	Examples
Iambic trimeter	/Its fleece/ was white/ as snow/
Iambic tetrameter	/As I/ was walk/ing past/ her house/
Trochaic trimeter	/London/ Bridge is/ broken/
Trochaic tetrameter	/London/ Bridge is/ falling/ down, oh/
Iambic pentameter	/Shall I/ compare/thee to/ a sum/mer's day?

[Note: a pyrrhic is sometimes substituted for an iamb.]

Dactylic hexameter	/This is the/ forest pri/meval, the/ murmuring/
	pines and the/ hemlocks

[Note: a spondee is sometimes substituted for a dactyl or an anapest.]

Anapestic tetrameter	/But we loved/ with a love/ that was more/ than
	love/

[Note: an iamb is sometimes substituted for an anapest.]

The number of lines to a STANZA (bundle of lines) determines, in part, its name — couplet, tercet, QUATRAIN, sestet, and so on.

The examples of metrical lines in these tables represent, for the most part, "pure" patterns; that is, in each line usually only one kind of foot appears. However, in many celebrated poems substitutions have been made — a trochee for an iamb, a spondee for a trochee. The substitutions have generally been regarded not only as acceptable but also as desirable to keep the dominant RHYTHM from sounding monotonous. Variety in sound-effects is also achieved by ending a line, now with a light (*feminine*) stress, now with a heavy (*mascu-*

line) stress; e.g., "énding"; "thé énd." Another device for achieving variety in a series of lines is that of carrying forward, from line to line, the sense of a sentence as opposed to ending a sentence at the end of a line of poetry. (See ENJAMBEMENT.)

Through the years certain meters and lines, along with the typical STANZA forms in which they occur, have enjoyed popularity. Nursery jingles, for example, which comprise perhaps the most popular and memorable verse, tend to use very short lines, whether trochaic ("Sing a song of sixpence"), or iambic ("As I looked out my window"), or dactylic ("Hickory, dickory, dock"). When iambic tetrameter in the first and third lines is alternated with iambic trimeter in the second and fourth lines, the result is the "common meter" of the BALLAD stanza. Dactylic hexameter was the original meter of the classical EPICS, although some translators have preferred to render them them into iambic pentameter. The latter meter, in fact, has proved far and away the most popular of all in English, perhaps because it comes close to sounding like the ordinary speech patterns of English. Iambic pentameter is the meter of the SONNET, the SPENSERIAN STANZA, the HEROIC COUPLET, and BLANK VERSE.

REFERENCES: Clement Wood, *A Rhyming Dictionary;* Alex Preminger *et al.* (eds.), *Encyclopedia of Poetry and Poetics;* Morris Halle and Samuel Keyser, "The Iambic Pentameter," in W. K. Wimsatt (ed.), *Comparative Prosody;* Samuel Keyser, "The Linguistic Basis of English Prosody," in David Reibel and Sanford Schane (eds.), *Modern English Studies;* P. F. Baum, *Principles of English Versification;* T. S. Omund, *A Study of Metre.*

metonym   An example of METONYMY.

metonymy   Literally, "name-changing." A device of figurative language in which the name of an attribute or associated thing is substituted for the usual name of a thing: *the blue* for *the sky, the White House* for *the President, the press* for *newspapermen, the campus* for *the school, the Crown* for *the King, the devil* for *mischief, the gas* for *accelerator pedal, eye* for *look at, finger* for *touch, stomach* for *digest, hammer* for *pound.* The names of places may be substituted for things associated with those places: *java* for *coffee, bermudas* and *bikini* for certain pieces of *apparel.* The names of people may be substituted for things associated with those people: *quisling* for *traitor, gerrymander* for *unfair political redistricting, boycott* for *deliberate avoidance, Romeo* for *lover, Helen* for *beautiful woman, Milton* for *poet.* (Compare EPITHET and ALLUSION.)

SYNECDOCHE, a special kind of metonymy, substitutes the name of a part for the name of a whole, or the other way round: *keyboard artist* for *piano player, hand* for *working man, wheels* for *automobile;* the name of a substance for the thing made of that substance: *iron* for *golf club, cotton* for *dress, pigskin* for *football;* or the name of a container for what it contains: drink a *bottle,* smoke two *packs,* count the *house.*

Like other figures of speech, metonymy contributes to semantic change. Words used as metonyms often become the familiar terms for the things they are used to name: *iron* for *device to press clothing, stamp* for *a device that stamps or is stamped.* (Compare FADED META-PHOR.)

metrical romance   Also known as **medieval romance.** A medieval narrative poem (sometimes a prose translation from the French) dealing with the chivalric adventures, loves, and famous deeds of Greek, Roman, Saxon, Anglo-Norman, English, and French figures. Familiar heroes of these romances are Alexander, Charlemagne, and Arthur. Among the celebrated titles are *The Romance of Alexander, The Romance of Charlemagne, Tristan and Iseult, Morte d'Arthur, Sir Gawain and the Green Knight,* and *Perceval* (compare the German *Parzifal*). Sometimes in these writings history predominates over romance, although most scholars distinguish between genuine romances and the mere celebration of famous exploits (see GESTES).

REFERENCES: George Ellis, *Specimens of the Early English Metrical Romances;* A. C. Taylor, *An Introduction to Medieval Romance;* Lewis Spencer, *A Dictionary of Medieval Romance and Romance Writers;* W. H. French and C. B. Hale (eds.), *Metrical Romances;* Roger Sherman Loomis, *The Development of Arthurian Romance;* W. P. Ker, *Epic and Romance;* J. A. Bennett and G. V. Smithers (eds.), *Early English Verse.*

metrics   The art of composition in, or the analysis of, METER.

middle term   See SYLLOGISM I A.

miles gloriosus   The braggart soldier; a stock character in the comedies of ancient Greece and Rome and in those of medieval and Renaissance England.

REFERENCE: Daniel Boughner, *The Braggart in Renaissance Comedy.*

milieu   Political, social, cultural, and intellectual environment, which Hippolyte Taine, in *History of English Literature,* posited as indispensable background to the understanding of an author and his works. Taine also attributed importance to race and "moment." Most scholars and philological critics of the late nineteenth and early twentieth centuries rooted their interpretations of literature in the milieu and the biography of the author. Louis Bredvold's *Intellectual Milieu of John Dryden,* for example, is a distinguished product of this kind of scholarship. The revolt against milieu was led by the NEW CRITICS, who, committed to the doctrine of AESTHETIC DISTANCE, put more emphasis on the work of art itself than on biographical, historical, and other "external" facts. A middle position—that a reader or critic may "keep one foot in each world," the world of background and the world of the text itself—has been proposed by the poet, playwright, and teacher Archibald MacLeish.

REFERENCES: Theodore Morrison, "Dover Beach Revisited," in Robert W. Stallman and R. E. Watters (eds.), *The Creative Reader;* Frederick C. Crews, *The Pooh Perplex;* Archibald MacLeish, *Poetry and Experience.*

mimes   From the Greek for "imitate." Pantomimes or dramatic skits that use gestures and other nonverbal means of communicating, sometimes in humorous imitation or burlesque of well-known people or types of people. (See COMMEDIA DELL'ARTE.)

mimesis   From the Greek for "imitation." 1. The imitation of life or "holding the mirror up to nature" in the literal sense that allowed early Greeks to explain "singing" as "imitation of the birds." 2. In literary criticism, artistic and SELECTIVE REPRESENTATION of reality as opposed to one-for-one representation. Compare, for example, the differences between a photograph (one-for-one representation) and a portrait (selective representation) or between a pedestrian photograph reflecting the photographer's unimaginativeness and an artistic photograph reflecting carefully selected subject and composition. Poets' talents for abstracting from the environment certain nonliteral, metaphorical (and in Plato's notion, spurious) ideas prompted the author of *The Republic* (Book 10) to ban poets from his ideal world and scene. Much friendlier to the arts was Aristotle in his concept of mimesis — and no doubt shrewder. In *The Poetics* (Chapter 4) he exposes Platonic Ideas as missing the point about true universals and addresses himself to mimesis as representation of man's dramatic actions (compare Kenneth Burke's DRAMATISM) as they unfold in the plot (*mythos*) of a drama or in the dramatic elements of a poem. According to Aristotle, the chief way in which artists inventively "make" (*poiein*) is through selecting for their plots and structures universally representative types on a new high order of abstraction. Aristotle's representative types, which modern critics like Eric Auerbach and Northrop Frye equate with ARCHETYPES, were unfortunately vulgarized as stereotypes (that is, as THEOPHRASTAN or STOCK CHARACTERS) by Aristotle's Roman successors. The discriminating modern critic Frye distinguishes between "high mimetic" (EPIC and TRAGEDY) and "low mimetic" (COMEDY and SATIRE), though he contends that tragedy and comedy are ultimately "lenses in one vision" (*Anatomy of Criticism,* 1957).

During the Renaissance the HUMANISTS' notion of mimesis was narrowly rhetorical: imitation of style. Cicero and Vergil, for example, were held up as paragons of style worth imitating. From the Renaissance until the twentieth century, mimesis received an almost incredible contrariety of interpretations, as Eric Auerbach has shown in his monumental study *Mimesis* (1946). Auerbach shows how each age, each culture, develops its own rhetoric or life style. And what is rhetoric or life style if it is not a way of representing one's reality? (Some contemporary linguists, in fact, define grammar as a system for structuring one's reality.) In short, literature is essentially mimetic.

It remained for the twentieth-century critic Kenneth Burke to reexamine Aristotle's mimesis and to gain from it inspiration, perhaps, for his own mimetic theory, which, in *A Grammar of Motives* (1945), he calls DRAMATISM (act, scene, agent, agency, purpose). Viewed in its own right, Burke's mimetic theory may yet accommodate our sensibilities about "where it's at" and "telling it like it is," may yet reconcile the apparent dichotomy in our alleged two cultures ("Pop" vs. Matthew Arnold's "high seriousness"), as Susan Sontag has observed in the essay "The Basic Unit of Contemporary Art Is Not the Idea but the Analysis and Extension of Sensations," in G. E. Stern (ed.), *McLuhan: Hot and Cool.*

REFERENCES: Plato, *The Republic,* Book 10; Aristotle, *The Poetics,* Chapter 4; Eric Auerbach, *Mimesis;* Kenneth Burke, *A Grammar of Motives;* Northrop Fry, "The Archetypes of Literature," in James Miller (ed.), *Myth and Method;* Mary McCarthy, "The Fact in Fiction," *Partisan Review* (Summer, 1960).

minor premise   See SYLLOGISM.

minor sentence   A sentence that makes sense, in its context and situation, without full predication (that is, without a complete subject-verb combination expressed).

Unlike the FRAGMENT, the minor sentence is a rhetorical device that often lends force to a thought, perhaps the force of brevity, as in proverb and maxim: "Easy come, easy go."

Much of conversation consists of minor sentences, each fully acceptable though not complete in predication. (See ELLIPSIS.) Minor sentences are normal in commands ("Sit down!"), in questions ("Anywhere?"), and in exclamations ("No, not in the judge's chair!"). Answers to questions also often take minor sentence form, since the question itself supplies sense-giving context: "Are you ready?" "*In a minute.*"

Many transitional phrases appear as minor sentences; even in the most staid formal writing: *So much for preliminaries. To get back to the story. Now for the main point.* (Compare SIGNPOST DEVICES.)

To set off a word or phrase as a minor sentence may give extraordinary emphasis to its content, and the device should not be used unless such emphasis is appropriate. Charles Dickens, an effective user of the minor sentence, begins *Bleak House:*

London. Michaelmas Term lately over, and the Lord Chancellor sitting in Lincoln's Inn Hall. Implacable November weather. As much mud in the streets, as if the waters had but newly retired from the face of the earth, and it would not be wonderful to meet a Megalosaurus, forty feet long or some, waddling like an elephantine lizard up Holborn Hill. Smoke lowering down from chimney-pots, making a soft black drizzle, with flakes of soot in it as big as full-grown snow-flakes—gone into mourning, one might imagine, for the death of the sun.

All predications sufficiently implied. No chance of misreading. Verbs like ostrich heads: unseen, but perfectly inferred.

miracle plays   Medieval plays based on the lives of saints and on the Biblical miracles, presented first in churches, later in churchyards, for the entertainment and edification of the parishioners. When the plays became too complex and elaborate to be offered by the Church, production was taken over by the crafts and trade guilds and sometimes, especially in France, by traveling professional players. The first miracle play, the "Quem Quaeritis" trope, was a brief dialogue sung at the end of the gradual in the mass on Easter Sunday. It re-enacts the story of the three Marys and the angel in front of the tomb after the Resurrection. (See TROPE 2.)

There has been some controversy over the use of the terms "miracle play" and "mystery play," some scholars preferring to apply the term "miracle play" to plays based on the lives of saints and on martyrdoms (customarily performed on the particular saint's day), while reserving the term "mystery play" for the CRAFT CYCLE PLAYS enacted by craft guilds on Corpus Christi. E. K. Chambers, however, believes that the term "miracle play" was used by the men of the Middle Ages to refer to all outdoor vernacular plays with religious subjects, and so prefers to use it for both plays about saints and the craft cycle plays.

REFERENCES: Alexander Franklin (ed.), *Seven Miracle Plays;* E. K. Chambers, *The Medieval Stage;* Hardin Craig, *English Religious Drama;* Karl Young, *Drama of the Medieval Church;* Harold C. Gardiner, *Mysteries' End;* Allardyce Nicoll, *Masques, Mimes and Miracles;* Arnold Williams, *The Drama of Medieval England;* A. P. Rossiter, *English Drama from Early Times to the Elizabethans; Cambridge History of English Literature,* Vol. V.

miscellany   An ANTHOLOGY, or collection, of literary pieces, the most celebrated being *Songs and Sonnets* (1557), selected by Richard Tottel and frequently referred to as *Tottel's Miscellany.* One of the anthologist's chief purposes is to give pleasure by tempting the reader's appetite with a smorgasbord representative of the fare. No sensible anthologist has ever intended his sampling to replace the main courses.

misplaced modifier   The misplacement of modifying elements causes remarkable trouble in English, even for accomplished writers. The fault produces an unwanted ambiguity, sometimes laughable but at other times simply misleading. Careful writers are constantly alert to the misplaced modifier that causes either laughter or confusion. "Look at that ridiculous lady's hat," writes the careless scribbler, producing what is either slanderous or slovenly. He redeems himself in the revision, however, making it "Look at that lady's ridiculous hat."

No serious trouble arises from a misplaced modifier that draws a laugh; for the laugh shows that the reader saw around the blunder and knows what was meant: "I want a car like the one I saw driven by the blonde with a convertible top and a flashy paint job." The writer is understood, but ridiculed. When the misplacement draws no laugh, the writer's meaning may be taken wrongly, and communication breaks down. What is a reader to make of "You can't charm a woman with money"?

Misplacement of modifiers is a perilous trap for the writer who may know what he intends, but who gives no thought to the reader. Even a great writer sometimes nods, as does William Faulkner in this example from *The Bear:* ". . . and he broke a plate-glass window that cost McCaslin forty-five dollars and hit a negro woman who happened to be passing in the leg. . . . " It was a pistol shot, not the plate-glass window, that hit the woman—and the woman was not "passing in the leg" but hit in the leg. (See SQUINTER.)

mixed metaphor   The thoughtless use of more than one METAPHOR in a context so that incongruous images are brought to mind; for example, "The critic hammered out a slashing review." Since hammers do not slash, the writer shows that he has not considered what he is saying. Often such mixtures involve CLICHÉS, or FADED METAPHORS, since the thoughtless writer is seldom original. An example from a newscaster's remarks: "Another of the Communists' red herrings has come home to roost."

mnemonics   Devices for assisting the memory. Mnemonics are often used by students who must remember detailed lists with each item in its proper place or order; for example, students of astronomy remember the order of stellar classifications by the sentence, "Oh, be a fine girl, kiss me right now, smack," in which the initial letters form the sequence O B A F G K M R N S. Mnemonics are also useful in remembering the correct spelling of many English words. (See SPELLING.)

mock epic   A poem that treats a trivial subject in an EPIC manner. The mock epic ridicules its subject, however fashionable, by contrasting obvious triviality of subject with grandeur of treatment; it is a form of SATIRE. Famous examples are Dryden's *Absalom and Achitophel,* Pope's *Rape of the Lock,* and Butler's *Hudibras.* Chaucer's "Nun's Priest's Tale" also contains elements of the mock epic. A broader synonym of mock epic is *mock heroic.*

REFERENCE: Richard P. Bond, *English Burlesque Poetry 1700–1750.*

mode   1. In grammar, a synonym for *mood.* 2. In literature, a general label for specific categories of treatment, such as romance, COMEDY, TRAGEDY, IRONY, ALLEGORY, POLEMIC, SATIRE. In contemporary literary criticism, mode is distinguished from GENRE, which pertains to such literary forms as NOVEL, PLAY, STORY. **3.** In Northrop Frye's theory of modes, romance, comedy, tragedy, and irony comprise, in that order, a hierarchy of complexity.

REFERENCES: Northrop Frye, *The Educated Imagination;* Arthur M. Clark, *Studies in Literary Modes;* Ashley Brown and J. L. Kinney (eds.), *Modes of Literature* (series); Lawrence S. Hall, "Modes," *A Grammar of Literary Criticism;* Austin Warren and René Wellek, *Theory of Literature.*

molossus   See METER.

monologue   An extended speech by one person; a passage or a work written to be spoken by one person only. (See DRAMATIC MONOLOGUE.)

morality play   A late medieval popular play in which the characters are virtues and vices personified, such as Temperance and Greed. The best-known morality play is *Everyman* (ca. 1500), in which the titular lead represents the common man, just as does Christian in Bunyan's allegory, *The Pilgrim's Progress.* In another morality play, *The Castle of Perseverance,* such characters as World, Flesh, and Devil (along with retinues of minor-vice characters) vie for the Soul (a separate character) of Man (another character).

REFERENCES: E. K. Chambers, *The Medieval Stage;* G. P. Oust, *Literature and Pulpit in Medieval England;* John Quincy Adams (ed.), *Chief Pre-Shakespearian Dramas;* A. P. Rossiter, *English Drama From Early Times To the Elizabethans.*

motif   A recurring symbol, expression, or feature (e.g., the love potion that redeems for humanity a person temporarily bestialized). See Stith Thompson, *Motif Index of Folk Literature.*

muse   In Greek mythology, any of the nine goddesses who preside over the arts and some of the sciences: Calliope (epic poetry), Clio (history), Erato (love lyrics), Euterpe (music and songs), Melpomene (tragedy), Polyhymnia (sacred songs), Terpsichore (dance), Thalia (comedy and pastoral poetry), and Urania (astronomy).

mystery play   See MIRACLE PLAY and CRAFT CYCLE PLAYS.

myth   **1.** A traditional narrative of unknown authorship concerning supernatural persons and events. Different from LEGEND (or debased history) and closer to FOLKLORE, myth tends to concentrate on explanations for natural phenomena (compare ANIMISM). Thus the stories about the Greek god Zeus (also the Roman Jupiter and the Norse Odin) seek to explain thunder and lightning; the stories of Ceres and Gaea, to explain spring and fertility; and the stories of Apollo and Daphne, to explain the sunrise following the dawn. (See also ARCHETYPE, especially regarding the seasons.) A whole series of myths attempts to account for certain constellations as deifications of former mortal heroes. PERSONIFICATION and ALLEGORY appear in almost all myth, as distinguished from SAGA, which deals with the exploits of more or less historical persons, and as distinguished from FABLE and fairy tale, which are designed to teach a moral lesson.

REFERENCES: Thomas Bullfinch, *Mythology* [Nordic as well as classical]; Robert Graves (ed.), *Larousse Encyclopedia of Mythology* [contains myths of many different cultures, especially Oriental]; Edith Hamilton, *Mythology;* Paul Harvey (ed.), *The Oxford Companion to Classical Literature;* James Frazer, *The Golden Bough* [a comparative study of different cultures and primitive religions with respect to one major myth and its variations—the myth of the birth, death, and resurrection of fertility, as symbolized in the search for the golden fleece]. The College English Association chapbook *On the Mythological,* edited by Kathleen Raine, contains a "Selected Bibliography of Myth in Literature" by James McPeek.

2. A second kind of myth, more recent than the first, and of identifiable authorship, is the "mythical system" or "mythical world" created mostly in fiction. This kind of world is characterized by moral assumptions (though not necessarily by DIDACTICISM) and its demigods and demigoddesses are endowed with more of the frailties and fewer of the heroic qualities of classical gods and goddesses. In Faulkner's mythical world of Yoknapatawpha County, for example, the Compsons and the Sartorises represent the decadent old aristocracy of the South, while the Snopeses represent first the poor whites, then the social-climbing and callous mercantile whites, lacking in agrarian grace, conscience, and sensibility. Similarly, Al Capp has created in his cartoons the mythical world of Dogpatch County, where L'il Abner and Daisie Mae predominate in the roles of back-country, half-literate satyr and nymph. Perhaps the subtlest creations of mythical worlds are those of J. R. R. Tolkien, a former Oxford professor of philology. In *The Hobbit* (1937) gnomelike creatures act out, almost as in an allegory, the all-too-human struggle between good and evil. Aside from the hierarchy of hobbits, dwarves, elves, trolls, and goblins, Tolkien's mythological worlds (among them "Middle Earth") are re-created out of an ingenious mix of contemporary and medieval language and symbols.

REFERENCES: David Miller, "The Moral Universe of J. R. R. Tolkien," *Mankato Studies in English* (Spring, 1967); John Steinbeck (ed.), *The World of L'il Abner;* Malcolm Cowley, "Faulkner's Mythical Kingdom," in the Introduction to *The Viking Portable Faulkner;* John B. Vickery (ed.), *Myth and Literature;* Paul Olson, *The Uses of Myth;* Ernest Cassirer, *Philosophy of Symbolic Forms;* Mark Schorer, "The Necessity of Myth," in Richard W. Lid (ed.), *Grooving the Symbol.*

3. In expository essays, especially those dealing with social and anthropological issues, the term *myth* is often used in a derogatory sense to describe certain popular superstitions—for example, "the myth of progress" and "the myth of success." Indiscriminate use of

the term can be explosive, however, since one person's "myth" may be another's religious conviction.

REFERENCES: W. G. Sumner, *Folkways;* Richard Chase, *Quest for Myth;* Claude Levi-Strauss, "Time Regained," *The Savage Mind.*

mythopoetics 1. In poetry and fiction, especially in a series of novels or poems, the creation by an author of a mythical world. The creation of such a mythical world, in which the cultural context helps to explain the behavior, assumptions, and the interrelatedness of the characters, usually requires a broad canvas, the extension of space and time in several novels, stories, or poems. William Faulkner created in his novels and short stories the world of Yoknapatawpha County. Smaller mythical universes have been created by Edgar Lee Masters (Spoon River), Sherwood Anderson (Winesburg, Ohio), Edwin Arlington Robinson (Tilbury Town), and the cartoonist Al Capp (Dogpatch County). Another kind of mythopoetic world is the complex system which the poet Yeats developed to explain human history, man, and his place in the universe. This system, which he outlined in *A Vision,* forms the basis of many of his later poems. The mythopoetic world that an author creates almost always reflects his social criticism and his VISION OF LIFE.

2. In literary criticism mythopoetics is the critic's interpretation (*a*) of the mythical world that an author has created—for example, Faulkner's Yoknapatawpha County; or (*b*) of certain ARCHETYPES consciously or unconsciously re-created—for example, the hero's JOURNEY on a boat or raft through a life of symbolic ordeals, as in *Moby-Dick, The Heart of Darkness,* and *The Adventures of Huckleberry Finn.* Freudian critics tend to interpret literary myths as mechanisms of *individuals'* wish-fulfillments; Jungian critics tend to interpret literary myths as reflections or echoes of the unconscious dreams of the whole human race. (See ARCHETYPE.) In literary criticism an interpreter may also call attention to an author's conscious or unconscious re-creation, in a character, of a classical mythological character. Thus a critic may well call Melville's *Billy Budd* a "modern myth," in which Billy is a re-creation of Apollo. For Billy shares with Apollo such characteristics as youth, physical attractiveness, innocence, aesthetic sensitivity, absolute purity of moral behavior—especially avoidance of vengeance except for automatic involuntary (and deadly) reaction to evil—the need for expiation of guilt-feelings, involuntary magnetism, and qualities of the NOBLE SAVAGE. Another interpreter may compare Billy with Jesus, especially in the final episode, in which Billy is executed and his shipmates take small chips and relics of the crucifix-like yardarm.

REFERENCES: Otto Rank, *The Myth of the Birth of the Hero;* Carl Jung,

Archetypes and the Collective Unconscious; Northrop Frye, "Archetypes of Literature," *In Fables of Identity;* Norman O. Brown, *Life Against Death;* Richard Chase, *Quest for Myth;* Maud Bodkin, *Archetypal Patterns in Poetry;* J. B. Vickery (ed.), *Myth and Literature: Contemporary Theory and Practice;* Hugh Dickenson, *Myth on the Modern Stage.*

N

name-calling   The pursuit of arguments, campaigns, or advancements by negative means, not by supporting one's own cause so much as by attacking that of an opponent or by attacking the opponent himself. The technique is to "smear" the opponent by attaching abusive labels to him and his cause: "Friends, don't be *taken in* by the *deceptive appearance* of my *fast-talking* opponent and his *gang* of *henchmen* from *out of town*. They have come *sneaking* down here to *conceal the truth* and *rob* us of all we hold dear." The name-caller may go as far as to label his opponent "Communist," "Fascist," "atheist," "misguided," or anything with an unfavorable connotation. (See PROPAGANDA DEVICES.)

narration   Storytelling. Perhaps the central method of literature, narration primarily reports action—focusing upon events in their concrete reality. The causes and the meanings of those events are, of course, necessary to the ultimate value of the story; but good narrative *presents* the action and does not merely *tell about* it.

Since no narrative can report all of life's events, narration depends for its success upon the writer's skill in selecting details and organizing them in a clear and meaningful sequence.

From the time of Aristotle the pattern of narration has been much discussed but little changed by writers and critics. It is generally agreed that a good story must have three parts—beginning, middle, and end. In the *beginning* the writer sets the stage and introduces all that the reader needs to know for full appreciation of the story—that is, he accomplishes the EXPOSITION. In the *middle* the writer builds tension and suspense through COMPLICATION. In the *end* the writer resolves the tension, bringing the events to some satisfactory conclusion, or DÉNOUEMENT. (See DRAMATIC STRUCTURE.)

Effectiveness in narration depends much upon proper choice and maintenance of a POINT OF VIEW—that is, a well-defined "window" through which the reader views the story's events. The window is, more properly, the mind and eye of a narrator—a person who sees and reveals the events of the story, often tempering them by his own attitudes and limitations.

In telling a story, a speaker or writer actually blends with narration some other forms of discourse—DESCRIPTION, EXPOSITION, even ARGUMENTATION occasionally. But always his focus is upon the events themselves in their vivid concreteness, and the descriptions and explanations are designed only to enhance the narrative.

Literary forms whose method is chiefly narration include the ANEC-DOTE (often the joke), the tale, the SHORT STORY, the NOVEL, the NOVELLA, the NOVELETTE, the narrative poem, the BALLAD, the EPIC, the news report, the historical report, the DIARY, and the BIOGRAPHY, including AUTOBIOGRAPHY. (Compare DRAMATIC STRUCTURE.)

REFERENCES: Caroline Gordon, *How to Read a Novel;* Gertrude Stein, *Narration;* Robert Scholes and R. Kellog, *The Nature of Narration;* Leo Braudy, *Narrative Form in History and Fiction.*

narrative hook   A device by which a writer initially catches the interest of his reader. Since a story (with people in action) normally catches interest most effectively of all literary forms, the writer or speaker who begins by relating an incident or ANECDOTE has a head start toward holding attention. The narrative hook is used by public speakers, teachers, ministers, writers of nonfiction—by virtually anyone who has an audience to capture, whether his form of discourse be chiefly NARRATION, EXPOSITION, or ARGUMENTATION. The device is typified (but not shown at its best) by the hackneyed opening, "A funny thing happened to me on my way to the . . . ."

naturalism   1. In philosophy, the ancient Greek beginnings of scientific realism. 2. In literature, especially fiction, the representation of life in its most depraved and sordid aspects, times, and places. Thus reading a naturalistic novel can sometimes be like riding through a sewer in a glass-bottomed boat. The chief tenet of the literary naturalists is that man is a helpless pawn of his environment, and their primary concern is with people from poor and ugly environments. The naturalistic movement in modern times is generally said to have started with the French novelist Emile Zola (1840–1902), author of *Nana* and *Germinal.* The novels of Theodore Dreiser (1871–1945) are prevailingly naturalistic, especially *An American Tragedy* and *Sister Carrie.* Upton Sinclair's *Jungle* and Sinclair Lewis's *Elmer Gantry* are other celebrated examples. Naturalism is to be distinguished from REALISM, with which it is sometimes confused. Realism, like naturalism, is often concerned with the more sordid sides of human existence, but not exclusively and not for the same reasons. Literary realists try to depict life as it is—both good and bad—and are not necessarily concerned with the importance of environment.

Naturalistic novelists and the more recent secular existentialists believe that environment and universe are indifferent, if not hostile, to mankind. But the existentialists, like the humanists, imply (as does Camus in *The Stranger* and *The Plague*) that man has a moral responsibility toward man. (See EXISTENTIALISM and HUMANISM.)

REFERENCES: Edward Stone, *What Was Naturalism?* Lars Ahnebrink, *The Beginnings of Naturalism in American Fiction;* Charles Walcutt, *The Rise of*

Literary Naturalism; William Kimball, "Naturalism in Some Representative American Authors," *Venture* (April, 1969); Gifford Davis, "The Spanish Debate over Idealism and Realism before the Impact of Zola's Naturalism," *PMLA* (October, 1969).

nature   1. The physical world—mountains, meadows, brooks, woods, birds, and so on—with which such authors as Wordsworth, Emerson, and Thoreau "commune"; also called *external nature.* Wordsworth, like many another romantic idealist, believed that by "communing with Nature," one could discover oneself. Thus he believed in Nature as a kind of teacher, or at least a source of inspiration: "One impulse from a vernal wood / May teach you more of man / Of moral evil and of good / Than all the sages can." In this respect Wordsworth was one of the spiritual ancestors of Ralph Waldo Emerson, who says in his essay "Nature": "Give me health and a day, and I will make the pomp of emperors ridiculous." Perhaps the most celebrated literary work in praise of the great out-of-doors and the simple life is Thoreau's *Walden* (1854). In it he says, "I went to the woods because I wished to live deliberately, to front only the essential facts of life, and see if I could not learn what it had to teach, and not, when I came to die, discover that I had not lived." 2. For notions related to "human nature," see HUMANISM and NOBLE SAVAGE. 3. In literary criticism "holding the mirror up to nature" is one aspect of MIMESIS.

REFERENCES: Joseph Warren Beach, *The Concept of Nature in Nineteenth-Century English Poetry;* A. O. Lovejoy, *The Great Chain of Being;* John Arthos, *The Language of Natural Description in Eighteenth Century Poetry.*

near-rhyme   The same as oblique-rhyme, off-rhyme, slant-rhyme. (See RHYME.)

negative to affirmative   See SYLLOGISM I H.

negative capability   A term introduced by the poet John Keats and used in several of his letters, especially those to his brothers George and Thomas and to his friends Benjamin Bailey and Benjamin Haydon. In the letter of December 21, 1817, Keats said, "I had not a dispute but a disquisition with [Charles] Dilke on various subjects; . . . at once it struck me what quality went to form a Man of Achievement, especially in Literature, and which Shakespeare possessed so enormously . . . I mean *Negative Capability;* that is, when a man is capable of being in uncertainties, mysteries, doubts, without any irritable reaching after fact and reason. . . ." Thus the term *negative capability* has all too often been misinterpreted to mean "a negative attitude toward ideas." But as Lionel Trilling has observed, Keats repeatedly used the term to refer to "a way of dealing with life"—"to make up one's mind about nothing—to let the mind be a thoroughfare for all thoughts"; to let the subconscious do its work and not "try too hard in coming at a truth." Another of Keats's ways of approaching experience—a way closely related to negative capability, as Aileen Ward has observed— was to let go of one's own preconceived notions and to "identify with the object . . . to imagine the inner life of the object itself. . . . This ability was not only the source of a great secret joy and the wellspring of his poetry but also the one thing sure among the uncertainty and incompleteness of experience."

REFERENCES: Lionel Trilling, "Introduction," *The Selected Letters of John Keats;* Aileen Ward, *John Keats, The Making of a Poet;* Walter Jackson Bate, *Negative Capability.*

Negro literature See BLACK LITERATURE.

Neo-Classicism The CLASSICISM of the RESTORATION and eighteenth century; a reaction against the extravagant theater and the lyrical brilliance of the RENAISSANCE. The period of Neo-Classicism closed with the beginnings of ROMANTICISM toward the end of the eighteenth century.

One of the chief differences between the classicism of the Renaissance and that of the Restoration and later was that the Restoration writers returned to classical models in an almost slavish imitation. (Renaissance classicists had used classical models as springboards for individualistic departures.) Another difference—and perhaps the fundamental philosophic difference undergirding all others—was in the attitude toward man. Whereas the Renaissance classicists had viewed man idealistically and humanistically as an individual with limitless possibilities, the Restoration and eighteenth-century Neo-Classicists viewed man, somewhat more realistically, as embodying evil and good, idleness and initiative, etc. The Neo-Classicists (among them, Dryden, Pope, and Swift) extolled such virtues—checks and balances—as Order, Discipline, Rules, Reason, Decorum, Good Taste, etc., which they did not hesitate to capitalize in their essays and verses. They also discouraged such suspect virtues as imagination, invention, innovation, emotion, and the like. As a consequence, intellect, METAPHYSICAL wit, and so on, in the late 1600s and the early 1700s became the rage. Classical models of prose and verse were openly imitated. Interest in design and form gained an ascendancy over interest in IMAGERY and emotional language with some few exceptions.

REFERENCES: Walter Jackson Bate, "Neoclassic Developments and Reactions," *Prefaces to Criticism;* George Sherburn, *The Restoration and the Eighteenth Century;* Louis Bredvold, *The Intellectual Milieu of Dryden;* James R. Sutherland, *A Preface to Eighteenth-Century Poetry;* Ian Jack, *Augustan Satire.*

New Critics Originally, such American writers as John Crowe Ransom, Allen Tate, R. P. Blackmur, Robert Penn Warren, and Cleanth Brooks (in England, T. S. Eliot, I. A. Richards, and William Empson), who revolted against the nineteenth-century school of biographical critics. Whereas the earlier critics had based their interpretations of literary masterpieces not only on the works themselves, but also on biographical and historical backgrounds (MILIEU) and other external influences, the new critics insisted on interpretations supported mostly by the literary works themselves ("close reading of the text"). The new critics rejected external "facts" and scientific positivism, insisting that a masterwork of literature creates its own facts, logic, and integrity — that form and content interact inextricably. Such criticism is no longer new, of course, and it claims numerous devotees. Nor do these writers regard themselves as "critics" so much as interpreters, "readers," and "explicators." Among the concepts of the new criticism: AESTHETIC DISTANCE, AMBIGUITY, BIOGRAPHICAL FALLACY, DRAMATISM, INTENTIONAL FALLACY, EXPLICATION DE TEXTE, and MYTHOPOETICS.

REFERENCES: John Crowe Ransom, *The New Criticism;* I. A. Richards, *Practical Criticism;* William Elton, *A Glossary of the New Criticism;* Ezra Pound, *The ABC of Reading;* Cleanth Brooks, *The Well-Wrought Urn;* Allen Tate, *On the Limits of Poetry;* R. P. Blackmur, *The Lion and the Honeycomb;* Cleanth Brooks and Robert Penn Warren, *Understanding Poetry* and *Understanding Fiction;* Kenneth Burke, *The Philosophy of Literary Form;* René Wellek and Austin Warren, *Theory of Literature;* Joel Spingarn, "The New Criticism," in B. S. Oldsey and A. O. Lewis, Jr. (eds.), *Visions and Revisions.*

New Humanism   A short-lived movement (ca. 1910–30) in literary criticism, led by Irving Babbitt, Paul Elmer More, and Norman Foerster, in reaction against NATURALISM, ROMANTICISM, and the kind of realism inspired by Freud and Marx. The patron saint of this movement was Matthew Arnold, especially the nostalgic models provided by "Dover Beach" and *Culture and Anarchy.* One of the leaders of this movement had branded the novels of Dreiser and Dos Passos as "cesspools." The New Humanists argued for a return to restraint and reason, but a humane reason as opposed to the cold reason of science and logical positivism. However, with the advent of the NEW CRITICISM, Freudian and Marxian ideas, and the fiction of the 1940s, 1950s, and 1960s, the New Humanism became hopelessly outmoded and almost forgotten. (Compare HUMANISM and EXISTENTIALISM.)

REFERENCES: Paul Elmer More, *Shelburne Essays;* Norman Foerster, *American Criticism;* Irving Babbitt, *Rousseau and Romanticism.*

Nobel Prize   Since 1901, an annual prize in literature (among other fields) of about $50,000 awarded by the Swedish Academy in Stockholm to a writer of "idealistic works." The award was established by Alfred Nobel (1833–96), a Swedish chemical engineer. Writers in English who have won the prize are Rudyard Kipling (1907), William Butler Yeats (1923), Bernard Shaw (1925), John Galsworthy (1932), T. S. Eliot (1948), Bertrand Russell (1950), Winston Churchill (1953), and six Americans—Sinclair Lewis (1930), Eugene O'Neill (1936), Pearl Buck (1938), William Faulkner (1949), Ernest Hemingway (1954), and John Steinbeck (1962). Other notable recipients have been Thomas Mann, André Gide, Albert Camus, and Boris Pasternak. Jean-Paul Sartre was awarded the prize in 1965, but declined to accept it. The Irish author Samuel Beckett, winner of the prize in 1969, was also exceptional, since his works were originally written in French, but were translated by him into English.

REFERENCES: Warren French, *American Winners of the Nobel Literary Prize;* Marshall McClintock (ed.), *The Nobel Prize Treasury;* Horst Frenz (ed.), *Nobel Prize Lectures in Literature (1901-1967).*

noble savage   **1.** The idol of Jean-Jacques Rousseau (1712–78) and certain romantic primitivists, who believed the savage in his innocence to be more admirable than the civilized man. **2.** A literary cult based on this creed. James Fenimore Cooper seems to have been a devotee of the noble savage, as reflected in *The Last of the Mohicans* and the other *Leatherstocking Tales.* In *Billy Budd* Herman Melville invests Billy with all the virtues of an unspoiled child of nature (Billy was a natural child in more ways than one) and depicts him as a foil against the villainous Claggart, the "civilized" officer unable to accept "natural perfectibility." (Compare and contrast PALEFACE AND REDSKIN.) For a citizen's savage attack on the "noble savage," read Irving Babbitt, *Rousseau and Romanticism.*

REFERENCES: Jean-Jacques Rousseau, *Emile;* Roy Harvey Pearce, *Savagism and Civilization;* Franz Boas, *Mind of Primitive Man;* Claude Levi-Strauss, *The Savage Mind;* Peter Collier (ed.), *Crisis: A Contemporary Reader.*

nonce word   A word coined for a specific occasion and not likely to be applicable again; one useful only for the nonce, for the present.

nonfiction   Such prose as articles, autobiography, biography, essays, history, and the like.

non sequitur   A conclusion that does not follow logically from its premises or from the evidence offered to support it. One kind of non sequitur is the POST HOC. (See CAUSAL REASONING.)

note-taking   See RESEARCH PAPER and DOCUMENTATION.

noun-banging   The stringing together of nouns used attributively. "The party platform committee rules argument" is the noun-banger's way of describing an argument over the rules of debate between members of a committee assembled to write the platform of a political party. In the hands of an expert noun-banger, "missile guidance center" may become, progressively, "missile guidance center personnel," "missile guidance center personnel office," "missile guidance center personnel office equipment," and even "missile guidance center personnel office equipment maintenance." Such compounds may be perfectly clear to those knowledgeable in the subject; but often what is gained in conciseness is canceled by an increase in ambiguity. (Compare NOUNIFICATION.)

nounification   1. The pretentious or thoughtless making of nouns by adding a suffix such as *-ion*, *-ance*, *-ment*, *-ness*, or *-ity* to verbs and other forms; and, generally, the use of more nouns than are needed. "State" becomes "make a *statement*"; "recognize" becomes "give *recognition* to"; "forgive" becomes "extend *forgiveness* to." Often a short noun is made verb by the adding of a suffix and then reconverted into noun by the adding of another suffix: "noun" becomes "nounify," then nounificate," then "nounification." The habit is characteristic of GOBBLEDYGOOK. 2. The awkward or ambiguous stringing together of nouns that end in *-ion;* for example, "complication of the production of solutions by the administration." One of the ways of clarifying such an utterance is to use definite agent-subjects and simple verbs; e.g., "Administrators complicate problems when they try to solve them." (See AGENT.)

novel   A long prose narrative comprising, usually, one hundred thousand words or more and seldom less than fifty thousand. Though prose narratives, LEGENDS, FABLES, and TALES were written and circulated from earliest times, the serious development of the novel started in eighteenth-century England with the rise of the mercantile middle class. Henry Fielding, author of *Tom Jones,* defined the novel as a "comic epic romance in prose." By "comic" he implied that it contained not only humor and WIT but also happy resolutions of problems. By "epic" he implied that its hero reflected the culture, customs, and aspirations of his nation or race. (See EPIC.) By "romance" he implied both amorous and heroic adventures. By "prose" he implied (*a*) that romance need not be confined, as it had been in previous centuries, to verse and (*b*) that this new form of fiction contained such nonfiction as essays and philosophic comment. Since the eighteenth century, novels have been more or less true to Fielding's definition, though many have experimented with STREAM OF CONSCIOUSNESS, PHYCHOLOGICAL INTROSPECTION, and so on. (See ANTINOVEL.)

Novels often nominated as "greatest" include *Tom Jones* (Henry Fielding), *Vanity Fair* (William Makepeace Thackery), *David Copperfield* (Charles Dickens), *The Scarlet Letter* (Nathaniel Hawthorne), *Moby-Dick* (Herman Melville), *Madame Bovary* (Gustave Flaubert), *War and Peace* (Leo Tolstoy), *Crime and Punishment* (Feodor Dostoevsky), *Middlemarch* (George Eliot), *The Return of the Native* (Thomas Hardy), *The Adventures of Huckleberry Finn* (Mark Twain),

The Red Badge of Courage (Stephen Crane), *The Wings of the Dove* (Henry James), *Sons and Lovers* (D. H. Lawrence), and *Ulysses* (James Joyce).

REFERENCES: Caroline Gordon, *How to Read a Novel;* Bradford Booth, "The Novel," in Lewis Leary (ed.), *Contemporary Literary Scholarship;* Cleanth Brooks and Robert Penn Warren, *Understanding Fiction;* Wayne Booth, *The Rhetoric of Fiction;* Edward Wagenknecht, *Cavalcade of the English Novel* and *Cavalcade of the American Novel;* Ernest Baker, *The History of the English Novel;* Ian Watt, *The Rise of the Novel;* Dorothy Van Ghent, *The English Novel;* Richard Chase, *The American Novel and Its Tradition;* Joseph Warren Beach, *The Twentieth Century Novel: Studies in Technique;* Frederick Karl, *The Contemporary English Novel;* Chester Eisinger, [*American*] *Fiction of the Forties;* John W. Aldridge (ed.), *Critiques and Essays on Modern Fiction;* Philip Stevick (ed.), *The Theory of the Novel;* Elizabeth Hardwick, "Reflection on Fiction," *The New York Review of Books* (February 13, 1969); Alain Robbe-Grillet, *For a New Novel: Essays in Fiction.*

novelette   A short novel (fifteen to fifty thousand words, approximately). A more serious art form than the novella, the novelette blends the unity of effect of the short story with a little more of the scope of the novel and much of its psychological introspection. Among the masterpieces of this form are *Benito Cereno* (Herman Melville), *The Death of Ivan Ilych* (Leo Tolstoy), *A Simple Heart* (Gustave Flaubert), *Notes from Underground* (Feodor Dostoevsky), *Abel Sanchez* (Miguel Unamuno), *The Heart of Darkness* (Joseph Conrad), *The Beast in the Jungle* (Henry James), *The Metamorphosis* (Franz Kafka), *Death in Venice* (Thomas Mann), *The Pastoral Symphony* (André Gide), *The Fox* (D. H. Lawrence), *Agostino* (Alberto Moravia), *The Old Man* (William Faulkner), *The Morning Watch* (James Agee), *The Old Man and the Sea* (Ernest Hemingway), and *Seize the Day* (Saul Bellow). One hesitates to add Katherine Anne Porter's *Noon Wine.* For—as distinguished from such terms as *short stories, long stories, short novels,* and *novels*—the term *novelette* (like the term NOVELLA 2) is controversial and strikes some people as a derogation. Miss Porter, for example, says in the Preface to her *Collected Stories* (1965), "Please do not call my short novels *novelettes* or even worse, *novellas. Novelette* is classical usage for a trivial dime-novel sort of thing; *novella* is a slack, boneless, affected word that we do not need to describe anything." Nevertheless, the term *novelette* persists in contemporary currency, for better or worse, as a synonym for *short novel.*

REFERENCES: Leo Hamalian and Edmond Volpe (eds.), *Ten Modern Short Novels;* Charles Neider (ed.), *Short Novels of the Masters;* R. C. Albrecht, *The World of Short Fiction.*

novella   1. In medieval and early Renaissance literature, a piece of fiction (about ten to fifteen thousand words) of Italian or French origin and mostly about adulterous intrigues. Representative collections of such *novelle* that later found their way into English translation are Boccaccio's *Decameron* (1353) and Margaret of Navarre's *Heptameron* (1558). Many a novella from the *Decameron* and the *Heptameron* appeared, for example, in William Painter's collection, *Palace of Pleasure* (1566). 2. In modern literature, a long story of about the same length as its Renaissance prototype (not a condensed novel). That it has "poetic insights" and "treats an unusual occurrence," as Goethe observed, hardly distinguishes it from other fictional genres, and Katherine Anne Porter has suggested abolishing the term altogether. (See NOVELETTE.)

O

obiter dicta   Casual but sophisticated comments or observations made in passing.

objective correlative   1. The image undergirding a metaphor or literary symbol. 2. That kind of artistic selectivity which re-creates an experience by means of referent objects and images rather than by subjective comment; a term introduced by T. S. Eliot to name a set of objects or chain of events selected by the artist to call up a particular emotion in his audience – an emotion appropriate to (correlative with) these objects. Thus Wordsworth instead of observing, "Oh, what a touching picture that reticent girl makes against that rock!" gives us "a violet by a mossy stone." And Shakespeare gives Lady Macbeth unwashable bloody hands to communicate her state of mind during her sleepwalking scene.

REFERENCES: T. S. Eliot, "Hamlet and His Problems," *Collected Essays;* David DeLaura, "Pater and Eliot: The Origins of the Objective Correlative," *Modern Language Quarterly* (September, 1965)

oblique rhyme   Same as near rhyme. (See RHYME.)

obscenity   In literature and the arts, a value judgment of whether a work can be demonstrated to be pornographic (from the Greek words *graphein,* "to write," and *porne,* "prostitute"); that is, whether a work can be demonstrated to be specifically and commercially designed to incite antisocial sexual acts. In courts of law the writer's *intention* is one of the chief criteria for deciding whether to ban or not to ban a book. The responsible attorney, whether prosecuting or defending, seeks evidence in answer to the question, "Does this book tend to make the normal reader (as distinguished from the pervert) more human or less human?" The question, echoing a tenet of Aristotle's theory of CATHARSIS, to say nothing of Freudian repression theory, is extremely difficult to answer. The answer, in fact, varies from time to time, from place to place, depending on the background of the judge; and a decision by one judge does not necessarily set an irreversible precedent.

However, the celebrated decision in 1933 by Judge John Woolsey of the United States District Court in New York (Southern District), lifting the ban on James Joyce's novel *Ulysses,* seems to have set a precedent in the interpretation of such criteria as *intention* and *normal reader.* Judge Woolsey exonerated *Ulysses* on the grounds that (*a*) its intention was "not pornographic – not dirt for dirt's sake" but rather "a serious and sincere attempt to devise a new literary method for the observation and description of mankind"; (*b*) the normal reader is "a person with average sex instincts . . . what the French would call *l'homme moyen sensuel* [average sensual man] who plays the same role . . . as does the 'reasonable man' in the law of torts. . . ." Judge Woolsey had, moreover, consulted two friends whose literary judgment he respected, and he

> was delighted to find [he wrote in his decision] that they both agreed . . . that reading *Ulysses* in its entirety, as a book must be read in such a test as this, did not tend to excite . . . lustful thoughts but that its net effect on them was only that of a somewhat tragic and very powerful commentary on the inner lives of men and women.

Notice that to the criteria mentioned above there is now added the criterion of a work "read in its entirety" and not of bits and pieces taken out of context. Thus the mere presence of sexual scenes and Saxon four-letter words in a literary work does not by itself necessarily mark the work as a whole obscene.

Another milestone case involving an interpretation of the intention criterion occurred in 1968, when the Supreme Court decided against the editor of *Eros* magazine on the grounds that his advertisements tended toward the obscenity of pandering. But perhaps the most celebrated court decision on the issue of obscenity was handed down in 1946 by Supreme Court Justice William O. Douglas in favor of *Esquire* magazine. Here is a key excerpt from the decision:

> Under our present system of government there is an accommodation for the widest varieties of tastes and ideas. What is good literature, what has educational value, what is refined public information, what is good art—each of these considerations varies with individuals as it does from one generation to another. There doubtless would be a contrariety of views concerning Cervantes' *Don Quixote,* Shakespeare's *Venus and Adonis,* or Zola's *Nana.* But a requirement that literature or art conform to some norm prescribed by an official smacks of an ideology foreign to our system.

Basic premises among cultivated people, finally, include the following: (1) The sex act can and should be treated in literature and life with a sense of responsibility. (2) Books and advertisements written specifically and commercially to incite antisocial sex acts are obscene. (3) Written pandering is as obscene as oral pandering. (4) Even more obscene crimes against humanity are bigotry, slavery, murder, genocide, and war.

REFERENCES: John McCormick and Mairi MacInnes (eds.), *Versions of Censorship: An Anthology;* Robert Downs (ed.), *The First Freedom;* Richard McKeon *et al.* (eds.), *The Freedom to Read: Perspective and Program; The Student's Right to Read* (NCTE pamphlet); Norman Podhoretz, "Our Changing Ideals," and Eric Larrabee, "Pornography Is Not Enough," in Irving and Harriet Deer (eds.), *The Popular Arts;* Anne Haight, *Banned Books;* James A. Farrer, *Books Condemned to Be Burned;* Richard Kuh, *Foolish Figleaves: Pornography In and Out of Court;* Lee Burress, "Foolish Figleaves," *The*

English Journal (January, 1969); Wayne Booth, "Censorship and the Values of Fiction," *The English Journal* (March, 1964); John Frank and Robert Hogan, *Obscenity, the Law, and the English Teacher;* Charles Rembar, *The End of Obscenity.*

occasional verse   Verse written for a specific occasion; sometimes by prescription, as by a POET LAUREATE on request, sometimes on the poet's own inspiration, as Milton's "Lycidas" or Spenser's "Epithalamion."

octameter   See METER.

ode   A poem in an elevated manner, usually written for a specific occasion. The odes of the ancient Greek poet Pindar were songs intended to celebrate the victories of athletes at the annual games, though these songs also concern themselves with nobility as a concept. They were sung by a choir to Pindar's own music, while dancers performed an intricate ballet. Although these odes consist generally of three parts—strophe, antistrophe, and epode—within the parts they are so complex and varied as to be more like symphonic music than like poems in stanzaic form. The Pindaric ode has been compared (by Horace) to a rushing mountain stream, swollen by rain and overflowing its banks. It is typically emotional, extravagant, bold, energetic, even at times incoherent. By contrast, the odes of Horace are—as befits the Augustan era in which they were written—more regular, quiet, and polished, though they can be moving nonetheless.

Both Horace and Pindar have inspired great odes in English. The seventeenth-century poet Abraham Cowley wrote some odes that his age called Pindaric, though they do not approximate the Greek poet's work in form. From the same period we have Andrew Marvell's beautiful "Horatian Ode upon Cromwell's Return from Ireland." Other celebrated odes include Milton's "On the Morning of Christ's Nativity," Wordsworth's "Ode on the Intimations of Immortality from Recollections of Early Childhood," Shelley's "Ode to the West Wind," and Keats's "Ode on a Grecian Urn."

REFERENCES: George N. Shuster, *The English Ode from Milton to Keats;* Carol Madison, *Apollo and the Nine;* Gilbert Highet, "The Renaissance and Afterwards: Lyric Poetry," *The Classical Tradition;* David Lee Rubin, "Toward a New View of Malherbe," *Papers of the Midwest MLA* (1969).

officialese   The woolly, impersonal, pedantic, and prolix style of writing often adopted by those who prepare office bulletins or official announcements. (See GOBBLEDYGOOK.)

off-rhyme   The same as near-rhyme, oblique-rhyme, slant-rhyme. (See RHYME.)

onomatopoeia   A sound-effect in which the words sound like what they describe: "The slap, slap, slap, of the lapping pond"; "The murmuring of innumerable bees amongst the immemorial elms."

open book 1. When pronounced /o˘ pən *bŭk* /, a FADED METAPHOR meaning "obvious" or "transparent": "That brother of mine is an open book."

2. When pronounced / *o˘ pən*-buk /, with high pitch and heavier stress on *open,* a synonym for "open-ended," or a work full of intentional AMBIVALENCE and AMBIGUITY, open to various interpretations. (Compare CLOSED.)

operational definition See DEFINING 4.

ottava rima A stanza of eight iambic pentameter lines rhyming *ababcc*. It was used by Ariosto in *Orlando Furioso* and by other poets of the Italian Renaissance, though with lines of eleven syllables. In English it has been used by Spenser, Milton, Keats, and, especially, Byron in *Don Juan:*

He that reserves his laurels for posterity	*a*
(Who does not often claim the bright reversion)	*b*
Has generally no great crop to spare it, he	*a*
Being only injured by his own assertion;	*b*
And although here and there some glorious rarity	*a*
Arise like Titan from the sea's immersion,	*b*
The major part of such appellants go	*c*
To—God knows where, for no one else can know.	*c*

outline A systematic statement of the content of a discourse. The jottings made preliminary to organizing a speech or written work may be a *rough outline,* perhaps loosely indicating the intended relationship and sequence of ideas. But the formal outline is carefully structured.

Outlines are of three types: (1) *topic,* (2) *sentence,* (3) *paragraph.*

1. The *topic outline* indicates the order and relationships of topics within a discourse, doing so by headings and subheadings rather than by full statements.

2. The *sentence outline* is similar in structure to the topic outline, but each of its entries is a complete sentence, affording a fuller development of the subject and the relationships of its parts.

3. The *paragraph outline* follows (or prescribes) the order of paragraphs in a discourse, ordinarily offering as items something very close to the topic sentences of the paragraphs of that discourse. It thus becomes a kind of PRÉCIS.

Each of these types follows a basic system of organization and structure, with topics and subtopics numbered or lettered by rank. Topics of highest rank are assigned Roman numerals I, II, III, ... Then follow items of rank in this order: capital letters, arabic numbers, lower-case letters, arabic numbers in parentheses, lower-case letters in parentheses, lower-case Roman numerals followed by closing parenthesis, and so on.

In skeleton the outline looks like this, each topic of equal rank indented to the same point:

Topic. . . .

I.

   A.

      1.

         a.

           (1)

              (a)

              (b)

           (2)

         b.

      2.

   B.

II.

When properly prepared, the formal outline follows a strict PARALLELISM—each of its items is couched in similar grammatical form. The proper outline also divides each topic or subtopic into *at least two* parts (or divides it not at all)—just as an apple cannot be cut into fewer than two parts. Thus, when I appears, II must also appear; when A appears, B must also.

REFERENCE: Ralph Loewe, *The Practical Writer.*

outlining for interpretive exposition   The following is a useful pattern for a short-statement outline:

Thesis statement: ....
Thesis question: ....
   Answer I: ....
      Support A ....
      Support B ....
      Support n...
   Answer II: ....
      Support A ....
      Support B ....
      Support n...
   Answer n: ....

Filled in, a model outline for a five-hundred-word exposition might look something like this:

Thesis: Lady Macbeth functions less as a believable woman than as Macbeth's own evil self.
Thesis question: How do we know this?
    Answer I: She keeps awakening in him mostly his hitherto unaroused evil desires.
        Support A: "Your face, my thane, is a book where men / May read strange matters."
        Support B: "Was the hope drunk / Wherein you dress'd yourself?"
    Answer II: She keeps egging on only his evil desires once they are aroused.
        Support A: "But screw your courage [to do evil] to the sticking place."
        Support B: "Wouldst thou have that / Which thou esteem'st the ornament of life / And live a coward in thine own esteem?"
    Answer n: She says and does little or nothing else that might identify her particularly as a woman.

overphrasing   See DEADWOOD.

overpredication   See DEADWOOD.

Oxford Movement   A nineteenth-century religious movement that started at Oxford University in 1833. The leaders — John Henry Newman (ultimately a convert to Roman Catholicism, and later a Cardinal), John Keble (author of *The Christian Year*), R. H. Froude (an historian), Charles Mariott, and E. B. Pusey (butt of the EPITHET "Puseyism") — sought to inject new life and spirit into what they regarded as an effete Established Church. They published a series of tracts, *Tracts of Our Times,* that aroused much controversy and that led to the synonym "Tractarian" for the movement. Because one of their chief pleas was for a return to some of the aesthetic rituals of the Roman Catholic Church, the members soon became identified as "Anglo-Catholics." Though this movement was primarily religious rather than literary, it did influence directly and indirectly many literary figures, among them (ultimately) T. S. Eliot.

REFERENCES: R. W. Church, *The Oxford Movement;* H. W. Stewart, *A Century of Anglo-Catholicism.*

oxymoron   Contradictory ideas expressed in as few words as possible; an abbreviated PARADOX. An oxymoron consists, usually, of a noun and its modifier; but the modifier seems to give the noun an attribute quite the opposite of what is normally associated with it. To call someone a *delightful bore* is to use oxymoron. Other examples: *acid sweetness, studied carelessness, eloquent silence, living death, cowardly hero.* For best effect the oxymoron's contradictory words should be immediate constituents, for if they are widely separated, they lose their sharp effect; and the Greek derivation (*oxy* = sharp, pointed; *moron* =

foolish—that is, pointed foolishness) seems to demand sharpness. The oxymoron may appear as an EPITHET when the attribute normally associated with the thing or person is twisted to an opposite: *all-seeing Milton* (for Milton was blind, though only optically); *Little Old New York* (for the city was among the biggest in the world even when the phrase was first used). (See ANTITHESIS.)

P

paean   A song in praise of a person or an event. (Compare DITHY-
RAMB.)

paeon   See METER.

paleface and redskin   Two polar types of writers, chiefly American,
represented on the one hand by Walt Whitman, a "redskin, full of energy," who gloried in his Americanism, and on the other hand by Henry
James, an EXPATRIATE, full of sensibility, who was somewhat ashamed
of his national origin. The following are some other tags of the two
polarities:

Palefaces	Redskins
patrician (highbrow)	plebeian (lowbrow)
civilized	frontier
drawing-room	open-air
lonely	gregarious
disciplined	free-wheeling
conservative	radical
humanistic	naturalistic

REFERENCES: Philip Rahv, "Paleface and Redskin," *Image and Idea;* Leslie
Fiedler, "Prototypes and Early Adaptations," *Love and Death in the American
Novel.*

palindrome   Whether read backward or forward, a palindrome reads
the same (e.g., *radar*). Though of doubtful value, palindromes and
their contrivance have provided brainteasers and parlor games. Among
the longest palindromes devised in English is the now well-known
"Able was I ere I saw Elba." (Compare DICHO.)

parable   An ANECDOTE or very SHORT STORY with an implied or expressed moral. The parables of Jesus are examples, especially those
of "The Prodigal Son" and "The Wise and Foolish Virgins." In modern literature a master of humorous parables has been the essayist
E. B. White. (See, for example, his "The Decline of Sport," in *The
Second Tree from the Corner.*)

REFERENCES: "Prose Forms: Parables," in Arthur Eastman *et al.* (eds.), *The
Norton Reader;* Joachim Jeremias, *The Parables of Jesus.*

paradox   A seeming contradiction; whatever sounds impossible yet
is in fact possible. "It's the little things in life that are colossal," said
G. K. Chesterton (1874–1936), the British essayist and master of
paradox. A paradox is a play on ideas, side-by-side contraries that seem
to clash and reconcile simultaneously. In "Canis Major" Robert Frost
calls the Big Dog constellation "that heavenly beast." (See OXYMORON.)

    Paradoxical ideas provide the theme for serious poetry, for poets
often set out to show that things are not what they seem — that death

is life, that love is hate. Richard Lovelace, in "To Althea, From Prison," writes, "Stone walls do not a prison make"—and in confinement that poet finds freedom. The underlying statement in much poetry is made, and can only be made, by paradox, as Cleanth Brooks observes:

> More direct methods may be tempting, but all of them enfeeble and distort what is to be said. . . . Many of the important things which the poet has to say have to be said by means of paradox:—most of the language of lovers . . . most of the language of religion: "He who would save his life, must lose it"; "The last shall be first."

Perhaps the best-known paradoxes occur in seventeenth-century METAPHYSICAL POETRY, especially that of John Donne. Examples: "that he may raise, the Lord throws down" and "when thou hast done, thou hast not done" (the last word a PUN, of course, on the poet's name).

Paradox brings freshness to otherwise trite truisms: "Youth is wasted on the young," said George Bernard Shaw. "Divorces are made in heaven," says an irreverent character in Oscar Wilde's *Importance of Being Earnest*. Here the shock value underscores the truth as the author sees it.

Nonsensical paradoxes are part of folk sayings, Mother Goose rhymes, riddles, and FOLK SONGS. Among the best-known nonsensical Irish folk paradoxes: "You can't rightly get there from here"; "I would not object to their noise if they would only keep quiet"; "I wouldn't be after parting with it [saucepan] if it wasn't to get money to buy something to put in it."

Paradoxical situations and IRONIES, finally, underlie the structure of great fiction—where, as in the phrasal paradox itself, opposing forces clash.

REFERENCES: Cleanth Brooks, "The Language of Paradox," *The Well-Wrought Urn;* Andrew Wanning, Introduction to the *Laurel Edition of Donne.*

paragraph   A group of sentences that relate to a single topic and are joined in meaningful order to support it. Though the ancient Greeks did not break their pages into indented blocks of type as we do today, the word "paragraph" derives from their habit of marking a turn of thought in writing by a short line in a text, a *paragraphos*—literally, "a writing beside." Today an indention serves the same purpose: to make the organization of thought visible on the printed page.

Good paragraphs are a matter of art rather than of rule; but certain principles underlie art. It is generally conceded that a good paragraph has at least these virtues: (1) *unity,* (2) *coherence,* (3) *adequate development.*

1. *Unity* means singleness of purpose. Traditionally, the paragraph is built upon a *topic sentence*—a presentation of the core thought. But that thought may lie hidden, implicit in the paragraph rather than

openly stated in a "sentence"; it may be only what a reader would say if he were asked to put the essential content of the paragraph into a sentence in his own words. Typically, it offers a generalization that is clarified and supported by the rest of the paragraph. Whether it appears first, last, or in the middle is of little import; the idea in the topic sentence must be narrow enough to be developed adequately in brief space and must form an essential part of the complete theme. A topic sentence is to a paragraph what the "thesis" is to the whole paper. Even when a paragraph contains no *stated* topic sentence, it contains or implies a topic question, a central question. And all or most of the statements that a paragraph does contain answer, or should answer, this topic question. As for appropriate length of a paragraph: it should be just long enough to answer the topic question it raises—and no longer.

2. *Coherence* begins with consistency—the holding to one point of view, one attitude, one tense (or a consistency of tenses); it implies an orderly joining of thought elements into a meaningful pattern. Progression of thought may be chronological, carrying the reader through a series of events in time; spatial, carrying the reader from part to part of a structure or landscape; logical, carrying the reader from a cause to its effects, from a generalization to specific cases, from particulars to a generalization, or from the less to the more important. Coherence is strengthened by artful repetition of syntactical structures (PARALLELISM, BALANCE, ANTITHESIS), of words (including substitution of synonyms or of pronouns for nouns), and even of sounds (ALLITERATION, ASSONANCE, CONSONANCE). Further, coherence is enhanced by careful use of words of TRANSITION and conjunction, so that the ideas in the paragraph are tied to one another through their development.

3. Since good paragraphs are the product of art more than of precept, no writer should inhibit his work by overzealous adherence to rules of *adequate development*. Yet it is helpful to be aware of some common types of paragraphs designed to do special jobs. Among them are paragraphs of (*a*) definition, (*b*) description, (*c*) comparison, (*d*) contrast, (*e*) illustration (by details or examples), (*f*) explanation of cause and effect, (*g*) argument (by evidence and conclusion), (*h*) classification and analysis (by division or enumeration), (*i*) negative detail (elimination of alternatives to an argument), (*j*) restatement, (*k*) transition (leading from one phase of a theme to another). The writer of effective paragraphs does not fear to mix one or more of these techniques in a single paragraph when to do so serves his purpose without violating unity of topic.

Just as the sentences in an effective paragraph relate to a single topic and are linked coherently, so the paragraphs in a theme relate to the

THESIS and are linked to one another like the elephants in a circus parade. Just as each elephant grasps in its trunk the tail of the preceding elephant, good paragraphs pick up the tails of the preceding paragraphs, preserving a parade of thought. Appropriate conjunctions and repeated words and phrases help the writer link his paragraphs. Paragraphs so linked contribute to a composition's unity, coherence, and adequate development.

REFERENCES: "The Expository Paragraph," *Purdue English Notes* (December, 1962); Cleanth Brooks and Robert Penn Warren, *Modern Rhetoric;* Malcolm Moore and Conrad Geller, *Paragraph Development.*

parallelism   The principle in sentence structure that elements of equal function should have equal form. Parallel structures are usually required for:

1. *Coordinates:*

We have *lecture on Monday* and *lab on Tuesday.*
My sister and *my father* will attend.
Will you *ride* or *walk?*
Most Americans see America *at thirty thousand feet* and *at six hundred miles an hour.*

2. *Correlatives:*

We must either *end the war* or *extend it.*
Vickie not only *cooked the meal* but also *washed the dishes.*
Tom is neither *bright* nor *dull*—just *average.*

3. *Compared elements:*

Horace is more *greedy* than *needy.*
Children like *to play games* as well as *to do chores.*

4. *Contrasted elements:*

Mike is *heavy* but not *fat.*
Marty loves to swim—not *in the lake,* but *in the ocean.*
The bed is *firm,* yet *comfortable.*

5. *Verbal noun complements:*

Reading is *understanding.*
To exercise is *to build* strength.

6. *Verbal appositives:*

The trick is *to hang on, to hold fast.*
Rod went *tumbling, sprawling.*

7. *Elements in series and outlines:*

Nancy, Sue, and *Jackie* are here.
They have *books, pens,* and *notepads.* They expect to *hear lectures* this

morning, *join discussions* this afternoon, and *attend the dance* tonight. They always enjoy *listening, talking,* and *dancing.*

Parallelism is both substance and ornament in effective writing and speech. It will be useful to illustrate with a prose passage from Robert Louis Stevenson ("On Some Technical Elements of Style in Literature"):

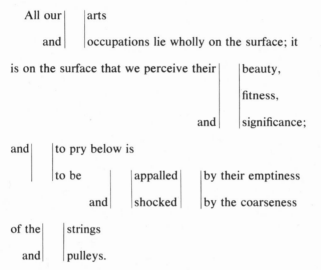

Faulty parallelism occurs when the elements joined in such structures, though they are intended to serve equal functions, do not have equal grammatical form. These examples are obviously faulty:

"He is *my friend* and *who will never let me down.*" (Noun phrase not parallel with adjective clause.)

"Cheryl tried *to memorize* lines and *repeating* them." "It's better *to get* the work done rather than *letting* it go." (Infinitives not parallel to gerunds.)

"The player *with experience* has advantage over the player *who has none.*" (Prepositional phrase not parallel with adjective clause.)

"*Loneliness* is more painful than *being without money.*" (Noun not quite parallel with gerund phrase. Improvement: "*Loneliness* is more painful than *poverty,*" or "*Being without company* is more painful than *being without money.*")

"Sydney traveled *through Europe, Africa,* and *in Asia.*" ("Noun not parallel with prepositional phrases. Improvement: ". . . through *Europe, Africa,* and *Asia.*")

(See also ANTITHESIS and BALANCE.)

paraphrase   A recasting of a passage so that the meaning and general tone of the original are retained although different words are used. A paraphrase may be useful as a test of understanding the original, but is not intended as an improvement or replacement of the original. Nor is a paraphrase a shortened version like a PRÉCIS, but only a version in different words. Paraphrasing a poem as a device for extracting "meaning" should be handled with extreme caution, as Cleanth Brooks warns in "The Heresy of Paraphrase," *The Well-Wrought Urn.* Susan Sontag disparages the paraphrase altogether in *Against Interpretation.*

parentheses   A pair of upright curves, ( ), used to set off an aside or an insertion having only an indirect connection with the rest of the sentence. Current practice has relegated the paired parentheses to infrequent use in standard prose, since careful writing makes necessary very little discontinuous or gratuitous comment. Some informative asides are acceptable (see the examples below—in addition to this one itself), but the cute remark in parentheses is considered a blemish on serious prose.

1. Enclose grammatically unrelated matter within a larger context, either internal or at the end of the main body, in parentheses. The parentheses do not alter the need for other normal sentence punctuation: "William Shakespeare (1564–1616) had reached popular success long before the year of Elizabeth's death (1603). Most accounts of his affairs (see Chapter IV) are obscure." (When the enclosed matter constitutes a full sentence or several sentences, the terminal period is placed inside the closing parenthesis.)

2. Enclose figures or letters that indicate divisions and are run into the text. In enumerating the reasons for the use of the parentheses, for example, each reason may be prefaced by (1), (2), (3), ...

3. Use a single parenthesis after lower-case Roman numerals in an OUTLINE: i), ii).

4. Enclose the dates of birth and death after a name: "Samuel Johnson (1709–1784)."

5. In FOOTNOTES, enclose the place and date of publication; in BIBLIOGRAPHIES, enclose the dates of periodicals. (See DOCUMENTATION.)

parody   An imitation or mimicking of a composition or of the style of a well-known artist. When a performer impersonates another performer, he offers a compliment, for the style being imitated is, if not original, at least the mark of a given artist. Ernest Hemingway's sentences, characteristically laconic, lend themselves to parody, as do William Faulkner's, which often twist and detour (by means of parentheses) for several pages. A modern parody of Shakespeare's *Macbeth* and at the same time a satire of "warhawks" is Barbara Garson's play *MacBird!* Especially unfortunate victims of parodists have been sentimental poems. Joyce Kilmer's "Trees" begins "I think that I shall never see / A poem lovely as a tree." In the parody by Ogden Nash, one of America's best-known writers of light verse, the poem becomes a protest against billboards: "I think that I shall never see / A billboard lovely as a tree. / Indeed, unless the billboards fall, / I'll never see a tree at all."

REFERENCES: Charles Kaplan (ed.), *The Overwrought Urn;* Dwight Macdonald (ed.), *Parodies;* A. L. Lazarus, *Entertainments and Valedictions.*

paronomasia   See PUN.

parsimony   Economy of reasoning, procedure, and expression; the opposite of bureaucratic procedures and expressions, according to *The Law and the Profits* by C. Northcote Parkinson. In philosophy the law of parsimony (which is similar to "Occam's razor" — the simplifying principle set forth by William of Occam) states that entities should not be multiplied beyond necessity; that is, eliminate the meaningless and the redundant. In speech and writing the law of parsimony has been applied whenever an idea is couched in the most economical and effective language. (See DEADWOOD.)

participating character   See FOCUS OF NARRATION.

Participles Anonymous   A writers' club, most leading writers of fiction belonging to it. Members of Participles Anonymous prefer the finite verb (e.g., *walked*) to the participle (e.g., *walking*) at the beginnings of sentences, although they indulge heavily in end-of-sentence absolute phrases — absolute phrases, that is, after the main clause. For example, most fiction writers avoid a sentence like this: "Walking across the porch, Tom heard the weathered planks creak under his boots," in preference to a sentence like this: "Tom walked across the porch, the weathered planks creaking under his boots." The last sentence is also an example, incidentally, of RENDERING details *after* the main clause.

REFERENCES: H. W. Fowler, "Participles" and "Sentry Participles," *Modern English Usage,* Second Edition, revised by Ernest Gowers; Francis Christensen, *Notes Toward a New Rhetoric;* Caroline Gordon and Allen Tate, *The House of Fiction;* R. V. Cassill, *Writing Fiction.*

particular statement   See SYLLOGISM I F.

particular to universal   See SYLLOGISM I H.

pastiche   Literally, "a patchwork." A jumble of literary styles, often a PARODY of the styles of well-known writers; in the play *Mrs. Moonlight,* for example, a serious attempt to imitate the best qualities of style of several master playwrights. James Joyce's *Ulysses* contains a pastiche of famous English prose styles in the chapter beginning "Deshil Holles Eamus," usually referred to as the "Golden Oxen of the Sun" chapter. One of the most entertaining and irreverent pastiches of the 1950s is Peter De Vries's *Tents of Wickedness,* in which the protagonist-author Charles Swallow attempts the styles, respectively, of Dreiser, Faulkner, Fitzgerald, Hemingway, Joyce, Kafka, Marquand, Proust, and Thurber. As against conscious and artful pastiche, there must be mentioned the hazard to young writers of unconsciously adopting and using the styles of respected authors without having created distinctive styles of their own. The effect is that of pastiche—a bit of one's own creation, a bit of Runyon, a bit of Faulkner, and so on.

pastoral   Pertaining to shepherds and the countryside. Most pastoral writing is the city-dweller's idea of country life. (See ECLOGUE.)

REFERENCES: Eleanor Terry Lincoln (ed.), *Pastoral and Romance: Modern Essays in Criticism;* Robin Magowan, "A Note on Genre," *College English* (April, 1969); William Empson, *Some Versions of Pastoral;* Richard Cody, *The Landscape of the Mind.*

pathetic fallacy   John Ruskin's phrase for the tendency of writers unconvincingly to attribute sympathetic human qualities to inanimate forces in nature; thunder and lightning, for example, warn Caesar's wife Calpurnia (in Shakespeare's *Julius Caesar*) of ominous dangers to his life. (The blizzards of MELODRAMA are not exactly sympathetic; they usually add obstacle and frustration to a heroine about to run for help.) When water is described as "cruel" or "kind," according to the mood of a character, the description is a pathetic fallacy.

REFERENCE: John Ruskin, Chapter VII, *Modern Painters.*

pedagogical novel   See DIDACTIC NOVEL.

pentad   See DRAMATISM.

pentameter   See METER.

Perennialism   See GREAT BOOKS.

period   When a sentence has rounded its full thought, the sentence is a period; that is, in the Greek sense of "a going around" or of coming full circle. The Greeks marked the rounded thought in writing by a dot or small circle. By association the dot itself came to be called a *period,* and the mark used to punctuate the end of a written declarative sentence. Today the period is also used for certain conventional purposes, including the marking of decimals and most abbreviations.

The period is used:

1. To mark the end of a declarative sentence; that is, a sentence that does not command, question, or exclaim.

2. To mark the end of an imperative sentence not intended to be emphatic: "Please turn in the assignment tomorrow." (Stronger commands are emphasized by the EXCLAMATION MARK.)

3. To mark the end of a question whose intent is mildly imperative: "Will you please send us three dozen pairs of nylons."

4. To mark the end of a MINOR SENTENCE the full meaning of which is made clear by context: "Good writing can be acquired only by wide

and intelligent reading. And in no other way whatsoever." — David Lambuth.

5. After initials in names: T. S. Eliot, H. G. Wells.

6. To punctuate many, but not all, abbreviations: A.M., Dr., e.g., etc., ibid., M.D., Mrs., St. Louis, U.S.

7. As a decimal point with numbers: 808.4, $43.02.

8. In a group of three (. . .) to mark an ellipsis.

When a period appears next to an end quotation mark, the period comes first: "Wait and see."

When an abbreviation comes at the end of a sentence, one period serves for the abbreviation and the sentence terminal: "Be here at 8 A.M."

In current established practice, the period is *not* used:

1. After display lines (such as titles, subheadings, or headlines), datelines (in correspondence), or signatures.

2. After most groups of capitalized initials and acronyms that have come into common usage: NATO, TWA, UCLA, UN.

3. After *per cent* (except at the end of a sentence).

4. After Roman numerals.

5. After certain scientific and scholarly abbreviations: H_2O, Fe (and other chemical symbols), MS (manuscript), OE, MHG (and other abbreviations for linguistic eras).

6. After contractions written with the APOSTROPHE: nat'l, sec'y (though these forms should be avoided in formal writing).

7. After 1st, 2nd, 3rd, *n*th.

period fault   See FRAGMENT.

periodic sentence   A sentence that delays its main idea until the end, or period, while presenting the subordinate ideas or modifiers first. The full sense of such a sentence is not realized until the period. (The periodic sentence thus contrasts with the LOOSE SENTENCE, whose message comes early, with modifiers and afterthoughts trailing.) The periodic sentence may be long or short, simple or complex. It ends with an indispensable main element — a subject, a verb, an object or other complement, or an essential (RESTRICTIVE) modifier.

Carefully handled, the periodic sentence, with its tight structure and delayed statement, is capable of dignity and emphasis. But it should be used with caution: Dignifying or emphasizing every thought shows poor planning just as surely as does emphasizing nothing. The formality and suspense of the periodic sentence may, if not relieved by variety of length and rhythm, seem artificial, even bombastic. "To end sentence after sentence with a thump would lead to maddening monotony," says F. L. Lucas in his classic essay "What Is Style?"

The periodic sentence was cultivated as the basis of a literary style by such seventeenth- and eighteenth-century writers as Joseph Addison, Samuel Johnson, Edmund Burke, and Edward Gibbon, all of whom modeled their prose style on the works of the Roman orator Cicero.

Current English tends toward informality and so shuns the heavily periodic style, finding it too "rhetorical." (See RHETORIC 4.) Yet the periodic sentence may have both modernity and ease, as in these examples:

Not to be troubled about anything over which one has no control, whether the oppression of tyrants or the peril of earthquakes — on the necessity of this also, Epictetus and I are as one. Yet, close as is the resemblance between our opinions, I could not help feeling, as I read, that Epictetus was wise in holding his opinions and that I, though holding the same opinions, was far from wise.
— ROBERT LYND, "On Not Being a Philosopher," *It's a Fine World.*

peripety   A turning point, usually a severe reversal, in which as a result of an unforeseen incident, but not a mere coincidence, a character moves from ignorance to sudden confrontation with reality. For example, in Sophocles' *Oedipus the King,* an ironic reversal occurs when the Messenger intending to bring Oedipus good news reveals the secret of the king's birth and, hence, incestuous marriage. (Compare DISCOVERY 1.)
REFERENCE: Caroline Gordon and Allen Tate, *The House of Fiction.*

periphrasis   A roundabout way of communicating, now generally avoided by writers and speakers. A periphrasis of "Our fathers founded a new nation here" might read: "A number of individuals related to us paternally organized a governmental setup here within the geographical bounds of what is now referred to as this country, as a kind of novel experiment, you might say." (See DEADWOOD 4.)
REFERENCES: James R. Masterson and Wendell B. Phillips, *Federal Prose: How to Write In and/or For Washington;* Dwight D. Eisenhower, "West Point Address," in Dwight Macdonald (ed.), *Parodies;* Ezra Pound, "Dichten = Condensare," *ABC of Reading.*

persona   1. Originally, a mask (with a megaphone built into the mouth) worn by classical Greek actors during performances in amphitheaters. 2. A character in a play, one of the *dramatis personae,* as in the plays of Shakespeare and in the dramatic poems of Robert Browning and Ezra Pound. 3. The "person" mentioned by St. Paul in his various Epistles: "God is no respecter of *persons.* There is neither Jew nor Greek nor Gentile [but that God sees through one's mask (*persona*) to the real person underneath]." Thus the King James scholars translated by transliteration the Greek and Latin word for "mask," *persona.* 4. Among recent critics influenced by the psychologist Carl Jung the persona is regarded as the special role, or "voice," or "mask," that a poet (especially Browning, Yeats, Eliot, Pound, and Frost) assumes in a given poem, rather than speaking as himself directly to the reader. One of the first questions that a reader or an explicator asks of a poem, then, is "Who is speaking?" or "What is the persona?" The answer is something more than what is on the surface; for instance, in a dramatic monologue like Browning's "My Last Duchess," the obvious speaker is the Duke. But the reader should ask, "What *role* is the Duke Playing?" (See SPEAKING VOICE.)

REFERENCES: John Hall Wheelock, "Four Voices," *What Is Poetry?;* T. S. Eliot, "The Three Voices of Poetry," *Collected Essays;* Walker Gibson, *Persona;* Ingmar Bergman, *Persona* (a film).

personification   A figure of speech attributing human qualities to inanimate objects or abstract ideas. Writers and speakers of earlier centuries often treated such abstractions as Truth (with a capital letter) as if they were sentient beings. For example, Samuel Johnson had Fame tell a tale and Victory hover over a general; and poets often addressed such beings as the *West Wind* or *Melancholy*. (See APOSTROPHE.) Today personification is likely to be indirect, seldom pretending to address the personified thing, yet giving it human capacities: "The boiled *cabbage leered* at him from the table"; "The *tires complained* aloud as he took the curve at high speed." When personification of the abstract is developed at great length in narrative, it may become ALLEGORY. The habit of personification perhaps grew out of man's habit of seeing all things as comparable to himself, or perhaps out of his psychological need for company, so that the rocks and trees, doors and chairs, hopes and fears became fellow creatures in his mind. When exaggerated and sentimentalized, personification may become an instance of what John Ruskin called PATHETIC FALLACY, a belief that natural objects and phenomena share the feelings of human beings. Personification is common in LEGEND, MYTH, and SAGA.

REFERENCES: C. S. Lewis, *Allegory of Love;* Morton W. Bloomfield, "A Grammatical Approach to Personification Allegory," *Modern Philology* (1962–63).

Petrarchan sonnet   See SONNET.

Philistinism   The worship of materialism; castigated by Schopenhauer, Matthew Arnold, Ralph Waldo Emerson, Henry David Thoreau, and H. L. Mencken. Also the inability to appreciate the more subtle and nonmaterial values of literature and art.

REFERENCE: Matthew Arnold, "Sweetness and Light," *Culture and Anarchy.*

philology   Literally, "love of language"; actually, love of learning, including literature as well as language. Both the term and what it represented were phenomena of the nineteenth century and earlier. A philologist studied Anglo-Saxon for its literature (e.g., *Beowulf*) as well as its language. Most scholars—E. K. Chambers, F. J. Child,

George Lyman Kittredge, Walter W. Skeat, Kemp Malone, for example — regarded language and literature as inextricably one whole. Today, because of extreme specialization, scholars tend to regard the study of literature and the study of language as two separate disciplines. The study of language now comes under the heading of "linguistics," a term that seems to have replaced "philology."

REFERENCES: Howard Mumford Jones, *One Great Society;* Jacques Barzun, *The House of Intellect;* Albert Marckwardt, *A Common Language.*

philosophic statement   The main idea, thematic predication, or conclusion, more often implied than expressed, to which a literary work leads the reader. In *The House of the Seven Gables* Hawthorne leads the reader to a philosophic statement like: "The sins of the fathers are visited upon the children." A philosophic statement is not always so Biblically moral, however. Katherine Anne Porter's story "Theft" leads the reader to a statement like: "A person who does not look out for himself gets stepped on." The philosophic statement expressed or implied in a literary work is likely to reflect the author's VISION OF LIFE. (See THESIS STATEMENT.)

REFERENCE: Monroe Beardsley, "Predication," *Aesthetics.*

picaresque novel   A novel containing (*a*) a *picaro,* or rogue, as a central character, (*b*) an episodic rather than a dramatic story-line, (*c*) a number of characters whom the rogue ruins, and (*d*) a wide range of adventures in "faraway" settings. Examples of picaresque novels are Thomas Nash's *Unfortunate Traveller, or the Life of Jacke Wilton* (1594), Alain René le Sage's *Gil Blas* (1715), Daniel Defoe's *Moll Flanders* (1722), Joseph Fielding's *Jonathan Wild* (1743), Tobias Smollett's *Peregrine Pickle* (1751), and Hervey Allen's *Anthony Adverse* (1933).

Pindaric ode   See ODE.

pirated edition   1. The unauthorized printing of a play or other work. Some of Shakespeare's plays were first published in pirated editions. 2. In modern times, the unauthorized publication of English books by printers in Russia, China (particularly on Formosa), and other countries that do not subscribe to international agreements on COPYRIGHT. 3. Any unauthorized publication. The pirating of books has been, since the institution of formal international agreements on copyright, episodic, and in the twentieth century has been limited in America to underground classics which, because of vagaries of American copyright law, could not be formally copyrighted here. D. H. Lawrence, in particular, suffered from pirated American editions of his novels.

plagiarism   The act of appropriating the ideas or writings of other persons and presenting them as one's own. (See DOCUMENTATION.)

plain folks   A propaganda device whose aim is to make an audience feel that the speaker (or candidate or product) is down-to-earth, simple, and honest—like the audience itself. The office-seeker who puts on overalls and pitches hay with the farmer-voters is using the plain-folks appeal. What it subtly conveys is the message, "I am one of you, so my ideas are your ideas; a vote for me is a vote for yourself." In advertising, the plain-folks appeal uses folksy language and associates the product with the customer's cherished values. (See PROPAGANDA DEVICES.)

platitude   Any commonplace statement of the dull or obvious. (See TRITENESS, BROMIDE, STEREOTYPE, and CLICHÉ.)

play   See COMEDY, COMMEDIA DELL'ARTE, DRAMATIC STRUCTURE, INNS OF COURT PLAYS, INTERLUDE, MASQUE, PROBLEM PLAY, THEATRE OF THE ABSURD, TRAGEDY.

pleonasm   See DEADWOOD.

plot   See DRAMATIC STRUCTURE.

poem, poetry   1. As distinguished from PROSE, poetry defies generalization. One cannot say that poetry has a special subject matter, for it has not. (In fact, the would-be poets who regard "beauty" and "moral lessons" as the special subject matters of poetry are the first to stultify it.) Nor can one say that emotion and RHYTHM are the preserves of poetry rather than of prose, though formal meters are indeed peculiar to poetry. Expository prose (but not fiction) communicates directly and with relatively little ambiguity, or tries to, whereas a poem suggests much more than it says and is purposefully indirect and ambiguous. Poetry is much richer in IMAGERY than is prose and usually views reality by means of METAPHOR. Metaphor is in fact at the heart of a poem.

2. As distinguished from DOGGEREL and LIGHT VERSE, a poem is a serious attempt, not necessarily without humor, to re-create an experience. The subject matter of poetry seems to be unrestricted, but the treatment rises above the trivial, transforms the matter, and transports the reader, so that a critic like John Ciardi would ask of a poem not "*What* does it mean?" but "*How* does it mean?" Thematic meaning is rooted in and arises from treatment. Treatment is almost everything. To attain the distinction of being a poem, moreover, the piece bears the unique mark of the poet himself, even though in his youth the poet may have steeped himself in the work of other poets. Only if the writer has digested, distilled, and freed himself of other writers' styles can he produce a poem of his own.

3. The chief kinds of poems are (*a*) the *narrative-dramatic,* including BALLAD, EPIC, METRICAL ROMANCE, and DRAMATIC MONOLOGUE; and (*b*) the *lyric,* including BALLADE, SONNET, ODE, MADRIGAL, RONDEL, and VILLANELLE.

REFERENCES: F. T. Palgrave, *The Golden Treasury; The Oxford Anthology of*

English Verse; Donald Hall *et al.* (eds.), *New Poets of England and America;* Louis Untermeyer (ed.), *Modern American Poetry* and *Modern British Poetry;* Judson Jerome, *Poetry: Unpremeditated Art;* John Ciardi, *How Does a Poem Mean?;* Lawrence Perrine, *Sound and Sense;* John Hall Wheelock, *What Is Poetry?;* Cleanth Brooks and Robert Penn Warren, *Understanding Poetry;* Karl Shapiro (ed.), *Prose Keys to Modern Poetry; The Poetry Index;* B. Stevenson (ed.), *The Home Book of Verse;* Alex Preminger *et al.* (eds.), *Encyclopedia of Poetry and Poetics.*

poeticism   A derogatory term applied to the contemporary use (unless in PARODY) of such archaic expressions as "o'er" for "over," "e'er" for "ever," "e'en" for "even," and the like.

poetic justice   In fiction and drama, especially MELODRAMA, the just rewards and punishments that the heroes and villains eventually receive. Though poetic justice prevails as a general rule in the novels of Dickens and the plays of Shakespeare, it fails to materialize in such EXISTENTIALIST novels as those by Dostoevsky, Kafka, and Camus and in such absurdist plays as those by Sartre, Anouilh, Cocteau, Giraudoux, Brecht, Dürrenmatt, and Ionesco.

poetic license   The poet's right to use language as he sees fit to serve his own purposes; thus he may occasionally wish to substitute a SPONDEE for an IAMB, to vary a traditional pattern like the VILLANELLE, or to make such experiments as the logic and structure of each poem dictate. Tennyson's "The blue fly sung in the pane" is an example of poetic license; to have substituted "sang" would have diminished the line poetically.

poet laureate   The poet honored by English royalty as more or less the official favorite. The laureateship lasts for the rest of the so-honored poet's life. The honor is not without its drawbacks, since the laureate is supposed to produce poems for certain occasions, regardless of whether the muse inspires him. Among the best-known laureates are John Dryden, William Wordsworth, Alfred, Lord Tennyson, and John Masefield. The present Poet Laureate is C. Day Lewis. Among poets who declined the honor were Thomas Gray and Sir Walter Scott. Rudyard Kipling is said to have been passed over because of the line in his poem "Recessional": "The captains and the kings depart." Most of the laureate poems written for occasions have fallen short of excellence.

point of view   1. The attitude, opinion, or set of values unifying oral or written argumentation. 2. In description, the physical point or vantage ground from which the observer views what he is describing. 3. In fiction and other narration, the FOCUS OF NARRATION.

REFERENCES: Percy Lubbock, "Point of View," *The Craft of Fiction;* James Moffett (ed.), *Points of View: An Anthology of Short Stories;* Wayne Booth, *The Rhetoric of Fiction.*

polyphonic prose   Literally, "many-sounding." Prose in essays and fiction, especially the fiction of James Joyce, which comes close to (is sometimes undistinguishable from) FREE VERSE. Examples range from the comparatively restrained "He saw the sea of waves, long dark waves rising and falling, dark under the moonless night" (*A Portrait of the Artist as a Young Man*), to the DITHYRAMBIC "O that awful deep down torrent O and the sea the sea crimson sometimes like fire" (*Ulysses*), to the experimental "Don Dom Dombdomb and wee fillyo!" (*Finnegans Wake*).

REFERENCE: W. Y. Tindall, *A Reader's Guide to Finnegans Wake.*

polysyndeton   The use of many *ands*—more often than not, too many. Children who relate an adventure ("I went out and I saw Billy and we got our bikes and we rode to the circus and we saw the elephants") use polysyndeton as a natural means of "getting on" with a story. The device may be used deliberately, of course, to create a desired effect. It appears with success in the King James Bible:

> And the earth was without form, and void; and
> darkness was upon the face of the deep. And the
> Spirit of God moved upon the face of the waters. . . .

Polysyndeton is often the rhetoric of the catalogue, as it is in the prose of Ernest Hemingway and in these verses by Walt Whitman:

> The early lilacs became part of this child,
> and grass and white and red morning-glories, and white
> and red clover, and the song of the phoebe-bird. . . .

Although overuse and inappropriate use of polysyndeton produce a noticeable mannerism, it can, like most devices of REPETITION, be used to achieve a tone of simplicity and power—as long as it is used with care. Its contrasting device is ASYNDETON.

pop literature   See MASS LITERATURE.

pornography   See OBSCENITY.

portmanteau words   Two or more words telescoped into one; for example, *brunch* (for *breakfast* and *lunch*). Many portmanteau words occur in *Alice in Wonderland*. (Compare ACRONYM.)

post hoc, ergo propter hoc   Literally, "after this, therefore on account of this." A CAUSAL FALLACY in which it is asserted that since B follows A, A must have caused B. For example, it is clearly fallacious to assume that because one eats dinner just before the sun sets, the eating of dinner causes the sun to set. (See INDUCTIVE REASONING 3.)

REFERENCE: Darrell Huff and Irving Geis, "Post Hoc Rides Again," in W. L. Anderson and Norman Stageborg (eds.), *Introductory Readings on Language.*

preamble   An introductory statement preceding a formal document, explaining the document's purpose. The most celebrated example is the Preamble to the Constitution of the United States.

precept   See APHORISM.

précis   A concise summary or digest of any literary work. It is not an outline; in fact, it is a complete composition in itself, with all the elaboration and illustration of the original work cut away. It omits all but the essential. The précis is also called an ABSTRACT. (Compare PARAPHRASE.)

preface   1. The page or two in which an author tells his readers why the book came to be written, for what purpose and audience, and under whose auspices (to whom he is indebted). Among the celebrated, if somewhat longer, prefaces is Samuel Johnson's to his *Dictionary* (1755), in which he observes, "Every other author may aspire to praise; the lexicographer can only hope to escape reproach." For a modern example of a model preface, see Samuel Eliot Morison's Preface to *Admiral of the Ocean Sea*. 2. A kind of informal, often satirical, essay in which the writer pretends to be presenting elementary matters, philosophic appetizers preliminary to a main course, but in fact makes a main course of the appetizers. A typical example is *A Preface to Morals* by Walter Lippman. A synonym for this kind of preface is *prolegomena*. (Compare INTRODUCTION.)
REFERENCES: Jacques Barzun, *The Modern Researcher;* H. L. Mencken, *Prefaces.*

prelude   1. In general, a long poem as a preface to a long prose work; e.g., the longer sections of James Russell Lowell's *Vision of Sir Launfal* begin with preludes. 2. A work complete in itself, an autobiography or aesthetic confession offered to audiences as a kind of introduction to, or explication of, the artist's other works; e.g., Wordsworth's *Prelude*.

premise   See SYLLOGISM (opening paragraph).

preposition at end   The belief that an English sentence should not end with a preposition is what Fowler calls a "cherished superstition." Many who listen to the language through ears of pedantry and prejudice cling to this belief—though their own speech, when candid, may abound with final prepositions. The schoolmarm's enjoinder to avoid the preposition at end probably arose from the common tendency to repeat a preposition unnecessarily—and inelegantly: "He had nothing *in* which to carry the fish *in*." Also common is the habit of attaching a preposition or an adverb needlessly: "Where have you been *at*?" When the preposition is not redundant, it falls at the end quite naturally in plain English. Little would be gained by recasting such expressions as these: "Oscar had much to live *for*," "Always know what you're working *with*," "She's had no experience to speak *of*." Fowler's advice is useful:

If a preposition falls naturally at the end and sounds comfortable, keep it there.

Pre-Raphaelites   A school of Victorian writers and artists including Dante Gabriel Rossetti, John Millais, Holman Hunt, Edward Burne-Jones, and William Morris. In revolt against VICTORIAN academism they advocated a return to art as they believed it to have been before the time of Raphael (1483–1520). The Pre-Raphaelites objected not just to Victorian prudery in particular, but also to what they regarded as the low standards of British art in general. One of their spokesmen was the celebrated critic John Ruskin, who came to their defense in *Pre-Raphaelitism* (1851) and in other works.

REFERENCES: William Gaunt, *The Pre-Raphaelite Tragedy;* John D. Hunt, *The Pre-Raphaelite Imagination.*

problem play   1. Broadly, any serious play in which certain aspects of the human condition are presented as a problem; e.g., Shakespeare's *King Lear.* 2. More specifically, a drama of ideas. In *A Doll's House* Henrik Ibsen dramatizes the issue of woman's role in modern society; in *Death of a Salesman* Arthur Miller dramatizes the issue of values in a mercantile society. These two playwrights, and George Bernard Shaw, are among those celebrated for their problem plays.

REFERENCES: Eric Bentley, *In Search of Theater;* Fred B. Millett and Gerald E. Bentley, *The Art of the Drama;* Frederic Litto (ed.), *Plays from Black Africa;* Ernest Schanzer, *Shakespeare's Problem Plays.*

proem   An introductory statement preceding a formal literary work or speech; a FOREWORD, PREFACE, or PRELUDE.

progress   1. Pronounced prō'-gress, in Elizabethan England a public procession made by the Queen and her retinue, usually to a house party given by a nobleman (for example, the Earl of Leicester at his Castle Kenilworth in 1575, the background of one of Scott's Waverley novels). 2. A philosophic concept — "the idea of progress" — that views the history of mankind as a series of gradual improvements interrupted by setbacks only temporarily.

REFERENCE: Charles Beard, "The Idea of Progress," in Cleanth Brooks and Robert Penn Warren, *An Approach to Literature.*

projective verse   Just as the speaker in a psychological "projective test" projects himself, through his responses, beyond the stimulus (usually a painting or picture), so the speaker in a projective poem projects himself — his thoughts, feelings, "breathing" (Robert Creeley's term) — beyond such stimuli and "artificial structures" as METER, LINE, FORM. The Projectivists (Robert Creeley, Charles Olson, Robert Duncan, Denise Levertov, LeRoi Jones, Alfred Hayes, and others) thus reject the doctrine of Marshall McLuhan and of the NEW CRITICS that form or "the medium" is "the message," that form disciplines meaning, that form helps one to "discover one's meaning" (Mark Schorer's theory).

REFERENCE: Donald M. Allen (ed.), *The New American Poetry*.

prolegomena   See PREFACE 2.

prolepsis   From the Greek for *anticipation*. Speaking figuratively of some anticipated event as if it had already happened. It may appear as a kind of exaggeration (see HYPERBOLE) in which the status of the moment is projected to its extreme result, as in "I'm frozen to death" or "We have won tomorrow's game." A famed example of prolepsis is Hamlet's remark as he lies wounded: "Horatio, I am dead." Prolepsis occurs also in such phrasing as "knock him flat" or "run her ragged," in which the anticipated result is indicated by an objective complement.

prolixity   See DEADWOOD.

prologue   1. A synonym of PRELUDE I. The best-known examples are Chaucer's Prologue to *The Canterbury Tales,* describing the various members making the pilgrimage to Canterbury, and such prologues as are prefixed to most of the tales, especially those of the Miller, the Reeve, the Cook, the Man of Law, the Shipman, the Prioress, the Monk, the Friar, the Clerk, the Summoner, the Pardoner, and the Wife of Bath. 2. In drama the prologue is a convention of RESTORATION and eighteenth-century plays, in which the stage manager (or other official) would preface a performance with an explanation of what it was all about. (Compare, in the modern theater, the servant's prologue in Robert Bolt's *Man for All Seasons* and the Stage Manager's in Thornton Wilder's *Our Town.*) The play prologue has its counterpart in the EPILOGUE.

propaganda devices   Methods of gaining advocates for an idea, a cause, a person, or a product—usually through a beguiling association of things. To persuade people that they should support, believe in, or buy, the propagandist (or advertiser or publicist) seeks to associate his idea, cause, person, or product with admired things (see GLITTERING GENERALITY, TRANSFER, TESTIMONIAL, PLAIN FOLKS). The propagandist may deal in bias by emphasizing arguments in favor of and ignoring arguments against what he seeks advocates for (see CARD-STACKING). He may persuade many to his view simply by pointing out (or at least asserting) that others hold this view (see BANDWAGON). And he may seek support for his own view by attacking his opponent (see NAME-CALLING and ARGUMENT AGAINST THE MAN). Other tendentious appeals, most of them covered by the terms already referred to, are known by the Latin terms for certain devices of rhetorical argument (see AD CAPTANDUM, AD HOMINEM, AD IGNORANTIAM, AD MISERICORDIAM, AD POPULUM, AD VERECUNDIAM).

REFERENCE: William Hummel and Keith Huntress, *The Analysis of Propaganda.*

prosaic A synonym for "dull," "humdrum," or "commonplace" — that is, a derogation, not ordinarily a neutral term. The neutral term pertaining to prose is PROSE; e.g., "prose fiction" or "prose narrative."

prose Most works that are not POEMS. Prose may be classified as (*a*) *utilitarian* or *documentary* — letters, bills of notice, legal advertisements, directions, encyclopedic information, news reports, etc. — and (*b*) *aesthetic* or *lyrical* — FICTION, ESSAYS, certain plays, etc. (See EXPOSITION, BELLES LETTRES, and POEM.)
REFERENCE: Arthur T. Quiller-Couch, "On the Capital Difficulty of Prose," *The Art of Writing.*

prosody The theory of versification. (See METER and RHYME.)

protagonist Hero or chief character. (See DRAMATIC STRUCTURE.)

Protestant ethic See CALVINISM.

provenience, provenance The origins or sources of a literary work. (See INFLUENCE.)

proverb See APHORISM.

pseudonym or **pen name** The fictitious name that an author uses, for various reasons, mostly until he is sure of having arrived. Mary Ann Evans used the pen name "George Eliot"; and Aurore Dupin "George Sand" to escape the onetime prejudice against women writers. Samuel Clemens picked up from his pilot days on the Mississippi the "Mark Twain" pen name by which he became widely known. "O. Henry" was really William Sidney Porter. Charles Dickens's early pen name, "Boz," which he soon abandoned, was the nickname of a pet younger brother. Other celebrated pseudonyms: Molière (Jean Baptiste Poquelin), Voltaire (François Marie Arouet), George Orwell (Eric Blair). Other synonyms for pseudonym and pen name are *nom de plume* and *nom de guerre.*

psychedelic Literally, "mind-expanding." **1.** Pertaining to the effects of certain drugs, notably lysergic acid (LSD), upon the consciousness. The vivid colors, fluid lines, and bizarre patterns characteristic of LSD-induced hallucinations have been adopted as the basis of a decorative style now widely disseminated throughout popular culture. The moving strobe-light effects produced on walls and ceilings during light shows are likewise meant to approximate the effects of consciousness-expanding drugs. **2.** Pertaining to contemporary art, cinema, and graphics influenced by the decorative style described in (1).
REFERENCES: Mordecai Marcus and Henry Salerno (eds.), "Popular Culture," *Cross Section: Essays on Contemporary America;* "The Aesthetics of the Popular Arts," in Irving and Harriet Deer (eds.), *The Popular Arts: A Critical*

Reader; Marshall Lee (ed.), *Psychedelic Art;* William Sparke and Clark Mc-Kowen, *Montage;* R. E. L. Masters and Jean Houston, *Varieties of Psychedelic Experience.*

psychic distance   In fiction, the use of a generalization like "the man" or "he" (instead of "Harry") and "the woman" or "she" (instead of "Helen") at the beginnings of narratives to attract the attention of the reader-as-bystander before engaging him with a more intimately rendered characterization. Examples can be found in the opening passages of Henry James's *Beast in the Jungle,* Joseph Conrad's "Lagoon," James Joyce's "Two Gallants," D. H. Lawrence's "Rocking Horse Winner," Katherine Anne Porter's "Noon Wine," Ernest Hemingway's "Snows of Kilimanjaro," and William Faulkner's "Spotted Horses." Occasionally (as in Hemingway's "Clean Well-Lighted Place" and Jack London's "To Build a Fire") psychic distance is maintained throughout with a concomitant focus on thematic values rather than on characterization.

psychoanalysis   **1.** A set of treatments, mostly confession and CATHAR-SIS, presided over by a psychoanalyst, a physician who studies not only conscious behavior, as do "behaviorist" psychologists, but also subconscious or unconscious human behavior. Such an analyst is a student of certain "depth psychologists," notably Freud, Jung, Rank, and Adler. According to Freud a person's behavior is motivated more by forces hidden beneath the consciousness than by those that are apparent. He called these hidden forces the "id"; the more conscious forces, the "ego" and "superego." To the superego he assigned the role of censor, ever ready to veto impulses originating in the id.

2. In literature, a synonym for "psychological introspection" — the art of the writer who portrays the thoughts and motivations of his characters, whether or not he echoes Freud or Jung or is even aware of them.

3. In literary criticism, an emphasis of interpretation, chiefly Freudian, developed by such writers as Edmund Wilson, Norman Holland, Lionel Trilling, Steven Marcus, and Leslie Fiedler. The magazine *Literature and Psychology* is the leading American exponent of the psycholanalytic school of literary criticism. (See LEVELS OF MEANING.)

REFERENCES: Sigmund Freud, *A General Introduction to Psychoanalysis;* Carl Jung, *Psychological Types;* Alfred Adler, *Understanding Human Nature;* Ruth Monroe, *Schools of Psychoanalytic Thought;* Carl Jung, *Archetypes and the Collective Unconscious;* Otto Rank, *The Myth of the Birth of the Hero;* Lawrence S. Hall, "Psychological Focus," *A Grammar of Literary Criticism;* Simon O. Lesser, *Fiction and the Unconscious;* Frederick J. Hoffman, *Freudianism and the Literary Mind;* Oscar Cargill, "The Theban Plague," *CEA Critic* (February, 1969); Albert Mordell, *The Erotic Motive in Literature;* Norman N. Holland, *The Dynamics of Literary Response;* Leon Edel, *The*

Psychological Novel (1900–1950); Frederick Crews, *Psychology and Literature* (MLA booklet); Alan and Sue Stone (eds.), *The Abnormal Personality through Literature.*

pulps, the   Journalists' JARGON for such magazines as *True Story, True Confessions, Popular Westerns,* and the like, which are printed on coarse, pulpy paper (slightly heavier than *newsprint*). The coarseness of the paper is often matched by the woodenness of the characters and of the contrived (*formula*) plots. (Contrast SLICKS.)

pun   A play on words, so that one utterance brings to mind two sound-alikes or two incongruous meanings of the same word. Condemned to death for punning, the court jester won pardon from the king – and greeted the reprieve with the pun, "No noose is good news." (Whether he was subsequently put to death depended, we suppose, upon the degree of the king's tolerance for low thresholds of originality.) Yet a pun need not be "the lowest form of wit" – a view held chiefly by those whose experience with puns has been confined to the shallows. Says Fowler, "The assumption that puns are *per se* contemptible . . . is a sign at once of sheepish docility and desire to seem superior. Puns are good, bad, indifferent, and only those who lack wit to make them are unaware of the fact."

Like the two poles of an electrical circuit, the elements of a pun may come together wastefully to make only sparks and sputters – or they may come together usefully to engender power and light. Max Eastman (in *Enjoyment of Laughter*) distinguished three sorts: *pointless puns, witty puns,* and *poetic puns.*

Pointless (often called bad, lame, feeble, or atrocious) are of the spark-and-sputter sort. They bring to mind two words, or two meanings of one word, only one meaning relevant, the other "dragged in." The tire manufacturer who advertises that "It's time to retire" has produced such a pointless pun: he intends "retire" in only one sense (buy a new tire) yet forces us to think of another sense that has no relevance unless to suggest subliminally "retire in peace."

Witty puns provide a double relevance: both members of the word-pun bear meaning for those who can bare it. They play not only upon words, but also upon ideas – ideas ranging from the simple/obvious to the complex/obscure. In the simpler range is the advertisement urging you to buy a certain mattress "for the rest of your life." More complex and obscure is this newsclip with comment from England's *Punch* magazine:

Died April 15th 1895, John, the son of Henry and Rachel
Longbottom, at the age of 2½ years.
Vita brevis est, ars longa.

To appreciate that pun requires a good ear, an unsheltered vocabulary, and some knowledge of Latin.

Poetic puns go beyond the merely humorous play upon words, as William Empson observes in *Seven Types of Ambiguity*. From Chaucer to Robert Frost and beyond, the pun has been turned to poetry's uses. In Dylan Thomas's "Do Not Go Gentle into That Good Night" the speaker refers to "grave men near death," a slyness that the running reader may miss altogether.

Punning and its appreciation sometimes depend upon PARONYMS, words having a common root. Knowledge of etymology provides a special delight in word play as when, for example, James Joyce says of a character, "He was astoneaged." Punning is also called PARONOMASIA. (See HOMONYM, HOMOPHONE.)

REFERENCES: William Empson, *Seven Types of Ambiguity;* Paul F. Baum, "Chaucer's Puns," *Chaucer, A Critical Appreciation;* Sister Miriam Joseph, *Shakespeare's Use of the Arts of Language;* Bennett Cerf, *Treasury of Atrocious Puns.*

punctuation   A system of signs and symbols to aid the reader in understanding grammatical and syntactical relationships, as well as intonation, as they are represented in written discourse. In the broadest sense even the space between words is a kind of punctuation, for it helps the reader to separate meaningful elements at a glance; in this sense CAPITALIZING, INDENTION, and PARAGRAPHING can be considered as kinds of punctuating. But punctuation is more narrowly and commonly considered the use of certain marks to *link, separate,* or *terminate* utterances in writing. In this book each mark of punctuation is treated in its separate article (see APOSTROPHE, BRACKETS, COLON, COMMA, DASH, ELLIPSIS, EXCLAMATION MARK, HYPHEN, PARENTHESIS, PERIOD, QUESTION MARK, SEMICOLON, VIRGULE).

Puritanism   1. A Calvinistic movement that acquired political power in England with the rise of Oliver Cromwell, who ruled the Commonwealth from 1649 to 1659. The Puritans succeeded in closing the London theaters ("pits of iniquity") in 1642, but were themselves suppressed after the RESTORATION of Charles II in 1660. 2. In the New England colonies, the prevailing Calvinist outlook of the settlers and the theocentric forms of government that this outlook inspired, especially under Increase Mather (1639–1723) and Cotton Mather (1663–1726). 3. Broadly, the attitude that unless one represses sexual desire one is doomed to eternal punishment. (See CALVINISM.)

REFERENCES: Bliss Perry, *Puritanism and Democracy;* Perry Miller, *The New England Mind;* Vernon L. Parrington, *Main Currents in American Thought* (Vol. I); Roy Harvey Pearce (ed.), *Colonial American Writing.*

purple passage   Any noticeably florid passage of a written work. The purple passage, or purple patch, differs markedly in tone from its context, making a sudden flourish with elaborate FIGURES OF SPEECH, IMAGERY, or rhetorical devices not congenial to the context. The term ordinarily implies unfavorable criticism, suggesting that the author has written the passage tastelessly.

purpose in communicating   See INTENTION and DRAMATISM.

pyrrhic   See METER.

Q

quatrain   A STANZA or poem of four lines.

question mark   The symbol "?" whose basic use is clearly indicated in its name. It is placed after a direct question, but not after an indirect question; and the writer must know which is which. A direct question is a seeking of information ("Have you read Spinoza?" "What else?" "Was he the topic of your paper?"), but an indirect question is *an utterance about* a question ("We want to know *whether you have read Spinoza*"; "Tell us *what else*"). Direct questions are followed by question marks; the utterances *about* questions are followed by periods. Sometimes the two are combined: a direct question is "quoted" within another utterance ("We asked him, 'What have you told the president?'") or is used appositively within another such utterance ("The burning question, How long will it last? consumed me"). No comma is used after the question mark.

Question marks are also used after items in a question series: "Did you remember your lunch? your money? your tickets?" The question marks, in place of commas, emphasize the items one by one.

If a full question is quoted, the closing quotation marks go outside the question mark ("What's the name of that song?"), but the question mark goes outside the quotation marks if what is quoted is not itself a question ("Have you read 'The Raven'?"). If our example were not itself quoted, it would be punctuated thus: Have you read "The Raven"? (See QUOTATION MARKS.)

Question marks in parentheses are sometimes used to indicate doubt or uncertainty or to question the accuracy of some bit of information: "John Marston (1575–1634), the dramatist, was born at Coventry(?)." No space is left between the challenged word or number and the parentheses.

Using the question mark in parentheses to convey IRONY may have a childish effect: "He entertained(?) with his color slides." It is one thing to challenge information, quite another to challenge an opinion — even the writer's own.

Question marks are never doubled. If a sentence is a question within a question and both end in the same place ("Did she ask, 'Where's Johnny?'"), one question mark will do. Extra question marks for emphasis ("Can you guess where we went???") may be appropriate in a personal letter, but not in serious EXPOSITION.

quip   A brief, witty remark, often sarcastic; a BON MOT, A JEU D'-ESPRIT.

quotation marks   Dictionaries sometimes define quotation marks as pairs of inverted commas (for opening quotes) and pairs of apostrophes (for closing quotes). Newspaper men call them simply "quotes" — and we have "put quotes around" the word. Quotation marks are used:

1. To enclose directly quoted matter, from a single word to many paragraphs. Direct quotations report the exact words spoken (or, in fiction, supposedly spoken).

"Where are you going?" she asked.
"On private business," he replied.

An indirect quotation is not the exact words of a speaker or writer, but a summary of his words, and is written without quotation marks.

She asked where he was going. He said that it was private business.

Indirect quotations usually appear as noun clauses, like those in the examples. In the formal quotation (as in a research paper) of long passages or of poetry, indention often takes the place of quotation marks. (See RESEARCH PAPER.)

2. To enclose words that deserve special notice. Quotation marks for this purpose should be used only when the words quoted really deserve the extra attention.

Perry was a "bright" boy, and that was his downfall.

3. Singly, to enclose quotations within quotations.

"Wasn't it Winston Churchill who said, 'We shall never surrender'?" Mary asked.
"Everybody had to memorize Bryant's 'Thanatopsis' or flunk Miss Bisby's English course."

4. To enclose titles of published works that are parts of larger units. Such titles include those of chapters, magazine or newspaper articles, short stories, and poems. Also enclosed in quotation marks are the titles of radio and television shows, songs and other short musical works, paintings and other art works. (See TITLES.)

When several paragraphs are quoted continuously, opening quotation marks appear at the beginning of each paragraph; but closing quotation marks appear only after the final paragraph.

Closing quotation marks usually appear next to other punctuation, such as COMMA, PERIOD, QUESTION MARK, or EXCLAMATION MARK. These are the patterns followed by most writers and editors:

1. Commas and periods always go inside the end-quotation marks.

"That," he pontificated, "is beyond question."
Write a comment on the Ramon Fernandez in Wallace Stevens's "Idea of Order at Key West."

2. Colons and semicolons always go outside quotation marks.

I saw two reasons for reading "Locksley Hall": it was considered "great literature"; it was sure to be expected on the examination.

3. The question mark and the exclamation mark go inside quotation marks if what is quoted is a question or an exclamation; otherwise, they go outside.

> Shelley asked, "If Winter comes, can Spring be far behind?"
> Wasn't that the last line of his "Ode to the West Wind"?
> The whole cast sang "Oklahoma!"
> How we all enjoyed hearing "Stardust"!

quotations, introducing   In expository essays, long quotations — even those by celebrated authorities — are better abstracted in the essayist's own words. But if a brief passage in the celebrity's words seems more appropriate than a paraphrase (perhaps because the revelation may be contrary to popular notions), the technique with which the writer introduces that direct quotation can heighten its effectiveness. Other than such introductory expressions as "Here is Alfred North Whitehead on this point" or "as Alfred North Whitehead has put it," there is the device of "keynoting" — of first summarizing in a brief statement the substance of what is about to be quoted so that the quotation corroborates and reinforces the point that both the writer and the authority are making. This quotation from the anthropologist (and authority) Franz Boas and the way in which the critic Richard Chase introduces it may serve as an example:

No people have ever been known to be without a literature. Tales and songs are worldwide, writes Professor Boas.

> The Bushman and the Eastern Eskimo, although poor in the production of art, are rich in tales and songs, of which they possess a well-nigh inexhaustible treasure. The poor hunter of the Malay peninsula and the Australian aborigines have their literature no less than economically advanced people.

—Richard Chase, "Myth as Literature," *The Quest for Myth.*

The critic has introduced the quotation, and at the same time advanced the logical flow of his own essay, with the keynote summary.

R

ratiocination   Often erroneously called "deduction" in reference to the way Sherlock Holmes and other celebrated detectives in fiction solve cases; more accurately, a process of inductive reasoning, since it starts with clues and proceeds from these specific data to "conclusions." Poe called "The Murders in the Rue Morgue" and "The Gold Bug" ratiocinative mysteries.

rationalism   **1.** The philosophic viewpoint associated with the Age of the Enlightenment in France (eighteenth century) — especially those aspects of the Enlightenment that rejected emotion and the cult of the noble savage, and preferred reason, restraint, and balance. One associates with this viewpoint such writers as Voltaire, Diderot, and Thomas Paine. **2.** A philosophic movement, akin to DEISM, which rejected, as a foundation for religious beliefs, pure faith unsupported by reason.

REFERENCES: W. E. H. Lecky, *History of the Rise and Influence of the Spirit of Rationalism in Europe;* John Dewey, *The Quest for Certainty;* George Santayana, *The Life of Reason.*

realism   **1.** In scientific philosophy, the belief that when you see or touch a table, the table is there ("it's real"), as distinguished from the belief that it is only your idea of the table that is real (idealism or Platonic realism). (For distinctions among such philosophic concepts as *Platonic realism, scientific realism, social realism, religious realism,* see Herbert E. Cushman, *A Beginner's History of Philosophy.*) **2.** In literature, especially fiction, the writer's philosophic emphasis on life-as-it-is (in his vision) rather than life-as-it-might-be. Such early realistic novels as *The Rise of Silas Lapham, Ethan Frome,* and *Washington Square* may thus be contrasted with such romantic novels as *Ivanhoe, The Last Days of Pompeii,* and *The Last of the Mohicans.* (Compare NATURALISM.)

REFERENCES: Joseph Warren Beach, *The Twentieth-Century Novel;* Walter Lawrence Myers, *The Later Realism;* Everett Carter, *William Dean Howells and the Rise of Realism;* Vernon L. Parrington, *Beginnings of Critical Realism in America (1860–1920);* Harold H. Kolb, Jr., *The Illusion of Life.*

red herring   In ARGUMENTATION, any attempt to draw attention from the main issue by raising another. The name of the device comes from the practice of using a smoked herring to train hunting dogs to follow a scent. If an arguer (or a propagandist) can lure his hearers into discussing or considering an irrelevant or false issue, they may forget entirely about the issue he wants to evade. (Also known as *smokescreen.*)

reductio ad absurdum   A form of conditional argument used to establish or refute a thesis by arguing that a proposition is true because its contrary is obviously false or absurd, or that a proposition is false because its contrary is obviously true.

To disprove, for example, that I do not exist:

Assume: I do *not* exist.

Deduce: If I do not exist, then I cannot think. But I *can* think (since this argument itself requires thinking).

Conclude: Since I have denied the alternative ("consequent"), I must conclude that the condition does not hold. Therefore, "If I do *not* exist" is false—and "I exist" must be true.

The reductio ad absurdum is more often used to refute an opponent's argument. In defending the accused, an attorney may set out to prove that his client did not commit the crime. The attorney may make his point by assuming the contrary—that his client *did* commit the crime. He then reasons that his client must have been at the scene of the crime; but he produces evidence that his client actually was elsewhere at the time. His conclusion: "If my client committed the crime, he was in two places at once—a condition that is obviously absurd; therefore, my client did *not* commit the crime."

redundancy   See DEADWOOD.

reduplication   The doubling of all or part of a word. In some languages the device has INFLECTIONAL effect, but in English it is used chiefly to indicate a diminutive or affectionate tone—as in *dada* and *mama,* or (the slang) *super-duper* and *whing-ding.* The affectionate tone is often achieved by doubling of names: President Kennedy's infant son was called *John-John.* In RHETORIC reduplication occurs when the end of one structure (word, phrase, clause, or verse) is repeated as the initial element of the next: "Now in the shadows she *lingers, / lingers* in silent repose."

referent   See SEMANTICS 1.

refrain   1. In popular songs, a synonym for "chorus" as distinguished from the seldom sung "introduction." 2. In poetry, especially BALLADS and other narrative verse, a line repeated verbatim or with variation at the end of each stanza. (Compare REPETEND, which usually carries more variation). The best-known example is Poe's refrain in "The Raven": "Quoth the raven, 'Nevermore!' " Following are the first and last stanzas of William Morris's ballad "Two Red Roses across the Moon":

> There was a lady lived in a hall,
> Large of her eyes and slim and tall;
> And ever she sung from noon to noon,
> *Two red roses across the moon.*

Under the may she stooped to the crown;
All was gold, there was nothing of brown,
And the horns blew up in the hall at noon,
Two red roses across the moon.

reification   The treatment of abstractions as though they were things. Reification helps to make the abstract idea concrete, more easily "realized" by the reader or listener. It often takes the form of METAPHOR ("Truth is a deep well"), though more strictly metaphor compares two concrete things rather than one abstract and one concrete.

Renaissance   1. Generally, any rebirth, the French word having been adopted in preference to the English *renascence*. (Compare Italian *rinascimento*.)

2. The rebirth of interest in Greek and Roman culture that took place first in Italy during the fourteenth and fifteenth centuries and gradually spread across the Continent, reaching England in the sixteenth and seventeenth centuries. Classical ideas and literary forms had been held up as models throughout the Middle Ages, but without a clear conception of their origins or of the vast differences that separated the ancient Greco-Roman world from the world of the medieval man. To the Middle Ages, Roman aristocrats were "knights"; a TRAGEDY was a story of a high person's fall, rather than a dramatic form; and RHETORIC, which had been such an integral part of public and forensic oratory in the ancient democracies, was a set of rules employed only for writing letters and poetry, since in a feudal society there was little occasion for anyone to write speeches. Classical authors—mainly Latin ones, as few medieval men knew Greek—were venerated for their antiquity, but the civilization of which they were a part was virtually unknown.

With the Renaissance came a sense of historical perspective, a curiosity about the past, and the excitement of discovering a rich cultural heritage. Italian interest in things classical received impetus in part from Byzantine scholars who fled to Italy at the fall of Constantinople (1453), bringing with them a knowledge of classical Greek texts that had been known previously only through hearsay and a very few scattered translations. But an interest in Greek language and literature was already being felt well before the middle of the fifteenth century, and Greek was becoming available by way of Byzantine and Greek-speaking Arabic visitors. Petrarch (1304–74), for example, had a Byzantine tutor, with whom he studied Homer.

In the arts and in architecture, as well as in literature, the rediscovery of classical masterpieces stimulated men to produce new works that were classical in spirit, but original in conception. The architecture of Andrea ("Palladio") di Pietro (1508–80), the inventions and paintings of Leonardo da Vinci (1452–1519), and the paintings and sculpture of Michelangelo Buonarroti (1475–1564) are among the most celebrated products of the Italian Renaissance. This was the age of great private collections of classical art and patronage of contemporary artists by noble families, such as the Medici of Florence.

The emergence of HUMANISM was another feature of the Renaissance. This is the idea that man has a potential for culture which distinguishes him from lower orders of beings, and which he should strive constantly to fulfill. What we now refer to as a "Renaissance man" is a person who, by long and varied training, has fulfilled as many of his potentials for culture as possible and has thereby attained the state of civilization. Michelangelo, for example, was a "universal" or Renaissance man in his ability to write sonnets, paint and sculpt great works of art, and design some of the architecture that has made Rome famous.

Finally, the Renaissance impulse cannot be dissociated from a passion for translation—from Greek into Latin, and from Latin into various vernacular languages. Translation and the invention of the printing press were the chief means by which classical culture was brought within the reach of a wide reading public across Western Europe. In the process of translation many Greek and Latin words found their way into the vernacular languages, particularly into French, English, and Spanish, strengthening and enriching them and making them better vehicles for sophisticated literature and philosophy.

REFERENCES: Gilbert Highet, *The Classical Tradition;* B. L. Ullman, *Studies in the Italian Renaissance;* Roberto Weiss, *The Dawn of Humanism in Italy;* Leonardo da Vinci, *Notebooks;* George F. Young, *The Medici;* John A. Symonds, *The Life of Michelangelo;* Carl J. Burckhardt, *The Civilization of the Renaissance in Italy;* Paul O. Kristeller, *Renaissance Thought: The Classic Scholastic and Humanistic Strains* and *Studies in Renaissance Thought and Letters;* R. R. Bolgar, *The Classical Heritage and Its Beneficiaries;* Erwin Panofsky, *Renaissance and Renascences in Western Art.*

3. The Renaissance in England is generally held to comprise the ELIZABETHAN and JACOBEAN eras. It was perhaps England's Golden Age, especially in literature. Among the giants were Shakespeare, Spenser, Jonson, Sidney, Marlowe, and Donne. Though the Renaissance is said to have arrived late in England, it was making headway in several fields long before the reign of King James I. Aside from the Italian influence on English art, architecture, and music, the ideals of the Renaissance gentleman as outlined in Castiglione's *The Courtier* (1518, English translation 1561) and other etiquette books were well known enough to become the butt of satire in Elizabethan and Jacobean plays. (See COURTESY BOOKS.) Poets and travelers like Wyatt and Surrey brought back from Italy the Petrarchan sonnet form and other literary souvenirs during the early 1500s. But perhaps one of the basic forces behind the English Renaissance was the classical

scholarship of William Grocyn (1446–1519), John Colet (1467–1519), and Thomas Linacre (1460–1524), who made translations possible. Grocyn introduced at Oxford the teaching of Greek. Colet, who studied in Italy and France, on his return collaborated with William Lily, first headmaster of St. Paul's School, and with the celebrated humanist Erasmus and Sir Thomas More in writing grammars and readers. Whatever "little Latin and less Greek" Shakespeare picked up as a schoolboy in Stratford-on-Avon he almost surely got from one or another of the instructional materials prepared by these classical scholars.

REFERENCES: J. V. Cunningham (ed.), *The Renaissance in England;* L. E. Elliott-Binns, *England and the New Learning;* Samuel Dresden, *Humanism in the Renaissance;* C. S. Lewis, *English Literature of the Sixteenth Century;* Douglas Bush, *English Literature of the Earlier Seventeenth Century* and *The Renaissance and English Humanism;* J. William Hebel and Hoyt H. Hudson (eds.), *Poetry of the English Renaissance (1509–1660);* James Ross and Mary McLaughlin (eds.), *The Viking Portable Renaissance Reader;* J. D. Huston and A. B. Kernan (eds.), *Classics of the Renaissance Theater.*

4. The American Renaissance was the age of Emerson, Thoreau, Hawthorne, Melville, and Whitman. Except for Whitman, who lived in New York, these writers lived for the most part in New England. Depending on the literary historian, the American Renaissance sometimes includes attention to Mark Twain, who lived most of his life away from the influences of Boston and New York literary circles. The phenomenon consisted chiefly of nineteenth-century New England developments in American literature, characterized by a departure from some few British traditions, by experimentation, and by individuality. Like the Italian and English Renaissances, the American Renaissance was not a movement but a phenomenon of a certain time and place. Though the giants of this era did join one movement or another, such as BROOK FARM, and all of them knew one another, each developed his own writings quite independently.

REFERENCES: F. O. Matthiessen, *American Renaissance;* Van Wyck Brooks, *The Flowering of New England;* Vernon L. Parrington, *The Romantic Revolution in America.*

rendering   1. In narration and description, the art of showing as opposed to telling or reporting; SCENE as opposed to summary; the art of using concrete details, images, and speech. Contrast these examples:

Reporting : Delia became angry with her brother.
Rendering: Delia glowered at her brother: "I hope you break a leg, you overgrown ox!"

Reporting : The waves hit the schooner and splashed over the men.
Rendering: White-capped combers gathered into moving walls, smashed into the hull, and crashed over the decks, soaking the sailors to their skins.

(See TEXTURE.)

2. In composition for beginners the term "rendering" is sometimes used in its culinary sense of "condensing" or "tightening" or "boiling off the fat and water." (See DEADWOOD.)

REFERENCES: Hart Day Leavitt and David Sohn, *Stop, Look and Write;* Walker Gibson, *Seeing and Writing;* Caroline Gordon, *The House of Fiction;* Allen Tate, "Techniques of Fiction," in Bernard Oldsey and Arthur Lewis, Jr. (eds.), *Visions and Revisions;* J. Patrick Creber, *Sense and Sensitivity;* Wallace Stegner (ed.), *The Writer's Art* and *Twenty Years of Stanford Short Stories;* Joseph Conrad, "Preface to *The Nigger of the Narcissus*"; Mark Schorer, "Technique as Discovery," in James Miller (ed.), *Myth and Method;* Francis Christensen, "The Cumulative Sentence," *Notes toward a New Rhetoric;* Wayne Booth, "The Story-Telling Distinction," *The Rhetoric of Fiction;* Leon Surmelian, *Techniques of Fiction Writing.*

repartee   See STICHOMYTHY.

repetend   A line of verse repeated, like a REFRAIN, at certain intervals, but each time with a slight variation bent to the context of its own stanza. Thus in Poe's "Annabel Lee," the initial "In a kingdom by the sea" becomes "In this kingdom by the sea" and "In her sepulcher there by the sea." For variety a repetend is sometimes placed irregularly among stanzas of a long narrative poem, as are Coleridge's in "Christabel."

repetition   **1.** In PROSE, repetition is often needless or awkward. But skillful writers do not hesitate to use repetition deliberately if necessary or appropriate for clarity or force. Where would be the force of Lincoln's Gettysburg Address, for example, had he said "government of, by, and for the people"? **2.** In poetry deliberate repetition is used in ALLITERATION, ASSONANCE, CONSONANCE, REFRAIN, RHYME, SESTINA, and so on. (Compare CACOPHONY and REDUNDANCY.)

research   Studious, diligent investigation aimed at verifying facts and drawing reasonable conclusions. (1) *Pure research* is that done chiefly by students and scholars, having as its aim the extension of man's knowledge in some limited way. (2) *Applied research* has as its aim the invention of useful products, the prediction of phenomena, the control of disease or of other aspects of man's environment.

Pure research is carried on in three distinct manners: (*a*) *academic* — investigation of documentary evidence, chiefly in libraries; (*b*) *scientific* — investigation by laboratory observation and experimentation; (*c*) *field* — investigation by interview, consensus, or observation of facts outside the laboratory or the library.

For the student and writer *academic research* is clearly the most common, and the RESEARCH PAPER in literary or humanistic studies is its chief result.

research paper   An extended piece of written EXPOSITION or ARGUMENTATION (or a combination of both) in which the results of investigation and reasoning that support a THESIS are presented. Such a paper almost always includes DOCUMENTATION. The tone and content of a research paper are usually more explanatory than argumentative, though the methods of argumentation are used to present the THESIS. The purpose of the research paper is to bring together old and new information and documented recent opinions that have not previously been brought together, and to use them as evidence in support of a thesis. The research paper, then, is (or should be) more than a rehash of what has been done before—more than a paraphrase of a few encyclopedia articles, though it may synthesize information and opinion from several articles and books.

Usually, the writer of a research paper follows these steps: (1) selecting a topic; (2) limiting the topic to an aspect that can be feasibly handled in the available time and with the available resources; (3) making a preliminary OUTLINE to guide the investigation; (4) compiling a working BIBLIOGRAPHY of potentially pertinent items from library catalogues, periodical indexes, reference works, and other published bibliographies in the topic field; (5) reading the materials; (6) notetaking, or selecting what is pertinent and useful from the materials; (7) ordering the notes and preparing the final outline; (8) writing the paper, with appropriate REVISING; (9) documenting by means of footnotes and final bibliography.

Note-taking and documenting are generally done at the same time to avoid retracing of steps. Ordering, or adjusting of the outline, may continue even through the step of writing and revising. (See DOCUMENTATION, OUTLINE, and REVISING.)

REFERENCES: Donald Sears, *Harbrace Guide to the Library and Research Paper;* J. K. Gates, *Guide to the Use of Books and Libraries;* John Nist, "Doing Research," *Speaking into Writing;* Saul Gallin and Peter Spielberg, *Reference Books: How to Select and Use Them;* D. F. Bond, *A Reference Guide to English Studies* [a revision of the bibliographical guide by Tom Peete Cross]; R. B. McKerrow and Henry M. Silver, *On the Publication of Research.*

Restoration   The period of English history from 1660 to 1688 (from the restoration of the Stuarts to the throne at the end of the Puritan Commonwealth and Protectorate) comprising the reigns of Charles II (1660–85) and James II (1685–88). It was an era characterized by the rise of NEO-CLASSICISM and libertinism in reaction to the Puritans. Among notables of the Restoration were the poet-critics John Milton and John Dryden; the dramatists Wycherly and Congreve; the Restoration wits and court poets, Rochester, Sedley, Dorset, and Cotton.

REFERENCES: George Sherburn, *The Restoration and Eighteenth Century;* Walter Jackson Bate, *From Classic to Romantic;* Louis Bredvold, *The Intellectual Milieu of John Dryden;* John Loftis (ed.), *Restoration Drama: Essays in Criticism;* D. M. Vieth (ed.), *Complete Poems by John Wilmot.*

restrictive   In a sentence, an essential (or defining) MODIFIER or AP-POSITIVE — one that cannot be taken from the context without altering the sense. "The fellow is my roommate" would leave a question — *What fellow?* Therefore a defining modifier seems needed: "The *tall* fellow" or "The fellow *on the diving-board*" or "The fellow *who is about to do a swandive*" (the italicized elements are restrictive modifiers). In "My brother likes poetry" the implication is that the speaker has but one brother; if he has more than one, the sentence needs a restrictive modifier, or a restrictive appositive, for *brother:* "My brother *at college*" (modifier) or "My brother *Ned*" (appositive). Restrictive elements are not set off by commas. (See COMMA FAULT 4.)

review   1. A notice of a literary work. According to the newspaper or magazine in which it appears, a review may be brief or lengthy, journalistic or literary, an expository article or an essay in literary criticism. Most literary journals (e.g., *Blackwood's* and the *Quarterly Review* in England; *The Atlantic, Harper's,* and *The New York Review of Books* in America) carry reviews of current literary works, as do a host of other journals ranging from such weeklies as *The Saturday Review, The Nation, The New Republic,* to such quarterlies as *The Kenyon Review* and the college reviews, from Antioch's to Yale's. Occasionally, a review makes history, as did J. G. Lockhart's review of one of Keats's poems in 1818 in *Blackwood's Magazine* and Poe's review of Hawthorne's *Twice-Told Tales* in the *North American Review.* A good review avoids mere summary, focuses upon one major aspect, and makes a value judgment. (See BOOK REVIEW.) 2. A periodical publication that prints reviews as well as other articles of information and comment.

revising   The art of improving a written piece of work without beating it to a fine dust. Writers who compose perfect copy — writers who "get it right" at first draft — are in a very small minority. The majority have revealed in their journals, as well as in various versions of a given literary work, or both, that they return again and again to early drafts, making an improvement here and an improvement there — sometimes rewriting altogether.

There is much to be said for both the nonsystematic and the systematic approaches to revising, though in the end each individual is on his own here. But almost every approach demands a "cooling-off" period between the white-hot heat of creating the first draft and that day or hour of reckoning known as the deadline. According to nonsystematic approaches, the writer reads his piece over casually and swiftly, if possible aloud and at one sitting, to test over-all impact. This system will also suggest specific elements that may need revising. In the more systematic approaches, the writer gives his manuscript *several* readings — once for content, once for structure or form, once for mechanics, and so on. Whatever the approach, the serious writer and student allow as much time as possible between the first and the last drafts. The conscientious also extend to their readers the courtesy of clean, legible copy. To do this may necessitate retyping the final draft.

REFERENCES: Louis Zahner *et al.,* "Revise It Yourself! A Checklist for Revising Your Compositions," in *The* [Harbrace] *English Language Series;* Max Shulman, "Ten Tips for Writers" and Joyce T. Smith, "Manuscript Preparation," in A. S. Burack (ed.), *The Writer's Handbook; MLA Style Sheet;* Karl Knight and Floyd Watkins (eds.), *Readings on the Craft of Writing;* Wallace Hildick; *Word for Word: The Rewriting of Fiction;* Walker Gibson (ed.), *Poems in the Making;* John Kuehl (ed.), *Creative Writing and Re-Writing; Contemporary American Novelists at Work;* Wallace Douglas, "Composition and the Editorial Process," in Gary Tate (ed.), *Reflections on High-School English;* Geneva Hanna, "Proofreading, a Panacea," *English Journal* (October, 1962); Daniel D. and Paula R. Pearlman, *Guide to Rapid Revision;* John Nist, "Checklist for Revisions," *Speaking into Writing.*

rhetoric   1. The art of effective communication in speaking and writing. For the ancient Greeks and Romans rhetoric was the art of the *rhetor* or orator, and since oratory so often lent itself to persuasion, rhetoric came to mean the art of persuasion through effective techniques of ARGUMENTATION. 2. In Medieval and Renaissance times the emphasis fell upon the more decorative aspects of discourse, so that rhetoric came to mean *elegant discourse,* and it often degenerated into EUPHUISM. 3. The modern world still shows certain effects of that sense of the term, but the study of rhetoric today, at least in the schools, is the study of composition — the principles of speaking and writing. In addition, rhetoric as a scholarly discipline has recently been re-examined for its contributions to the illumination of all the language arts. The very word *rhetoric* included in a literary or linguistic study today tends to give that study a prestigious aura — as it does in such titles, for example, as *The Rhetoric of Fiction, A Generative Rhetoric of the Paragraph,* and *The Transformational Density of Dickinson's Rhetoric.* Analogous with NEW [literary] CRITICISM and with the new grammars, there are several "new rhetorics" competing for attention, as Daniel Fogarty shows in his *Roots for a New Rhetoric.* Perhaps one of the new rhetorics with promise of permanence is Walker Gibson's, the SPEAKING VOICE. 4. Depending on the context (e.g., in a discussion of a poet's style) and on whether it is coupled with the derogatory qualifier "mere," the term rhetoric sometimes means "bad writing." (See DARTMOUTH CONFERENCE, DICTION, SPEAKING VOICE, STYLE.)

REFERENCES: Walker Gibson, *Tough, Sweet, and Stuffy;* Francis Christensen, *Notes Toward a New Rhetoric;* Dudley Bailey (ed.), *Essays on Rhetoric;* Edward Corbett (ed.), *Classical Rhetoric for the Modern Student;* Kenneth Burke, *A Rhetoric of Motives;* Richard Weaver, *The Ethics of Rhetoric;* I. A.

Richards, *The Philosophy of Rhetoric;* Leo Rockas, *Modes of Rhetoric;* J. E. Connor and Marcelline Krafchick (eds.), *Speaking of Rhetoric;* Richard Cook, "Swift as Tory Rhetorician," *Texas Studies in Literature and Language* (Spring, 1962).

rhetorical question   A device (particularly useful in ARGUMENTATION) by which a writer or speaker lures his audience into hearing an answer that he himself is about to provide — or perhaps into providing an obvious answer for themselves. The asker of the rhetorical question does not expect an overt answer from his audience. A famed example is Patrick Henry's "Is life so dear, or peace so sweet, as to be purchased at the price of chains and slavery?"

rhyme, rime   The repetition of sounds, usually at the ends of lines in verse; ordinarily avoided in prose: "make / shake"; "miss / criss." Monosyllabic rhymes are called *masculine* rhymes; disyllabic rhymes — "ranches / branches" — are called *feminine* rhymes. (*Note:* Masculine and feminine *rhymes* are to be distinguished from masculine and feminine *lines*. See METER.) When a rhyme occurs inside a line of verse, it is called *internal* rhyme: "He gave his rain and Cain." In humorous verse, often by surprise, there occurs a rhyme achieved by a pair of words: "crystal" rhymed with "missed all." The latter is also an example of *near-rhyme* (also called *slant rhyme, oblique rhyme,* and *wrenched rhyme*), a device often used deliberately by a poet wishing to depart from close, "sing-song" rhyme. Emily Dickinson frequently uses slant rhyme, as in "pavement / bereavement" and "crumb / home."

As language and pronunciation change in time and place, certain words which once rhymed may no longer do so. A case in point is Pope's (eighteenth-century) rhyme "pine / join"; he and his contemporaries pronounced the second word "jine."

Rhyme schemes in poems are conventionally described by assigning the letters *a, b, c, d,* etc., to the rhyme words at the ends of successive lines. Thus the familiar jingle "Mary had a little lamb" is described as rhyming "*abcb*," the second and fourth lines (*bb*) rhyming "snow / go," the first and third lines (*ac*) not rhyming.

REFERENCES: Clement Wood, *The Complete Rhyming Dictionary and Poet's Craft Book;* Lawrence Holofcener, *A Practical Dictionary of Rhymes;* Babette Deutsch, *Poetry Handbook.*

rhyme royal   A seven-line stanza in iambic pentameter rhyming *ababbcc.* It was used by Chaucer in *Troilus and Criseyde,* among other poems; by Shakespeare in *The Rape of Lucrece;* by William Morris in *The Earthly Paradise;* and by John Masefield in *Dauber.* The following is a representative stanza from *The Earthly Paradise:*

Dreamer of dreams, born out of my due time,	*a*
Why should I strive to set the crooked straight?	*b*

Let it suffice me that my murmuring rime   *a*
Beats with a light wing against the ivory gate,   *b*
Telling a tale not too importunate   *b*
To those who in the sleepy region stay,   *c*
Lulled by the singer of an empty day.   *c*

rhythm   1. The occurrence and recurrence of words and word groups, now with strong stress, now with weak stress, in any speech-stream or in written works. As distinguished from METER, rhythm is a cadence not ordinarily measured by speaker or writer, and in that narrow sense rhythm may be considered the raw material of meter. 2. In a broader sense, rhythm is a pristinely natural and poetic phenomenon, a cyclic recurrence shared by all living creatures (e.g., birth, mating, death) and even by inorganic matter—for example, the tides, the lightning-thunder-rain, the seasons, phenomena contributing to, if not the very stuff of, ARCHETYPE and MYTH.

REFERENCES: George Saintsbury, *A Historical Manual of English Prosody* and *A History of English Prose Rhythm;* P. F. Baum, *The Other Harmony of Prose;* Jacques Barzun and H. F. Graff, "Right Emphasis and Right Rhythm," *The Modern Researcher;* Joost Meerloo, *Along the Fourth Dimension;* David Kaarfalt, "Some Comments on the Principles of Rhythm in a Generative Rhetoric," *Journal of English Teaching* (Fall, 1969).

rococo   1. In the fine arts, a style developed in France in the eighteenth century and characterized by graceful, somewhat feminine, curvilinear designs; for example, foliage, scrolls, and shells. This florid style in art (also in music) succeeded the somewhat more masculine baroque of the previous century. 2. In literature rococo refers to works, especially those of the eighteenth century, characterized by deft lightness of touch, wit, and a tone at once colloquial and sophisticated; such works, for example, as Pope's "Rape of the Lock," Voltaire's *Candide,* and Laurence Sterne's *Tristram Shandy.* (Compare BAROQUE.)

REFERENCE: Peter Demetz, "Reflections on the Use of Rococo as a Period Concept," *The Disciplines of Criticism.*

rock verse   From "rock 'n' roll" music. Popular songs and ballads of love, protest, alienation, personal identity, and related themes, set to the music of "pure rock" and "folk rock." Some of the writers are leading Hippies and members of "The [cultural revolutionary] Movement." Most of them are also performers in such commercially successful groups as The Beatles, The Rolling Stones, The Jefferson Airplane, and Simon and Garfunkel.

Among the best-known composers and lyrics of *pure rock* are:

John Lennon and Paul McCartney (of The Beatles): "Norwegian Wood," "In My Life," "Eleanor Rigby," "Penny Lane," "Strawberry Fields Forever," "A Day in the Life."

Mick Jagger and Keith Richards (of The Rolling Stones): "Get Off of My Cloud," "Nineteenth Nervous Breakdown," "Ruby Tuesday," "Street Fighting Man."

Grace Slick (of The Jefferson Airplane): "White Rabbit," "Somebody to Love."

Best known for *folk rock* are:

Bob Dylan: "Blowing in the Wind," "Don't Think Twice, It's All Right," "Mr. Tambourine Man," "Like a Rolling Stone," "Desolation Row," "Sad-Eyed Lady of the Lowlands."

Arlo Guthrie: "Alice's Restaurant," "Motorcycle Song."

Paul Simon: "The Sound of Silence," "The Dangling Conversation," "59th Street Bridge Song (Feelin' Groovy)," "America."

Joni Mitchell: "Both Sides Now," "Chelsea Morning."

Leonard Cohen: "Suzanne," "Dress Rehearsal Rag."

Although most of these songs are not ungrammatical (judged by the criteria of the new linguists), they often use nonstandard usage and the dialects of whatever subculture they wish to be identified with—now Appalachian, now Liverpudlian, now general Hippie. Bob Dylan deliberately used Appalachian in his early period, for example, to repudiate his middle-class urban origins.

The lexicon commonly associated with the rock movement is truly "something else," although some writers use this lexicon deliberately for literary effect (e.g., Paul Simon's half-satirical use of the word "groovy" in the "59th Street Bridge Song"). A representative list of the "mind-blowing" expressions includes the following: "bent out of shape" (under external and internal pressure), "cop out" (let someone down), "dig" (understand), "do your thing" (express yourself the way you feel best for you), "fuzz" (the police), "groove" (feel euphoric), "groovy" (really nice), "hang loose" (relax), "hang in there" (stay with it), "hash" (opium), "pad" (sleeping place), "pot" and "grass" (marijuana), "the scene" (the place to be if you're under thirty), "tell it like it is" and "tell what's going down" (tell the truth), "tighten up" (pull yourself together), "trip" (hallucinogenic experience), "turned on" (interested or excited—the antonym, of course is "turned off"), "where it's at" (where important things are happening).

REFERENCES: Jonathan Eisen (ed.), *The Age of Rock: Sounds of the American Cultural Revolution;* John Gabree, *The World of Rock;* Richard Goldstein (ed.), *The Poetry of Rock;* J. Marks and Linda Eastman, *Rock and Other Four Letter Words;* Albert Goldman, "The Emergence of Rock," *New American Review* (1968). *Note:* For this entry we are indebted to Edmund Guertin, Purdue University.

roman à clef   Literally, "key novel." A popular kind of romance in seventeenth- and eighteenth-century France and England in which certain characters were supposed to be transparencies of prominent

people, though "keys" had to be published as adjuncts to satisfy appetites of readers eager for gossip. These key novels carried on the traditions of love casuistry (i.e., love according to the rules of COURTLY LOVE)
and turned out to be bridges between medieval romance and the sentimental novels of the eighteenth and nineteenth centuries. They also
had their counterparts in *key plays* (*drames à clef*). (Both *"clefs"*
were satirized by Molière in *Les Précieuses Ridicules*.) A very popular
key novel, written by Madeleine and (her brother) George de Scudéry,
was *Clelie . . .* (1654–60) in ten volumes. Others were Honoré d'Urfé's
(anglicized as Durfey) *Astrée* (1607–19), Mme. de la Fayette's *Prin-
cess of Cleves* (1678), Mrs. Mary Manley's *Power of Love* (1720),
and Eliza Haywood's *Philidore and Placentia* (1727), the latter two
considerably less courtly and more sentimental. Of the more realistic
key novels of the nineteenth century, the most celebrated were Thomas
Peacock's *Headlong Hall* (1815) and Nathaniel Hawthorne's *Blithedale Romance*. Certain "key" aspects are attributed to such modern
novels as Aldous Huxley's *Point Counter Point,* Evelyn Waugh's
Loved One, Ernest Hemingway's *Sun Also Rises,* and Simone de Beauvoir's *Mandarins.*

REFERENCE: Earle Wallridge, *Literary Characters Drawn from Life.*

romance   1. One of the MODES. 2. One of the GENRES. (See CHIVALRIC
ROMANCE, GOTHIC NOVEL, METRICAL ROMANCE, ROMAN À CLEF.)

romanticism   In English literature, the poetic movement led by Wordsworth, Coleridge, Keats, Shelley, and Byron between 1795 and about
1830. The Romantic poets were concerned mainly with (*a*) the need to
fabricate a new mythology to explain the universe and the individual's
place in it; (*b*) emotion over reason (in this they had much in common
with the German STURM-UND-DRANG movement of the 1770s); (*c*)
spontaneity over "art," although the Romantic poets' letters, journals,
and revisions of poems now being re-examined reveal that they did not
entirely resist technique and form; and (*d*) a realistic rather than an
idealistic view of nature, even if this approach led such poets as Wordsworth and Shelley into certain tenets of idealism (for example, the idea
of progress and ultimate perfectibility).

By 1798, when Wordsworth published his Preface to the *Lyrical
Ballads,* a kind of manifesto for the Romantic movement, the concept
of the GREAT CHAIN OF BEING seemed no longer adequate to explain
the makeup of the universe; the eighteenth-century poetry based on
that idea no longer seemed relevant to the turn-of-the-century mood.
Eighteenth-century poetry had not assumed progress or ultimate perfectibility; it had been more concerned with the place of abstract
"Man" in the "Chain" and with how to live the good life. In contrast

to this attitude, the Romantic poet was concerned with self-discovery; he looked within himself and asked, "Who am I?" (One can hardly imagine Samuel Johnson asking such a question.)

Moreover, the Romantic poets, intent on expressing themselves in what Wordsworth called "language really used by men," were less concerned about making contact with their audience than with the need for self-expression; the poet must express the spirit within him, audience or not. In turning away from NEO-CLASSICAL notions about "ideal Nature" the Romantics preferred to seek their reality through spontaneous and personal acts of the IMAGINATION. As Keats said in a letter, "I am certain of nothing but the holiness of the heart's affection and the truth of Imagination." He could not perceive how anything could be known except through "personal identity." (See NEGATIVE CAPABILITY.) They also sought their reality through the RENDERING of personal experience, especially through IMAGERY, the concrete particular ("a violet by a mossy stone," "the lone and level sands," "those caves of ice!"). (See OBJECTIVE CORRELATIVE.)

Among other characteristics of the Romantics: They preferred the countryside (the Lake Windemere country, for instance) to the materialistic city ("Getting and spending, we lay waste our powers"); preferred longing or mysterious aspiration (as reflected in Keats's "Ode on a Grecian Urn") rather than fulfilled desire. They attempted to connect, indeed to fuse, certain worlds—Truth and Beauty for Keats; the Platonic paradise and the realm of concrete phenomena for Shelley. Wordsworth sought to incorporate the object—the external world of nature—into himself, the subject.

What almost every poet of the Romantic movement shared was a desire to bring nature, God and man, the finite and the infinite, the familiar and the mysterious, into unity through the shaping power of the individual's imagination. In this context, then, the term *Romanticism* is to be distinguished from the more popular notion, "romantic love."

REFERENCES: Meyer Abrams, *The Mirror and the Lamp;* John Livingston Lowes, *The Road to Xanadu;* C. M. Bowra, *The Romantic Imagination;* Clarence D. Thorpe *et al.* (eds.), *Major English Romantic Poets;* Frank Kermode, *Romantic Image;* Geoffrey Hartman, *The Unmediated Vision;* Northrop Frye (ed.), *Romanticism Reconsidered;* Margaret H. Nicholson, *Mountain Gloom and Mountain Glory;* Robert Gleckner and Gerald Enscoe (eds.), *Romanticism: Points of View;* David Perkins (ed.), *English Romantic Writers;* Lilian Furst, *Romanticism.*

rondeau   A French verse pattern or variations thereon used by many English poets. The traditional rondeau consists of fifteen tetrameter lines divided into three STANZAS, with lines 9 and 15 being short RE-

FRAINS. Except for the refrains there are only two rhymes in the poem. Following is the traditional rhyme scheme, in which *c* represents the refrain lines: *aabba aabc aabbac*. There are also many free variations of the pattern. Perhaps the most celebrated English "Rondeau," a free variation, is this, by Leigh Hunt:

> Jenny kissed me when we met,
>> Jumping from the chair she sat in;
> Time, you thief, who love to get
>> Sweets into your list, put that in;
> Say I'm weary, say I'm sad,
>> Say that health and wealth have missed me,
> Say I'm growing old, but add,
>> Jenny kissed me.

REFERENCE: Nigel Wilkins (ed.), *One Hundred Ballades, Rondeaux, and Virelais.* . .

rondel A French lyric pattern, or variation on it, something like the RONDEAU, its predecessor; it consists of thirteen or fourteen lines in iambic pentameter. These usually rhyme *abbaabab abbaab*, with the first two and the last two lines REFRAINS. As in most French lyrics like the rondel and rondeau there are no more than three rhymes in the poem, a convention that not only challenges the poet but also tends to predetermine a TOUR DE FORCE. As with the rondeau and other French models, English poets have taken all sorts of liberties, especially in shortening the refrain lines. Chaucer begins but does not finish a rondel ("Now welcome, summer, with thy sun [so] soft") in his *Parliament of Fowls*. Perhaps the best-known "Rondel" in English—quite a free variation on the French form—is this, of Swinburne:

> Kissing her hair I sat against her feet,
> Wove and unwove it, wound and found it sweet;
> Made fast therewith her hands, drew down her eyes,
> Deep as deep flowers and dreamy like dim skies;
> With her own tresses bound and found her fair,
>> Kissing her hair.
>
> Sleep were no sweeter than her face to me,
> Sleep of cold sea-bloom under the cold sea;
> What pain could get between my face and hers?
> What new sweet thing would love not relish worse?
> Unless, perhaps, white death had kissed me there,
>> Kissing her hair?

roundel A variation of the RONDEAU and RONDEL, running on only two rhymes, with the refrain taken from the first line. Perhaps the best-known example in English poetry is Swinburne's "The Roundel."

roundelay   A variation of the RONDEL.

run-on sentence   Two or more sentences written without punctuation to separate them. The run-on sentence is normally considered a fault in formal writing—especially in school and in college—since it seems to show that the writer does not know when he has completed a sentence. The term *run-on* is also applied to a pair of sentences written with only a comma (no conjunction) between them, but that error is more often called a COMMA FAULT or comma splice.

S

saga 1. Loosely, a history transmitted orally as well as in writing: "the saga of the American West." Also a related series of tales or novels: *The Forsyte Saga* by John Galsworthy. 2. Old Norse, Icelandic, or Scandinavian folk EPIC in prose or verse with a legendary hero, orally transmitted during the eleventh and twelfth centuries, thereafter written. Among the best known are Snorri Sturluson's *Starlunga Saga* and *Heimskringla* and also *Frithiof's Saga* (thirteenth century), based on an Icelandic myth about a Norwegian king and his beautiful daughter, Ingeborg. (Compare LEGEND 2.)

REFERENCES: Knut Liestol, *Origin of the Icelandic Family Sagas;* Halvdan Koht, *The Old Norse Sagas;* A. S. Hoffman, *Book of the Sagas;* Loftur Bjarnason, "Land of Song and Saga," *Brigham Young University Studies* (Winter, 1969).

sarcasm Scornful, taunting, contemptuous language. The word derives from the Greek *sarkazein,* "to tear flesh," and the metaphor is reflected in the expression "cutting remark" and "biting jibe." A villain like Polyphemus in *The Odyssey* sneers at Ulysses, "you puny, good-for-nothing little runt" (Book IX). Sarcasm may or may not be coupled with IRONY. Ironic sarcasm is often apparent praise that really condemns: "You're the best secretary who ever used to work here," says employer to employee. According to Gilbert Highet, in *The Anatomy of Satire,* sarcasm is irony "whose true underlying meaning is both so obvious that it cannot be misunderstood and so wounding that it cannot be dismissed with a smile."

satire From *satura,* "a lavish assortment of fruits." A term often misunderstood in literary studies, since it is both a GENRE and a MODE. 1. A genre developed mainly by the Roman poets Horace and Juvenal, and the Roman prose writers Petronius and Lucan. These Roman satires sometimes did, sometimes did not, ridicule the follies of their day. 2. In any genre (poem, play, novel, tract) a mode of literary ridicule, which sets the work's tone and meaning. As a mode, satire works through subtle attack or through biting wit on a person, place, event, issue, philosophy, system, or institution. The satirist's purpose is to correct, for he assumes and is committed to certain moral standards from which the person or institution satirized has departed. The satirist is concerned with showing the incompatibility, in fact, between *his* standards ("the good old days," the Roman republic, the Golden Age, or whatever) and the misguided present. Through IRONY, pretended innocence, and other voices, his aim is to lead us into seeing familiar phenomena and conditions as if for the first time or as though they were from another planet, another place, another time. He may depict these phenomena in distorted or even perverted shapes so that we tend to judge and condemn them first, and only later recognize their resemblance to the conditions in our own system of government, our own way of life. This is the method used by Swift in *Gulliver's Travels* (1726), in which the more admirable creatures, a race of rational horses called Houyhnhmns, demonstrate a greater sense of justice than do the vicious and bestial Yahoos, who look very much like human beings.

Another approach, also found in Swift, is to introduce into the actual world some unsophisticated person and give us through his artless comments a glimpse of how we look through the eyes of first innocence. The satirist thus strips from the things satirized the veil of familiarity that normally reconciles us to them, and he makes us see them as they really are.

Still another approach, one used by Cervantes and especially by Voltaire, is to introduce into the actual world some naive protagonist (Don Quixote or Dr. Pangloss) and ridicule that person's philosophic position. In *Candide,* for instance, Voltaire debunks the naive Pangloss's conviction that "this is the best of all possible worlds." (Dr. Pangloss is generally regarded, incidentally, as a transparency of the German idealist Leibnitz.) In Cervantes' *Don Quixote,* which is at least in part satirical, the protagonist, trying to correct what he regards as social and moral blemishes, tilts against windmills; that is, he fights senseless ("quixotic") battles.

The butts of satire accord with the satirist's VISION OF LIFE. Thus Cervantes and Voltaire satirize romantic idealists, whereas Swift castigates social realists for their lack of humane idealism. But whatever the world-view, and however the satirist tries to restore in us a sense of right reason as he sees it, the main tool is IRONY. And this irony, which is intended to enlighten and correct, is to be distinguished from SARCASM, which is intended merely to wound. In fact, the Romans distinguished between the ironic, laughing satirist (the "Horatian") and the sarcastic, didactic satirist (the "Juvenalian"). Both kinds of satire have afforded the writer a means of expressing his irreverence and subversiveness.

The best-known satires, besides those mentioned above, include the medieval *Tyl Eulenspiegel* and *Reynard the Fox* (see FABLES and FABLIAUX); Butler's *Hudibras,* an attack on puritanism; Byron's *Don Juan;* Gilbert and Sullivan's operettas, most of them attacks on imperialism; the plays of Oscar Wilde and of George Bernard Shaw, full of attacks on middle-class values; the fiction of Mark Twain, especially *The Mysterious Stranger;* the novels of Sinclair Lewis, especially *Babbitt;* and Barbara Garson's play *MacBird!,* which combines satire with PARODY.

REFERENCES: Gilbert Highet, *The Anatomy of Satire;* W. O. S. Sutherland, *The Art of the Satirist;* Alvin Kernan (ed.), *Modern Satire;* Edgar Johnson (ed.), *A Treasury of Satire;* David Worcester, *The Art of Satire;* Jan Jack, *Augustan Satire;* Northrop Frye, "The Nature of Satire," *University of Toronto Quarterly* (1944); Maynard Mack, "The Muse of Satire," *Yale Review* (1951); E. G. V. Knox, *The Mechanism of Satire;* Robert Elliott, *The Power of Satire;* Hugo Reichard, "Pope's Social Satire," *PMLA* (June, 1952); Jacob Adler, *The Reach of Art;* see also *Satire Newsletter,* a quarterly.

saw   See ADAGE.

scansion   The counting of poetic feet. (See METER.)

scenario   **1.** An outline or a summary of the plot of a play or other dramatic work. (Compare SYNOPSIS.) **2.** A fully elaborated script for the making of a motion picture, with dialogue and actions of the actors, descriptions of settings, and directions for photographing.

scene   **1.** In the theater of ancient Greece the *skene* was the place (literally, the "tent") in or near which an action or DIALOGUE took place. Today the *scene* is the setting as well as the whole of a unified action (including dialogue), whether defined by the rise and fall of curtain or lights—as in a play—or defined by a distinct change of characters or change of locale in any work of fiction. **2.** A term in Burke's pentad. (See DRAMATISM.)

scene and summary   In a typical story or novel, part of what happens is reproduced with a sense of immediacy by means of action and DIALOGUE; part is reported only by one or another of the characters or by the narrator or by the author himself. In distinguishing between those two major fictional processes, writers and critics refer to the first as scene, to the second, as summary.

selective representation   A term suggested by Aristotle (*Poetics,* I and II) in his MIMESIS ("imitation of life"); the term, still argued by scholars and translators, and perennially reiterated by critics, seeks to distinguish "genuine" art, which is highly selective, from "mere" reporting or photography, which are comparatively less selective, if not always indifferently "random" representation. The dialogue in a literary work—*Sunrise at Campobello,* for example—may *sound* like the speech or dialect of actual persons (for example, the Roosevelts) but it actually only approximates or suggests it, as comparison with real-life tape recordings reveals. The playwright has thus selected certain utterances, utterance-patterns, pet words and expressions, characteristic pronunciations, etc., of his real-life models. He has assembled *selective* rather than random or photographic representations. *Note:* Because dialects of characters in literary works are selective rather than random representations, many a linguist rejects them, perhaps justifiably, as appropriate data for laboratory study and for purposes of linguistic atlases. For most other purposes, however, the dialects of a Huck Finn or an Eliza Doolittle are not only *selective* but also (on a higher level of abstraction) *faithful* representations of their regional and cultural contexts. Linguists and other scientists sometimes delude themselves about their "objectivity," as C. P. Snow and others have shown. Scientists use subjective as well as objective, deductive as well as inductive processes.

REFERENCES: Erich Auerbach, *Mimesis;* Hazard Adams, "Imitation and Creation," *The Interests of Criticism;* J. D. Boyd, *The Function of Mimesis and Its Decline;* Joyce Cary, *Art and Reality;* Mario Praz, *Mnemosyne.*

semantics   The study of meanings as distinguished from structures, forms, or appearances. Semanticists (much more than linguists, psychologists, and psycholinguists) regard language as a vast resource of meanings, as a source of pluralistic possibilities of meanings, depending on CONTEXT. In this respect several semanticists gravitate toward literary criticism. The main tenets in semantics are: (1) there are countless more things (concrete objects and other "referents") than there are names for them; there are simply not enough words to go around for things; (2) the word is not the same as the thing but only symbolically represents the thing—e.g., the word *desk* is not the actual thing we sit at but only one convenient symbolic representation that we have invented or pulled out of ("abstracted from") the thing-in-itself; (3) for all abstractions there is a staircase or "ladder," going from the *less abstract to the more abstract,* as illustrated below:

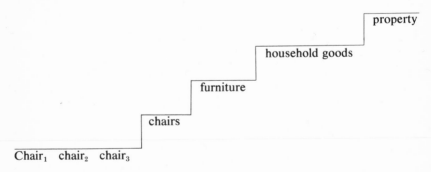

(4) if a speaker or writer uses a higher-level abstraction indiscriminately, he runs the risk of sounding irresponsible—for example, condemning all furniture or even all chairs because of the bad performance of one or two chairs; (5) language is thus not only a part of human behavior, it also affects human behavior; (6) language suggests meaning; it almost always suggests more than it says in so many words. One must therefore read between the lines, as they say; one must ask, "What does the total context imply and assume?"

REFERENCES: S. I. Hayakawa, *Language in Thought and Action;* C. K. Ogden and I. A. Richards, *The Meaning of Meaning;* Marshall McLuhan, *Understanding Media;* "Language-Learning Objectives," in Alton C. Morris *et al.* (eds.), *College English: The First Year;* Alfred North Whitehead, *Symbolism, Its Meaning and Effect* [discusses semantics and symbolic logic]; Kelly Thurman, *Semantics;* Donald Hayden and E. P. Alworth (eds.), *Classics in Semantics;* Edward Hall, *The Silent Language.*

semicolon   Among the "stop" or "separator" devices of punctuation, the semicolon (;) indicates a separation between elements of equal rank, usually between the independent clauses of a compound sentence. The semicolon is used:

1. To separate the major parts of a compound sentence when no *and, or, but, so, for, or, yet* is used between them.

The victory was in view; none of the generals doubted it.

If *and* were used, the comma would be the normal punctuation.

The victory was in view, and none of the generals doubted it.

2. To separate the major parts of a compound sentence when *however, therefore, hence* (or another conjunctive adverb) is used between them.

They knew we opposed them; moreover, they knew we would defeat them.

3. To separate the major parts of a compound sentence even when *and* (or other such conjunction) is used — if any one of those parts is long and involved or already contains commas.

His attitude, already widely censured, grew more offensive with every session; yet he could not temper it.

4. To separate major items in a series when commas are used within those items.

The Cabinet members present included Artuosi, Labor; Dillahunt, Treasury; Pierce, Commerce; and Nedden, Interior.

5. To set off items of example introduced by *namely, that is, for example* (or other such conventional phrases).

He had many tricks to learn; for instance, how to ask for money without mentioning his poverty.

Inexperienced writers sometimes confuse the semicolon (;) with the colon (:), using it improperly to introduce something (Dear Mr. Smith;) when proper punctuation demands the colon (Dear Mr. Smith:)

Senecan tragedy   English plays with plots hinging on violence; the actions of tyrants; madness, ghosts, poison, suicide, incest, and other striking and spectacular themes, which imitated, or were influenced by, the plays of the Roman writer Seneca. Seneca, though using many of the myths of the Greek dramatists, had brought the action indoors and made great use of secrecy and concealment. His plays are filled with bloodshed, elaborate description, sententious DIALOGUE, and thunderous diatribe. His main themes are the cares of empire, the fickleness of fortune, the uncertainty of popular favor, the cruelty of war, and the rashness of youth. All these elements appear in *Gorboduc* (1562), the first of the true Senecan tragedies in English. Another famous one was Kyd's *Spanish Tragedy,* which took from Seneca the ghost, the revenge theme, and the soliloquy, elements which were also used to good effect in Shakespeare's *Hamlet.*

REFERENCES: John W. Cunliffe, *The Influence of Seneca on Elizabethan Tragedy;* Howard Baker, *Induction to Tragedy* [qualifies assumptions about Seneca's influence on Elizabethan tragedy]; F. L. Lucas, *Senecan and Elizabethan Tragedy.*

sensibility   1. In eighteenth-century literature an agrarian, anti-urban, and antimercantile life style reflected in sentimental drama (see SENTIMENTALISM), the SENTIMENTAL NOVEL, and the poetry of the "School of Sensibility." Although many a minor poet who belonged willy-nilly to that school wrote odes to sensibility, three of the best-known poems associated with sensibility are Joseph Warton's *Enthusiast; or Lover of Nature* (1744), William Collins's "Ode to Simplicity" (1746), and Thomas Gray's "Elegy Written in a Country Churchyard" (1750) — with its "lowing herds" and "homely joys . . . far from the madding crowd's ignoble strife." Oliver Goldsmith's long poem *The Deserted Village* also celebrates the charms of agriculture and laments the ravages of commercial trade. Similarly, William Cowper's long poem *The Task* (1784), though opening as a TOUR DE FORCE on the evolution of the sofa, shifts into profuse tributes to gardening and the delights of rural life. Because of its emphasis on tender feelings (the boy in the EPITAPH of Gray's "Elegy" "gave to Misery all he had, a tear") and on overt emotional responsiveness as opposed to stoicism and hard-shelled reticence, eighteenth-century sensibility has usually been regarded as incipient ROMANTICISM. But this notion is perhaps unfair, each movement having an integrity of its own. A revival of eighteenth-century sensibility, along with many of its tenets, can be seen in the work of the BEAT POETS and the Hippie movement and in the poetry of Allen Ginsberg (1926–   ). Ginsberg — unlike Walt Whitman, with whom he is often compared — has been inclined to "howl" against many aspects of mercantilism that Whitman was willing to accept and even celebrate (e.g., in "Carol of Occupations").

2. In twentieth-century literary criticism, sensibility is a synonym for sensitivity or the aesthetic mix of sensuous and intellectual response to experience. In 1921 T. S. Eliot, for example, regretted in Milton's poetry a "dissociation of sensibility," a failure of "unification" or in-

tegrity between feeling and thought. Most of Eliot's successors in criticism have rejected Eliot's assumptions, however, as being too simplistic whether or not he misread the psychology of Remy de Gourmont (1885–1915), an apologist for the SYMBOLISTS. Contemporary critics seem readier to accept the sensitivity theory of Charles Baudelaire (1821–67), a theory that seems to have stood up remarkably well over the years. In his essay "The Painter of Modern Life," in *Romantic Art* (1869), Baudelaire observed that the first-rate artist responds to (and is "drunk with") experience through all his senses, much as a child who discovers something for the first time, although the genius then selectively refines these first impressions and shapes them into "exquisitely sensitive" expression. Modern poets, with a few exceptions, while accepting the truth of Baudelaire's observations, have tended to shy away from letting the public see their "intoxications," whether initial or refined. In fiction, however, the prose that most reflects Baudelairian sensitivity (probably initial as well as refined) is that of Marcel Proust (in *Remembrance of Things Past*, 1913–27) and James Joyce (notably in *Ulysses*, 1922, and *Finnegans Wake*, 1939).

REFERENCES: Bonamy Dobrée, "The Claims of Sensibility," *Humanitas* (Spring, 1946); F. W. Bateson, "Dissociation of Sensibility," in "Contributions to a Dictionary of Critical Terms," *Essays in Criticism;* William Van O'Connor, *Sense and Sensibility in Modern Poetry;* Northrop Frye, "Towards Defining an Age of Sensibility," *E*(nglish) *L*(iterary) *H*(istory), *XXIII* (1956).

sentence fault   See FRAGMENT.

sentence fragment   See FRAGMENT.

sentimental novel   Also called novel of sensibility. A novel or a work of episodic prose fiction in which the characters overreact emotionally and in which the author bumptiously assumes an extravagant amount of empathy by his readers. The classic example is Henry Mackenzie's *Man of Feeling* (1771). In this work the hero, young Harley, becomes ill when he hears that his beloved Miss Walton is about to marry a rival; when she visits him to deny the rumor and declare her love for him, he expires. In Mackenzie's own words:

He seized her hand – a languid color reddened his cheek – a smile brightened faintly in his eye. As he gazed on her, it grew dim, it fixed, it closed. He sighed and fell back. . . . Miss Walton screamed at the sight – His aunt and the servants rushed into the room – They found them [sic] lying motionless together. – His physician happened to call at that instant. Every art was tried to recover them – With Miss Walton they succeeded. – But Harley was gone forever.

As casual structurally as *The Man of Feeling,* but more sanctimonious in its moral assumptions, *Pamela, or Virtue Rewarded* (1740), Samuel Richardson's EPISTOLARY NOVEL, chronicles the episodes in which

Pamela keeps the eligible "Mr. B." chasing her until he is caught in marriage. The agrarian SENSIBILITY and sentimentality of this work, along with its moral hypocrisy, were urbanely satirized in the skit *Shamela; or an Apology for the Life of Mistress Shamela Andrews* (1741), the work almost certainly of Henry Fielding. Fielding made another hit, the next year, with the novel *Joseph Andrews,* of which the first part depicts Joseph escaping attacks on his virtue by Lady Booby (compare the Old Testament Joseph dodging the advances of Potiphar's wife).

Richardson's *Pamela* seemed to elicit a host of sentimental novels, the best known of which included Laurence Sterne's *Tristram Shandy* (1760-67), whose sentimentality is often relieved by humor; Oliver Goldsmith's *Vicar of Wakefield* (1766), which assumed the reader's sentiments to be on the side of huge families and agrarian, as opposed to urban, prejudices; Fanny Burney's *Evelina, or a Young Lady's Entrance into the World* (1778); William Godwin's half-believable *Caleb Williams* (1794); and Maria Edgeworth's melodramatic *Castle Rackrent* (1801).

A death blow to the sentimental novel was intended by Jane Austen in the novels *Love and Friendship* [sic] (1790) and *Sense and Sensibility* (1811). But her attack proved too subtle—judging from the sentiment that gushed from fiction (to say nothing of MELODRAMA) in England and America during the rest of the 1800s and early 1900s. Even an otherwise great novelist like Charles Dickens indulged in sentimentality, especially in *Oliver Twist* (1837-38), *Nicholas Nickleby* (1838-39), and *The Old Curiosity Shop* (1840-41).

In the New World, Richardsonian sentimentalism was emulated in the very first American novel, William Hill Brown's *Power of Sympathy* (1789). Other sentimental American novels included Charles Brockden Brown's *Wieland* (1798), which was also one of the first American GOTHIC NOVELS, and Hugh Henry Brackenridge's *Modern Chivalry,* published in installments between 1792 and 1815.

Perhaps the best known, though not necessarily the worst offender, among sentimental fiction writers in America was James Fenimore Cooper (1789-1851). The sentimentalism and other excesses in the Leatherstocking Tales—especially in *The Last of the Mohicans* (1826) and *The Pathfinder* (1840) and most disastrously in *The Deerslayer* (1841)—were mercilessly attacked by Mark Twain in 1895 in an article in the *North American Review* entitled "Fenimore Cooper's Literary Offenses." Like Dickens, however, Cooper had created enough credible people and scenes to win immortality in spite of his sentimentalism.

Although the corrective—novels of REALISM—began to appear in

America as early as the 1880s (for example, William Dean Howells's
Rise of Silas Lapham, 1885), the sentimental novel persisted into the
early 1900s with such CLOAK AND SWORD exemplars as George Barr
McCutcheon's *Graustack* series, 1901–14. The sentimental novel
finally disappeared under the onslaught of realism, NATURALISM, and
the fiction of psychological introspection, especially the prolific output
of Henry James (1843–1916), which achieved much of its momentum
posthumously. (See SENSIBILITY, SENTIMENTALISM, MELODRAMA.)

REFERENCES: Robert M. Lovett and Helen Hughes, *The History of the Novel
in England;* Alan D. McKillop, *The Early Masters of English Fiction;* Ronald
Crane, "Suggestions Toward a Genealogy of the Man of Feeling," *English
Literary History* (Vol. 1, 1934); Louis Bredvold, *The Natural History of
Sensibility;* Virginia Woolf, "Mr. Bennett and Mrs. Brown," *The Common
Reader;* H. R. Brown, *The Sentimental Novel in America;* Mark Twain,
"Fenimore Cooper's Literary Offenses," in Edmund Wilson (ed.), *The Shock
of Recognition;* Leslie Fiedler, "Cross the Border, Close the Gap," *Playboy*
(December, 1969).

sentimentalism   1. In general, a synonym for sentimentality or over-
indulgence in emotion. 2. In particular, an aesthetic flaw in any literary
piece that makes extravagant emotional appeals or unwarranted claims
on the reader's emotions. Well-known examples in verse are the works
of Edgar Guest, James Whitcomb Riley, Thomas Gray, and Oliver
Goldsmith. But even a generally restrained and understating poet like
Emily Dickinson occasionally indulges in sentimentalism, as in her
poem, "If I can stop one heart from breaking." The trouble with sentimentalism is not that it asks us to feel but that it asks us to feel more
than what the depicted situation itself elicits. It is as if the author, ob-
truding between the piece itself and his audience, is persuading us to
shed a tear or two. And this persuasion can misfire. Rather than shed a
tear we may smile if, in addition to the feeling that we are supposed to
be experiencing, we give in to the slightest but stubbornest bit of
thinking. For example, even Emily Dickinson unconsciously obtrudes
with her word "stop," which in the context of her poem is all too
vulnerable to a second meaning—the manipulative ("tear-jerking")
device on a pipe organ. MELODRAMAS and similar plays of the nineteenth and early twentieth centuries gained popularity no doubt because their sentimentalism elicited not only tears but also smiles from
the sophisticated. Similarly, certain eighteenth-century plays—e.g.,
Richard Steele's *Conscious Lovers* and George Lillo's *London Merchant; or, The History of George Barnwell*—relied heavily on sentimentality, as did such prose pieces as Laurence Sterne's *Sentimental
Journey* and Henry MacKenzie's *Man of Feeling.* Though moods and
styles change from time to time, place to place, and audience to audience, it is safe to observe that most literature that has stood the tests

of time and place has resisted sentimentalism. (Compare PATHETIC FALLACY.)

REFERENCES: H. R. Brown, *The Sentimental Novel in America;* Arthur Sherbo, *English Sentimental Drama.*

sequel   A literary work that continues a narrative from its setting and previous chronology in another work. In Cooper's *Leatherstocking Tales, The Last of the Mohicans* (1826) is a sequel to *The Deerslayer,* though the latter was not published until 1841. Similarly, in Faulkner's mythical Yoknapatawpha County, *Sanctuary* (1931) is a sequel to *The Reivers,* which was not published until many years later.

series   Three or more items, consecutive and in the same grammatical form, within a sentence; for example: " . . . government *of the people, by the people,* and *for the people.* . . . " The three or more items may be single words, PHRASES (as in the example), or CLAUSES (independent or subordinate). The series is normally punctuated by a comma after each item except the last (see COMMA 2). It is worth noting that *two* items joined by *and* are not considered a series; no comma is used in "time and tide," but commas would be needed if there were three or more items, as in "time, tide, and temptation."

sesquipedalianism   The use of big words; that is, of words "a foot and a half long."

sestina   A complex French form of poetry now coming back into fashion. Arnaut Daniel, a twelfth-century poet and TROUBADOUR, is generally credited with the invention of the sestina. The form was popular in Provençal and, in Italy, became known through the sestinas of Dante and Petrarch. The sixteenth-century English courtiers Wyatt and Surrey imported the form along with the sonnet. Between then and the twentieth century very few English poets—with the exception of Swinburne (a Victorian)—wrote sestinas. In the twentieth century the most distinguished sestinas have been written by Ezra Pound, T. S. Eliot, and W. H. Auden.

The sestina consists of six six-line STANZAS plus a three-line ENVOI, all in iambic pentameter. Unlike the VILLANELLE, the sestina has no REFRAIN. In fact, it uses no RHYME, preferring that the sound effects emanate from the repeated end-words. This repetition follows a fixed pattern, as illustrated in the following well-known sestina by W. H. Auden:

Hearing of Harvests Rotting in the Valleys
Hearing of harvests rotting in the valleys,
Seeing at end of street the barren mountains,
Round corners coming suddenly on water,
Knowing them shipwrecked who were launched for islands,

We honor founders of these starving cities,
Whose honor is the image of our sorrow.

Which cannot see its likeness in their sorrow
That brought them desperate in the brink of valleys;
Dreaming of evening walks through learned cities,
They reined their violent horses on the mountains,
Those fields like ships to castaways on islands,
Visions of green to them that craved for water.

They built by rivers and at night the water
Running past windows comforted their sorrow;
Each in his little bed conceived of islands
Where every day was dancing in the valleys,
And all the year trees blossomed on the mountains,
Where love was innocent, being far from cities.

But dawn came back and they were still in cities;
No marvelous creature rose up from the water,
There was still gold and silver in the mountains,
And hunger was a more immediate sorrow;
Although to moping villagers in valleys
Some waving pilgrims were describing islands.

"The gods," they promised, "visit us from islands,
Are stalking head-up, lovely through the cities;
Now is the time to leave your wretched valleys
And sail with them across the lime-green water;
Sitting at their white sides, forget their sorrow,
The shadows cast across your lives by mountains."

So many, doubtful, perished in the mountains
Climbing up crags to get a view of islands;
So many, fearful, took with them their sorrow
Which stayed them when they reached unhappy cities;
So many, careless, dived and drowned in water;
So many, wretched would not leave their valleys.

It is the sorrow; shall it melt? Ah, water
Would gush, flush, green these mountains and these valleys
And we rebuild our cities, not dream of islands.

Notice the virtuosity with which the poet plays his key end-words
(valleys, mountains, water, islands, cities, and sorrow) across his poem.
He deliberately creates a shifting to suggest the shifting and flowing
of men from one "ideal" place to another. Notice, also, the pattern
that the poet contrives—the system of repetition. *Valleys,* the end-word
of the first line of the first stanza is repeated in each of the other stanzas, respectively in lines 2, 4, 5, 3, 6; and in the envoi, line 2. *Moun-*

tains, the end-word of line 2 of the first stanza, is repeated in each of the other stanzas, respectively in lines 4, 5, 3, 6, 1; and in the envoi, not as an end-word at all but rather as part of the second line "these mountains and these valleys." *Water,* the end-word of line 3 in the first stanza, is repeated as an end-word in each of the other stanzas, respectively in lines 6, 1, 2, 4, 5; and in the envoi, line 1. *Islands,* the end-word of line 4 in the first stanza, is repeated as the end-word in each of the other stanzas, respectively in lines 5, 3, 6, 1, 2; and in the envoi, line 3. In short, with the exception of the envoi, each stanza uses each of the end-words in a unique position; in each stanza, each end-word occurs in a new line and in a subtly different new light. Within the envoi, finally, can be found all six end-words.

setting   The time, place, and MILIEU, or cultural context, in a story, novel, or play. The SHORT STORY, like most dramas, tends to have a single setting, whereas a novel allows for more scope in time and space.

seven arts, the   (Also called the *classical liberal arts.*) The *trivium* (grammar, LOGIC, and RHETORIC) and the *quadrivium* (arithmetic, astronomy, geometry, and music). During the Middle Ages studying the *trivium* led to the B.A. degree; the *quadrivium,* to the M.A. degree.

seven deadly sins   *Pride, envy, anger, laziness, greed, gluttony,* and *lust.* Each of these takes its hierarchic place in the circles of Hell described by Dante in *The Inferno.* Intellectual pride, including betrayal of friends, is the most deplorable and its punishments the most severe. The seven deadly sins have been assumed as standard realities not only by medieval writers, who personified them in the MORALITY PLAYS, but also by writers as modern as T. S. Eliot (in *The Cocktail Party* and *Murder in the Cathedral*); Graham Greene (in *Brighton Rock, The Heart of the Matter,* and *The End of the Affair*); and Edward Albee (in *Tiny Alice*).

REFERENCE: Angus Wilson, Edith Sitwell, *et al., The Seven Deadly Sins;* Morton Bloomfield, *The Seven Deadly Sins.*

shifting definition   See EQUIVOCATION.

short-short story   (Also known as *short-short.*) A tightly knit narrative of about a thousand words, with all the strictures and challenges of the SHORT STORY and with even less leeway for RENDERING, so that the writer must adhere ruthlessly to "singleness of effect." (See SHORT STORY.)

short story   A comparatively short fictional prose narrative (usually about five thousand words, but also as short as three thousand and as long as ten thousand) with a short time-span and very few characters and scenes, in which all the elements—plot, characterization, theme, etc.—aim toward a *single effect* or *impact,* a single mood or emotional atmosphere (Edgar Allan Poe's concept). Somerset Maugham demanded of a short story that it have "unity of impression" and that it invite reading within a "single sitting." Though episodic tales were told all over the world and written down for many centuries before the nineteenth, the dramatic narrative containing unity of effect (i.e., a single setting or locale, a single conflict, a single moment of decision or character-change) was predominantly an American enterprise, if not the invention, of such writers as Poe, Hawthorne, Irving, and Melville. Even the prolific French writer Maupassant acknowledged his indebtedness, in this genre, to the Americans.

Before the advent of movies and television, short stories were published in many magazines. But today very few magazines publish fiction. Among the few that do, the best fiction can be read in the *Atlantic, The New Yorker, Mademoiselle, Literary Cavalcade,* the LITTLE MAGAZINES, and *Seventeen* (which offers an annual prize for the best story written by a teen-ager). Some of the best collections of short stories are listed below. A glance through the tables of contents of these collections reveals the comparatively few writers well thought of. Among the British: Robert Louis Stevenson, Sir Arthur Conan Doyle, Rudyard Kipling, Joseph Conrad, Katherine Mansfield, Virginia Woolf, D. H. Lawrence, James Joyce, H. G. Wells, Elizabeth Bowen, Kay Boyle, Frank O'Connor, and Kingsley Amis. Among the Americans: Mark Twain, Bret Harte, O. Henry, Jack London, Henry James, Willa Cather, Sherwood Anderson, Pearl S. Buck, F. Scott Fitzgerald, Ernest Hemingway, William Faulkner, John Steinbeck, William Saroyan, Katherine Anne Porter, Eudora Welty, Jesse Stuart, Richard Wright, Ralph Ellison, J. D. Salinger, John Cheever, John Updike, Philip Roth, James Baldwin, Flannery O'Connor, and Shirley Anne Grau. (Compare NOVELLA and NOVELETTE.)

REFERENCES: Ralph Singleton (ed.), *Two and Twenty;* James Moffett (ed.), *Points of View;* Alton C. Morris *et al.* (eds.), *College English: The First Year;* Arthur Mizener (ed.), *Modern Short Stories;* Barbara McKenzie (ed.), *The Process of Fiction;* Robert Scholes, *Elements of Fiction;* J. B. Hall (ed.), *The Realm of Fiction: 61 Short Stories;* Jarvis Thurston (ed.), *Reading Modern Short Stories;* Robert Penn Warren and Albert Erskine (eds.), *Short Story Masterpieces;* Winifred Lynskey (ed.), *Reading Modern Fiction;* Edith Mirrielees, *Story Writing;* "The Importance of Irrelevancies," in A. S. Burack (ed.), *The Writer's Handbook* (1968); Robert Freier *et al.,* "The Short Story," *Adventures in Modern Literature;* William Abraham (ed.), *The O. Henry Prize Stories Annual;* William Saroyan *et al.,* "International Symposium on the Short Story," *Kenyon Review* (January, 1969); Helmut Gerber (ed.), *The English Short Story in Transition* (1880–1920).

Siamese sentence   See RUN-ON SENTENCE.

signpost devices   Just as signposts on highways are courtesies to travelers, so signposts (also called *guideposts*) in written works are courtesies to the reader. They tell him where he is, where he has come from, and where the road leads, should he care to follow. Signposts in their most mechanical form consist of such indispensables as writer's name, title of paper, page numbers, etc. But in the longer expository paper (term paper, library paper, etc.) they also consist of such thoughtful markers as (1) *a statement of the chief purpose,* preferably in the opening paragraph; (2) *summary statements* at the ends of main sections, especially if a contrariety of information and ideas has been presented; (3) *subsidiary statements of purpose* at the beginnings of sections. The latter statements can also serve as TRANSITIONS. For example: "The previous section was devoted to the main characteristics of X. . . . I now turn to a brief history of their development and a discussion of some of their possible causes." Of course, such signpost statements can be disabused of their tediousness if the writer capitalizes on specific expressions peculiar to his particular paper. And decisions on such matters of style hinge on whether the paper is intended as (a) a *record* of research, addressed to one's associates, or (b) a *product* of research (i.e., an article or essay) addressed to a broader outside audience, for example, in a magazine.

REFERENCE: "The Question of Audience," *MLA Style Sheet.*

simile   An explicit comparison of *two unlike things,* ordinarily using the words *like* or *as;* for example, in "Auto Wreck" Karl Shapiro writes that the ambulance comes with its "ruby flare / Pulsing out red light *like an artery.*" The light is compared to blood pulsing from an artery; the simile says that the one is *like* the other, not that the two are almost identical—and that is simile's (and metaphor's) distinction from prosaic comparison. For simile draws a comparison between things that are normally not thought of as related or alike. "A child is like a man" is no simile, for the child and the man are too nearly alike in actuality. But the utterance "a child is like a balloon" is indeed simile (and "a child is a balloon" is metaphor), calling our attention to imaginative similarities between two actually unlike entities (child and balloon). Reading similes or creating them calls for imaginative insight—a readiness in sensing similarities and relationships that escape the literal mind. (See EPIC SIMILE and compare METAPHOR.)

skeltonic verse   Short-lined verse, sometimes racy, sometimes DOGGEREL, originally developed by John Skelton (1460–1529). Among his best-known verses is "Philip Sparrow," which contains this representative stanza:

> When I remember again
> How my Philip was slain,
> Never half the pain

Was between you twain,
Pyramus and Thisbe,
As then befell to me:
I wept and I wailed
The tear-es down hailed—
But nothing it availed
To call Philip again,
Whom Gib our cat hath slain.

slanting 1. In poetry, the use of *slant-rhyme* or NEAR-RHYME. 2. In journalism, the bending of an editorial (or even a news report, unfortunately) to influence a particular audience. Some slanting is always with us, though many of the popular media have begun to exercise some self-discipline. In the early 1900s slanting the news was common practice among journalists, particularly the "yellow journalists." 3. In free-lance writing the term has a somewhat less derogatory connotation. When a writer speaks of his work as "slanted" toward a given "market," he has more often than not "analyzed the market" to see which audience his piece seems best directed toward. (See AUDIENCE.)

slant rhyme See RHYME.

slapstick 1. A stick with a hinged slat that makes a slapping sound when someone is struck with it. In ancient comedies—for example, those of the Greek Menander (343–291? B.C.) and of the Romans Plautus and Terence (second century B.C.)—the hits that a master administered with a walking-stick to a slave or servant (later, king to jester) who talked too cleverly or out of turn or both. 2. In medieval times, in some of the CRAFT CYCLE PLAYS and MORALITY PLAYS, scenes which contained similar "stage business." Noah's wife, for example, was traditionally portrayed as a shrew who hit him over the head with household objects; the devils in scenes of hell often ran away, vanquished, with firecrackers popping from the rear of their devil-suits. 3. In modern times, the same kind of humor. In *The End of the Beginning,* a play by Sean O'Casey, two foolish idlers turn a farmhouse into a shambles while trying to tie down a cow with a rope through a fireplace chimney. 4. In third-rate movies and television programs, such horseplay as pie-throwing and pratfalls.

slash See VIRGULE.

slicks, the Journalists' jargon for such magazines as *Harper's, The Atlantic, Saturday Review, Life,* and so on, which are printed on "slick," glossy paper (as opposed to the coarse paper of the PULPS). While the label "slick" carries with it a kind of "sour grapes" connotation (at least when used by writers who wish they could be published in the slicks), it does not include the most sophisticated magazines.

Such magazines as *The Nation, The New Republic, The Christian Century,* and so on, even if not slick, publish many "think pieces" that editors of the slicks tend to reject.

sock   The low shoe, the conventional attire of actors of ancient comedy; contrasted with the BUSKIN used in tragedy.

solecism   Narrowly defined, any violation of standard usage ("Where's the car at?") or grammar ("They come yesterday"). Broadly defined, a solecism may be any mistake, impropriety, or incongruity in the use of language—CATACHRESIS, MALAPROPISM, MIXED METAPHOR, mispronunciation, DANGLER. It must be remembered, however, that *what is a solecism in one company may be respectable usage in another.*

soliloquy   A solo speech, usually in serious drama, in which a character thinks out loud. The classic examples are in Shakespeare's *Hamlet,* especially the speech beginning "To be or not to be."
REFERENCE: Wolfgang Clemen, *Shakespeare's Soliloquies.*

sonnet   From the Italian *sonetto,* "a little sound or song." A fourteen-line lyric poem in iambic pentameter with a variety of stanza forms and rhyme schemes but generally conforming to the Italian or Petrarchan pattern (an *octave* rhyming *abbaabba* and a *sestet* rhyming *cdecde* or *cdcdcd*) or to the Shakespearian pattern (three *quatrains* and a *couplet* with the rhyme scheme *abab cdcd efef gg*). The label "English sonnet" usually refers to the Shakespearian pattern, but it is somewhat loosely applied since English sonnet forms also embrace the Spenserian (*abab bcbc cdcd ee*), the Miltonic-Wordsworthian (*abbaabba cdecde*), and variations through the centuries to Dylan Thomas.

In his sonnets to Laura, Petrarch (1304–74) used a *volta,* or turn of thought, between the octave and the sestet, the octave developing a problem that the sestet resolves. An example in an English sonnet is John Milton's "On His Blindness," in the octave of which the speaker expresses a feeling of helplessness, a feeling that is resolved in the sestet, which concludes, "They also serve who only stand and wait." Although Petrarch's work had been known to scholars at the universities, its wider introduction to England is credited to two of King Henry VIII's young ambassadors to Italy—Thomas Wyatt (1503?–42) and Henry Surrey (1517?–47). Both of these courtiers led politically stormy and all too brief lives (Surrey was executed), but their creative vitality is reflected in the large number of their poems posthumously reprinted in *Tottel's Miscellany* (1557). Aside from scores of other poems (including Surrey's BLANK VERSE), Wyatt had translated ten of Petrarch's sonnets, for example, and had composed twenty-one of his own. Although he retained the Petrarchan octave, he experimented—within the sestet—with a closing couplet. Surrey introduced the pattern that was to be adopted by Shakespeare in his sequence of one hundred and fifty-four sonnets dedicated to a "W.H." This is the sequence that begins "From fairest creatures we desire increase / That thereby beauty's rose might never die." and ends "Love's fire heats water, water cools not love." It is the sequence that contains one of the most poignant love sonnets — number seventy-three:

> That time of year thou mayst in me behold
> When yellow leaves, or none, or few, do hang
> Upon those boughs which shake against the cold,
> Bare ruin'd choirs, where late the sweet birds sang.
> In me thou seest the twilight of such day
> As after sunset fadeth in the west;
> Which by and by black night doth take away,
> Death's second self, that seals up all the rest.
> In me thou seest the glowing of such fire
> That on the ashes of his mouth doth lie,
> As on the death-bed whereon it must expire,
> Consumed with that which it was nourished by.
> > This thou perceiv'st, which makes thy love more strong,
> > To love that well which thou must leave ere long.

Other sixteenth-century and early seventeenth-century poets who seemed to have been as taken as were Wyatt and Surrey with the possibilities of the sonnet were Philip Sidney (1554–86); Edmund Spenser (1552–99), who invented the Spenserian form described above; and John Donne (1572–1631), whose "crown" of seven "Holy Sonnets" used the last line of each of the first six sonnets as the first line of each succeeding sonnet. But toward the end of the seventeenth century — after Milton, who died in 1674 — and for most of the eighteenth century the sonnet suffered a decline — with some few exceptions like those of Cowper, Gray, and Warton.

It took a giant like William Wordsworth (1770–1850) to revive interest in the form. He wrote over five hundred sonnets, of which at least three seem destined for immortality: "Milton! thou shouldst be living at this hour," "The world is too much with us," and "Earth has not anything to show more fair." Two other romantic poets — Percy Bysshe Shelley (1792–1822) and John Keats (1795–1821) — wrote considerably fewer sonnets but have done better than Wordsworth as far as ratios of anthologized titles are concerned. For Shelley's "Ozymandias" and Keats's "On First Looking into Chapman's Homer" continue to be the two sonnets most widely reprinted.

The best-known nineteenth-century English sonnets include Elizabeth Barrett Browning's "How do I love thee? Let me count the ways," Matthew Arnold's "Shakespeare," Dante Gabriel Rossetti's "A sonnet is a moment's monument," and Gerard Manley Hopkins's "God's Grandeur" (which uses that poet's SPRUNG RHYTHM).

The best-known twentieth-century English sonnets include Thomas Hardy's "If but some vengeful god would call to me," William Butler Yeats's "Leda and the Swan," Rupert Brooke's "The Soldier," and Dylan Thomas's "Altarwise by owl-light in the halfway house" (with its TRANSFERRED EPITHETS).

The best-known American sonnets include Henry Wadsworth Longfellow's "Three Silences"; Edwin Arlington Robinson's "Calvary"; Robert Frost's "The Silken Tent," "Acquainted with the Night," and "Once by the Pacific"; Edna St. Vincent Millay's "Euclid alone has looked on Beauty bare"; e. e. cummings's "I like my body when it is with your / body"; W. H. Auden's "They wondered why the fruit had been forbidden"; Merrill Moore's "The Noise That Time Makes" (one of a thousand in his book *M*); and X. J. Kennedy's "Nothing in Heaven Functions As It Ought." (See also SONNET SEQUENCE.)

REFERENCES: Robert Bender and Charles Squier (eds.), *The Sonnet: A Comprehensive Anthology of British and American Sonnets from the Renaissance to the Present;* Arthur Quiller-Couch (ed.), *The Oxford Book of Sonnets;* William Wiatt, "Sir Thomas Wyatt's Word Play," *Annuale Mediaevale.*

sonnet sequence Also called **sonnet cycle.** A series of sonnets developing a single theme or addressed to one person. In most of these sequences each sonnet retains its independence even though it may appear like a stanza in the longer literary work to which it contributes. The prototype was Petrarch's *Sonnets to Laura in Life* (ca. 1330). The best-known English sonnet sequences include Philip Sidney's *Astrophel and Stella* (1584); Edmund Spenser's *Amoretti* (1595); Shakespeare's *Sonnets* (1609); John Donne's "Holy Sonnets" (1633); William Wordsworth's *Ecclesiastical Sonnets* (1822); Elizabeth Barrett Browning's *Sonnets from the Portuguese* (1850); and Dante Gabriel Rossetti's *House of Life* (1881). Best-known American sequences include Henry Wadsworth Longfellow's "Divina Commedia" (1867), a sequence of six Petrarchan sonnets added to his translation of Dante's *Divine Comedy;* Arthur Davison Ficke's *Sonnets of a Portrait Painter* (1914); William Ellery Leonard's *Two Lives* (1925); Elinor Wylie's *One Person* (1928); Edna St. Vincent Millay's *Fatal Interview* (1931); and W. H. Auden's *Quest* (1944).

REFERENCE: L.C. John, *Elizabethan Sonnet Sequences.*

sound effects Most of these devices are treated in separate articles in this glossary. See ALLITERATION, ASSONANCE, CACOPHONY, CONSONANCE, DISSONANCE, EUPHONY, ONOMATOPOEIA, and RHYME.

sorites See SYLLOGISM IJ.

southern gothic A style of fiction associated with certain writers from the southern United States, among whom are Carson McCullers, Shirley Ann Grau, and Flannery O'Connor. Short stories and novels in this mode deal with themes of incest, insanity, sexual perversion, religious manias, and various other extreme psychological disturbances. The characters are frequently concerned with family history, and they live in houses that echo with reminders of the family's past. (See GOTHIC NOVEL.)

speaker   A narrator or a person; to be distinguished from PERSONA or SPEAKING VOICE.

speaking voice   In the new rhetoric, the role that the speaker assumes or "makes like" — reporter, novelist, teacher, preacher, lawyer, doctor, and so on. Whatever a speaker says in a given role controls the rhetoric, the style or manner, of his saying it. Even in such a tour de force as the reading of names from a telephone directory the assumed role of the speaker, the speaking voice, can be projected and understood. In the EXPLICATION of poetry the teacher usually asks not only "Who is speaking?" but also "What is his speaking voice — his role — in this particular poem?" (Compare VOICE 1.)

REFERENCES: Walker Gibson, *Tough, Sweet, and Stuffy;* Yvor Winters, "Problems for the Modern Critic of Literature, "*Hudson Review* (Autumn, 1956); Wayne Booth, "The Author's Many Voices," *The Rhetoric of Fiction;* Edith Wylder, *The Voice of the Poet: Emily Dickinson's Manuscripts.*

spelling   Any communication containing more than one or two misspelled words *looks* illiterate and hence can retard the misspeller's social or economic progress. (There is the occasional exception, of course, of the millionaire rancher or oilman who can sign only with an "X.") Learning to spell remains an individual problem, and there are two major reasons for this. First, almost everyone tends to spell the way a word sounds to him, even though the correspondence between sounds and letters in modern English is notoriously unreliable, and this aside from regional or dialectal pronunciations. Second, the regularities discovered by linguists (rules that do indeed apply to most of the words *in dictionaries*) and the more popular rules (like "*i* before *e* except after *c*," "double the consonant before adding -ed unless the word is accented on the first syllable," and so on) *do not work for most of the two or three hundred words most frequently misspelled.*

The most frequently misspelled words are listed in almost every high school and college English handbook, and some of them are listed here. We also know the trouble spots (shown in italics) in these words. Many surveys, including one made recently by the writer of this article, reveal that most business and professional leaders, among them teachers and professors of English, rely for their own spelling on *mnemonics* (memorization devices). Though some mnemonics are given below, they are not usually as reliable as the mnemonics an individual invents and uses for himself. Of course, one consults a dictionary for the spelling of a word unusual to his particular working vocabulary. But here, along with some illustrative mnemonics, are some of the most widely used words that are frequently misspelled:

Words and trouble-spots	Suggested mnemonics
acciden*tally*	Tally ho! accidenTALLY
attend*ance*	Dance at ten. At ten dance.
bar*gain*	Gain from the deal . . . barGAIN.
bene*fit*ed	ED keeps FIT. BENE! BENE FIT ED.
cem*et*ery	E, E, E. cEmEtEry.
chang*e*able	Able + change . . . changeABLE.
com*pet*ition	PET . . . two PET words: comPETition
re*pet*ition	and rePETition
*de*scription	DE. Script + DE . . . DE Scription
des*s*ert	SS . . . two s's . . . you like a second helping of s in that kind of deSSert.
di*sapp*ear	DIS + Appear . . . DIS Appear
di*sapp*oint	DIS + Appoint . . . DIS Appoint
dis*sa*tisfied	DIS + Satisfied . . . DIS Satisfied
embar*ra*ssed	RR. Railroad RR into embaRRassed.
envi*ron*ment	IRON. Put an IRON into envIRONment.
indi*spensab*le	DIS PEN . . . I'm in DIS PEN because of a SABLE . . . in DIS PEN SABLE . . . She couldn't do without a SABLE . . .
le*i*sure	Hawaiian LEI is SURE to spell LEI SURE.
lic*e*nse	LICE make no sense in one's LICEnse.
loo*s*e, lose	FootLOOSE and fancy free before we LOse one O.
main*ten*ance	The MAIN idea is to put TEN in the middle . . . Main TEN ance.
obs*ta*cle	Don't ticle it; TACle it without a K.
par*allel*	ALL EL . . . If you're up to PAR, you can give your ALL . . . par ALL el
po*sse*ss	SS . . . SS . . . poSSeSS
princi*pal*, -*ple*	PAL is CHIEF; chief is PAL . . . principal. -le is like the -le on the end of ruLE.
re*comm*end	MM! One C, and you'll say MM! reCoMMend . . .
secr*et*ary	SECRET. You can't keep a SECRET from your SECRETary
sep*a*rate	A-RATE. RATE an A with an A before the RATE . . . sep A RATE . . .
simi*lar*	LAR . . . Don't make a liar out of LAR . . . simiLAR
station*ary*	StAnding still . . . stationAry.
station*ery*	WritEr puts pEn to stationEry.
than, then	thEn answers whEn; compAre with thAn.
th*ere*	thEre answers whEre
th*ey're*	they + are = they're
th*eir*	the HEIR takes possession . . . tHEIR

t*o*, t*oo*	To market, to market! If you come, too, it won't cost too much!
vill*age*, vill*ain*	the viLL AGE vill AIN has LAIN for AGES.
*wei*rd	WE . . . WEird . . . aren't WE all . . .
wo*man*	Wo, MAN! (singular . . . man) woman
wo*men*	wo, MEN! (plural . . . men) women

REFERENCES: "The Purdue Survey on Spelling," NCTE *Councilgram* (November 1967), p. 13; James Kavanagh (ed.), "The Nature of Writing Systems," in *Communicating by Language* (U.S. Government Printing Office); J. N. Hook, *Spelling 1500;* Joseph Mersand, *Spelling Your Way to Success.*

Spenserian stanza The nine-line STANZA popularized by Edmund Spenser (1552–99) in *The Faerie Queene.* The first eight lines are iambic pentameter; the last line is an ALEXANDRINE (iambic hexameter). The rhyme scheme is *ababbcbcc:*

> It was an hill placed in an open plain,
>> That round about was bordered with a wood
> Of matchless height, that seemed th'earth to disdain,
>> In which all trees of honor stately stood,
>> And did all winter as in summer bud,
> Spreading pavilions for the birds to bower,
>> Which in their lower branches sung aloud;
> And in their tops the soaring hawk did tower,
> Sitting like king of fowls in majesty and power.

Among the celebrated poems subsequently written in Spenserian stanza are Robert Burns's "The Cotters' Saturday Night," Shelley's "Adonais," Keats's "The Eve of St. Agnes," and Byron's "Childe Harold."

split infinitive The infinitive in English consists ordinarily of two words: *to prepare, to ask, to follow.* When something is put between the *to* and its verb-like form, the structure is split—and is called a split infinitive: "One must learn *to* properly *prepare* his lessons"; "It is courteous *to* always *ask* permission"; "What is worse than *to* blindly *follow* an unworthy leader?"

Whether the split infinitive is a fault depends always upon the specific utterance—its rhythm and its meaning. Some splits are awkward; others tax the understanding; some few are needful, being the best way to say what is intended. *"To prepare his lessons properly"* is quite an improvement; *"to follow* an unworthy leader blindly" is not much better than *"to* blindly *follow;"* and *"to ask* permission always" distorts the meaning of *"to* always *ask* permission."

What can be done with the split infinitive in "I am expected *to* really *do* my best"? Placed elsewhere, the adverb *really* will drift from its proper work. What is most effective here is to keep the infinitive split. It is generally considered weak, however, to split the infinitive too broadly asunder: "Don't forget *to* (when you get to London next week) *write* us all about it," or "He made it a ritual *to* every morning before breakfast *take* a swim"—these are simply slipshod. Attention to the natural rhythms of English and to the problems readers have in mentally knitting up a raveled thought will help the writer avoid unfortunate splitting.

spondee   See METER.

spoonerism   By a slip of the tongue the sounds of a phrase may be transposed: "He's back in the outyard growing the mass" for "He's out in the backyard mowing the grass." This kind of slip is called a spoonerism, named for The Rev. William A. Spooner (1844–1930) of New College, Oxford, in whose speech such transpositions were frequent. Spoonerisms have become a device of conscious word-play for humorous effect, whole stories and essays being written (or revised) for the fun of spoonerisms—such as "The Pea Little Thrigs" and "How to Sty a Frake in Your Own Outfire Doorplace," which, the humorist contends, is not so difficult as some thinkle seem to peep.

sprung rhythm   1. Loosely, any ACCENTUAL VERSE. 2. Specifically, the term Gerard Manley Hopkins (1844–1889) invented for his own accentual verse; in Hopkins's system sprung rhythm counts only the heavily, not the lightly, stressed syllables. Hence in practice, where two or two and a half *trochees* (heavily stressed syllables) surprise the reader in an otherwise *iambic* line, the effect is tantamount to syncopation. In one of Hopkins' best-known poems, "God's Grandeur," the reader begins the iambic line "And all is seared with trade . . . " and is suddenly surprised with the *epitrite* "bleered, smeared, with toil." (See METER.)

REFERENCES: Gerard Manley Hopkins, "Preface" to *Poems* (1876–1889) and his "Letters" (especially those to R. W. Dixon) in William H. Gardner (ed.), *The Penguin Poets Series.*

squinter   A disconcerting utterance that looks two ways at once; the receiver cannot be sure which way is meant. For example: "Girls who cry *often* get little sympathy." (Do they often *cry,* or do they often *get little sympathy?* Avoiding that kind of squinter takes a less ambiguous placement of the modifier: "Girls who often cry" or "Often, girls who cry. . . . ") Another example: "Danley decided *when the war was over* not to enlist again." (Did he *decide* when the war was over, or did he decide earlier?) The careful writer would shift the *when* clause to the very beginning or very end of the sentence. (Compare MISPLACED MODIFIER, DANGLER, and REFERENCE OF PRONOUNS.)

stanza   See METER and METRICS; also BALLAD, OTTAVA RIMA, SPENSER-IAN STANZA, and TERZA RIMA.

statement   1. A synonym for declarative assertion. (See SENTENCE.) 2. In the SYLLOGISM a *premise* or *conclusion* in one or another of several forms. (See DEDUCTIVE REASONING.)

statement of fact   Any assertion, true or false, that can be operationally tested. For example: (*a*) "There are thirteen eggs in this carton." (*b*) "There are five major stresses in this line of the poem." (*c*) "Nat Turner had been promised his freedom."

statement of opinion   Any assertion, true or false, that cannot be op-erationally tested but that may well be supported by argumentation. (See THESIS STATEMENT.) For example: (*a*) "Shakespeare was a real-ist." (*b*) "T. S. Eliot writes tough poetry." (*c*) "William Styron's *Confessions of Nat Turner* is an incendiary novel."

statistical induction   See INDUCTIVE REASONING 2.

stereotype   In language, any conventional usage, whether a salutation in a letter ("Dear Sir") or ready-made phrase ("It may interest you to know" or "hale and hearty"). The stereotype is thus a kind of triteness. (Compare CLICHÉ.) In literature, the stereotype extends to characters and plots that offer only the conventional and expected. A stereotyped character is one whose attitudes, actions and reactions, words, and dress fall in with a widely held idea of what such a "type" of person is like; he does not grow, change, or do the unexpected thing. Similarly, a stereotyped plot is one in which the story-line is conventional and known to most readers.

stichomythy, stichomythia   1. In Greek drama, quick dialogue; brief sentences exchanged in rapid sequence by two characters, often in the form of questions and answers. Elements of IRONY and of the riddle are characteristic of tragic stichomythy. 2. In the theater generally, from ancient to modern times, any fast repartee or conversational ping-pong. SENECAN TRAGEDY was especially fond of stichomythy, using it as a means of heightening suspense. In comedy stichomythy has always lent itself to PUNS and other word play. Here is an example from George Farquhar's *Beaux' Strategem* (1707):

CHERRY: Then, friend, good night.
ARCHER: I hope not.
CHERRY: You may depend upon't.
ARCHER: Upon what?
CHERRY: That you're very impudent.
ARCHER: That you are very handsome.
CHERRY: That you're a footman.

REFERENCES: George Thomson, *Aeschylus in Athens;* Allardyce Nicoll, *Development of the Theater;* Kenneth Macgowan, *A Primer of Playwriting.*

stipulative definition   See DEFINING 8.

stock character   In a story or a play, a character with very few individualistic and many stereotyped traits; e.g., the braggart soldier, the gossiping maid, the overbearing butler, and so on.

stock epithet   See EPITHET 3.

storm and stress   See STURM UND DRANG.

story-line   See DRAMATIC STRUCTURE and NARRATION.

stream of consciousness   A narrative technique in which a character seems not only to be thinking out loud, but also to be manifesting symptoms of subconscious experience. In the creating of this illusion the novelist dispenses with normal sentences and punctuation and instead runs words, notions, feelings, images, and vestiges from deep within the psyche's past together in one continuous stream, a technique also called "interior monologue," though with certain fine distinctions. Perhaps the best-known example is Molly Bloom's monologue (the "Penelope" passage) at the end of James Joyce's *Ulysses.* Other users of this technique have been Virginia Woolf, in *The Waves,* and William Faulkner, in *The Sound and the Fury.*

In examining Joyce's novel *Ulysses* for legal purposes, preparatory to deciding whether or not it violated OBSCENITY laws, Judge John Woolsey made an incidental but nonetheless keen analysis of the stream-of-consciousness technique:

Joyce has attempted [observed Judge Woolsey] . . . to show how the screen of consciousness with its ever-shifting kaleidoscopic impressions carries . . . not only what is in the focus of each man's observation of the actual things about him, but also in a penumbral zone, residua of past impressions, some recent and some drawn up by association from . . . the subconscious. He shows how each of these impressions affects the life and behavior of the character he is describing . . . what he seeks is not unlike the results of a double or . . . a multiple exposure on a cinema film which would give a clear foreground with a background visible but somewhat blurred and out of focus in varying degrees . . . and [Joyce reveals] an honest effort to show exactly how the minds of the characters operate.

REFERENCES: Robert Humphrey, *Stream of Consciousness in the Modern Novel;* R. A. Brower, "Virginia Woolf," *The Fields of Light;* T. S. Eliot, *Introducing James Joyce;* Frederick Karl, *The Contemporary English Novel;* Melvin J. Friedman, *Stream of Consciousness: A Study in Literary Method;* Leon Edel, *The Psychological Novel, 1900–1950.*

strophe   See ODE.

Sturm und Drang   Literally, "storm and stress." A romantic youthful movement of the 1770s in revolt against traditional classicism. Founded by J. G. Herder (1744–1803), the movement attracted such artists as Goethe (d. 1832) and Richard Wagner (d. 1883). In the novel *The Sorrows of Young Werther* Goethe recognized in the younger generation of his time an attitude of *Weltschmerz*, or satiety with life, brought on, he felt, by the suppression of individuality, the requirement that all forms of thought be useful and practical, and the general restraint that eighteenth-century society imposed upon youthful enthusiasm. The problem, as Goethe saw it, was youth's lack of any object in which to have faith. The RATIONALISM of the age had seemingly explained away all aspects of religion that could not be supported by logic, and with them much of the emotional and intuitive satisfaction of Christianity. Goethe's hero Werther turned to affairs of the heart for the spiritual satisfaction that had been denied him in rationalistic religion. His combination of physical attraction with spiritual love stood in marked contrast to the established attitudes of the time, which placed physical attraction in the category of frivolity. The adherents of this movement let their emotions run hard, as did Goethe in *Werther,* which was later satirized by Thackeray in *The Yellowplush Papers* (1838).

REFERENCES: Goethe's Letters to Herder in Thomas Mann (ed.), *The Permanent Goethe;* Roy Pascal, *Storm and Stress.*

style   1. Graphic mechanics as described in the "style book" of a newspaper, printing press, or publisher; the *MLA Style Sheet* of the Modern Language Association and *A Manual of Style* of the University of Chicago Press are pre-eminent examples. Certain periodicals, such as the Kansas City *Star* and *The New Yorker* magazine, have from time to time issued style sheets for the private use of their staff members. The style sheet of the Kansas City *Star,* for example, is reputed to have nurtured Hemingway on succinct sentences, active verbs, and economy of vocabulary. (See Charles Fenton, *The Apprenticeship of Ernest Hemingway.*)

2. A subjective label for "literary elegance" or the lack of it. "Style is the man himself," said the celebrated French critic Buffon (1707–88). "I am not satisfied to let it go with the aphorism that style is the man," said Robert Frost. "Rather, his style is the way he carries himself toward his ideas and deeds. . . . It is the mind skating circles round itself as it moves forward" ("Letter to Louis Untermeyer" in Lawrance Thompson [ed.], *Selected Letters of Robert Frost,* p. 299). William Golding, author of *Lord of the Flies,* said at the NCTE Conference in San Francisco in 1963 that style is the end result of "pristine clarity" and cited as examples the closing sentences of Richardson's *Clarissa.* Many NEW CRITICS — among them Allen Tate and Robert Penn War-

ren—refer again and again to the French novelist Flaubert as a master stylist insofar as narrative RENDERING is concerned.

3. An attempt at objective analysis of style has been made by John Carroll, among others, in order to "program" computers and accommodate other devices of "quantifying." Among the measurements Carroll has proposed (in Sebeok, cited below) are the following:

number of paragraphs
number of sentences
sentence length(s)
clause complexity
number of noun clauses
number of adjective clauses
number of adverbial clauses
number of parenthetical phrases
number of appositives
number of phrases
number of words to a sentence
number of words to a phrase
number of words to a clause
number of syllables in word(s)
number of words with Latin
 affixes
number of verbal modifiers
number of attributive ad-
 jectives
number of complements

number of verbs
number of transitives
number of intransitives
number of actives
number of passives
number of copulatives
mean tense
entropy of tense
number of proper nouns
number of common nouns
number of determiners
number of definite articles
number of indefinites
number of pronouns
number of personal pronouns
number of impersonals
number of prepositions
number of numbers

Carroll then lists some "subjective" measures of style, which he hopes can ultimately be either "quantified" or else described operationally enough to be useful to stylistic analysis:

meaningful – meaningless
precise – vague; clear – hazy
profound – superficial (trivial)
subtle – obvious
concrete – abstract
succinct – wordy
graceful – awkward
vigorous – flaccid
lush – austere
earnest – flippant
intimate – remote
elegant –uncouth
natural – affected

personal – impersonal
masculine – feminine
varied – monotonous
complex – simple
rational – emotional
vivid – pale
ordered – chaotic
opinionated – impartial
original – trite
pleasant – unpleasant
good – evil
strong – weak
interesting – boring

REFERENCES: Richard Bridgman, *The Colloquial Style in America;* Monroe Beardsley, "Style: Semantic and Phonetic," *Aesthetics;* Thomas Sebeok (ed.), *Style in Language;* Northrop Frye, "Manual of Style," *The Well-Tempered Critic;* F. L. Lucas, "What Is Style?" in Barnet Kottler and Martin Light (eds.), *The World of Words;* Paul C. Wermuth (ed.), *Modern Essays on Writing and Style;* Arthur Eastman (ed.), "An Album of Styles," *The Norton Reader;* Glen Lore and Michael Payne (eds.), *Contemporary Essays on Style;* Nona Balakian, "Style and the New Economy," in H. Mitgang (ed.), *America at Random;* Carl Klaus, *Style in English Prose;* Donald Hall (ed.), *The Modern Stylists;* W. F. Irmscher, *Ways of Writing;* Frederick Candelaria, *Perspectives on Style;* Raymond Queneau, *Exercises in Style;* John Knott and Reeve Parker (eds.), *The Triumph of Style.*

subordination   The couching of less important ideas in less important structures of language. Subordination is a device both for EMPHASIS and ECONOMY, helping to push secondary matters into the background and to reduce wordage. In terms of sentence structure, *subordinate* contrasts with *independent;* whatever is put into a structure other than an independent clause is *subordinated.* In order of importance, the subordinating structures are (1) subordinate clause, (2) absolute phrase, (3) phrase, (4) word, (5) segmental morpheme.

To illustrate: in the context "The little duck that belonged to the girl had no mother, and it died," one of the two clauses may be made subordinate: "Because the little duck that belonged to the girl had no mother, it died." Further, the adjective clause may be reduced to the possessive: "The *girl's* little duck." The phrase *little duck* may be reduced by the *-ling* morpheme for *little:* "The girl's *duckling.*" The revision with its several subordinations: "Because the girl's duckling had no mother, it died."

Beyond the sentence structures, subordination may be achieved by placement of elements—the least important ideas being treated in less emphatic position. The end of a context is normally the most emphatic position, the beginning the next most emphatic, and the middle the least emphatic. What is to be subordinated, then, may well be placed in the middle of a sentence, of a paragraph, or of a larger work.

surrealism   Just as in the antirational paintings of Salvador Dali legs are apt to grow out of eyes or ears, fingers out of furniture, and so on, so in certain contemporary poetry and fiction there can be seen, from time to time, similarly incongruous IMAGES and scenes. Though hardly any writer creates these "automatically," as some critics have claimed, the writer may operate as a kind of medium to his dreams, his subconscious, even his hallucinations (not necessarily induced by drugs). Such depth imagery (compare DEEP IMAGES) is not exactly unrealistic, since it does create an ILLUSION OF REALITY. But it is not conventionally realistic either. It has come to be called *sub*realistic or, more often, surrealistic, a term invented in 1917 by the French poet and painter Guillaume Apollinaire (1880–1918). The two best known surrealist poets are René Char of France and Pablo Neruda of Chile. There are also elements of surrealism in the fantasy-folklore-fiction of the British writer J. R. R. Tolkien; in Dylan Thomas's *Portrait of the Artist as a Young Dog* and *Adventures in the Skin Trade;* and in the Walpurgis night episode of James Joyce's *Ulysses.* The United States can claim several well-known surrealist poets, among them Kenneth Patchen, Michael McClure, and Kenneth Koch, as well as many poets who occasionally write surrealist poems. Nathaniel West's *Dream Life of Balso Snell* is an example of surrealist fiction, as are the stories of Kenneth Patchen. Surrealist elements are also present in Carson McCullers's short novel *Reflections in a Golden Eye,* and in Djuna Barnes's novel *Nightwood.*

REFERENCES: Roger Shattuck, "Guillaume Apollinaire," *The Banquet Years;* André Breton, *Manifestoes of Surrealism;* Herbert Gershman, *The Surrealist Revolution in France;* J. H. Matthews, *Surrealism and the Novel;* Ferdinand Alquie, *The Philosophy of Surrealism;* Pablo Neruda, *A New Decade: Poems 1958–1967* [translated by Ben Bellitt and Alastair Reid].

sweeping generalization   An emotional assertion frequently unsubstantiated by, and contrary to, factual evidence, yet asserted as though a statement of fact: e.g., "Women drivers are the world's worst." (*Note:* Insurance statistics show that most reckless driving is done by males in their early twenties.) Such generalizations ("All Jews are. . . ." "All Catholics are. . . ." "All Negroes are. . . .") suffer from failure to discriminate among individuals. Sweeping generalizations are also known colloquially as *sweepers* and are usually derogatory, as contrasted with GLITTERING GENERALITIES.

REFERENCE: Lionel Ruby, "Are All Generalizations False?" *The Art of Making Sense.*

syllabication   Strictly, the dividing of words into syllables; here considered for its importance in the dividing of words between one line and the next in writing and printing. For printers the problem is momentous, since typesetters must *justify,* or space out, each line to a predetermined, uniform length, as is done in this book. For the writer in script or at the typewriter, the problem is less, for he may leave a ragged right margin. Thus the writer may, if he chooses, avoid the problem of dividing words entirely by dividing none whatsoever.

For compositors, who must meet the problem, and for writers who choose to do so, there are a number of rules that are of help. The fundamental rule is *divide between syllables.* What is or is not a syllable then becomes the critical problem. In American English, a syllable is determined by the pronunciation and not, as in England, by the etymology. Pronunciation, even without a dictionary, will usually provide a correct syllabication, but there need be no doubt if a good dictionary is consulted, for every dictionary of value indicates syllabication.

Knowledge of syllabication alone, however, will not be sufficient to determine whether a word *may* be divided in composition. A cardinal principle is that the initial component of the divided word should accurately reflect both the desired pronunciation and the expected sense; in short, the part left at the end of the line should suggest the whole word. For example, "I pro-duce this prod-uce" and "We pro-ject for this proj-ect." The rules given here are intended to be applied in conjunction with the use of a dictionary, and are mostly negative elaborations of the basic rule.

1. Never divide a one-syllable word: *touched, through, shipped, prism*.

2. Never divide a word of less than six letters, regardless of the number of syllables: *unity*, not *uni-ty; party*, not *par-ty; iota*, not *io-ta*.

3. Never leave a single-letter syllable on the first line: *usu-ally*, not *u-sually; imag-inary*, not *i-maginary*.

4. Never leave less than three letters on the second line: *pointed*, not *point-ed; mother*, not *moth-er; re-lated*, not *relat-ed; em-panel*, not *empan-el; emer-gency*, not *emergen-cy*.

5. Never divide within a prefix or suffix; divide after the prefix or before the suffix: *over-optimistic*, not *overop-timistic; inter-act*, not *in-teract; super-natural*, not *su-pernatural; celes-tial*, not *celesti-al; reli-gious*, not *religi-ous*.

6. Never divide abbreviations or contractions: A.M., not A.-M.; *haven't*, not *have-n't; doesn't*, not *does-n't*.

7. Never divide month and day from year in dates.

8. Never divide proper names or separate initials from a surname.

9. Never divide the last words of more than two successive lines.

10. Never divide the last word of a paragraph.

11. Divide words already containing a hyphen only after the hyphen; never insert a second hyphen in such words: *cross-section*, not *cross-sec-tion; tax-supported*, not *tax-sup-ported*.

12. When a vowel alone forms a syllable, divide after the vowel: *credu-lous*, not *cred-ulous; exhila-rate*, not *exhil-arate*.

13. When a syllable has a silent vowel, do not leave that syllable standing alone: *prin-ciple*, not *princi-ple; chuckle*, not *chuc-kle; bristle*, not *bris-tle*.

14. Never divide a number of less than 10,000 and avoid dividing larger numbers; if the division is unavoidable, divide after a comma: 1,873,-974.

syllabus A brief statement or listing of the main points to be covered in a course of study. Some syllabi include a list of books to be read and dates by which the student should have read them. The very idea of a

syllabus has been rejected or resisted by the "bored school" of edu-
cationists. (See, for example, Neil Postman and Charles Weingartner,
Teaching as a Subversive Activity.)

syllepsis   The use of a word to do double duty within an utterance so
that it appears to shift its meaning unexpectedly. Syllepsis is ordinarily
effective (in English, at least) only as humor. Some examples (with the
shifty words in italics): "We *shot* one deer and lots of photographs";
"He writes *with* enthusiasm and red ink"; "Walter *ran for* the relay
team and class prexy"; "She's *engaged* for the evening and to Charles."
As the examples show, syllepsis is not the same thing as a pun, in which
the word-play depends more upon sound than upon mere shifting of
idiom or usage. (Compare ZEUGMA.)

syllogism   A formal argument chiefly in DEDUCTIVE REASONING,
couched in rigid form and observing rules that ensure the validity of
the conclusion. A typical syllogism consists of three statements, as
follows:

a) Major premise — e.g., All cows are females.
b) Minor premise — e.g., Bessie is a cow.
c) Conclusion — e.g., Bessie is a female.

In this article the following kinds of syllogism will be discussed: (1)
categorical, (2) *conditional,* (3) *alternative,* and (4) *disjunctive.*

   1. *The categorical syllogism* is so called because each of its statements is categorical, or absolute, with no *ifs* or other limitations. Understanding of the principles of valid reasoning in the categorical syllogism
requires a knowledge of the parts of the syllogism — their names, their
aspects, and their functions.

   a) Term: each of the things named in a syllogism. In the syllogism
about Bessie the cow, the *terms* are *cows, females,* and *Bessie.* Every
categorical syllogism has three terms: the *major term* (the term in the
predicate of the conclusion), the *minor term* (the term in the subject
of the conclusion), and the *middle term* (the term that appears in both
premises but not in the conclusion).

   b) Class: each term refers to (or names) a group whose members
share certain characteristics. *Cows* are a *class; females* are a *class;
Bessie* is a *class* — this time a class with but one member, or "a class
of one."

   c) Statement: a subject-predicate assertion every syllogism contains three. Each *statement* contains two terms — one the *subject* of
the statement, the other the *predicate-complement* of the statement.
The two terms are linked by a verb — usually a state-of-being verb
like *is* or *are.* When some other verb appears, the statement usually

can be translated into an *is* or *are* statement; for example, if we assert that "All cows give milk," we must understand that *milk* is not a term in the statement, but *milk-giving animals* is the correct term, and we translate the statement as, "All cows *are* milk-giving animals." Statements in the syllogism do not imply equality. "All cows are females" does not assert that cows *equal* females; it asserts, rather, that the class called cows is *included* in the class called females. Syllogistic statements *include* or *exclude;* they do not equate.

d) Premises: the first two statements in a syllogism, the major premise containing the major term, the minor premise containing the minor term.

e) Conclusion: the final statement in a syllogism. It draws an inference based upon the two premises — and, when valid, justified by them.

f) Four forms of statement. To understand how statements work in the categorical syllogism, we must consider two special aspects — *quality* and *quantity.*

In the context of deductive logic, *quality* concerns whether a statement is affirmative or negative. The statement "Bessie is a cow" is *affirmative;* it *affirms* that Bessie is a cow. The statement "No cats are cows" is *negative;* it *denies* that cats are cows.

In the context of deductive logic, *quantity* concerns whether a statement is universal or particular. The statement "All cows are females" is *universal;* it refers to *all* of its subject class — *all* cows. The statement "Some birds are robins" is *particular;* it refers to only part of its subject class — *some* birds.

These aspects make possible *four forms of statement,* designated by the symbols as A, E, I, O:

"A" form: the universal-affirmative (*All X is Y*)
"E" form: the universal-negative (*No X is Y*)
"I" form: the particular-affirmative (*Some X is Y*)
"O" form: the particular-negative (*Some X is not Y*)

These four forms of statement may be combined in several patterns to produce a syllogism — as long as their combination does not produce any violate of the rules of validity.

g) Distribution: the *all* or *some* aspect of a term. Terms refer to classes of things; but when a term appears in a statement, it may refer to *all* members of a class or only to *some* members of the class. A term that refers to *all* members of its class is a *distributed* term; a term that refers only to *some* members of its class is an *undistributed* term. It is helpful to know the pattern of distribution of terms in the four forms of categorical statement:

FORMS OF CATEGORICAL STATEMENT IN DEDUCTIVE SYLLOGISMS

Statement form		Distribution	
		Subject	Predicate
"A" form:		D	U
"E" form:		D	D
"I" form:		U	U
"O" form:		U	D

Reference to the diagrams will show that a term whose circle is entirely shaded or entirely unshaded is a *distributed* term; a term whose circle is *partly* shaded is an *undistributed* term.

In the statement "All cows are females" we are discussing *all* cows; *cows* is a *distributed* term. But we are not discussing all females — only a few of them, the females that are also cows; therefore, *females* is an *undistributed* term. A few moments of study with the diagrams as aid will clarify the matter of distribution of terms.

h) *Fallacy:* an error in the form or process of a syllogism. The most common fallacies in the categorical syllogism are these:

1) *Undistributed middle.* The middle term in a categorical syllogism must be distributed *once* — and only once. Consider:

All x is y.
All z is y.
Therefore . . . ?

No valid conclusion is possible, since the middle term, y, is undistributed in both of its appearances: It never refers to *all* members of its class. Also consider:

All p is q.
No r is p.
Therefore . . . ?

Again, no valid conclusion is possible, since the middle term, p, is distributed both times it appears.

2) *Four terms.* Every syllogism must have *three* terms, and *only* three. Consider:

All c is d.
All e is f.
Therefore . . . ?

No conclusion is possible, since the minor premise is entirely irrelevant to the major premise.

3) *Two particulars.* Every syllogism must have at least one *universal* premise. Consider these

Some Americans are men.
Some girls are Americans.
Therefore . . . ?

It is invalid to conclude that some girls are men, since girls may be among the Americans not mentioned in the first premise. Neither premise is a *universal* statement.

4) *Two negatives.* Every syllogism must have at least one *affirmative* premise. Consider these:

No mothers are men.
Some grandparents are not men.
Therefore . . . ?

It would be invalid to conclude any relationship between grandparents and mothers. Neither premise is an *affirmative* statement.

5) *Particular switched to universal.* If either premise is a particular, the conclusion must also be a particular. Consider:

All natives are citizens at birth.
Some natives are of foreign parentage.
Therefore, all who have foreign parentage are citizens at birth.

The conclusion is invalid, for it is an *all* statement when one of the premises was a *some* statement.

      6) *Negative switched to affirmative.* If either premise is negative, the conclusion must also be negative. Consider:

No voters are aliens.
Some citizens are voters.
Therefore, some citizens are aliens.

The conclusion is invalid, for it is affirmative although one of the premises was negative. The conclusion becomes valid if we convert it to negative: "Some citizens are *not* aliens."

      7) *Undistributed switched to distributed.* Any term that is undistributed in a premise must also be undistributed if it appears in the conclusion. Consider:

Some Texans are Democrats.
No Democrats are Republicans.
Therefore, some Republicans are not Texans.

The conclusion is invalid, for the term *Texans* is distributed in the conclusion although it was undistributed in the major premise. The conclusion becomes valid if we convert it to "some Texans are not Republicans," leaving the term *Texans* in undistributed form.

      i) *Enthymeme:* an elliptical syllogism. A valid conclusion may be drawn although not all the stages of syllogistic reasoning have been made explicit. Consider:

All lazy students are underproducers;
Therefore, Tim is an underproducer.

The argument has moved directly from a major premise to a conclusion, omitting the minor premise, "Tim is a lazy student."

      j) *Sorites:* a series of interlaced syllogisms in which the conclusion of one syllogism becomes a premise of another, so that the chain leads to a conclusion connecting the subject of the first statement to the predicate of the last.

      2. The *conditional syllogsim* is so called because its initial premise is introduced by an "if" clause—a conditional clause. This "if" clause (called the *antecedent*) is followed by a "then" clause (called the consequent):

If he goes to the game, then he cannot study.
   (*antecedent*)   (*consequent*)

Conditional arguments depend for their validity upon the proper application of a second premise, which must be in one of two modes:

      a) *affirming the antecedent* (*modus ponens*), in which the second premise affirms that the "if" clause, the condition, is true: "He goes to the game";

b) *denying the consequent* (*modus tollens*), in which the second premise denies that the "then" clause is true: "He can study."
Either of these forms will produce a valid conclusion:

If he goes to the game, then he cannot study.
He goes to the game (*modus ponens*).
Therefore, he cannot study.

If he goes to the game, then he cannot study.
He can study (*modus tollens*).
Therefore, he does not go to the game.

Fallacies of the conditional syllogism occur when either of these modes is violated. The fallacies are *affirming the consequent* and *denying the antecedent*. For example, a second premise saying "He cannot study" would not permit a conclusion that "he does not go to the game"—because it is possible that he cannot study, *for other reasons*. And a second premise saying "He does not go the game" would not permit a conclusion that "he can study"—because the initial premise did not say anything about what might happen if he does not go to the game. (*See also* REDUCTIO AD ABSURDUM.)

3. *The alternative syllogism* offers in its major premise an alternative in the "either-or" form: "Either we eat, or we starve." One of the alternatives *must* be true; therefore, if we show that one of them is false, we prove that the other is true. A valid argument reads:

Either we eat, or we starve.
We do not starve.
Therefore, we eat.

The major premise is an alternative (*either-or*) statement. The minor premise and the conclusion are both categorical statements, the minor premise *denying* one of the alternatives and the conclusion *affirming* the other. If the minor premise *affirms* an alternative ("we eat"), a fallacy appears:

Either we eat, or we starve.
We eat.
Therefore, we do not starve.

Odd as it may seem in the given context, the conclusion is not valid, for there is nothing in the premises to assure us that we cannot eat and *also* starve. The second premise commits the fallacy of *affirming an alternative*.

4. *The disjunctive syllogism* has a major premise in the "not both . . . and . . ." form: "Men are *not both* dishonest *and* happy." One of the two conditions *must* be false; therefore, if we show that one of them is true, we show that the other must be false. A valid argument reads:

> We cannot both eat our cake and have it;
> We have eaten our cake;
> Therefore, we cannot have it.

The major premise is disjunctive; the minor premise and the conclusion are both categorical—the minor premise *affirming* one of the two disjunctive conditions. If the minor premise denies one of those conditions, the argument commits the fallacy of *denying a disjunctive*.

REFERENCES: John Sherwood, *Discourse of Reason: A Brief Handbook of Logic and Semantics;* Morris Raphael Cohen, *Introduction to Logic.*

symbol   1. In general, and loosely, a synonym for *sign;* e.g., the dollar sign ($), a proofreader's mark (#), a musical notation (⌒), a mathematical notation (+), and the like, usually translatable with a single meaning.

2. In SEMANTICS, which defines language as symbolic process, any word at all (e.g., *furniture*) is symbolic in the sense that it is only more or less representative of, and has been abstracted from, a comparatively more concrete object or REFERENT (e.g., *table* or *chair*) and hence cannot be the object itself, but only a symbol of it.

3. In RHETORIC and in some literature a symbol shares the characteristics of definitions 1 and 2 above, but in addition carries a *conventional* or broadly accepted and understood representation, especially in PROVERB and CLICHÉ. For example, in the expression "The pen is mightier than the sword," the sword has conventionally symbolized or stood for war or violence; the pen, peace or conciliation or arbitration and the like. Similarly, in the expression "Every man has his cross to bear," cross by ALLUSION as well as by convention symbolizes painful burden or misery or misfortune and the like. Well-known rhetorical and literary symbols with conventional representations include the *cellar* (of bottomness), the *woods* (of inextricability; but compare its nonconventional representations in a poem like Frost's "Stopping by Woods"), the *cornucopia* (of plenty), the *tower* (of strength), the *wheel* (of fortune), the *spiral* (of gradations, as in Dante, Yeats, and Eliot), and the *mountain* (as an object of conquest; but compare the nuances of even that kind of mountain in Dante's *Divine Comedy,* Mann's *Magic Mountain,* and Hemingway's "Snows of Kilimanjaro").

4. In literature and literary criticism an *unconventional* symbol is any object or image capable of representing several different ideas or experiences, even within one context, and often with diametrically different emotional values and impacts for different characters and readers. For example, the Christian cross may represent the hope of salvation or the power of the Church for characters wearing that symbol, whereas the same symbol may represent oppression to the victims in a poem, drama, or narrative about a pogrom or inquisition, to say

nothing of a crucifixion. (For the victim of a crucifixion the cross can ambivalently represent oppression *and* salvation.) In short, an unconventional literary symbol is "an object or image outside ourselves, which represents something inside ourselves," as Erich Fromm observes; it generates a variety of sensory and emotional responses. One of the memorable examples of an unconventional symbol in literature is the white whale in Melville's *Moby-Dick*. The reader may well remember the variety of emotional responses and associations that this whale elicits, not only as whale, but also as symbol to Captain Ahab, as distinguished from its meanings for other members of the crew. There is of course the danger of "reading in" more symbolic meanings than an author may have intended. There is also the misguided practice of jumping so far ahead to find symbolic representations as to leap-frog over very important literal representations; for example, in *Moby-Dick,* the whale is a whale and the rope is a guideline or instrument of safety, as Terence Martin has observed.

REFERENCES: Erich Fromm, "The Nature of Symbolic Language," in Richard W. Lid (ed.), *Grooving the Symbol, A Contemporary Reader;* Maurice Beebe (ed.), *Literary Symbolism;* J. E. Cerlot, *A Dictionary of Symbols;* Monroe Beardsley, "Representation and Abstraction," *Aesthetics;* Kenneth Burke, "Symbolic Action," *The Philosophy of Literary Form;* R. Z. Temple, *The Critic's Alchemy;* Mary McCarthy, "Settling the Colonel's Hash," in R. E. Knoll (ed.), *Contrasts;* Terence Martin, *The Instructed Vision.*

symbolism   A literary movement that developed first in France in the 1800s and that extended the revolt of ROMANTICISM against REALISM. Such French *symbolistes* as Baudelaire, Rimbaud, Mallarmé, and Verlaine – and, later, such English symbolists as Yeats, Joyce, and Eliot – made poetry "even more a matter of the senses than did the Romanticists," said Edmund Wilson in the "Symbolism" chapter of *Axel's Castle*. But sensory experience and the use of imagery are not, of course, the special preserve of symbolist poets. (Almost all poets suggest more than they say directly, and almost all of them appeal to the emotions through IMAGES and SYMBOLS.) What does come closer to pinpointing the symbolist vision, the special symbolist use of imagery and sensory experience, is perhaps best understood in Yeats's discussion of "Dove or Swan" in *A Vision* (Book 5) and in Baudelaire's *Flowers of Evil,* especially in the poem "Correspondences": "Nature is a temple from whose living columns / Commingling voices emerge at time; / Here man wanders through forests of symbols / Which seem to observe him with familiar eyes / . . . Colors, scents, and sounds correspond. / There are fragrances fresh as the flesh of children, / . . . Possessing the pervasiveness of everlasting things / . . . Which the raptures of the senses and the spirit sing." [Translated by Kate Flores, *The Anchor Anthology of French Poetry,* Doubleday, 1958.] For the symbolists another world—either imagined (as by Baudelaire) or constructed (as by Yeats)—exists beyond the world ordinarily visible. And the symbolist poet tries to make that world known to himself and others by means of images and image-clusters that stand for, that translate, that world. The early symbolist movement was carried on by the French poets Corbière and Laforgue (who in turn influenced T. S. Eliot), by the playwright Maurice Maeterlinck, by the composer Debussy, by the critic Remy de Gourmont, and by such writers as Marcel Proust, James Joyce and Gertrude Stein. (Compare IMAGIST, OBJECTIVE CORRELATIVE.)

REFERENCES: Angel Flores (ed.), *The Anchor Anthology of French Poetry from Nerval to Valéry;* W. B. Yeats, "The Symbolism of Poetry," *Essays and Introductions;* René Wellek and Austin Warren, "Image, Metaphor, Symbol, Myth," *The Theory of Literature;* Enid Starkie, *Baudelaire and Arthur Rimbaud;* C. M. Bowra, *The Heritage of Symbolism;* Arthur Symons, *The Symbolist Movement in Literature;* Nicholas Perella, *The Kiss Sacred and Profane.*

symbolists, symbolistes   See SYMBOLISM.

syncope   The compression of a word by the dropping of a letter, sound, or syllable from the middle: "ne'er for "never," "gen'ral" for "general," "e'er" for "ever." (See POETICISM.)

synecdoche   A kind of METONYMY, or name-changing, in which a part stands for the whole. We use synecdoche when we say *hand* for man ("a hired hand" and "all hands on deck"), *wheel* for bicycle or automobile, *bread* for food ("the breadwinner"), or *door* for house ("Run next door"). Synecdoche may also name an individual for a class ("mute inglorious *Miltons*" for unsung geniuses or poets), an ingredient for something containing it (*nickel* for a five-cent coin, *oil* for a painting, *wood* or *iron* for a golf club), a container for the thing contained ("keep the pot boiling," "drink a cup with me," or "good house" for a large audience).

On the analogy of FADED METAPHOR, expressions like "write a paper" and "bake a cake" may be thought of as faded synecdoches, since we have come to take for granted that "paper" in the above context is only a part of what we write, and baking only a part of what we do when we make a cake.

synesthesia   In IMAGERY, the use of one sense to convey the experience of another sense; for example, the image "coolness of blue" contains a transfer appeal between the senses of sight and touch. Compare also "piercing yellow," "loud necktie," "salty music."

synopsis   A brief and general overview of a long literary work, usually of a novel. (Compare PRÉCIS.).

synthesis   See DIALECTIC 3.

T

table of contents A list (or main topic outline) of the sections or chapters of a book, with the numbers of the pages on which these begin.

tale **1.** Loosely, a synonym for narrative or story. **2.** Strictly, a folk form, especially the *tall tale,* such as those narrating the exploits of Paul Bunyan, Johnny Appleseed, Pecos Bill, John Henry, and so on. REFERENCES: Martha Pappas (ed.), *Heroes of the American West;* Milton Rugoff (ed.), *A Harvest of World Folk Tales;* Stith Thompson (ed.), *One Hundred Favorite Folk Tales.* See also the references under FOLKLORE.

tanka A classic Japanese verse form in five unrhymed lines of, respectively, five, seven, five, seven, and seven syllables. Like the HAIKU, the tanka is characterized by a tight unity of mood, event, and imagery. The chief difference between the two, aside from form, is that the tanka usually builds on an event that would be too difficult to encompass in the three-line haiku. Another difference is that a season is less likely to be established in the tanka. An example of a tanka by Saigo Hoshi:

> Now we know, alas,
> that when we said "Remember,"
> when we vowed as much,
> it was in "We must forget"
> our true hearts had their meeting.
>   Translated Tadami Takenori

REFERENCE: Sanford Goldstein and Seishi Shimoda (trans.), *Tangled Hair.*

tautological argument See BEGGING THE QUESTION 3.

tautology **1.** Unnecessary repetition: "bibliography of books," "vocabulary words." (See DEADWOOD.) **2.** In LOGIC, a statement necessarily valid by its logical structure alone: "Either it is snowing or it is not snowing."

technique **1.** Loosely, a synonym for STYLE. **2.** In general, an artist's working method—in fiction, drama, poetry, and the other arts—which is at the same time a kind of control. One of Vladimir Nabokov's techniques in *Lolita* is the "diary first-person." In Joyce's *Ulysses* the symbolic journey is one of the chief techniques. **3.** In particular, one such device that may not be chief but only incidental, as is the STREAM-OF-CONSCIOUSNESS technique in *Ulysses.* Similarly, in the play *Strange Interlude,* O'Neill uses the technique of the above-the-stage voice to represent a character's thinking.

According to Mark Schorer, a writer's techniques—or a given one—may well become the discipline that leads him to discover what he wants to say. As Marshall McLuhan has put it, what the artist has to say is largely the way he says it ("the medium is the message").

REFERENCES: Mark Schorer, "Technique as Discovery," *The Hudson Review* (Spring, 1948); Marshall McLuhan, *Understanding Media;* Allen Tate, "Techniques of Fiction," in B. S. Oldsey and A. O. Lewis, Jr. (eds.), *Visions and Revisions.*

tension 1. In ARGUMENTATION, the force gravitating between an argument and its rebuttal; a proposition and its opposite; a THESIS and its ANTITHESIS (see DIALECTIC). 2. In a literary work the emotional atmosphere, now serious, now comic, generated by two dynamic opposing forces, meanings, or values—much like counterpoint in music. Examples: the literal vs. the symbolic; a character vs. a FOIL; a plot and its subplot; a GENRE vs. its PARODY; strophe and antistrophe (see ODE); MASQUE and antimasque; HYPERBOLE VS. UNDERSTATEMENT; rhetoric vs. silence; CONSONANCE VS. DISSONANCE; the DONNÉE and the implied; the fact vs. the METAPHOR; form and content. Each force by itself is only a kind of cloud until it clashes with its opposite—to make lightning.

REFERENCE: Judson Jerome, *The Poet and the Poem.*

term See SYLLOGISM 1a.

term paper See RESEARCH PAPER.

terza rima The iambic pentameter, three-lined stanza of Dante's *Divine Comedy,* with the "chain riming" *aba, bcb, cdc,* etc. According to John Ciardi, Dante managed to preserve in the terza rima the flavor of the spoken language. Terza rima was introduced into English by Thomas Wyatt (sixteenth century). It was used by Shelley in "Ode to the West Wind," from which we quote the first two stanzas (*aba, bcb*):

> O wild West Wind, thou breath of Autumn's being,
> Thou, from whose unseen presence the leaves dead
> Are driven, like ghosts from an enchanter fleeing.
>
> Yellow, and black, and pale, and hectic red,
> Pestilence-stricken multitudes: O thou,
> Who chariotest to their dark wintry bed . . .

Terza rima has been used by Milton, Byron, Browning, Eliot, MacLeish, and Auden.

testimonial The argument that, because a well-known person praises, uses, or advocates a thing or idea, the thing or idea must be worthy. The sceptical consumer will ask, "Is the person who is making the testimonial an expert in this particular field?" (See PROPAGANDA DEVICES.)

tetrameter See METER.

text 1. The actual written or printed form of a literary work. 2. In the view of some critics, the literary work before it is experienced by a reader. (See LEVELS OF MEANING.)

texture 1. In RHETORIC, the "transformational density" of an utterance; that is, the measure of succinct modifiers that have been embedded in it and of the specifiers that have been added. For example, in a rich-textured sentence like "Ulysses sailed the wine-dark sea," there is embedded the modifier "wine-dark," which derives consciously or intuitively from some such utterance as "the sea was wine-dark." (That last utterance was reduced to its essence, "wine-dark," and was then embedded as a modifier in the sentence "Ulysses sailed the sea.") As an example of add-ons—especially of absolute phrases (noun-participle, noun-adjective, and so on)—the texture of the sentence "Ulysses sailed the wine-dark sea" may be enriched by such end-phrases as "the men working the oars, the water washing from the wood," one phrase riding piggyback on its predecessor. Although nineteenth- and twentieth-century critics disparaged the Latinate absolute phrase (which almost always occurred at the beginning rather than at the end of a main clause), they seem to have had a blind spot about the position of word groups. Except for a generalization like "the best words in their best order" (Coleridge), these critics' observations on style, especially on texture, are now eclipsed by the observations and insights of contemporary rhetoricians and linguists. The texture-enriching absolute phrase is used extensively by the most celebrated writers, as Francis Christensen has shown—especially by Conrad, Joyce, Faulkner, and Hemingway. These writers have preferred to use it as a terminal add-on, however, rather than as a front-door sentry. (The "sentry participle" was disparaged by Fowler even if it did not dangle. See "participles" in Fowler's *Modern English Usage*.) Using the absolute phrase add-on gives an utterance a cumulative texture similar to that of the LOOSE SENTENCE. (See RENDERING.)

2. In literature, the depth or richness of a literary piece (as measured by its LEVELS OF MEANING) as opposed to nontexture or flimsiness. A flimsy piece tends to have only one meaning—the literal or surface meaning—and tends to communicate prosaically. A sentimental poem like Emily Dickinson's "If I can stop one heart from breaking," for example, noble as its sentiment may be, is said to have a thin texture because its meaning is communicated directly from the surface and because it has no deeper layers of meaning. In contrast, the same poet's "I Heard a Fly Buzz When I Died" can be said to have a rich texture because much of its meaning is signaled indirectly and beneath what is given literally. (Of course, all literary pieces have to start with some

"given," as Henry James observes in "The Art of Fiction.") Similar contrasts are evident between such fiction as Conrad's "Youth" (thin-textured) and *The Heart of Darkness* (rich-textured); between Melville's "Bartleby" (thin-textured) and *Benito Cereno* (rich-textured).

REFERENCES: Francis Christensen, *Notes Toward a New Rhetoric;* Owen Thomas, *Transformational Density in Emily Dickinson's Poetry;* Laurence Perrine, "Bad Poetry," *Sound and Sense;* Wyndham Lewis and Charles Lee, *The Stuffed Owl;* Henry James, "The Art of Fiction," in James Miller (ed.), *Myth and Method.*

Theater of the Absurd   The drama of Samuel Beckett, Eugene Ionesco, Edward Albee, Jack Gelber, Harold Pinter, Jean Genêt, and other contemporary playwrights, whose attempts to show the absurdities, inconsistencies, and bewildering complexities of twentieth-century man have resulted in extravagant symbolical plays. These defy traditional stage conventions of time, place, plot, and characterization; hence, they are occasionally termed *anti-plays*. The attempt to show man as irrational, solitary, and incapable of understanding his condition often divorces the stage action from any context of conventional reality. The dialogue—often absurd and full of CLICHÉS and gibberish—frequently contradicts the action. The very title of Arthur Kopit's *Oh Dad, Poor Dad, Mama's Hung You in the Closet and I'm Feeling So Sad* is representative of the Absurdist language. The characters often lack individuality and consistency, no doubt intentionally so. Midway in Beckett's *Waiting for Godot,* the master and the slave suddenly reverse their roles. (Beckett is, of course, trying to tell us something here.) The laws of nature are disregarded, denied existence, or are even satirized. In Ionesco's *Amédée* a corpse offstage suddenly enlarges until a mammoth foot crashes through the door onto the stage—suggesting, perhaps, that academic circles pay too much attention to the dead, and not enough to the living. The characters in Arthur Adamov's *Ping-Pong* argue the economics and aesthetics of pinball machines with almost religious fervor. The themes of these plays often seem senseless to all but the most confirmed secular EXISTENTIALISTS. In terms of conventional dramatic structure, the anti-play has no beginning or end—no rising action, CLIMAX, or DÉNOUEMENT (see DRAMATIC STRUCTURE). The audience is kept in suspense, not by the progressive unraveling of a problem to its final solution, as in traditional drama, but rather by successive, apparently random, clues as to the "meaning" of the play—the meaning almost always left open-ended. (See IMMEDIATE THEATER.)

REFERENCES: Martin Esslin, *Theatre of the Absurd;* Jan Kott, *Theatre Notebook: 1947–1967;* George Kernodle, *Introduction to the Theater.*

theme   1. A subject that recurs throughout a literary work, though it cannot be said to be the single focus of the author's attention. Any novel is likely to contain several themes — greed, friendship, family involvement in the affairs of its members. A writer develops such themes by offering more than one example for the reader to compare; for instance, the friendship of A and B (lasting) in contrast to the friendship of X and Y (destroyed by circumstances). In this sense a theme is comparable to a MOTIF. **2.** The unifying statement, express or implied, in a literary work; e.g., "A person who does right as he sees it, no matter how unpopular, ultimately wins respect, even from his enemies." In this sense theme is more or less synonymous with "thesis" or "predication" or "author's philosophic statement" or "what the author seems to be saying here." **3.** As loosely used by students and teachers, a synonym for "composition," "paper," or "essay."

REFERENCES: Monroe Beardsley, "Interpretation of Literature," *Aesthetics;* Harry Levin, "Thematics and Criticism," in Peter Demetz *et al.* (eds.), *The Disciplines of Criticism;* Palmer Bovie, "The Amphitryon Theme from Plautus to Pinter," *Minnesota Review* (Fall, 1967); Michael Allen, "The Chase: Development of a Renaissance Theme," *Comparative Literature* (Fall, 1968); Ruth Taylor Todasco, "Theme and Imagery in *The Golden Bowl,*" *Texas Studies in Literature and Language* (Summer, 1962); Evon Nossen, "The Beast-Man Theme in the Work of Steinbeck," *Ball State Forum* (Spring, 1966).

Theophrastan characters   Character sketches of conventional types of people in conventional walks of life, broadly generalized if not stereotyped: "The Scolemaster," "the milkmaid," "The Scrivener," the bore, the flatterer, etc. Best-known collections: Joseph Hall, *Characters of Vertues and Vices* (1608) and Thomas Overbury, *A Wife and Twenty-one Other Characters* (1614). The name "Theophrastan" was adopted in recognition of the third-century B.C. character-sketch writer Theophrastus. Aside from influencing Washington Irving (compare "The Morose Scolemaster" and "Ichabod Crane"), these sketches are often cited as contributing to the early development of English prose fiction.

REFERENCES: C. N. Greenough, *A Bibliography of the Theophrastan Character in English;* P. A. Smith, *Our English Seneca;* Wilbur Cross, *History of the English Novel;* "Prose Forms: Characters," in Arthur Eastman *et al.* (eds.), *The Norton Reader;* Warren Anderson, *The Characters of Theophrastus.*

thesis   **1.** A formal paper, *term paper,* or RESEARCH PAPER for an academic degree (Bachelor of Arts, Master of Arts, etc.); also a "dissertation," the synonym usually preferred for the Ph.D. opus. **2.** An idea or statement-of-opinion, usually with an argumentative edge or an original interpretation, which the writer or speaker proposes to develop or defend. (See DIALECTIC 4.)

REFERENCES: Monroe Beardsley, "Interpretation of Literature," *Aesthetics;*

Sheridan Baker, "Thesis," *The Practical Stylist;* Edgar Roberts, *Writing Themes about Literature;* William J. Brandt *et al., The Craft of Writing.*

thesis question A question like "How do we know this?" or "In what ways?" or "What *are* these?" A question one puts to a THESIS STATE-MENT to elicit answers. The answers thus elicited serve as main heads in an OUTLINE and main points in an article or expository essay. REFERENCE: Harry H. Crosby and George Estey, "The Controlling Concept," *The Rhetorical Imperative.*

thesis statement The statement of the major idea in an article or expository essay; it answers the question, "What do I want to say here — mainly?" or "What is the central point of this essay — what does it add up to?" An interpretive essay related to a study of *Macbeth*, for example, may yield a thesis statement like the following: "Lady Macbeth functions less as a believable woman than as Macbeth's own evil other self." Characteristics of viable thesis statements: (1) They are statements, not topics or questions. (2) They are statements of opinion rather than of fact — they do not rehash what is already given (DONNÉE) in the primary work being interpreted. Thus, if the statement goes something like this: "Lady Macbeth keeps egging Macbeth on," it is too factual — too close to what is given in the play — to qualify as a statement of opinion, even if later this statement of fact may be quite usable as a supporting point. (3) They go out on a limb of commitment. (4) They can be supported by details in the primary text. (See THESIS QUESTION and OUTLINING.)

REFERENCES: Sheridan Baker, *The Practical Stylist;* W. J. Brandt *et al., The Craft of Writing;* Gary Tate and E. P. J. Corbett (eds.), *Teaching High School Composition;* Edgar Roberts, *Writing Themes about Literature;* Alan Casty and D. J. Tighe, *Staircase to Writing and Reading;* Richard Dodge and George Wykoff, *Handbook of College Composition.*

title The name given to a specific piece of writing. Since the title is ordinarily what a reader sees first, it ideally performs one or more of the following functions: (1) attracts attention, (2) establishes the topic, (3) hints at the THEME, (4) predicts MODE and TONE, (5) serves as a memorable name for the work.

Some writers fail to distinguish between a title and a *label*: "My Vacation" or "Food Preparation," for example, will not do; the one is too vague, the other too general, and both are too trite. The vacation piece might be titled, "Where the Bears Are," and as for food preparation a title such as "How to Cook an Armadillo" would at least attract some attention. Literary titles are often ALLUSIONS: *For Whom the Bell Tolls, Gone With the Wind, That Evening Sun.*

Titles referred to in RESEARCH PAPERS have special typographical requirements. Titles of major works (books, plays, operas, magazines, newspapers, pamphlets, and movies) are printed in ITALICS, and indicated in a manuscript by UNDERLINING. Titles of shorter works (usually included within the major ones), such as articles, short stories, chapters, and poems, are in roman type and are enclosed within QUOTATION MARKS. (See DOCUMENTATION and RESEARCH PAPER.)

tone   1. A synonym for "tone of voice," or the attitude of the speaker or of the writer toward his material or audience. **2.** More strictly, the attitude of the author toward his material or subject—an attitude that will then determine the material's MODE (SATIRE, COMEDY, TRAGEDY, ROMANCE, etc.). **3.** Loosely, a synonym for *voice, mask,* or PERSONA— "the way the poet takes himself" (Robert Frost's definition). Tone is directly or indirectly tied to the author's purpose—to inform or instruct; to entertain, delight, or amuse; to convince or persuade; to inspire; etc. **4.** Tone in ESSAYS is largely linguistic and tied to usage. Essays can thus usually be distinguished as either "formal in tone" (expository essays); or "informal in tone" (imaginative, personal, familiar essays).
REFERENCE: Richard D. Altick, "Tone," *Preface to Critical Reading;* Laurence Perrine, "Tone," *Sound and Sense;* Walker Gibson, *Tough, Sweet and Stuffy;* Edward M. White (ed.), *The Writer's Control of Tone.*

topic outline   See OUTLINE.

topic sentence   See PARAGRAPH.

tough literature   A contemporary label for high-quality imaginatively rendered literature—mostly poetry, drama, and fiction; the opposite of "pop" or low-brow and of mass (or middle-brow) literature, which tend to be superficial and ephemeral. The word "tough" suggests in part its informal sense of "difficult" but even more so its formal sense of complexity, especially complexity of TEXTURE. Besides being rich in texture, tough literature tends to be multidimensional in one or another of such features as LEVELS OF MEANING, DRAMATIC STRUCTURE, ARCHETYPES, SYMBOLISM, IRONY, PARADOX, PERSONA, or in a combination of these aspects. Nor does tough literature consist exclusively of the CLASSICS (literature that has survived the centuries); it includes many modern works (works less than a century old). Certain tough novels by such writers as Dostoevsky, Flaubert, Melville, Mark Twain, Henry James, Conrad, Joyce, Faulkner, and Hemingway, for example, have become the subjects of lifelong studies by scholars and of book-length EXPLICATIONS by critics. (Contrast MASS LITERATURE.)
REFERENCES: Leslie Fiedler, "The Discovery of High Culture," *The Art of the Essay;* Henry James, "The Art of Fiction" and Joseph Conrad, "Preface to *The Nigger of the Narcissus*," in James Miller (ed.), *Myth and Method;* John Ciardi, *How Does a Poem Mean?;* George Boas, *Vox Populi: Essays in the History of an Idea;* Walker Gibson, *Tough, Sweet, and Stuffy.*

tour de force   1. An ingenious, sometimes farfetched, feat by an author or artist. In this sense the term is derogatory. 2. A remarkable achievement unlikely to be equaled; for example, Melville's *Moby-Dick* or Laurence Durrell's *Alexandria Quartet.*

Tractarian movement   See OXFORD MOVEMENT.

tragic flaw   A tragic PROTAGONIST's key trait, such as jealousy, greed, overweening ambition, credulousness, that makes him his own worst enemy. (See DRAMATIC STRUCTURE.)

tragic irony   See IRONY.

tragedy   1. A major MODE. 2. A drama in which the PROTAGONIST falls from happiness to misfortune as a result of his own "hamartia" or TRAGIC FLAW. According to Aristotle, in *The Poetics,* the falling protagonist who elicits from the audience most pity and terror occupies from the beginning a high station of authority. But Aristotle's and his contemporaries' ethos was in this respect the opposite of that of today's audiences, who rather enjoy seeing the mighty fall and who identify more compassionately with the common man, as for example, the protagonist in Arthur Miller's *Death of a Salesman.* Ancient Greek tragedy (ca. sixth century B.C.) whose religious origins are not fully known, reached its literary glory in the fifth century B.C. in the works of Aeschylus, Sophocles, and Euripides. *The Complete Greek Tragedies,* edited by David Greene and Richard Lattimore, contains seven plays by Aeschylus (including the Oresteian trilogy of *Agamemnon, The Libation Bearers,* and *The Eumenides*); seven plays by Sophocles (including *Oedipus the King, Electra,* and *Antigone*); and nineteen plays by Euripides (including *Medea, Iphigenia in Taurus, Helen, The Trojan Women,* and *The Bacchae*). Many more Greek tragedies, among them some prize-winners in the annual competitions, are now lost to us; we know of them chiefly through references by historians. Greek tragedy was characterized by adherence to the UNITIES of time, place, and action; by a tragic hero who usually sacrificed himself (e.g., Oedipus) to salvage posterity; by a CHORUS that made philosophic comments, sometimes serving as the playwright's mouthpiece; by a fatalistic VISION undergirding themes of retribution and the displeasure of the gods. Above all, the language of Greek tragedy was formal and poetic.

When compared with Greek tragedy, Roman tragedy seems second rate—especially the blood-and-thunder tragedies of Seneca, even if they did follow the unities and certain other mechanics. In the Middle Ages tragedy practically disappeared except for elements in certain of the MIRACLE PLAYS (those concerned, for example, with the Passion of Christ).

Tragedy rose to prominence again during the English RENAISSANCE. The first English tragedy was *Gorboduc* (1562) by Sackville and Norton. During the reign of the Tudors such tragedies as those by Kyd (*The Spanish Tragedy*), by Marlowe (*The Jew of Malta*), and by Shakespeare (*Hamlet, Othello, King Lear, Macbeth*) carried forward some conventions of the Greek tragic hero (e.g., high station) and further developed certain distinctions between those who sacrificed themselves (Hamlet) and those who fought life forces and were overcome by them (Macbeth). But Elizabethan tragedy dared to depart from the classical unities and added COMIC RELIEF—an element that the ancient Greek playwrights would no doubt have considered incongruous in tragedy.

In the seventeenth century, classical tragedy was revived in France by the playwrights Corneille (d. 1684) and Racine (d. 1699). But during the Neo-Classical seventeenth and eighteenth centuries in England such "heroic tragedies" as those by John Dryden (*All for Love*), Thomas Otway (*Venice Preserved*), and Joseph Addison (*Cato*) reflected only a slavishness to classical mechanics. In fact, in some of these plays—especially in Otway's *Orphan*—there can be seen the beginnings of melodrama. (See MELODRAMA and SENTIMENTALISM.)

In modern times tragedy seems to have waned as a dramatic form. Popular preferences have gravitated more to comedy, perhaps as an escape from the real-life tragedy all around us (war, hunger, disease, ignorance, air pollution, water pollution, and so on). Nevertheless, some notable exceptions are the tragedies of J. M. Synge (*Riders to the Sea*), Sean O'Casey (*The Plough and the Stars*), Eugene O'Neill (*Mourning Becomes Electra*), and Arthur Miller (*The Crucible*). (See CATHARSIS, DRAMATIC STRUCTURE, TRAGIC FLAW, SENECAN TRAGEDY, PERIPETY.)

REFERENCES: David Greene and Richard Lattimore (eds.), *The Complete Greek Tragedies;* Aristotle, *The Poetics;* Lily Bess Campbell, *Shakespeare's Tragic Heroes, Slaves of Passion;* Friedrich Nietzsche, *The Birth of Tragedy;* Herbert J. Muller, *The Spirit of Tragedy;* Richard Levin (ed.), *Tragedy: Plays, Theory, and Criticism;* H. D. Saunder (ed.), *Man and the Gods;* Cleanth Brooks (ed.), *Tragic Themes in Western Literature;* Oscar Mandel, *A Definition of Tragedy;* Geoffrey Brereton, *Principles of Tragedy;* Clifford Leech, *Tragedy;* M. E. Pryor, *The Language of Tragedy.*

Transcendentalism   1. The philosophy of Immanuel Kant (1724–1804), and of certain other German idealists, that reality resides in knowledge, ideas, and ideals, transcending mere sensory experiences. 2. The literary philosophy of Ralph Waldo Emerson (1803–82) and of other Americans who gravitated to BROOK FARM; rooted in Kantian fundamentals, the philosophy emphasized the spiritual (that is, the intuitive) and the individualistic nature of man.

REFERENCES: Ralph Waldo Emerson, "The Transcendentalist," *Nature Addresses and Lectures;* Bliss Perry (ed.), *The Heart of Emerson's Journals;* Odell Shepard, *Pedlar's Progress;* F. O. Matthiessen, *American Renaissance;* Van Wyck Brooks, *The Flowering of New England;* George Whicher (ed.), *The Transcendentalist Revolt Against Materialism;* Myron Simons and Thornton Parsons (eds.), *Transcendentalism and Its Legacy.*

transfer   A propaganda device that works upon the theory that favorable attitudes toward one thing may be transferred to another thing if the two are shown or named together. If the viewer likes the pretty girl in the picture, he may transfer that attitude to the gasoline; if he admires manliness, he may admire Goopy, the he-man's shaving cream. Since people readily form their opinions by association of ideas or symbols, a propagandist or an advertiser may win favor for his cause or his product by linking it, through words or pictures, with things already held in esteem by the public. (See PROPAGANDA DEVICES.)

REFERENCES: William Hummel and Keith Huntress, *The Analysis of Propaganda.*

transferred epithet   See EPITHET.

transition   The leading from one phase to another within a discourse; the bridging between sentences, groups of sentences, paragraphs, and larger sections of a work. Transitional words and phrases show the relationships among those elements—relationships of time, space, cause and effect, part and whole. Among transitional devices are conjunctions, especially the conjunctive adverbs *therefore, consequently, hence, thus, accordingly, however, nevertheless, furthermore, finally, in the same way, on the contrary, moreover.* Transitions between paragraphs may also be achieved by (1) repetition at the beginning of a paragraph of a word or phrase used at the end of the preceding paragraph; (2) use of demonstrative pronouns or demonstrative adjectives *this, that, these, those, such;* but hese words are best used not alone (leaving their reference broad and uncertain), but with some repetition or summary of the things they refer to: "These victories [already named in preceding paragraph] led to new ambitions on the part of military commanders"; (3) summarizing in a subordinated phrase or clause an idea already established: "*Because none of the battles had been wholly successful so far,* the command sought a new strategy for the remaining campaign."

For addition: *again, also, and, and then, besides, equally, first (second, etc.), finally, further, furthermore, in addition, in conclusion, last, likewise, moreover, next, similarly, then*

For contrast: *and yet, after all, at the same time, although, but, for all that, however, in contrast, nevertheless, nonetheless, notwithstanding, on the contrary, on the other hand, still, yet*

For comparison: *in like manner, in the same way, likewise, similarly*

For purpose: *for this reason, for this purpose, to this end*
For illustration: *for example, for instance, indeed, incidentally, in fact, in other words, to illustrate, that is*
For result: *accordingly, as a consequence, as a result, consequently, hence, then, therefore, thus*
For passage of time: *afterward, before that, at length, immediately, in the meantime, meanwhile, soon, then, thereafter, while*
For summary: *in brief, in short, on the whole, to sum up, to summarize*

Usually considered weak and ineffective are the transitional "numbering" devices—*first, in the first place, secondly, next, and then, finally*—though these are preferable to no transitions at all.

tribrach   See METER.

trilogy   A group of three literary works treating one continuous theme. For example, Aeschylus's *Oresteia* (*Agamemnon, The Libation Bearers,* and *The Eumenides*); Shakespeare's *King Henry VI* (which consists of three parts); John Dos Passos' *U.S.A.* (*The 42nd Parallel, Nineteen Nineteen,* and *The Big Money*); James T. Farrell's *Studs Lonigan* (*Young Lonigan, The Young Manhood* . . . , and *Judgement Day*); and Sigrid Undset's *Kristin Lavransdatter* (*The Bridal Wreath, The Mistress of Husaby,* and *The Cross*).

trimeter   See METER.

triteness   Whatever lacks freshness of expression is *trite*. Even original ideas may be couched in trite phrasing that robs them of sparkle. When triteness becomes more noticeable than mere lack of freshness, we may call the style *hackneyed*—for to travel by hackney cab is to hire a readymade conveyance, not to go on one's own; and the extremely hackneyed usage may be called *threadbare*. (For special sorts of trite phrasing, see CLICHÉ, BROMIDE, PLATITUDE, STEREOTYPE; see also TRUISM.)

trochee   See METER.

trope   1. In rhetoric, any figure of speech or figurative use of a word. (See FIGURATIVE LANGUAGE.) This term has also had the more specialized meaning apparent in the Greek *tropos,* "a turn." A trope is thus a "turn of speech" or a turning of a word to uses it does not ordinarily have. For instance, trope attaches an adjective to a noun that the adjective does not logically modify: "*ripe* October" is so described because October's *crops* are ripe; "*dreamy* night" declares that *men* are dreamy on such a night; and Horace Walpole mentions "the gentleman with the *foolish* teeth"—not because the teeth were foolish but rather because the *grin* (or the gentleman himself) was foolish. In this sense, a trope is much the same as a transferred EPITHET.

2. In medieval drama, a term for a musical interpolation in Gregorian chants—words added to the wordless series of notes which were

sung on the last syllable of the last Alleluia in the mass. These verbal additions or "turns" became a form of dialogue, an important step in the development of liturgical drama. The earliest trope was the dramatic dialogue "Quem Quaeritis" sung on Easter Sunday. In this trope the three Marys come to Christ's tomb, where they find angels. *"Quem quaeritis?"* ("Whom are you seeking?"), the angels ask. The Marys reply, *"Jesum Nazarenum crucifixem"* ("Jesus of Nazareth who was crucified"). *"Non est hic; surrexit, sicut praedixerat"* ("He is not here; he is risen just as he foretold"), the angels tell them.

REFERENCE: John Quincy Adams, "Sources of the Liturgical Drama," *Chief Pre-Shakespearian Drama.*

troubadours   From Old French *trobar,* "to seek or invent." Inventive lyric poets of Provence during the twelfth and thirteenth centuries. Many troubadours were attached to the royal courts. (See COURTLY LOVE.) Other troubadours, like the ROCK lyricists of the 1960s, were wandering minstrels and satirists. (See GOLIARDIC VERSE.) For representative troubadour lyrics, see Anthony Bonner (ed.), *A Troubadour Anthology.*

REFERENCES: Maurice Valency, *In Praise of Love;* F. V. Grunfeld, "The Troubadours," *Horizon* (Summer, 1970); James Wilhelm, *Seven Troubadours.*

truism   A statement of obvious or self-evident truth. One may assert, "Blind men do not see" — but the assertion is hardly worth the effort. An essay that begins, "There are many different kinds of animals," usually has little to say that is cogent. Truisms are often tautological (see TAUTOLOGY), either explicitly ("Poison is dangerous because it can kill you") or implicitly ("Nobody can swim across the Pacific from the mainland to Hawaii"). (For some fine distinction of terms see AXIOM, BROMIDE, PLATITUDE, STEREOTYPE, and TRITENESS.)

tu quoque   Literally, "You, too." The phrase is used to indicate the device of extenuating guilt by spreading it to the accuser or to the audience. "If I am guilty, you are guilty too," says the *tu quoque* arguer. In its baldest form the *tu quoque* argument appears in the well-known Third Knight's speech in T. S. Eliot's *Murder in the Cathedral,* in which the knight rationalizes the killing of Becket: "We have been instrumental," he says to the audience, "in bringing about the state of affairs that you approve. We have served your interests; we merit your applause; and if there is any guilt whatever in the matter, you must share it with us."

U

ubi sunt   Literally, "Where are they [now]?" A perennial motif in POEMS and SHORT STORIES that ask directly or implicitly the nostalgic question, "Where are the . . . of times now past?" (Supply *girls, boys, men, women, heroes, leaders, places, things.*) The best-known poem built on this motif is Dante Gabriel Rossetti's translation of François Villon's BALLADE, "But where are the snows of yester-year?" A humorous takeoff on this MOTIF is George Starbuck's poem "Water Under the Bridge."

underlining   In preparing manuscripts for print (or for submission to teachers), use underlining to indicate matter to be printed in ITALICS. Italics are used for:

1. Emphasis, especially in calling attention to a portion of matter being quoted:

That is *exactly* what I wanted to hear.
Note the unusual use of words by Edmund Waller in the line, "When I *resemble* her to thee."

Note: Good writers avoid indiscriminate emphasis.

2. Words, letters, and figures used as names of themselves:

A misplaced *only* may twist your meaning.
Are there two *l*'s in *tranquillity*?
There are two *2*'s in *220*.

3. Titles of books, plays, newspapers, periodicals, essays, long poems (printed separately), motion pictures, and television programs:

Absalom, Absalom	*Self-Reliance*
Cat on a Hot Tin Roof	*Hiawatha*
The New York Times	*Citizen Kane*
Toledo *Blade*	*High Noon*
Fortune magazine	*The Ed Sullivan Show*

Exceptions: Do not underscore: Bible, or books of the Bible; Koran; Prayer Book, Book of Common Prayer, or other books of worship; Constitution, Declaration of Independence, Magna Carta, statute books, or other books of acts and legislative enactment.

4. Operas, operettas, and symphonies:

Rigoletto	*Harold in Italy*
The Student Prince	Prokofiev's *Classical Symphony*

Exceptions: Do not underscore the names of songs, short musical compositions, or other works identified only by number or key.

5. Foreign words and expressions:

Her singing is full of *joie de vivre.*
It is a matter of *chacun à son gout.*
The concept of *Der Ubermensch* has wrought terror in the modern world.

6. Latin abbreviations used in documentation and in running text:

cf.	*loc. cit.*
et al.	*N.B.*
et seq.	*op. cit.*
ibid.	*q.v., qq.v.*
id., idem.	*v.*

Exceptions: Do not underscore i.e., e.g., etc., viz.

7. The names of ships, airplanes, and spacecraft:

S.S. *United States*	*Spirit of St. Louis*
U.S.S. *Enterprise*	*Yankee Clipper*

Exceptions: Do not underscore such things when known by model or serial designations: DC-3, Boeing 747, Apollo 11.

8. Subheadings, usually at the beginnings of paragraphs, but sometimes as separate lines above sections of a manuscript.

underscoring   See UNDERLINING.

understatement   The saying of less than what is merited by the facts of the case; a way of "playing down" or underemphasizing a statement. However, if the statement clearly implies the full meaning—without actually stating it—understatement is a device for achieving especially strong emphasis. It is thus a kind of psychological approach that works by stirring the imagination of the reader or listener so that he supplies his own "build-up"—often more effective than any statement the writer or speaker could possibly make. The victorious athlete who passes off his success by saying "I was lucky" may show modesty, but he also effectively emphasizes the extent of his achievement. The remarkable contrast between an event and the understated report of it (man's first flight to the moon referred to as "an excursion") invariably says more than a report that bears a host of strong adjectives. Exaggeration (see HYPERBOLE) tends to lose effectiveness, and understatement tends to gain effectiveness—perhaps because people appreciate being treated as intelligent enough to understand. Understatement may serve to soften a harsh or offensive idea. (See EUPHEMISM.) Understatement often involves IRONY (*asserting* the opposite of what is intended) and LITOTES (*denying* the opposite of what is intended). Understatement is as common in good literature as it is absent in bad literature. Shakespeare, a master of all the tricks, often makes little things and words carry great weight. In the midst of the terrors in King Lear the ragged and crazy Tom enters and says "Poor Tom's a-cold"—it is enough to make the audience, aware of so much more than the damp chill of the countryside, actually shiver.

undistributed middle   A fallacy in the deductive SYLLOGISM, in which the middle term ("sports cars" in the example below) is undistributed (that is, it refers to *all* as opposed to *certain ones*) in both of its appearances. Given, for example, the syllogism:

All Mustangs are sports cars.
All Ferraris are sports cars.
Therefore Ferraris are Mustangs.

the absurdity of the conclusion is obvious with respect to sports cars. But alas for less obvious conclusions and undiscriminating notions in certain social and political aspects of life!

unities   1. Aristotle's three unities—of time, place, and action—described the Greek playwrights' practice of limiting, in most of their plays, the time to one day, the place to one city-state or even one palace, and the action to one unified story-line (with a beginning, rising action, middle or climax, falling action, and end). Although Aristotle had emphasized only the unity of action, several of his successors extended and rigidified the other two unities (see DRAMATIC STRUCTURE). 2. Poe's "unity of effect," as expounded in his critical review of Hawthorne's *Twice-Told Tales,* posits the theory that everything in a SHORT STORY—the story-line, the SETTING, the characterization, the mood, or tone, the very words—should lead to *one effect:* horror, or beauty, or mystery, etc.
REFERENCES: Monroe Beardsley, "Unity and Related Concepts," in *Aesthetics;* Aristotle, *The Poetics.*

unity   The quality of singleness of purpose and treatment in a literary work. Unity depends first upon the selection of *one* topic, then upon the treatment of that topic in a coherent and self-contained work without digression into irrelevancy. (See UNITIES.)

University Wits, the   Tudor English intellectuals like Marlowe, Lyly, Lodge, and Greene. The term *wit* meant *knowledge* or *sophistication* rather than cleverness. (See WIT.)

utilitarian writing   Lists, inventories, receipts, applications, memoranda, class notes, social notes, business letters, classified advertisements, etc., mainly devoted to personal order and growth, and to carrying forward the world's work. (Compare EXPOSITION.)
REFERENCES: E. Glenn Griffin, *Effective Business Writing;* Herman Estrin (ed.), *Technical and Professional Writing;* J. S. Krey et al., *Effective Writing for Business;* Leo Bogart and W. F. Massy, *Strategy in Advertising.*

Utopia   1. The title of a book (1516) by Sir Thomas More. In this political romance with specifications for an ideal state, the setting is an imag-
inary island, Utopia. 2. Hence, any ideal state, wherein everything is
perfect, as the author envisions perfection, in people, government, education, health, and general welfare. The connotation of a "never-never
land" is implicit in the derivation of *utopia*—from the Greek *ou*, not,
and *topos*, place. The best-known utopias are described in the following
books: Plato's *Republic* (ca. 400 B.C.), St. Augustine's *City of God*
(A.D. 411), Dante's *On Monarchy* (ca. 1300), Campanella's *City of the
Sun* (1623), Bacon's *New Atlantis* (1627), Butler's *Erewhon* (1874),
Bellamy's *Looking Backward* (1888), William Morris' *News from
Nowhere* (1890), H. G. Wells's *Modern Utopia* (1905), Aldous Huxley's *Brave New World* (1932), and B. F. Skinner's *Walden Two*
(1948).

REFERENCES: Frederic R. White (ed.), *Famous Utopias of the Renaissance;*
Karl Mannheim, *Ideology and Utopia.*

V

vagueness   Generally, imprecision of meaning, haziness, lack of clarity. But that definition leaves vagueness nearly synonymous with AMBIGUITY—and the terms need to be distinguished. To distinguish them, Monroe Beardsley (in *Thinking Straight*) has offered a more useful definition: "In vagueness, you know what the sense is, all right; but you don't know *how much* there is of the quality referred to." Thus *hot* and *cold* are vague words: *how* hot? *how* cold? *Long, heavy, good, bald, wet, populated, rare, common*—all these are vague words, their meanings being matters of unspecified degree. But vagueness has its benefits: It keeps us from having to be precise when precision is of no useful consequence. We may refer to a "crowded room" without finding it necessary to specify the size of the room or the number of persons in it. When the need to be specific is great, as it often is in scholarly work, vagueness may destroy the worth of a writer's THESIS.

variety   Even a good thing too often repeated or too long continued loses its hold upon the mind, and variety is among the spices of language as well as of life. In writing or speech the notable style arises not from relentless insistence upon one manner (sentence pattern, length, rhythm, or structure), but upon a variety in which one manner dominates and is made continually delightful by the differences that set it off. Effective writing achieves variety of: (1) DICTION—not switching indiscriminately from one level of diction to another, but always selecting the appropriate yet unexpected word; (2) sentence structure and length; (3) word order and sentence pattern—varying position of subjects, objects, complements, and modifiers; (4) RHETORIC—avoiding any overuse of such devices as BALANCE, PARALLELISM, PERIODIC SENTENCES, IMAGERY, and FIGURATIVE LANGUAGE; (6) sound and rhythm. Variety, however, should not be sought for its own sake. What is simple and natural can be repeated more readily than what is remarkable and contrived: A simple "he said" is better repeated than varied to "he bellowed" and "he pointed out." The fault to be avoided is often called ELEGANT VARIATION—the precious searching for needless SYNONYMS and cute EPITHETS.

verbiage   See DEADWOOD.

verbosity   See DEADWOOD.

verisimilitude   A striking illusion of reality achieved by the writer's painstaking selection and description of details that give the reader the sensation "you are there." A classic example is Defoe's *Journal of the*

Plague Year (1722), which is primarily fiction, though based on historical facts.

REFERENCES: Monroe Beardsley, "Phenomenal Objectivity" and "Representation and Abstraction," *Aesthetics;* Benedetto Croce, "The Probable," *Aesthetics* (pp. 32–33); Erich Auerbach, *Mimesis.*

verse   1. A term generally used for non-PROSE writing. Even if it rhymes and scans (has METER), verse does not come up to the quality of serious poetry. Verse is more informal than poetry in TONE and language. Usually called "verse" rather than "poetry" are *nursery rhymes, jingles, limericks,* and other humorous lines (*light verse*). (Compare POEM; see LIGHT VERSE.) 2. A single line of poetry.

REFERENCE: Wyndham Lewis and Charles Lee (eds.), *The Stuffed Owl: An Anthology of Bad Verse.*

vers de societé   See LIGHT VERSE.

vers libre   See FREE VERSE.

victorian   1. Pertaining to the era (1837–1901) when Queen Victoria reigned in England. 2. Pertaining to the artifacts, customs, morals, and pastimes of that period. 3. Sometimes a derogatory EPITHET—especially when prefaced by "mid"—suggesting *strait-laced, prim, prudish,* etc. Among the best-known poets of the Victorian era: Robert Browning (1812–89) and his wife, Elizabeth (1806–61); Alfred, Lord Tennyson (1809–92); Dante Gabriel Rossetti (1828–82) and his sister Christina (1830–94); William Morris (1834–99); Algernon Swinburne (1837–1909); Gerard Manley Hopkins (1844–89); Francis Thompson (1859–1907); Rudyard Kipling (1865–1936) (also famous for his fiction); and A. E. Housman (1859–1936). In this era there were also scores of minor poets famous for one or two memorable poems.

Among the best-known novelists: Charles Dickens (1812–70), George Eliot (1819–80), William Makepeace Thackeray (1811–63), Robert Louis Stevenson (1850–94), George Meredith (1828–1909), and Thomas Hardy (1840–1928), who now seems to be emerging also as a major poet.

Among the major essayists: Thomas Carlyle (1795–1881), whose reputation seems to have suffered an eclipse; T. B. Macaulay (1800–59); Matthew Arnold (1822–88), also a poet and the critic who remains the giant of his age; John Ruskin (1819–1900); John Henry (Cardinal) Newman (1801–90); John Addington Symonds (1840–93); and Andrew Lang (1844–1912).

Among the best-known playwrights: Oscar Wilde (1856–1900); James M. Barrie (1860–1937); Arthur W. Pinero (1855–1934); and the team of William S. Gilbert (1836–1911) and Arthur Sullivan (1842–1900), who wrote satirical light operas. (George Bernard Shaw was born in 1856, but he did not produce his major plays until after the turn of the century.)

REFERENCES: William Irvine, *Apes, Angels, and Victorians;* W. E. Houghton, *The Victorian Frame of Mind;* Lytton Strachey, *Eminent Victorians;* Gordon Haight (ed.), *The Portable Victorian Reader;* G. B. Woods (ed.), *Poetry and Prose of the Victorian Period;* A. W. Ward and Alfred Waller (eds.), *The Cambridge History of English Literature,* Vols. 12–14; Bonamy Dobree, *The Victorians and After;* Philip Appleman et al., *1859: Entering an Age of Crisis;* Austin Wright (ed.), *Victorian Literature: Modern Essays in Criticism;* George Levine and William Madden (eds.), *The Art of Victorian Prose;* Vineta Colby, *The Singular Anomaly;* Gerald Kaurar and Gerald Sorensen (eds.), *The Victorian Mind.*

villanelle   An intricate French verse pattern of nineteen lines (five *tercets* and a final four-line STANZA) with only two rhymes throughout—*aba aba aba aba aba abaa*—and at least eight of the nineteen lines repeating a REFRAIN. Austin Dobson (1840–1921) is generally credited with having introduced into England the villanelle along with such other French patterns as the BALLADE and the RONDEL.

The following poem by Austin Dobson, "On a Nankin Plate," is representative of the playful tone as well as of the metrics of the villanelle:

On a Nankin Plate
"Ah me, but it might have been!
Was there ever so dismal a fate?"
Quoth the little blue mandarin.

Such a maid as was never seen!
She passed, though I cried to her "Wait"—
Ah me, but it might have been!

I cried, "O my Flower, my Queen,
Be mine!" "Twas precipitate"—
Quoth the little blue mandarin—

But then . . . she was just sixteen,
Long-eyed—as a lily straight—
Ah me, but it might have been!

As it was, from her palankeen,
She laughed—"You're a week too late!"
(Quoth the little blue mandarin.)

That is why, in the mist of spleen,
I mourn on this Nankin Plate.
"Ah me, but it might have been!"
Quoth the little blue mandarin.

virgule   Hardly another mark of punctuation (/) has so many names—*slant line, slash, bar, shilling sign.* And despite its not being a mark of sentence punctuation, it has more miscellaneous uses than it has names. The virgule is used:

1. To indicate addition or alternative, meaning *and* or *or:* "He traveled on the Continent in 1842/43." *Note:* The use of "and/or" is shunned by logically inclined grammarians.

2. To abbreviate certain much-used words and phrases: *c/o,* for *in care of; w/o,* for *without; N/A,* for *not available* or *not applicable.*

3. To mark the end of a line of poetry when part of a poem is quoted in run-on format: "Note the irony in the Shakespearean lines: 'If this be error and upon me proved, / I never wrote, nor no man ever loved.' "

4. To separate numerator and denominator in rational numbers: 2/3, 5/8, 15/32.

5. To signify dates reckoned by different calendars, the Old Style (Julian) and the New Style (Gregorian): "George Washington was born on February 11/22, 1732."

6. To signify year-dates reckoned from different New Year's days: "The Charter of Massachusetts Bay dates from March 4, 1628/29."

7. To indicate shillings in the sterling monetary system: 10/6.

8. To separate proofreading symbols that refer to errors in a single line on a printer's proof: tr/#/cap

9. In pairs, to enclose symbols in phonemic transcription: In New York City, *bird* is not pronounced "boyd," but/bəyd/.

vision of life   An author's philosophic attitude toward his material; this attitude is usually conscious, though it may also be unconscious. It is sometimes consistent, if not systematic, throughout the author's works, but it more usually varies from work to work. Theodore Dreiser consistently reflects in all his novels one vision of life — NATURAL-ISM. In Faulkner's novels, though many of the characters and actions are morally degraded, there is enough "saving grace" to support Faulkner's view that "man will prevail," that man's best qualities will "endure." The works of Shakespeare, on the other hand, do not reflect a single view of life, so that the reader can only say that in play "X" the vision is REALISTIC, in play "Y" the vision is ROMANTIC; in play "Z" the reflection is of a tragic vision of life."

REFERENCES: Ruben A. Brower, "The Twilight of the Double Vision," *The Fields of Light;* Richard Chase, *The Democratic Vista;* B. S. Oldsey and A. O. Lewis (eds.), *Visions and Revisions;* Donald Watt, "Vision and Symbol in Huxley's *Island,*" *Twentieth Century Literature* (October, 1968).

voice   In literature there are, according to T. S. Eliot and John Hall Wheelock, at least three distinguishable voices. (1) The first voice is the PERSONA, or mask-voice, that a poet wears for a particular poem. This voice at its most recognizable level may belong to a character-narrator like the Duke in Browning's "My Last Duchess," and is thus several removes from the poet himself. More often, the persona-voice is not that far away from the poet himself, is in fact only one of his voices, one aspect of his personality. Thus, the flame-snatching rebel voice of the speaker in Frost's "Canis Major" is in quite a different key from the chastened voice of the speaker in "Stopping by Woods. . . ." In short, the persona-voice expresses TONE or mood or attitude in one particular poem. (2) The second kind of voice is more cumulative; it is the trademark voice we have come to recognize and associate with a celebrated poet—the conversational voice of Frost, the understatement of Emily Dickinson, the rhetoric of Whitman, and so on. This voice is one of the key characteristics of a poet's style and is so well known as to make itself the easy butt or adulation of PARODY. It can also be heard as a derivative echo in the first attempts of prospective poets. (3) Finally, there is the rarest, least artful voice—something eternal and universal that comes almost effortlessly from the poet's psyche. This is the ARCHETYPAL voice, for which the poet has only served as a kind of medium. Two examples that come to mind are Coleridge's "Kubla Khan" and Yeats's "Sailing to Byzantium," poems for which these poets served as "compulsive midwives," as Northrop Frye has put it. Dante called this voice the ANAGOGICAL, or mystical (*The Banquet*, I, 1). It is a quality that has no doubt assured the immortality of "The Song of Songs" and of Shakespeare's sonnet "That time of year thou mayst in me behold."

REFERENCES: T. S. Eliot, *The Three Voices of Poetry;* John Hall Wheelock, *What Is Poetry?* (*Note:* Mr. Wheelock divides the above-mentioned three into four voices.)

volta   See SONNET.

vulgate   1. A Latin translation of the Bible, made by St. Jerome in the fourth century; the authorized version of the Roman Catholic Church. 2. Old French romances in prose, from which Malory borrowed for the *Morte D'Arthur* (1471).

W

Walpurgisnacht   1. Walpurgis Night, the night preceding May 1, the Feast of St. Walpurga (710?–777), an English missionary nun who helped St. Boniface in Germany. 2. Witches' annual holiday on the Brocken in the Harz Mountains, an extravagant celebration at midnight with bonfires and elaborate religious and sexual rites. In Goethe's *Faust,* Part I, Mephistopheles conducts Faust to a Walpurgisnacht. Similarly, the Devil conducts Hawthorne's Goodman Brown to a comparable, if less elaborate, witches' sabbath. 3. More broadly, a satirical term for any wild or extravagant midnight ball or party.
REFERENCE: Jules Michelet, *Satanism and Witchcraft;* George Lyman Kittredge, *Witchcraft in Old and New England.*

Weltanschauung   Literally, "world view." 1. A comprehensive conception of the world and events in which all is viewed within a consistent philosophical system to explain purpose and meaning. 2. In a more restricted sense, VISION OF LIFE.

Weltschmerz   World-weariness; satiety with life. (See STURM UND DRANG.)

whichmire   James Thurber's term for overly long sentences bogged down in their own *which* clauses; for example, "In this old house, which we owned, which was in a town, which had a name, which I shall not mention. . . ." The chief remedy for a whichmire is to recast completely, perhaps into two or more sentences. If only two which clauses are involved, one of them can be recast into an appositive: "In this old house, our very own" or "In this old house of ours." More often than not, a *which* or two may be expendable altogether: "a name I shall not mention" or "a name I need not mention." In his essay "Ladies' and Gentlemen's Guide to Modern English Usage" Thurber satirized whichmires as bogs where readers were likely to be lost and "never heard from again."

Whitsunday   See HOLIDAYS.

wit   1. Cleverness or brilliance. A witty person or character is quick with words. (Thus the expression "quick-witted" is a redundancy even if it is accepted idiom.) Dr. Samuel Johnson (1709–84) defined wit as "the discovery of occult resemblances in things apparently unlike." 2. In Shakespeare's works and in those of his contemporaries, wit usually means *sophistication* or *knowledgeability,* a definition close in meaning to the Anglo-Saxon and German roots *witan* and *wissen,* "to know." (See METAPHYSICAL POETS and CONCEIT.)
REFERENCE: James B. Leishman, *The Monarch of Wit.*

wordiness   The use of more words than necessary; verbosity. (See DEADWOOD.)

working bibliography   See DOCUMENTATION and RESEARCH PAPER.

wrenched rhyme   The same as slant rhyme. (See RHYME.)

Z

Zen   A Buddhist philosophy based on the central belief that enlightenment comes through the renunciation of materialism and through the concentration on things of the spirit. The three "pillars" of Zen, undergirding Salvation (*Gedatsu*) are (1) work (*Samu*), (2) dialogue (*Monto*), and (3) contemplation (*Meiso*), in that order, although the practice properly begins and ends in *Meiso*.

REFERENCES: Philip Kapleau (ed.), *The Three Pillars of Zen;* William Barrett (ed.), *Zen Buddhism: Selected Writings of D. T. Suzuki;* Alan Watts, *Beat Zen, Square Zen, and Zen.*

zeugma   Literally, "yoking." "Her hair is red, her eyes blue" conveys meaning clearly enough, but causes the grammarian's eyebrow to go up, for it seems to imply "her *eyes is* blue." The fault is an example of zeugma, a construction in which the writer has too optimistically assumed that one of his predicates or modifiers is going to do double duty, when it really cannot. The result is inadvertent, often bumptious, nonsense. Other examples (with the offending constructions in italics): "The silly girl has her head *filled* with straw and her *face* with paint," "No *amount of* money or *people* can influence me," "Did you *drink* all the milk and *the sandwiches*?" Zeugma may not always be a fault; it is sometimes a deliberate feat, as it is in Alexander Pope's line: "feared to stain her honor or her new brocade." (Compare SYLLEPSIS.)

A
GLOSSARY
OF
LANGUAGE

A Note About This Glossary

This glossary of English grammar and linguistics is for the beginning student. The descriptions are of terms and topics as they are used in their most frequent and familiar senses in beginning and intermediate courses in the field. The main concern of this glossary is with facts about grammar and linguistics; thus the terms are not labeled as to their parts of speech, and pronunciations are not given. Frequently, though not with complete consistency, the terms have been treated in their noun forms.

In one sense this is more than a glossary, for there is a good deal of encyclopedic description, information about the referent rather than merely a description of words. The list includes, then, not only terms but also topics (DISTINCTIVE FEATURES), events (THE FIRST CONSONANT SHIFT), and laws (VERNER'S LAW). The subject orientation is toward language history, phonemics, dialects, and grammar with much the heaviest emphasis on the latter, since it is the most frequent aspect of linguistics in school and college curricula. One of the major purposes of this glossary is, wherever possible, to contrast descriptions from the three grammars that receive most attention in introductory courses: conventional school grammar and structural and transformational grammars. Such items as ADJECTIVE and RULE OF GRAMMAR are thus defined from three points of view. Several models of transformational grammar are represented in the description of terms. An effort has been made to treat those models that are found in textbooks available at the time of composition of the glossary. Thus, while there is consideration of early terms and models, there is also an attempt to reflect more recent systems.

Symbols and Abbreviations

Because some of the terms in this glossary are defined from the point of view of more than one kind of grammar, these three abbreviations are used throughout: *CG*: As defined in conventional school grammar; *Str*: As defined in structural grammar; *TG*: As defined in transformational grammar.

Listed below are the conventional symbols and abbreviations used in this glossary, with accompanying explanations.

↔	"agreement between subject and verb." EXAMPLE: N ↔ V
→	(1) "can be rewritten as/expanded into." EXAMPLE: S → NP + VP means "Sentence can be rewritten as/expanded into Noun Phrase + Verb Phrase." (2) This arrow is also used in the more traditional sense of "becomes." EXAMPLE: Indo-European *bh* → Germanic *b*
⇒	"can be transformed into." EXAMPLE: NP + V + Pred ⇒ V + NP + Pred means "the order of the string of symbols to the left of the arrow is transformed into the order of the string of symbols to the right of the arrow"
( )	When this parenthesis appears in a rule of grammar it means "the element inside the parenthesis is optional; you do not have to choose it." EXAMPLE: S → NP + VP (Adv) means "Sentence is rewritten as Noun Phrase + Verb Phrase + an optional adverb"
{ }	(1) In a syntactic rule this means "choose one of the obligatory elements inside the braces." EXAMPLE:

$$N \rightarrow \begin{Bmatrix} N_{pr} \\ N_{com} \end{Bmatrix}$$

means "nouns are either proper or common; you must choose either one or the other, but not both at the same time."

(2) Morphemes are placed within braces. EXAMPLE: $\{-s_2\}$ means "plural morpheme"

[ ]	(1) In a syntactic rule this means "the elements within brackets share the element that follows." EXAMPLE:

$$\begin{bmatrix} stay \\ remain \end{bmatrix} + \text{Predicate}$$

means "both *stay* and *remain* can be followed by a predicate."

(2) Brackets enclose phonetic transcription. EXAMPLE: [pʰ].

(3) Brackets enclose a list of distinctive features. EXAMPLE:

walk

$$\begin{bmatrix} +VB \\ +V \\ +action \end{bmatrix}$$

⟨ ⟩	Angle brackets are used to enclose graphemes and single distinctive features. EXAMPLES: ⟨a⟩ ⟨+VB⟩
*	(1) Preceding a sentence, the asterisk means that the sentence is unacceptable. EXAMPLE: *What ignored Joe was Mary. (2) Preceding a word or the transcription of a word, the asterisk indicates a hypothetical or reconstructed form. EXAMPLES: Primitive Germanic* [bro: θer]; Indo-European *kmtom
–	When the macron is over a written symbol, usually a vowel, it means length. EXAMPLE: habēre
:	After a transcribed vowel, the colon means length. EXAMPLE: [e:]
↑	Rising intonation. EXAMPLE: Is she here ↑
↓	Falling intonation. EXAMPLE: She's here ↓
→	Level intonation. EXAMPLE: She's a nice girl → but. . . .
~	Phonologically conditioned alternation
∞	Morphologically conditioned alternation
Adj	Adjective
Adv	Adverb
Af	Affix. EXAMPLE: Noun + Af = Boy + s
ART	Article
AUX	Auxiliary verb
C	TG: Complement construction following a verb. EXAMPLE: likes living there
CG	Conventional school grammar
(COMP)/ (N-COMP)	TG: The open position after a noun which can be filled by a transformed insert sentence which modifies the noun
COMP	CG: The complement of the verb
D/Det	Determiner. EXAMPLE: a, the, several of the, many of the
{-d₁}	The past tense morpheme
DO	Direct Object
ed/en	The past tense morpheme as it is represented in the terminal string of a phrase structure grammar
ing	The progressive aspect morpheme
IO	Indirect Object
LOC(ATIVE)	An adverb of location. EXAMPLE: there, at the corner
LV	Linking Verb
M	Modal Auxiliary
MOT	Adverb of motion. EXAMPLE: ran into the house
MV	Main Verb
N	Noun
N°	Number; either singular or plural
N$_{human}$	Human noun. EXAMPLE: man, boy, girl

NEG	Negative particle. EXAMPLE: *not, 'nt*
Nom	Nominal
NP	Noun Phrase
OV	Object complement verb. EXAMPLE: *elected* Bob President
PRE-ART	Pre-article. EXAMPLE: *some of, all of, many of*
Pred	Predicate
s	The plural morpheme in a string
S	Sentence
$\{-s_2\}$	the noun plural morpheme
Str.	Structural Grammar
TG	Transformational Grammar
V	Verb
V_b	Any other verb besides BE in the rule

$$MV \rightarrow \begin{Bmatrix} BE + Predicate \\ V_b \end{Bmatrix}$$

V_{be}	The verb *be*
V_c	Any linking verb except *be*
V_i/V_{int}	Intransitive verb
V_{iL}/V_L	Verbs like *sit* that are usually followed by adverbials of location EXAMPLE: sit *at the table*
V_{iM}	Verbs like *run* that are usually followed by adverbials of motion EXAMPLE: run *into the house*
V_t/V_{tr}	Transitive verb
VP	Verb Phrase
$\emptyset$	(1) A morphologically conditioned allomorph. EXAMPLE: plural of *sleep, deer* (2) No suffix

The Phonemic Transcription

The phonemic transcription used in this glossary is a very slightly modified version of the Pike-Fries system found on pages 450–51. The pronunciations are those of the Northern Dialect of American English. See pages 401–2.

VOWELS

/i/	beat				
/ɪ/	bit	/ɨ/	candid	/u/	too
/e/	bait	/ər/	sir, butter	/ʊ/	put
/ɛ/	bet	/ə/	but	/o/	note
/æ/	bat	/a/	pot	/ɔ/	law

CONSONANTS

Stops		Affricates		Fricatives		Nasals		Lateral	
/p/	pin	/č/	church	/f/	fan	/m/	met	/l/	live
/b/	bin	/j/	jump	/v/	van	/n/	net		
/t/	tin			/θ/	thin	/ŋ/	ring		
/d/	din			/ð/	then				
/k/	kin			/s/	sip				
/g/	give			/z/	zip				
				/š/	ship				
				/ž/	rouge				
				/h/	help				

GLIDES
/r/ run
/y/ yes
/w/ win

DIPHTHONGS
/ai/ sigh
/au/ how
/ɔi/ boy

In addition, two symbols are included in the historical entries which represent sounds no longer in English:

/x/ voiceless velar fricative as in German "Nacht," "Buch"; the closest approximation in English is the initial sound in "cool"

/ɣ/ voiced velar fricative. The same sound as /x/ except it is voiced. It is similar to /g/ except that it has friction. It is the medial g in Spanish *rogar*

ablaut   The changes that occur in a vowel sound as a result of variations in pitch in the parent language and in the stress accent of languages that evolve from this parent language. The vowel thus goes through a series of changes. *Nest,* for example, is ultimately related to Indo-European **nizdo,* "sitting-down place." The prefix *ni-* means "down" and *-zd-* is related to Germanic *-st-.* The vowel *o* was lost because of lack of stress in Indo-European, leaving *nizd,* which appears in Germanic languages as *nest.* Verb forms such as *ring, rang, rung* and *strike, streak, stroke, stricken* are evidences of ablaut, a series of vowel changes. (See GRADATION.)

absolute construction   This is composed of a noun in the common case, or a pronoun in nominative or objective case, followed by a nonfinite verb or an adjectival. This construction has no syntactic relationship with the rest of the sentence but serves as a sentence modifier. Examples:

> *His hand in a sling,* he grabbed the beer.
> *Her arm being broken,* she wore it in a sling.
> *The work being completed,* we went home.
> *He being boss,* I did what he said.
> We felt sad, *the house having collapsed.*
> He kissed Matilda, *his face sorrowful.*

abstract noun   *CG:* A noun that names a quality, condition, action, or anything that cannot be perceived by the senses: *love, sickness, running, justice. Str:* Abstract nouns generally do not take the plural suffix. Some of them pattern in the singular without the determiner:

_____ is common.

TG: An abstract noun names an abstract quality. Most of these nouns can occur in subject position opposite a noun clause or noun phrase in a sentence with the verb *be:*

> *Opposite Noun Clause:* The *problem* is that I don't know him.
> *Opposite Noun Phrase: Happiness* is to love.

(See LEXICAL PROPERTIES.)

accidence   A term describing changes in the form of a word when it is inflected for gender *(he/she),* number *(boy/boys),* case *(I/me),* tense *(burn/burned).* (See CONJUGATION, DECLENSION, INFLECTION, PARADIGM.)

accusative   A term from the grammar of classical languages designating the word that is the object of the verb. English has six distinctive pronoun forms that are used as objects: *me, her, him, us, them,* and, less frequently, *whom.* Since nouns have no distinctive forms to show that they are the objects of verbs and prepositions, this function is indicated in English by word order. But nominal direct objects are sometimes called accusative. (See CASE, DIRECT OBJECT, OBJECT.)

acoustic phonetics   The study of significant speech sounds as they are heard by the listener. (Compare with ARTICULATORY PHONETICS: see DISTINCTIVE FEATURES.)

REFERENCES: N. Chomsky and M. Halle, *The Sound Pattern of English* (New York: Harper & Row, 1968); M. Halle, "On the Bases of Phonology," in J. A. Fodor and J. J. Katz (eds.), *The Structure of Language, Readings in the Philosophy of Language* (Englewood Cliffs: Prentice-Hall, 1964); _____, "Phonology in Generative Grammar," in *ibid.;* R. T. Harms, *Introduction to Phonological Theory* (Englewood Cliffs: Prentice-Hall, 1968); R. Jakobson and M. Halle, *Fundamentals of Language* ('s-Gravenhage: Mouton, 1956); _____, C. G. M. Fant, and M. Halle, *Preliminaries to Speech Analysis* (Cambridge, Mass.: MIT Acoustics Laboratory, 1952); P. Postal, *Aspects of Phonological Theory* (New York: Harper & Row, 1968); B. M. H. Strang, *Modern English Structure,* 2nd ed. (New York: St. Martin's Press, 1968).

active voice   When the subject of the verb is the actor or is in a condition named by the verb, the verb is said to be in the active voice.

    Actor: Bill threw the ball.
    Condition: He slept for eight hours.

actor-action-goal construction   A grammatical construction in which the order of words indicates their grammatical relationships. *John scared the dog* and *The dog scared John* both show the same grammatical action, but actor and goal in the second construction signal a reversed meaning.

additive allomorph   The allomorph of a suffix added to a base. The past-tense morpheme {-d₁} has three phonologically conditioned allomorphs that are additive: /-ɨd~ -d ~-t/ are added to bases to form /sitɨd simd læft/. The plural morpheme {-s₂} has three phonologically conditioned allomorphs and two morphologically conditioned allomorphs, all of which are additive; /-ɨz~ -z~ -s∞ ɨn~∅/ are added to bases to form the plurals /bičɨz dɔgz kæts aksɨn šip/. (See ALLOMORPH, MORPHOLOGICAL CONDITIONING, PHONOLOGICAL CONDITIONING, REPLACIVE ALLOMORPH.)

adjective   *CG:* A word used to limit, describe, or qualify a noun or noun equivalent. *Str:* Adjectives, when used in comparison, can be inflected with *-er* or *-est.* The base form of most polysyllabic adjectives, when they are used in comparison, is preceded by *more* or *most,* in which case there is no inflection. Adjectives pattern between the article and the noun modified or after nouns as part of larger constructions:

a *larger* house
a house *larger* than I thought

Predicate adjectives follow *be* and linking verbs. *TG:* In one model of this grammar an adjective is a modifier derived from a transformed insert sentence that is embedded into a matrix sentence:

Matrix:	Joe is a man (COMP).
Transformed Insert:	Joe is old ⇒ who is old ⇒ w̷ho i̷s̷ old
Embedded Result:	Joe is an old man.

In a more recent model of this grammar adjectives are considered to be in some ways similar to verbs in the DEEP STRUCTURE of sentences. They are, thus, verbals that are marked ⟨+VB⟩ and ⟨−V⟩. (See INSERT SENTENCE; LEXICAL PROPERTIES; VERBAL.)

adjectival   An adjective, noun, participle, adverb, or syntactic construction that is in a shared position usually filled by adjectives:

Adjective:	*green* house
Noun:	*telephone* office
Participle:	*burning* house
	burned steak
Adverb:	the *upstairs* room
Syntactic Construction:	*very old* man

(See POSITION CLASS.)

adjective clause   A clause that occurs after a noun and modifies it:

car *that I drove*

(See RELATIVE CLAUSE.)

adjective complement   Another term for PREDICATE ADJECTIVE.

adverb   *CG:* An adverb modifies, describes, or limits a verb, adverb, or adjective. *Str:* Many adverbs are adjectives or participles plus the ending *-ly: poorly, dashingly.* Like adjectives, adverbs can be compared with *-er, -est* or *more, most.* They express such concepts as time, place, degree, manner, and number, and they can occur in various positions in a sentence without changing its meaning. Some frequent positions occupied by adverbs in English are before the sentence (*Now* it's time to run.), after the subject (He *actually* thinks about it.), after the auxiliary or first auxiliary (I will *seldom* eat that.), after the verb (He drives *recklessly*. She is *always* a lady.), after the Subject Complement (He will be pitcher *tomorrow*.), after the Object Complement (He will be elected captain *tomorrow*.), after the Direct Object (He will play baseball *tomorrow*.). (See PRO-FORM.)

adverb clause   A dependent clause modifying a verb, adverb, adjective, or sentence. It expresses notions such as time, place, cause, manner, concession, condition, comparison, purpose, and result.

> *Verb Modifier:* I will go *when I am ready.*
> *Adverb Modifier:* He runs faster *than Joe does.*
> *Adjective Modifier:* She is younger *than her sister is.*
> *Sentence Modifier: When he is ready,* we'll go to town.

adverbial   This term describes single words, phrases, and clauses that fill adverb positions in sentences.

> *Single Word:* He fell *down.*
> *Phrase:* He fell *down the stairs.*
> *Clause:* He fell *while he was running.*

affix   A general term describing bound morphemes that are prefixes (*re*-run), infixes (man:m*e*n), or suffixes (quick*ly*). (See BOUND MORPHEME, MORPHEME.)

affix transformation   An obligatory transformation upon a terminal string. It rearranges affixes (Af) and verbs (V) within the auxiliary:

$$Af + V \Rightarrow V + Af:$$
$$en + break \Rightarrow broken$$
$$ed + burn \Rightarrow burned$$
$$s + break \Rightarrow breaks$$
$$ing + break \Rightarrow breaking$$
$$\emptyset + can \Rightarrow can$$

where Af = -en, -ed, -s (third singular present tense), -ing, $\emptyset$ (zero affix on modal auxiliaries). Here is an illustration of how this transformation operates on a terminal string:

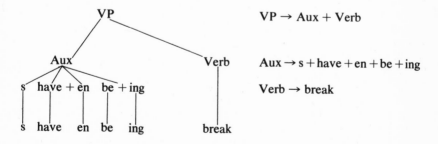

After the obligatory affix transformation has been applied, the result is

has been breaking

(See OBLIGATORY TRANSFORMATION, SIMPLE TRANSFORMATION, TERMINAL STRING.)

affricate   A meaningful sound consisting of two types of articulation, a stop followed by a fricative. English has a voiceless affricate /č/, the first and last sounds in *ch*ur*ch,* and a voiced affricate /ǰ/, the first sound in Jim.

agglutinative language   A language like Swahili, Hungarian, or Turkish, in which words are made up of parts that are whole syllables and have lexical meanings. Affixes are attached to invariable and independent bases. Consider Swahili *atanipenda,* "he will like me," *atakupenda* "he will like you," *atanipiga* "he will beat me," where the affixes have lexical meaning: *ata = he; ni = me; ku = you; penda = like; piga = beat.* Contrast this with English *books,* in which the base *book* has lexical meaning, but the affix *s* means plural and is not a syllable.

agnate   *TG:* Sentences that are agnate have a traceable relationship. *I saw the man* and *The man ran away* combine to form *I saw the man who ran away.* They combine, are related, through a series of transformational rules, thus they are agnate.

agreement   *CG:* Sometimes called *concord,* this is a formal correspondence between two parts of speech. Subject and verb agree in number:

> He is here.
> They are there.

Demonstrative pronouns generally agree in number with the nouns they precede:

> this dog
> those shoes

Pronouns agree in number and gender with their noun antecedents:

> *Number:* I saw the *planes* and liked *them.*
> *Gender :* I saw *Mary* and liked *her.*

allomorph   One of the related forms that belong to the same morpheme. These related forms have the same meaning and are in complementary distribution. For example, the past tense morpheme {-d₁} has the phonologically conditioned allomorphs /-d/: rubb*ed;* /-t/: stopp*ed;* /+d/: heat*ed.* (See ADDITIVE ALLOMORPH, COMPLEMENTARY DISTRIBUTION, MORPHEME, REPLACIVE ALLOMORPH.)

allophone   One of the individual sounds comprising a phoneme; a positional variant of a phoneme. For example, [kʰ], the initial sound in *king,* and [k⁼], the final sound in *book,* are, respectively, aspirated and unaspirated allophones of /k/. Aspiration is a puff of air that can follow the articulation of any consonant sound.

alveolar stop   A significant speech sound. English has two: /t/ and /d/. (See STOP.)

ambiguity   Two or more meanings in a word or construction. Ambiguities are either lexical or structural. In lexical ambiguity the multiple meaning is in the words themselves:

The Reverend Smith was congratulated on getting his *parish plastered.*

Structural ambiguity results from a mistake in the structure — the arrangement of words — of an utterance or written sentence:

Her thoughts were interrupted as the door swung open and a young woman carrying a baby and her husband entered.

REFERENCE: N. C. Stageberg, "Some Structural Ambiguities," in H. B. Allen (ed.), *Readings in Applied English Linguistics,* rev. ed. (New York: Appleton-Century-Crofts, 1964).

analogy   This is the name for the natural, unconscious tendency among speakers to make their language more regular than it may be. New words are formed by the same processes that have formed existing ones, "irregular" constructions are regularized into more frequently occurring patterns. An example of the first process is the Anglicization of plurals of Latin words into English plurals: *stadium-stadiums.* Past-tense forms of "irregular" verbs are frequently analogized to regular *-ed* forms: *drive-drived.* Analogy is a powerful and intuitive force in the process of language change.

analytic language   One in which the relationships among words, thus their functions, depend upon the order of words and the use of prepositions and auxiliary verbs. Modern English is an analytic language, as is French. Modern German, Latin, and Old English are SYNTHETIC LANGUAGES. (See INFLECTIONAL LANGUAGE, SYNTHETIC LANGUAGE.)

Anglo-Saxon   A highly inflected ancestor language of Modern English spoken in the British Isles in the period c. A.D. 500–1000.

REFERENCES: A. Campbell, *Old English Grammar* (Oxford: Clarendon Press, 1959), J. W. Clark, *Early English* (New York: Norton, 1957); S. Moore and T. A. Knott, *The Elements of Old English,* 8th ed. (Ann Arbor: Wahr, 1940); R. Quirk and C. L. Wrenn, *An Old English Grammar,* 2nd ed. (London: Methuen, 1958).

animate noun   *CG:* Animate nouns name living things: *dog, man, boy,* etc. *TG:* Animate nouns are a subclass of concrete nouns. Those nouns that must occur as subjects with such verbs as *breathe* and *play. Dog, man, boy, poet* are animate nouns. (See LEXICAL PROPERTIES.)

anomolous verbs   *Be, go, do,* and *will* are called anomolous verbs because their forms come from different verbs rather than from one.

Be has forms from three Old English infinitives: *beon, is,* and *wesan; go* used the preterit *ēode* but now employs *went,* the preterit of *wend.*

antecedent   That word or group of words to which a pronoun refers.

I saw *Fred* while *he* was at home.   *To see Fred again; that* excites me.

apocope   The loss of a final sound during the process of language change. For example, Old English *singan* became Modern English *sing.*

apposition   Two constructions or words that are next to each other and refer to the same person or thing.

Our teacher, Mr. Smith, is a good one.

appositive   The second of two words or constructions in apposition is usually called the appositive. In the example above, *Mr. Smith* is the appositive.

archaism   A word, construction, or expression that is in infrequent current use and is recognized as being from an earlier period of the language. Examples are *forsooth, durst* (for *dared*).

argot   The name given to words and expressions that are peculiar to a particular class or group, mainly in the criminal underworld. The term was originally used in the nineteenth century to describe the talk of thieves who wished to disguise or conceal meanings. It still describes criminal language such as *yellow* (a telegram), *apple* (the victim), *to light a rag* (to run away), *to play the C* (to operate a confidence game).

article   *The* is the definite article; *a, an* are indefinite articles. Articles are frequently considered a subclass of adjectives. (See DETERMINER.)

articulative intrusion   The process by which sounds are added to words at any time during their course of development or use. These additional sounds come into words as a result of the mechanics of articulation. (See INTRUSIVE CONSONANT.)

articulatory phonetics   The study of the production of speech sounds. This study is based upon the manner of production and points of articulation of speech sounds, and establishes classifications among these sounds. (See ACOUSTIC PHONETICS, AFFRICATE, CONSONANT, FRICATIVE, GLIDE, LATERAL, STOP, VOWEL.)

REFERENCES: A. Bronstein, *The Pronunciation of American English* (New York: Appleton-Century-Crofts, 1960); C. F. Hockett, *A Manual of Phonology* (Baltimore: Williams and Wilkins, 1955); J. S. Kenyon, *American Pronunciation,* 10th ed. (Ann Arbor: Wahr, 1950); H. Kurath, *A Phonology and Prosody of Modern English* (Ann Arbor: University of Michigan Press, 1964); G. L. Trager and H. L. Smith, Jr., *An Outline of English Structure* (Washington: ACLS, 1963 [reprint]).

aspect   A term sometimes used to describe the nature of the action of a verb. Aspect does not refer to the time of an action but rather to whether the action is completed (punctual aspect):

> I wrote. I had written.

is not yet completed (durative or progressive aspect):

> I am writing.

has recently begun (inchoative aspect):

> He got going.
> Let's get moving.

is repeated (repetitive aspect):

> We keep moving from house to house.

or is emphasized (emphatic aspect):

> He did *too* win it.

(See PROGRESSIVE TENSE.)

aspiration   A puff of air, represented by /ʰ/, that can follow the articulation of any consonant sound. Aspiration is not phonemic in English; it is a predictable allophonic feature of the voiceless stop consonants /p t k/ in certain positions. For example, these three consonants are aspirated in initial positions before a vowel: *pin* /pʰɪn/, *tin* /tʰɪn/, *can* /kʰæn/. In final word position, aspiration is a nonpredictable allophonic feature in free variation with lack of aspiration in the same phoneme: *lap* /læpʰ/ or /læp/; *rat* /rætʰ/ or /ræt/; *lack* /lækʰ/ or læk/. The glottal fricative /ʰ/ does not follow another consonant phoneme before a vowel and thus does not represent phonemic aspiration. Some English words spelled with initial *ph* (*photo*), *th* (*Thomas*), and *kh* (*khaki*) probably reflect aspirated initial consonants in the languages from which they were borrowed or an analogy with which they were spelled: Greek, Latin, Hindi.

assimilation   The phonetic process by which one sound changes to resemble or become identical with a sound near it. There are two kinds of assimilation: voice assimilation and place assimilation. (1) Voice assimilation occurs when a sound becomes voiced or voiceless to resemble one of the sounds surrounding it. The word *north* ends with a voiceless *th*. When we add *ern* to *north, northern,* the *th* becomes a voiced sound to resemble the voiced sound, *er,* which now follows it. This is also known as phonological conditioning. (2) Place assimilation is of two kinds. (*a*) In the first, two sounds come to resemble each other in that they are articulated in the same part of the mouth. The two pronunciations spelled *strength* and *strenth* illustrate this. The sound of *ng* in the first pronunciation comes to resemble the sound of *n* in the second. The second one is easier to pronounce because both the *n* and the *th* are articulated in the front of the mouth. In *ngth*, the tongue is in the back of the mouth for *ng* and moves to the front of the mouth for *th*. In *strenth*, then, we have a pronunciation shortcut; the sound of *ng* has been assimilated to, has been made like, the sound of *n*. (*b*) In the second, one sound becomes identical with another. An example of this can be found in the pronunciation of *horseshoe*. The usual pronunciation might be spelled *horshoe*. Here the final *s* of *horse* is assimilated to, has become identical with, the *sh* sound of *shoe*. This standard pronunciation is a shortcut; it reduces the movements of the tongue from two to one at this point in the pronunciation of the word.

attribute   *CG:* The same as a HEADWORD.

attributive   *CG:* An adjective in position before or after a noun: *small* house; house *dark* and *dreary*. A noun modifying another noun is used attributively: *telephone* operator.

auxiliary verb   Sometimes called a helping verb; the term describes a verb used with the infinitive or participial form of the main verb to form a verb phrase. *Be, do* and *have* are used most frequently as auxiliary verbs:

> I *am* going.
> I *didn't* want it.
> He *has* gone.

Can, could, may, shall, will, must, should, would, might, and *ought (to)* are also frequent in this use in American English. *TG:* In this grammar, auxiliary material includes tense, which is obligatory, plus optional modals and/or *have* and/or *be*. The auxiliary rule can be written this way:

$$\text{Aux} \rightarrow \text{Tense (Modal) (have - ed) (be - ing)}$$

This rule accounts for all sixteen active voice auxiliary phrases in English. (See VERB PHRASE.)

B

back formation   A process of word formation that is the reverse of the usual method in English. It is the formation of a word from one that looks like its derivative. Centuries ago the verbs *peddle* and *beg* were formed from the nouns *peddlar* and *beggar*. The modern verb *televise* has been back-formed from the noun *television* on the analogy with pairs such as *supervise-supervision, revise-revision*. (See ANALOGY.)

back vowel   A vowel articulated at the back of the mouth. (See VOWEL.)

base   A term used in the study of morphemes. A *base* morpheme is the one that carries the principal meaning in structures like *cats*, *friend*ly. Bases are of two kinds: free and bound. Most bases in English are free; they can occur alone. *Cat* and *friend* are free bases. Many bound bases in English come from Latin and Greek; they can occur in English only with affixes. Thus, they are bound to affixes and cannot occur alone. The italicized bound bases in the following words illustrate this: *dict*ate, contra*dict*, in*spect*, *spect*acles; *port*able, re*port*; in*spire*, re*spire*.

base form   When the linguist wishes to make statements about the variations, or allomorphs, of a morpheme, he chooses one allomorph as the base form and considers the others as describable variations of it. Thus the English noun plural morpheme $\{-s_2\}$ has three phonologically conditioned allomorphs $/\text{-z} \sim \text{-s} \sim \text{-ɨz}/$ (son*s*, cake*s*, glasse*s*), any one of which might be considered as the base form at a given time.

base rules   Base rules are one of the two types of syntactic rules that relate deep structure and surface structure. Base rules are rewrite rules of the form

$$S \rightarrow NP + VP$$

and they are represented by a tree diagram:

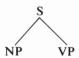

In relating surface structure with its meaning, its deep structure, base rules function in several ways. The elements of the surface structure

the + man + feed + PAST + the + dog

are arranged one after the other, in linear order, by base rules. Changing this linear order yields an ungrammatical surface structure such as

dog + the + the + PAST + feed + man

or a sentence which differs from the original:

the + dog + feed + PAST + the + man

In addition, base rules group elements together to form units of meaning like *the + man, feed + PAST,* and *feed + PAST + the + dog*. Two other functions of base rules can be understood by looking at this tree diagram:

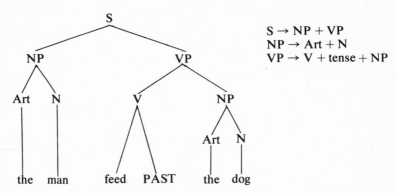

$$S \rightarrow NP + VP$$
$$NP \rightarrow Art + N$$
$$VP \rightarrow V + tense + NP$$

As native speakers of English we can intuitively group these elements in units like *the + man* and *feed + PAST + the + dog*. But these groupings do not show what kind of units, constituents, these sequences are. The labelled node points (S, NP, VP, etc.) show us what kind of constituent a given group is. The shape of the tree diagram is prescribed by the base rules to the right of it which, then, label the constituents. The base rules also group constituents into related hierarchies of varying size. The constituents *V* and *NP* (*feed + PAST* and *the dog*), for example, are parts of the larger constituent *VP* which is itself a constituent of *S*. Consider a more complicated diagram:

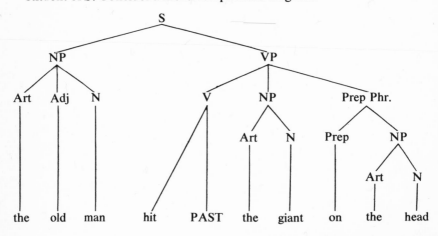

This diagram illustrates another function of base rules—they account for similar constituents of varying complexity. We see that *the giant* and *the old man* can function as noun phrases as can even more complex structures like *the old man who lives down the street*. Similarly, a verb phrase can be a single word like *hit* or it may be more complex like *hit the giant* or *hit the giant on the head*. All of these constituents are labelled either NPs or VPs because they function as noun phrases or verb phrases. Though some are more complex than others, they are all governed by the same sets of base rules for NPs and VPs. In relating deep and surface structures, then, base rules arrange morphemes in a linear order, group elements together into meaningful units, label the constituents in a tree diagram, group constituents into related hierarchies of varying size, and account for the similarity of constituents of varying complexity. (See PHRASE STRUCTURE RULES, REWRITE RULE, RULE OF GRAMMAR, TREE DIAGRAM.)

be-verb   The verb *be* comprises a single-member class. Syntactically, it is similar to the transitive verb, the mid-verb, and *become, stay,* and *remain* in that all of them can be followed by a noun phrase. It is most like *become, stay,* and *remain* since the predicate noun phrase of both must refer to the same person or thing as the subject:

> *Become:*   The man became chairman.
> *Be:*   The man is chairman.

Be also resembles linking verbs in that both can be followed by a predicate adjective that modifies the subject; but linking verbs can be followed only by adjectivals:

> *Linking Verb:*   The man appeared strong.
> *Be:*   The man is strong.

Be is like intransitive verbs in that both can be immediately followed by an adverbial:

> *Intransitive Verb:*   The boy sleeps in the bed.
> *Be:*   The boy is in the bed.

Be is different from the intransitive verb, however, in that *be* must be followed by a completing element:

> *Intransitive Verb:*   The boy sleeps.
> *Be:*   *The boy is.

Be has at least seven forms: I *am;* you, we, they *are;* he, she, it, noun *is.* In the past tense the singular form is *was,* plural *were.* Participles are the present *being* and the past *been. Ain't* is a frequent form with the negative. Infrequent archaic forms are the present thee/thou *art,* past indicative thee/thou *wast,* and past subjunctive thee/thou *wert.*

Be is an auxiliary verb as well as a full, or main, verb. (See AUXILIARY VERB.)

bilabial stop   A consonant made by a momentary stoppage, then release, of air by the lips. (See STOP.)

binary construction   *SG:* One that is considered to be built with a hierarchy of twosomes. A binary morphological construction may be illustrated by the word *ungentlemanly,* in which the word is divided into two parts in succeeding steps down to its smallest individual parts:

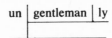

A binary syntactic construction is one in which word groups become successively smaller while undergoing this bipartite division:

Boys	who	ride	bicycles	will	go	to	the	park
							b₁	b₂
		a	b		a			b
	1		2		1			2
A			B	A				B
I								II

Many, though not all, English word groups can be divided into two constituent parts. (See IMMEDIATE CONSTITUENT.)

blending   A process of word formation in which, usually, the first part of one word is combined with the last part of another:

> *slip + glide = slide*
> *squeeze + crash = squash*
> *motor + hotel = motel*
> *smoke + fog = smog*
> *squall + squeak = squawk*

(See NONCE WORD.)

bound morpheme   One type of bound morpheme is that which can occur only with bases or stems. They are inflectional suffixes that have meanings such as "past tense," "plural," and "continuous action":

> burn*ed*   boy*s*   runn*ing*

or they are derivational suffixes:

> slow*ly*   advis*er*   act*ion*

or prefixes:

*un*kind   *in*capable   *re*hire

Some words contain two bound morphemes: a bound base and an affix:

tele|*vise*   *hydro*|*phone*

(See BASE, FREE FORM.)

breaking   A process, noted in the study of language history, in which vowels are diphthongized, or "broken" into two vowels. For example, in Old English the front vowels / æ ǣ ɛ ɪ i/ were "broken" by the effect of a following *h* or consonant cluster with *r* or *l*. These vowels became, respectively, the diphthongs / æ æə ɛo ɪo io/. We can notice breaking in process in Modern English too. In the northern and western parts of the United States the historical vowels /e o/ are preserved, but they have become "broken," diphthongized, into two vowels in parts of the East Coast:

Northern	*Eastern*
/de/ "day"	/dei/
/et/ "eight"	/eit/
/se/ "say"	/sei/
/əgo/ "ago"	/əgou/
/kot/ "coat"	/kout/
/so/ "so"	/sou/

C

cant   A kind of slang used to exclude outsiders. It is the familiar, conversational language used and generally understood solely by members of a specified occupation, trade, profession, class, age group, or interest group. (See ARGOT, JARGON.)

case   In inflected languages like German, Old English, and Latin the nouns, pronouns, articles, and adjectives exhibit endings that signal nominative, accusative, genitive, and dative cases. These case endings are important in establishing grammatical relationships among words in a sentence. In English, a few case markers survive. The -*s* ending for plural and genitive (possessive) case of nouns is distinguished only in writing: boy*s*, boy'*s*. Otherwise, nouns have a common form: *boy.* The personal pronouns exhibit three cases: nominative, genitive, and, except for *it* and *you,* accusative: *I, my, me; he, his, him; we, our, us,* etc. (See ACCUSATIVE, DATIVE, GENITIVE, NOMINATIVE, VOCATIVE CASE.)

central vowel   A vowel articulated in the central part of the mouth. (See VOWEL.)

centum languages   These constitute one of the divisions of the Indo-European family of languages. The centum group is composed of the Tocharian, Hellenic, Italic, Celtic, and Germanic languages. In these languages the consonant /k/, as in Latin *c*entum, "hundred," was not palatalized to /s/ as it was in the satem language group. The /k/ remained as in Indo-European **kmtom,* Celtic *cant* or, in the Germanic group of languages, shifted to *h* in the First Consonant Shift: Old English *hund.* (See FIRST CONSONANT SHIFT, PROTO-INDO-EUROPEAN, SATEM LANGUAGES.)

checked vowel   A vowel followed by a voiceless consonant in the same syllable. English vowels are shorter — checked — before voiceless consonants than before voiced consonants: compare *seat* vs. *seed;* shorter when followed by /m n ŋ l/ + voiceless consonant than when a voiced consonant follows these four sounds: compare *rumple* vs. *rumble, seamstress* vs. *seam, kilt* vs. *killed.*

clause   *CG:* A sequence of words consisting of a subject and a predicate. An independent clause is a complete sentence; a dependent, or subordinate, clause is a word group that is part of a larger sentence. It is a word group that does not make complete sense standing alone, that depends for its completed meaning on one or more independent clauses. Dependent clauses can serve the grammatical functions of noun, adjective, adverb. *TG:* This term refers only to "relative clause" and "that-clause"; otherwise "sentence pattern" equates with the conventional meaning of *clause*. (See ADJECTIVE CLAUSE, ADVERB CLAUSE, INDEPENDENT CLAUSE, NOUN CLAUSE.)

clipping   A process of word formation in which the beginning or end of a word, or both, are cut off, leaving the part to stand for the whole. This remainder is called a clipped word: *lab, dorm, prof, pike* (road), *cello, Bert.* The clipping of the end of a noun is the most common process.

closed syllable   One that ends in a consonant. (See OPEN SYLLABLE, SYLLABLE.)

close(d) vowel   A high vowel, made with a relatively small opening of the mouth and the tongue raised toward the palate: oo /u/ is more closed than aw /ɔ/. (See HIGH VOWEL, VOWEL.)

cognate   Words related to each other by being descended from the same original word: German *essen:* English *eat;* Old Irish *brāthir:* English *brother.* The first two words are descended from Germanic **etan.* The second two come from Proto-Indo-European **bhrāter.*

collective noun   A noun whose singular form indicates a group of people, acts, things. Some common collective nouns are *army, contents, crowd, public,* etc. When a collective noun names the whole group, it agrees with a singular verb and a singular pronoun:

The *flock* ha*s* found *its* place to graze.

When the noun names the individuals of the group it takes a plural verb and a plural pronoun:

The *team have* found *their* uniforms.

The rules for using collective nouns are complicated because some of them have regular plural forms (*band/bands*) and some do not (*contents, mankind*). Further, some collectives habitually take singular verbs (*mankind, crowd*), while others more commonly take the plural verb form (*people*).

colloquial   Denoting a level of spoken and written usage. The level consists of familiar words and idioms used in informal speech and writing, but not considered formal enough for business correspondence or public speaking. (See USAGE.)

common noun   A noun that may refer in common to any or all the members of a group of persons, places, or things: *tree, dogs, magazine,* etc. (See PROPER NOUN.)

comparative degree   The comparative degree of a monosyllabic adjective or adverb ends in -er and is used when speaking or writing of two things:

> Bill is fast*er* than Joe.
> Bill runs fast*er* than Joe.

More indicates the comparative degree of polysyllabic adjectives and adverbs: *more important, more slowly.* (See COMPARISON, SUPERLATIVE DEGREE.)

comparison   Refers to adjectives and adverbs when they are used to indicate degrees of quantity, intensity, or superiority in quality. Three degrees of comparison are recognized: (1) the positive, which is indicated by the base form of the word: *fine;* (2) the comparative, which is indicated by -er added to the base: *finer;* (3) the superlative, which is indicated by -est added to the base: *finest. More* and *most* preceding polysyllabic adjectives and adverbs indicate comparative and superlative degrees, respectively: *more acrimonious, most acrimonious.* (See COMPARATIVE DEGREE, SUPERLATIVE DEGREE.)

compensatory lengthening   The lengthening of a vowel to compensate for the loss of a following consonant. In Old and Middle English *knight* is spelled *cniht* and *kniȝt* and pronounced with a voiceless velar fricative /x/ before *t:* /knɪxt/. When the velar fricative was lost in pronunciation, the vowel was lengthened and eventually became the diphthong: /nait/.

compensatory shortening   The shortening of a vowel when a consonant that follows it is doubled: Latin *lītera* → *littera.*

competence   *TG:* Describes what the speakers of a language are *competent* to produce rather than what they actually do produce. A transformational grammar can be described as a competence model since it describes a native speaker's abstract ability to produce an infinite number of different sentence structures and this speaker's ability to understand sentences that he has never heard before. (See TRANSFORMATIONAL GRAMMAR.)

complement   *CG:* A grammatical complement is usually thought of as (*a*) the direct object or (*b*) the indirect and direct object of a transitive verb. The complement of a linking verb is (*c*) a predicate adjective that modifies the subject or (*d*) a predicate noun that means the same thing as, is equivalent to the subject, and, like the predicate adjective, completes the meaning of the sentence.

> (*a*) John eats *steak.*
> (*b*) John gave *Bill a dog.*
> (*c*) John felt *sick.*
> (*d*) John is *chairman.*

A noun complement after linking verbs is also known as subject complement, the predicate nominative, and the predicate noun. *TG:* The optional noun complement position immediately follows an NP. It may be filled by an insert sentence transformed into a *that*-clause:

the car *that Joe drives*

Transformations that convert basic sentences into inserts to be embedded after NPs are called complementizer transformations. The *that* transformation illustrated above is one kind of complementizer transformation. (See COMPLEMENTIZER TRANSFORMATION.)

complementary distribution   The distribution of two similar items is complementary when they occupy different territories that do not overlap. Thus, the noun-plural morpheme {-s₂} has among its allomorphs /s/ and /z/ which are in complementary distribution: /s/ follows voiceless sounds, /z/ follows voiced sounds.

complementary infinitive   *CG:* An infinitive that occurs in the verb complement position: I'm willing *to invite* her.

complementizer transformation   *TG:* A transformation that converts basic sentences into inserts to be embedded after NPs. There are three frequent kinds of complementizer transformations.

1. The *that complementizer* inserts *that* before an insert sentence that does not have an NP in common with the main sentence. This is different from the *relative that* transformation.

Main Clause Sentence: The car is wrecked.
Insert Sentence: Joe drives.
Transformation: The car *that Joe drives* is wrecked.

2. The *infinitive complementizer* inserts *for* before the first NP of an insert sentence and *to* after it.

Main Clause Sentence: There is something.
Insert Sentence: John reads.
Transformation: There is something *for John to read.*

3. The *gerunditive complementizer* attaches *'s* to the first NP of an insert sentence and *-ing* to the verb.

Main Clause Sentence: John completed his requirements.
Insert Sentence: John passed the examination.
Transformation: *John's passing* the examination completed his requirements.

Complementizer transformations also convert sentences into inserts to be embedded after verbs that take complements.

Main Clause Sentence: The man knows SOMETHING.
    Insert Sentence: The book is good $\Rightarrow$ the book to be good.
    Transformation: The man knows *the book to be good.*

In the example above, the *infinitive nominal transformation* changes the insert sentence so that it can fill the complement position marked by the pro-form SOMETHING. The verb *know* can also take a *that*-clause nominal (The man knows *that the book is good.*), a *wh-word* nominal (The man knows *what* is good.) or a *verb-based noun* nominal (The man knows *its avoidance of bad style.*). The verb *know* cannot take a *gerund nominal* (*The man knows *its being good.*), but *prevent* can take a *gerund nominal* as its direct object (The man prevents *its being good.*). Some other complement verbs are *expect, believe, try, want, find, avoid, imagine,* etc. The conventional complements of transitive and linking-type verbs are accounted for in the base rules of transformational grammar. These rules specify that complements follow the verb:

$$MV \rightarrow \begin{Bmatrix} BE + pred \\ \cdot \quad \cdot \quad \cdot \quad \cdot \quad \cdot \end{Bmatrix} \quad \text{and} \quad V \rightarrow \begin{Bmatrix} V_{int} \\ V_{tr} \quad + Nom \end{Bmatrix}$$

(See OBJECT COMPLEMENT, RULE OF GRAMMAR.)

complex sentence   *CG:* A sentence that consists of one independent clause and any number of dependent clauses. The dependent clause or clauses may occur before the independent clause at the beginning of the sentence:

When I get home, I'll read to you.

after the independent clause:

I'll read to you *when I get home.*

or inside the independent clause. When it is inside the independent clause, the dependent clause can serve as a modifier:

The man *who came to dinner* is my uncle.

as a subject:

Whoever wins the election confronts problems.

or as an object:

We know *what you are supposed to do.*

(See SUBORDINATION.)

complex transformation   *TG:* The process by which an insert sentence is embedded into a main-clause sentence.

The man knows S

The man forgot his coat ⇒ that he forgot his coat

Readout: The man knows that he forgot his coat.

This is a general term for the process of forming complex sentences. (See MULTIPLE COMPLEX TRANSFORMATION, TRANSFORM.)

compound sentence   *CG:* A sentence that consists of at least two independent clauses joined by at least one coordinating conjunction or a semicolon: *John ran and Bill walked. John ran, Bill walked, but Sue rode her horse. John ran home; Bill walked.*

compound-complex sentence   *CG:* A sentence made up of two or more independent clauses and at least one dependent clause:

I don't know *what he wants* and I don't care.
          Dep. Clause

compound word   Words printed either as one word or hyphenated: *birdhouse, inside, father-in-law.* Morphemically, a compound word is a free form consisting of two or more free forms. Some compound words must be differentiated from grammatical constructions consisting of the same free forms. This is done by stress patterns. For example, the following contrasts are common in American English:

Compound Word	*Grammatical Construction*
bluebird	blue bird
greenhouse	green house
bull's-eye	bull's eye

(See STRESS.)

concatenation   *TG:* An operation that forms strings of symbols. This operation is symbolized by +. Thus, we have the free and bound morphemes *the, dog, s, ed, jump* which appear concatenated in this string of symbols:

the + dog + s + ed + jump

(See TERMINAL STRING.)

concord   Another word for AGREEMENT.

concrete noun   *CG:* Nouns that name persons, places, or things that can be perceived by the senses: *water, grass, tree,* etc. *TG:* Concreteness is a property of some nouns. The two subclasses of concrete nouns are *animate* and *inanimate* nouns. (See LEXICAL PROPERTIES.)

conditioning   See MORPHOLOGICAL CONDITIONING, PHONOLOGICAL CONDITIONING.

conjoining transformation   A simple transformation that joins two or more basic sentences with conjunctions such as *and, but, or, nor, either . . . or, neither . . . nor, both . . . and,* and *not only . . . but also.* For example:

> The plane took off *and* they all cheered.
> *Either* you take the exam *or* you fail the course.

conjugation   A conjugation represents a series of changes in a verb by means of prefixes, suffixes, or infixes. These changes represent such factors as person, number, tense, voice, mood. Here is a conjugation of the Old English strong verb *singan* "to sing."

PRESENT		PRETERIT	
Indicative		*Indicative*	
Singular	*Plural*	*Singular*	*Plural*
1. singe	1. singað	1. sǫng	1. sungon
2. singest	2. singað	2. sung	2. sungon
3. singeð	3. singað	3. sǫng	3. sungon

Optative		*Optative*	
1–3. singe	1–3. singen	1–3. sunge	1–3. sungen

Imperative	
2. sing	2. singað

Infinitive. singan
Gerund. tō singanne
Pres. Ppl. singende   *Past Ppl.* (ge)sungen

(See ACCIDENCE, INFLECTIONAL SUFFIX, PARADIGM.)

conjunction   A conjunction connects words, phrases, and clauses. (See CONJOINING TRANSFORMATION, COORDINATORS, CORRELATIVES, SUBORDINATION, SUBORDINATOR.)

conjunctive adverb   *CG:* A connective word or phrase used with adverbial force between independent clauses. This connects the first clause to a qualifying clause: "He writes forcefully; *however,* he needs to check his facts." Most common conjunctive adverbs, besides *however,* include *therefore, nevertheless, still, thus, yet, moreover, besides, consequently, as a result, on the other hand.*

consonant   A speech sound produced by some kind of an obstruction to the flow of breath. A momentary stoppage and then a release of the breath produces /p, t, k, b, d, g/. A stoppage at one place and then escape at another produces /m, n, ŋ, l/. Forcing the breath through a loosely closed or narrow passage produces /f, v, s, z, š, ž, θ, ð, h/. A stop plus friction produces /č, ǰ/. /y, r, w/ are made by gliding the tongue between vowel sounds. Consonants are produced variously with and without the voice. The term consonant is also used rather loosely to mean a character in the alphabet that represents any of the above sounds or combinations of them.

consonant shift   See FIRST CONSONANT SHIFT.

constituent   Any word or construction that is part of a larger construction. Constituents of a phrase can be words, as in

the| boy

or constructions, as in the first two constituents of this sentence:

The boy| walked home.

The concept of constituents is useful in parsing sentence structure. (See IMMEDIATE CONSTITUENT.)

constituent sentence   See INSERT SENTENCE.

construction   A syntactic construction is any group of words that are knit together in grammatical relationships. A complete sentence is a construction, as are subordinate sentences and word groups with verbs, nouns, adjectives, and prepositions as their headwords. Morphological constructions are those which consist of a combination of free morphemes or of a free morpheme and one or more bound morphemes:

fire|man   cat|s   un|tie   un|man|li|ness

The concept of syntactic constructions is useful in analyzing the internal grammatical structure of the constituents of a sentence. (See HEADWORD, IMMEDIATE CONSTITUENT, SYNTACTIC CONSTRUCTION.)

consumer sentence   See MAIN-CLAUSE SENTENCE, MATRIX SENTENCE.

contact clauses   Two or more independent clauses written together to form a sentence without any connecting words between them are called contact clauses:

He came, he saw, he conquered.

continuant   A speech sound in which there is a continuous, uninterrupted flow of air. This classification includes vowels and some consonants. (See FRICATIVE, GLIDE, LATERAL, NASAL.)

contraction   The written form of words which indicate colloquial pronunciation by substituting an apostrophe for one or more letters of the standard spelling:

hasn't: has not   he's: he is   won't: will not

co-occurrence   The term describes a feature basic to linguistic structure. A number of grammatical relationships can be considered co-occurrence relationships, relationships that exist between two or more classes of words and/or constructions that occur in easily described positions in sentences.

The first kind of co-occurrence relationship is *simple dependence* between two or more classes. In this relationship, the occurrence of one class requires the occurrence of other(s), but not vice versa. For example, in sentences like

He walked slowly.
She walked in the garden.

the presence of an adverb or prepositional phrase in the predicate requires the presence of a verb, but the presence of a verb does not require the occurrence of an adverb or prepositional phrase:

He walked.
She walked.

The second kind of co-occurrence relationship is *mutual dependence* between two or more classes. In this relationship, one class always occurs with the other(s), and vice versa. For example, in sentences like *He walked. She walked.* the subject pronoun and the verb always co-occur. For these sentences to be grammatical, the occurrence of both of these classes is obligatory. In other words, the following are not English sentences: *walked, She.*

The third kind of co-occurrence relationship is a *mutually exclusive* one, either between two or more classes or between some members of one class and some members of another. For an example of the first type, in which the members of two or more classes can never co-occur in one position, observe that pronouns and nouns never co-occur in the subject position, nor do two pronouns or two nouns:

*he Tom walks
*he she walks
*Tom Mary walks

For an example of the second kind of mutually exclusive co-occurrence relationship, in which some members of one class never co-occur with some members of another, observe that certain nouns cannot be the object of certain verbs:

*The woman frightened the tree.
*The man killed the gun.

(Adapted from A. Koutsoudas, *Writing Transformational Grammars* (New York: McGraw-Hill Book Co., 1966), pp. 95–96.)

coordinate clause   *CG:* Another name for INDEPENDENT CLAUSE.

coordination   Two or more words, phrases, or clauses that are equivalent in morphological or grammatical construction and are joined by a coordinating conjunction are said to be in coordination:

running and jumping
to run and to jump
who were running and who were jumping

coordinators   Coordinating conjunctions, words that join items of equivalent grammatical construction; *and, but, for, nor, or, yet* are examples.

copulative verb   *TG:* These comprise one of the three large classes of English verbs, the other two being transitive and intransitive verbs. There are four subclasses of copulative verbs:

(1) *Sense verbs: taste, smell, feel,* etc.
(2) *Appearance verbs: appear, seem, look,* etc.
(3) *Action verbs: grow, turn,* etc.
(4) *Existential verbs: become, stay, remain.*

Sense verbs can be followed by adjectives:

This beer *tastes* good.
This plate *feels* cold.

These verbs have homophones that are transitive verbs and are thus followed by direct objects:

John *tasted* the beer.
He *felt* the pitcher.

In American English appearance verbs are not usually followed by nominals and, unlike sense verbs, they can take abstract nouns as subjects:

His patriotism *seems* strong.

They can also be followed by the infinitive *to be:*

He appears *to be* strong.

Action verbs can be followed by manner adverbs, whereas the previous two subclasses cannot be:

He *turned* green slowly.
Bill *grew* angry quickly.

Unlike most other copulative verbs, *become* can be followed by a nominal:

Joe *became* president.

Like action verbs, *become* can also be followed by a manner adverb:

Joe became president *unexpectedly.*

When *stay* and *remain* are used as copulative verbs, they share the characteristics of the verb *be*. They can be followed by nominals, adjectivals, and adverbs of location and time:

> Joe *stayed/remained* president.
> Joe *stayed/remained* happy.
> Joe *stayed/remained* in the bar.
> Joe *stayed/remained* in the bar for three days.

(See LINKING VERB.)

correlatives   Coordinators used in pairs. The most common are *both . . . and; either . . . or; neither . . . nor; not so . . . as; not only . . . but (also); whether . . . or.* (See CONJOINING TRANSFORMATION.)

count noun   A subclass of concrete nouns, count nouns have singular and plural forms and name objects that may be counted as separate units. They may be distinguished in their plural forms from mass nouns, which go with *how much: how much gold, how much coffee,* but not **how much dogs.* Count nouns in the plural go with *how many: how many dogs, how many boats,* but not **how many gold.* (An exception occurs in ELLIPSES: *How many red sunsets; how many gold?*) Count nouns generally do not stand alone in the singular, and can be preceded by the indefinite article in their singular form. (See MASS NOUN.)

counter-word   An automatic, often one-word response of like or dislike, acceptance or rejection. These words are usually overused, sometimes meaningless fad words creating a common bond of self-defense within a subgroup. Some slang counter-words for rejecting an outsider are *boob, creep, dope, drip, jerk, square.* For acceptance we can list words such as *gas, George, the greatest, nice, smooth, way out.*

creole language   One that has been expanded in grammar and vocabulary from a pidgin language from which it is immediately derived. Further, a creole language has speakers for whom it is a native language. It is not a dialect of any one of its parent languages since it is not mutually intelligible with other dialects of these parent languages. Examples of creole languages are the Creole French of Haiti and one of the co-existent varieties of English in Hawaii. (See PIDGIN LANGUAGE.)

cultural level of usage   Cultural levels of usage are based on the socio-economic and educational background of the speakers of a language. There are generally two levels: *nonstandard* and *standard. Nonstandard cultural level* is identified by illiterate speech, ungrammatical speech and writing, excessive and unskillful slang, careless use of vocabulary. *Standard cultural level* is identified by cultivated language, clear, grammatical writing. Cultural level is to be contrasted with FUNCTIONAL VARIETY OF USAGE. Both of these concepts were formulated by John Kenyon. (See FUNCTIONAL VARIETY OF USAGE, USAGE.)

D

dangling modifier   *CG:* A modifier "dangles" when it is in a position to modify a word that it cannot logically modify. Dangling modifiers are most frequently participles. The subject of the main clause seems to be, but is not, the subject of the participle:

Being only eight years old, his father drove him to school.

Infinitive phrases may be dangling modifiers:

To run the mile, your stopwatch must be accurate.

So may prepositional phrases:

At fifteen, his family took a long trip.

TG: A sentence modifier is derived, by transformation and embedment, from an insert sentence that has the same subject as a main-clause sentence.

Main-Clause Sentence: John heard the storm.
Insert Sentence: John was opening the door → opening the door
Readout: Opening the door, John heard the storm.

Dangling modifiers result from two conditions. (1) When the insert sentence is ungrammatical:

Main-Clause Sentence: The day was rainy.
Insert Sentence: The day was looking out the window → looking out the window
Readout: Looking out the window, the day was rainy.

(2) When two grammatical sentences are joined and give an illogical result:

Main-Clause Sentence: Jane is an old grouch.
Insert Sentence: Jane is a sweet girl → being a sweet girl
Readout: Being a sweet girl, Jane is an old grouch.

(See EMBEDMENT.)

dative case   In inflected languages the dative case endings signal the indirect object. But English has no distinctive form for the dative case, thus it can hardly be said to have this case. In English, nouns that are indirect objects are in the common case form, and pronouns are in the objective case form. Thus, indirect objects in English are indicated by word order, the indirect object being the first of two nouns or noun equivalents after a transitive verb:

He gave *Tom* the book.
He gave *him* the book.

Or the indirect object is indicated by function words like *to* and *for:*

> He gave the book *to Tom.*
> He did it *for him.*

In *CG* the last two italicized phrases are called prepositional phrases. (See CASE, PERIPHRASTIC CONSTRUCTION.)

declension In inflected languages, the change in form of nouns, pronouns, and adjectives to show number, gender, and case. English nouns can hardly be said to have declension since they have only the genitive and plural inflected forms. There are variations in English pronouns, but they are irregular. Thus, Modern English does not have declension, at least in the sense that Latin and German have it. Old English, on the other hand, had many such inflections.

declarative sentence One that conveys information; it makes a statement. (See MOOD.)

deep grammar *TG:* The same as PHRASE STRUCTURE GRAMMAR. In this grammar the PHRASE STRUCTURE RULES operate.

deep structure *TG:* These two sentences appear, at first glance, to be the same:

> Lou is easy to please.
> Lou is eager to please.

By "at first glance" we mean "on the surface." But notice how different they are when they are transformed into *It-Expletive* sentences:

> It is easy to please Lou.
> *It is eager to please Lou.

Superficially, these sentences are the same. Yet, they are different somehow. Linguists have posited that sentences have a *deep structure* and a *surface structure;* the two are related by transformations and by lexical rules. Further, deep structure may be the same as or different from surface structures. The deep structure of the simple, active, declarative sentence *He saw Suzie* is the same as its surface structure. On the other hand, the surface structure of the sentence *I know the girl who lives there* has a deep structure consisting of *I know the girl* and *The girl lives there.* Notice that the information implied in the structure *who lives there* is conveyed by the second deep structure sentence, *The girl lives there.* Thus it is said that the deep structure of a sentence contains its real meaning. In transformational grammar the deep structure of sentences is produced by the phrase-structure rules, which generate terminal strings, and by rules of affix transformation,

which change terminal strings into basic sentences. (See INTER-
MEDIATE STRUCTURE, SURFACE STRUCTURE, TERMINAL STRING.)

degree   See COMPARISON.

delayed subject   See **expletive.**

deletion transformation   A transformation that enables us to delete
words or phrases from sentences. The deletion transformation accounts
for shortened sentences in English. For example, when two kernel
sentences are joined to produce

I like Joe and I like Lou.

a deletion transformation can remove the second *I like* to produce

I like Joe and Lou.

The "short answer" is the result of a deletion transformation:

Question: Are you going to Denver?
Short Answer: Yes, I am.

Here, *going to Denver* is deleted to produce the "short answer."

demonstrative   This refers to the singular pronouns *this, that,* and
their plurals *these, those,* which indicate or point out.

dental consonant   This describes /d t n s/, sounds made by placing the
tongue tip against the back of the upper teeth. (See ALVEOLAR STOP,
FRICATIVE, NASAL)CONSONANT.)

dependent clause   *CG:* One that cannot stand alone and convey a
complete meaning. Dependent clauses are frequently introduced by
relative words and function as nouns:

That you like pie is obvious.

as adjectives:

The man *who likes pie* is here.

and as adverbs:

I study *when I can find quiet.*

TG: Transformed insert sentences are dependent clauses. They are
introduced into main-clause sentences by an embedment transformation:

Main-Clause Sentence: SOMETHING is obvious.
Insert Sentence: You like pie ⟹ That you like pie $\Big\}$ ⟹
Result Sentence: That you like pie is obvious.

Main-Clause Sentence: The man (comp) is here.
Insert Sentence: The man likes pie ⟹ Who likes pie } ⟹
Result Sentence: The man who likes pie is here.

Main-Clause Sentence: I study SOMETIME.
Insert Sentence: I can find quiet ⟹ When I can find quiet } ⟹
Result Sentence: I study when I can find quiet.

(See RELATIVE CLAUSE.)

derivation   The process of forming words from bases by adding one or more derivational suffixes or by changing one or more sounds. *Boy-ish, badly, reword, unbend* are derived by adding affixes (suffixes and prefixes). *Strength* and *deem* are derived from *strong* and *doom* by sound change in the vowel. (See ETYMOLOGY.) *TG:* The process of producing a basic sentence from the phrase-structure rules:

Phrase-Structure Rules	*Derivation*
S → NP + VP	NP + VP
VP → Aux + MV	NP + Aux + MV
MV → V (Adv)	NP + Aux + V (Adv)
$V \to \begin{Bmatrix} V_1 \\ V_{tr} + NP \\ V_C + Adj \end{Bmatrix}$ (Adv)	NP + Aux + V_{tr} + NP (Adv)
NP → (D) + N	(D) + N + Aux + V_{tr} + (D) + N (Adv)

Lexical Rules	*Application of Lexicon*
D → the, a	The + N + Aux + V_{tr} + a + N (Adv)
N → boy, ball	The + boy + Aux + V_{tr} + a ball (Adv)
Aux → can	The + boy + can + V_{tr} + a ball (Adv)
V_{tr} → throw	The + boy + can + throw + a + ball (Adv)
Adv → now	The + boy + can + throw + a + ball (now)

(See LEXICON, RULE OF GRAMMAR.)

derivational suffix   In Modern English derivational suffixes include noninflectional endings that derive nouns from verbs (govern*ment,* play*er*), adjectives from nouns (use*ful,* act*ive*), and verbs from adjectives (social*ize,* sharp*en*). Derivational suffixes differ from inflectional suffixes in that (1) they do not end a word; inflectional suffixes can be added on after derivational suffixes (player*s,* sharpen*ing*); (2) derivational suffixes form words of a different class or new words of the same class. (See DERIVATION.)

descriptive grammar   As contrasted with prescriptive grammar, this grammar is concerned with describing the sounds, the word forms of, and the grammatical relationships within a language at a given stage in its development.

determiner   *SG:* Determiners are words like *a, an, one, this, that, any, no, some, their;* they pattern like *the.* These function words, and others like them, determine that sooner or later a noun will follow them.

>   *the* man
>   *a* big dog
>   *that* gray stone house

TG: A determiner is either an ARTICLE like *the, a, that, this, these, those,* or a PRE-ARTICLE + an ARTICLE: *some of* + *the, all of* + *the, several of* + *the.* The base rule for determiners is

D → (PRE-ART) ART

(See POSTDETERMINER, PREDETERMINER.)

diachronic   Refers to a long period of historical time. Many linguists use the term as synonymous with "historical." (See SYNCHRONIC.)

diacritic, diacritical mark   A mark added to a letter or character to give it a particular phonetic value. In linguistics diacritics are used to indicate varying degrees of stress: ′ ∧ ‵ ◡. Other frequent diacritical marks are the dieresis (coöperate), and the cedilla (façade). (See STRESS.)

diagram   Systems of diagramming are used to represent, graphically, various structures encountered in the study of English syntax. There are three major conventions of diagramming:

Transformational:

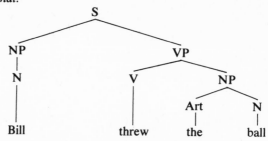

When we wish to represent an embedded sentence but are not interested in the details of its structure, we use a triangle:

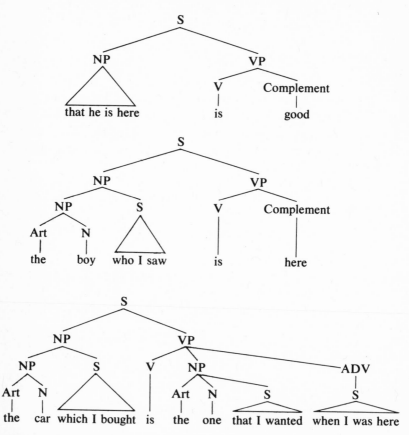

(See TREE DIAGRAM.)

REFERENCE: H. A. Gleason, *Linguistics and English Grammar* (New York: Holt, Rinehart and Winston, 1965), pp. 142–167.

dialect   Any one of the mutually comprehensible social or regional varieties of a language. Distinguishing features of a dialect are found in its pronounciation, grammar, and word-choice. (See MIDLAND DIALECT, REGIONAL DIALECT, SOCIAL DIALECT, PRESTIGE DIALECT.)

REFERENCES: H. B. Allen, and G. Underwood, *Readings in American Dialectology* (New York: Appleton-Century-Crofts, 1970); E. B. Atwood, *A Survey of Verb Forms of the Eastern United States* (Ann Arbor: University of Michigan Press, 1953); H. Kurath, *Word Geography of the Eastern United States* (Ann Arbor: University of Michigan Press, 1949); H. Kurath and Raven McDavid, *The Pronunciation of English in the Atlantic States* (Ann Arbor: University of Michigan Press, 1961); R. W. Shuy, *Discovering American Dialects* (Champaign: NCTE, 1967).

dialectology   The study of social and geographical dialects. (See DIALECT, LINGUISTICS, REGIONAL DIALECT, SOCIAL DIALECT.)

dictionary   The word list of a language. Although it is difficult to characterize all dictionaries since they vary in quality and kind, ten major items of information are usually found in a good, abridged desk dictionary:

1. *Main Entry:* The main entries follow one another in alphabetic order and are set in heavy black letters called **boldface type.**

2. *Pronunciation:* Pronunciations are shown by means of a system of phonetic transcription whose symbols are listed. Variant pronunciations are usually indicated.

3. *Function Labels:* Labels in *italics* indicate at least one of the eight parts of speech to which a given word belongs.

4. *Inflectional Forms:* Plurals of nouns, principal parts of verbs, and comparative and superlative forms of adjectives and adverbs are listed.

5. *Etymology:* The etymology traces an entry as far back as possible in English, tells what language a word came from into English, and traces the pre-English source as far back as possible.

6. *Vocabulary Entry:* The vocabulary entry defines and identifies a word.

7. *Status Labels:* Status labels indicate the temporal, stylistic, or regional status of a word.

8. *Usage Notes:* Usage notes, when they occur, provide information about the use of a word and, thus, further modify it.

9. *Cross References:* Cross references are of various kinds and serve to establish word relationships; they are usually given in SMALL CAPITAL letters.

10. *Synonyms:* Synonyms are generally found in a separate paragraph following the vocabulary entry.

TG: A dictionary is one of the two parts of the semantic component of a transformational grammar, the other part being projection rules, rules that show the relationship among dictionary meanings. This dictionary provides the meaning for each word in the sentence, for example, *dog:* its *syntactic properties* ("noun," "animate," "common," "count"); its *semantic properties* ("animal," "male," or "female"); its *phonological properties* in the form of distinctive features; its *distinguishers* ("a variable, carnivorous, domesticated mammal," "a worthless fellow," "a mechanical device for holding or fastening," "ruin"); and its selection restraints: the word *dog* has at least four meanings, each of which has certain restraints of selection on it. These allow the various readings to occur; (1) This dog is a good pet. (2) That man is a dog. (3) Tighten the dogs on the hatch. (4) Tom is going to the dogs. Selection restraints are, obviously, contextual features. (See DISTINCTIVE FEATURES, LEXICAL PROPERTIES, TRANSFORMATIONAL GRAMMAR.)

REFERENCES: P. B. Gove, *The Role of the Dictionary* (Indianapolis: Bobbs-Merrill, 1967); J. H. Sledd and W. R. Ebbitt, *Dictionaries and THAT Dictionary* (Chicago: Scott, Foresman, 1962); D. Starnes and G. E. Noyes, *The English Dictionary from Cawdrey to Johnson* (Austin: University of Texas Press, 1954).

digraph   A combination of two written letters representing one sound: *ph*one, *th*ing, *th*en, *pi*ece, *ea*t.

diphthong   A bundle of sounds connected by a tongue glide. The three phonemic diphthongs of American English are /au/, /ai/, /ɔi/ as in *cow, sigh,* and *boy,* respectively.

direct object   The person or thing receiving the action of the transitive verb. The direct object is the verbal, noun, pronoun, or noun clause following the verb:

> *Verbal:*   I like *swimming.*
> *Noun:*   I like *pie.*
> *Pronoun:*   I like *it.*
> *Noun Clause:*   I like *what he makes.*

discontinuous constituents   *SG:* Parts of the same grammatical construction whose continuous, common-order sequence is changed by the intrusion of other linguistic units:

The man *can walk : Can* the man *walk*?

dissimilation   A phonetic process in which two neighboring sounds that were once alike become different. In the words derived in English, Italian, and French from Latin *peregrinus* the first *r* has become dissimilar to the second one by changing to *l: pilgrim.* Sometimes one of the neighboring sounds will disappear completely. This kind of dissimilation is illustrated in the common pronunciations of *library, February, secretary* in which the first *r* is lost in each word.

distinctive features   Speech is heard as a chain of successive segments of sound. This auditory impression provides the linguist with an acoustic (contrasted with *articulatory*) basis for segmentation of sounds. It is on this acoustic basis that a good deal of phonetic analysis is now being done. Acoustic phonetics, a discipline based on the use of the Acoustic Spectograph which produces an exact visible record of speech, provides for a description of precisely what the ear hears. Speech sounds are described by their distinctive features, characteristics organized into bundles to form sounds. In this presentation of features we will consider each classification of sound variables as a set of binary, "yes/no," choices. Further, since an attempt has been made greatly to simplify the description, we will describe each feature on the basis of its acoustic or articulatory characteristics. In two instances we will resort to both bases for description. There are two large classes, and a number of subclasses, of distinctive features. One of the two main classes consists of *sonority features,* which are characterized by "the amount and concentration of energy in the [frequency] spectrum and in time." We will describe seven of the nine sonority features here. They are *Vocalic/Non-vocalic* Acoustic: the presence or absence of a sharply defined frequency differentiation. Vowels have a distinctive set of pitches. *Example:* /u/ vs. /k/. Articulatory: the mouth is open for vocalic sounds. *Consonantal/Non-consonantal* Articulatory: the presence or absence of an obstruction in the vocal tract. *Example:* /k/ vs. /l/. *Compact/Diffuse* Acoustic: a higher or lower concentration of energy in the central region of the frequency spectrum accompanied by an increase in the total amount of energy. *Example:* /ɛ/ vs. /ɪ/. *Nasal/Oral* Articulatory: the oral resonance chamber supplemented by the nasal one versus exclusion of the nasal resonance chamber. *Example:* /m/ vs. /p/. *Tense/Lax* Articulatory: greater versus lesser tensing, deformation of the tongue muscles from their position of rest. *Example:* /ɪ/ vs. /æ/. *Interrupted/Continuant* Articulatory: the rapid turning on or off of sound either by closure-release or by one or more tongue taps versus absence of such an on-off mechanism. *Example:* /b/ and trilled /r/ vs. /l/. *Strident/Mellow* Acoustic: higher intensity noise versus lower intensity noise. *Example:* /s/ vs /θ/.

The other main class of features consists of *Tonality Features.* Here are two of the three. *Grave/Acute* Acoustic: predominance of the lower versus the upper end of the frequency spectrum. Articulatory: *Grave* consonants or vowels are pronounced with a larger, less-divided oral cavity; *Acute* consonants or vowels are pronounced with a smaller,

	p	b	m	f	v	k	g	t	d	θ	ð	n	s	z	č	ǰ	š	ž	ʊ	o	a	ɔ	ɪ	ɛ	æ	ə
Vocalic/Non-vocalic	−	−	−	−	−	−	−	−	−	−	−	−	−	−	−	−	−	−	+	+	+	+	+	+	+	+
Consonant/Non-consonant	+	+	+	+	+	+	+	+	+	+	+	+	+	+	+	+	+	+	−	−	−	−	−	−	−	−
Compact/Diffuse	−	−	−	−	−	+	+	−	−	−	−	−	−	−	+	+	+	+	−	+	+	+	−	+	+	−
Grave/Acute	+	+	+	+	+	+	+	−	−	−	−	−	−	−					+	+	+	+	−	−	−	+
Flat/Plain																				+		+				
Nasal/Oral			+									+														
Tense/Lax	+	−		+	−	+	−	+	−	+	−		+	−	+	−	+	−								
Continuent/Interrupted	−	−		+	+	−	−	−	−	+	+		+	+	−	−	+	+	+	+	+	+	+	+	+	+
Strident/Mellow				+	+	−	−	−	−	−	−		+	+	+	+	+	+	−	−	−	−	−	−	−	−

Adapted from R. Jakobson, C. G. M. Fant, and M. Halle. *Preliminaries to Speech Analysis* (Cambridge, Mass.: MIT Acoustics Laboratory, 1952), p. 43.

(See ACOUSTIC PHONETICS.)

more divided cavity. *Grave* phonemes are back vowels and labial and velar consonants; *Acute* phonemes are front vowels and dental and palatal consonants. *Examples: Grave:* /m a/; *Acute:* /n ɪ/. *Flat/Plain* Articulatory: these features result from variations in lip-rounding or contraction of the pharyngeal tract: lip-rounding versus less rounding with concomitant increase in length of lip constriction; pharyngeal contraction versus less contraction. *Examples:* rounding: /ʊ/ vs. /ə/; contraction: /a/ vs. /æ/. This "yes/no" arrangement can be used to characterize the phoneme pattern of English.

do transformation   *TG:* A transformation associated with the yes/no question transformation. It is necessary to apply the do transformation when the tense affix is not followed by a verb or auxiliary word such as *have, be*, or by a modal auxiliary. The *do* form is added to carry tense. Here is an example:

> *Basic Sentence:*   Bill -s- show his paintings.
> *Yes/No Question Transformation:*   s- Bill show his paintings.
> *Do-Transformation:*   Does Bill show his paintings?

The rule for the do-transformation can be written this way:

$$\begin{Bmatrix} \varnothing \\ s \\ ed \end{Bmatrix} \Big/ \begin{array}{l} \text{in contexts other than} \\ + \text{VERB, HAVE, BE,} \\ \text{MODAL} \end{array} \Big/ \Rightarrow \begin{Bmatrix} \varnothing \\ s \\ ed \end{Bmatrix} + \text{DO}$$

(See EMPHATIC ASPECT, NEGATIVE TRANSFORMATION.)

double-base transformation   *TG:* One of the names for a transformation that operates on two or more basic sentences:

> *Main-Clause Sentence:*   Joe is a man (comp). ⎫
> *Insert Sentence:*   Joe is old ⇒ who is old ⎬ ⇒
> *Result Sentence:*   Joe is a man who is old. ⎭

(See COMPLEX TRANSFORMATION, DEPENDENT CLAUSE.)

double negative   The use of two negative words in the same statement to express a single negation:

> I have*n't* got *none*.
> She is *not* sure she *won't* be here.

doublet   One or the other of two words derived from the same source through different routes of transmission (for example, *cattle* and *chattel* derive from Latin *capitalis* via Middle English and Old French).

dual number   Identifies two persons, in contrast with singular (one) and plural (more than two), in the first- and second-person pronoun paradigms of Old English. The dual number pronouns of Old English are

	First Person		*Second Person*
Nom.	*wit* (we two)	Nom.	*git* (ye two)
Gen.	*uncer* (of us two)	Gen.	*incer* (of you two)
Dat.,		Dat.,	
Accus.	*unc* (us two)	Accus.	*inc* (you two)

These pronoun forms were used in Late Old English (tenth century) and Early Middle English (eleventh–twelfth centuries). All trace of the dual number was lost after the thirteenth century. (See PARADIGM, PRONOUN.)

E

ellipsis, elliptical construction   A construction in which an element existing in a related construction is missing:

Are you going to Minneapolis? Yes, I am [going to Minneapolis].

(See DELETION TRANSFORMATION.)

embedment   A transformational operation in which an insert sentence is embedded into, added to, a main clause sentence. This transformation is the source of subordinate clauses and adverb and adjective modifiers in English. An example of embedment is given with the definition of DOUBLE-BASE TRANSFORMATION.

emphatic aspect   *CG:* The insertion of the verb *do* in a statement to put emphasis in the statement. The *do* verb then takes strong stress and indicates tense:

He *does* drive.
He *did* drive.

(See DO TRANSFORMATION.)

endocentric construction   A word group that functions in the same manner as its headword. *Old man* has a noun headword *man,* and the word group functions as a noun. *Very old* has an adjective headword *old,* and the word group functions as an adjective modifying a noun. (See EXOCENTRIC CONSTRUCTION, HEADWORD.)

epenthesis   An articulatory process by which an extra sound is inserted within a word, such as /p/ in *warmth, something* or /t/ in *sense.* The extra sound in the pronunciation is called excrescent. Most frequently after /m/ an excrescent /p/ may occur before voiceless consonants /t k f θ s š/. This process is further illustrated by the excrescent /p/ in *dreamt, comfort, Sampson.*

epithesis   An articulatory process by which an extra consonant is added to the end of a word. This extra consonant occurs after /s/ or /n/. After /s/, /t/ is added in some pronunciations of *once:* /wənst/, *across* /əkrɔst/. The word *midst* had the form *middes* in the fourteenth century. After /n/, /d/ is added. The words *bound* and *sound* were spelled *boun* and *soun* in the fourteenth century. (See ETYMOLOGY for the spellings of *sound.*)

eth   The written symbol ð, a modification of *d,* adopted in Old English times. It occurred within words and indicated both voiced and voiceless *th* sounds as in *thin* and *thine;* e.g., *oðer, cweðan.* (See THORN.)

etymology   The origin and development of the form of a word. The term also means the description of a word's etymology, tracing it back through history by means of historical and comparative linguistics. Here, as a sample, is the etymology of the word *sound* (the Roman numerals indicate the century of first recorded usage):

> **SOUND**   (saund) that which is or may be heard, auditory effect. xiii (Cursor M.). ME. *sun, son, soun* — AN *sun, soun,* (O)F. *son* = Pr. *son, so,* Sp. *son,* Pg. *som,* It. *suono:* -L. *sonu-s* (whence also OE. *son,* ON. *sonn*). So *sound* vb. cause to make a sound xiii; emit a sound xiv. ME *sune, sone, soune* — AN. *suner,* OF. *soner* (mod. *sonner*) = Pr., Sp. *sonar,* Pg. *soar,* It. *sonare:* — L. *sonare,* f. *sonus.* ¶ The form with -d appears xv, and is established xvi.†
>
> REFERENCE: C. T. Onions *et al., Oxford English Dictionary* (Oxford: Clarendon Press, 1933).

exocentric construction   A word group whose function is different from that of any of its constituents. *Bill sleeps* is neither a nominal expression like *Bill* nor a verbal expression like *sleeps.* In *to the house* the constituents are the preposition *to* and the noun phrase *the house,* yet the word group functions as an adverb of motion. (See ENDOCENTRIC CONSTRUCTION.)

excrescent sound   An INTRUSIVE CONSONANT.

expletive   In English the two expletive words are *it* and *there,* as they are used to get a sentence started. They have no explicit grammatical function in or connection with the rest of the sentence.

> *It* is raining.
> *There* is a man outside.

In the second construction *a man* is called the "delayed subject" because it comes after the verb with which it agrees. (See THERE TRANSFORMATION.)

eye dialect   A dialect perceived by the eye. It is a false phonetic respelling of common words to suggest nonstandard pronunciation. But it actually suggests the standard English pronunciation of many of the words it spells: *bekuz, nite, wuz, sez.*

† From C. T. Onions (ed.), *The Oxford Dictionary of English Etymology* (Oxford: The Oxford University Press, 1966), p. 848.

F

factive nominal   *TG:* A construction composed of *that + sentence,* which can be subject or object in certain kinds of sentences:

That he is honest is true.
I thought *that he would come home.*

factitive verbs   That small subclass of transitive verbs that make their two complements refer to the same person or thing. Factitive verbs are themselves of two classes: those that take two nominals as their complements

They *elected* Geoff president.
I *called* him an ape.
She *thought* him a fool.

and those that take a nominal and adjective as their complements:

He *painted* his house white.
I *consider* Eve good.

Factive verbs are also called OBJECT COMPLEMENT verbs.

Family Tree Theory   A theory, characteristic of historical linguistics, in which a parent language such as Indo-European is regarded as having split into various different, yet related languages. The theory is useful in a general sort of way, and it has undergone considerable refinement in the last fifty years. The family tree diagram is a kind of gross representation of the theory. Here is a diagram suggesting the relationships among the various branches of Indo-European and the subdivisions of the Germanic branch.

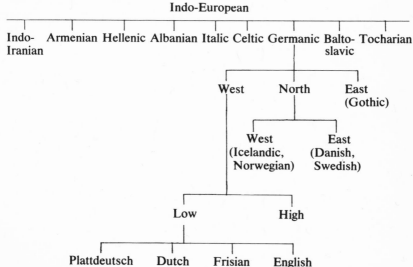

(See GLOTTOCHRONOLOGY, WAVE THEORY.)
REFERENCES: L. Bloomfeld, *Language* (New York: Holt, Rinehart & Winston, 1933); Morton W. Bloomfield, "A Brief History of the English Language," in *The American Heritage Dictionary* (Boston: Houghton Mifflin, 1969).

Features of Words   See LEXICAL PROPERTIES.

finite verb   A verb limited in person by a pronoun or other subject nominal, in time by its tense form, or in number by the singularity or plurality of its subject. Finite verbs are contrasted with "nonfinite" forms of verbs, which are not limited in person or number: infinitives (*see, to see, to have seen*) and participles (*learning, learned*). The participle forms are also used as gerunds. Finite verbs are usually main verbs in sentences: *He runs. They ran.* Nonfinite verb forms combine with auxiliaries to form verb phrases that function as finite forms: He *was to have seen* it. They *had been learning.* (See NOMINAL.)

First (or **Great**) **Consonant Shift**   This was described by the German philologist Jacob Grimm in 1822. He observed a regular pattern of shift of certain Indo-European consonants in the Germanic languages. The Indo-European voiceless stops *p, t, k* became the Germanic voiceless fricatives *f, th, h.*

> *Example:*   I-E *p* = Latin *p* : L. *p*ater → Gmc. *f*ather
> I-E *t* = Latin *t* : L. *t*res → Gmc. *th*ree
> I-E *k* = Latin *c* : L. *c*ent → Gmc. *h*undred

The Indo-European voiced stops *b, d, g* became the Germanic voiceless stops *p, t, k.*

> *Example:*   I-E *b* = Latin *b* : L. canna*b*is → Gmc. hem*p*
> I-E *d* = Latin *d* : L. *d*uo → Gmc. *t*wo
> I-E *g* = Latin *g* : L. *g*enus → Gmc. *k*in

The Indo-European voiced aspirated stops *bh, dh, gh* became the voiced stops *b, d, g.*

> *Example:*   I-E *bh* = Latin *f* : L. *f*rater → Gmc. *b*rother
> I-E *dh* = Latin *f* : L. *f*oris → Gmc. *d*oor
> I-E *gh* = Latin *h* : L. *h*ortus → Gmc. *g*arden

Each of these sound changes took place only once. (See GRIMM'S LAW, INDO-EUROPEAN, VERNER'S LAW.)

flapped r   An allophone of /r/ in which the tongue tip momentarily touches the alveolar ridge once. It is heard in the British English pronunciation of *worry,* and in some dialects in the United States in which it sounds somewhat like /d/ or /t/. (See TRANSCRIPTION.)

focal area   An area whose economic, social, or cultural prestige has led to the spread of its linguistic forms into other areas. Focal areas in the eastern United States are Boston, Philadelphia, New York City, Richmond, and Charleston. The dialect features of focal areas are likely to have prestige when they are used by younger or more sophisticated speakers. (See DIALECT, RELIC AREA.)

folk etymology The changing of the forms of words to fit what people think these words mean; the changing of the unfamiliar to the familiar by people who do not know the real etymology of a word. Words borrowed from other languages are particularly subject to the process of folk etymology. The Old French word *crévis/crévice* became Middle English *crevis(se)*, but has since been changed to *crayfish/crawfish* because the "meaningless" *-vis(se)* could easily be changed to the apparently similar native *-fish*. Other examples are Old French *primerole* → English *primerose;* Old French *mousseron* → English *mushroom.* Native words can also be altered in form and sometimes in meaning by folk etymology. *Hangnail* is derived from Old English *angnægl,* "tight or painful nail," in the sense of a growth like a corn in the foot. Now the form has been changed and the word is associated with fingernail. Other native folk etymologies include *bridegroom* from Old English *brȳdguma* "bride-man"; *hiccough* from earlier echoic forms such as *hickop, hicket.*

form class word *Str:* A form class consists of words that share characteristic forms and pattern in the same ways in sentences. For example, nouns share the plural and possessive inflectional suffix *s,* a number of derivational suffixes such as *-er, -ment, -ness,* etc., and they pattern in generally similar ways with determiners, before and after verbs, and in constructions after prepositions. From the structural point of view, the four form classes are nouns, verbs, adjectives, and adverbs. There is some disagreement about pronouns, some of which show changes in form, some of which do not. (See FUNCTION WORD.)

fortis When the stopped energy of the breath stream is great, the resulting stop consonant is a strong, or fortis, sound. Articulation and aspiration are usually stronger in the voiceless stops /p t k/ than in the voiced stops /b d g/. And these voiceless stops are, in English, fortis when they are in the initial position in a word. (See LENIS, STOP.)

free form Free forms are bases and stems that carry lexical meaning and can stand alone: *boy, girlishness.* (See BOUND MORPHEME.)

free variation Two sounds are said to be in free variation with each other when they can alternate in the same position in a word. Thus, /d/ and /t/ are in free variation with each other in the pronunciation of the past tense and past participle of the verb *burn:* burned/burnt. For some non-native speakers of English in Southeast Asia /s/ and /d/ are in free variation with each other in the pronunciation of the past tense of English verbs, both forms meaning the past tense: burne*d*/burn*s*. (See COMPLEMENTARY DISTRIBUTION.)

fricative A consonant produced by friction caused by the air moving through a narrowed air passage in the mouth. Thus, audible friction is heard as the air is expelled. Fricatives are articulated at the meeting of the upper teeth and lower lip (voiced /v/, voiceless /f/); at the meeting of the tongue tip and the upper and lower teeth (voiced /ð/, voiceless /θ/; at the point of proximity of the tongue tip to the alveolar ridge (voiced /z/, voiceless /s/); at the point of proximity of the tongue tip to the palatal region just behind the alveolar ridge (voiced /ž/, voiceless /š/); and by the breath rushing through the vocal cords when they are constricted (voiceless /h/). (See CONTINUANT.)

fronting A change in a vowel or consonant caused by moving the point of articulation further forward toward the front of the mouth. An example would be /u/ becoming /i/. (See UMLAUT.)

front vowel A vowel articulated in the front of the mouth. These vowels are /i ɪ e ɛ æ /. (See VOWEL.)

functional shift This term describes the ability of many words in English to be used, to function, as more than one part of speech. The manner in which a word is used in a given context determines its functional classification. Notice, for example, how *out* can be used in five different functions and can, consequently, be classified as five different parts of speech.

Noun:	He made the third *out*.
Adjective:	We saw only the *out*side of the house.
Adverb:	He ran *out*.
Part of two-word verb:	He dropped *out* of school.
Preposition:	He looked *out* the window.
	He was scared *out of* his skin.

functional variety of usage Functional varieties of usage are based upon the function for which the usage is intended. John Kenyon posits two functional varieties of usage: *familiar-colloquial* and *formal-public*. The familiar-colloquial variety is identified by familiar conversation, private correspondence, informal conversation, and familiar public address. The formal-public variety is identified by pulpit or platform speech, public reading, worship, belles-lettres, and legal, scientific, or other expository prose writing. Martin Joos, in *The Five Clocks* (*International Journal of American Linguistics,* April 1962), discusses the "four usage-scales of native central English." These scales, all of which are influential in spoken and written usage, are Age, Style, Breadth, and Responsibility. Joos discusses five styles of usage: frozen, formal, consultative, casual, intimate. The frozen style is characteristic of print and declamation. It is characterized by the absence of authoritative intonation in the text and by the fact that the reader or hearer cannot cross-question the author. The purpose of formal style is to inform. It is characterized by the absence of participation on the part of the hearer and by the fact that neither the speaker nor the text is "involved"; the style is an objective one. The consultative, casual, and intimate styles are all characteristic of the colloquial mode. The consultative style is the norm for coming to terms with strangers. It is characterized by the fact that the speaker assumes no background information on the part of his listener; he supplies all this information. Further, the person who is addressed in this style is continuously participating in the discussion. The casual style is used with friends; it is the style for "insiders." This style uses ellipsis and slang. The intimate style is that used in an intimate group, usually between two people. It is characterized by the extraction of small units of wording or intonation from what in other situations would be longer lengths of discourse. These small units of wording or intonation are frequently a kind of code between two people. (See CULTURAL LEVEL OF USAGE, USAGE.)

function word   A term from structural grammar. Most function words, in their citation forms, have no lexical meaning. They lack inflectional forms and perform the syntactic function of connecting form-class words and sentences. The main function words are prepositions, conjunctions, determiners, auxiliary verbs, interrogative words, expletives, and some pronouns. (See FORM CLASS WORD.)

future tense   The tense that refers to time after the present. It is formed in the active voice by *shall*, more frequently *will*, plus the infinitive form of the verb:

> I shall go → I'll go.
> I will see → I'll see.

or by the present tense form of the verb plus an adverb:

> He graduates tomorrow.
> She goes next week.

Future time is also indicated by adverbials following verb phrases containing modal auxiliary verbs:

> We may leave soon.
> We must leave tomorrow.

and by adverbials following the uninflected form of the verb:

> We leave tomorrow.

Very frequently, the future is expressed by *going to:*

I'm going to leave (tomorrow).
We're going to leave (tomorrow).

future perfect tense   The tense that refers to a time after the simple present and before the simple future. It is formed in the active voice by *will* plus the infinitive form of *have* plus the past participle:

will have turned
will have gone

In the passive voice it is formed by *will* plus the infinitive of *have* plus the past participle of *be* and the main verb:

will have been turned
will have been gone

The future perfect tense is generally used in a context with the simple future:

I will have gone by the time you will go.

and with the present:

I will have gone by the time you go.

G

gemination   The process of lengthening or doubling, especially of consonant sounds. In West Germanic, for example, a single consonant other than *r* doubled (was geminated) when it was preceded by a short vowel and followed by *j*. Later the *j* changed the quality of some of the preceding vowels and finally disappeared. Thus, Germanic **cunja-* → W. Germanic **cunnja* → Old English *cynn;* Germanic **saljan* → W. Germanic **salljan* → Old English *sellan*. From the preceding examples it is obvious that gemination is indicated in writing by the doubling of a letter.

gender   English has what is called *natural gender*. The gender of nouns in English is masculine, feminine, or neither, according, literally and figuratively, to the sex or sexlessness inherent in the item the noun names. In English, then, gender is generally determined by the meaning of a word: *man, girl, rooster, hen, doe,* etc. The few exceptions to this statement are words that exhibit *grammatical gender*, a feature almost wholly lost in English by the fourteenth century. Pronouns such as *he, she, it* and a few nouns with feminine endings (*-ess, -ix, -euse*) and masculine endings (*-or, -us, -eur*) are the only remnants of grammatical gender in English. Grammatical gender is very much alive in inflected languages like French and German which have inflections for masculine, feminine, and neuter nouns and for articles and adjectives modifying them.

generative grammar   A term sometimes used to name transformational grammar, which actually consists of two parts: the generative and the transformational grammars. The generative grammar, while distinctly different from the transformational, is closely related to it. The generative grammar selects parts of speech and their subclasses on the bases of their co-occurrence and distinctive features, and puts them together to produce basic sentences consisting of a NOUN PHRASE and a VERB PHRASE:

The man   walked home.

NP   +   VP

Basic sentences are sometimes called deep structure sentences. Transformations produce complex sentences from basic sentences. (See CO-OCCURRENCE, DEEP STRUCTURE, KERNEL SENTENCE, TERMINAL STRING, TRANSFORMATIONAL GRAMMAR.)

genitive case   In its best-understood use, the genitive case indicates possession in English by the -'s/s' inflection on nouns, by the personal pronoun possessive forms *my, your, his, her, its, our, their,* and in part by the noun-replacive pronouns *mine, yours, hers, ours, theirs.* In many instances the genitive can be replaced by a prepositional phrase, usually with *of,* and sometimes by the uninflected form of a noun:

the report of the committee; the committee report
the cage of the bear; the bear cage

Besides representing possession, the genitive represents other relationships. (1) The *descriptive genitive* is evidenced in phrases such as *Chicago's new buildings, car's speed.* (2) The *subjective* and *objective genitive* occur with nouns naming an action. The subjective genitive is shown in *Joe's run* (Joe ran), *the scientist's discovery* (the scientist discovered). The objective genitive is illustrated by the *treasure's discovery* (someone discovered the treasure), *the robber's release* (someone released the robber). (3) Another genitive measures quality (*a dollar's worth*), space (*a stone's throw*), and time (*an hour's wait*). (4) The genitive of origin is illustrated by *Shakespeare's plays, duck's eggs.* (5) The partitive genitive establishes the relation of the part to the whole; this is expressed by of: *some of us, piece of pie.* (6) The appositive genitive employs *of.* It is sometimes used to show the relationship between two nouns or noun phrases that stand together, the second noun describing the first: *the state of Minnesota, the office of chairman.* (See CASE, POSSESSIVE INFLECTION.)

gerund   The verb form ending in *-ing;* when it is used as a noun, it is also called a verbal noun:

Swimming is fun.
I like *swimming.*
He did lots of *swimming.*

glide   In one sense, glide is the name for the phonemes /y r w/. In the second sense, a glide is a non-phonemic transitional sound made by the vocal organs in passing to or from the articulatory position for a speech sound. It is an *on-glide* if it precedes the sound [ʸe]; it is an *off-glide* if it follows the sound [eʸ]. (See CONTINUANT.)

glottal stop   This voiceless sound is the result of the compression and sudden release of air at the glottis. It is symbolized by /ʔ/. The glottal stop in English occurs initially before stressed vowels:

↓I run.

sometimes between vowels, when the second vowel begins a stressed syllable:

tri↓umphant

and sometimes as a transition from a final to an initial vowel:

India ↓ office

glottochronology   A statistical technique in which vocabulary similarities and differences permit deductions about the family relationship of languages as well as the probable dates when the branches of a given family separated from the common parent language. (See FAMILY TREE THEORY.)

REFERENCES: C. D. Chrétien, "The Mathematical Methods of Glottochronology," *Language,* 38 (1962): 11–37; S. C. Gudschinsky, "The ABC's of Lexicostatistics," *Word,* 12(1956): 175–210; M. Swadesh, "Lexicostatistic Dating of Prehistoric Ethnic Contacts," *Proceedings of the American Philosophical Society,* 96(1952): 452–63.

gradation   A change in vowel quality to one of the central vowels /ə ɨ ər/ when stress is reduced to weak stress. Consider these examples:

Strong Stress	Weak Stress	Gradation
John /ǽnd/ Jim	John /ǝn/ Jim	/æ/ – /ə/
He came /tú/	came /tǝ/ town	/u/ – /ə/
/əwé/	/ɔlwɨz/	/e/ – /ɨ/
/fɔ́r/	/fər/ you	/ɔr/ – /ər/

(See ABLAUT.)

grammar   From the popular point of view the meaning of the term *grammar* is consonant with "correct usage," "linguistic etiquette." From the point of view of linguistics, grammar means the principles of operation of a language, or the study and description of these principles. When the structural linguist speaks of *grammar,* he means the morphology and syntax of a language. The transformational linguist describes *grammar* as a finite set of rules that generates an infinite number of grammatical sentences of a language, and no ungrammatical ones. This finite set of rules assigns to each sentence its correct structural description.

grammatical   In one of its meanings this word describes the morphological and syntactic portions, or "levels," of a structural grammar, the "grammatical level," as opposed to the "phonological level." The other sense of the term, "grammatical sentence," is very difficult to define. Clearly, this meaning has something to do with our intuitions about what is "structurally acceptable," but the various meanings of "intuition" and instances of "borderline" cases confuse the issue. *"The men is there" is clearly ungrammatical, but "The child seems sleeping" seems to be a borderline case.

grammatical meaning   That meaning which is conveyed by contrasting differences in word forms and grammatical structures. For example, the difference between *runs* and *ran* is the difference between the third-person singular present tense and the common form of the past tense. This term is contrasted with LEXICAL MEANING.

grapheme   Generally, any one of the written or printed alphabetic characters of a language. As a phoneme is a family of allophones and a morpheme is a family of allomorphs, so a grapheme is a family of ALLOGRAPHS, different shapes of the same letter. Thus A, a, *a,* and *A* are four different allographs of the same grapheme which is written as ⟨a⟩. There are thirty-seven segmental graphemes of standard English writing or printing. They are classified in two groups:

(1) Twenty-six LETTERS OF THE ALPHABET: ⟨a, b, c, d . . . z⟩
(2) Eleven PUNCTUATION MARKS: ⟨, ; : . ? ! ' " - — ( )⟩

Members of the series a b c d . . . z are called LOWER CASE. Members of the series A, B, C, D . . . Z are called CAPITALS. Space can also be included as a sort of zero grapheme since it is what bounds written words on either side, thus defining them for most literate people. Adapted from W. Nelson Francis, *The Structure of American English* (New York: The Ronald Press Co., 1958), pp. 436–437.

REFERENCES: I. J. Gelb, *The Study of Writing* (Chicago: University of Chicago Press, 1952); R. A. Hall, Jr., *Sound and Spelling in English* (Philadelphia: Chilton, 1961).

Grassman's Law   Grassman's Law is a phonetic statement to the effect that when two related languages have aspirated stops at the beginning of two successive syllables, the first of the two stops becomes unaspirated in the later of the two languages.

pre-Greek	Greek
*[phewthomai]	[pewthomai]
*[thithe:mi]	[tithe:mi]
*[thrikha]	[trikha]

Great Vowel Shift   The change in pronunciation of accented long vowel sounds that took place from the late Middle English period (1400) until about 1750. The following chart describes these changes, showing a written representation of these sounds at two periods and a phonemic representation at three periods in the history of the English language. See VOWEL for a description of the vowel phonemes and the ways in which they are represented by phonemic transcription.

Late Middle English (1400)	Early Modern English (after 1500)	MnE
mīn /i:/———————————→/əy/—————————→/ai/ mine, fire		
wē /e:/————————————→/e/—————————→/i:/ we, east		
ēst /æ:/		
moūs /u:/————————————→/əw/————————→/au/ mouse		
tō /o:/————————————→/u:/—————————→/u:/ to		
stōn /ɔ:/————————————→/o:/—————————→/o:/ stone		
nāme /a:/————————————→/æ:/ > /ɛ:/————→/e:/ name		

Grimm's Law   The description of the shift in pronunciation in the Germanic languages of nine Indo-European consonants. (See FIRST CONSONANT SHIFT.)

H

headword   The word that is grammatically central in a construction because all other words in the construction modify it.

Noun Headword:	my old *friend; friend* of mine
Verb Headword:	sometimes quietly *talked; arrived* noisily yesterday
Adjective Headword:	exceedingly *cold; good* for nothing
Adverb Headword:	rather *slowly,* sometimes *outside;* a yard *away; away* for a month

(See ATTRIBUTE, CONSTRUCTION, NOUN-HEADED CONSTRUCTION, VERB-HEADED CONSTRUCTION.)

helping verbs   See AUXILIARY VERB.

high vowel   The vowel produced with the tongue raised toward the roof of the mouth. (See CLOSED VOWEL, VOWEL.)

homonym, homophone   These terms describe a word that is identical in pronunciation with another word whose meaning is different. Examples are *plain-plane; beet-beat.*

human noun   *TG:* Human nouns are a subclass of animate nouns that can co-occur with the pronouns *who/whom:*

who is the *boy*
man whom I saw

(See LEXICAL PROPERTIES.)

I

ideogram, ideograph   A symbol or group of symbols representing a word or phrase, but not representing the phonemes of the word or phrase. Examples from our own alphabetic writing are *5, +, $.* (See PICTOGRAM.)

idiolect   An individual's characteristic way of using his language; the distinctive features of his pronunciation, grammar, and word-choice.

immediate constituent   The two parts into which every word group can be divided. These parts are constituent because they constitute the word group, and they are immediate because they are directly related to one another. ICs may be word groups

> *The boys played yesterday*

or single words

> *the boys* and *played yesterday*

For a description of the morphemic ICs, the immediate constituents of words, see the definition of CONSTRUCTION.

REFERENCE: C. C. Fries, *The Structure of English* (New York: Harcourt, Brace & World, 1952).

imperative mood   The mood of the verb used in giving a command or making a request. Normally, there is no subject of the verb in this construction:

> Close the door.
> Go away.

TG: The prevailing school grammar description of this sentence type still speaks of the "understood subject *you.*" While this is not a precise description of this construction, there is an important, intuitive perception of grammatical process underlying it. Transformational rules should probably derive the imperative from a related sentence containing the modal auxiliary verb *will* so that we can account for imperative sentences such as

> Close the door, will you?

The imperative transformation, then, might operate, first, by deleting *will,* then the subject *you,* from the basic sentence:

> You will open the window ⟹You open the window ⟹Open the window.

It can now be seen that "understood subject *you*" can be interpreted as the result of an automatic deletion transformation. (See DELETION TRANSFORMATION.)

imperfect aspect   *CG:* The imperfect or durative aspect is frequently termed the imperfect tense. The imperfect notes an action or state of being that is still in progress in reference to some point in time, particularly the past. It is expressed in a number of ways in English. Among them are the progressive:

> He is/was running.

the present or past form of the verb plus present participle as predicate:

> He continues/continued running.

or by the addition of *on* or *on and on:*

> He walked on alone.
> He went on and on.

(See PROGRESSIVE TENSE.)

inanimate noun   *TG:* Inanimate nouns are a subclass of count nouns. They are those nouns that refer to inanimate objects and that can occur only as the subjects, not objects, of verbs like *surprise, frighten,* and *confuse:*

> The *house* surprised the man.
> The *mountain* frightened the explorer.
> The *puzzle* confused Norman.

House, mountain, and *puzzle* refer to inanimate objects and cannot occur as objects of these verbs. (See LEXICAL PROPERTIES.)

indefinite pronouns   Pronouns that do not indicate one particular person or thing but, rather, any one or more of a class or persons or things. They have no explicit antecedent. *All, any, each, some, everyone, few, nobody,* and *you* and *we* in some of their uses are indefinite pronouns.

independent clause   A clause that can stand alone and convey a complete meaning. Independent clauses may be complete sentences:

> The man is here.

or parts of sentences:

> *The man is here* because he came home.

(See DEPENDENT CLAUSE.)

indicative mood   The mood of the verb that expresses a statement of fact. (See IMPERATIVE MOOD, INTERROGATIVE MOOD.)

indirect object   With verbs of giving, telling, etc., there is frequently an object that names the receiver of the thing or message. This indirect object is the first of two nominals after a transitive verb:

I gave *the man* a dollar.
He told *me* a story.

(See DATIVE CASE, PERIPHRASTIC CONSTRUCTION.)

indirect question   A question in which its substance, but not its exact words, is stated. The question clause is introduced by an interrogative word:

I wonder whether he has the car.
He asked if they saw the fire.

indirect statement   A quotation summarized or paraphrased in the writer's own words rather than being quoted as it was originally stated or written:

He said that he wouldn't arrive until tomorrow.

Indo-European   The term describes languages belonging to the large group of related languages of which English is a member. The abbreviation is IE. (See PROTO-INDO-EUROPEAN.)

REFERENCES: L. Bloomfield, *Language* (New York: Holt, Rinehart & Winston, 1933); S. Robertson and F. G. Cassidy, *The Development of Modern English* (Englewood Cliffs: Prentice-Hall, 1954).

infinitive   The infinitive is the stem form of the verb which is not limited in tense, person, mood, or number. *Run* is an infinitive. The form of the infinitive preceded by *to, to run,* is called the *marked infinitive.*

infinitive phrase   *To* plus the verb stem is also called the infinitive phrase. Infinitive phrases function as nouns:

He tried *to go.*
To drive is his idea of fun.

as adjectives:

John has time *to think.*

and as adverbs:

He's going home *to see* his parents.

infix   An inflectional or derivational affix inserted within a word rather than at its end or beginning. In English, infixes can indicate past tense (st*oo*d, h*u*ng) or plural (m*e*n, g*ee*se).

inflection   The same as an INFLECTIONAL SUFFIX.

inflectional language   An inflectional language, also known as a SYNTHETIC LANGUAGE, is one in which the relationships among words, thus their functions, depend mainly upon inflections. For example, the Latin sentence *Agricola amat puellam* has the same meaning—"The farmer loves the girl"—no matter what the order of words is. The *-a* ending on *agricola* and the *-am* ending on *puellam* designate, respectively, the subjective (nominative) and objective (accusative) functions. Changing the word order makes no difference in meaning, as long as the endings remain the same; *Agricola puellam amat* still means "The farmer loves the girl." In Modern English, an ANALYTIC LANGUAGE, a change in the order of words makes a difference in meaning: *The farmer loves the girl : The girl loves the farmer.* Old English, like Latin and Modern German, was synthetic in its grammatical structure. (See ANALYTIC LANGUAGE, SYNTHETIC LANGUAGE.)

inflectional suffix   Affixes that occur with the stems of form-class words. They show number and possession in nouns:

> *Noun Plural:*   dog*s*, cat*s*, wom*en*
> *Possession:*   boy'*s*, girl'*s*

number and tense and person in verbs:

> *3rd Singular Present Tense:*   she shop*s*, it burn*s*
> *Past Tense:*   shopp*ed*, burn*ed*
> *Present Continuous Tense:*   shopp*ing*, burn*ing*

and comparative and superlative degrees in adjectives and adverbs:

> *Comparative:*   slow*er*
> *Superlative:*   slow*est*

insert sentence   *TG:* A basic sentence that is embedded, introduced, into a main clause sentence by processes of transformation:

> *Main-Clause Sentence:*   Joe is a man (COMP) ⎱
> *Insert Sentence:*   Joe is old ⟹ who is old⎰ ⟹
> *Result Sentence:*   Joe is a man who is old.
> *Deletion Transformation:*   Joe is a man w~~ho~~ ~~is~~ old.
> *Adjective Rearrangement:*   Joe is an old man.

(See ADJECTIVE.)

intensifier   See QUALIFIER.

intensive pronoun   See PRONOUN.

intermediate structure   *TG:* A structure intermediate between a deep structure and a surface structure; it is a tree representing a deep structure on the way to being transformed into a surface structure. The following example shows an intermediate structure in which a sentence, on the way to becoming a relative clause, is being embedded after an NP, *the dog.* Notice that a relative word, *that,* has been substituted for a determiner, *the,* as part of the transformation.

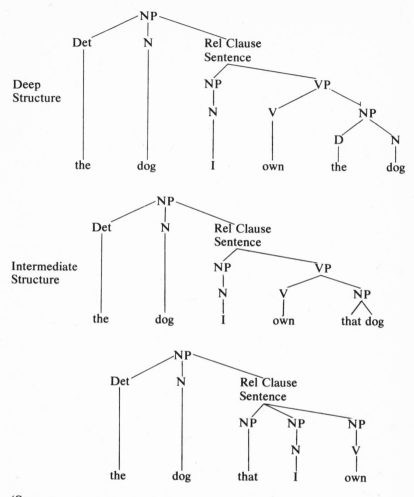

(See DEEP STRUCTURE, SURFACE STRUCTURE.)

International Phonetic Alphabet   See TRANSCRIPTION.

interrogative mood   The mood of the verb that expresses a question. (See QUESTION for the forms that express the interrogative mood.)

interrogative pronoun   Pronouns used to ask questions. They are *who, whom, whose, what, which*. (See INTERROGATIVE WORD.)

interrogative sentence   See QUESTION.

interrogative word   A term that designates a broader class of interrogators than just pronouns. Sometimes they are called *wh-words*. Interrogative words ask questions: *who, whom, whose, what, when, where, why, which, how,* etc. (See WH-QUESTION.)

intervocalic   Literally, "between vowels." Consonants and groups of consonants are intervocalic: me*t*er, chi*ldr*en.

intonation   Loosely, "way of talking." Linguists use the term to indicate distinctive speech patterns. (See INTONATION CONTOUR.)

REFERENCES: K. L. Pike, *The Intonation of American English* (Ann Arbor: University of Michigan Press, 1944); J. H. Sledd, *A Short Introduction to English Grammar* (Chicago: Scott, Foresman, 1959); N. C. Stageberg, *An Introductory English Grammar* (New York: Holt, Rinehart & Winston, 1965).

intonation contour   The intonation contours of English are phonemic combinations of pitch and terminal juncture that characterize various kinds of utterances:

Statement:	[2]He has a [3]cold[1] ↓
	The intonation contour is 231 ↓
Yes/No Question in Statement Form:	[2]He has a [3]cold[3] ↑
	The intonation contour is 233 ↑
Wh-Question:	[2]Who [3]is it[1] ↓
	The intonation contour is 231 ↓

(See PITCH LEVELS, SUPRASEGMENTAL PHONEME, TERMINAL JUNCTURE.)

intransitive verb   *CG:* A verb that does not take an object. *Go, sleep, look, laugh* are intransitive verbs. Many verbs may be used either intransitively or transitively. *Str:* Intransitive verbs cannot take an object in the active voice. Thus, they are complete predicates in themselves. They usually have no passive voice form. Intransitive verbs are words like *run, stop, sink, rise, lie, appear,* etc. *TG:* Intransitive verbs can be divided into three subclasses: (1) verbs like *sleep,* which may have no post-verbal element; (2) verbs like *sit,* which usually select adverbs of location after them; (3) verbs like *run,* which may select adverbs of motion after them (He *ran into the house*). In certain circumstances intransitive verbs require either adverbs of motion or adverbs of location, but not both. The expansion rule for intransitive verbs attempts to show such restriction. (C) allows for the optional development of an additional element in the complement:

$$V_{int} \longrightarrow \left\{ \begin{array}{l} V_i \\ \begin{bmatrix} V_{iL} + LOC \\ V_{iM} + MOT \end{bmatrix} \quad (C) \end{array} \right\}$$

intrusive consonant   A consonant that comes into a word as a result of the process of articulation; this consonant is not found in the etymology of the word. The intrusive *r,* found in the speech of many "r-less" areas of the United States, particularly in the east, occurs most often after /ə/ and links one word with another: *lawr office, idear of, sawr a girl.* Intrusive *d* and *t* occur after *n* and before *s.* As the tongue moves from the alveolar position of /n/ to the open position of /s/ it releases air, producing an excrescent /d/ or /t/. Compare your pronunciations of *bands : bans, finds : fins* and *cents : sense, prints : prince* to hear these excrescent sounds. (See ARTICULATORY INTRUSION, EPENTHESIS, EPITHESIS.)

inversion   Grammatical inversion consists of placing a verb before the subject as in the question pattern *Are you going?* or *Did he go?* Inverted word order was a common feature of declarative sentences in the early stages of the development of the English language:

> *Old English:*   þā cwǣdon þā cristenan, "then said the Christians"
> *Middle English:*   Speke we now of wikked conseil

irregular verb   Irregular verbs in English are in contrast with regular verbs, which form their past tense and past participle by adding *-ed* to the infinitive. Irregular verbs, the "strong verbs" of Old English, form their past tense and past participle through change in the root vowel:

Infinitive	*Past Tense*	*Past Participle*
fall	fell	fallen
lie	lay	lain
ride	rode	ridden
see	saw	seen
spring	sprang	sprung

isogloss   A line on a dialect map connecting points at which a specific feature of pronunciation, grammar, or vocabulary exists. A number of isoglosses that generally delineate the same area is considered to be a dialect boundary. Where the dialectologist finds that one pronunciation or word is used almost entirely in one area, he draws a line, an isogloss, which marks the boundary of the use of that item. The map below shows the isoglosses marking the distribution of *frijoles* (pinto beans) and *pilón* (something extra) in Texas:

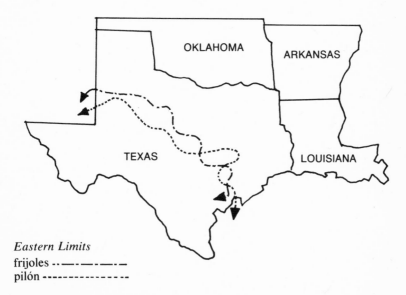

From E. Bagby Atwood, *The Regional Vocabulary of Texas* (Austin: University of Texas Press, 1962), map 116, p. 246.

REFERENCE: H. B. Allen, "The Primary Dialect Areas of the Upper Midwest," in H. B. Allen (ed.), *Readings in Applied English Linguistics,* rev. ed. (New York: Appleton-Century-Crofts, 1964).

isolating language   A language like Chinese that consists of invariable, usually monosyllabic, root words. The relation between words is expressed by word order or by variations in tonal pattern. An isolating language is similar to an ANALYTICAL LANGUAGE.

J

jargon The technical "shop talk" or, in some instances, the secret vocabulary of a specific occupation, trade, profession, class, age group, etc. (See ARGOT, CANT.)

juncture A feature of spoken utterances that describes the various kinds of transitions of pitch and pause within a complete utterance and between utterances. (See SUPRASEGMENTAL PHONEME, TERMINAL JUNCTURE.)

K

kernel sentence   *TG:* The kernel, or basic, sentence is simple, active, declarative, affirmative. Kernel sentences are generated by phrase structure rules and by obligatory simple transformations. They are the sentences upon which optional simple and complex transformations operate.   (See GENERATIVE GRAMMAR, SIMPLE TRANSFORMATION.)

L

labeled-tree diagram   See TREE DIAGRAM.

labial consonant   Consonants in whose formation the lips play the important functions of stopping or stopping and releasing the flow of air. /b p m/ are labial consonants.

labio-dental consonant   These are made by friction of the air passing through a point at which one lip is in contact with the cutting edge of the teeth. /v f/ are labio-dental consonants.

language   A system of arbitrarily chosen vocal sounds by which a group of people communicate with one another. Some languages have a roughly or closely corresponding set of arbitrarily chosen symbols that constitute a writing system. Natural languages, then, are those thousands of systems of vocal sounds that have developed in the course of human history. The term *language* is also applied to artifical systems such as Esperanto, to systems of written or printed symbols such as Fortran IV (a computer "language"), to systems of communication used by animals and insects, and to systems such as signs and colors in various media.

langue   A concept of the Swiss linguist Saussure (1857–1913). It is that part of the system of language which is inherited; it is the complete grammatical system used by the speakers of a language. It is contrasted with PAROLE, an individual speaker's utterance of the language. (See COMPETENCE, PAROLE.)

REFERENCE: F. Saussure, *A Course in General Linguistics,* Wade Baskin, trans. (New York: McGraw-Hill, 1966).

lateral sound   A consonant sound produced by the air flowing laterally off one or both sides of the tongue. The tip of the tongue is pressed against the alveolar ridge to stop the flow of air. /l/ is a lateral. (See CONTINUANT.)

lax vowel   A vowel articulated with relatively little tension of the tongue muscles. Compare the lax vowels /ɪ/ and /ɛ/ against the tense vowels /i/ and /e/.

lenis   When the stopped energy of the breath stream is relatively slight, the resulting stop consonant is a weak, or lenis, sound. Articulation and aspiration are usually weaker in the voiced stops /b d g/ than in the voiceless stops /p t k/. (See FORTIS, STOP.)

leveling of inflections   A process that takes place as a result of NEU-TRALIZATION and ANALOGY. In Old English one of the vocalic declension noun classes had the following inflectional endings:

MASCULINE		NEUTER
	Singular	
-		-
es		es
e		e
	Plural	
as		u
a		a
um		um

In Middle English these endings are leveled to:

Singular	*Plural*
-	es
es	es
(e)	es

In Modern English further leveling has taken place:

Singular	*Plural*
-	s
-	s
-	s

(See ANALOGY, NEUTRALIZATION.)

REFERENCE: S. Robertson and F. G. Cassidy, *The Development of Modern English* (Englewood Cliffs: Prentice-Hall, 1954).

levels of usage   See CULTURAL LEVEL OF USAGE, USAGE.

lexeme   A meaningful speech form, a word or a stem. It is an item in the vocabulary of a language.

lexical meaning   English nouns, verbs, adjectives, and adverbs have lexical meaning, — a meaning that can be found in a dictionary. These four classes of words can be contrasted with FUNCTION WORDS, most of which have no meaning until they connect words in a sentence. (See GRAMMATICAL MEANING.)

lexical properties   *TG:* Every speaker of English has an innate knowledge of the properties of words, a kind of internalized dictionary that determines the ways in which words go together in the DEEP STRUCTURE of sentences. This internalized dictionary is part of the lexical entry in the LEXICON, or DICTIONARY, of a TRANSFORMATIONAL GRAMMAR. The properties of words in the lexicon are represented as sets of features. The presence of a feature is shown by a plus (+) sign, the absence of a feature by a minus (−) sign. NOUNS have many different properties. They may be *common* ("boy") or *proper* ("Joe"). Common nouns have the feature ⟨+common⟩; proper nouns have the feature ⟨−common⟩. Common nouns are either *concrete* ("tree") or *abstract* ("luck"). Concrete nouns have the feature ⟨+concrete⟩; abstract nouns have the feature ⟨−concrete⟩. Concrete nouns are either *animate* ("puppy") or *inanimate* ("mountain"). Animate nouns show the feature ⟨+animate⟩; inanimate nouns show the feature ⟨−animate⟩. Animate nouns are either *human* ("girl") or *nonhuman* ("horse"). Human nouns and nonhuman nouns show the features ⟨+human⟩ and ⟨−human⟩. The noun *man* is listed in the lexicon like this:

$$
\text{man}
\begin{bmatrix}
+\text{N} \\
+\text{common} \\
+\text{concrete} \\
+\text{animate} \\
+\text{human}
\end{bmatrix}
$$

The entry for *luck* looks like this:

$$
\text{luck}
\begin{bmatrix}
+\text{N} \\
+\text{common} \\
-\text{concrete} \\
-\text{animate} \\
-\text{human}
\end{bmatrix}
$$

These features can be an important influence in the choice and arrangement of words in the deep structure of sentences. In the following sentences, for example, the distinction between ⟨+animate⟩ and ⟨−animate⟩ explains part of the ungrammaticality of the starred sentence:

The mountain frightened the man.
*The man frightened the mountain.

$$
\begin{bmatrix}
\langle+\text{common}\rangle \\
\langle+\text{concrete}\rangle \\
\langle+\text{animate}\rangle
\end{bmatrix}
\qquad
\begin{bmatrix}
\langle+\text{common}\rangle \\
\langle+\text{concrete}\rangle \\
\langle-\text{animate}\rangle
\end{bmatrix}
$$

Some noun features can be ⟨+⟩ or ⟨−⟩ for the same word, depending on its syntactic environment. Most English nouns can be *singular* (⟨+singular⟩) or *plural* (⟨−singular⟩) in the same sentence:

The boy likes to run.
The boys like to run.

But some nouns like *gold* and *dirt* can be only ⟨+singular⟩. Nouns can also be *definite* (⟨+definite⟩) or *indefinite* (⟨−definite⟩) depending on whether they are preceded by the definite article *the* in the singular and plural or by the indefinite articles *a, an* in the singular or by no article at all in the indefinite plural. Personal PRONOUNS have features of number, person, gender, and case. These features can be summarized in this way:

Number	Person and Gender	Case
⟨+singular⟩	⟨+I⟩	⟨+accusative⟩ *me*
		⟨−accusative⟩ *I*
	⟨+II⟩ *you*	
	⟨+III⟩ ⟨+male⟩	⟨+accusative⟩ *him*
		⟨−accusative⟩ *he*
	⟨+III⟩ ⟨+female⟩	⟨+accusative⟩ *her*
		⟨−accusative⟩ *she*
	⟨+III⟩ ⟨−male⟩ ⟨−female⟩ *it*	
⟨−singular⟩	⟨+I⟩	⟨+accusative⟩ *us*
		⟨−accusative⟩ *we*
	⟨+II⟩ *you*	
	⟨+III⟩	⟨+accusative⟩ *them*
		⟨−accusative⟩ *they*

Examples of pronouns with their features marked are

$$
\text{her} \quad
\begin{bmatrix}
+N \\
+\text{pronoun} \\
+\text{III} \\
+\text{singular} \\
+\text{accusative} \\
+\text{female}
\end{bmatrix}
\qquad
\text{they} \quad
\begin{bmatrix}
+N \\
+\text{pronoun} \\
+\text{III} \\
-\text{singular} \\
-\text{accusative}
\end{bmatrix}
$$

A recent, though not universally accepted, theory is that VERBS and ADJECTIVES are not wholly different constituents in the DEEP STRUCTURE of sentences. Instead, they are considered as *verbals* (⟨+VB⟩) and their differences are marked by the features ⟨+V⟩ for verbs and ⟨−V⟩ for adjectives. Thus, "run" and "good" would be marked in these ways:

$$
\begin{bmatrix}
\text{run} \\
+\text{VB} \\
+\text{V}
\end{bmatrix}
\qquad
\begin{bmatrix}
\text{good} \\
+\text{VB} \\
-\text{V}
\end{bmatrix}
$$

Verbs and adjectives seem to share some properties. For instance, as there are action verbs and non-action verbs like "walk" and "own," so there are action and non-action adjectives like "honest" and "short." The difference between action (⟨+action⟩) and non-action (⟨−action⟩) verbals (verbs and adjectives) can be seen in several ways. First, only action verbals can occur in imperative sentences. Non-action verbals cannot:

walk down the street
be *honest*
*own the dog
*be short

Second, only action verbals may take the progressive aspect. Non-action verbals cannot:

> the man is *walking* down the street
> he is being *honest*
> *the man is *owning* the dog
> *he is being *short*

Third, action verbals can occur in some embedded sentences in which non-action verbals cannot occur. This restriction depends upon the verb. Consider sentences with the verb *ask:*

> He asked the girl to *walk* away.
> He asked Jim to be *honest.*
> *He asked the girl to *own* the cat.
> *He asked Jim to be *short.*

The features for the four verbals above would be:

$$
\begin{bmatrix} \text{walk} \\ +\text{VB} \\ +\text{V} \\ +\text{action} \end{bmatrix}
\begin{bmatrix} \text{own} \\ +\text{VB} \\ +\text{V} \\ -\text{action} \end{bmatrix}
\begin{bmatrix} \text{honest} \\ +\text{VB} \\ -\text{V} \\ +\text{action} \end{bmatrix}
\begin{bmatrix} \text{short} \\ +\text{VB} \\ -\text{V} \\ -\text{action} \end{bmatrix}
$$

Adapted from R. Jacobs and P. S. Rosenbaum, *English Transformational Grammar* (Waltham, Mass.: Blaisdell Publishing Co., 1968), pp. 63–64. (See *syntactic markers* under DICTIONARY.)

REFERENCES: N. Chomsky, *Aspects of the Theory of Syntax* (Cambridge, Mass.: MIT Press, 1965); C. J. Fillmore and I. Lehiste, *Working Papers in Linguistics,* No. 2 (Columbus: The Ohio State University, 1968); J. J. Katz, *The Philosophy of Language* (New York: Harper & Row, 1966); J. J. Katz and J. A. Fodor, "The Structure of Semantic Theory," in J. A. Fodor and J. J. Katz (eds.), *The Structure of Language, Readings in the Philosophy of Language* (Englewood Cliffs: Prentice-Hall, 1964).

lexicon   A list or book containing the words of a given language; it is a DICTIONARY. *TG:* The lexicon is the second part of a phrase-structure grammar. It is the source of words that are substituted for the abstract symbols in the TERMINAL STRING. For an example of the application of the lexicon, see DERIVATION. Substitution of words from the lexicon is one of several ways of interpreting a terminal string. (See DICTIONARY, TERMINAL STRING.)

lexicography   A branch of the discipline of linguistics having to do with the making of dictionaries.

linguist   A person whose task it is to analyze and classify the facts of language; a specialist in linguistics. Popularly, a linguist is a person who has command of several languages.

linguistics   A term that denotes the systematic and, frequently, scientific study of language. This discipline has numerous branches such as psycholinguistics, historical (diachronic) linguistics, descriptive (synchronic) linguistics, comparative linguistics, dialectology, and lexicography.

linguistic atlas   A set of maps and tables that report the dialect of a particular geographic region. Examples are *The Linguistic Atlas of New England* and *The Linguistic Atlas of the Upper Midwest*. (See ISOGLOSS, MIDLAND DIALECT.)

REFERENCE: H. Kurath *et al.*, *Linguistic Atlas of New England* (Providence: Brown University, 1939–43).

linking verb   *CG:* A verb that functions mainly in connecting its subject with a predicate adjective or predicate noun. The most common linking verb is *be* when it is used as a full verb:

He *is* fine.
He *is* president.

Other high-frequency linking verbs are *become, remain, seem, look, sound*. *Str:* Linking verbs are those for which *be* can be substituted without change in the structure meaning of the sentence:

milk *becomes* sour : milk *is* sour
but not
he *found* my dog : he *is* my dog

TG: Linking verbs, like *be*, can be followed by a range of predicate words; these must generally agree in number with the subject noun. Linking verbs, unlike *be*, cannot be inverted to form yes/no questions; thus they are a separate class of verbs from *be*:

He *is* fine : *Is* he fine?
but not
He *remains* tired : **Remains* he tired?

Further subdivision of this conventional class is possible. *Stay* and *remain* differ from *become*, which cannot be immediately followed by adverbs of location:

**He becomes there.

Thus, in transformational grammar, only those verbs that have adjectives immediately after them are linking verbs:

The man *felt* tired.
His face *turned* blue.
The boys *appeared* strong.

Two transformational rules that express these restrictions follow. The first rule separates *be* from all other classes of verbs:

$$MV \rightarrow \left\{ \begin{array}{l} BE + \text{Predicate} \\ V_b \end{array} \right\}$$

The second rule expands V_b (all other verbs) by stating how *stay* and *remain, become,* linking verbs, and all other verbs (V) that are left over from this division are distinct from one another:

$$V_b \rightarrow \left\{ \begin{array}{ll} \begin{bmatrix} \text{stay} \\ \text{remain} \end{bmatrix} & +\text{predicate} \\ \text{become} + & \text{Adj} \\ & \text{Nom} \\ V_L + \text{Adj} \\ V \end{array} \right\}$$

(See COPULATIVE VERB.)

loan word Words that come into a language through the process of borrowing, a process by which one language absorbs words and expressions from other languages and adapts them to its own particular use. English is one of the world's "borrowingest" languages. Loan words from Latin (exemplified by *animal*), from Greek (*church*), from French (*cattle*), and from the Scandinavian languages (*husband*) are most frequent in English. Minor borrowings into English are exemplified by *clan* from Gaelic, *spook* from Dutch, *paprika* from Hungarian, *vodka* from Russian, *yogurt* from Turkish, *manna* from Hebrew, *chess* from Persian, *algebra* from Arabic, *shampoo* from Hindi, *zebra* from Congolese, *sugar* from Sanskrit, *tea* from Chinese, *kapok* from Javanese, *ketchup* from Malay, *ukulele* from Hawaiian, and so on.

REFERENCES: O. Jespersen, *Growth and Structure of the English Language* (Garden City: Doubleday, 1955; Anchor A46); M. S. Serjeantson, *A History of Foreign Words in English* (London: Routledge and Kegan Paul, 1961; New York: Barnes and Noble, 1961).

localism A word restricted to a given geographical area. Thus, *cabinet* is a localism in the Narragansett Bay area of southern New England meaning what elsewhere would be called a milkshake, a frosted, a frappe, etc. *Gum band* in the Pittsburgh area describes what is in many other parts of the country a rubber band.

locative *TG:* An adverbial of place, of location: *in the house, there, at the party*. The pro-form indicating location is SOMEPLACE. In some models of tranformational grammar locative adverbs are introduced in the BASE RULE that expands the main-verb:

$$\text{MV} \rightarrow \text{V (Adv)}$$

(See PRO-FORM.)

low vowel A vowel produced with the tongue low in the mouth, which is relatively wide open. (See OPEN VOWEL, VOWEL.)

M

main clause sentence   *TG:* A basic sentence that can be expanded by receiving an insert sentence through the process of embedment transformation.

> *Main Clause Sentence:*   Joe is a man (COMP) ⎫ ⟹
> *Insert Sentence:*   Joe is old ⟹ who is old ⎬
> *Result Sentence:*   Joe is a man who is old. ⎭

(See CONSUMER SENTENCE, MATRIX SENTENCE.)

marker   A marker can be considered as a morpheme or a morpheme-combination that indicates the class or grammatical function of a word that includes it. Thus, *-est* indicates the form-class adjective when attached to an adjective base like *grand; -ing* indicates, marks, the form-class verb when attached to a verb base like *eat.* Conjunctions such as *and, or* mark a relationship between two form-classes; thus they are markers. *The* and *a* are markers in that they identify a following noun. Auxiliary verbs such as *must, can* mark following main verbs. Qualifiers like *very, too* mark following adjectives and adverbs. (See PHRASE MARKER, DETERMINER, QUALIFIER.)

mass noun   *CG:* The names of materials in general: *gold, coffee, water,* etc. *TG:* A subclass of concrete nouns that are not counted as separate units or as singular or plural. Thus, they do not take the *-s* plural suffix. Some mass nouns are abstract; they name a quality or concept rather than an object: *love, intelligence, honor,* etc. Mass nouns go with *how much* : *how much water, how much intelligence.* Many of them cannot be preceded by the indefinite article in the singular: **a blood, *a gold.* (See COUNT NOUN.)

matrix sentence   The same as MAIN CLAUSE SENTENCE, CONSUMER SENTENCE.

metalinguistics   In one sense, a branch of linguistics that deals with the relationship between language and such other kinds of culturally determined behavior as gestures. In another sense, metalinguistics refers to the technical language used in making logical and scientific statements about such things as mathematics, philosophy, and language itself.

metathesis   The transposition of speech sounds, of a consonant and a vowel. In English the most common metathesis occurs between /r/ and a following vowel: *pretty* /pərti/; *hundred:* /həndərd/; *apron:* /epərn/; *pronounce:* /pərnauns/. Examples of other frequent metatheses in English are *tragedy:* /trædəji/; *relevant:* /rɛvələnt/; *ask:* /æks/. In word history metathesis has been responsible for changing some spellings and pronunciations over the centuries:

Middle English (1100–1400)	*Modern English*
brid	bird
thridda	third
gærs — græs	grass
clapsen	clasp
drit	dirt

Middle English   The term describes a period in the development of the English language and the language within that period, c. 1100 to 1400.

REFERENCES: J. W. Clark, *Early English: A Study of Old and Middle English* (New York: Norton, 1957); A. MacLeish, *The Middle English Subject-Verb Cluster* ('s-Gravenhage: Mouton, 1969); S. Moore, *Historical Outlines of English Sounds and Inflections,* rev. by A. H. Marckwardt (Ann Arbor: Wahr, 1957); F. Mossé, *A Handbook of Middle English,* J. A. Walker, trans. (Baltimore: The Johns Hopkins Press, 1952); T. F. Mustanoja, *A Middle English Syntax, Part 1: Parts of Speech* (Helsinki: Société Néophilologique, 1960); J. Wright and E. M. Wright, *An Elementary Middle English Grammar* (London: Oxford University Press, 1932).

Midland dialect   A dialect of the English language during the Middle English period. Its boundary was the same as that of the Mercian dialect of Old English, roughly between the Thames River on the south and the Humber River on the north, and from the English Channel to

Adapted from Samuel Moore, *Historical Outlines of English Sounds and Inflections,* rev. by Albert H. Marckwardt (Ann Arbor: Wahr, 1960), p. 112.

Wales. It existed in two distinctly different parts, East and West Midland. Because it was the dialect of London, the East Midland Dialect
became the predominant dialect of England. It is the ancestor dialect
of American English.

In the study of American English dialects, scholars have delineated
the Midland area of America as one of three main dialect regions:

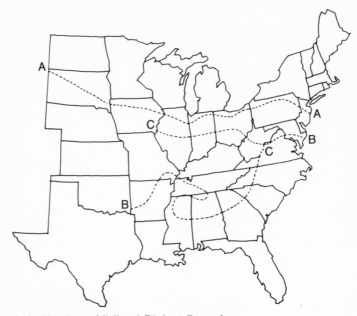

A-A: Northern-Midland Dialect Boundary
B-B: Midland-Southern Dialect Boundary
C-C: North Midland-South Midland Dialect Boundary

The dialect boundaries on this map are the result of work done on the
dialects of the Atlantic states by Hans Kurath and Raven I. McDavid,
Jr., on *The Linguistic Atlas of New England* edited by Hans Kurath,
on the Linguistic Atlas of the North-Central States under the direction
of Albert H. Marckwardt, on the Linguistic Atlas of the Upper Midwest under Harold B. Allen, and of work done on Southern dialects by
Gordon R. Wood.

REFERENCES: H. B. Allen, "The Primary Dialects of the Upper Midwest," in
H. B. Allen (ed.), *Readings in Applied English Linguistics,* rev. ed. (New York:
Appleton-Century-Crofts, 1964); S. Moore, S. B. Meech, and H. Whitehall,
Middle English Dialect Characteristics and Dialect Boundaries (Ann Arbor:
University of Michigan Press, 1935).

mid verb   *TG:* The mid verbs stand somewhere amidst transitive,
intransitive, and linking verbs and the verb *be.* They are a small class

of a dozen or so verbs like *cost, have, weigh, lack,* which exhibit the following characteristics:

(1) they must be followed by a noun phrase: *It costs a dollar.*
(2) they cannot be passive like transitive verbs: **A dollar was cost by it.*
(3) they cannot be modified by adverbs of number: **It cost a dollar slowly.*
(4) they differ from *be* and linking verbs in that the number of the noun-object is not controlled by the number of the subject: *He lacked shoes/a shoe.*
(5) they differ from transitive verbs in that they cannot be followed by an *of* construction:

Transitive verb: Joe's building *of the house* delighted her.
Mid verb: *Its costing *of a dollar* delighted her.

minimal pair   The term describes a pair of words that differ in only one phoneme: /pɪt/ : /bɪt/ ; /pæt/ : /pat/. (See PHONEME.)

modal auxiliary   There are ten modal auxiliaries:

can	could
may	might
shall	should
will	would
must	ought to

In sentences they precede verb stems and give them special shades of meaning such as futurity, possibility, volition, probability, permission, necessity, etc. Most frequently, they express a notion of futurity as well as nuances of meaning exclusive of time.

You *ought* to go.   *May* I help you?
You *must* run.   *Will* you come over?
Could I come over?   *Would* you come over?
Can you go away?   You *ought to* be careful.

(See AUXILIARY VERB.)

Modern English   The term describes the English language from c. 1500 to the present. Early Modern English, the language of Shakespeare, means English from c. 1500 to 1750. Late Modern English refers to English from c. 1750 to the present.

REFERENCES: For Early Modern English see: E. A. Abbott, *A Shakespearian Grammar* (London: Macmillan, 1888; New York; Dover, 1966); T. Pyles, *The Origins and Development of the English Language* (New York: Harcourt, Brace & World, 1964), Chs. 7, 8; M. Schlauch, *The English Language in Modern Times (Since 1400)* (Warsaw: Pánstwowe Wydawnictwo Naukowe, 1959); for Present-day English, see titles under MORPHOLOGY, SENTENCE PATTERN, STRUCTURAL GRAMMAR, SYNTAX, TRADITIONAL GRAMMAR, TRANS-FORMATIONAL GRAMMAR, VERB.

modification   The function performed by MODIFIERS, which describe or limit the word they are related to.

modifiers   Words of several classes (adjectives, adverbs, verbs, determiners, qualifiers) and word groups that function as these words. Modifiers limit and make more precise the meanings of HEADWORDS:

> *Adjective:* *blue* boat
> *Adverb:* walk *slowly*
> *Verb:* *burned* steak, *running* water
> *Determiner:* *these* men
> *Qualifier:* *very* good
> *Word Group:* kitten *in the basket*
> man *whom I saw*

monophthong   A phoneme produced as a single sound. Many vowels and consonants that have a single articulatory position are monophthongs. Compare with DIPHTHONG.

mood   (Sometimes *mode.*) The construction or function of the verb that indicates whether a writer or speaker regards his utterance as a statement (indicative mood), a question (interrogative mood), a command (imperative mood) or an expression of wish, doubt, or possibility (subjunctive mood).

morpheme   A word or part of a word that conveys grammatical or lexical meaning, that cannot be subdivided into smaller meaningful elements, and that occurs in various contexts with a relatively stable meaning. It is often defined as the minimum meaningful unit of language. The morphemes in *unmanly* are *un-*, *man,* and *-ly.* (See ALLOMORPH, BASE, BOUND MORPHEME, FREE MORPHEME, STEM.)

morphographemic   The term that describes spelling changes that result from a combination of written or printed allomorphs. For example, when *-est* is added to *holy,* the final *y* changes to *i,* resulting in the spelling *holiest;* when *-d* is added to *lay,* the root vowel *a* changes to *ai* and *y* disappears, resulting in the spelling *laid.* These are morphographemic changes. (See GRAPHEME, MORPHOPHONEMIC.)

morphological conditioning   This is largely the result of historical development. For example, the plural morpheme {-s₂} has the morphologically conditioned allomorphs /ɪn/ and /Ø/ which are in complementary distribution. The occurrence of these allomorphs is not determined by phonological environment, but rather by the history of the words with which they occur. /ɪn/ occurs today only on *oxen.* The *-en* plural comes from the Old English weak plural ending *-an.* /Ø/ allomorph marks the plural on animal words: *swine, sheep, deer, pike,* etc. *Swine,* for example, had only a plural in the genitive case in Old English *swyna.* With the leveling of inflections, this genitive plural disappeared and the word did not take on a nominative and accusative plural /s/ by analogy. (See COMPLEMENTARY DISTRIBUTION, PHONOLOGICAL CONDITIONING.)

morphology   That part of a language concerned with the structure and form of words, with the way in which their morphemes are arranged and related to each other. (See GRAMMAR, MORPHEME.)

REFERENCES: G. O. Curme, *Parts of Speech and Accidence* (Boston: Heath, 1935); H. Marchand, *The Categories and Types of Present-Day English Word-Formation* (Wiesbaden: Harrassowitz, 1960).

morphophonemic   A term that describes a change, or changes, in sound resulting from a combination of allomorphs. For example, when the *-an* of *woman* becomes the plural allomorph *-en, women,* the first vowel changes in pronunciation from /ʊ/ to /ɪ/; when the plural allomorph *-s* is added to *knife,* the consonant /f/ changes to /v/, resulting in the pronunciation /naivz/.

multiple-complex transformation   *TG:* The process in which, when two or more positions are open in a main-clause sentence, two or more insert sentences can be introduced into this main-clause sentence:

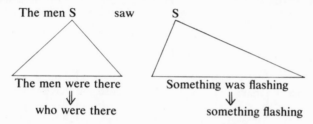

Readout: The men who were there saw something flashing.

(See RECURSIVE COMPLEX TRANSFORMATION.)

mutation   See UMLAUT.

N

nasal consonant   Nasal consonants are articulated like stops, but because the velum is open, the sound is emitted through the nasal cavity. The nasal consonants of English are /m/, the bilabial nasal, /ŋ/, the alveolar nasal, and /n/, the velar nasal. (See CONTINUANT.)

negative transformation   *TG:* A transformation by which a negative sentence is derived from a non-negative sentence by attaching the negative particle *not/n't* to an auxiliary verb. If the source sentence does not have an auxiliary verb (modal, *have*, or *be*), then the verb *do* is introduced to carry tense and the negative particle unless the main verb of the sentence is *be:*

John past see the car ⇒ *John past NEG see the car* ⇒ *John do past NEG see the car* ⇒ *John didn't see the car* (not **John sawn't the car*); but, also, *John present be a car* ⇒ *John present NEG be a car* ⇒ *John isn't a car.*

Any English sentence can be made negative by this simple transformation. The rule looks like this:

$$\text{NP} + \text{tense} + \left\{ \begin{array}{l} \text{Modal} \\ \text{have} \\ \text{be} \end{array} \right\} + \text{VP} \Rightarrow \text{NP} + \text{tense} + \left\{ \begin{array}{l} \text{Modal} \\ \text{have} \\ \text{be} \\ \text{do} \end{array} \right\} + \text{NEG} + \text{VP}$$

neutralization of vowels   Before the end of the Old English period, every unstressed *a, e, o,* and *u* tended to become a vowel, usually spelled *e* and pronounced as /ə/. Thus, all of these unstressed vowels were neutralized. Since the sixteenth century, all English unstressed vowels have been neutralized to either /ə/ or /ɨ/. (See GRADATION.)

node   *TG:* The nodes of a labeled-tree-diagram are the points from which branchings occur.

Nodes are said to "dominate" the construction branching from them; thus the S node dominates the NP node and the VP node, etc.

nominal   A noun, pronoun, adjective, adverb, verb participle, or a syntactic construction in a shared position usually filled by nouns. These shared positions are called *subject of the verb, object of the*

verb, object of the preposition, subjective complement, object comple-
ment, indirect object.

Noun:	John ran; saw *John;* of *water.*
Pronoun:	*He* is; likes *her,* of *it.*
Adjective:	*Red* is; likes *red;* of *red.*
Adverb:	*Steadily* is the best way to work.
Participles:	*Swimming* is fun; likes *swimming;* of *swimming.*
Construction:	*That he is here* is obvious. I see *that you are here.*

nominative case   A term from the grammar of classical languages
designating a word that is the subject of a verb. English has six distinctive pronoun forms that are used as subject: *I, he, she, we, they,* and
who. Since nouns have no distinctive forms to show that they are subjects of verbs, this function is indicated in English by word order. (See
CASE, EXPLETIVE, SUBJECT.)

nonce word   A word coined to suit a particular occasion, often by
different writers or speakers, but not generally accepted into the vocabulary. Nonce words are generally here today and gone tomorrow.
Many blends are nonce words. (See BLENDING.)

nonhuman nouns   *TG:* A subclass of animate nouns that generally
co-occur with the pronouns *that/which.*

dog *that* I saw
animal *which* I saw

(See LEXICAL PROPERTIES.)

nonrestrictive modifier   Nonrestrictive words, phrases, or clauses add
descriptive detail about a noun but do not limit or specify its meaning.
These modifiers are usually set off by commas and can be omitted from
the sentence without changing its basic meaning:

My father, *who was here yesterday,* is fine.
My father, *hale and hearty,* was here yesterday.

A modifier that follows a proper noun is considered to be nonrestrictive, since the name itself limits the person or place:

Bill, *who is standing in the corner,* is fine.
Jamestown, *my home town,* is a pretty place.

(See RESTRICTIVE MODIFIER.)

normative grammar   A prescriptive grammar based on the assumption
that there is a universal standard of correctness for all speech and
writing.

noun   *CG:* A noun names a person, place, idea, or thing. *Str.* and *TG:*
A form-class word that can be inflected for plural with *-s* (cat*s*) and for
the possessive with *-'s* (boy*'s*). It can be derived from other words by

suffixes such as *-ment* (agree*ment*), *-ity* (abil*ity*), *-ness* (friendli*ness*), and *-ism* (national*ism*.) Nouns exhibit number concord with finite verbs, with determiners, and with some noun modifiers: (*boy works, those men, woman driver/women drivers*). Nouns pattern after determiners (*the/ a man*), after single word modifiers (*tall tree*), before finite verbs in declarative sentences (*The old man lives*), after prepositions (*of water*), and sometimes before other nouns (*telephone operator, dog kennel*). (See LEXICAL PROPERTIES.)

noun adjunct A noun used in an adjectival position: *telephone* operator, *stone* wall. (See ADJECTIVAL.)

noun clause A dependent construction, with a subject and predicate, that functions as a noun. Many noun clauses are introduced by a relative connector like *that, which, who, what, why, when,* etc. Noun clauses without these relative words are *reduced noun clauses.*

Subject:	*That he succeeded* pleased him.
Object:	He knows *what he likes.*
Object of Preposition:	She's going to *where she came from.*
Appositive:	The idea *that he should study* is strange to him.
Reduced Clause:	I know the man *you saw yesterday.*

(See DEPENDENT CLAUSE, RELATIVE CLAUSE.)

noun complement position *TG:* The noun complement position is immediately after a main-clause noun. It may be filled only by an insert sentence having the same noun as the one to be complemented. The noun complement position is an optional one, that is, it does not have to be filled.

He saw the man S

The man stole the car ⇒ who stole the car

Readout: He saw the man who stole the car.

noun-headed construction *Str:* This denotes a construction in which a noun is the headword: my old *friend;* my old *friend* whom I saw yesterday. (See HEADWORD.)

noun of quantity A count noun of quantity names collections, measures, and parts of objects. These nouns occur before *of:*

Collections	Measures	Parts
a *crowd* of people	a *quart* of milk	a *piece* of cake
a *gang* of thieves	a *pound* of butter	a *slice* of pie
a *group* of boys	a *yard* of silk	a *cut* of meat

noun phrase   *CG:* A group of grammatically related words that has the syntactical function of a noun:

Subject: *The old man* walked home.
Object: I saw *the old man.*

TG: A construction in the phrase structure portion of transformational grammar. It consists of an optional determiner, a noun, and the singular or plural number of the noun. This is the rewrite rule for the noun phrase, abbreviated NP:

$$NP \rightarrow (D) + N + N°$$

An NP can be symbolized by a diagram:

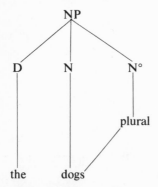

noun replacives   Possessive pronouns that can replace NOUN-HEADED constructions indicating possession. Noun replacives are *mine, your, his, hers, ours, theirs.*

This is my book ⟹ This is *mine.*
This is Jane's book ⟹ This is *hers.*

number   In English, the difference in word form that shows whether one or more than one person or thing is being referred to. Plural number is usually indicated by -*s:* tree*s,* river*s.* Singular number is indicated by lack of an ending: tree, river. (See PLURAL INFLECTION.)

O

object   A noun, noun phrase, or other nominal that can be replaced by a personal pronoun in the objective case. Objects follow verbs and prepositions.

Direct Object:	I hit *the man* ⟹ I hit *him.*
Indirect Object:	John gave *the boy* a penny ⟹ John gave *him* a penny.
Object of Preposition:	John gave it to *the boy* ⟹ John gave it to *him.*

(See ACCUSATIVE, CASE.)

objective case   See ACCUSATIVE.

object complement   The second of two nominals following a factitive, or object complement, verb. Object complements in American English can be nouns, adjectives, and infinitive phrases:

They elected John *president.*
They painted the house *white.*
They ordered John *to go.*

(See FACTITIVE VERB, OBJECT.)

obligatory transformation   *TG:* Only the affix transformation is obligatory. (See AFFIX TRANSFORMATION.)

oblique case   A case other than the nominative or vocative. In Classical languages the vocative case indicates the person who is addressed. (See CASE.)

obstruent   A consonant articulated by an obstruction to the flow of air. AFFRICATES, FRICATIVES, and STOPS are obstruents.

Old English   See ANGLO-SAXON.

open syllable   A syllable ending in a vowel sound. (See CLOSED SYLLABLE, SYLLABLE.)

open vowel   The same as a LOW VOWEL. (See LOW VOWEL, VOWEL.)

optative mood   The mood that expresses desire. (See SUBJUNCTIVE MOOD.)

optional element   *TG:* An optional element is enclosed within parentheses; it is an element that does not have to be chosen. For example, the rule

$$S \rightarrow NP + VP \ (Adv)$$

means "Sentence is rewritten as Noun Phrase + Verb Phrase + an optional adverb." This rule, then, accounts for either *He runs* or *He runs slowly.*

optional transformation   *TG:* All transformations except the affix transformation are optional; they are not necessary in generating a grammatical sentence.

oral sound   A sound in which the stream of air is directed into the mouth and which is resonated in the mouth. (See NASAL CONSONANT.)

orthography   The conventional representation of a spoken word in alphabetic writing.

P

palatal sound   Any kind of consonant articulated by placing the tongue front near or against the hard palate: /š ž č j y/ are palatals; /g k ŋ/ are palatalized velar sounds.

palatalization   The adaptation of the point of articulation of a consonant to the place of articulation of a front vowel near it. /k/ can be articulated at the velum when it is followed by a back vowel as in *cool*. It can be palatalized, articulated forward near the palate, when it is followed by a front vowel as in *keel*. Contrast velar /g/ in *goose* with palatal /g/ in *geese*. During the historical development of English, palatalization took place in the south of England more frequently than in the north. Thus, we still find unpalatalized northern forms contrasting with palatalized southern standard forms. Some examples follow.

Northern English	*Standard English*	*Palatalization*
kirk	church	/k/ → /č/
garth	yard	/g/ → /y/
scoot (U.S.)	shoot	/sk/ → /š/

paradigm   A set of related words having a common base and all the affixes that may be attached to it. Paradigms are of two kinds. The words in the paradigm may differ according to the derivational affixes that are attached. An example of this is a paradigm built on the Latin base *vide*: *pro + vide, pro + vis + ion, vis + ion, vis + ible, in + vis + ible, in + vis + ibil + ity, vis + abil + ity*, etc. The words in the second kind of paradigm may differ according to the inflectional affixes that are added. This kind of paradigm is usually associated with the "conjugation" of principal parts of regular and irregular verbs:

Infinitive	*3rd Sing. Present*	*Past Tense*	*Past Participle*	*Present Participle*
sing	sing*s*	s*a*ng	s*u*ng	sing*ing*
laugh	laugh*s*	laugh*ed*	laugh*ed*	laugh*ing*

A paradigm of nouns might look like this:

Singular	*Singular Possessive*	*Plural*	*Plural Possessive*
girl	girl*'s*	girl*s*	girls'
child	child*'s*	child*ren*	children*'s*

Quite obviously, pronouns, adjectives, and adverbs also exhibit both derivational and inflectional paradigms.

parole   An individual's use of language. This concept contrasts with LANGUE. (See IDIOLECT, PERFORMANCE.)

REFERENCE: F. Saussure, *A Course in General Linguistics,* Wade Baskin, trans. (New York: McGraw-Hill, 1966).

parsing   To parse a sentence is to divide it into its component parts, or constituents, and to describe the grammatical functions of and relationships among these parts. The process of parsing is illustrated graphically by diagrams. (See DIAGRAM.)

participle   The present participle ends in *-ing.* The past participle of "regular," or "weak," verbs ends in *-ed;* "irregular," or "strong," verbs make their past participle by changing the root vowel and sometimes by adding *-en: sang-sung; chose-chosen.* Participles may function as part of a verb phrase:

he is runn*ing*

as adjectives:

the runn*ing* boy

as adverbs:

rav*ing* mad

and as sentence modifiers:

Driv*ing* fast, he went over the hill.

In conventional grammar the term denotes *verb + ing* or *verb + ed* when they are used as adjectives: burn*ing* house/burn*ed* steak. (See GERUND, PRINCIPAL PARTS.)

participial phrase   A word group lacking a finite verb and introduced by a participle: He walked in, *reading a newspaper.*

part of speech   Grammatical functions in sentences are performed by certain classes of words. Generally, each function is performed by a distinctive part of speech. Parts of speech are nouns, verbs, adjectives, adverbs, pronouns, prepositions, conjunctions, determiners, qualifiers, expletives, etc. In *CG* a word's part of speech depends upon its use in the sentence; in *Str* a word's part of speech depends on its form and position.

particle   Uninflected parts of speech. In English they are prepositions, conjunctions, interjection words, and some adverbs like *no, not.*

passive transformation   The passive transformation switches the position of the subject and object noun phrases of a transitive verb, introduces the verb *be* as an auxiliary, changes the main verb to the past participle, and adds *by* optionally in the adverbial position.

The men repair the house ⟹   The house is repaired (by the men).

$$NP_1 + Aux + V_t + NP_2 \Rightarrow NP_2 + Aux + be + en + V_t + (by + NP_1)$$

(See PASSIVE VOICE.)

passive voice   *CG:* In the passive voice the subject is acted upon. *Str:* The passive voice verb phrase consists of some form of the verb *be* followed by the past-participle form of the verb:

> He *is elected.*
> The house *was repaired.*

(See ACTIVE VOICE, PASSIVE TRANSFORMATION.)

past participle   Past participles of verbs have several forms. The most frequent forms end in *-ed, -t, -d,* and *-en:* dream*ed,* caugh*t,* bi*d,* begu*n,* aris*en.* The past participle is used with *have, had, has,* and *having* to form verb phrases.

> *have* dream*ed*
> *had* bi*d*
> *has* caugh*t*
> *having* beg*un*

The past participle is also used as an adjective: burn*ed* steak, was burn*ed.* (See PARTICIPLE, PRINCIPAL PARTS.)

past perfect tense   The tense that indicates a time before the simple past. This tense is marked by *had* plus the past participle of the main verb:

> He *had* depart*ed*
> They *had been*
> He *had* been ask*ed*

(See PERFECT TENSE.)

past tense   These forms of verbs regularly end in *-ed:* pass*ed,* pleas*ed,* part*ed.* Their forms for irregular or strong verbs are many: *shrunk/ shrank, kept, led, began, rode, knew,* etc. The past tense occurs alone, not in combination with the forms of *have.* It *shrank.* He *kept* it, etc. (See PAST PARTICIPLE, PRINCIPAL PARTS.)

perfect tense   The three perfect tenses in English are made with a form of the verb *have* followed by the past participle of the main verb. (See PRESENT PERFECT, PAST PERFECT, FUTURE PERFECT.)

performance   A performance grammar, like structural grammar or the grammar of a foreign language in a textbook, describes what we actually produce at a given moment rather than our abstract ability to produce an infinite number of different sentences. (See COMPETENCE.)

periphrastic construction   A construction that accomplishes its purpose by means of a phrase using function words. (This function would otherwise be indicated by word order or inflections.)

Inflected Genitive:	The man's car.
Periphrastic Genitive:	The car *of* the man.
Word-Order Indirect Object:	He gave *the man the money.*
Periphrastic Indirect Object:	He gave the money *to* the man.

person   In English, the division of pronouns into three classes to indicate whether the subject is speaking (first person: *I* run), is spoken to (second person: *You* run), or is spoken of (third person: *he/she/it/ they* run(s)).

philology   The study of written and printed texts in order to interpret the linguistic data in them. The philologist re-creates the history of a language from its written documents. Among the most prominent philologists of the nineteenth century were F. Bopp (1791–1867), R. Rask (1787–1832), and J. Grimm (1785–1863). The latter two are often thought of as the founders of scientific historical linguistics. Rask wrote the first systematic grammar of Old Norse and Old English (1811, 1830), and Grimm's *Deutsche Grammatik* (*Germanic Grammar*) (1819–37) is called the start of Germanic linguistics. Bopp, in his *Comparative Grammar* (1833), discovered the principles of comparative grammar. Wilhelm von Humboldt (1767–1835), one of the profoundest thinkers on general linguistic matters, contributed to the theory of the typological development of language in his *Origin of Grammatical Forms and Their Influence on the Development of Thought* (1822). Probably the most influential mid-nineteenth-century figure in linguistics was A. Schleicher (1821–68) who postulated the *Stammbaumtheorie,* or geneological tree model of the relations between the parent language and the known Indo-European languages. (See FAMILY TREE THEORY, WAVE THEORY.)

REFERENCES: E. Mätzner, *An English Grammar,* C. J. Crece, trans. (London: J. Murray, 1880–85); H. Pedersen, *The Discovery of Language,* J. W. Spargo, trans. (Bloomington: Indiana University Press, 1962); R. Peters, *A Linguistic History of English* (Boston: Houghton Mifflin, 1968); T. Pyles, *The Origin and Development of the English Language* (New York: Harcourt, Brace & World, 1964); S. Robertson and F. G. Cassidy, *The Development of Modern English* (Englewood Cliffs: Prentice-Hall, 1954); R. Stevick, *English and Its History* (Boston: Allyn and Bacon, 1968); E. H. Sturtevant, *An Introduction to Linguistic Science* (New Haven: Yale University Press, 1947).

phone   Any speech sound considered as the result of the physical event of articulation without any thought given to how this sound fits into the sound structure of the language. (Contrast with PHONEME.)

phoneme   A speech sound that makes a difference in meaning. It is symbolized within slant lines: /p/. Thus, /p/ and /b/ are phonemes: *p*it : *b*it; they make a difference in meaning. A phoneme is a family of one or more sounds; allophones are varieties of a given phoneme. They are phonetically similar and in complementary distribution. Present-day English has a total of thirty-nine segmental phonemes: vowels, consonants, etc. The suprasegmental phonemes of English are varieties of stress, pitch, and pause. (See ALLOPHONE, MINIMAL PAIR, PHONEMIC TRANSCRIPTION, SEGMENTAL PHONEME, SUPRASEGMENTAL PHONEMES.)

REFERENCES: W. N. Francis, *The Structure of American English* (New York: Ronald Press, 1958); K. L. Pike, *Phonemics* (Ann Arbor: University of Michigan Press, 1947).

phonemic transcription   A graphic record of speech that uses one symbol for each phoneme. Phonemic transcription, then, recognizes only the meaning-changing sounds of a language: /fonimɪk trænskrɪpšən/. A system of transcription is necessary because there is not a 1:1 ratio between the sound system and the writing system of Modern English. For example, there are fourteen ways to spell the phoneme /i/, the vowel in *see*: ee, ie, ea, e, e-e, ei, ey, ay, eo, ae, oe, eau, i, and i-e. (See PHONEME, TRANSCRIPTION.)

phonetics   See ACOUSTIC PHONETICS, ARTICULATORY PHONETICS.

phonetic assimilation   See ASSIMILATION.

phonetic/phonemic transcription   See TRANSCRIPTION.

phonological conditioning   When the allomorphs of a phoneme are in complementary distribution and this distribution is determined by a phonological environment, these allomorphs are said to be phonologically conditioned. As an example, consider the allomorphs /-s~-ɨz~-z/ of the plural morpheme {-s₂}. /s/ is added to singular nouns ending with the phonemes /p t k θ f: *maps* /mæps/; *pets* /pɛts/; *kicks* /kɪks/; *moths* /mɔθs/; *muffs* /məfs/. /ɨz/ is added to singular nouns ending in /s z š ž č ǰ/: *kisses* /kɪsɨz/; *roses* /rozɨz/; *lashes* /læšɨz/; *garages* /gəražɨz/; *churches* /čərčɨz/; *judges* /ǰəǰɨz/. /z/ is added to singular nouns ending in any other phoneme: *pills* /pɪlz/; *sums* /səmz/; *pains* /penz/; *rugs* /rəgz/; *beds* /bɛdz/; *labs* /læbz/; *pies* /paiz/; *toes* /toz/. The phoneme with which a noun ends determines which of the three allomorphs is added to make that noun a plural. Thus we say that these allomorphs are phonologically conditioned; their selection is the result of phonological conditioning. (See ALLOMORPH, COMPLEMENTARY DISTRIBUTION, MORPHOLOGICAL CONDITIONING, PLURAL INFLECTION, SANDHI FORM.)

phonology   The sound system of a language or the study of this system. The sound system of a language consists of (1) the inventory of sounds—its phonetic system; (2) the distribution of these sounds—the rules of order—its phonotactic system; (3) the distribution of allophones of phonemes—its phonemic system; (4) the rules for altering the phonemic shape of morphemes in combination (knife-knives)—its morphophonemic system. *CG:* Phonology means "pronunciation" or "phonetics." *SG:* Phonology is the foundation of the grammatical system, the first "level" of the discovery procedure that leads to morphology and on to syntax. *TG:* Syntax is the foundation of the grammatical system, while phonology is one of several ways of representing the surface structure of a sentence.

phrase   *CG:* A word group without a subject-predicate sequence. *Str:* A syntactic construction that is not a structure of predication; it is not a clause or a "sentence pattern." *TG:* A basic sentence consists of two phrases, a noun phrase (NP) subject and a verb phrase (VP) predicate. (See CONSTRUCTION, NOUN-HEADED CONSTRUCTION, VERB-HEADED CONSTRUCTION, GENERATIVE GRAMMAR.)

phrase marker   *TG:* A labeled-tree diagram that represents the immediate constituent structure of a string. This phrase marker, or tree, has labeled nodes and labeled or unlabeled lines that tell us where parts of the string come from. (See TERMINAL STRING, TREE DIAGRAM.)

phrase structure grammar   Another name for GENERATIVE GRAMMAR.

phrase structure rules   See BASE RULES, RULE OF GRAMMAR.

pictogram   A complete or simplified picture representing an act or object—prehistoric cave paintings, for example.

pidgin language   A language characterized by a simplified grammar and vocabulary when compared with the language on which it is based. Further, a pidgin language has no native speakers. One of the major co-existent varieties of English in Hawaii offers an example of a pidgin language. People who speak the pidgin variety of English in Hawaii speak another language as their native tongue: Chinese, Ilicano, Korean, Japanese, Spanish. And this variety of English has a grammar somewhat more simplified than the grammar of Standard English: (1) There is no verb *be* in equational sentences ("This man sick" : "This man *is* sick"); (2) there is a lack of articles ("I want ball" : "I want *the/a* ball"); (3) there is no possessive inflection on nouns ("He see Tom brother" : "He sees Tom's brother"); (4) the simple morphological structure is further evidenced by lack of inflectional endings for plural and tense ("He like three beer" : "He like*s* three beer*s*"); (5) there is a reduction in the number and use of prepositions ("I go Tom house" : "I go *to* Tom'*s* house"). Viewed in another way, this pidgin variety can be identified with the English of immigrants whose native language is other than English. Adapted from a discussion in S. Tsuzaki, "Hawaiian English: Pidgin, Creole, or Dialect?", *Pacific Speech* (December, 1966), pp. 25–28. (See CREOLE LANGUAGE.)

REFERENCES: R. A. Hall, Jr., *Hands Off Pidgin English!* (New York: Albert Daub, 1956); _____, *Pidgin and Creole Languages* (Ithaca: Cornell University Press, 1966).

pitch levels   Pitch is the quality of speech sounds determined by frequency of vibration of sound waves reaching the ear. High and low pitch are relative, and linguists define four levels from high to low: 4 is extra-high; 3 is high; 2 is normal (most utterances move up or down in pitch from this level); 1 is low (the usual pitch at the end of a statement).

^{2}I ^{3}see the man^1

(See SUPRASEGMENTAL PHONEMES.)

pluperfect tense   The same as the PAST PERFECT TENSE.)

plural inflection   The plural form of most nouns is made by adding the written letter *s* to the singular form: *nouns + s = nouns*. Depending upon the sound that precedes *s*, this inflection can be pronounced in three ways: /z/: fan*s*; /ɨz/: dish*es*; /s/: rat*s*. Three nouns in English preserve very old plural forms in *-en* and *-ren*: ox*en*, child*ren*, breth*ren*. A few nouns make their plural by changing the vowel of the singular form: *goose/geese; man/men; tooth/teeth; mouse/mice,* etc. A small class of nouns naming animals has no plural inflection: *sheep, deer, bear, fowl;* etc. Some nouns from Latin, like *genus,* preserve their Latin plurals, *genera,* though most of these plurals are Anglicized by the general public: *stadium/stadiums.* One class of nouns in common use frequently preserves the gender distinction in both singular and plural: *alumnus/alumni* (masc.): *alumna/alumnae* (fem.). (See MORPHOLOGICAL CONDITIONING, PHONOLOGICAL CONDITIONING.)

portmanteau word   A result of BLENDING. (See also NONCE WORD.)

position   *Str:* The position of a word in a syntactic construction is the privilege of occurrence that this word has with respect to its environment. Positions are *shared* or *unshared.* A shared position may be one such as prenominal "the _____ house," This position can be shared by nouns (*stone*), adjectives (*gray*), verbs (*burning/burned*), and by inflected nouns (*man's*). An unshared position like "She spoke _____ quickly" can be filled only by qualifiers like *very, too, extremely.* The position is not shared by other word classes.

position class   *Str:* This describes the syntactic class of forms and word groups that occupy shared or unshared positions in sentences. Words and word-groups that fill a position most frequently occupied by nouns are called *nominals*. This position

The _____ is good

can be occupied by nouns (*man*), adjectives (*red*), an indefinite pronoun (*other*), a verb with *-ing* (*meeting*), and by a word group such as *fast runner*. Any word or word group filling the position in the test sentence is a nominal. Words and word groups filling

The _____ ladies are pretty

are *adjectivals*. *Verbals* fill the position

The boy has been _____ happily

Adverbials can fill many positions. One of them is

He reads books _____.

(See POSITION.)

REFERENCE: J. H. Sledd, *A Short Introduction to English Grammar* (Chicago: Scott Foresman, 1959).

positive degree   See COMPARISON.

possessive inflection   The possessive form of most nouns is made by adding the written *'s* for the singular and *s'* for the plural. Depending upon the sound that precedes *'s* or *s'*, they can be pronounced in three ways: /z/: *dog's/dogs'*; /ɪz/: *judge's/judges'*; /s/: *book's/books'*. There are no irregular formations as there are in the plural. The use of the apostrophe in this inflection came about in Shakespeare's time. A word like *boy's* was spelled *boys* or *boyes*. Some writers got the mistaken notion that *the boyes ball* was a contracted form of a construction common in the early seventeenth century, *the boy his ball*. Thus, they used an apostrophe to show that *hi-* had been left out.

postdeterminer   Postdeterminers follow determiners and precede adjectives. This class of words consists of ordinal numbers (the *second* large house), cardinal numbers (the *four* green boats), the possessive of common nouns (the *winter's* last snow) and the following: *every, few, less, little* (quantity), *many (a), more, most, other, same, several, single, such (a):*

his *every* last wish	those *same* old men
the *many* fine books	any *such* bad jokes
some *other* good guys	Joe's *few* old friends
much *more* coal smoke	the *little* chocolate cake remaining

Not all postdeterminers follow all determiners, but each one may follow at least one determiner. (See DETERMINER, PREDETERMINER.)

postnominal modification   This refers to structures of modification that follow nouns:

> structure of *modification*
> payment *larger than I thought*
> money *to burn*
> meat *cooking slowly*

(See NOUN-COMPLEMENT POSITION.)

predeterminer   A small group of modifiers that pattern before determiners. Predeterminers are words like

> *all* the young boys
> *both* the old men
> *half* the cake
> *double* the money

Phrases like *a few of, none of, one of, some of, pieces of, yards of,* etc., frequently predetermine noun phrases: *a few of those fish, none of the girls, one of the cars,* etc. The word *of* used in this position is called a predeterminer *of*; it is always the last word in a predeterminer. (See DETERMINER, POSTDETERMINER.)

predicate   A structure consisting of at least one or more finite verbs. Objects, complements, and modifiers of the verb are also part of the predicate: *run, run and swim; run and swim all day; gave John a ride in my car yesterday; is well today,* etc.

predicate noun   Also known as predicate nominative, this is a noun that appears after *be* and some linking verbs. This is called the predicate position: He is *president;* He remains *manager;* He seems a *friend.*

predicate adjective   A predicate adjective is an adjective that appears after *be* and many linking verbs: He is *sick;* It smells *sour;* It tastes *bad;* It sounds *good;* etc.

predicate objective   The same as OBJECT COMPLEMENT.

predication   The function of a full verb in a sentence or clause. One of the SYNTACTIC structures. (See PREDICATE.)

prefix   Prefixes are bound morphemes that are attached before bases. There are about seventy-five prefixes in English, and their meanings are frequently like those of prepositions and adverbs: *anti*climax, *co*-pilot, *contra*dict, *de*value, *in*secure, *un*wary, *sub*way, etc.

preposition   Prepositions are a class of function words in English. They are usually followed by a noun, personal pronoun, or a construction, all of which are called the object of the preposition. The most frequently used prepositions are *at, by, for, from, in, of, on, to,* and *with.* Of these, the most frequent are *of, in, to.* Two-syllable prepositions are words like *after, behind, except, inside, under,* etc. Compound, or phrasal, prepositions are constructions like *together with, out of, away from, because of, in spite of, by way of, in reference to, by means of,* etc.

preposition adverb   These are words conventionally classified as prepositions which can also function as adverbs of place: *in, on, out, up, down, over, under, inside, around.*

prepositional phrase   A construction consisting of the preposition and its object. Prepositional phrases can function as adverbials of motion:

ran *into the house*

as adverbs of manner:

ran *with his shoes off*

as adverbs of place:

stood *on the grass*

as noun modifiers:

girl *with a smile;* man *on the street;* bucket *of water*

as predicate nouns:

He was *of the same opinion.*

as noun-subjects:

Under the table was where we found Norman.

prescriptive grammar   The grammar found in many school grammar books. This grammar requires strict adherence to a set of rules that is supposed to be necessary for correctness. Many prescriptive grammars do not discriminate between grammar, in the narrower sense, and usage; thus they also contain prescriptive attitudes toward usage. (See NORMA- TIVE GRAMMAR.)

present participle   Present participles of verbs end in *-ing.* The present participle is used with *am, is, are, was, were, be, been* to form verb phrases: *were going, been walking,* etc. Present participles are also used as adjectives: *crying* baby, was *sleeping.* (See PRINCIPAL PARTS.)

present perfect tense   The tense that indicates a time before the present but after the simple past. This tense is marked by *has* or *have* plus the past participle of the main verb:

He *has* departed.
They *have* departed.
He *has* been asked.

(See PARTICIPLE, PERFECT TENSE.)

present tense   The present tense of the verb is indicated by the stem form *(depart)* for all persons except the third person singular, which is inflected with *s* (depart*s*). This *s* inflection has the same three phonologically conditioned allomorphs as the plural and possessive morphemes on nouns: /s/: *departs;* /z/: *burns;* /ɨz/: rush*es.*

prestige dialect   The dialect within a speech community which is considered to be "standard" and which is used by cultured speakers within that community. The evaluation "prestige" is cultural and social; it does not mean that one dialect is more systematic than any other. (See DIALECT, USAGE.)

preterit tense   The tense that indicates action in the past without any implication as to its duration. For example: We *swam* there last summer.

preterit-present verbs   These Germanic verbs are irregular. They are called preterit-present because the present tense of each was formerly a strong preterit that lost its preterit meaning and acquired a present meaning. To compensate for this loss of preterit meaning, the new present form acquired an accompanying new weak preterit and past-participle form. Preterit-present verbs retained in Modern American English are *can, shall, may, ought,* and *must.* The last two have no separate preterit form; the other three have *could, should* and *might* as preterit forms. (But see MODAL AUXILIARY.)

primary stress   See STRESS, SUPRASEGMENTAL PHONEMES.

principal parts   The principal parts of verbs can be illustrated in the verb paradigm. Verbs have three, four, or five forms for their principal parts. Verbs with four forms are most frequent.

Stem	Pres. 3rd Sing.	Pres. Ppl.	Past Tense	Past Ppl.
set	sets	setting	set	set
walk	walks	walking	walked	walked
see	sees	seeing	saw	seen

For the use of the principal parts see PRESENT TENSE, PRESENT PARTICIPLE, PAST TENSE, PAST PARTICIPLE.

pro-form   *TG:* In an early model of the grammar, a device used in complex transformations to indicate the place in a main-clause sentence that can be filled by a transformed insert sentence. PRO-forms thus suggest a relationship between a main-clause sentence and one or more insert sentences. They are fillers that indicate the general content of insert sentences when we lack the specific information that these insert sentences contain.

There are three kinds of PRO-forms: those that fill nominal positions, those that fill the noun-complement position, and those that fill adverbial positions. Nominal positions that can be filled by transformed insert sentences are subject, direct object, indirect object, subject complement, object complement, and object of the preposition. The PRO-forms that fill these positions are SOMETHING and SOMEONE.

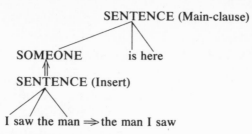

Readout: The man I saw is here.

The noun-complement position immediately follows the noun and permits modification of it. The PRO-form that indicates the possibility of noun phrase expansion is N-COMP.

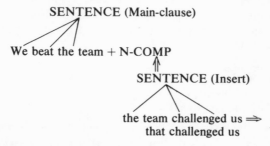

Readout: We beat the team that challenged us.

PRO-forms that indicate adverbial concepts are SOMEPLACE, SOMETIME, IN-SOME-MANNER, IN-SOME-DIRECTION, FOR-SOME-DISTANCE, FOR-SOME-DURATION, WITH-SOME-FREQUENCY, UNDER-SOME-CONDITIONS, etc.

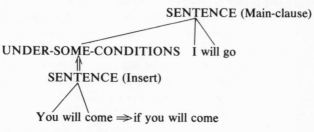

Readout: If you will come, I will go.

From another point of view a PRO-FORM is the pronoun which remains after the reduction of an identical element in an embedded sentence or in conjoined sentences. For example, when two identical noun phrases occur in the same sentence a Pronominalization reduces the second one to a pronoun, a PRO-FORM.

Tom saw the car and Joe drove the car ⟹ Tom saw the car and Joe drove *it*.

An embedded clause may be reduced to *this, that,* or *which.* Consider the sentence

Joe drove the car and that Joe drove the car displeased Tom.

The embedded clause *that Joe drove the car* is, except for *that,* identical to the first clause in the sentence. Because of this identity, the embedded clause can be reduced to a PRO-FORM *this:*

Joe drove the car and *this* displeased Tom.

(See NOUN-COMPLEMENT POSITION, COMPLEX TRANSFORMATION, INSERT SENTENCE, DEPENDENT CLAUSE, MULTIPLE-COMPLEX TRANSFORMATION.)

progressive tense   The tense that represents continuing action, in contrast with a habitual or completed action. The progressive tenses are signaled by some form of *be* and the present participle of the main verb:

I am going
She was going
We have been going
They will be going

Some linguists use the term *aspect* instead of *tense* in describing the progressive construction. From this point of view, the idea expressed is not so much one of the time of action as it is the notion that the action is incomplete (*durative aspect*) or completed (*punctual aspect*). (See ASPECT.)

pronoun   Some pronouns are used in place of nouns. Pronouns are of many subclasses: *personal pronouns* with their subject, object, and possessive forms (*I, me, my; we, us our,* etc.), *relative pronouns* (*that, which,* etc.), *noun-replacive* forms of personal pronouns (*mine, yours, theirs,* etc.), *interrogative pronouns* (*who, when,* etc.), *intensive* and *reflexive pronouns* (*myself, himself,* etc.), *demonstrative pronouns* (*this, those,* etc.), and *indefinite pronouns* (*someone, anyone,* etc.). For the most part, pronouns are a form class; that is, they are inflected. In sentences the subject and object personal pronoun forms and the noun-replacives function as nouns:

Tom saw John $\Rightarrow$ *He* saw *him.*
Joan is your girl $\Rightarrow$ *She* is *yours.*

The possessive forms of personal pronouns pattern like the noun determiners *the* and *a: my* book, *his* desk, *your* pen. *Who* is also a relative pronoun along with *what, that, which:*

Who he is I don't know.
man *who* is outside.

Intensives (He *himself* said so!) and reflexives (He hit *himself* with a hammer) refer to a noun or pronoun already mentioned at least once. (See LEXICAL PROPERTIES.)

proper noun   The name of a particular person, place, or thing: *Joe, Minneapolis, Mardi Gras*. Proper nouns cannot be preceded by either the definite or the indefinite article. (See COMMON NOUN.)

proto-   This word, used in combination, designates the earliest known form of a word of language or the artificially reconstructed original of a word of language. *[swepnos] is a reconstructed word in Proto-Indo-European. (See PROTO-INDO-EUROPEAN.)

Proto-Indo-European   A hypothetical, reconstructed language regarded as the common ancestor of all languages in the Indo-European family. It has been reconstructed from related languages that are apparently its ancestors. (See INDO-EUROPEAN.)

psycholinguistics   The examination of the relationship between the descriptive and the behavioral approaches to the study of language. Psycholinguistics attempts to relate the work of the descriptive linguist, who formulates the rules for generating sentences, with the work of the psychologist, who attempts to determine what factors cause a person to say something in a certain way at a certain time.

punctuation   A system of eleven marks that are written substitutes for the suprasegmental features of speech. (See GRAPHEME, SUPRASEGMENTAL PHONEME.)

Q

qualifier   Sometimes called *intensifiers,* these are words that pattern like *very*. They modify adjectives: *very* good, *too* happy, *pretty* bad. Adverbs are frequently modified by qualifiers: *rather* quickly, *very* slowly. In conventional grammar these words are called adverbs, though they clearly do not pattern as adverbs in position after the verb: "He ran *quickly*" but not "He ran *very*."

question   An interrogative sentence that can be answered either by *yes* or *no* or by furnishing information relating to *What? Why? When? Where? Who? How?* etc. Yes/No questions can occur grammatically in statement form with a rising intonation: ²You're going³ hóme³↑ or they can occur with subject and verb inverted, usually with rising intonation: ²Are you going³ hóme³↑. If the verb is not a modal auxiliary, *have* or *be,* then *do* asks the question: ²Did he go³ hóme³↑. Information questions are signaled by any one of the "*Wh*-words" listed above: ²Who is³ going¹↓ ; ²Where³ are you¹↓ . *TG:* Both the Yes/No question and the *WH*-question derive from basic sentences by way of a simple transformation: You're going home ⇒ Are you going home?; John is going ⇒ Who is going?; You are there ⇒ Are you there? ⇒ Where are you? (See QUESTION TRANSFORMATION, YES/NO QUESTION, WH-QUESTION.)

question transformation   *TG:* For Yes/No Questions the transformational rule is as follows:

The information question takes many forms since we can question the subject, the object, or other predicate elements. The easiest way to describe this question transformation is to say that it has two parts.

(1) The basic sentence is transformed into a Yes/No Question.
(2) The appropriate *Wh*-word is substituted for the item to be questioned and then put into the initial position in the sentence.

Here are some examples:

(1) Questioning the Subject:
    Basic Sentence: *John* will go.
       Yes/No Q: Will *John* go?
    Wh-word Q: *Who* will go?
(2) Questioning the Object:
    Basic Sentence: John reads *the book.*
       Yes/No Q: Does John read *the book?*
    Wh-word Q: *What* does John read?

(See MODAL AUXILIARY, QUESTION, WH-QUESTION.)

R

received standard pronunciation   The pronunciation of English that is "accepted" among educated people in Britain.

reconstruction   In linguistics the process of determining the original, unwritten form or state of a parent language by comparing written and spoken forms or languages descended from the original. PROTO-INDO-EUROPEAN is a reconstructed language. (See RESIDUE FORMS.)

REFERENCE: H. Hoenigswald, *Language Change and Linguistic Reconstruction* (Chicago: University of Chicago Press, 1960).

recursiveness   A basic quality of the system of any language; it enables the grammar of a language to produce an infinite number of sentences. A language is made up of a relatively small number of basic sentence types that are used recursively, over and over again, to produce complex sentences. A recursive rule, then, is one that enables us to trace our way through a grammar an infinite number of times. In the next definition there is an example of recursiveness. Note that the term *sentence* is itself recursive and that all the rules below the level of *sentence* recur. (See RECURSIVE COMPLEX TRANSFORMATION.)

recursive-complex transformation   The quality of recursiveness, discussed in the definition above, can be illustrated by showing how a complex sentence is formed. Consider this sentence:

John cleaned the shop after he was done so that he could start another job.

It is made up of three simple, basic sentences:

(1) John cleaned the shop SOMETIME FOR-SOME-PURPOSE.
(2) He was done.
(3) He could start another job.

Sentences (2) and (3) are transformed so that they can become sub-sentences, parts, of sentence (1). We can diagram the recursive complex sentence like this (notice, first, that the term SENTENCE is recursive; it is used, it recurs, three times):

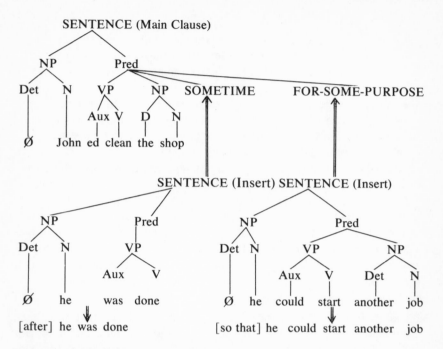

Readout: John cleaned the shop after he was done so that he could start another job.

Notice also the recursiveness in the rules by which the constituents of the three sentences are constructed. The rule NP → D + N recurs four times. The rule VP → Aux + V recurs three times. At an even lower level of construction the rewrite rule for determiner occurs five times:

$$D \rightarrow \begin{Bmatrix} \varnothing \\ \text{the} \\ \text{another} \end{Bmatrix}$$

And so on. (See RECURSIVENESS, REWRITE RULES.)

redundancy   This term means "something that is said more than once." Languages have redundancy in their grammars and between their grammars and intonation contours. An example of grammatical redundancy can be seen in the sentence *The dog barked at the top of his voice.* The verb *barked* is redundant because its meaning—"make a vocal noise like a dog"—includes the meanings given in the sentence by *dog* and *voice.* A more obvious example can be seen in the duplication of plural signals in the expression *those dogs.* This phrase is marked twice as plural—by the plural pronoun *those* and by the noun-plural ending *-s* on *dog.* Intonation contours and grammar can also be redundant. For example, the intonation features and word order of one type of Yes/No question are redundant—we can predict the intonation contour by knowing the word order. Both intonation and word order perform the function of asking a Yes/No question: ²Are you³ going³↑. Thus, linguistic redundancy is the excess of linguistic signals above the minimum necessary to convey meaning. When redundancy is present, we can often predict one meaning signal by the presence of another. The built-in redundancies of language are to be distinguished from more controllable redundancies in rhetoric.

reduplication   The process by which languages construct a derivative form or an inflected form by doubling a specified syllable. Illustrations may be found in Tagalog: [ta: wa], "a laugh," reduplicated [ta: ta: wa], "one who will laugh"; Thai reduplicated *dang-dang,* "red, reddish"; Latin *cado,* "I fall," reduplicated *cecidi,* "I fell." Sometimes reduplication is merely euphonic; it has no meaning. For example, in Swedish the usual rejoinder to [tăk], "thanks," is the reduplicated [tăk:tăk], which serves as a euphonious substitute for "You're welcome."

reference of pronouns   See ANTECEDENT.

regional dialect   The major regional dialect boundaries that have been established to date in the United States indicate nine major dialect areas: *Eastern New England* (eastern Massachusetts, eastern Connecticut, Rhode Island, Vermont, Maine); *New York City; Eastern Virginia; Eastern Southern* (eastern North and South Carolina, southern Georgia, southeast Alabama, Florida); *Central Southern* (southeastern Alabama, Mississippi, southern Arkansas, Louisiana, East Texas, southern Oklahoma); *Western Southern* (West Texas); *South Midland; North Midland; Northern.* (See DIALECT, MIDLAND DIALECT.)

relative adverb   These are words like *as, after, before, when, where.* They occur after nouns, introducing a relative clause that functions as an adjective:

the place *where* I saw him
the time *when* he won the game
the house *after* the one you live in

(See RELATIVE CLAUSE.)

relative clause   A clause subordinate to the main clause with which it occurs and to which it is connected by a relative word such as *that, which, what, who, whom.* Relative clauses function as adjectives:

man *whom I saw*

as nouns:

What you don't know won't hurt you.

or as adverbs:

He went *when the sun set.*

(See RELATIVE ADVERB, RESTRICTIVE MODIFIER, NONRESTRICTIVE MODIFIER.)

relative pronouns   These are used to relate and connect relative clauses to one another and to main clauses. They are words like *who, which, that, whom, what,* etc. (See RELATIVE CLAUSE.)

relic area   The area in which geographical or cultural isolation and relative lack of prestige have caused retention of older dialect forms or have prevented the spread of dialect forms characteristic of the area. Relic areas in the United States are northeastern New England, the eastern shore of Chesapeake Bay, and eastern North Carolina. Dialect forms in these areas lack prestige, especially when they are used by older or less sophisticated speakers. (See DIALECT, FOCAL AREA.)

replacive allomorph   Replacive allomorphs contrast with additive allomorphs. Consider the allomorphs of the past-tense morpheme $\{-d_1\}$ which replace the vowels in /sɪŋ tɛr bait gro spik tek/ to produce the past tense forms /sæŋ tɔr bɪt gru spok tʊk/. Thus, we can consider / æ ɔ ɪ u o ʊ/ as some of the replacive allomorphs of $\{-d_1\}$. (See ADDITIVE ALLOMORPH.)

residue forms   These occur during historical reconstruction. After laws of phonetic correspondence among several languages have been postulated, there will remain word forms whose existence cannot be accounted for by these laws. These word forms, then, are residues from the application of the laws of phonetic correspondence. These residual forms that do not fit into recognizable types of phonetic correspondence may be accounted for by the fact that while they may be descendants of a common ancestral form, they may be deviant because we have not correctly determined the phonetic correlation. An instance of this was the supposed deviancy between Sanskrit [bo:dha:mi] and English *bid* before the discovery of GRASSMAN'S LAW concerning the disappearance of aspiration in the first of two successive aspirated stops. Or residue forms may not be descendants of a common ancestral form at all. In this case the resemblance between the residue and a group of apparently related languages may be due to accident: Latin *dies* and English *day* do not represent an etymology that falls within any known set of correlations; nor do Malay [*mata*], "eye" and Greek [*máti*]. Resemblance may be due to borrowing of cultural or technical words in general distribution. English-Finnish *abstract-abstraktinen, architect-arkkitehti* exhibit a relationship which is only apparent; there is no kinship between Finno-Ugrian and Indo-European. Sometimes apparent correlations may be due to partial morphological resemblances of word forms in the parent language; Latin *habēre* and English *have* may be descendants of two stems which were morphologically similar in Indo-European. Finally, residue forms may appear resemblant for reasons other than descent from a common prototype. Latin *dentālis* and English *dental,* while they look alike, do not exhibit the Latin *d:* English *t* correspondence indicated of common Indo-European prototypes by the FIRST CONSONANT SHIFT. The reason for the resemblance is that *dental* is an English speaker's pronunciation of the Latin word; there is no prototypical relationship. (See GRASSMAN'S LAW, FIRST CONSONANT SHIFT.)

restrictive modifier   Restrictive words, phrases, or clauses limit or specify the meaning of the nouns they modify, providing information that is essential to the meaning of the sentence. Restrictive modifiers are not set off by commas from the rest of the sentence:

> The man *over here* is the one.
> The car *that I bought yesterday* is newer than my other one.

(See NONRESTRICTIVE MODIFIER.)

retroflex *r*   Speakers of American English pronounce the retroflex r before stressed vowels (*ród, erúpt*), and initially before unstressed vowels (*rèfér, rèmínd*). The tip of the tongue is turned upward toward the hard palate so that it points to, but does not touch, the palatal area immediately behind the alveolar ridge.

rewrite rule   *TG:* The means of representing expansion and/or change. An arrow is used to indicate the operation of rewriting; it is an instruction that the symbol or string of symbols to the left of the arrow is to be rewritten as the string to the right. Thus, the arrow also suggests a relationship between the string on the left and the string on the right. In the phrase structure rules a single-shafted arrow shows the relation "is rewritten as" or "is expanded into." For example, the arrow in the rule $NP \rightarrow D + N$ indicates that a noun phrase (NP) is rewritten as, or is, a Determiner (D) and a Noun (N). Thus, rewrite rules can expand linguistic units. In the transformational portion of the grammar the double-shafted arrow indicates the relationship "is changed into," "is derived from." For example, the rule $X + X \Rightarrow Y + X$ indicates that $X + Y$ is changed into $Y + X$, that the relationship between $X + Y$ and $Y + X$ is that $Y + X$ is "derived from" $X + Y$. The passive transformation is an example of a rewrite rule in the transformational grammar:

$$NP_1 + V_t + NP_2 \Rightarrow NP_2 + BE + ed + V_t + (by + NP_1)$$

(See RULE OF GRAMMAR.)

rhotacism   See VERNER'S LAW.

root   See BASE.

rounded vowels   Rounded vowels, like the ones in *boot* and *put,* are produced with a rounding of the lips. In most standard American English dialects the back vowels are round and the front and central vowels are unround. (See VOWEL.)

rule of grammar   Different grammars demand different notions as to what a rule of grammar is. Generally speaking, we can make the following broad distinctions. *CG:* The rule is deductive and prescriptive in its formulation. That is, the rule prescribes linguistic conduct on the basis that there is, somewhere, a standard of correct usage in speech and writing that all levels and varieties of English should adhere to. "Avoid the split infinitive" is an example of this kind of rule. To really write well, one should avoid this construction. Another kind of prescriptive, deductive rule is based on the logical fallacy that the laws of language reflect the logic of the universe outside language. "Never use two negatives, because they make a positive" is an example of this kind of rule. But one can never be sure that he is not using the double negative. A third kind of prescriptive rule is based on rhetoric, not usage or logic: "Avoid the passive voice." Another prescriptive rule is the groundless, sheerly negative prescription "Never end the sentence with a preposition." Sir Winston Churchill once remarked that this was the kind of pedantic interference up with which he would not put. Some rules of this grammar are syllogistic in nature: "Every*one* should put on *his* coat." *Str:* The rules of structural grammar are largely inductive and descriptive. That is, the rule objectively describes a linguistic phenomenon on the basis of wide observation, but it does not attempt to prescribe the "correctness" of a particular usage. Structural rules describe the forms of words and the patterns in which they occur in sentences. An example of a rule describing the forms of words is the following: "English nouns are characterized by what is called the possessive form: *man's, teacher's, Tom's.*" An example of a "pattern" rule is the following: "Some characteristic noun positions are 'The _____ is ugly,' 'I saw their _____,' 'a glass of _____.' Any word occurring in these positions is a nominal." *TG:* The rewrite rules of transformational grammar are deductive in their application; that is, the rules must apply every time the prescribed syntactic conditions occur and the rules must be applied in a fixed sequence. There are two kinds, phrase structure rules and transformation rules. The phrase structure rules expand elements in the phrase structure grammar. They are of the type exemplified by $NP \rightarrow D + N$, which states that a noun phrase is composed of a determiner and a noun. Rules of transformation are of the type exemplified by $X + Y \Rightarrow Y + X$, which states that $X + Y$ is changed to $Y + X$, that the relationship between $X + Y$ and $Y + X$ is that $Y + X$ is derived from $X + Y$. These two types of rules are the syntactic rules of transformational grammar. Their purpose is to describe and account for all and only the grammatical sentences of a language. The rules of conventional and structural grammar parse sentences *after* they have been produced; thus these rules can analyze only a few of the sentences of a language. (See REWRITE RULE.)

runic writing   Runes are characters of the alphabet used by Germanic peoples from approximately the third century A.D. The earliest remaining writings of Old English are written in the runic alphabet. The Old English characters *thorn* (þ) and *wynn* (ƿ) are runic.

S

sandhi form   The modification of the sound of a morpheme, of a word, or of an affix. These modifications are conditioned by the phonological context in which the morpheme is uttered. Sandhi variants can be illustrated by the pronunciations of *the* as /ðə/ in *the boy* and as /ði/ in *the old man;* by the pronunciations of plural *s* as /s/ in *cats,* as /z/ in *dogs,* and as /ɨz/ in *dishes;* by the pronunciations of *not* as /nt/ in *can't* and as /nat/ in *cannot.* (See PHONOLOGICAL CONDITIONING.)

satem languages   These constitute one of the divisions of the Indo-European family of languages. The satem group is composed of the Indo-Iranian, Armenian, Balto-Slavic, and Albanian languages. In these languages the consonant /s/ — as in Avestan *s*atem, Lithuanian *š*im̃tas, and Old Slavic *s*ŭto, all meaning "hundred" — represents a palatalization of the /k/ found in the centum languages: Latin *c*entum, "hundred." (See CENTUM LANGUAGES, PALATALIZATION.)

school grammar   The name given to the prescriptive statements found in most school grammar books. (See PRESCRIPTIVE GRAMMAR.)

schwa   The name of a mid-central unstressed vowel. In phonetic transcription it is symbolized by /ə/. Schwa is probably the most frequently occurring vowel in American English. It can be heard in words such as *o*ccur, ang*e*l, *a*side.

segmental phoneme   Segmental phonemes are segments of sound, the phonemes arranged in sequence in an utterance, the vowels and consonants. They are contrasted in linguistic description with SUPRA-SEGMENTAL PHONEMES.

semantics   In one of its meanings, a branch of linguistics. The term refers to a theory, study, or system of meanings underlying a word, phrase, sentence, or language. These linguistic meanings of the term are different from its meaning in the term GENERAL SEMANTICS. See *TG* definition under DICTIONARY, LEXICAL PROPERTIES.

sememe   The semantic meaning of a morpheme. (See MORPHEME.)

semivowel   Semivowels are articulated in consonantal positions in the mouth. They are in the same syllable with a full vowel, which is the nucleus of the syllable. Their duration is brief; they consist of a rapid movement of the articulators from a characteristic initial position to the position of the vowel that follows. Or the movement is the reverse, from the position of the preceding vowel to a characteristic final position. Semivowels are sometimes called GLIDES. /w/ is the voiced and voiceless labiovelar semivowel. It is formed by raising the tongue back toward the velum and then moving it rapidly to the position for the next vowel. The degree of lip-rounding depends upon the following vowel. /r/ is the voiced and voiceless apico-alveolar retroflex semi-vowel. The American /r/ is formed in various ways in different dialects. (See RETROFLEX *r*.) /y/ is the voiced fronto-palatal semivowel. It is formed by bringing the tongue front close to the palate where it joins the alveolar ridge, with the tongue tip pointing toward the upper teeth or resting against the lower front teeth. The tongue is then moved rapidly down into the position of the following vowel.

sentence   A sequence of words forming a unit. Actually, there is no simple, clear statement that takes into account the various points of view as to just what a sentence is. More specifically, a sentence is a structure of predication consisting of a noun-phrase subject and a verb-phrase predicate. This structure of predication makes sense to a native speaker and is not contained within another sentence. *CG, Str:* In conventional and structural grammars sentences are classified as simple (consisting of one structure of predication), compound (consisting of two or more coordinate structures of predication), complex (consisting of one independent structure of predication and one or more dependent structures of predication), or compound-complex (two or more coordinate independent structures of predication and at least one dependent structure of predication). Further, structural grammar describes a sentence as a verbal sequence that ends with either a falling terminal juncture, He went home↓ (statement), or a rising terminal juncture, He went home↑ (question). A written sentence is, conventionally, an acceptable structure of predication that begins with a capital letter and ends with a period, exclamation mark, or question mark, and is bounded by space. *TG:* In transformational grammar a sentence (S) is rewritten as a noun-phrase plus a verb-phrase: $S \rightarrow NP + VP$. A sentence generated by rules in the phrase structure grammar is a simple, active, indicative, affirmative sentence. It is called a basic sentence. All other sentences are derived from basic sentences by simple and complex transformations.

sentence pattern   A basic sentence type is composed of elements in a left-to-right sequence. *Str:* Structural grammar considers a number of sentence patterns based upon the number and kind of elements following the verb and, in part, upon the kind of verb. Six structural sentence patterns may be summarized as follows:

N ↔ V:	Dogs bark.
N ↔ LV Adj:	Elephants seem large.
N ↔ V N:	Monkeys eat bananas.
N ↔ LV N:	Horses are animals.
N ↔ V N N:	John gave Bill a bicycle.
N ↔ OV N N:	John called Bill a fool.

In these patterns, LV is a linking verb, and OV is an object complement verb. An object complement verb is one that makes the two words after it name the same thing. *TG:* Basic sentence patterns in transformational grammar are differentiated by the nature of the verb in the pattern. These are four basic patterns defined in this way:

NP + be + Pred   + (Adv):   Bill is happy (today).
NP + V_i + O   + (Adv):   Bill sleeps (soundly).
NP + V_t + NP   + (Adv):   Bill ate steak (yesterday).
NP + V_c + Comp + (Adv):   Bill seemed sick (last night).

Sentence patterns in *TG* are further determined by the kinds of transformations (changes) these basic sentences can undergo. For example, only the pattern with V_t, the transitive verb, can be changed into a passive sentence. On the basis of subclassifying these four types of verbs and then seeing the kinds of transformations they can undergo, we would probably get ten or twelve basic sentence types. In the representation above, V_i is an intransitive verb, V_t is a transitive verb, and V_c stands for all linking verbs except *be*, which is in the first pattern. The parentheses around (Adv) mean that an adverbial element is optional.

REFERENCES: Paul Roberts, *Patterns of English* (New York: Harcourt, Brace & World, 1956); _____, *English Sentences* (New York: Harcourt, Brace & World, 1962).

sibilant   A fricative consonant. In the production of fricatives, the tongue comes into contact with the hard palate. Sibilants are /s/ (*s*ee), /z/ (*z*est), /š/ (*sh*ip), /ž/ (rou*ge*), /č/ (*ch*ur*ch*),   ǰ/ (*j*oke).

simple sentence   A simple sentence has one subject-predicate combination that is an independent clause: *Lions roar.* (See COMPOUND SENTENCE, COMPLEX SENTENCE, COMPOUND-COMPLEX SENTENCE.)

simple transformation   A simple transformation operates on one basic sentence or on a terminal string of morphemes, as contrasted with a complex transformation, which operates on two or more basic sentences. All simple transformations are optional except the affix transformations. Some other simple transformations are *passive* (He saw the game ⟹ The game was seen by him), *negative* (He saw the game ⟹ He didn't see the game), *Yes/No Question* (*He is nice* ⟹ Is he nice?), *Wh-Question* (He is here ⟹ Where is he?), *There-Expletive* (The boy is here ⟹ There is a boy here), *Imperative* (You will close the door ⟹ Close the door!). (See AFFIX TRANSFORMATION, NEGATIVE TRANSFORMATION, PASSIVE TRANSFORMATION, THERE-EXPLETIVE TRANSFORMATION, QUESTION TRANSFORMATION.)

singular form   The form that denotes "one." Among nouns that form plurals, the singular form is the one without the plural ending.

slang   Slang is composed of a large body of words and expressions which are intelligible to and frequently used by a large portion of the speakers of a language, though it is not accepted as formal usage. Slang is derived mostly from cant, jargon, and argot words, and its use suggests that both speaker and listener enjoy a kind of mutual understanding. (See ARGOT, CANT, JARGON.)

REFERENCE: H. Wentworth and S. B. Flexner (eds.), *Dictionary of American Slang* (New York: Crowell, 1960).

social dialect   A cultural or technical variant of the language of a speech community. A cultural variant can be exemplified by contrasting the speech of educated speakers with the speech of uneducated speakers. A technical variant can be exemplified by contrasting the technical speech of space scientists, engineers, etc., with the speech of the layman. Social dialects differ from one another in their vocabulary, pronunciation, and grammar. Each speaker of a language probably commands more than one social dialect. (See DIALECT.)

REFERENCES: E. Evertts (ed.), *Dimensions of Dialect* (Champaign: NCTE, 1967); J. L. Fischer, "Social Influences on the Choice of a Linguistic Variant," in H. B. Allen (ed.), *Readings in Applied English Linguistics* (New York: Appleton-Century-Crofts, 1964); W. Labov, "Stages in the Acquisition of Standard English," in R. W. Shuy (ed.), *Social Dialects and Language Learning* (Champaign: NCTE, 1964); _____, *The Study of Nonstandard English* (Champaign: NCTE, 1970); R. I. McDavid, Jr., "American Social Dialects," *College English* 26 (1965):10–16; _____, "Some Social Differences in Pronunciation," in Allen (ed.), *op. cit.;* _____ and Virginia G. McDavid, "The Relationship of the Speech of American Negroes to the Speech of Whites," *American Speech,* 26 (1951):3–17; L. A. Pederson, "Social Dialects and the Disadvantaged," in *Language Programs for the Disadvantaged* (Champaign: NCTE, 1965); W. A. Stewart, *Non-standard Speech and the Teaching of English* (Washington: Center for Applied Linguistics, 1964); _____, "Non-standard Speech Patterns," *Baltimore Bulletin of Education,* 43 (1966–67):2–4, 52–65.

sound change   The term, an historical concept, describes changes in a speech sound or phoneme which are brought about because of characteristics of the sound itself or by influence of nearby sounds. (See ABLAUT, FIRST CONSONANT SHIFT, UMLAUT, VERNER'S LAW.)

source sentence   See CONSTITUENT SENTENCE, INSERT SENTENCE.

spelling pronunciation   An attempt to make pronunciation conform closely to spelling. But spelling is not an infallible guide to pronunciation because of the many irregularities of English orthography. Consider, for example, words like *come/home; move/shove; friend/fiend/ sieve.* Spelling pronunciations frequently came about in the course of the historical development of a word. For example, *alter, fault, vault,* and *Walter* had the thirteenth- and fourteenth-century Middle English spellings *auter, faut(e), vaute,* and *Wat(te).* Thus, they were like the "l-less" Old French words from which they derive. The *l* came into these words through the influence of Latin spelling. They became *vault* in the fifteenth century, and *alter, fault,* and *Walter* in the sixteenth century. In the seventeenth century these words were pronounced irregularly with and without /l/ on the analogy with the varied pronunciations of native words like *malt* and *salt.* Thus, a spelling pronunciation was established, and the pronunciations with /l/ became regular by the eighteenth century.

REFERENCES: J. S. Kenyon, "Spelling Pronunciation," in *American Pronunciation,* 10th ed. (Ann Arbor: Wahr, 1950); A. MacLeish, "Do You Pronounce It As It's Spelled?" in N. C. Stageberg and W. Anderson, *Introductory Readings on Language,* rev. ed. (New York: Holt, Rinehart & Winston, 1970).

spirant   See FRICATIVE.

split infinitive   A grammatical construction in which an adverb occurs between *to* and the verb: *to quietly go, to easily see.* (See RULE OF GRAMMAR.)

Standard English   A term applied to an item of usage or a dialect of English that is acceptable to educated, cultivated speakers of the language. Standard English is the English used to carry on the daily business of the nation.

stem   A linguistic form to which an inflectional suffix can be attached: run/run*s;* beautify/beautif*ied;* aggreeableness/agreeablenesse*s.*

stop   A consonant sound formed by a stoppage and, in many instances, a release of breath. The voiceless stops are /p t kʔ/. The voiced stops are /b d g/. /p/ and /b/ are bilabial stops; they are formed by the lower lip meeting the upper one and stopping the breath. The vocal cords vibrate when /b/ is sounded, thus it is a voiced bilabial stop; /p/ is a voiceless bilabial stop. When /p/ and /b/ occur at the beginning and middle of words, as in *pin, bin, spin, number,* the lips open and release the breath, though with much less force with /b/ than with /p/. When /p/ and /b/ occur at the end of words, as in *stop* and *tub,* the lips stay closed and the breath is unreleased. /t/ and /d/ are alveolar stops. They are formed by the tongue tip coming into contact with the alveolar ridge (the ridge just behind the upper gums) and stopping the breath. The vocal cords vibrate when /d/ is sounded, thus it is a voiced alveolar stop. /t/ is a voiceless alveolar stop. When /t/ and /d/ occur at the beginning and middle of words, as in *top, dog, stop, ladder,* the lips open and release the breath, though with much less force with /d/ than with /t/. When /d/ and /t/ occur at the end of words, as in *sad* and *hot,* the lips stay closed and the breath is unreleased. /k/ and /g/ are velar stops. They are formed by raising the tongue back against the velum, thus stopping the breath. The vocal cords vibrate when /g/ is sounded, thus it is a voiced velar stop. /k/ is a voiceless velar stop. When /k/ and /g/ occur at the beginning and middle of words, as in *kin, go, skin, stagger,* the lips open and release the breath, though with much less force with /g/ than with /k/. When /g/ and /k/ occur at the end of words, as in *beg* and *lick,* the lips stay closed and the breath is unreleased. /ʔ/ is a glottal stop. It is made when the vocal cords, located in the glottis, are pressed shut so that no air can get through. This sound is heard as the first sound in words beginning with a stressed vowel: *apple, only, each,* etc. It is the first sound we hear in each word in the phrase "oh, oh."

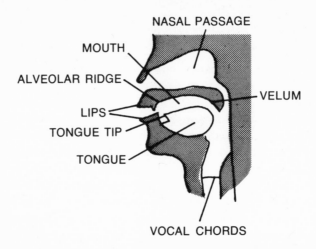

stress   The relative loudness with which speech sounds are uttered. There are four stress phonemes, or relative degrees of loudness: primary ◌́, secondary ◌̂, tertiary ◌̀, and weak ◌̆. Three degrees of stress can occur on one word: *désĭgnàte.* Primary and secondary stress are illustrated in the modifier + noun combinations *hôt hoúse, blâck bírd. dârk roóm.*

string   See TERMINAL STRING.

strong verb   See IRREGULAR VERB.

structural grammar   A system of linguistic description characterized by attention to form and distribution, to the spoken language rather than to writing, to description rather than to prescription. Structural grammar is mainly concerned with phonology (sounds) and morphology (word structure), less with syntax. The study of structural linguistics began in Europe about 1900 with the discovery of the principle of the phoneme and extended to the United States about 1930 with the discovery of the principle of the morpheme. Structural linguistics reached its fullest development in the 1950s with the development of notions of constructions and immediate constituent syntax and with the publication of textbooks for schools and colleges.

REFERENCES: L. Bloomfield, *Language* (New York: Holt, Rinehart and Winston, 1933); W. N. Francis, *The Structure of American English* (New York: Ronald Press, 1958); C. C. Fries, *American English Grammar* (New York: Appleton-Century-Crofts, 1940); _____, *The Structure of English* (New York: Harcourt, Brace & World, 1952); H. A. Gleason, *Linguistics and English Grammar* (New York: Holt, Rinehart and Winston, 1965); A. A. Hill, *Introduction to Linguistic Structures, From Sound to Sentence in English* (New York: Harcourt, Brace & World, 1958); C. F. Hockett, *A Course in Modern Linguistics* (New York: Macmillan, 1958); Paul Roberts, *Patterns of English* (New York: Harcourt, Brace & World, 1956); E. Sapir, *Language* (New York: Harcourt, Brace & World, 1921; Harvest Book HB7); James Sledd, *A Short Introduction to English Grammar* (Chicago: Scott, Foresman, 1959); N. C. Stageberg, *An Introductory English Grammar* (New York: Holt, Rinehart and Winston, 1965); R. Wells, "Immediate Constituents," *Language,* 23 (1947: 81–117.

structure group word   See FUNCTION WORD.

subject   The subject of a sentence is the noun, pronoun, or nominal structure that usually agrees in number with the verb and, except in inverted sentence order, stands before the verb. The subject is the actor in the active-voice sentence. (See NOMINATIVE CASE.)

subjective complement   A noun or adjective that completes the meaning of a linking verb, and in so doing, modifies, or complements, the subject of that verb: He is *sick*. Bill seems *nice*. Lou became *chairman*.

subjunctive mood   Expressions of wish, doubt, or possibility are said to be in the subjunctive mood.

> I wish you *were* here.
> If he *were* here, we could leave.
> *Be* it said that he is a good man.

(See MOOD.)

subordinate clause   See DEPENDENT CLAUSE, SUBORDINATION.

subordination   *CG:* The notion that one clause in a sentence has a less important meaning than another clause or clauses in the same sentence. For example, if we want to suggest that the men's beer drinking is less important than their loud singing, we might write a COMPLEX SENTENCE:

> The men *who drink beer* sing loudly.
> Subord. Clause

The function of subordination is indicated by the word *who*. Three kinds of words indicate subordination in English. Relative pronouns introduce subordinate clauses. *Who* in the sentence above is an example; others are *whose, whom, which, that.* Certain adverbs connect subordinate clauses with main clauses by modifying a word in the main clause. Examples are *when, where, how, whenever, why,* etc.

The men sing loudly *whenever they drink beer.*
Subord. Clause

Subordinating conjunctions also introduce subordinate clauses. These are conjunctions like *since, because, unless, as, for so.*

Because the men drink beer, they sing loudly.
Subord. Clause

(See DEPENDENT CLAUSE, COMPLEX SENTENCE.)

REFERENCE: James Sledd, "Coordination Faulty and Subordination Upside Down," *College Composition and Communication* (December, 1956).

subordinator   Subordinators are words like *because, until, if, since, that* whose major function is to subordinate sentences so that they become parts of larger sentences:

I can't go *because* I don't have any money.
Until you get it you won't come.
I saw *that* she was ill.

substantive   Nouns, pronouns, and word groups that function as nouns.

suffix   A bound morpheme that attaches to the end of a stem, thus forming a new word or word form. Modern English suffixes are either derivational or inflectional. (See DERIVATIONAL SUFFIX, INFLECTIONAL SUFFIX.)

superfix   A meaningful combination of stresses, the stress pattern on a word or phrase:

gréenhoùse

grêen hóuse

superlative degree   The superlative degree of an adjective or adverb is expressed by attaching the suffix *-est* to short words, while long words are preceded by *most: softest, greatest, most agreeable, most comfortable.* Some words, like *happy,* can form the superlative degree either way: *happiest, most happy.* (See COMPARISON, COMPARATIVE DEGREE.)

suppletion   This describes the complete change of stems in a paradigm. *Go* and *be* illustrate suppletion. In the paradigm for *go*

go   goes   going   went   gone

we would expect the past tense form to be *goed.* Instead, the stem /go-/ has been replaced by a different stem /wɛn-/. This change is called suppletion, and *went* is the suppletive form. Looking at the paradigm for *be*

be   am/is/are   being   was/were   been

we note that *am, is, are, was, were* are the suppletive forms. (See PARADIGM.)

suprasegmental phoneme   A term that designates the phenomena of pitch and juncture which are marked above the segments of sound in phonemic transcription. (See INTONATION CONTOUR, PITCH, TERMINAL JUNCTURE.)

surface structure   Surface structure is an abstract string of morphemes which is interpreted into speech or writing. Underlying a surface structure is a deep or conceptual structure that may be the same as or different from the surface structure. The simple, active, declarative surface structure *the + man + see + PAST + Suzie* is related to the identical deep structure through the choice of lexical items and through syntactic rules that arrange the morphemes in a linear order and enable us to cluster these morphemes together in groups, constituents, like *the + man* and *see + PAST*. Surface structures that are different from deep structures can be illustrated by (1) *Suzie was seen by the man* and (2) *Shut the door!* The deep structure of (1) is *The man saw Suzie*. These different surface and deep structures are connected by syntactic rules that rearrange the subject and object. Noun Phrases in the surface structure, add a form of the verb *be* and the preposition *by,* and substitute the past participle *seen* for the past tense form *saw*. The deep structure of (2) is *You will shut the door*. The surface structure (2) is connected to the deep structure by syntactic rules that delete *you* and *will*. Surface structures can be interpreted by phonological rules to produce utterances. Or surface structure can be changed into writing by the application of morphographemic rules. These relationships between surface and deep structure on the one hand and between surface structure and speech and writing can be depicted by this diagram:

Deep Structure

| Choice of Lexical Items |
| Syntactic Rules
  1. Base Rules
  2. Transformation
    Rules |

↕

Surface Structure

| Phonological Rules
  1. Distinctive Features
  2. Nondistinctive
    Features
  3. Intonation | | Morphographemic Rules |

↕   ↓

Speech   Writing

(See DEEP STRUCTURE.)

syllable   A group of phonemes consisting of a vowel alone or a vowel combined with one or more consonants. This group of phonemes is a unit of the word in which it occurs and has its peak of sonority, its carrying power, on the vowel. Here are some English words with their syllabic peaks underlined:

One Syllable: *me*   /mi̱/
Two Syllables: *receive*   /rɪ̱si̱v/
Three Syllables: *receiving* /rɪ̱si̱vɪ̱ŋ/
Four Syllables: *disenchantment*   /dɪ̱sə̱ncæntmə̱nt/
Five Syllables: *unbelievingly* /ə̱nbɨ̱li̱vm̩li̱/

(See CLOSED SYLLABLE, OPEN SYLLABLE.)

syllabic consonant   There are four syllabic consonants in English which have sufficient peaks of sonority, carrying power, to occur as syllables by themselves in some pronunciations in which they occur. /m/ is syllabic in the pronunciation of *rob 'em,* in which lips are closed for /b/ and remain closed for /m/: /rabm̩/. /n/ is syllabic in the pronunciation of *glutton,* in which the tongue, in contact with the alveolar ridge for the articulation of /t/, remains there for the articulation of /n/: /glə̩tn̩/. /ŋ/ is syllabic in the pronunciation of *and* in *Jack and Bill,* in which the tongue back, held against the velum for the pronunciation of /k/, remains there as the velum is lowered to produce the syllabic velar nasal phoneme /ŋ/: /jækŋ̩bɪl/. /l/ is syllabic in the pronunciation of *battle,* in which the tongue tip, held against the alveolar ridge for the articulation of /t/, remains there for the pronunciation of /l/: bætl̩/. (See SYLLABLE.)

synchronic   In linguistics this term denotes the description of a language at a certain limited time in its development, regardless of its past history. (See DIACHRONIC.)

syncopation   This term describes the loss of a sound in a word during the course of its historical development. In Modern English the words *dogs, cats, wishes* are pronounced /dɔgz kæts wɪšɪz/ with three different endings. In the Late Middle English of Chaucer's time they were all pronounced with the same ending: /dɔgəs katəs wɪšəs/. Between Late Middle English and Modern English times the vowel /ə/ syncopated because it occurred in an unstressed syllable, the usual cause of syncopation. The ending *th* for the third-person singular present indicative of verbs, *mākth,* "maketh," *bērth,* "beareth," syncopated during Old English and Middle English times. The verb preterit ending *-ed:* /ɨd/ syncopated after all phonemes except /t/ and /d/ in the fifteenth century. The fact that /ɨd/ was once widely used is indicated by its continued presence in *aged, blessed,* and *learned* when they are used as adjectives: /ejɨd blɛsɨd lərnɨd/.

syntactic construction   A grammatical sequence having only words as its immediate constituents. (See CONSTRUCTION, IMMEDIATE, CONSTITUENT.)

syntax   *CG, Str:* The description of actual written or spoken sentences; a description of the system by which words combine into phrases and clauses and of the ways that these combine into sentences. In structural grammar, phonology is basic, with syntax being the last level of description. *TG:* Syntax is the base of the grammar; it is a part of a theory of grammar. This base consists of three sets of rules: (1) Phrase structure rules, which generate basic sentences rewritten as complex symbols:

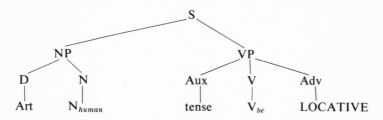

(2) Lexical rules of selection, which substitute words for the complex symbols in the phrase structure string:

Art → the V_{be} → be
N_{human} → man   LOCATIVE → in the house
tense → Present

Lexical rules also assign properties to nouns, pronouns, adjectives, and verbs.

(3) Transformational rules, which add to, rearrange, and subtract from the phrase structure string:

> *Add:*   The old man is in the house.
> *Rearrange:*   Is the old man in the house?
> *Subtract from:*   Yes, the old man is.

(See COMPLEX TRANSFORMATION, SIMPLE TRANSFORMATION, TRANSFORMATION, LEXICAL PROPERTIES.)

REFERENCES: *CG:* M. Bryant, *A Functional English Grammar* (Boston: D. C. Heath, 1950); G. O. Curme, *Syntax* (Boston: D. C. Heath, 1931); R. B. Long, *The Sentence and Its Parts* (Chicago: University of Chicago Press, 1961); *Str:* C. C. Fries, *The Structure of English* (New York: Harcourt, Brace & World, 1952); W. N. Francis, *The Structure of American English* (New York: Ronald Press, 1958); *TG:* See readings under TRANSFORMATIONAL GRAMMAR.

synthetic language   A language in which the relationships among words in a sentence depend mainly upon inflections, the endings on words. Latin, Old English, and modern German are synthetic languages. (See ANALYTIC LANGUAGE, INFLECTIONAL LANGUAGE.)

T

T-unit   A "minimal terminable unit . . . one main clause expanded at any of many different points by structures that are modifiers or complements or substitutes for words in the main clause" (K. W. Hunt, *Grammatical Structures Written at Three Grade Levels* [1965]).

tagmeme   A unit of grammatical arrangement resulting from a slot-class correlation. A *slot* is a grammatical position or function (subject, verbal, object) that is filled by mutually substitutable items, members of a word *class* (nouns and verbs). The utterance *I'd walk* consists of features of the subject-verb slot order, of the classes of words that fill these slots (nouns and verbs), and of phonetic modification – the substitution of *'d* for *would*. Taken alone, none of these three elements has any meaning. But "correlated" they make up a tagmeme whose meaning is that the subject expression "performs" the action of the verb expression.

REFERENCES: W. A. Cook, *Introduction to Tagmemic Analysis* (New York: Holt, Rinehart & Winston, 1969); B. Elson and V. B. Pickett, *Beginning Morphology-Syntax* (Glendale, California: Summer Institute of Linguistics, 1960); R. E. Longacre, "Some Fundamental Insights of Tagmemics," *Language*, 41 (1965) 65–76; Kenneth Pike, *Language in Relation to a Unified Theory of the Structure of Human Behavior* (Glendale, California: Summer Institute of Linguistics, 1954–1960).

tag question   An elliptical inversion of a preceding declarative or imperative sentence which turns the whole sentence into a yes/no question. If the preceding sentence is positive or imperative, the tag question is negative: John has gone, *hasn't he?* Come in, *won't you?* If the preceding declarative sentence is negative, the tag question is positive: John hasn't gone, *has he?* The verb of the tag question is the same as the finite verb of the preceding sentence, if that verb is *be, do,* or a modal auxiliary verb. If a finite verb other than these is used in the preceding sentence, the tag question uses *do:* He likes it, *doesn't he?* He has it, *doesn't he?*

tapped *r*   See FLAPPED *r*.

taxeme   A simple feature of grammatical arrangement; a minimum grammatical feature such as the *order* of words or morphemes (verb follows subject; *-ing* follows *turn*), *selection* (selecting *-ly* to follow *quick* in forming an adverb), *modulation* (strong stress on the first syllable of *quickly;* the rising pitch at the end of "He's walking home?"), or *phonetic modification* ("I would → I'd"). (See TAGMEME.)

tense   A verb form or combination of verb forms indicating that the time of an action or state of being is past, present, or future. Tense is also an indication of agreement between a finite verb and its subject. This agreement can be in person (*I have; she has*), number (*she has; they have*), or time (*she has; she had*). Traditional grammar describes many phrasal tenses. (See FUTURE TENSE, FUTURE PERFECT TENSE, PAST TENSE, PAST PERFECT TENSE, PRESENT TENSE, PRESENT PERFECT TENSE, PROGRESSIVE TENSE.)

tense vowel   The high vowels /i/ b*ee*t and /u/ p*oo*l are articulated with tense tongue muscles. Lower front and back vowels are lax. (See VOWEL.)

terminal juncture   Junctures are combinations of pitch and pause that signal the connection between parts of a complex utterance or the termination of an utterance. There are three terminal junctures in English. The first one, indicated by ↓ , signals the fadeaway of the voice to silence at the end of a statement: *John eats pie* ↓ . The second terminal, indicated by ↑ , signals the slight rise in pitch at the end of a yes/no question: *Are you here* ↑ . The third terminal, indicated by → , is the sustained terminal. It can be most easily recognized as connecting long subjects with their verb: *Most of the people at the game* → *were thrilled by his run* ↓ . It also occurs after introductory statements, indicating that the speaker has more to say: *She's a nice girl* → *but.* . . . The predominant characteristic of terminals within utterances is the lengthening of the stressed syllable that precedes them. Contrast the length of time it takes to pronounce *game* in these two sentences:

The game was over ↓
Most of the people at the game → were thrilled by his run

(See INTONATION CONTOUR, SUPRASEGMENTAL.)

terminal string   *TG:* The string of free and bound morphemes produced by application of rewrite rules in the phrase structure grammar. The string is terminal because its symbols cannot be further expanded by any rule in the grammar.

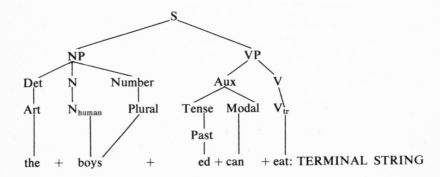

The next step is to apply the obligatory AFFIX TRANSFORMATION:

ed + can $\Rightarrow$ can + ed $\Rightarrow$ could

that-clause   In conventional school grammar a *that-clause* is called a noun clause: *I knew that he was sick*. In *TG*, insert sentences are nominalized with *that* for insertion into subject, object, or noun-complement positions in the main sentence.

S is strange   I saw S

He is here $\Rightarrow$ That he is here   He was running $\Rightarrow$ that he was running

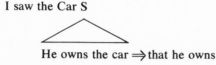

I saw the Car S

He owns the car $\Rightarrow$ that he owns

(See DEPENDENT CLAUSE, FACTITIVE NOMINAL.)

there transformation   This transformation derives from sentences such as *A man is in the house* a sentence with inverted subject and verb and the expletive word *there* in initial position: *There is a man in the house*. A simplified form of the transformation rule looks like this:

NP + BE + LOCATIVE ADVERB $\Rightarrow$
There + BE + NP + LOCATIVE ADVERB

This transformation is useful in distinguishing the verb *be* from the linking verbs (*seem, become,* etc.), which cannot be directly followed by a locative adverb, and from other intransitive verbs, which, though they can be followed by a locative adverb (*The man sleeps here*), cannot undergo the there-transformation: **There sleeps a man here*.

thorn   Thorn is the written symbol þ, a rune used in Old English writing. Thorn represented both the voiced and voiceless *th* sound in the initial position, alternating with ð. It disappeared in Late Middle English times, being replaced by *th*. (See ETH, RUNIC WRITING.)

traditional grammar   See SCHOOL GRAMMAR for the usual synonym for this term. There are also the grammars of the scholarly tradition, which reached its peak in Europe in the early years of the twentieth century. The great taxonomic grammars of Otto Jespersen (*A Modern English Grammar*, 7 Vols, 1909–1949), E. Kruisinga (*A Handbook of Present-Day English*, 3 Vols, 1931), H. Poutsma (*A Grammar of Late Modern English*, 5 Vols, 1926–29), and Henry Sweet (*A New English Grammar*, 1891–98) exemplify this tradition. The work of George Curme (*Parts of Speech and Accidence*, 1935; *Syntax*, 1931) reflects this tradition in America. R. W. Zandvoort, *A Handbook of English Grammar* (3rd ed., 1966), and G. Scheurweghs, *Present-Day*

English Syntax: A Survey of Sentence Patterns (1959), are the most recent works in this illustrious genre of grammars.

transcription   The conversion of the sounds of speech into writing, into a written form in which each letter stands for only one sound. There are two types of transcription, phonetic and phonemic. Phonetic transcription notes all the allophones, variants, of a given phoneme. In phonetic transcription, phones are written within brackets [   ]. For example, the allophones of the phoneme /r/ are written

trilled:	[ř]	Scottish *red*
voiced fricative:	[ɹ]	U.S. *dream*
voiceless fricative:	[ɹ̥]	*tree*
devoiced:	[ɾ̥]	*pray*
flapped:	[ɾ]	British *hurry*

In phonemic transcription, the kind used in this glossary, we use the same character for all the allophones of a given phoneme, and the phonemes are written within slant lines; *r* and all its allophones are written /r/. There are four major systems of phonemic transcription: the system used in *Webster's Third International Dictionary* (1961); the system developed by K. L. Pike and C. C. Fries of the University of Michigan (about 1947); the system used by Trager and Smith in *An Outline of English Structure* (1951); and the International Phonetic Alphabet. These systems are compared below. The IPA Alphabet given here is that found in Kenyon and Knott, *A Pronouncing Dictionary of American English* (10th edition). This version is the widest dissemination of the IPA in a form adapted to the sounds of American English.

Webster 3	Pike-Fries	Trager-Smith	IPA	
ē	i	i	i	
i	ɪ	ɪ	ɪ	
ā	e	e	e	
e	ɛ	ɛ	ɛ	
a	æ	æ	æ	
ə	ə	ə	ə	VOWELS
ər	ər	ɚ	ɚ	AND
ä	a	a	a	DIPHTHONGS
ü	u	u	u	
u̇	ʊ	ʊ	ʊ	
ō	o	o	o	
ȯ	ɔ	ɔ	ɔ	
ī	aɪ	ay	aɪ	
au̇	aʊ	aw	aʊ	
ȯi	ɔɪ	oy	ɔɪ	

Webster 3	Pike-Fries	Trager-Smith	IPA	
p	p	p	p	
b	b	b	b	
t	t	t	t	
d	d	d	d	
k	k	k	k	
g	g	g	g	
ch	č	č	tʃ	
j	j	j	dʒ	
f	f	f	f	
v	v	v	v	CONSONANTS
th	θ	θ	θ	
th	ð	ð	ð	
s	s	s	s	
z	z	z	z	
sh	š	š	ʃ	
zh	ž	ž	ʒ	
h	h	h	h	
m	m	m	m	
n	n	n	n	
ŋ	ŋ	ŋ	ŋ	
l	l	l	l	
r	r	r	r	
y	y	y	j	GLIDES
w	w	w	w	

transform   *TG:* A transform is a structure that is the result of the process of transformation and is, thus, related to the sentence from which it is derived. Sometimes a transform is another sentence. For example, the passive sentence

<blockquote>The dog was patted by the man.</blockquote>

is a transform derived from the active voice sentence

<blockquote>The man patted the dog.</blockquote>

Sometimes a transform is only part of a sentence. *The man's patting the dog* is a gerund transform derived from *The man patted the dog.* When a transform is part of a sentence it can be embedded in a main-clause sentence:

Readout: The man's patting the dog is good.

(See COMPLEX TRANSFORMATION, MULTIPLE-COMPLEX TRANSFORMATION.)

transformation   *TG:* The process that derives from one syntactic structure a different yet related one. Transformations are of two kinds, simple and complex. (For examples of simple transformations see AFFIX TRANSFORMATION, DO-TRANSFORMATION, IMPERATIVE MOOD, NEGATIVE TRANSFORMATION, PASSIVE TRANSFORMATION, SIMPLE TRANSFORMATION, THERE-TRANSFORMATION. For examples of complex transformations see COMPLEX TRANSFORMATION, CONSTITUENT SENTENCE, DEPENDENT CLAUSE, DOUBLE-BASE TRANSFORMATION, MULTIPLE-COMPLEX TRANSFORMATION, NOUN-COMPLEMENT POSITION, PRO-FORM, RECURSIVE-COMPLEX TRANSFORMATION.) Transformations are one of the three parts of the syntactic component of a transformational grammar. The other two parts are the set of basic sentences and the lexicon. (See DICTIONARY, LEXICON, SENTENCE PATTERN, SYNTAX, TRANSFORMATIONAL GRAMMAR.)

transformational grammar   In one sense, this is a theory of grammar that suggests the abstract ability of a native speaker to produce an infinite number of sentences. This grammar predicts all of the grammatical sentences available to the native speaker. Transformational grammar differs from conventional classroom grammar and structural grammar in that it neither analyzes particular sentences nor describes speech production. The complete theory of transformational grammar consists of a syntactic component (phrase-structure, lexicon, transformations), a semantic component (a dictionary and rules that show the relationships among dictionary meanings), and a phonological component, which consists of pronunciation and spelling rules. This model of the grammar dates from the publication of Noam Chomsky's *Syntactic Structures* (1957) and has more recently been modified by Chomsky (*Aspects of the Theory of Syntax,* 1965) and others. (See DICTIONARY and the references under GENERATIVE GRAMMAR and TRANSFORMATION.)

REFERENCES: E. Bach and R. T. Harms (eds.), *Universals in Linguistic Theory* (New York: Holt, Rinehart and Winston, 1968); N. R. Cattell, *The New English Grammar* (Cambridge, Mass.: MIT Press, 1969); J. A. Fodor and J. J. Katz (eds.), *The Structure of Language: Readings in the Philosophy of Language* (Englewood Cliffs: Prentice-Hall, 1964), pp. 50–118, 119–136, 211–245, 384–389, 547–578; R. A. Jacobs and P. S. Rosenbaum, *English Transformational Grammar* (Waltham, Mass.: Blaisdell, 1968); J. J. Katz, *The Philosophy of Language* (New York: Harper & Row, 1966); _____ and P. M. Postal, *An Integrated Theory of Linguistic Descriptions* (Cambridge, Mass.: MIT Press, 1964); A. Koutsoudas, *Writing Transformational Grammars* (New York: McGraw-Hill, 1966); G. Lakoff, *Irregularity in Syntax* (New York: Holt, Rinehart and Winston, 1970); R. W. Langacker, *Language and Its Structure* (New York: Harcourt, Brace and World, 1968); D. T. Langendoen, *Essentials of English Grammar* (New York: Holt, Rinehart and Winston, 1969); R. B. Lees, *The Grammar of English Nominalizations* (Bloomington, Ind.: Indiana University, 1963); P. M. Postal, *Constituent Structure: A Study of Contemporary Models of Syntactic Description* (The Hague: Mouton, 1964); _____, "Underlying and Superficial Linguistic Structure," *Harvard Educational Review,* 34 (Spring, 1964): 246–66; J. Emig, J. Fleming, and H. Popp (eds.), *Language and Learning* (New York: Harcourt, Brace and World, 1966), pp. 153–175; R. Stockwell, B. Partee, *et al., Integration of Transformational Theories on English Syntax.* 2 vols. (Los Angeles: UCLA Bookstore, 1969); J. M. Williams, *The New English* (New York: The Free Press, 1970).

transformational rule   See RULE OF GRAMMAR, REWRITE RULE.

transitive verb   A verb that takes a direct object (Jim drinks *milk*), an indirect object (John gave *Bill* the key), and object complements (They elected Andy *president*). (See FACTITIVE VERB, OBJECT COMPLEMENT.)

transposition   This describes a kind of word order pattern, found mainly in the poetry and prose of earlier historical stages of English, in which objects are transposed before verbs (*A sorry song we might all sing*) or verbs are transposed before auxiliary verbs (*The people assembled were*). (See INVERSION.)

tree diagram   *TG:* This represents the syntactic structure of a sentence. It shows the word order of the sentence, indicates the relationship among the constituents of the sentence, and explicitly labels these constituents.

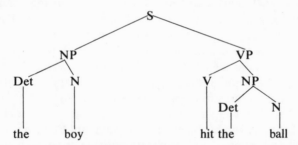

(See DIAGRAM, INTERMEDIATE STRUCTURE, PHRASE MARKER.)

trilled *r*   The trilled *r* is made by several taps of the tongue tip against the alveolar ridge, as in Scottish, Welsh, Spanish, and the Slavic languages, or by the back of the tongue against the uvula, as in German. (See TRANSCRIPTION.)

U

ultimate constituent   *Str:* In morphology the ultimate constituents are the morphemes of which a word is composed:

$$\underline{\text{life} \mid \text{less} \mid} \text{ness}$$

In syntax the ultimate constituents are usually the individual words of the utterance. (See IMMEDIATE CONSTITUENT.)

umlaut   The change in an accented low or back vowel (*a, o, u*) brought about by anticipation of a high front vowel such as /i: ɪ y/ in the following syllable. Evidences in Modern English of this "i-umlaut" can be seen in the pairs *goose : geese, man : men.* The presence of *i* in the second syllable of the Primitive Germanic **gosiz* brought about the fronting of /o:/ eventually to /i:/. The presence of *i* in the second syllable of Primitive German **manni* eventually brought about the fronting of /a/ to /ɛ/. The pair *louse : lice,* from Old English *lūs : lȳs,* illustrates the fronting of /u:/ to /y:/. Umlaut should not be confused with ABLAUT. (See FRONTING.)

usage   The customary manners of speaking or writing a language; the lexical, grammatical, and phonological choices we make. The term also denotes a particular example of a customary manner of speaking or writing, such as the use of the double negative. While a description of levels and varieties of usage is very complex (See John S. Kenyon, "Cultural Levels and Functional Varieties of English," in Harold B. Allen [ed.], *Readings in Applied English Linguistics* [2nd ed., 1964], pp. 294–301), we can say that there are two general varieties of English usage, Standard and Nonstandard. Standard English is that used by educated, cultivated people to communicate in speech and writing. Because it is the language of influential people, its use is socially advantageous. There are three general varieties of Standard English: *formal* (used in serious writing and in formal speeches), *informal* (used in books and magazines intended for the general reader), and *colloquial* (conversation and in writing where the conversational idiom is desired). The dividing line between Standard and Nonstandard English is not clear, since usage is frequently shared between the two. Nonstandard English is infrequently used by Standard English speakers, since some of its expressions, such as the double negative, put the speaker at a social and economic disadvantage. But the fact that the dividing line between Standard and Nonstandard English is not always clear should caution us to regard Nonstandard usage as different from, and not necessarily inferior to, Standard usage. (See CULTURAL LEVEL OF USAGE, FUNCTIONAL VARIETY OF USAGE.)

REFERENCES: M. Bryant, *Current American Usage* (New York: Funk & Wagnalls, 1962); M. Joos, *The Five Clocks* (Bloomington, Indiana: *International Journal of American Linguistics* 28(1962), No. 2; New York: Harcourt, Brace & World, 1968); Bergen and Cornelia Evans, *A Dictionary of Contemporary American Usage* (New York: Random House, 1957).

usage label   The purpose of usage labels, which sometimes appear with definitions in dictionaries, is to identify the general nature of the context in which the word is ordinarily used. Usage labels are usually of three kinds: stylistic (*slang, nonstand.*), temporal (*archaic, obs.*), and regional (*dial., dial. Brit., New. Eng., Midland*). (See DICTIONARY.)

V

velar stop   /k/ and /g/ are velar stops. (See STOP.)

verb   *CG:* A verb names an action or state of being. Verbs are of two kinds: auxiliary (helping) and full (main). *Str., TG:* The verb is a part of speech class whose members exhibit certain formal, distributional, and semantic characteristics.

(1) *Formal* (*a*) Inflection: the verb is capable of inflection for the present tense third person singular {-s} *learns;* past tense {-d} *learned;* past participle {-d} *learned* or *-en chosen;* and the present participle {-ing} *learning.* (*b*) Derivation: verbs may be derived from bound stems, nouns, and adjectives by the addition of derivational suffixes such as *-ate* (orchestrate), *ize* (idolize), *-fy* (beautify), *-ish* (furnish), *-en* (blacken). (*c*) Agreement: the finite verb exhibits the tense and person or number concord with its subject in the present or past tense. The present and past participles do not show concord with a subject because the tense marker attaches to the first verb in the verb phrase, whether the phrase contains only a main verb (*He runs*) or one or more auxiliaries: *He will run, He has run, He is running,* etc.

(2) *Distributional:* the verb patterns after the noun phrase subject. (See the transformational grammar description of SENTENCE PATTERN.) On the basis of the kind of complement a verb requires, the kinds of transformations a sentence can undergo, and the freedom with which a sentence can accept verbs, there are at least five kinds of verbs: transitive, intransitive, mid, linking, and *be.*

(3) *Semantic:* The semantic characteristics of the verb tell what the subject does, is, or has. The semantic characteristic describes an action or state of being. But it is frequently difficult to define verbs by their semantic characteristics alone. (See INTRANSITIVE VERB, LEXICAL PROPERTIES, TENSE, TRANSITIVE VERB.)

REFERENCES: M. Joos, *The English Verb: Form and Meanings* (Madison: University of Wisconsin Press, 1964); A. G. Juilland and J. Macris, *The English Verb System* ('s-Gravenhage: Mouton, 1962); J. Svartik, *On Voice in the English Verb* ('s-Gravenhage: Mouton, 1966); W. F. Twaddell, *The English Verb Auxiliaries* (Providence: Brown University Press, 1960).

verb-headed construction   *Str:* This term denotes a construction in which a verb is the headword: quickly *ran* : quickly *ran* home yesterday; has quickly *run* the race. (See HEADWORD.)

verb phrase   *CG:* This consists of the main verb and its auxiliary verb(s). *TG:* This is composed of auxiliary material and the main verb: VP → Aux + MV. The auxiliary consists of present or past tense and, optionally, a modal verb and/or *have* and/or *be:* Aux → Tense (modal) (have + en) (be + ing). The main verb can be variously subclassified. (See MID-VERB, VERB.)

verbal   *CG:* This term denotes the infinitives of verbs and the verb + *ing* and the verb + *ed* when they function as nouns and adjectives. The *gerund* is the verb + *ing* in its noun function: *Skiing* is fun. He likes *swimming*. The participle is the verb + *ing* and verb + *ed* in its adjective function: We heard *running* water. *Used* in several ways, the verb is an *interesting* word. The base form of the verb preceded by *to* is called the *infinitive*. Infinitives are also verbals and function as nouns (*To learn* is good), adjectives (John had a wish *to travel*), and adverbs (He waited *to see* Sue). *TG:* It is apparent that verbs and adjectives have some properties in common in the deep structure of sentences. They are both considered as verbals, marked ⟨+VB⟩, and their differences are marked by the features ⟨+V⟩ for verbs and ⟨−V⟩ for adjectives. (See LEXICAL PROPERTIES.)

Verner's Law   Like Grimm's Law, Verner's Law is a simple statement describing systematic changes in pronunciation. In 1875 Karl Verner, a Danish scholar, explained the presence of the voiced fricative sounds *b, d, g* in Germanic languages in which, according to Grimm's Law, we should expect to find voiceless sounds, *p, t, k*. Verner also explained the principle of *rhotacism* (r-ing) in which the Indo-European *s* develops in Germanic to *z* and *r*. The following diagram will show Verner's modification of one stage of Grimm's Law:

GRIMM			*VERNER*	*EXAMPLE*
I-E	*Gmc*		*Gmc*	
p	→ f	→	b = OE /v/	a li*f*e/ to li*v*e
				a grie*f*/ to grie*v*e
t	→ þ (th) →		d	dea*th*... dea*d*
k	→ x (h) →		g	Example may be found in the two pronunciations of the Modern English *exit*: /ɛksɪt/; /ɛgzɪt/

Rhotacism can be stated as follows:

I-E	*Gmc*	
s	⟶ s → z → r	OE wæ*s*, wæ*r*on → MnE wa*s*, we*r*e

Verner concluded that these voiced sounds occurred because stress was not on the first syllable, that this voicing occurred before the Germanic stress shift to the first syllable. (See FIRST CONSONANT SHIFT, GRIMM'S LAW.)

vocative case   *CG:* In fully inflected languages the case that marks the person being addressed. In the Latin *miserere, Domine* ("have mercy, O Lord") *Domine* is marked for the vocative case. Even in relatively uninflected languages like English, school grammar books sometimes consider *Joe* in *Joe, come here* as being in the vocative case.

voice of verbs   See ACTIVE VOICE, PASSIVE VOICE.

voiced voiceless   A voiced sound is one made when breath forced from the lungs vibrates the vocal cords. All vowels are voiced sounds, as are some consonants (m, n, b, d, g, z, etc.). Voiceless sounds are those made without vibration of the vocal cords. Some consonants are voiceless (s, t, k, p, etc.). (See STOP, VOWEL.)

vowel   Voiced sounds produced by the breath passing through the opened mouth with relatively little obstruction by the speech organs. The term also names the written letters *a, e, i, o, u.* Generally speaking, vowels are characterized according to the height of the tongue in the mouth and according to its front-back position in the mouth. Thus, high vowels are produced with the tongue relatively high in the mouth; low vowels have the tongue relatively low, and mid vowels have the tongue between high and low position. Front, central, and back vowels are produced with the tongue in these positions from the front to the back of the mouth. All of this can be represented on what is called a vowel quadrangle. This is a representation of the tongue positions in the mouth:

	FRONT	CENTRAL	BACK
HIGH	i ɪ	ɨ	u ʊ
MID	e ɛ	ər ə	o
LOW	æ	a	ɔ

/i/ = beet	/ɨ/ = candid	/u/ = too
/ɪ/ = bit	/ər/ = sir	/ʊ/ = put
/e/ = bait	/ə/ = but	/o/ = note
/ɛ/ = bet	/a/ = pot	/ɔ/ = law
/æ/ = bat		

(See DISTINCTIVE FEATURES.)

W

wave theory   In 1872 Johannes Schmidt postulated the *wave hypothesis*. Schmidt demonstrated that similarities can be found between any two branches of Indo-European, and these similarities are most frequent in the case of branches that lie geographically nearest to each other. Thus, languages that originate from a parent language spread from this parent in all directions, and changes in languages spread in the same way—like waves moving out from the point at which a stone lands in a pool. In accounting for linguistic differentiations, the wave theory stands in contrast to the splitting process implied by the FAMILY TREE THEORY. (See FAMILY TREE THEORY, GLOTTOCHRONOLOGY.)

wh-clause   *TG:* A Wh-clause is a sentence which has been transformed to contain a wh-word so that this sentence can be inserted into a nominal, noun-complement, or adverbial position in a main-clause sentence.

S is right

He says it ⇒ *What* he says

Readout: What he says is right.

The boy S is asleep.

You know the boy ⇒ *who* you know

Readout: The boy who you know is asleep.

He stays S

He lives there ⇒ *where* he lives

Readout: He stays where he lives.

Any structure in an insert sentence can be changed to a wh-word and moved to the front of the sentence to produce a wh-clause. But notice that the use of wh-words to make nominal, noun-complement, or adverbial clauses does not cause inversion of the subject and finite verb since these clauses do not produce questions. (See WH-QUESTION, WH-WORD.)

wh-question   *Str., TG:* So-called because it begins with a word containing the letters *w* and *h: who, whom, whose, what, which, why, where, when, how,* and sometimes their compounds ending in *-ever.* The *wh-*question is an information question, that is, it requires information rather than *yes* or *no* for an answer. Any element, any structure, in a yes/no question can be changed to a *wh-*word and moved to the front of the sentence to produce an information question:

Yes/No Question: Will John give his paper in the seminar tomorrow?
Question the Subject: Who will give his paper in the seminar tomorrow?
Question the Object: What will John give in the seminar tomorrow?
Question the Determiner of the Object: Whose paper will John give. . . ?
Question the Locative Adverb: Where will John give his paper tomorrow?
Question the Time Adverb: When will John give his paper in the seminar?

(See QUESTION.)

wh-word   See WH-QUESTION.

word   In writing, a word is understood to be a sequence of letters with or without a hyphen, sometimes with space within it (as in *snow tires*), always with space before it and after it. From the point of view of morphemics, a word is said to be a free form (it can be used alone, uncombined with any other forms) having only one base, either free (*annoy*ance) or bound (dis*sent*). Compound words consist of two or more bases (*baseball, brother-in-law, bluebird*). (See BASE, BOUND MORPHEME, FREE MORPHEME.)

word order   This term describes the order in which words may occur in a phrase (*gave him the car*) or in a sentence (*The dog barked ferociously*). (See INVERSION, TRANSPOSITION.)

wynn   The runic character ꝥ used in Old English writing. It represented /w/. (See RUNIC WRITING.)

Y

yes/no question   Yes/no questions are so-called because they elicit an answer *yes* or *no*. They are of two kinds. The yes/no question in statement form asks the question by means of the intonation contour 233↑: ²You're³ here³↑. The yes/no question in question form has the same intonation contour but the question is signaled by grammar—the inversion of subject and verb: ²Are you³here³↑. (See INTONATION CONTOUR, TERMINAL JUNCTURE, QUESTION, WH-QUESTION.)

yogh   A written symbol. In Old English times its shape was ȝ and it stood for the voiced velar stop /g/ before consonants (*glæd*), initially before back vowels (*gōs*), and initially before mutated front vowels (*gēs*). In the combination *ng* (*bringan*) it represented the sound in Modern English *linger:* /ŋg/. Initially before *e, i,* and *y,* yogh represented /y/ (*gecoren, giftian, gydd*). In other positions in Old English yogh represented the voiced velar fricative /ɤ/: /draȝan/. In Early Middle English its shape was ȝ and it was used for the sound of *y* (ȝeld-de(n)) and for the voiceless velar fricative /x/; *cniȝt,* spelled *gh* in the Late Middle English of Chaucer's time and in Modern English.

Z

zero allomorph   A variant of a morpheme. If no actual sound change is evident, if there is zero variation in sound, the zero allomorph has been added. For example, the plural of *bear* and *deer* is identical with the singular. When these words are used as plurals, it is said that the plural is formed by the addition of a zero allomorph of the plural morpheme {-s}. (See ALLOMORPH, MORPHOLOGICAL CONDITIONING.)